European Union Law in a Global Context

Text, Cases and Materials

Trevor C. Hartley

London School of Economics

CAMBRIDGE
UNIVERSITY PRESS

PUBLISHED BY THE PRESS SYNDICATE OF THE UNIVERSITY OF CAMBRIDGE
The Pitt Building, Trumpington Street, Cambridge, United Kingdom

CAMBRIDGE UNIVERSITY PRESS
The Edinburgh Building, Cambridge CB2 2RU, UK
40 West 20th Street, New York, NY 10011–4211, USA
477 Williamstown Road, Port Melbourne, VIC 3207, Australia
Ruiz de Alarcón 13, 28014 Madrid, Spain
Dock House, The Waterfront, Cape Town 8001, South Africa

http://www.cambridge.org

First published 2004

Printed in the United Kingdom at the University Press, Cambridge

Typeface Swift 9.5/12.5 pt. and Formata   *System* LATEX 2$_\varepsilon$ [TB]

A catalogue record for this book is available from the British Library

Library of Congress Cataloguing in Publication data
Hartley, Trevor C.
European Union law in a global context : text, cases and materials /
Trevor C. Hartley
    p. cm.
Includes bibliographical references and index.
ISBN 0 521 82030 8 – ISBN 0 521 52730 9 (pbk.)
1. Law – European Union countries. 2. Law – European Union countries – Cases.   I. Title.
KJE947.H368   2004
341.242′2 – dc21   2003055281

ISBN 0 521 82030 8 hardback
ISBN 0 521 52730 9 paperback

The publisher has used its best endeavours to ensure that the URLs for external websites
referred to in this book are correct and active at the time of going to press. However, the
publisher has no responsibility for the websites and can make no guarantee that a site will
remain live or that the content is or will remain appropriate.

Contents

Preface

The purpose of this book is to give a picture of how the European Union operates as part of the world system. Instead of just *saying* what happens, it lets you see for yourself. It does this by presenting edited versions of the cases in which major decisions were given. You can read them, and decide for yourself whether they are right. To make this easier, the background is first explained. Treaties and other sources of law are set out in panels, so you can refer to them to check the arguments.

Why study the European Union? And why in a global context? The reason is globalization. This is the process that takes away from individual States the ability to control day-to-day activities within their territories. With globalization, a country is no longer "an island unto itself". It is part of a larger unit – the world system. For European countries, the advent of the European Union is the most striking element in this process. In the UK, the government tells us almost every day that it cannot do this or that because it is a matter for the EU. Almost all aspects of our lives now seem to depend on some directive from Brussels. Shops are forbidden to sell goods in pounds and ounces. Our passports have "European Union" on the front cover. Across the Channel, marks and francs have been displaced by the euro – something that may happen in the UK too. The result is that democratic institutions are losing power and influence, while international institutions – diplomatic, bureaucratic or judicial – are in the ascendant.

Some people say that the EU is unique – that it resembles no other entity and, in its concept and design, owes nothing to anything found anywhere else. That is not true. Although the breadth and depth of its powers put the EU in a special position, this is merely a matter of degree. The EU is simply the foremost among a whole pack of international bodies that have the power to control what countries do. The Council of Europe is another. It is the parent organization of the European Court of Human Rights, the body responsible for the government's decision to ban corporal punishment in British schools. When bombs rained down on Belgrade in 1999, it was NATO, another international organization, that decreed that this should happen, though it is unlikely that this provided much consolation for the citizens on whom they fell. When a factory is closed in the UK because it cannot compete with foreign imports, the cause may lie with the World Trade Organization, though this body is also responsible for more affordable goods in the shops.

The international system, therefore, consists of much more than the European Union. For Europeans, however, the EU is the most important part of it. For this reason, the European Union constitutes the centrepiece of this book. However, the EU is described in the context of the international system of which it is a part. This allows us to do two things. First, we can understand it better by comparing it with other organizations of a similar kind. Secondly, we can gain greater knowledge of the international system by examining the way the EU operates in it. The materials presented in this book enable you to do both.

Many years ago, a friend of mine asked a senior colleague (who subsequently became a judge on the European Court) whether he should take up the study of European Community law. "Oh, no, you don't want to do that", he was told, "EC cases are about nothing more interesting than the price of semolina." Though exaggerated, this reply was not totally unfair. Many EC cases are about technical matters unlikely to engage the interest, let alone enthusiasm, of anyone not an expert. The aim of this book is to avoid all cases about "semolina". To achieve this, a policy of ruthless selectivity has been adopted. The chapters that follow are focused clearly on topics that can genuinely be called "fundamental". These are the topics that anyone – from inside or outside the Union – would want to know about. Can the EU pass laws? If so, what are the limits to its powers? Can international courts enforce their judgments against States? Is there legal redress for the victims of torture? Must national courts apply international treaties? What if they conflict with national law? Can the EU sign treaties with other countries? Does this stop Member States from signing treaties? How are free-trade rights balanced against other concerns? These are just some of the issues covered in the pages that follow.

I hope you find them interesting.

Trevor Hartley
4 February 2004

Acknowledgements

Chapter 2 is based on Chapter 1 of my book, *Constitutional Problems of the European Union* (Hart Publishing, Oxford and Portland, OR, 1999). I have also reused material from the following pages: pages 18–21, 27–29, 59–61, 86 and 152–153. I would like to thank Richard Hart for generously granting permission to do so.

The Comment on the *Matthews* case in Chapter 17 is taken from pages 31–35 of my article, "International Law and the Law of the European Union – A Reassessment" (2001) 72 BYIL 1. I am grateful to the editors of the *British Yearbook of International Law* for their permission to reuse it here.

Paragraphs 19–27 and 35 of the English translation of the decision of the *Bundesverfassungsgericht* in the *Internationale Handelsgesellschaft* case, which first appeared in [1974] 2 CMLR 540, are reproduced with permission from Sweet & Maxwell, publishers of the *Common Market Law Reports* (editor, Dr Neville March Hunnings).

Finally, I would like to thank the Incorporated Council of Law Reporting for England and Wales for permission to reproduce extracts from the following cases: *Thoburn v. Sunderland City Council* [2002] 3 WLR 247 (Div. Ct); *Salomon v. Commissioners of Customs and Excise* [1967] 2 QB 116 (CA); and *Attorney General for Canada v. Attorney General for Ontario* [1937] AC 326 (PC).

How to use this book

This book has been carefully structured for ease of use.

How to find a case

The cases are listed alphabetically by name in the Table of Cases. Cases decided by the European Court are, in addition, listed by case number. Case numbers are assigned to each case at the beginning of the proceedings. They are normally in the form "Case 79/87", in which the two digits after the oblique stroke (slash) indicate the year. Cases decided under certain special provisions – for example, Article 300(6) [228(6)] EC – are called "Opinions" and are separately numbered. We list all cases/opinions for the same year together. Within each year, they are listed according to the number before the oblique stroke, "Opinions" being listed before "Cases". The Table of Cases gives the page number where the case is set out.

How to find a provision in a treaty, convention, statute or other instrument

All major legislative provisions discussed in the text are set out in panels, either on the page in question, on the facing page or on the next available page. These panels are numbered consecutively. The digits before the dot indicate the chapter. Thus Panel 12.2 is the second panel in Chapter 12. There is a Table of Panels, which lists all the panels in order and gives the page references. There is also a Table of Treaties and Other Instruments, which lists all provisions in treaties, etc. that are set out in this book. The list is alphabetical by instrument. Within each instrument, the individual provisions are listed by number. Page references are given. Thus if you know the number of the panel you want, you look in the Table of Panels. This is useful because references in the text give the panel number. If you know the instrument you want, you look in the Table of Treaties and Other Instruments.

The Treaty of Amsterdam renumbered the Articles in the EC Treaty and the Treaty on European Union (Maastricht Agreement). Although this made the treaties look neater, it created problems for those using them. Judgments of the European Court given prior to the date on which the Treaty of Amsterdam took effect (1 May 1999) use the old numbering. To avoid confusion, references in this book to Articles in these two treaties will be to the new numbering with the old numbering in square brackets. Thus "Article 10 [5] EC" means the Article originally numbered 5 and now numbered 10. The text of judgments given before 1 May 1999 has been altered to conform to this system. If no bracketed Article is given for the EC Treaty or the Treaty on European Union, this means that the provision is of recent origin and there is no equivalent under the old system. Likewise, if only a bracketed Article is cited, this means that the provision in question has now been deleted or substantially amended.

How to find where a topic is discussed

There is an Index at the end of the book, which you can use to find where topics are discussed.

Further developments

Developments since the publication of this book are covered on its website, www.cambridge.org/Hartley

Table of cases

Only cases set out, or discussed in some detail, are listed.

Numerical table of ECJ cases

The number after the oblique stroke (slash) represents the year. Cases are listed here first by year, and then by the number before the oblique stroke. "Opinions" are listed before "Cases" for the same year. Only those cases set out, or discussed in some detail, are included.

Case 10/61, Commission v. Italy, [1962] ECR 1   *336*

Case 25/62, Plaumann v. Commission, [1963] ECR 95   *362*

Case 26/62, Van Gend en Loos v. Nederlandse Administratie der Belastingen, [1963] ECR 1; [1963] CMLR 105   *145*

Case 6/64, Costa v. ENEL, [1964] ECR 585   *151*

Case 48/65, Lütticke v. Commission, [1966] ECR 19; [1966] CMLR 378   *378*

Cases 8–11/66, Cimenteries v. Commission (Noordwijks Cement Accoord case), [1967] ECR 75; [1967] CMLR 77   *357*

Cases 2 and 3/69, Sociaal Fonds voor de Diamantarbeiders (Diamond Workers case), [1969] ECR 211; [1969] CMLR 335   *395*

Case 29/69, Stauder v. Ulm, [1969] ECR 419   *297*

Case 11/70, Internationale Handelsgesellschaft Case, [1970] ECR 1125   *300*

Case 22/70, Commission v. Council (ERTA/AETR case), [1971] ECR 263; [1971] CMLR 335   *228*

Case 42/71, Nordgetreide v. Commission, [1972] ECR 105   *379*

Cases 21–23/72, International Fruit Company v. Produktschap voor Groenten en Fruit (Third International Fruit case), [1972] ECR 1219; [1975] 2 CMLR 1   *239*

Case 4/73, Nold v. Commission, [1974] ECR 491   *301*

Case 8/73, Hauptzollamt Bremerhaven v. Massey-Ferguson, [1973] ECR 897   *53*

Case 181/73, Haegeman v. Belgium, [1974] ECR 449; [1975] 1 CMLR 515   *252*

Case 8/74, Procureur du Roi v. Dassonville, [1974] ECR 837   *398*

Case 41/74, Van Duyn v. Home Office, [1974] ECR 1337; [1975] 1 CMLR 1   *166*

Case 43/75, Defrenne v. Sabena, [1976] ECR 455   *153*

Opinion 1/76, Laying-Up Fund for Inland Waterway Vessels, [1977] ECR 741   *232*

Cases 83 and 94/76 and 4, 15 and 40/77, HNL v. Council and Commission (Second Skimmed Milk Powder case), [1978] ECR 1209; [1978] 3 CMLR 566   *383*

Case 106/77, Amministrazione delle Finanze dello Stato v. Simmenthal, [1978] ECR 629; [1978] 3 CMLR 263   *152*

Cases 116 and 124/77, Amylum and Tunnel Refineries v. Council and Commission (Second Isoglucose case), [1979] ECR 3497   *386*

Table of treaties and other instruments

Charter of Fundamental Rights of the European Union

Charter of the United Nations

Constitution

See under name of State concerned

Convention on Consular Relations

See Vienna Convention on Consular Relations

EC Treaty

Protocol on the Application of the Principles of Subsidiarity and Proportionality

Euratom Treaty

European Community

See EC Treaty

European Convention on Human Rights

Protocol No. 1

Statutes

For national legislation, see under name of State concerned

Treaty establishing the European Community

See EC Treaty

Treaty on European Union

United Kingdom

European Communities Act 1972

Civil Procedure Rules

United Nations

See Charter of the United Nations

United States

Constitution

Uruguay Round Agreements Act 1994

Vienna Convention on Consular Relations 1963

Vienna Convention on the Law of Treaties 1969

Table of panels

Abbreviations

AD	anti-dumping (NAFTA)
AG	Advocate-General (EC)
AJIL	*American Journal of International Law*
BYIL	*British Yearbook of International Law*
CMLR	*Common Market Law Reports*
CMLRev.	*Common Market Law Review*
COREPER	Committee of Permanent Representatives (EC)
CVD	countervailing duty (NAFTA)
DSB	Dispute Settlement Body (WTO)
DSU	Dispute Settlement Understanding (WTO)
EC	European Community
ECB	European Central Bank (EC)
ECJ	European Court of Justice (EC)
ECOSOC	Economic and Social Committee (EC)
ECR	*European Court Reports*
ECSC	European Coal and Steel Community (no longer in existence)
EEA	European Economic Area
EEC	European Economic Community (now renamed "European Community")
EFTA	European Free Trade Association
ELRev.	*European Law Review*
EP	European Parliament (EC)
EU	European Union
Euratom	European Atomic Energy Community
FTC	Free Trade Commission (NAFTA)
ICJ	International Court of Justice
ILM	*International Legal Materials*
JIEL	*Journal of International Economic Law*
LQR	*Law Quarterly Review*
NAFTA	North American Free Trade Area
NILR	*Netherlands International Law Review*
OJ	*Official Journal* (EC)
RTDE	*Revue Trimestrielle de Droit Européen*
TEU	Treaty on European Union (Maastricht Agreement)
WTO	World Trade Organization

Latest development: the proposed Constitution for Europe

This book tries to state the law as it existed in April 2003, though it covers the accession of the new Member States in May 2004. Since the book was written, the most important developments have been the drafting by the "European Convention" of a Constitution for the European Union[1] and the collapse of the Inter-Governmental Conference convened in December 2003 for its adoption.

The proposed Constitution was contained in a draft treaty. Parts of it were submitted to the European Council, meeting in Thessaloniki (Salonika) on 20 June 2003. The final text was submitted to the President of the European Council in Rome on 18 July 2003.[2] Italy, which held the Presidency from July to December 2003, then had the task of brokering agreement among the twenty-five Member States.[3] The process reached its climax at a summit meeting of the Heads of State or Government held in Brussels on 12 and 13 December 2003.[4] The meeting ended in disarray. A terse statement was issued on Saturday 13 December that the Member States had failed to reach agreement.

This is not necessarily the end of the Constitution. However, it is unlikely that progress will be made for some time. Moreover, even if agreement is eventually reached, the Treaty will have to be ratified by each Member State in accordance with its constitutional requirements, a process that will entail referendums in many countries. For this reason, the draft Constitution will be considered here in broad outline only. It is nevertheless of interest both because it may one day come into effect and because it is an indication of thinking on the most important problems facing the EU.

The draft is in four Parts. Part I contains the most basic and important provisions. Part II deals with fundamental rights and is mainly taken up with the Charter of Fundamental Rights. Part III deals with more detailed matters and consists mainly of modified provisions of the EC Treaty. Part IV contains general and final provisions. At present, the Articles in Parts II, III and IV are numbered according to the Part in which they are found. Thus Article II-3 is in Part II and Article III-3 in Part III.[5] Articles not prefixed by a Roman numeral are in Part I. In the discussion that follows, the proposals will be dealt with

---

1 For the background, see p. 14, below.
2 CONV 850/03. At the time of writing (December 2003), it is available on http://european-convention.eu.int.
3 The ten new Member States played a full part in the negotiations, even though they were not formally to join the Community until May of the following year.
4 At the time of writing, details of this are available on http://ue.eu.int/igc.
5 In the following pages, references to provisions of the proposed Constitution will be to the Articles as numbered in CONV 850/03. The numbering may be changed in the future.

according to the chapters of this book to which they relate. The explanation will be easier to understand if it is read after each chapter.

Chapter 1

The new treaty would repeal the EC Treaty and the Treaty on European Union,[6] though, curiously, the Euratom Treaty would remain.[7] The European Community would be abolished. All the activities of the EC, and those previously coming directly under the EU, would be activities of the European Union, an entity that would be re-established by the Constitution.[8] The European Union would take over all the rights and obligations of the EC as well as those that were previously applicable to the EU.[9] This would simplify the structure outlined in Chapter 1.

Chapter 3

One of the most controversial proposals was for the creation of a new post of President of the European Council.[10] (The European Council, it will be remembered, consists of the Heads of State or Government of the Member States. It is the highest-level decision-making organ in the EU, and would be given the status of a separate institution by the proposed Constitution.) Under the proposal, the President would be elected by the European Council by qualified majority for a period of two and a half years, renewable once. He would have the job of chairing the European Council and "driving forward" its work. This was intended to be a heavyweight appointment and could rival the President of the Commission in importance. The smaller countries were unhappy about it because they thought it would enhance the influence of the big States.

There was also a proposal to appoint a Union Minister for Foreign Affairs, who would chair the Council of Ministers in its Foreign Affairs formation and would be one of the Vice-Presidents of the Commission.[11] He would be appointed by the European Council (acting by a qualified majority) with the agreement of the President of the Commission. He would be responsible for representing the Union with regard to the common foreign and security policy.[12]

---

6 Art. IV-2.
7 For amendments, see the Protocol Amending the Euratom Treaty.
8 Art. 1.
9 Art. IV-3.
10 Art. 21.
11 Arts 27 and 23(2).
12 Art. III-197(2). There is some uncertainty as to how his functions would fit in with those of the President of the European Council. According to Art. 21(2), the President would ensure the external representation of the Union on issues concerning its common foreign and security policy, though this is to be without prejudice to the responsibilities of the Minister for Foreign Affairs. However, according to Art. 27, the Minister for Foreign Affairs will conduct the Union's common foreign and security policy and be responsible for handling external relations. It is also unclear to what extent he would be responsible to the Council and to what extent to the Commission.

The most controversial proposal was for the radical recasting of the system of qualified-majority voting in the Council of Ministers, a proposal that would have taken effect only from 1 November 2009.[13] Under the proposal, the votes of the Member States would no longer have been weighted. Instead, a measure would be passed if it was supported by a majority of Member States representing at least 60 per cent of the total population of the Union. The proposal was vehemently opposed by Poland and Spain, both of which have disproportionate voting power under the system that would otherwise apply. This is the system in the Treaty of Accession 2003, which will apply from 1 November 2004 (see Panel 3.12). Under it, Poland and Spain both have 27 votes, while Germany, which has twice the population of either State, has only 29. The result is clearly unfair to Germany. When Germany insisted on the new proposal and Poland was adamant that it would not accept it, the summit meeting collapsed.

A new system for the appointment of the Commission was proposed.[14] Under the proposal, the European Council (acting by a qualified majority) would nominate its candidate for President of the Commission. The candidate would then have to be elected by the European Parliament, acting by a majority of members. If he did not receive the required support, a new candidate would have to be put forward within a month. Once the President was elected, the next step would be for each Member State to put forward three names (one of which would have to be a woman) as their Commissioner. The President would choose one. Under the proposal, only thirteen Commissioners would be entitled to vote. They would be styled "European Commissioners".[15] The remainder (called simply "Commissioners") would have no vote. The voting members of the Commission, known as the "College", would thus consist of fifteen persons: the President, the Minister for Foreign Affairs and the thirteen European Commissioners. The reduction of the Commission to fifteen voting members would have come into force only on 1 November 2009 and then only if the European Council so decided.

It is good to see that the draft includes proposals to give the Member-State parliaments a role in the Union's affairs.[16] Unfortunately, this is mainly limited to ensuring that they are informed in good time of proposed legislation. The Commission would, however, be required to reconsider proposed legislation if a third of the Member-State parliaments considered that it infringed the principle of subsidiarity.[17] There is also an obscurely worded provision under which proceedings could be brought to annul legislative acts on the ground that they infringed the principle of subsidiarity. The proceedings would be brought by a

---

13 Art. 24.
14 Arts 25 and 26.
15 A European Decision adopted by the European Council would determine how it would be decided which Member States would get a European Commissioner. However, Art. 25(3) states that there must be strict equality between Member States. Consequently, if a given Member State failed to get a European Commissioner on one occasion, it would be bound to get one next time round.
16 Protocol on the Role of National Parliaments in the European Union.
17 Protocol on the Application of the Principles of Subsidiarity and Proportionality, Art. 6. The actual rule is more complicated since it allows individual chambers of national parliaments to vote separately. Unicameral parliaments are given two votes and chambers of bicameral parliaments get one vote each.

Member State on its own behalf or on behalf of its national parliament or a chamber thereof.[18] It is unclear whether the national governments would be *obliged* to bring proceedings if so requested by the national parliament or chamber.[19]

Chapter 4

The proposed Constitution would adopt a new classification of legal acts.[20] Instead of the five measures set out in Panel 4.1, there would be a more complicated system. The primary division would be between legislative acts and non-legislative acts. This distinction would not be based on the nature of the measure or on what it did, but on how it was adopted. Legislative acts would normally be adopted jointly by the European Parliament and the Council of Ministers.[21] They would be of two kinds: European laws and European framework laws. The former would be like old-style regulations. They would be of general application, binding in their entirety and directly applicable in the Member States. The latter would be like old-style directives. They would be binding, as to the result to be achieved, upon the Member States to which they were addressed, but would leave the national authorities "entirely free" to choose the form and means of achieving that result.

Non-legislative acts would also be of two kinds: European regulations and European decisions.[22] Their purpose would be to put into effect (implement and, where so provided, supplement or amend) legislative acts and certain specific provisions of the Constitution. European regulations would normally be adopted by the Commission, acting under a power granted to it by a legislative act or by the Constitution. Confusingly, they would be either like old-style regulations or like old-style directives. European decisions would be like old-style decisions. They would be binding only on the addressees. They would be adopted mainly by the Council and the Commission. Recommendations and opinions would continue as before.

There would also be a clearer system for the division of powers between the Union and the Member States. The foundation of the system would still be the principle of conferred powers: competences not conferred on the Union would remain with the Member States.[23] Union competence would be divided into three categories: exclusive competence, shared competence and special cases. In areas in which the Union enjoyed exclusive competence, it alone would be able to adopt legally binding acts. Member States would be able to do so only where

18 *Ibid.*, Art. 7.
19 It is hard to see the point of the provision if they would not be obliged. However, the statement in Art. 7 that the proceedings must be brought "in accordance with their national legal system" suggests that it might depend on national law.
20 Art. 32.
21 Art. 33(1). Where so provided by the Constitution, they could also be adopted by the Parliament with the participation of the Council of Ministers, or by the Council of Ministers with the participation of the Parliament: see Art. 33(2).
22 Arts 32 and 34 to 36.
23 Art. 9(1) and (2).

they were empowered by the Union or where they acted in order to implement Union acts.[24] Where competence was shared, either the Union or the Member States would be able to adopt legally binding acts. However, the latter would be able to do so only if the Union had not already exercised its competence or if it had ceased to do so.[25] There would also be certain special cases: for example, the Union would have competence to promote and co-ordinate the economic and employment policies of the Member States, in particular by adopting broad guidelines.[26] The areas of exclusive Union competence are expressly set out in the draft Constitution.[27] They are fairly limited. All areas of Union competence not expressly stated to fall into another category would be shared.[28]

Chapter 5

If the proposals were accepted, the Court of Justice of the European Communities (European Court) would be renamed the "European Court of Justice".[29] The Court of First Instance would become the "High Court". The European Court of Justice, the High Court and any specialized courts that might be created would together make up the "Court of Justice". It is also proposed to establish a panel to vet candidates for appointment as judge or advocate general in the European Court of Justice or the High Court.[30] It would consist of seven persons chosen from among former members of the European Court of Justice and the High Court, members of national supreme courts and lawyers of recognized competence.

Chapter 8

The legal basis of the new Constitution would be exactly the same as that of the treaties it replaces. It would be established by a new treaty, the Treaty Establishing a Constitution for Europe, which would be a treaty just like any other. Its legal validity in each Member State would depend on the fact that it was ratified by that Member State as a treaty. Consequently, the general principles discussed in Chapter 8 would remain just as valid as before. Moreover, the new Constitution would make explicit that each Member State is free to leave the Union in accordance with the requirements of its own Constitution.[31] Normally, there would be an agreement between the Member State and the Union setting out the arrangements for withdrawal. The withdrawal would take effect

---

24 Art. 11(1).
25 Art. 11(2).
26 Art. 14.
27 Art. 12.
28 Art. 13(1).
29 Art. 28.
30 Art. III-262.
31 Art. 59.

when that agreement came into force. If no such agreement was concluded, it would take effect two years after the date on which the Member State notified the European Council of its intention to withdraw.

Chapter 9

It is proposed to have an express provision that the Constitution, and law adopted by the Union institutions acting within the powers conferred on them, would have primacy over Member State law.[32] The question who decides whether the Union institutions are acting within their powers would still be unresolved. The European Court would no doubt continue to take the view that it had the final say. The Member-State courts would disagree.

There is nothing new on direct effect; so the old law would probably continue to apply.

Chapter 12

The European Union would be given legal personality.[33] Under Article III-225, it would have competence to conclude an international agreement in the following cases:

- where the Constitution so provided;
- where the conclusion of an agreement was necessary in order to achieve, within the framework of the Union's policies, one of the objectives fixed by the Constitution;
- where there was provision for it in a binding Union legislative act; or
- where it affected one of the Union's internal acts.

Article 12(2) states that the Union's competence to conclude such an agreement would be exclusive in the following cases:

- where its conclusion was provided for in a legislative act of the Union;
- where its conclusion was necessary to enable the Union to exercise its internal competence;
- where its conclusion would affect an internal Union act.

Presumably, the Union would also have exclusive competence to conclude an international agreement in those areas in which it had exclusive internal competence — for example, the common commercial policy. Where the conclusion of the agreement fell within Article III-225 but not within Article 12, the power would be shared with the Member States.[34]

---

32 Art. 10(1).
33 Art. 6.
34 This would occur where the conclusion of the agreement was "necessary in order to achieve, within the framework of the Union's policies, one of the objectives fixed by the Constitution" (Art. III-225), but it was not "necessary to enable the Union to exercise its competence internally" (Art. 12(2)).

Chapter 13

It is proposed to state expressly that one of the objectives of the Union is to contribute to the strict observance and development of international law.[35]

Chapters 14–17

It is proposed that the Charter of Fundamental Rights should be legally binding on the European Union.[36] It is also proposed that the Union should seek accession to the European Convention on Human Rights.[37]

Chapter 18

A number of reforms are proposed regarding annulment actions (at present, Article 230 [173] EC).[38] The most significant concern the right of private persons to bring proceedings.[39] The first change would do away with the requirement that the applicant must establish that the challenged act is in substance a decision. All that would have to be established is that it was either addressed to him or was of direct and individual concern to him. As will be seen from Chapter 18, this simply follows the European Court's most recent case law.

Another proposal would, however, change the law with regard to the requirement of individual concern. Although private applicants would in general still have to establish individual concern, there would be an exception in the case of a "regulatory act". With regard to such an act, a private applicant would merely have to establish two things: that it was of direct concern to him and that it did not entail implementing measures. The former requirement has existed all along. The latter is new. It presumably means that the act must affect the applicant independently of any implementing measures.

Implementing measures would normally be adopted by the national authorities.[40] If the national authorities had a choice in the matter, the existence of such a choice (discretion) would mean that there was no direct concern (unless the authority had already exercised its choice). In such a case, standing would be excluded on the ground that the applicant was not directly concerned. Even if there was no choice (or if the national authority had already exercised its choice), the mere fact that implementing measures were necessary would mean that the applicant could no longer rely on the new rule. He would then

---

35 Art. 3(4). See also Art. III-193.
36 Art. 7(1).
37 Art. 7(2).
38 Art. III-270.
39 It is also proposed that acts of bodies and agencies of the Union intended to produce legal effects *vis-à-vis* third parties should be subject to judicial review.
40 Art. 36(1). In some cases, however, they may be adopted by the Commission or even the Council: Art. 36(2).

have to establish individual concern. The rationale of this is that if there are implementing measures, he can always challenge those. If, as would normally be the case, the implementing measures were adopted by the national authorities, the challenge would be in the national courts. In order to ensure that he could challenge them, another provision in the proposed Constitution[41] would require Member States to provide "rights of appeal"[42] sufficient to ensure effective legal protection in the field of Union law.

What are "regulatory acts"? It will be remembered from what was said above (with regard to Chapter 4) that it is proposed to set up a new system for the classification of Union acts. The primary division would be between legislative and non-legislative acts. Under the new proposals for annulment actions, private persons would still have to establish direct and individual concern if they wanted to challenge a legislative act. Non-legislative acts fall into two classes: European regulations and European decisions. It seems that "regulatory acts" would mainly consist of European regulations.[43] They would normally be adopted by the Commission. Their purpose would be to implement (and sometimes supplement) legislative acts.

Another difficulty is the meaning of "implementation". The problem is made clearer if one takes a couple of examples.

Example 1. Assume that a European regulation adopted by the Commission provides that wine may not be sold under a given designation. The sale of wine in a Member State under that designation, though in some sense unlawful, would nevertheless not constitute a criminal offence under Member-State law unless an appropriate national provision was adopted. Could a trader challenge the European regulation in the European Court without having to show individual concern? This would depend on whether the European regulation entailed implementing measures. Could one say that it did, because it could not be effectively enforced without Member-State legislation?

Example 2. Assume that a European law provides that fruit cannot be imported into the Union without an import licence. The licence is issued by the Member-State authorities but the European law empowers the Commission to give them directions as to when they should issue licences. Acting under this power, the Commission adopts a European regulation instructing the national authorities not to issue licences with regard to imports from a particular non-member State. The Member-State authorities then refuse to grant applications for imports from the State in question. Could an importer challenge the European regulation in the European Court without having to show individual

---

41 Art. 28(1) (second paragraph).
42 The phrase "rights of appeal" is a poor translation of the French "*voies de recours*". A better phrase would be "legal remedies". Judicial review would be the normal remedy.
43 It is not clear why the term "regulatory acts" was adopted in Art. III-270, when this is not one of the terms used in Art. 32. The Legal Experts Group at the IGC has said that it assumes that "regulatory acts" was intended to refer to non-legislative acts of general application. This would cover two classes of act: (a) regulations and (b) decisions without addressees. It therefore proposes that in the French text (the only one at present available) "*actes réglementaires*" (regulatory acts) be replaced with "*règlements ou décisions n'ayant pas de destinataires*" (regulations or decisions having no addressees) (see Doc. CIG 4/03 of 6 October 2003, pp. 428-429).

concern? This would depend on whether the refusal to issue the licence could be regarded as an "implementing measure".

It will be seen from these examples that it is not easy to say when an act does not "entail implementing measures".

It seems likely that the proposed amendments were the result of the *UPA* case. If so, the theory behind them is probably that the applicant must be given a remedy *either* in the European Court *or* in the national courts. If this is the rationale, it would make sense to say that a Union act entails implementing measures whenever it requires some measure on the part of the national authorities that the applicant could reasonably be expected to challenge in the national courts. The effect of Article 28(1) would be to impose a Union-law obligation on the Member States to permit such a challenge. This argument would suggest that a wide meaning should be given to "implementing measure", a meaning that would cover the situation in the two examples given above. If such an interpretation were adopted, the standing of private parties to bring annulment actions would be increased to only a limited extent.[44]

Conclusions

Despite the fanfare that accompanied its adoption, the draft Constitution was less ambitious than it looks. It is true that it would bring about major theoretical and conceptual changes. These would include:

- the abolition of the European Community and the establishment of the European Union as the vehicle for European integration;
- the reclassification of the legislative powers of the Union;
- the specification of the division of powers between the Union and the Member States;
- the acceptance that national parliaments have a role to play in the EU constitutional system; and
- the recognition that Member States have a right to withdraw.[45]

Other changes, however, would do no more than put down in the official text what has already been decided by the European Court. The statement that Union law prevails over Member-State law is an example.

If we look at the practical changes, it seems that, though significant, they would be no greater than those effected by many of the previous treaties. Most of them would be institutional. The establishment of the post of President of the European Council, and that of the Union Minister for Foreign Affairs, are examples. The new system of qualified majority voting in the Council and the reduction in the number of voting members of the Commission are even more

---

44 A case like *UPA* would not be affected by it, since, under the new system, the challenged measure would have been adopted in the form of a legislative act. (The regulation in *UPA* was adopted under Art. 37[43] EC. The equivalent provision in the proposed Constitution would be Art. III-127, which requires a European law or framework law.)

45 In practice, this has been the position all along.

important, though they were not scheduled to take effect until 2009. However, they were little more than a response to obvious defects in the present structure, defects that are in particular need of a remedy in view of the accession of the new Member States in 2004. All in all, it is probably fair to say that clarification, rather than innovation, was the most important feature of the proposals.

1 Introduction

With globalization, States are no longer the only actors on the world scene: they share the stage with international organizations. An international organization may be defined as an association of States that is created by international treaty and has personality under international law.[1] (Legal personality is the capacity to enjoy rights, enter into transactions and claim legal redress.)[2] Several international organizations have important roles in this book. Here, we introduce some of them.

The European Union[3]

Pride of place must be given to the EU. Some people feel that it is not an international organization at all, since its powers are so much greater than the general run of such organizations. They prefer to call it a "supranational" organization, to indicate that it does not merely operate in relations *between*[4] States, but has power *over*[5] them.

There is no general agreement as to what it means when one says that an organization is supranational, but the easiest way of explaining it is to say that the organization itself must have significant powers that can be exercised independently of its member states. The organization must be more than the member states acting together. It must be a force on its own. The EC bureaucracy, the Commission, has such powers. In contrast, the United Nations is supranational only to a small degree. Its Secretary General can do little without the support of major powers, such as the United States.

---

1 For a more refined definition, see that proposed by Sir Gerald Fitzmaurice in his report on the law of treaties presented to the International Law Commission in March 1956. He defined an international organization as "a collectivity of States established by treaty, with a constitution and common organs, having a personality distinct from that of its Member States, and being a subject of international law with treaty-making capacity". See [1956] II *Yearbook of the International Law Commission* 104 at 108. See also Bowett's *Law of International Organizations* (5th ed., 2001, by Philippe Sands and Pierre Klein), p. 16.
2 States also have personality under international law, but they are not created by treaty: their origin lies outside international law, though international law recognizes their existence.
3 Main website: http://www.europa.eu.int.
4 In Latin, *inter* means "between".
5 In Latin, *supra* means "above" or "over".

Panel 1.1 Member States of the European Union	
Member State	**Date joined**
Belgium	original member
Czech Republic	2004
Denmark	1973
Germany	original member
Estonia	2004
Greece	1981
Spain	1986
France	original member
Ireland	1973
Italy	original member
Cyprus	2004
Latvia	2004
Lithuania	2004
Luxembourg	original member
Hungary	2004
Malta	2004
Netherlands	original member
Austria	1995
Poland	2004
Portugal	1986
Slovenia	2004
Slovakia	2004
Finland	1995
Sweden	1995
United Kingdom	1973

Notes:
[1] The original members joined the ECSC in 1952, when the ECSC Treaty came into force, and the other Communities in 1958, when the EEC and Euratom Treaties came into force.
[2] The order in which the States are listed is alphabetical according to the name of each country in its own language. Thus, Belgium ("Belgique" in French or "België" in Dutch) comes before Austria ("Österreich" in German). This is the official EU way of doing it.

It is a mistake, however, to think that "supranational" is opposed to "international". Supranational organizations are one special kind of international organization, just as jet aircraft are one special kind of aircraft. The opposite of "supranational" is "intergovernmental", a word implying that the activity is carried out by a coalition of States without any supranational element.

The Member States of the European Union are listed in Panel 1.1. It is made up of two (originally, three) "Communities", and certain other activities. The Communities are: the European Coal and Steel Community (ECSC), which came into existence in 1952 and died a natural death in 2002;[6] the European Community (EC), originally called the "European Economic Community" (EEC), which began life in 1958;[7] and the European Atomic Energy Community, usually called "Euratom", which was created at the same time as the EC. The EC and Euratom are still very much in existence. The ECSC was established to deal with coal and steel, Euratom with atomic energy, and the EC with everything else. When the ECSC ceased to exist, the EC took over its activities. Both these Communities enjoy legal personality and, as we shall see, can enter into treaties. In this book we shall be concerned almost exclusively with the EC, the entity at the core of the EU.

In addition to the Communities, there are two activities that fall outside the scope of the Communities but are carried on within the framework of the EU. These are the common foreign and security policy (CFSP), and police and judicial co-operation in criminal matters.

A number of features distinguish the EU from international organizations of the traditional kind:

6 It was created by the Treaty Establishing the European Coal and Steel Community (ECSC Treaty, or Treaty of Paris), which was signed in 1951 and came into force in 1952. The treaty was concluded for a period of fifty years (Art. 97); therefore the ECSC ceased to exist in 2002.
7 It was created by the Treaty Establishing the European Economic Community (the famous Treaty of Rome), which was signed in 1957 and came into force in 1958. It was concluded for an unlimited period: Art. 312 [240].

- It can pass legislation, in many cases even if its Member States are not unanimous.
- This legislation is binding on the Member States and has to be applied by their courts.
- Its judicial organ, the European Court (officially known as the "Court of Justice of the European Communities"), can give rulings in cases originating in Member-State courts.
- The Member States are themselves subject to the compulsory jurisdiction of the Court in cases concerning the Treaties or Community legislation.

The institutions of the Community are located in Brussels, Luxembourg and Strasbourg. All the official languages of the Member States are official languages of the Community. In theory, all are equal. In practice, French and English are most used.

The Council of Europe[8]

The Council of Europe is often confused with the European Union. This confusion is made worse by the fact that when the most important organ of the EU, the Council, is meeting at its highest level (Heads of State or Government), it is called the "European Council". The Council of Europe is, however, quite distinct from the European Council and from the EU as a whole. It is older.[9] It was the original European organization and its foundation was partly inspired by Winston Churchill. It came into existence three years before the ECSC, the first of the European Communities, and its membership is much wider (over forty States, including Russia). All fifteen EU Member States are members of the Council of Europe. Its headquarters are in Strasbourg, and its official languages are English and French.

To a large extent, the Council of Europe keeps a low profile. One of its achievements is of such importance, however, that it puts it in the forefront of international organizations. This is the European Convention on Human Rights, the most significant international instrument of its kind in the world. Its noteworthy feature is that it is actually respected – not completely, it must be admitted, but to a large extent. This is due to two features. The first is that it has its own court, the European Court of Human Rights, to whose jurisdiction the Contracting States are subject. The second is that individuals who think a Contracting State has infringed their human rights can go directly to the court to bring proceedings against that State. This latter feature, the right of individual petition, is what makes the Convention effective. It is one of the great advances in international adjudication and constitutes the main supranational element in the Council of Europe. Even the European Union's court, the European Court of Justice, cannot hear complaints from individuals against

---

8 Main website: http://www.coe.int.
9 It was founded in 1949.

Member States. The European Convention on Human Rights and the European Court of Human Rights will be discussed in detail in Part V of this book.

The North Atlantic Treaty Organization[10]

NATO was founded with the adoption of the North Atlantic Treaty in 1949. It was an alliance between North America (the United States and Canada) and Western Europe. Its purpose was to prevent the Soviet Union from overrunning Western Europe. The fact that it never went into action against the USSR is an indicator of its success. When the Cold War ended, it changed its role.[11] It now acts as a self-appointed international policeman. Its most significant operations so far have been in Yugoslavia, where it has helped to stabilize the situation in Bosnia, following the civil war between Bosnians, Serbs and Croats. It has also intervened in Kosovo where it forced Serbia to withdraw its troops. It has no significant supranational element.

The World Trade Organization[12]

The foundations of the present world trading system were laid in 1947 when twenty-two States negotiated the General Agreement on Tariffs and Trade.[13] The GATT was intended to be merely temporary – until the International Trade Organization was established.[14] Unfortunately, the latter event never happened. Therefore the GATT – which in theory was just an agreement, not an international organization[15] – expanded to fill the gap. It did this with great success for almost half a century until the World Trade Organization was established in 1995.[16]

Today the WTO has over 140 members (including China and Taiwan, which joined in 2001) and is acknowledged as a major force in the world economy. It is steadily breaking down trade barriers so that one day the whole world will perhaps be one big common market. It is thus trying to achieve on a global scale what the EU has attained on a regional basis.

The main supranational element in the WTO is its dispute-settlement system, which provides for compulsory and binding arbitration of trade disputes between Member States. There is an appeal from the findings of arbitral panels

---

10 Main website: http://www.nato.int.
11 It also started admitting former Warsaw-Pact countries. Its members are now (April 2003): Belgium, Canada, Czech Republic, Denmark, France, Germany, Greece, Hungary, Iceland, Italy, Luxembourg, Netherlands, Norway, Poland, Portugal, Spain, Turkey, United Kingdom and United States. Seven more countries are expected to join shortly: Bulgaria, Estonia, Latvia, Lithuania, Romania, Slovakia and Slovenia.
12 Main website: http://www.wto.int. See also: http://www.gatt.org.
13 Opened for signature on 30 October 1947.
14 Technically, the GATT never actually came into force, but was given effect by a Protocol of Provisional Application.
15 The Agreement itself contains no mention of a secretariat.
16 The GATT was revamped and brought under the WTO.

to a permanent Appellate Body. The workings of this system will be considered in Chapter 5.

The North American Free Trade Agreement[17]

The NAFTA came into effect in 1994. The parties are Canada, Mexico and the United States. It is a development of the earlier free trade agreement between Canada and the US. It is less ambitious than the EC, aiming at the establishment of a free trade area rather than a common market,[18] and has a limited institutional structure. There is a Free Trade Commission, composed of cabinet-level representatives of the three countries, and a Secretariat to administer the dispute-resolution system. The latter is the main supranational element and is based on arbitration similar to that under the WTO. It too will be discussed in Chapter 5.

The United Nations[19]

The UN is the premier world organization. Membership is open to all countries and it deals with a wide range of matters. Its shortcomings are well known, but few would want to see it disappear. Its main organs are the General Assembly, where all Member States are represented and have equal voting rights, and the Security Council. The latter consists of fifteen members. Ten are elected by the General Assembly. The remaining five – China, France, Russia, the United Kingdom and the United States – are permanent members. They are guaranteed a seat and, in addition, have the right of veto.

The primary task of the Security Council is to maintain peace and security. It can take decisions by a majority vote, provided that none of the permanent members casts a veto. During the Cold War period, and to a lesser extent since then, the veto system has paralysed it, since most proposed actions are vetoed by one or other of the permanent members. Owing to a misjudgment by the Soviet Union, the Security Council was able to adopt a resolution in 1950 on the Korean War, when it lent its authority to action by the United States and its allies to prevent North Korea from overrunning South Korea. More recently, it has undertaken operations in, for example, Kuwait/Iraq, Somalia, Yugoslavia and East Timor. The UN headquarters are in New York.

The International Court of Justice[20] is the principal judicial organ of the UN. It has its seat in The Hague and is a continuation of the Permanent Court of International Justice, which was established in 1922 and functioned until 1946,

---

17 NAFTA secretariat website: http://www.nafta-sec-alena.org.
18 A free trade area aims to ensure that goods produced in one member state can move freely to the other member states. A common market goes further. In particular, it aims to ensure that goods imported into one member state can be freely re-exported to the other member states. This requires it to have common rules on imports from the outside.
19 Main website: http://www.un.org.
20 Main website: http://www.icj-cij.org.

Panel 1.2   International organizations, international courts and their acronyms

CoE = Council of Europe

Court of Justice of the European Communities: official name of the European Court of Justice

EAEC = European Atomic Energy Community

EC = European Community

ECJ = European Court of Justice

ECSC = European Coal and Steel Community

ECtHR = European Court of Human Rights

EEC = European Economic Community

EU = European Union

Euratom = European Atomic Energy Community

European Atomic Energy Community: part of the European Union

European Coal and Steel Community: until July 2002, part of the European Union

European Court of Human Rights: interprets and enforces the European Convention on Human Rights

European Court of Justice: judicial organ of the European Union

European Economic Community: former name of the European Community

European Community: part of the European Union

GATT = General Agreement on Tariffs and Trade

General Agreement on Tariffs and Trade: now falls under the WTO

ICJ = International Court of Justice

International Court of Justice: principal judicial organ of the United Nations

NAFTA = North American Free Trade Agreement

NATO = North Atlantic Treaty Organization

UN = United Nations

WTO = World Trade Organization

when it was replaced by the International Court of Justice. It can hear cases only if the parties consent to its jurisdiction. As we shall see in Chapter 6, its judgments are not always obeyed.

The focus of this book

The international organizations mentioned in this chapter are listed in Panel 1.2. They all play important roles in the world today. The pages that follow will not, however, attempt to cover them all. We shall focus on the European Union and on those organizations that are closely related to it, either geographically or functionally.

Further reading

Bowett's *Law of International Organizations* (Sweet & Maxwell, London, 5th ed., 2001, by Philippe Sands and Pierre Klein).

PART I
THE EUROPEAN UNION

2

Origins

The beginning

The Community enterprise began on 18 April 1951 when the six original Member States – three large countries[1] and three small[2] – met in Paris to sign the Treaty Establishing the European Coal and Steel Community (ECSC).[3] The Treaty was the result of a French initiative, the "Schuman Plan", the announcement[4] of which by the French Foreign Minister, Robert Schuman, marked a change in French policy towards Germany from one of attempted subordination to one of friendship.[5] Right from the start, the Community was based on a Franco-German partnership: the Schuman Plan expressly envisaged a pooling by France and Germany of their coal and steel resources. Other countries were invited to join, but only Germany was mentioned by name.

It is also clear that, at least in Schuman's eyes,[6] the fundamental purpose of the Plan was political. The Schuman Declaration emphasised that it constituted the first step towards a European federation, the establishment of which was "indispensable for the preservation of peace". It also said that the pooling of production that would occur under the ECSC would show that "any war between France and Germany would become, not merely unthinkable, but physically impossible".

There were various reasons why coal and steel were chosen for the new project. Then known as "heavy industry", this sector of the economy was regarded as the foundation on which other sectors, including armaments, rested. A major employer, it was in economic difficulties. Its geographical distribution meant that a common approach made particular sense.[7] Moreover, the

---

1 Germany, France and Italy.
2 Belgium, the Netherlands and Luxembourg.
3 It entered into force on 23 July 1952 and terminated fifty years later, in 2002. For the background, see William Diebold, *The Schuman Plan: A Study in Economic Co-Operation, 1950–1959* (Praeger, New York, and Oxford University Press, 1959).
4 On 9 May 1950.
5 For the full text, see Margaret Carlyle (ed.), *Documents on International Affairs, 1949–1950* (Oxford University Press, London, 1953), pp. 315–317.
6 It seems that the Plan was conceived hurriedly and in some secrecy; it was agreed by the Cabinet after only a brief discussion: Diebold, note 3 above, p. 8.
7 Geographically fairly compact but divided between four states, the industry was concentrated in southern Belgium, Luxembourg, northern France, Lorraine, the Saar and the Ruhr. Schuman was himself from Lorraine and had grown up at a time when that territory was ruled by Germany.

Panel 2.1 Key dates in the history of the European Union	
1950	Schuman Declaration
1951	ECSC Treaty signed in Paris
1952	ECSC Treaty in force
1957	EEC and Euratom Treaties signed in Rome
1958	EEC and Euratom Treaties in force
1973	Denmark, Ireland and the United Kingdom become members
1981	Greece becomes a member
1986	Spain and Portugal become members
1992	Treaty on European Union (Maastricht Agreement) signed
1993	Treaty on European Union in force
1995	Austria, Finland and Sweden become members
1997	Treaty of Amsterdam signed
1999	Treaty of Amsterdam in force
2000	Treaty of Nice signed
2002	The euro becomes the currency of twelve Member States
2002	ECSC Treaty expires (ECSC functions transferred to the EC)
2003	Ten new Member States agree to join

idea of an international solution had political advantages both with regard to the Saar, a territory of importance for these industries which was then in contention between France and Germany,[8] and to the policy of rebuilding the German economy, a policy supported by the United States and the United Kingdom but until then opposed by France.[9] Boldly conceived, the Schuman Plan thus operated on three levels: it solved political and economic problems in the short term; it provided a sound basis for France's relations with Germany in the medium term; and it laid the foundations for a new Europe in the long term. Although the ECSC was limited to a comparatively small sector of the economy, its creation was of lasting significance because the European Union of today is based on the blueprint of 1951, a blueprint which made an original contribution to the solution of international problems through the establishment of an international organization.

At that time, international organizations generally had an institutional structure designed to provide a framework for intergovernmental co-operation. One might therefore expect some sort of council, where the member states were represented, together with a secretariat to prepare the ground for meetings of the council and to carry out its decisions. The normal rule was that member states were not bound by decisions of the organization unless they consented. Consequently, decisions of the council had to be unanimous if they were to be binding, though there might be provision for majority voting if dissidents were free to declare that they would not accept the outcome.[10]

As soon as one looks at the structure of the Community, however, it is apparent that its founders rejected this concept. From its very inception, the Community was intended to be more than a traditional intergovernmental organization. It is equally clear, on the other hand, that the federal model was also rejected. The basic principle of a federation is that there is a democratic

---

8 It was reunited with Germany in 1957.

9 The International Agreement on the Ruhr (1949) provided (at French insistence) for Allied supervision of the coal and steel industry of the Ruhr through an international institution, the International Authority for the Ruhr, on which the US, the UK, France and Germany had three votes each and the Benelux countries one each. However, this did not function effectively, because the Germans were naturally against it, and the British and Americans doubted the wisdom of trying to keep Germany indefinitely in a position of subordination. The ECSC provided an acceptable substitute; indeed, prominent German politicians had called for such an alternative as early as 1948: Diebold, note 3 above, pp. 35–37.

10 NAFTA and the WTO are still based on this pattern.

legislature, elected by the people of the federation, which enacts its laws. There is an executive, which is either chosen by the legislature, or elected by the people. An essential feature of a federation is that the federal institutions exercise power independently of the states, a feature that is acceptable because they obtain their legitimacy directly from the people.

The distinguishing characteristic of the Community is that it is founded on neither of these models. The framers of the ECSC Treaty found a third way, one in which the Community was governed by an institution, the High Authority, which was independent of the Member States but which did not derive its power from democratic elections. This was acceptable because the Treaty itself laid down the programme it was to pursue and the objectives it was to attain. The Member States agreed to these when they signed the Treaty. Having done so, they were not at liberty to block the implementation of the programme, even though particular aspects might be contrary to their interests. True enough, there was a Council of Ministers, in which the Member States were represented, and which looked like the deliberative body of a typical intergovernmental organization; but this was intended to deal with unforeseen problems and major crises. The day-to-day running of the Community was in the hands of the High Authority, the members of which, though chosen by the national governments, were independent of them during their terms of office.

Since the High Authority was independent of the national governments and was not subject to direct democratic control, it was necessary to have some alternative mechanism to prevent it from abusing its authority. A Court of Justice was therefore established with the power to annul any act of the High Authority that was contrary to the Treaty and generally to ensure that the law was observed. Provision was also made for an Assembly, the members of which were to be designated by the national parliaments from among their members. It was largely without power, and in no way resembled the legislature of a federation, but it could force the resignation of the members of the High Authority if a motion of censure was passed by a two-thirds majority.[11] However, if it exercised this power – which it never did – it had no say in the appointment of their successors; moreover, the existing members would remain in office until the Member States made new appointments.[12]

The EEC and Euratom

When it became clear that the ECSC was a success, the Member States applied the same formula to the remaining sectors of the economy. Instead of merging the ECSC into a wider Community, however, they created two new Communities operating alongside the ECSC – Euratom, covering atomic energy, and the European Economic Community (EEC), which covered all other areas of the

11 Art. 24 ECSC.
12 Art. 10, last paragraph, ECSC.

economy.[13] The result was that there were three separate Communities, each with its own powers and functions.

The two new Communities had the same structure as the ECSC, the High Authority being replaced by a body known as the Commission.[14] The aim of the EEC, however, was much wider and less precisely defined than that of the ECSC, partly because its area of operation was so much broader and partly because its objectives could be attained only in the long term. As a result, its institutions had to be given wider and more general powers. Since the Member States were unwilling to confer such powers on a body they could not control, the position of the Council was enhanced at the expense of the Commission: while in the ECSC the High Authority was the main law-making organ, the EEC Treaty provided for legislation to be adopted by the Council on a proposal from the Commission. The result was to dilute the supranational character of the Community at the same time as its scope was widened.

It might be thought that the shift in power from the Commission (High Authority) to the Council would have solved the problem of legitimacy, since the Council consisted of representatives of the national governments, which were themselves subject to democratic control at the national level. At first, this may have seemed to be the case. However, as ever-increasing areas of policy were taken over by the Community, it became apparent that the effect on the national governmental systems was to transfer power from the national par-liaments to the national executives, since decisions that had previously been taken by the parliaments were now taken by the national governments meet-ing in the Council. Moreover, the *method* of decision making was also different. Debate in the national parliaments has traditionally been open and widely reported in the press. Discussions in the Council, on the other hand, were con-ducted in strict secrecy, which meant that the public could not always be sure which side their own government had supported. This led some governments to see the handing over of policy areas to the EEC as a convenient means of avoiding the blame for unpopular decisions. A government could even oppose a policy in public but secretly support it in the privacy of the Council chamber. It could then claim to have been forced to give in by pressure from the oth-ers. In these circumstances, *ex post facto* control by the national parliaments was difficult: once made, a diplomatic deal in the Council could not easily be overturned. Moreover, the rule that Community law prevails over national law, a rule not found in the Treaties but laid down by the European Court, ensured that legislation adopted by the Council could not be challenged at national level. This shift in the method of legislating from open debate in the national parliaments to the secret bargaining sessions of the Council is one

---

13 The EEC and Euratom Treaties were signed in Rome on 25 March 1957 and entered into force on 1 January 1958.
14 At first, the High Authority continued in existence to run the ECSC, and two new bodies – both called "the Commission" – were created to run the EEC and Euratom. Subsequently, these three bodies were merged into one body, called "the Commission". This was done by a new treaty, the Merger Treaty 1965 (officially, the Convention Establishing a Single Council and a Single Commission of the European Communities). The Treaty also merged the original three Councils into one. Right from the start, there has been only one Court and one Assembly (Parliament).

of the causes of the popular conception that the Community is the enemy of democracy.[15]

The European Court too changed its role. As we have seen, its original function was to control the High Authority. It retained this role, being given the power to hear actions against Community institutions, in particular the Commission and Council, when they infringed Community law. However, it was also given the function of controlling the Member States. As we shall see, it can hear actions against them when they infringe Community law. The problem of enforcing these judgments is considered in Chapter 6.

An ever closer union

Since the EEC and Euratom Treaties came into force, nine new States had joined the Community by 2003. Ten more are expected to join in 2004. There have been twelve major Community treaties,[16] which have either given new powers to Community institutions or provided for the admission of new Member States. The deepening (greater powers) and widening (new members) of the Community has thus been continuous ever since it was established. No doubt it will continue in the future, in line with the Preamble to the EEC Treaty, which said that the Member States were then laying the foundations of "an ever closer union among the peoples of Europe". Unlike a normal international organization, therefore, the Community is not something that exists in more or less the same form over an extended period of time, so that once a country has come to terms with it, it can turn its attention to other things: the Community is constantly developing and the process of adjustment must also be continuous. Moreover, these developments are not the result only of Treaty amendments accepted by the Member States. Some have been engineered by the European Court, which has moulded the law to hasten the process of integration.

The Community and the Union

The Treaty on European Union (Maastricht Agreement) brought about changes in nomenclature. The European Economic Community (EEC) was renamed "the European Community" (EC),[17] a term which had previously been applied

---

15 Whether the problem can be solved by the grant of greater powers to the European Parliament is considered below.
16 The Merger Treaty 1965; the First Budgetary Treaty 1970; the First Accession Treaty 1972 (by which Denmark, Ireland and the United Kingdom joined the Community); the Second Budgetary Treaty 1975; the Second Accession Treaty 1979 (by which Greece joined the Community); the Third Accession Treaty 1985 (by which Spain and Portugal joined the Community); the Single European Act 1986; the Treaty on European Union 1992 (Maastricht Agreement); the Fourth Accession Treaty 1994 (by which Austria, Finland and Sweden joined the Community); the Treaty of Amsterdam 1997; the Treaty of Nice 2000; and the Fifth Accession Treaty 2003 (by which Cyprus, the Czech Republic, Estonia, Hungary, Latvia, Lithuania, Malta, Poland, Slovakia and Slovenia are due to join). If the Act (annexed to Council Decision 76/787) concerning the election of the representatives of the Assembly by direct universal suffrage, OJ 1976, L278/1, is to be regarded as a treaty, there have been thirteen major treaties since the EEC and Euratom Treaties.
17 Art. 8 [G(1)].

(unofficially) to the whole European enterprise. The EEC Treaty then became the EC Treaty. Two new areas of activity were put on a firmer footing – the Common Foreign and Security Policy, and Co-operation in the Fields of Justice and Home Affairs (renamed in the Treaty of Amsterdam "Police and Judicial Co-operation in Criminal Matters"). Activities in these two areas are conducted on an intergovernmental basis: the Court is generally prohibited from interfering and the Commission and Parliament are largely onlookers. The European enterprise is now seen as having a tripartite structure: the first "pillar" consists of the Communities (originally three – EC, ECSC and Euratom – but, since the demise of the ECSC in 2002, now only two); the second pillar is the Common Foreign and Security Policy; and the third pillar is Police and Judicial Co-operation in Criminal Matters. As we have seen, these three pillars together constitute the European Union, an entity created by the Treaty on European Union.[18]

The Community today

On 1 January 2002, a single currency, the euro, was introduced in twelve of the Member States. Most of the former Communist countries in Central and Eastern Europe – though not Russia, Belarus and the Ukraine – are lining up to join. Though one cannot foresee the future, there is no doubt that the enterprise begun so hesitantly fifty years ago has been a success.

The latest development is the so-called "European Convention", also known as the "Convention on the Future of Europe".[19] This body, which consists of representatives of the Member States and the applicant Member States, the national parliaments (including those of the applicants), the European Parliament and the Commission, is chaired by Valéry Giscard d'Estaing, former President of France. Its task is to draw up a draft Constitutional Treaty to propose to the Member States. The most recent developments in this regard are summarized on pp. xxxviii *et seq.* above.

A Community of interests

A joint enterprise, whether political or economic, flourishes only if it is based on a community of interests. What is the community of interests that makes the European Community possible? Since it was originally a French idea, we shall start with France.

France ✓

For France, the greatest prize has always been political: the ending of what the Schuman Declaration called the century-old conflict between France and

---

18 Art. 1 [A] TEU.
19 Here "convention" does not mean "treaty", but instead refers to a "meeting" or "congress".

Germany. Three times in the previous hundred years, France had fought Germany. Defeated by Prussia in 1870, France was able – with British assistance – to hold the German advance in 1914, and ultimately, when the United States entered the war, to gain victory – though at a terrible cost in lives. She then pursued a policy towards Germany whose harshness was regarded by some as partly responsible for the rise of Hitler, an event that in turn led to the attack of 1940, when France surrendered and was occupied. Although Germany was eventually defeated, this was achieved by the Soviet Union, the United States and the United Kingdom: (Free) France played only a minor role.

After World War II, it was clear to those Frenchmen far-sighted enough to see such things that in the long term France could not contain Germany by military means alone. That had been tried and had failed. Divided and defeated, with her industry in ruins, Germany might not have seemed a threat in 1950; nevertheless, her potential – economic, military and political – was inevitably greater than that of France. Today, this potential has been realized: stronger economically and financially than France, and with a significantly greater population, Germany is the leading nation of Western Europe. Only in the military sphere, where the possession of nuclear weapons still gives her the advantage, can France claim pre-eminence.

In this situation, France could have allied herself with the United Kingdom and the United States against Germany. This was the policy that had been pursued during the two World Wars. In 1950, however, the United States and the United Kingdom saw the Soviet Union as the main enemy and needed Germany's support to meet the Communist threat; they were not, therefore, disposed to join with France in an anti-German alliance. In these circumstances, Schuman's idea of not merely forming an alliance with Germany, but of seeking to merge France and Germany in a European federation, whose institutions France hoped to control, was masterly. If successful, it would permanently eliminate the German threat and eventually allow Europe to act independently of both the United States and the Soviet Union.

Though France's confidence in this strategy has fluctuated over the years – de Gaulle believed in partnership with Germany,[20] but was hostile to European supranationalism – it has nevertheless brought rewards. Without the German relationship, France's influence in the Community would be diminished; without the Community, France would carry less weight in the world. Moreover, France has been able to shape the Community to her own advantage. French is the working language of the Community institutions, and the emphasis in the early days on agriculture was particularly beneficial to France, the largest agricultural producer in the Community. The only anxiety in the long term is that the partnership with Germany may not survive the shift in the balance of power between the two countries.

---

20 This was cemented by the Franco-German Treaty of Co-operation, signed in 1963 by de Gaulle and Adenauer.

Germany

It is easy to see why Germany accepted the Schuman Plan. In 1950, West Germany was not a fully sovereign state: her territory was occupied by the United Kingdom, France and the United States, and her government was subject to restrictions, both military and political. The legacy of Nazism still determined the way other countries looked at her. Germany was not a normal country, accepted as such by the community of nations. Regaining this position was one of her foremost objectives. When Schuman proposed the ECSC, the German coal and steel industry was subject to international control. The ECSC was also a form of international control, but in it Germany was treated as a normal country, not as an outcast. Indeed, the French made clear that politically Germany had a special status as France's partner. Joining the ECSC was thus a step on the road towards normality.

Today, circumstances have changed. Germany has regained her position in the international community and the long search for respectability is over. However, all the old suspicions would rise up again if Germany modified her pro-European stance. Moreover, Community membership serves German interests in other ways: Germany is now the dominant country in Western Europe and, together with France, leads the Community; the Community is thus an instrument that can be used to exert influence over other countries, both in the Community and outside it. Given her power and position, it is more an instrument she can use than an instrument that can be used against her. Moreover, as the dominant industrial and financial power in Europe, she derives particular benefit from the single market. Thus, though some Germans may resent the extent to which the financial burden of the Community has come to rest on their shoulders, pro-European sentiment is still the prevailing orthodoxy.

United Kingdom

The United Kingdom is a country that has not been invaded by a foreign army for a thousand years. She does not fear Germany, as France does. Her traditional policy has been to maintain a balance of power among the major continental states, so that no one country could become sufficiently strong to constitute a threat. Thus, when Napoleon was striving for hegemony, the United Kingdom supported the anti-French alliance of Germany and Russia; when first the Kaiser and then Hitler sought dominance, she supported the anti-German powers, France and Russia. Beyond this, the United Kingdom has traditionally sought to avoid continental entanglements; instead, she has looked overseas to the English-speaking countries she founded and which were originally peopled by British emigrants. In the past, the Commonwealth formed the ideal trading area, the overseas countries supplying food and raw materials in exchange for British manufactures. In two World Wars, Commonwealth and British soldiers fought side by side in Europe, Africa and Asia.

After World War II, however, this relationship began to break down. The Commonwealth countries started developing their own manufacturing industry and introduced tariffs to protect it. The "special relationship" with the United States weakened as the disparity in power between the two countries became more marked. When the Commonwealth ceased to be a meaningful entity, the United Kingdom, which had spurned the Community when it was first established, began to rethink her policy.

As a major exporter and traditional protagonist of free trade, the United Kingdom did not want to be excluded from one of the world's foremost trading blocs. Since joining the Community, she has enthusiastically embraced its free market aspects. Other aspects, however, have not been to her liking. Since she is a major food-importing country, the Common Agricultural Policy has been against her interests. Under it, continental – mainly French – producers are doubly subsidized by the UK: the UK consumer subsidizes them by paying higher prices for food, and the UK taxpayer subsidizes them by paying for grants and the buying up of unwanted produce. The Community fisheries policy has been harmful to the UK fishing industry. Moreover, since the Community is run by Germany and France, the UK has felt an outsider. For these reasons, she has been a rather unenthusiastic Member State. Reluctant to leave, she has been cool towards further integration. Ideally, she would like the supranational side of the Community to be limited to free trade.

The Netherlands

It is interesting to compare British attitudes with those in the Netherlands. In some ways, they could not be more different: the Netherlands (together with Belgium and Luxembourg) is probably the strongest supporter of European federalism; the UK (together with Sweden and Denmark) is its strongest opponent. Yet, in many ways, the two countries have much in common. Both are seafaring nations; both had overseas empires, which they once saw as the focus for their foreign investment; and both are mercantile countries living by international trade.

However, the Netherlands is a continental country. Her law is based on that of France – Napoleon imposed the French Civil Code on her when he conquered the Netherlands – and her culture is much less distinct from that of other continental countries than that of the UK. She lacks the strong overseas links that Britain has. She was overrun by Germany in World War II, an event made all the more traumatic by the fact that she had successfully remained neutral in World War I and had given refuge to the Kaiser after Germany's defeat. As a small but highly developed country, her economy is much more integrated with that of her neighbours than is the case with the UK. Economic links with Germany are especially close.

The Dutch, therefore, see the Community not only as a new trading area to replace their lost empire, but also as a means by which they can avoid becoming a satellite of Germany, with less influence than a German *Land*. A

Community run by France and Germany would not have this effect. Only a federal Europe run by independent supranational institutions would produce the desired result. As a small country, her freedom of action would be limited even if there were no Community. A truly federal Europe would not limit that freedom much more, while it would prevent the bigger countries from throwing their weight around. From the Dutch point of view, the ideal would be a European federation in which the Federal Republic of Germany ceased to exist and the German *Länder* were Member States in their own right.

Thus, her smaller size, her proximity to Germany (both geographical and economic), her closer ties with her continental neighbours and the absence of links of kinship and culture with non-European countries comparable to those enjoyed by the UK – these are the reasons why her policy towards the Community has taken a different course from that of the UK. It is possible that, when the UK first sought to join the Community, the Dutch hoped she would join them in fighting for a federal Europe as a way to counteract Franco-German domination. If they entertained this hope, they must have been sadly disillusioned.

Other countries

Belgium and Luxembourg are in a similar position to the Netherlands. Sweden has something (though certainly not everything) in common with the UK. Other countries have other interests and combinations of interests. For some, Community membership is prized as an indication that they are accepted as part of the West. For others (for example, Ireland and Greece), EU grants and subsidies are important. For Finland and some of the applicants from Eastern Europe, Community membership is a means of safeguarding their independence from Russia.[21] For all Member States, membership of an organization that is demonstrably successful, and which – at least until recently – has been seen as the gateway to economic growth, cannot be other than attractive. If the Community is destined to be the major force in Europe, it is better to be inside than outside.

Further reading

Diebold (William), *The Schuman Plan: A Study in Economic Co-Operation, 1950–1959* (Praeger, New York, and Oxford University Press, 1959).

---

21 Finland was ruled by Russia from 1807 to 1917, and relations with Russia have dominated Finnish foreign policy ever since.

3

Legislative institutions

The basic mechanism of the EC is the bipolar relationship between the Council and the Commission. The Parliament was an afterthought, though it is coming to play a greater role today. The interplay between the Council, representing the individual Member States, and the Commission, which is supposed to represent the common interest, makes the Community system unique. In this chapter and the next we shall consider this relationship, together with the role of the Parliament. These three bodies are the legislative institutions of the European Union.[1]

The Commission

We start with the Commission, because this is where the legislative procedure starts. The Commission has two main roles (see Panel 3.1). The first is to initiate new policies and the legislation needed to put them into effect. The second is to administer legislation once it is adopted. This gives it a certain law-enforcement role.[2] It also gives it a legislative role of another kind, since Community measures often delegate power to the Commission to adopt implementing measures, a kind of subordinate legislation intended to provide for the operation of the original measure.

These are the traditional roles of the Executive in most States, and the Commission's size (at present twenty) is not unlike that of a modern Cabinet. However, unlike the Executive in a democratic State, the Commission is chosen neither by the Parliament nor by the people. Before the Treaty of Nice, it was chosen by the Member States. Now, it is chosen by the Council, but these are the same people acting in a different capacity. The European Parliament must approve, but in practice the Parliament's influence has not so far been significant. The procedure will be explained below, when we come to discuss the Council.

---

1 There is also an Economic and Social Committee (ECOSOC), which represents trade unions, employers' organizations, consumers' organizations, etc., and a Committee of the Regions, which represents regions within Europe, but they do not have the status of institutions and their functions are purely advisory.
2 This role should not be exaggerated. Apart from ensuring that Member States comply with Community law (discussed in Chap. 6), it is limited to a small number of policies, of which the most important is competition (antitrust) law.

Panel 3.1   The Commission's functions

EC Treaty

Article 211 [155]

In order to ensure the proper functioning and development of the common market, the Commission shall:

- ensure that the provisions of this Treaty and the measures taken by the institutions pursuant thereto are applied;
- formulate recommendations or deliver opinions on matters dealt with in this Treaty, if it expressly so provides or if the Commission considers it necessary;
- have its own power of decision and participate in the shaping of measures taken by the Council and by the European Parliament in the manner provided for in this Treaty;
- exercise the powers conferred on it by the Council for the implementation of the rules laid down by the latter.

Panel 3.2   When Commissioners cease to hold office

EC Treaty

Article 215 [159]

Apart from normal replacement, or death, the duties of a Member of the Commission shall end when he resigns or is compulsorily retired.

A vacancy caused by resignation, compulsory retirement or death shall be filled for the remainder of the Member's term of office by a new Member appointed by the Council, acting by a qualified majority. The Council may, acting unanimously, decide that such a vacancy need not be filled.

In the event of resignation, compulsory retirement or death, the President shall be replaced for the remainder of his term of office. The procedure laid down in Article 214(2) [158(2)] shall be applicable for the replacement of the President.

Save in the case of compulsory retirement under Article 216 [160], Members of the Commission shall remain in office until they have been replaced or until the Council has decided that the vacancy need not be filled, as provided for in the second paragraph of this Article.

Article 216 [160]

If any Member of the Commission no longer fulfils the conditions required for the performance of his duties or if he has been guilty of serious misconduct, the Court of Justice may, on application by the Council or the Commission, compulsorily retire him.

Note: See also Art. 217(4), Panel 3.6, below (resignation at the request of the President).

Although the Council appoints the members of the Commission, it has no power to dismiss them during their term of office (five years). Only the European Parliament can do that. As we shall see below, this is carried out by a motion of censure. If passed, such a motion forces the whole Commission to resign – though they remain in office until their successors are appointed. The Parliament cannot force individual Commissioners to resign. However, if an individual Commissioner is no longer able to fulfil his duties, or if he is guilty of serious misconduct, the European Court can make him retire. This procedure is set in motion by either the Council or the Commission itself. The relevant provisions are to be found in Articles 215 [159] and 216 [160] EC, set out in Panel 3.2.

An amendment brought in by the Treaty of Nice provides that a Commissioner must resign if so requested by the President of the Commission,

Panel 3.3 Membership of the Commission

EC Treaty

Article 213 [157]

1. The Commission shall consist of 20 Members, who shall be chosen on the grounds of their general competence and whose independence is beyond doubt.

The number of Members of the Commission may be altered by the Council, acting unanimously. Only nationals of Member States may be Members of the Commission.

The Commission must include at least one national of each of the Member States, but may not include more than two Members having the nationality of the same State.

2. The Members of the Commission shall, in the general interest of the Community, be completely independent in the performance of their duties.

In the performance of these duties, they shall neither seek nor take instructions from any government or from any other body. They shall refrain from any action incompatible with their duties. Each Member State undertakes to respect this principle and not to seek to influence the Members of the Commission in the performance of their tasks.

The Members of the Commission may not, during their term of office, engage in any other occupation, whether gainful or not. When entering upon their duties they shall give a solemn undertaking that, both during and after their term of office, they will respect the obligations arising therefrom and in particular their duty to behave with integrity and discretion as regards the acceptance, after they have ceased to hold office, of certain appointments or benefits. In the event of any breach of these obligations, the Court of Justice may, on application by the Council or the Commission, rule that the Member concerned be, according to the circumstances, either compulsorily retired in accordance with Article 216 [160] or deprived of his right to a pension or other benefits in its stead.

provided that the latter has obtained the approval of the Commission as a whole (Article 217(4) EC, set out in Panel 3.6, below). This could be used where a Commissioner was guilty of incompetence or mismanagement, or where his activities were politically unacceptable.

Commissioners are not agents of their home States. They are not supposed to consult with their national governments to ask what policies they should support, nor are Member States supposed to give them instructions. This is set out in Article 213(2) [157(2)] EC (Panel 3.3). This principle is not always observed. In the nature of things, secret consultations do not normally become public knowledge.

Structure

The Treaty[3] says that there must be twenty Commissioners, at least one (but not more than two) from each Member State (Panel 3.3). The Council (acting unanimously) may increase the number of Commissioners and it is assumed that it will do so when the new Member States join in 2004. At present (2003), there are two Commissioners from each of the five largest States (France, Germany, Italy, Spain and the United Kingdom) and one from each of the others. When the new Member States join, Poland will probably get two Commissioners and the others one each. There will then be twenty-six Commissioners.

A Commission with twenty members is manageable, but if it gets too big, it will not function effectively. The Treaty of Nice lays down a two-stage plan

---

3 Art. 213(1) [157(1)] EC.

Panel 3.4 Composition of the Commission under the Treaty of Nice: first stage

Treaty of Nice: Protocol on the Enlargement of the European Union

Article 4

1. On 1 January 2005 and with effect from when the first Commission following that date takes up its duties, Article 213(1) [157(1)] of the Treaty establishing the European Community and Article 126(1) of the Treaty establishing the European Atomic Energy Community shall be replaced by the following:
    "1. The Members of the Commission shall be chosen on the grounds of their general competence and their independence shall be beyond doubt.
    The Commission shall include one national of each of the Member States.
    The number of Members of the Commission may be altered by the Council, acting unanimously."

Panel 3.5 Composition of the Commission under the Treaty of Nice: second stage

Treaty of Nice: Protocol on the Enlargement of the European Union

Article 4

2. When the Union consists of 27 Member States, Article 213(1) [157(1)] of the Treaty establishing the European Community and Article 126(1) of the Treaty establishing the European Atomic Energy Community shall be replaced by the following:
    "1. The Members of the Commission shall be chosen on the grounds of their general competence and their independence shall be beyond doubt.
    The number of Members of the Commission shall be less than the number of Member States. The Members of the Commission shall be chosen according to a rotation system based on the principle of equality, the implementing arrangements for which shall be adopted by the Council, acting unanimously.
    The number of Members of the Commission shall be set by the Council, acting unanimously."
    This amendment shall apply as from the date on which the first Commission following the date of accession of the twenty-seventh Member State of the Union takes up its duties.

3. The Council, acting unanimously after signing the treaty of accession of the twenty-seventh Member State of the Union, shall adopt:

– the number of Members of the Commission;

– the implementing arrangements for a rotation system based on the principle of equality containing all the criteria and rules necessary for determining the composition of successive colleges automatically on the basis of the following principles:

   (a) Member States shall be treated on a strictly equal footing as regards determination of the sequence of, and the time spent by, their nationals as Members of the Commission; consequently, the difference between the total number of terms of office held by nationals of any given pair of Member States may never be more than one;

   (b) subject to point (a), each successive college shall be so composed as to reflect satisfactorily the demographic and geographical range of all the Member States of the Union.

4. Any State which accedes to the Union shall be entitled, at the time of its accession, to have one of its nationals as a Member of the Commission until paragraph 2 applies.

---

to deal with this. The plan is set out in a protocol[4] to the Treaty of Nice, the Protocol on the Enlargement of the European Union. The first stage, provision for which is made by an amendment to the relevant treaty provisions laid down by Article 4(1) of the Protocol (Panel 3.4), is to restrict all States to one Commissioner each. As a *quid pro quo*, the larger States will get more votes in the Council (as explained below). The amendment will apply to the first new Commission to take up its duties after 1 January 2005. However, it cannot come into operation without a decision to this effect by the Council, acting

---

4 A protocol is an additional text added to a treaty. As regards the parties to it, it has the same force and effect as the treaty. All the Member States are parties to the Protocol on the Enlargement of the European Union.

Panel 3.6   Operation of the Commission

EC Treaty

Article 217

1. The Commission shall work under the political guidance of its President, who shall decide on its internal organisation in order to ensure that it acts consistently, efficiently and on the basis of collegiality.

2. The responsibilities incumbent upon the Commission shall be structured and allocated among its Members by its President. The President may reshuffle the allocation of those responsibilities during the Commission's term of office. The Members of the Commission shall carry out the duties devolved upon them by the President under his authority.

3. After obtaining the approval of the College, the President shall appoint Vice-Presidents from among its Members.

4. A Member of the Commission shall resign if the President so requests, after obtaining the approval of the College.

Article 218

1. The Council and the Commission shall consult each other and shall settle by common accord their methods of co-operation.

2. The Commission shall adopt its Rules of Procedure so as to ensure that both it and its departments operate in accordance with the provisions of this Treaty. It shall ensure that these rules are published.

Article 219

The Commission shall act by a majority of the number of Members provided for in Article 213 [157].
   A meeting of the Commission shall be valid only if the number of Members laid down in its Rules of Procedure is present.

---

unanimously. One Member State could, therefore, block it, though there would be repercussions if it did.

If the European Union enlarges to at least twenty-seven Member States, the second stage will come into operation. Provision for this is made by an amendment to the relevant treaty provisions laid down by Article 4(2) of the Protocol (Panel 3.5). Under it, Member States will no longer have a right to even one Commissioner. A system of rotation will apply. However, the Council, acting unanimously, must take a decision to bring it into force. It remains to be seen whether this will ever happen.

Operation

The internal workings of the Commission are laid down in Articles 217 [161] to 219 [163] EC (Panel 3.6). The Commission takes decisions by a simple majority, provided there is a quorum.

The Treaty of Nice strengthens the position of the President. It states that he decides on its internal organization – it is made up of various departments, called Directorates General – and that he gives individual Commissioners their responsibilities. In practice, this happened previously. The President has also been given the power to require a Commissioner to resign, though the Commission as a whole[5] must approve. This is intended to provide a means of removing Commissioners who engage in disreputable activities, or fail to do

---

5 This is the meaning of "the College" in Art. 217(4) EC.

their jobs properly. It is simpler than bringing formal proceedings before the European Court, something that has so far never happened.

Legislative powers

Delegated legislation. Although the Council is the main legislative organ of the Community, the Commission also enacts legislation. Most of it is delegated. Many regulations adopted by the Council do no more than lay down the principles and policies to be followed. The regulation will then delegate to the Commission the power to adopt implementing measures to fill in the details (see Article 202 [145] EC, set out in Panel 3.8, below). For example, an agricultural regulation may provide for a price-support system for a given category of produce, and lay down the formula to determine the price level at which the Community will intervene. The Commission will have the job of deciding when that level has been reached and of taking the necessary measures. This will be done by means of delegated legislation adopted by the Commission. Such a system is essential if the Community is to respond rapidly to changing economic circumstances. However, since the Council does not want to lose all control, the original regulation will often provide for a committee of representatives of the national governments to monitor what the Commission does.[6]

These committees go by various names – consultative committees, management committees or regulatory committees – depending on their powers. In all cases the Commission will be obliged to put proposed measures before the committee for its opinion. The effect of a negative opinion by the committee will depend on which variant of the system has been adopted. It may have no effect; it may simply allow the Council to override the Commission's measure; or it may bar the Commission from acting unless the Council has been invited to act and has not done so.[7]

Original Legislation. There are a small number of cases in which the EC Treaty gives the Commission original (non-delegated) legislative power. The nature of these powers was considered by the European Court in our first case.

> *European Union*
> **France, Italy and the United Kingdom v. Commission**
> **COURT OF JUSTICE OF THE EUROPEAN COMMUNITIES**
> Cases 188–190/80, [1982] ECR 2545; [1982] 3 CMLR 144

Background

Article 86 [90] EC concerns the application of Community rules on competition and State subsidies to monopolies and publicly owned industries. Its third paragraph provides:

---

6 See Council Decision 99/468/EC, OJ 1999 L184/23.
7 This system is jokingly referred to as "comitology", hence the nickname of the case, *European Parliament v. Council*, Case 302/87, [1988] ECR 5615, mentioned in Chap. 7.

The Commission shall ensure the application of the provisions of this Article and shall, where necessary, address appropriate directives or decisions to Member States.

Acting under this provision, the Commission adopted a directive, which was intended to ensure transparency (openness) in government subsidies for such undertakings. France, Italy and the United Kingdom brought proceedings to annul it. The United Kingdom put forward the argument that, under the system on which the Treaties were based, the Council was the legislature of the Community and the Commission was the executive. In most States, the executive has only limited legislative powers. It can adopt measures to give effect to existing laws, but cannot enact new laws: this is the province of the legislature. From this, the United Kingdom concluded that when Article 86 [90] gives the Commission power to adopt directives, its powers are limited to measures that concern the application of existing legislation in particular cases. Such measures would be executive in substance. Since the directive before the court sought to impose entirely new obligations, the United Kingdom considered that it was beyond the powers of the Commission.

Judgment

4. According to the United Kingdom, by adopting the contested Directive the Commission committed a breach of the very principles which govern the division of powers and responsibilities between the Community institutions. It is clear from the Treaty provisions governing the institutions that all original law-making power is vested in the Council, whilst the Commission has only powers of surveillance and implementation. That division of powers is confirmed by the specific enabling rules in the Treaty, virtually all of which reserve to the Council the power to adopt regulations and directives. The same division of responsibilities is to be found in particular in the rules on competition. Those provisions themselves confer functions of surveillance on the Commission, whereas it can legislate only within the limits of a specific and express power delegated to it by a measure of the Council.

5. Again according to the United Kingdom, the provisions of the Treaty which exceptionally confer on the Commission the power to issue directives must be interpreted in the light of the foregoing considerations. Commission directives are not of the same nature as those adopted by the Council. Whereas the latter may contain general legislative provisions which may, where appropriate, impose new obligations on Member States, the aim of the former is merely to deal with a specific situation in one or more Member States. As for Article 86(3) [90(3)], such a limited aim is suggested by the very wording of the provision, which states that the Commission is to "address" appropriate directives or decisions to Member States.

6. There is, however, no basis for that argument in the Treaty provisions governing the institutions. According to Article 7 [4], the Commission is to participate in carrying out the tasks entrusted to the Community on the same basis as the other institutions, each acting within the limits of the powers conferred upon it by the Treaty. Article 211 [155] provides, in terms which are almost identical to those used in Article 202 [145] to describe the same function of the Council, that the Commission is to have its own power of decision in the manner provided for in the Treaty. Moreover, the provisions of the chapter which lays down general rules concerning the effects and content of measures adopted by the institutions,

in particular those of Article 249 [189], do not make the distinction drawn by the United Kingdom between directives which have general application and others which lay down only specific measures. According to the first paragraph of that Article, the Commission, just as the Council, has the power to issue directives in accordance with the provisions of the Treaty. It follows that the limits of the powers conferred on the Commission by a specific provision of the Treaty are to be inferred not from a general principle, but from an interpretation of the particular wording of the provision in question, in this case Article 86 [90], analysed in the light of its purpose and its place in the scheme of the Treaty.

7. In that regard, it is not possible to draw any conclusions from the fact that most of the other specific provisions of the Treaty which provide a power to adopt general measures confer that power on the Council, acting on a proposal from the Commission. Nor can any distinction be drawn between provisions providing for the adoption of directives according to whether they use the word "issue" or "address". According to Article 249 [189], the directives as well as decisions, both of the Council and of the Commission, are addressed to parties which, in so far as directives are concerned, are necessarily Member States. In the case of a provision providing for the adoption of both directives and decisions addressed to Member States, the word "address" therefore simply constitutes the most appropriate common expression.

Comment

In this case, the European Court gave judgment in accordance with the strict wording of the treaties, rejecting any attempt to interpret them on the basis of their underlying scheme. As we shall see in Chapter 7, however, the European Court is all too happy to adopt this method when it suits its purpose.[8]

European Union
Germany, France, Netherlands, Denmark and United Kingdom v. Commission
COURT OF JUSTICE OF THE EUROPEAN COMMUNITIES
Cases 281, 283–285, 287/85, [1987] ECR 3203[9]

Background

Under what was then Article [118] EC[10] (see Panel 3.7), the Commission was given the task of promoting close co-operation with the Member States in certain social fields, including employment. To achieve this, the Commission was to arrange consultations with the Member States. Nowhere, however, did Article [118] give the Commission any legislative power. Despite this, it adopted Decision 85/381, which concerned immigration from outside the Community. The decision required Member States to provide the Commission with information on their policies and to enter into consultations. The decision was challenged by a number of Member States on various grounds. One ground was that Article [118] did not cover immigration. The European Court, however, ruled that, though it did not cover immigration as such, it did cover employment. Since migration from outside the Community can have an impact on

---

8 *Parti Ecologiste "Les Verts" v. European Parliament*, Case 294/43, [1986] ECR 1339.
9 For a comment, see Hartley, "The Commission as Legislator under the EEC Treaty" (1988) 13 ELRev. 122.
10 This provision has been both amended and renumbered. However, as the present version is significantly different, we will refer to it by the number it had at the time of the case. The square brackets indicate that this is not its present number.

Panel 3.7   Tasks of the Commission (original version)

EC Treaty (text applicable to *Germany, etc. v. Commission*)

Article [118]

Without prejudice to the other provisions of this Treaty and in conformity with its general objectives, the Commission shall have the task of promoting close co-operation between Member States in the social field, particularly in matters relating to:

– employment;

– labour law and working conditions;

– basic and advanced vocational training;

– social security;

– prevention of occupational accidents and diseases;

– occupational hygiene;

– the right of association, and collective bargaining between employers and workers.

To this end, the Commission shall act in close contact with Member States by making studies, delivering opinions and arranging consultations both on problems arising at national level and on those of concern to international organisations . . .

---

employment in the Community – for example, by driving down wage rates – Article [118] did to this extent cover immigration. The European Court, therefore, held that most parts of the decision fell within the field covered by Article [118]. The Member States, however, argued that Decision 85/381 was still invalid, since Article [118] did not give the Commission the power to adopt legislation.

Judgment

27. Since the contested decision falls only partly outside the social field covered by Article [118], it must be considered whether the second paragraph of Article [118], which provides that the Commission is to act, *inter alia*, by arranging consultations, gives it the power to adopt a binding decision with a view to the arrangement of such consultations.

28. In that connection it must be emphasized that where an Article of the EEC Treaty – in this case Article [118] – confers a specific task on the Commission it must be accepted, if that provision is not to be rendered wholly ineffective, that it confers on the Commission necessarily and *per se* the powers which are indispensable in order to carry out that task. Accordingly, the second paragraph of Article [118] must be interpreted as conferring on the Commission all the powers which are necessary in order to arrange the consultations. In order to perform that task of arranging consultations the Commission must necessarily be able to require the Member States to notify essential information, in the first place in order to identify the problems and in the second place in order to pinpoint the possible guidelines for any future joint action on the part of the Member States; likewise it must be able to require them to take part in consultations.

29. Indeed, the collaboration between Member States required by Article [118] is only possible within the framework of organized consultations. In the absence of any action to initiate it that collaboration might remain a dead letter, even though provision is made for it in the Treaty. Since the Commission was specifically given the task of promoting such collaboration and arranging it, it is entitled to initiate consultation procedures within the social field referred to in Article [118].

30. It must be borne in mind that that power of the Commission must be confined to arranging a procedure for the notification of information and consultation and that in the present stage of development of Community law the subject-matter of the notification and consultation falls within the competence of the Member States. It must also be pointed out that the power which the Commission seeks to exercise under Article [118] is simply a procedural one to set up the notification and consultation machinery which is to result in the adoption of a common position on the part of the Member States.

The court concluded by annulling certain provisions of the decision, but upheld most of it.

Comment

In the previous case, the court refused to listen to theories about the system of the Treaty as a means of discerning what the Member States intended. It simply applied the letter of the law. Here, however, it adopts a different approach. It applies a theory of reasonableness to determine what the Member States must have had in mind. The result is to give the Commission wider powers than those expressly laid down in the Treaty. Note how it did this. First, it said that if the Commission is given a task, it must by implication have the powers that are "indispensable" in order to carry it out, something that most people would regard as reasonable. In the next sentence, it changes "indispensable" to "necessary", a slightly weaker word. It then decides that it was necessary for the Commission to have legislative powers in order to promote co-operation.

By its very nature, however, co-operation must be voluntary. If it is done under compulsion, it is no longer co-operation. Admittedly, the Commission decision merely required the Member States to give it advance notice of their plans and to consult with it,[11] which presumably meant that they had to attend meetings. No doubt, it was highly desirable that the Member States should do these things, but was it necessary – still less indispensable – for them to be under a legal obligation to do so? The framers of the Treaty presumably thought not; otherwise, they would have given the Commission this power.

Assessment

In the early days, Commission officials were often idealists, who devoted themselves to Europe as a means of making the world a better place. Today, things have changed. Working for the Commission, with its low tax rates,[12] special perks[13] and security of tenure,[14] is regarded as a good career, especially by people from the poorer regions of the Community. In all too many cases, idealism

11 It actually went slightly further in that it attempted to lay down the outcome of the co-operation, but this part of the decision was annulled by the European Court.
12 Commission officials do not pay Member-State income tax. There is a special Community tax, but the rate is low. There are also various ways of obtaining goods, such as new cars, more cheaply than the ordinary citizen can do.
13 There are various special allowances, which can be manipulated to the official's benefit.
14 Any attempt to discipline a Commission official usually results in a lawsuit in the European Court. There is also a strong union movement, which insists on the right of officials to regular promotions, regardless of merit.

Panel 3.8 Functions and composition of the EC Council

EC Treaty

Article 202 [145]

To ensure that the objectives set out in this Treaty are attained the Council shall, in accordance with the provisions of this Treaty:

 – ensure co-ordination of the general economic policies of the Member States;

 – have power to take decisions;

 – confer on the Commission, in the acts which the Council adopts, powers for the implementation of the rules which the Council lays down. The Council may impose certain requirements in respect of the exercise of these powers. The Council may also reserve the right, in specific cases, to exercise directly implementing powers itself. The procedures referred to above must be consonant with principles and rules to be laid down in advance by the Council, acting unanimously on a proposal from the Commission and after obtaining the Opinion of the European Parliament.

Article 203 [146]

The Council shall consist of a representative of each Member State at ministerial level, authorised to commit the government of that Member State.

 The office of President shall be held in turn by each Member State in the Council for a term of six months in the order decided by the Council acting unanimously.

Article 204 [147]

The Council shall meet when convened by its President on his own initiative or at the request of one of its members or of the Commission.

Treaty on European Union

Article 4 [D]

The European Council shall provide the Union with the necessary impetus for its development and shall define the general political guidelines thereof.

 The European Council shall bring together the Heads of State or Government of the Member States and the President of the Commission. They shall be assisted by the Ministers for Foreign Affairs of the Member States and by a Member of the Commission. The European Council shall meet at least twice a year, under the chairmanship of the Head of State or Government of the Member State which holds the Presidency of the Council.

 The European Council shall submit to the European Parliament a report after each of its meetings and a yearly written report on the progress achieved by the Union.

---

has been replaced by arrogance. Corruption is not unknown.[15] Non-elected officials think they know what is best for the citizens of Europe, and tell them so in no uncertain terms. The Commission is supposed to represent the Community interest, but sometimes it seems more concerned with its own interest – its power and status – than that of the Community, which is really just the collective interest of the Member States and their peoples.

The Council

The Council represents the Member States. The national governments can choose whom they send to Council meetings, but the person chosen must have ministerial rank (Article 203 [146] EC, Panel 3.8). The choice will normally

---

15 Allegations that they tolerated large-scale fraud and corruption forced the resignation of the whole Commission in 1999 (see below). The official who blew the whistle on these malpractices, an accountant in the internal audit department, was subsequently given a formal reprimand for leaking sensitive documents.

depend on the subject matter on the agenda. If it is agriculture, for example, ministers of agriculture will be asked to go. If it is law, ministers of justice – in the case of the UK, the Secretary of State for Constitutional Affairs (Lord Chancellor) – will be sent. These specialized meetings of the Council are sometimes called "sectoral", "specialized" or "technical" Councils, as distinct from the "general" Council, which is attended by foreign ministers and is not limited to a specialist agenda. In law, there is only one Council, irrespective of who is attending. Politically, however, the general Council can be regarded as operating at a higher level, since matters that cannot be settled in the specialized Councils go up to the general Council where a trade-off between different sectors is possible. Thus, for example, the UK may give way to France on an agricultural matter in exchange for a concession in the financial area. The highest level of all is the European Council, which consists of the Heads of State or Government.[16] It is mainly concerned with basic policy issues (see Article 4 [D] TEU, set out in Panel 3.8).

A body called "COREPER" (officially, the Committee of Permanent Representatives)[17] carries on the functions of the Council, at one level below it. COREPER consists of the Member States' permanent representatives (ambassadors) to the Community. Its function is to prepare the ground for Council meetings. If agreement is reached in COREPER, the result is adopted in the Council without further discussion.

The Member States take it in turns to hold the presidency of the Council, which rotates at six-monthly intervals. The State with the presidency chairs meetings of the Council and all Council committees. It also acts for the Community in dealings with the outside world. Since the Member State holding the presidency sets the agenda for the next six months, that State has the opportunity to advance the policies it regards as most important. If it promoted its own self-interest too vigorously, however, it would be subject to criticism.

Voting

Voting is a perennial problem in all international organizations. A one-State-one-vote system would give Luxembourg the same voting power as the United States. If voting rights were based on population, however, China could outvote the whole of Europe and the United States together. The solution adopted by the United Nations is, as we have seen, to give States equal voting rights in the General Assembly, but to give veto rights to the permanent members in the Security Council.

The European Union has adopted a different compromise. The theoretical principle, laid down by Article 205(1) [148(1)] EC (Panel 3.9), is that each Member

---

16 France is represented by its Head of State, the President, and all the others by their Heads of Government. Thus the UK is represented by the Prime Minister (not the Queen) and Germany by the Federal Chancellor (not the President). This is because the French President is a political figure, while all the other Heads of State are above politics.
17 "COREPER" is the acronym of the French version of this name.

Panel 3.9   Voting in the Council (until 31 October 2004)

EC Treaty (as amended by Article 26 of the Act of Accession 2003)

Article 205 [148]

1. Save as otherwise provided in this Treaty, the Council shall act by a majority of its members.

2. Where the Council is required to act by a qualified majority, the votes of its members shall be weighted as follows:

       Belgium 5
       Czech Republic 5
       Denmark 3
       Germany 10
       Estonia 3
       Greece 5
       Spain 8
       France 10
       Ireland 3
       Italy 10
       Cyprus 2
       Latvia 3
       Lithuania 3
       Luxembourg 2
       Hungary 5
       Malta 2
       Netherlands 5
       Austria 4
       Poland 8
       Portugal 5
       Slovenia 3
       Slovakia 3
       Finland 3
       Sweden 4
       United Kingdom 10

For their adoption, acts of the Council shall require at least:

—88 votes in favour where this Treaty requires them to be adopted on a proposal from the Commission,

—88 votes in favour, cast by at least two-thirds of the members, in other cases.

3. Abstentions by members present in person or represented shall not prevent the adoption by the Council of acts which require unanimity.

Article 206 [150]

Where a vote is taken, any member of the Council may also act on behalf of not more than one other member.

State has one vote, and decisions are taken by a simple majority. This is not, however, the real rule. The Treaty says that this system applies only if there is no provision to the contrary, and the Treaty almost always does provide for something different. The most common system is qualified-majority voting, under which the larger States have more votes than the smaller ones (though not fully in proportion to their population), and a specified number of votes (a little more than two-thirds) is required to adopt a proposal. The details are set out in Panel 3.9. The other system, required by certain provisions of the Treaty, is unanimity. This applies to particularly important decisions, such as the admission of new Member States. Unanimity does not, however, mean that every Member State must be in favour. It simply means that no State must

Panel 3.10 The Luxembourg Compromise

I. Where, in the case of decisions which may be taken by majority vote on a proposal of the Commission, very important interests of one or more partners are at stake, the Members of the Council will endeavour, within a reasonable time, to reach solutions which can be adopted by all the Members of the Council while respecting their mutual interests and those of the Community, in accordance with Article 2 [2] of the Treaty.

II. With regard to the preceding paragraph, the French delegation considers that where very important interests are at stake the discussion must be continued until unanimous agreement is reached.

III. The six delegations note that there is a divergence of views on what should be done in the event of a failure to reach complete agreement.

oppose the measure.[18] This is the same as "consensus" in the WTO. Whenever the Treaty gives the Council the power to take a decision, it specifies which system is to apply.

The legal position, therefore, is that there are three systems: the theoretical position (one State, one vote), which applies only when the framers of the Treaty forgot to provide otherwise; the normal system (qualified-majority voting); and the system for particularly important decisions (unanimity). In practice, however, the position is more complicated because political considerations impose a certain constraint on qualified-majority voting. Since the weighting of the votes does not truly reflect either population or political importance – for example, Greece and Portugal (combined population approximately 20 million) together have the same number of votes as Germany (population over 80 million) – the larger countries feel the system is unfair.

In 1965, France began a boycott of Council meetings, partly in protest against qualified-majority voting. The result was a document usually called the "Luxembourg Compromise"[19] (Panel 3.10). In the main, it was an agreement to disagree. It says that where very important interests of a Member State are at stake, an attempt should be made to reach a solution satisfactory to all concerned. All agreed to this. France's view was that if this was not possible, the objector could block further action. The other Member States did not accept this. Despite what the document says, however, the French view prevailed in practice for many years.

How is one to determine whether very important interests of a State are at stake? For a long time, it seemed to be accepted that it was enough if the State concerned *said* that this was so. This meant that a State could abuse the system by using the Luxembourg Compromise to block a proposal, not because it had any special objection to that proposal, but in order to put pressure on the others to agree to something completely different. However, the UK tried this once too often in 1982. It tried to block an agricultural price increase to force the others to agree to a reform of the financial system, which put an unfair burden on the UK. In what appears to have been a pre-planned

---

18 Art. 205(3) [148(3)] EC. The Member State abstaining must, however, be present or represented by another State. If a State deliberately boycotts meetings, it can block all decisions requiring unanimity. This was a policy pursued by France for a time in 1965. It ended with the "Luxembourg Compromise", discussed below.
19 Also known as the "Luxembourg Accords".

Panel 3.11 The Ioannina Compromise

Council Decision on Qualified Majority Decision-Making (OJ C105/1 of 13 April 1994 as amended by OJ C1/1 of 1 January 1995)

Article 1

If Members of the Council representing a total of 23 to 25 votes indicate their intention to oppose the adoption by the Council of a Decision by qualified majority, the Council will do all in its power to reach, within a reasonable time and without prejudicing obligatory time limits laid down by the Treaties and by secondary law, such as in Articles 251 [189 B] and 252 [189 C] of the Treaty establishing the European Community, a satisfactory solution that could be adopted by at least 66 votes. During this period, and always respecting the Rules of Procedure of the Council, the President undertakes, with the assistance of the Commission, any initiative necessary to facilitate a wider basis of agreement in the Council. The Members of the Council lend him their assistance.

move, the chairman called for a vote. The measure was passed by a qualified majority. As there was no legally binding obligation on the others to accept the UK's veto right, there was nothing the UK could do. Since then, less has been heard of the Luxembourg Compromise. However, it still exists to the extent that the majority of States are willing to accept it. This would depend on how much sympathy they felt for the objector.

Where qualified-majority voting is applied, a State can still block a measure if it garners sufficient votes to ensure that a qualified majority is not attained. This is known as a "blocking minority". In 2003, with fifteen Member States, a qualified majority was 62. Since the total number of votes was 87, a blocking minority was 26. Three big States or two big States and a couple of smaller ones were sufficient. The problem from the point of view of the big States is that as more countries keep joining the Community, a blocking minority, which remains more or less stable as a proportion of the total, keeps getting larger in absolute terms. Thus, before Austria, Finland and Sweden joined, a blocking minority was only 23. The UK, France and Ireland, acting together, for example, could block any measure. This was no longer true after Austria, Finland and Sweden joined.

When negotiations were being conducted for the accession of Austria, Finland and Sweden, it was proposed by the UK and Spain that a blocking minority should remain at 23. The other Member States rejected this, but another compromise was agreed, this time embodied in a decision of the Council. It was called the "Ioannina Compromise" (Panel 3.11). It accorded a special status to a group able to muster 23 to 25 votes, but fell short of giving them the right to block the measure.

The Accession Treaty of 2003[20] sweeps all this away, and provides for a new voting system, to come into operation on 1 November 2004 (Panel 3.12). All States are given more votes, but the larger ones get proportionately more. The States benefiting the most are actually Spain and Poland, which are not the largest. The four largest States (France, Germany, Italy and the United Kingdom)

20 Art. 12 of the Act of Accession 2003. Art. 3 of the Protocol on the Enlargement of the European Union (Treaty of Nice) is repealed.

Panel 3.12   Voting in the Council (from 1 November 2004)

EC Treaty (as amended by Article 12 of the Accession Treaty 2003)

Article 205 [148]

1. Save as otherwise provided in this Treaty, the Council shall act by a majority of its members.

2. Where the Council is required to act by a qualified majority, the votes of its members shall be weighted as follows:

> Belgium 12
> Czech Republic 12
> Denmark 7
> Germany 29
> Estonia 4
> Greece 12
> Spain 27
> France 29
> Ireland 7
> Italy 29
> Cyprus 4
> Latvia 4
> Lithuania 7
> Luxembourg 4
> Hungary 12
> Malta 3
> Netherlands 13
> Austria 10
> Poland 27
> Portugal 12
> Slovenia 4
> Slovakia 7
> Finland 7
> Sweden 10
> United Kingdom 29

Acts of the Council shall require for their adoption at least 232 votes in favour cast by a majority of the members where this Treaty requires them to be adopted on a proposal from the Commission.
   In other cases, for their adoption acts of the Council shall require at least 232 votes in favour, cast by at least two-thirds of the members.

3. Abstentions by members present in person or represented shall not prevent the adoption by the Council of acts which require unanimity.

4. When a decision is to be adopted by the Council by a qualified majority, a member of the Council may request verification that the Member States constituting the qualified majority represent at least 62% of the total population of the Union. If that condition is shown not to have been met, the decision in question shall not be adopted.

also gain proportionately, though not as much as Spain and Poland. The voting power of the others States is reduced.

The Netherlands, which previously had the same number of votes as Belgium, now pulls ahead – a reflection of its greater population. On the other hand, Germany (population: over 80 million) still has the same number of votes as the other three large countries, despite their smaller populations (all under 60 million). This was largely at French insistence. It will be remembered from Chapter 2 that France treated Germany as an equal in the early days of the Community, despite the fact that it was a defeated nation. The French expect Germany to do the same for them now that it has become dominant. The difference in voting power is so anomalous, however, that it cannot continue indefinitely.

From 1 November 2004, a qualified majority will be 232 votes out of a total of 321. This is just over 72 per cent, only slightly more than under the previous

---

Panel 3.13   Appointment of Commissioners

EC Treaty

Article 214 [158]

1. The Members of the Commission shall be appointed, in accordance with the procedure referred to in paragraph 2, for a period of five years, subject, if need be, to Article 201 [144].
   Their term of office shall be renewable.

2. The Council, meeting in the composition of Heads of State or Government and acting by a qualified majority, shall nominate the person it intends to appoint as President of the Commission; the nomination shall be approved by the European Parliament.
   The Council, acting by a qualified majority and by common accord with the nominee for President, shall adopt the list of the other persons whom it intends to appoint as Members of the Commission, drawn up in accordance with the proposals made by each Member State.
   The President and the other Members of the Commission thus nominated shall be subject as a body to a vote of approval by the European Parliament. After approval by the European Parliament, the President and the other Members of the Commission shall be appointed by the Council, acting by a qualified majority.

---

system. However, attaining 232 votes, though necessary, will no longer be sufficient. In all cases, there will have to be at least a majority of States in favour. If the act is not adopted on a proposal from the Commission, there will have to be a two-thirds majority of States in favour.[21] Both these rules benefit the smaller States and partially balance the greater voting power of the larger ones. The third rule is that the States in favour must constitute at least 62 per cent of the *population* of the Union.[22] This rule protects the larger States and partially balances the fact that the smaller ones have more votes relative to population.

Appointment of the Commission

The Treaty of Nice made an important change in the method of appointing the members of the Commission (Panel 3.13). Previously, the Member States made the appointments. They had to be unanimous. Now the European Council (the Council composed of Heads of State or Government) makes the appointments, acting by a qualified majority.

The first step is for the Council, acting by a qualified majority, to nominate the person it intends to appoint as President. This nomination must be approved by the European Parliament. The Council then nominates the other members of the Commission, by a qualified majority and by common accord with the nominee for President. This means that the Council (acting by a qualified majority) *and* the President-elect have to agree to each nomination. Then the President-elect and the other members have to be approved as a body by the European Parliament. The Parliament can reject the whole Commission, but cannot reject an individual Commissioner. It has to be all or none. Finally, the President-elect and other nominees are appointed by the Council acting by a qualified majority.

This new system prevents an individual Member State from blocking an appointment wanted by the majority. However, the second-last paragraph of

---

21 This latter rule applied under the previous system as well.
22 This rule applies only if a member of the Council requests verification of this fact.

Article 214(2) [158(2)] EC says that the list of persons the Council intends to appoint as members of the Commission is "drawn up in accordance with the proposals made by each Member State". This must mean that each Member State nominates the person it wants as its Commissioner.[23] This list is then put to the vote and, if adopted by a qualified majority (and the President-elect agrees), it goes forward to the Parliament. Thus individual Member States can still decide whom they want – the other Member States cannot impose someone on them – but they can no longer block the candidates put forward by other Member States. Only a "blocking minority" can do that.[24] The end result in this respect is not so very different from the situation in practice under the old system. However, the position is different with regard to the nomination of the President. The person wanted by the majority can now be nominated even if one Member State objects. Nor can that State threaten to block the appointment of the Commission as a whole. That too is done by a qualified majority.

The European Parliament

According to Article 189 [137] of the EC Treaty (Panel 3.14), the European Parliament consists of "representatives of the peoples of the States brought together in the Community". This recognizes that Europe consists of a number of different peoples (nations). There is no European nation. Some people say that the Parliament constitutes the democratic element in the EU system. As we shall see below, however, it cannot really do this.

Composition

Originally, the members of the European Parliament were selected by the Member-State Parliaments from among their own members. It was only after much wrangling that it was finally agreed in 1976 that they would be directly elected. The elections take place on fixed dates every five years.[25] The electoral system is, however, different in each Member State, since it has so far proved impossible to reach agreement on a uniform system.[26] It is hoped to do this one day: see Article 190(4) [138(4)] EC (Panel 3.14).

The present (2003) number of seats allocated to each Member State is set out in Article 190(2) [138(2)] EC (Panel 3.14). It is not proportionate to population. Small States get more than they are entitled to on a population basis. For example, the population of Germany is approximately 191 times that of Luxembourg. Yet, Germany gets only 16.5 times as many seats (99 to Luxembourg's 6). If 6 seats

---

23 There must be at least one Commissioner from each Member State: Art. 213(1) [157(1)] EC.
24 If this happened, it would seem that the whole process would have to start again. A new list would have to be drawn up on the basis of the proposals put forward by each Member State. If they put forward the same persons and they were again rejected, there would be deadlock. This could also have occurred under the old system, under which each appointment had to be approved by every Member State.
25 Council Decision 76/787 and annexed Act, OJ 1976, L278/1. The first direct elections were held in 1979.
26 In the past, the United Kingdom has used the first-past-the-post system, the same as in national elections, but it is intended to go over to a form of proportional representation in future.

Panel 3.14   Composition of the European Parliament (until 2004)

EC Treaty

Article 189 [137]

The European Parliament, which shall consist of representatives of the peoples of the States brought together in the Community, shall exercise the powers conferred upon it by this Treaty.

The number of Members of the European Parliament shall not exceed 732.

Article 190 [138]

1. The representatives in the European Parliament of the peoples of the States brought together in the Community shall be elected by direct universal suffrage.

2. The number of representatives elected in each Member State shall be as follows:

Belgium 25
Denmark 16
Germany 99
Greece 25
Spain 64
France 87
Ireland 15
Italy 87
Luxembourg 6
Netherlands 31
Austria 21
Portugal 25
Finland 16
Sweden 22
United Kingdom 87

In the event of amendments to this paragraph, the number of representatives elected in each Member State must ensure appropriate representation of the peoples of the States brought together in the Community.

3. Representatives shall be elected for a term of five years.

4. The European Parliament shall draw up a proposal for elections by direct universal suffrage in accordance with a uniform procedure in all Member States or in accordance with principles common to all Member States.

The Council shall, acting unanimously after obtaining the assent of the European Parliament, which shall act by a majority of its component members, lay down the appropriate provisions, which it shall recommend to Member States for adoption in accordance with their respective constitutional requirements.

5. The European Parliament, after seeking an opinion from the Commission and with the approval of the Council acting by a qualified majority, shall lay down the regulations and general conditions governing the performance of the duties of its Members. All rules or conditions relating to the taxation of Members or former Members shall require unanimity within the Council.

are right for Luxembourg, 1,149 would be the correct number for Germany. If 99 seats are right for Germany, Luxembourg ought to have half a seat. As things stand, the vote of one Luxembourger is equal to that of approximately 11.5 Germans. Equality of voting rights does not apply in the EU.

In 2004, the position will be even worse. As new States join the Community, they will have to be given representation. If the Parliament gets much bigger, however, it will become unwieldy. Therefore, the Treaty of Accession 2003 provides for a reduction in the representation of all the existing Member States (Panel 3.15).[27] Not quite all existing Member States, however. Germany retains

---

27 Art. 11 of the Act of Accession 2003. It takes effect from the start of the 2004–2009 parliamentary term. The position between the date of accession and the start of the 2004–2009 parliamentary term is laid down in Art. 25 of the Act of Accession 2003.

Panel 3.15   Composition of the European Parliament (2004)

EC Treaty, as amended by the Treaty of Accession 2003

[With effect from the start of the 2004–2009 parliamentary term, in Article 190(2) [138(2)] EC the first subparagraph will be replaced by the text below.]

The number of representatives elected in each Member State shall be as follows:

Belgium 24
Czech Republic 24
Denmark 14
Germany 99
Estonia 6
Greece 24
Spain 54
France 78
Ireland 13
Italy 78
Cyprus 6
Latvia 9
Lithuania 13
Luxembourg 6
Hungary 24
Malta 5
Netherlands 27
Austria 18
Poland 54
Portugal 24
Slovenia 7
Slovakia 14
Finland 14
Sweden 19
United Kingdom 78

the same number of seats as before, something that is justified by the fact that the ratio of seats to population is worse in the case of Germany than in the case of any other State. Luxembourg also retains the same number of seats. Since Luxembourg already has the most favourable ratio of seats to population of any existing Member State, this means that its advantage over all other States except Germany will become even greater. This is because Luxembourg insists that six is the smallest possible number that allows fair representation to all its political parties. However, Northern Ireland has a population that is approximately four times greater and is more diverse politically; yet it has to make do with fewer seats than Luxembourg. The fact that Northern Ireland is not a State is irrelevant, since the European Parliament does not represent States, but peoples.

Some compromise between equality of States and equality of population is legitimate in the case of the Council, since it represents States. However, if the Parliament is meant to supply the democratic element in the Community, the votes of all citizens should be of the same value. Equality of voting rights is an essential constituent of democracy.

Activities and powers

The activities of the Parliament are summarized in the provisions set out in Panel 3.16. MEPs sit according to their political party, not their State. The

---

Panel 3.16   European Parliament: operation and powers

EC Treaty

Article 191 [138a]

Political parties at European level are important as a factor for integration within the Union. They contribute to forming a European awareness and to expressing the political will of the citizens of the Union.

The Council, acting in accordance with the procedure referred to in Article 251 [189b], shall lay down the regulations governing political parties at European level and in particular the rules regarding their funding.

Article 192 [138b]

Insofar as provided in this Treaty, the European Parliament shall participate in the process leading up to the adoption of Community acts by exercising its powers under the procedures laid down in Articles 251 [189b] and 252 [189c] and by giving its assent or delivering advisory opinions.

The European Parliament may, acting by a majority of its Members, request the Commission to submit any appropriate proposal on matters on which it considers that a Community act is required for the purpose of implementing this Treaty.

Article 197 [140]

The European Parliament shall elect its President and its officers from among its Members.

Members of the Commission may attend all meetings and shall, at their request, be heard on behalf of the Commission.

The Commission shall reply orally or in writing to questions put to it by the European Parliament or by its Members.

The Council shall be heard by the European Parliament in accordance with the conditions laid down by the Council in its Rules of Procedure.

Article 198 [141]

Save as otherwise provided in this Treaty, the European Parliament shall act by an absolute majority of the votes cast.

The Rules of Procedure shall determine the quorum.

Article 201 [144]

If a motion of censure on the activities of the Commission is tabled before it, the European Parliament shall not vote thereon until at least three days after the motion has been tabled and only by open vote.

If the motion of censure is carried by a two-thirds majority of the votes cast, representing a majority of the Members of the European Parliament, the Members of the Commission shall resign as a body. They shall continue to deal with current business until they are replaced in accordance with Article 214 [158]. In this case, the term of office of the Members of the Commission appointed to replace them shall expire on the date on which the term of office of the Members of the Commission obliged to resign as a body would have expired.

---

political parties are supposed to be pan-European, but in fact they are alliances of national parties. Selection of candidates and fighting elections are a matter for the national parties, but, once elected, they group together in "European" parties. Thus, MEPs from the British Labour Party sit with their European colleagues in the Socialist grouping.

At present, MEPs receive the same pay as their national counterparts. This means that there are considerable variations in the pay received by different MEPs, a source of some resentment. To make up for this, however, they are given enormous allowances, which they can easily divert into their own pockets. Secretarial allowances can be paid to one's wife (regardless of her secretarial competence) and travel allowances can be claimed for trips not actually made. At least in the past, the Parliament had a policy of never checking up.

Panel 3.17 Powers of the European Parliament

Legislative
- Advisory opinions in certain cases
- Assent in certain cases
- Special role under Articles 251 [189b] and 252 [189c] EC
- Special role in the budgetary procedure

Political
- Assent to appointment of Commission (Art. 214 [158] EC)
- Censure of Commission (Art. 201 [144] EC)
- Assent to certain matters, e.g. admission of new members (Art. 49 [O] TEU)

Investigatory and informative
- Set up committees of inquiry (Art. 193 [138c] EC)
- Hear petitions (Art. 194 [138d] EC)
- Appoint Ombudsman and receive his reports (Art. 195 [138e] EC)
- Ask questions (Art. 197 [140] EC)
- Hold debates

Article 189 [137] EC says that the Parliament will exercise the powers conferred on it by the Treaty. Provisions conferring powers on the Parliament are scattered all over the treaties. Panel 3.17 summarizes the most important. Those concerning legislation will be discussed in Chapter 4. Most of the remainder are self-explanatory. The one exception is the power to force the resignation of the Commission by a vote of censure.

Under Article 201 [144] EC, the Parliament can force the resignation of the Commission by passing a motion of censure. Such a motion must be passed by a two-thirds majority of votes cast.[28] There must also be an absolute majority (i.e. a majority of members) in favour.[29] This power can, however, be used only against the Commission as a whole. The Parliament has no power to censure individual Commissioners. Moreover, if the Commission is forced to resign, its members remain in office until their successors are appointed.

In January 1999, there was a motion of censure against the Commission headed by Jacques Santer. It had been subject to widespread criticism for failing to take effective action against fraud and corruption by Commission officials. The motion failed to achieve a two-thirds majority, but the Commission had to accept the appointment of an independent committee of experts. When this produced a highly critical report, the whole Commission resigned in March 1999. However, the Member States failed to appoint a new Commission. So the existing Commissioners remained in office until their terms expired in January 2000.[30]

---

28 This means that the votes in favour must be at least twice the votes against.
29 This means that more than half of all members must vote in favour. In other words, the votes in favour must be greater than the votes against plus the votes that could have been cast by those who were absent or were present but did not cast a vote.
30 See Tomkins, "Responsibility and Resignation in the European Commission" (1999) 62 MLR 744.

Opinion: democracy and the EU

In the constitutional systems of the Member States, the national parliaments provide a mechanism under which the opinions, values and attitudes of the electorate can influence government policy. Admittedly, this mechanism functions imperfectly and is distorted in various ways. Nevertheless, it *does* function. In the UK, for example, there are a number of parties represented in Parliament, one of which usually has an overall majority and forms the government. The government then runs the country for a number of years. At the next election, the electorate holds that party responsible for what the government has done: if it approves, it will reward it by voting for it; if it does not, it will punish it by voting for some other party. Under this system, the party in power knows that it will have to answer to the electorate, and the Members of Parliament in that party will act accordingly. In most other Member States, the position is similar to that in the UK, except that the government is usually a coalition of two or more parties. The national parliaments thus constitute a mechanism under which public opinion constrains government action.

In the Community, on the other hand, there is no government, or, if one regards the Commission as the government, it is not a party government. No party holds power; consequently, no party is responsible for government policy. If things go well, no party can take the credit; if they go badly, no party need take the blame. The result is that when elections are held, the voters do not vote according to the governing party's record, nor indeed according to the opposition parties' promises as to what they will do if elected. In the UK at least, voters use European elections to express approval or disapproval of what their *national* government is doing: if there is a Labour Government in the UK and British voters want to express their dissatisfaction with it, they will vote Conservative in the European election. This means that nothing the parties do, or do not do, in the European Parliament will affect their chances of re-election; so they are not constrained in their actions by any consideration of public opinion. As a result, the European Parliament fails to provide a mechanism for popular opinion to influence Community policy. It is perhaps for this reason that turn-out is usually so low in European elections.

It might be thought that this problem could be solved by giving the European Parliament greater powers, in particular by making the Commission responsible to it in the same way that most national governments are responsible to the national parliaments. There are, however, reasons why this will not work. Democracy presupposes that most members of the electorate think of other voters in some sense as being "one of us". This is usually expressed by a phrase such as "one nation". The terminology is not important, but what matters is that the voters as a whole should have a sense of group loyalty and belonging: they must share the same fundamental values and attitudes. Only then will the minority be willing to give in to the majority on particular points of disagreement. Since both start from the same fundamental premises, they can reason with one another, and it will always be possible that today's minority will become tomorrow's majority. The minority parties know that they could win next time and the majority party knows that it could lose next time.

If, on the other hand, the electorate is split into segments with fundamentally different values, these expectations will not apply. This occurs particularly where there are national or religious differences regarded as so important by the persons concerned that they eclipse all other considerations. In such a situation, members of the opposing group are no longer "us", but "them". Sectarian parties spring up, catering exclusively for a particular group. If the whole political system becomes "tribalized" in this way, democracy will no longer work. Ethnic minority parties can never become the government because they can never win a majority of votes: except in the case of ethnic cleansing or mass immigration, they are doomed to be a permanent opposition. In such a situation, they will call for a separate state – one in which they constitute the majority. This is why democracy has never worked properly in Northern Ireland. When the whole of Ireland was part of the United Kingdom, Irish nationalists felt alienated and demanded separation. Ulster Protestants, however, were unwilling to accept a united Ireland, even if they were guaranteed democratic rights, because they knew they would be in a permanent minority within it. For similar reasons, Ulster Catholics have always felt that democratic rights in the Northern Ireland political system are not enough to satisfy their aspirations.

The relevance of this for Europe is that the European Union is made up of a number of separate nations, which have only a limited sense of being "European". Citizens of other Community countries are "them", not "us". There is no feeling of being one nation. There is no European public opinion, except perhaps among the narrow elite who actually run the Community. If there were a European Government responsible to the European Parliament, voters would feel just as alienated as they do at present. Each nation would regard itself as being in a permanent minority: there would be no sense of belonging. Voters would not feel that the European President spoke for them. They would not regard the European Government as *their* government.[31]

The problem is well known. The phrase "democratic deficit" is used to refer to it. This does not, however, mean that the European Parliament serves no useful purpose. It makes the Community system more open; it allows interest groups to influence policy through lobbying; and it imposes a check on the Commission and Council. The European Union nevertheless remains as undemocratic as ever. The same is true of other supranational organizations.[32] By their very nature, supranational organizations are made up of many States.

[31] This has been pointed out by a number of writers: see, for example, Dashwood, "States in the European Union" (1998) 23 ELRev. 201 at 216.
[32] See Stein, "International Integration and Democracy: No Love at First Sight" (2001) 95 AJIL 489.

These States may be democratic, but how is the organization itself to be made democratic? So far, no one has come up with a convincing answer.[33]

Further reading

Bradley, "Institutional Design in the Treaty of Nice" (2001) 38 CMLRev. 1095.

Hayes-Renshaw (Fiona) and Wallace (Helen), *The Council of Ministers* (Macmillan Press, Houndmills, Basingstoke, 1997).

Jacobs (Francis), Corbett (Richard) and Shackleton (Michael), *The European Parliament* (Cartermill International, London, 3rd ed., 1995).

Ress (George), "Democratic Decision-Making in the European Union and the Role of the European Parliament" in Deirdre Curtin and Ton Heukels (eds.), *Institutional Dynamics of European Integration: Essays in Honour of Henry G. Schermers* (Martinus Nijhoff, Dordrecht, Boston and London, 1994), vol. 2, p. 153.

Schmitter (Philippe C.), *How to Democratize the European Union . . . And Why Bother* (Rowman and Littlefield, Lanham, MD, 2000).

Stein, "International Integration and Democracy: No Love at First Sight" (2001) 95 AJIL 489.

Weiler (J. H. H.), *The Constitution of Europe* (Cambridge University Press, Cambridge, 1999), Chapter 8 (for earlier versions of this essay, see J. H. H. Weiler, "European Models: Polity, People and System" in Paul Craig and Carol Harlow (eds.), *Lawmaking in the European Union* (Kluwer Law International, London, The Hague and Boston, 1998) 3; and Weiler, Haltern and Mayer, "European Democracy and its Critique" (1995) 18 *West European Politics* 4).

---

[33] In the case of the European Union, a step in the right direction could be taken by giving the national parliaments a significant role. There could be a rule that important decisions of the Council would have to be ratified by the national parliaments, acting together. The votes of the parliaments would have to be weighted, perhaps according to the system applicable to the European Parliament, and there would have to be a majority, or even a two-thirds majority, of votes in favour of the decision.

4 Legislative powers

The European Union is unique among international organizations in the breadth and depth of its legislative powers. These powers form the subject matter of this chapter.

Our starting point must be the principle that the Community and its institutions possess only such powers as are conferred upon them by the Treaties. This principle of conferral, which is sometimes also called the principle of limited powers (competences), is laid down in Article 5 [E] TEU and Article 5 [3b] EC. The former reads:

> The European Parliament, the Council, the Commission, the Court of Justice and the Court of Auditors shall exercise their powers under the conditions and for the purposes provided for, on the one hand, by the provisions of the Treaties establishing the European Communities and of the subsequent Treaties and Acts modifying and supplementing them and, on the other hand, by the other provisions of this Treaty.

Article 5 [3b] EC reads:

> The Community shall act within the limits of the powers conferred upon it by this Treaty and of the objectives assigned to it therein.

In order to discover the legislative powers of the Community we must, therefore, look at the provisions of the Treaties.

Subject to one partial exception (discussed below),[1] the Treaties do not confer any general legislative powers. Instead, there are provisions granting the power to legislate with regard to specific matters, such as agriculture or free movement of workers. This gives rise to one of the perennial problems of Community legislation, the question of "legal basis". This refers to the Treaty provision under which a piece of legislation is adopted. Say, for example, that the Community wants to adopt a measure giving developing countries preferential trading terms. Should this be done under the Treaty provision concerning international trade or that concerning aid to developing countries? There has been much litigation on issues of this kind. Some of the cases will be set out below.

It might be thought that as long as the relevant institution has the power under some provision or other, it does not matter very much if it uses the

---

1 Article 308 [235] EC.

Panel 4.1   Community acts

EC Treaty

Article 249 [189]
In order to carry out their task and in accordance with the provisions of this Treaty, the European Parliament acting jointly with the Council, the Council and the Commission shall make regulations and issue directives, take decisions, make recommendations or deliver opinions.
   A regulation shall have general application. It shall be binding in its entirety and directly applicable in all Member States.
   A directive shall be binding, as to the result to be achieved, upon each Member State to which it is addressed, but shall leave to the national authorities the choice of form and methods.
   A decision shall be binding in its entirety upon those to whom it is addressed.
   Recommendations and opinions shall have no binding force.

---

wrong one. This is not so. The reason is that the provisions granting legislative power differ from one another in significant ways. The elements that could differ include:

* the institution that adopts the measure (the Council acting alone, the Council acting jointly with the Parliament, or the Commission);
* the voting procedure in the Council (qualified majority or unanimity);
* whether the Parliament must give its opinion; and
* the kind of measure adopted (legal form).

If the wrong legal basis is used, the measure may, for example, be adopted by the wrong institution; the institution may vote according to the wrong system; the rights of some other institution may be disregarded; and the wrong kind of measure may be adopted. This is why disputes as to legal basis are so important.

Types of Community acts

Article 249 [189] EC specifies five types of measures that may be adopted by the legislative institutions of the Community (Panel 4.1). Two of these (recommendations and opinions) have no binding force. This leaves us with three types of measure that are legally binding: regulations, directives and decisions.[2]

   Regulations are similar to UK statutes. They apply to everybody and lay down general rules. The Treaty says that they are directly applicable, which means that they are automatically part of the law of the land in every Member State. Directives are intended to be weaker instruments. They are binding on the Member States as to the result to be achieved, but allow each State to choose the appropriate way of achieving that result. As we shall see in Chapter 10, however, the European Court has not approved of this approach and has modified it. Nevertheless, the idea in the Treaty is that the Community will adopt

---

2 In *Commission v. Council (ERTA* case), Case 22/70, [1971] ECR 263; [1971] CMLR 335 (set out below in Chap. 12), the European Court held that this list is not exhaustive: it is possible to have other kinds of legally binding measures that are neither regulations, directives nor decisions. However, it did this for a particular purpose, and such acts *sui generis* do not normally play a significant role.

Panel 4.2   Form of Community acts

EC Treaty

Article 253 [190]
Regulations, directives and decisions adopted jointly by the European Parliament and the Council, and such acts adopted by the Council or the Commission, shall state the reasons on which they are based and shall refer to any proposals or opinions which were required to be obtained pursuant to this Treaty.

Article 254 [191]
1. Regulations, directives and decisions adopted in accordance with the procedure referred to in Article 251 [189b] shall be signed by the President of the European Parliament and by the President of the Council and published in the *Official Journal of the European Union*. They shall enter into force on the date specified in them or, in the absence thereof, on the twentieth day following that of their publication.

2. Regulations of the Council and of the Commission, as well as directives of those institutions which are addressed to all Member States, shall be published in the *Official Journal of the European Union*. They shall enter into force on the date specified in them or, in the absence thereof, on the twentieth day following that of their publication.

3. Other directives, and decisions, shall be notified to those to whom they are addressed and shall take effect upon such notification.

---

a regulation when it wants to lay down the rule itself, and will resort to a directive when it wants the Member State to lay down the rule. The advantage of the former is that there is a uniform rule throughout the Community. The advantage of the latter is that it allows the rule to be adapted to suit local conditions and to fit in with the legal system of the Member State in question. Problems arise, however, if a Member State fails to adopt a measure to give effect to the directive.

Decisions are more executive in character, though they can also fulfil a legislative role. They are fully binding, but only on the person to whom they are addressed. This may be a Member State or an individual or company. Thus a regulation may provide that all steel manufacturers must pay a levy at a certain rate. The regulation may then require the Commission to collect the money and give it the power to adopt decisions addressed to particular manufacturers determining how much they must pay. Thus the regulation would lay down the general rule and the decision would apply it to a particular case. This would be a typical example. In practice, however, things are not always as neat as this.

Some Treaty provisions simply empower the Council to adopt appropriate measures. In such a case, it can adopt regulations, directives or decisions, as it thinks fit. In other cases, however, the Treaty specifies the type of measure to be adopted. Thus, if the Treaty permits the Council to adopt only directives, it cannot adopt a regulation.

Articles 253 [190] and 254 [191] EC (Panel 4.2) lay down the formalities to be followed when the Community adopts legislative measures. The most important are the requirement to state the reasons for the measure, something that does not apply to Acts of Parliament in the UK, and the requirement that they be published.

Panel 4.3 Commission proposals

EC Treaty

Article 250 [189a]

1. Where, in pursuance of this Treaty, the Council acts on a proposal from the Commission, unanimity shall be required for an act constituting an amendment to that proposal, subject to Article 251(4) and (5) [189b(4) and (5)].

2. As long as the Council has not acted, the Commission may alter its proposal at any time during the procedures leading to the adoption of a Community act.

Legislative procedures

Most Community legislation is adopted either by the Council acting alone or by the Council and the Parliament jointly.[3] There are special procedures for the budget.

The basic procedure

The basic legislative procedure – for many years, virtually the only legislative procedure – is that under which the Commission makes a proposal, the Parliament gives its opinion, and the Council adopts the measure, usually by a qualified majority.

Under this procedure, each of the three legislative institutions has a role to play. The Commission's role is that it initiates the procedure. The Treaty provides that the Council can amend a Commission proposal only if it is unanimous (Article 250 [189a] EC, set out in Panel 4.3). This means that even if the Council can adopt the proposal on the basis of a qualified majority, it cannot amend it if a single Member State is opposed. In such a case, the majority will have to choose between adopting the Commission's version (which may not be entirely to their liking) or getting no measure at all. Thus, if it has the support of just one Member State, the Commission can force its policies on the majority. This is a great deal of power for a non-elected bureaucracy. In the early days of the Community, it was not a problem, since the Commission would readily amend its proposal to gain majority support. Today, things are not so simple.

Under the basic procedure, the Parliament's role is purely advisory. It has a right to give its opinion, but the Council does not have to follow it. Our next case considers what is involved in this right.

> ***European Union***
> **Roquette Frères v. Council**
> **COURT OF JUSTICE OF THE EUROPEAN COMMUNITIES**
> **Case 138/79, [1980] ECR 3333**

---

3 The exceptional cases in which the Commission has original (non-delegated) legislative powers were discussed in the previous chapter.

Background

Regulation 1293/79 (which amended Regulation 1111/77) was adopted under Article 37 [43] EC, a provision which enables the Council to enact legislation concerning agriculture on a proposal from the Commission and after consulting the European Parliament. The Council sent a draft of Regulation 1293/79 to the Parliament and asked it for its opinion. The draft was sent in March 1979, and the Council asked the Parliament to consider it during its April session, so that the regulation could enter into force on 1 July 1979. The Parliament asked its agricultural committee to consider the regulation. The committee considered it and proposed a resolution. The resolution was, however, rejected by the Parliament in plenary session. This meant that it had to go back to the agricultural committee for reconsideration. By this time, however, the session was at an end. The Parliament was due to be dissolved prior to new elections – the first direct elections – which were to take place on 17 July 1979. The Parliament was prepared to hold an extraordinary session; however, the Council made no such request. Instead, it adopted the regulation. The preamble to the regulation was changed to say that the Parliament had been "consulted", rather than that it had given its opinion.

Roquette, a French company, which was affected by the regulation, brought proceedings before the European Court under Article 230 [173] EC to annul part of the regulation. The Parliament intervened in the proceedings, and argued that the Council's failure to obtain an opinion from the Parliament constituted an infringement of an essential procedural requirement, a ground for annulment under Article 230 [173].

Judgment

32. The applicant and the Parliament in its intervention maintain that since Regulation No. 1111/77 as amended was adopted by the Council without regard to the consultation procedure provided for in the second paragraph of Article 37 [43] of the Treaty it must be treated as void for infringement of essential procedural requirements.

33. The consultation provided for in the third subparagraph of Article 37(2) [43(2)], as in other similar provisions of the Treaty, is the means which allows the Parliament to play an actual part in the legislative process of the Community. Such power represents an essential factor in the institutional balance intended by the Treaty. Although limited, it reflects at Community level the fundamental democratic principle that the peoples should take part in the exercise of power through the intermediary of a representative assembly. Due consultation of the Parliament in the cases provided for by the Treaty therefore constitutes an essential formality disregard of which means that the measure concerned is void.

34. In that respect it is pertinent to point out that observance of that requirement implies that the Parliament has expressed its opinion. It is impossible to take the view that the requirement is satisfied by the Council's simply asking for the opinion. The Council is, therefore, wrong to include in the references in the preamble to Regulation No. 1293/79 a statement to the effect that the Parliament has been consulted.

35. The Council has not denied that consultation of the Parliament was in the nature of an essential procedural requirement. It maintains however that in the circumstances of the

present case the Parliament, by its own conduct, made observance of that requirement impossible and that it is therefore not proper to rely on the infringement thereof.

36. Without prejudice to the questions of principle raised by that argument of the Council it suffices to observe that in the present case on 25 June 1979 when the Council adopted Regulation No. 1293/79 amending Regulation No. 1111/77 without the opinion of the Assembly the Council had not exhausted all the possibilities of obtaining the preliminary opinion of the Parliament. In the first place the Council did not request the application of the emergency procedure provided for by the internal regulation of the Parliament although in other sectors and as regards other draft regulations it availed itself of that power at the same time. Further the Council could have made use of the possibility it had under Article 196 [139] of the Treaty to ask for an extraordinary session of the Assembly especially as the Bureau of the Parliament on 1 March and 10 May 1979 drew its attention to that possibility.

Result: Regulation 1293/79 annulled.

QUESTION

Does this judgment mean that the Parliament can hold a measure up indefinitely by just not giving an opinion on it?[4]

European Union
European Parliament v. Council (Road Transport case)
COURT OF JUSTICE OF THE EUROPEAN COMMUNITIES
Case C-388/92, [1994] ECR I-2067

Background

In this case, the Parliament did give its opinion. Subsequently, however, the measure was amended. Did it have to go back to the Parliament for an opinion on the amendments?

Judgment
10. The Court has consistently held that the duty to consult the European Parliament in the course of the legislative procedure, in the cases provided for by the Treaty, includes a requirement that the Parliament be reconsulted on each occasion when the text finally adopted, viewed as a whole, departs substantially from the text on which the Parliament has already been consulted, except where the amendments essentially correspond to the wish of the Parliament itself . . .

QUESTION

How do you know whether the amendment is "substantial"?

---

4 See *European Parliament v. Council*, Case C-65/93, [1995] ECR I-643.

The co-operation procedure

The co-operation procedure was introduced in 1986 by the Single European Act in order to give the Parliament a greater role.[5] When it applied, the Council voted according to the qualified-majority procedure, except that if the Parliament rejected the measure, the Council could adopt it only if it was unanimous. The Parliament plus one Member State could, therefore, block the measure. The co-operation procedure has, however, been largely superseded by the co-decision procedure. So we will pass on directly to that.

The co-decision procedure

The co-decision procedure, which is laid down in Article 251 [189b] EC (Panel 4.4), provides for legislation to be adopted jointly by the Council and the Parliament. It fits on to the end of the basic procedure, described above. In other words, the Commission makes the proposal, the Parliament is consulted, and the measure comes back to the Council. If the Parliament does not propose any amendments, or if the Council accepts any such amendments, the measure is simply adopted.[6] In such a case, the co-decision procedure is no different from the basic procedure.

The differences begin if the Parliament makes amendments that the Council does not accept. The Council then adopts what is called a "common position", which is simply a statement of its preferred form of the measure.[7] At this point, the Parliament can kill the measure by rejecting it. It must do this by a majority of its members. If it does that, there is no way the Council can adopt it. If, on the other hand, the Parliament favours a measure of some kind, but wants a different version from that proposed by the Council, it can amend the common position, but must do so by a majority of its members.

If these amendments are not accepted by the Council,[8] something called a "conciliation committee" is set up. This consists of an equal number of representatives of the Parliament and of the Council (those of the Council may in fact consist of the Council's entire membership). Its job is to find a solution acceptable to both institutions. The two sides of the conciliation committee vote separately (the Council representatives by a qualified majority and the parliamentarians by a majority of representatives), and a solution cannot be adopted unless it is accepted by both sides. If this is done, the measure as modified by the conciliation committee still has to be adopted by the Parliament (now acting by a majority of votes) and the Council (acting by a qualified majority). If all this is not possible, the measure fails.

5 It was originally laid down in Art. 149(2) EC. See now Art. 252 [189c].
6 This is done by a qualified majority, except that the Council must be unanimous to accept amendments proposed by the Parliament that are rejected by the Commission. This follows from the rule in Art. 250 [189a] EC, discussed above.
7 This is done by a qualified majority, subject to the rule in Art. 250 [189a] EC.
8 If the amendments are approved by the Commission, they can be accepted by the Council by a qualified majority; otherwise, the Council must be unanimous. This follows from the rule in Art. 250 [189a] EC (Panel 4.3, above).

Panel 4.4 The co-decision procedure

EC Treaty

Article 251 [189b]

1. Where reference is made in this Treaty to this Article for the adoption of an act, the following procedure shall apply.

2. The Commission shall submit a proposal to the European Parliament and the Council.
The Council, acting by a qualified majority after obtaining the opinion of the European Parliament:

– if it approves all the amendments contained in the European Parliament's opinion, may adopt the proposed act thus amended,

– if the European Parliament does not propose any amendments, may adopt the proposed act,

– shall otherwise adopt a common position and communicate it to the European Parliament. The Council shall inform the European Parliament fully of the reasons which led it to adopt its common position. The Commission shall inform the European Parliament fully of its position.

If, within three months of such communication, the European Parliament:

(a) approves the common position or has not taken a decision, the act in question shall be deemed to have been adopted in accordance with that common position;

(b) rejects, by an absolute majority of its component members, the common position, the proposed act shall be deemed not to have been adopted;

(c) proposes amendments to the common position by an absolute majority of its component members, the amended text shall be forwarded to the Council and to the Commission, which shall deliver an opinion on those amendments.

3. If, within three months of the matter being referred to it, the Council, acting by a qualified majority, approves all the amendments of the European Parliament, the act in question shall be deemed to have been adopted in the form of the common position thus amended; however, the Council shall act unanimously on the amendments on which the Commission has delivered a negative opinion. If the Council does not approve all the amendments, the President of the Council, in agreement with the President of the European Parliament, shall within six weeks convene a meeting of the Conciliation Committee.

4. The Conciliation Committee, which shall be composed of the members of the Council or their representatives and an equal number of representatives of the European Parliament, shall have the task of reaching agreement on a joint text, by a qualified majority of the members of the Council or their representatives and by a majority of the representatives of the European Parliament. The Commission shall take part in the Conciliation Committee's proceedings and shall take all the necessary initiatives with a view to reconciling the positions of the European Parliament and the Council. In fulfilling this task, the Conciliation Committee shall address the common position on the basis of the amendments proposed by the European Parliament.

5. If, within six weeks of its being convened, the Conciliation Committee approves a joint text, the European Parliament, acting by an absolute majority of the votes cast, and the Council, acting by a qualified majority, shall each have a period of six weeks from that approval in which to adopt the act in question in accordance with the joint text. If either of the two institutions fails to approve the proposed act within that period, it shall be deemed not to have been adopted.

6. Where the Conciliation Committee does not approve a joint text, the proposed act shall be deemed not to have been adopted.

7. The periods of three months and six weeks referred to in this Article shall be extended by a maximum of one month and two weeks respectively at the initiative of the European Parliament or the Council.

There are two important points about this procedure. The first is that the Parliament cannot be forced to accept the measure without its amendments. Provided it can muster a majority of its members, it can put the Council (and the Commission) in the position of having to choose between accepting its amendments or getting no measure at all. It is by virtue of this feature that the measure is said to be adopted jointly by the Council and the Parliament, though there is not in fact any requirement that the Parliament must positively approve the measure. Secondly, the rule that a Commission proposal cannot be amended by the Council unless the latter is unanimous, a rule which continues to apply throughout the procedure up until the moment when a conciliation committee is formed, ceases to apply once this occurs. The conciliation committee is, therefore, a means by which the Council and the Parliament, acting together, can break the Commission's stranglehold on the legislative process. In this way, a qualified majority in the Council and a majority of members in the Parliament can override the Commission and its supporters in the Council.

The budgetary procedure

There is a special procedure for adopting the Community budget.[9] A preliminary draft budget is drawn up by the Commission on the basis of estimates provided by each of the institutions. The Council then adopts the draft budget, acting by a qualified majority. In doing this, the Council is not bound by the Commission's proposals. The rule that a proposal by the Commission cannot be amended unless the Council is unanimous does not apply under the budgetary procedure. The draft budget is then sent to the Parliament.

Beyond this point the procedure gets complicated. We shall confine ourselves to the salient features. The first is that the Parliament can reject the entire budget, provided it does so by a two-thirds majority of votes and a majority of members. If it does not positively reject it in this way, and if it makes no amendments, it is deemed to have accepted it. If the budget is rejected, a new budget must be prepared. In the meantime, the Community can spend each month one-twelfth of what it was entitled to spend under the previous year's budget. A rejection is not, therefore, quite as catastrophic as might be thought.

The second salient feature is that the Parliament's power to make amendments depends, in the final analysis, on a distinction between what is known as "compulsory" and "non-compulsory" expenditure. Compulsory expenditure is that which is required by existing law. Non-compulsory expenditure is all other expenditure. The greater part of the budget is usually made up of compulsory expenditure, but non-compulsory expenditure is not insignificant. Although the Parliament can propose changes with regard to both kinds of expenditure, the Council (acting by a qualified majority) has the last word in the case of compulsory expenditure.[10] In the case of non-compulsory expenditure, on the other hand, the Parliament can make its view prevail in the end. To do so, however, it must be able to muster a majority of members and a three-fifths majority of votes. There is also a limit to the extent to which the Parliament can increase non-compulsory expenditure each year. This is based on a formula derived from increases in GNP, Member-State budgets and inflation in the Community.

9 The relevant provisions are Arts. 268–280 [199–209a] EC.
10 There is, however, a joint declaration of the Parliament, the Council and the Commission, which gives the Parliament an opportunity to express its views (through a kind of conciliation committee) when legislation is being adopted which has appreciable financial implications. This allows the Parliament to influence compulsory expenditure in advance. See the Joint Declaration of 4 March 1975, OJ 1975, C89/1.

Panel 4.5   Article 308 [235]

EC Treaty

Article 308 [235]

If action by the Community should prove necessary to attain, in the course of the operation of the common market, one of the objectives of the Community and this Treaty has not provided the necessary powers, the Council shall, acting unanimously on a proposal from the Commission and after consulting the European Parliament, take the appropriate measures.

The problem of legal basis

We are now in a position to deal further with the problem of legal basis. It will be seen from the discussion above that the use of the wrong legal basis can have serious consequences, particularly for the Parliament. Our first case introduces this problem and also provides an opportunity to consider Article 308 [235] EC.

> *European Union*
> **Hauptzollamt Bremerhaven v. Massey-Ferguson**
> **COURT OF JUSTICE OF THE EUROPEAN COMMUNITIES**
> Case 8/73, [1973] ECR 897

Background

The issue in this case was the validity of a Community measure, Regulation 803/86. It had been adopted under Article 308 [235] EC (Panel 4.5), a provision which enables the Council to adopt any measure it likes, provided action by the Community is necessary to attain one of its objectives. This comes close to a general legislative power, but is subject to two qualifications. The first is that the need to legislate must arise in the course of the operation of the common market. The second is that some other provision of the Treaty has not provided the necessary powers.

Under Article 308 [235], the measure must be adopted by the Council on a proposal from the Commission and after consulting the Parliament (basic procedure). There is, however, one special feature. The Council must be unanimous. In view of this, it might be thought that the open-ended nature of the power does not matter. Since all the Member States have to agree, is it not like an amendment to the Treaty? This is not so. A treaty amendment has to be ratified according to the constitutional requirements of each Member State, a procedure which usually entails parliamentary approval. If Article 308 [235] did not exist, the measures in question would have to be adopted at the national level, which would also require parliamentary approval. Article 308 [235], therefore, allows Member State governments to take power away from the national parliaments. It is thus another element in the "de-democratization" of Europe.

This was not, however, the issue in the *Massey-Ferguson* case. The case arose when Massey-Ferguson challenged a customs duty on goods imported by it into Germany from outside the Community. The duty was imposed under Regulation 803/86, which established a uniform way of determining the value of goods, so that customs duties would be the same throughout the Community. In the course of the proceedings, Massey-Ferguson raised the question whether the Community was entitled to adopt the Regulation under Article 308 [235]. One of the arguments it put forward was that various other provisions of the Treaty (Articles 23 [9], [27], 26 [28], [111] and 133 [113]), if interpreted broadly, might provide the necessary power. The German court referred the matter to the European Court.

Judgment

2. By the first question it is asked whether the necessary authority for the validity of the Regulation is to be found in Article 308 [235] of the Treaty, on which it is based, or in any other provision of the Treaty.

3. The first recital in the Preamble to the Regulation declares that it is adopted by virtue of "the Treaty establishing the European Economic Community, and in particular Article 308 [235] thereof". Thus it is proper to examine first of all whether this Article constitutes a sufficient legal basis.

Article 308 [235] authorizes the Council to take the appropriate measures if action by the Community should prove necessary to attain, in the course of the operation of the Common Market, one of the objectives of the Community and if the Treaty has not provided the necessary powers.

The establishment of a customs union between the Member States is one of the objectives of the Community under Article 3(a) and (b) [3(a) and (b)] of the Treaty. The functioning of a customs union requires of necessity the uniform determination of the valuation for customs purposes of goods imported from third countries so that the level of protection effected by the Common Customs Tariff is the same throughout the whole Community . . .

[passage omitted]

4. If it is true that the proper functioning of the customs union justifies a wide interpretation of Articles 23 [9], [27], 26 [28], [111] and 133 [113] of the Treaty and of the powers which these provisions confer on the institutions to allow them thoroughly to control external trade by measures taken both independently and by agreement, there is no reason why the Council could not legitimately consider that recourse to the procedure of Article 308 [235] was justified in the interest of legal certainty. This is the more so as the Regulation in question was adopted during the transitional period.

By reason of the specific requirements of Article 308 [235] this course of action cannot be criticized since, under the circumstances, the rules of the Treaty on the forming of the Council's decisions or on the division of powers between the institutions are not to be disregarded.

5. No one has disputed the fact that on the adoption of Regulation No. 803/68 the procedure prescribed by Article 308 [235] was carried out in the proper manner.

6. Consequently, as the authority for this Regulation is to be found in Article 308 [235] of the Treaty, examination of the question raised has exposed no factor which is capable of affecting its validity.

Result: regulation held valid.

Comment

In this judgment, the court admits (paragraph 4) that the other provisions mentioned might provide appropriate authority for the measure. However, it holds that the Council was justified in using Article 308 [235] because it could not be certain of this. This course of action was all the more justified, said the court, in view of the fact that the regulation was adopted during the transitional period.[11] The significance of this is that during this period the other provisions mentioned also provided for the Council to act by unanimity. In other words, the Council would have voted by unanimity whichever legal basis was used. This is the significance of the phrase "the rules of the Treaty on the forming of the Council's decisions".

QUESTIONS

1. What do you think is meant by the phrase "the division of powers between the institutions" at the end of paragraph 4 of the judgment?
2. Why must neither this nor the voting system in the Council be disregarded?

European Union
Commission v. Council (Tariff Preferences case)
COURT OF JUSTICE OF THE EUROPEAN COMMUNITIES
Case 45/86, [1987] ECR 1493

Background

This was an action by the Commission against the Council under Article 230 [173] EC for the annulment of two regulations adopted by the Council on a proposal from the Commission. In each case, the Commission proposal had contained, in the preamble, the words "Having regard to the Treaty establishing the European Economic Community and in particular Article 133 [113] thereof", but the Council (acting unanimously) had deleted the reference to Article 133 [113]. The result was that the legal basis given in the preamble was to the Treaty in general, without a reference to any specific provision. It was on this ground that the Commission wished to annul the measure.

The Commission considered that the failure to state a precise legal basis was contrary to Article 253 [190] EC (Panel 4.2, above), which requires regulations to state the reasons on which they are based. A violation of this provision constitutes an infringement of an essential procedural requirement, a ground for nullity under Article 230 [173]. In addition, the Commission considered that a violation of the Treaty had occurred by reason of the fact that the Council had actually adopted the measure under Article 308 [235] and had therefore

---

11 The transitional period was the period at the beginning of the Community when the Treaty was not fully in force. Certain of its provisions, including those on qualified majority voting, did not become effective until after the transitional period had ended.

operated on the basis of unanimity. If it had acted under Article 133 [113], a qualified majority would have been sufficient, the transitional period now having expired.

The regulations in question provided for the importation of goods from developing countries at preferential tariff rates. The Commission considered that Article 133 [113] was the appropriate legal basis since the regulations concerned tariffs and trade. The Council, however, disagreed. It considered that the purpose of the regulations was not merely commercial but also developmental (aid); therefore some additional legal basis had to be found. It had opted for Article 308 [235], though it had not expressly said so.

Judgment
[After referring to the requirements of Article 253 [190], the court continued:]

6. It is therefore necessary to consider whether the contested regulations satisfy those requirements.

7. In that connection the Council contends that, although the indication of the legal basis is not precise, the recitals in the preambles to the regulations, taken as a whole, provide sufficient alternative information as to the aims pursued by the Council, that is to say both commercial aims and aims of development-aid policy.

8. However, those indications are not sufficient to identify the legal basis by virtue of which the Council acted. Although the recitals in the preambles to the regulations do refer to improving access for developing countries to the markets of the preference-giving countries, they merely state that adaptations to the Community system of generalized preferences have proved to be necessary in the light of experience in the first 15 years. Moreover, according to information given the Court by the Council itself, the wording "Having regard to the Treaty" was adopted as a result of differences of opinion about the choice of the appropriate legal basis. Consequently, the wording chosen was designed precisely to leave the legal basis of the regulations in question vague.

9. Admittedly, failure to refer to a precise provision of the Treaty need not necessarily constitute an infringement of essential procedural requirements when the legal basis for the measure may be determined from other parts of the measure. However, such explicit reference is indispensable where, in its absence, the parties concerned and the Court are left uncertain as to the precise legal basis.

10. In answer to a question put by the Court the Council has stated that when it adopted the contested regulations it intended to base them on both Articles 133 [113] and 308 [235] of the EEC Treaty. It has explained that it departed from the Commission's proposal to base the regulations on Article 133 [113] alone because it was convinced that the contested regulations had not only commercial-policy aims, but also major development-policy aims. The implementation of development policy goes beyond the scope of Article 133 [113] of the Treaty and necessitates recourse to Article 308 [235].

11. It must be observed that in the context of the organization of the powers of the Community the choice of the legal basis for a measure may not depend simply on an institution's conviction as to the objective pursued but must be based on objective factors which are amenable to judicial review.

12. In this case, the argument with regard to the correct legal basis was not a purely formal one, since Articles 133 [113] and 308 [235] of the EEC Treaty entail different rules

regarding the manner in which the Council may arrive at its decision. The choice of the legal basis could thus affect the determination of the content of the contested regulations.

13. It follows from the very wording of Article 308 [235] that its use as the legal basis for a measure is justified only where no other provision of the Treaty gives the Community institutions the necessary power to adopt the measure in question.

14. It must therefore be considered whether in this case the Council had the power to adopt the contested regulations pursuant to Article 133 [113] of the Treaty alone, as the Commission maintains.

[The court considered this question and concluded that it did. It continued:]

21. It follows that the contested regulations are measures falling within the sphere of the common commercial policy and that since the Council had the power to adopt them pursuant to Article 133 [113] of the Treaty, it was not justified in taking as its basis Article 308 [235].

22. It is clear from the foregoing that the contested regulations do not satisfy the requirements laid down in Article 253 [190] of the Treaty with regard to the statement of reasons and that, moreover, they were not adopted on the correct legal basis. Consequently, they must be declared void.

QUESTIONS
1. Must the legal basis be specified in all cases?
2. Why did the court annul the measure in this case, but not in the previous one? Was there not just as much doubt as to whether the alternative provision provided an adequate legal basis?

European Union
Commission v. Council (Commodity Coding case)
COURT OF JUSTICE OF THE EUROPEAN COMMUNITIES
Case 165/87, [1988] ECR 5545

Background

This was an action by the Commission to annul a decision, Decision 87/369, adopted by the Council to conclude an international convention on commodity description and coding. The Commission considered that Article 133 [113] provided an adequate legal basis, but the Council amended the preamble to specify in addition Articles 26 [28] and 308 [235].

Judgment
[The court began by saying that the convention dealt with two matters, tariff nomenclature and statistical nomenclature. The first of these was covered partly by Article 133 [113] and partly by Article 26 [28]. It rejected the Commission's view that Article 133 [113] alone was sufficient. It then continued:]

10. The Commission's argument that the scope of Article 26 [28] is covered by that of Article 133 [113] of the Treaty must therefore be rejected.

11. It may be added that where an institution's power is based on two provisions of the Treaty, it is bound to adopt the relevant measures on the basis of the two relevant provisions.

[passage omitted]

13. Articles 26 [28] and 133 [113] of the Treaty thus together constitute the appropriate legal basis for the establishment of a tariff nomenclature and consequently for the conclusion of an international convention on that subject.

[The court next turned its attention to the other matter covered by the Convention, statistical nomenclature. It held that this was fully covered by Article 133 [113]. After discussion of certain other questions, it continued:]

18. It follows from the foregoing that since the Council had power to take the contested decision under Articles 26 [28] and 133 [113] of the Treaty, it was not entitled to base it on Article 308 [235].

19. However, when the contested decision was adopted before the entry into force of the Single European Act, Article 26 [28] of the Treaty, like Article 308 [235], required unanimity in the Council; the illegality found to exist is therefore only a purely formal defect which cannot make the measure void.

[Note: the Single European Act changed the procedure under Article 26 [28] from unanimity to qualified-majority voting.]

20. It is true that in contrast to Article 26 [28], Article 308 [235] requires the European Parliament to be consulted, and such consultation, which took place in the present case, is likely to affect the substance of the measure adopted. Nevertheless, although disregard of the obligation to consult makes the measure concerned void [*Roquette Frères v. Council*, above], consultation of Parliament, which the Council is always entitled to do, cannot be regarded as unlawful even if it is not mandatory.

Result: measure held valid.

European Union
Commission v. Council (Titanium Dioxide case)
COURT OF JUSTICE OF THE EUROPEAN COMMUNITIES
Case C-300/89, [1991] ECR I-2867

Background

This was an action to annul Directive 89/428, a measure adopted unanimously by the Council to lay down Community-wide manufacturing standards to reduce pollution caused by the titanium dioxide industry. The Commission proposal had given Article 95 [100a], a provision dealing with the internal market, as the legal basis, but the Council proceeded under Article 175 [130s], a provision on the environment.

The Council's view was that the measure was primarily concerned with environmental protection. The Commission, on the other hand, considered that it was really concerned with fair competition between firms in different Member States, since it harmonized the rules on the production of titanium dioxide so that they would be the same throughout the Community. Previously, anti-pollution standards had varied from one country to another, which meant that production costs were greater in those Member States with higher standards.

The important difference between these two provisions was that Article 95 [100a] required that the co-operation procedure be applied, while Article 175 [130s] required unanimity in the Council with the Parliament merely being consulted. It will be remembered from the discussion above that the main feature of the co-operation procedure is that, though the Council otherwise votes by a qualified majority, it must be unanimous if it wishes to adopt the measure over the objections of the Parliament.

Judgment
[The court considered the purpose of the directive and decided that it had two aims. One was to protect the environment and the other was to establish fair competition. It then continued:]

16. It follows that, in view of its aim and content, the directive at issue displays the features both of action relating to the environment with which Article 175 [130s] of the Treaty is concerned and of a harmonizing measure which has as its object the establishment and functioning of the internal market, within the meaning of Article 95 [100a] of the Treaty.

17. As the Court held in [the *Commodity Coding* case, above], paragraph 11, where an institution's power is based on two provisions of the Treaty, it is bound to adopt the relevant measures on the basis of the two relevant provisions. However, that ruling is not applicable to the present case.

18. One of the enabling provisions at issue, Article 95 [100a], requires recourse to the co-operation procedure provided for in Article 252 [189c, originally149(2)] of the Treaty, whereas the other, Article 175 [130s], requires the Council to act unanimously after merely consulting the European Parliament. As a result, use of both provisions as a joint legal basis would divest the co-operation procedure of its very substance.

19. Under the co-operation procedure, the Council acts by a qualified majority where it intends accepting the amendments to its common position proposed by the Parliament and included by the Commission in its re-examined proposal, whereas it must secure unanimity if it intends taking a decision after its common position has been rejected by the Parliament or if it intends modifying the Commission's re-examined proposal. That essential element of the co-operation procedure would be undermined if, as a result of simultaneous reference to Articles 95 [100a] and 175 [130s], the Council were required, in any event, to act unanimously.

20. The very purpose of the co-operation procedure, which is to increase the involvement of the European Parliament in the legislative process of the Community, would thus be jeopardized. As the Court stated in its judgments in [*Roquette Frères v. Council*, above] and [second citation omitted], that participation reflects a fundamental democratic principle that the peoples should take part in the exercise of power through the intermediary of a representative assembly.

21. It follows that in the present case recourse to the dual legal basis of Articles 95 [100a] and 175 [130s] is excluded and that it is necessary to determine which of those two provisions is the appropriate legal basis.

[The court then considered the matter and decided that Article 95 [100a] (fair competition) was the appropriate legal basis. It then concluded:]

25. In view of all the foregoing considerations, the contested measure should have been based on Article 95 [100a] of the EEC Treaty and must therefore be annulled.

QUESTION

Why was the ruling in the *Commodity Coding* case not applicable in the present case?

Opinion: the Court's approach

The rules for qualified-majority voting do not say that there must be *exactly* a qualified majority. They say that there must be *at least* a qualified majority. So if the Council is unanimous, there is of necessity a qualified majority. This is the way most courts would consider the matter, but the European Court does not think in these terms. Its argument is that if the Council proceeds on the basis that unanimity is necessary, it might adopt a watered-down version of the proposal in order to gain the acceptance of those Member States that are doubtful about the measure. If it had adopted the measure on the basis of qualified-majority voting, on the other hand, it might have passed it in a stronger form. This shows that the court's concerns are political, rather than legal. It is not concerned with protecting the minority, but with protecting the majority. It also wants to help the Commission: it is easier for the Commission to get its measure passed if qualified-majority voting is used.

The *Titanium Dioxide* case is the most bizarre product of the court's approach. In that decision, it annulled a measure because it had been adopted on the basis of the *correct* treaty provision. It did this simply in order to preserve the full force of the Parliament's newly acquired rights under the co-operation procedure. It wanted to make the Council act by a qualified majority so that the Parliament's power to force it back to unanimity would actually be noticed. What, one wonders, has become of the principle enunciated in the *Massey-Ferguson* case that, in the interests of legal certainty, the Council is to be given a certain latitude in its choice of legal basis? How could the Council possibly have known in advance that it was not allowed to act under Article 175 [130s]?

Subsidiarity

Subsidiarity[12] is a general political and organizational theory, which appears to have originated in the teachings of the Catholic Church,[13] though it has no

---

12 This word was not current in English until recently. It was imported from the German (*Subsidiarität*) to make it possible to discuss the new theory on the distribution of powers between the European Union and the Member States.

13 See the Papal Encyclical, *Pacem in Terris* (Pope John XXIII, 1963), para. 140.

particular link to religious doctrine. In a nutshell, subsidiarity requires that decisions be taken at the lowest possible level in an organization, unless there is a good reason for them to be made at a higher level. As applied to relations between the European Union and the Member States, subsidiarity requires that legislation be adopted at the Member-State level, unless there is a good reason for adopting it at the Community level. The Community is made up of diverse peoples with diverse cultures, living in diverse conditions. What is good for one Member State may not be good for another. One can therefore approach closer to the greatest good for the greatest number by taking decisions at the Member-State level.[14] This should be departed from only if there is a special reason for acting at the Community level.

The theory of subsidiarity was given legal form by the Treaty on European Union, which added a new provision, Article 5 [3b], to the EC Treaty (Panel 4.6). The first paragraph of this requires the Community to keep within the limits of its powers (principle of limited powers, discussed above). The second paragraph deals with subsidiarity, and the third paragraph says that the Community must not go beyond what is necessary to achieve the objectives of the Treaty, a reference to the principle of proportionality. Proportionality is a principle of German law (*Verhältnismässigkeit*). It is based on the idea that the State should intervene in the lives of citizens only to the minimum extent necessary to attain its purposes. These three principles link up, in theory at least, to impose limits on Community activity.

Unfortunately, the legal effect given to subsidiarity in Article 5 [3b] is extremely limited. It cannot be used to question the granting of powers to the Community by the Treaties, but only the *exercise* of those powers by the passing of particular measures.[15] Moreover, it applies only in areas that do not fall within the exclusive jurisdiction of the Community. It is thus limited to areas in which the Community and the Member States share jurisdiction. The EC Treaty does not specify which those areas are.[16] The Commission has issued a list of areas that it regards as falling within the exclusive jurisdiction of the Community and therefore outside the scope of subsidiarity.[17] It covers a great deal of ground.[18] Moreover, the Commission considers that the list will lengthen as time goes on.[19]

---

14 Similar arguments could lead one to favour devolution to regional or local levels within a Member State; but this is not a matter for the European Union.
15 See para. 3 of the Protocol on the Application of the Principles of Subsidiarity and Proportionality (set out in Panel 4.6).
16 Commentators have expressed divergent views. Toth considers that *all* the areas of power granted to the Community under the EEC Treaty as originally concluded are exclusive: Toth, "The Principle of Subsidiarity in the Maastricht Treaty" (1992) 29 CMLRev. 669 at 1091 *et seq.*; Steiner, on the other hand, suggests that the only areas in which the Community has exclusive competence for the purpose of Art. 5 [3b] are those in which it has already legislated: Steiner, "Subsidiarity under the Maastricht Treaty" in David O'Keeffe and Patrick M Twomey (eds.), *Legal Issues of the Maastricht Treaty* (1994), p. 49 at pp. 55–58; see also Emiliou, "Subsidiarity: Panacea or Fig Leaf?" in *ibid.*, p. 65 at pp. 74–75; and Schilling, "A New Dimension of Subsidiarity: Subsidiarity as a Rule and a Principle" (1994) 14 YEL 203 at 217 *et seq.* (this last analysis is probably the most closely reasoned).
17 See *The Principle of Subsidiarity*, Com. Doc. SEC(92) 1990, 27 October 1992, p. 5.
18 The areas are: the removal of barriers to the free movement of goods, persons, services and capital; the common commercial policy; the general rules on competition; the common organization of agricultural markets; the conservation of fisheries resources; and the essential elements of transport policy.
19 *The Principle of Subsidiarity*, Com. Doc. SEC(92) 1990, 27 October 1992, p. 8.

Panel 4.6 Subsidiarity

EC Treaty

Article 5 [3b]

The Community shall act within the limits of the powers conferred upon it by this Treaty and of the objectives assigned to it therein.

In areas which do not fall within its exclusive competence, the Community shall take action, in accordance with the principle of subsidiarity, only if and in so far as the objectives of the proposed action cannot be sufficiently achieved by the Member States and can therefore, by reason of the scale or effects of the proposed action, be better achieved by the Community.

Any action by the Community shall not go beyond what is necessary to achieve the objectives of this Treaty.

EC Treaty: Protocol on the Application of the Principles of Subsidiarity and Proportionality

(3) The principle of subsidiarity does not call into question the powers conferred on the European Community by the Treaty, as interpreted by the Court of Justice. The criteria referred to in the second paragraph of Article 5 [3b] of the Treaty shall relate to areas for which the Community does not have exclusive competence. The principle of subsidiarity provides a guide as to how those powers are to be exercised at the Community level. Subsidiarity is a dynamic concept and should be applied in the light of the objectives set out in the Treaty. It allows Community action within the limits of its powers to be expanded where circumstances so require, and conversely, to be restricted or discontinued where it is no longer justified.

(4) For any proposed Community legislation, the reasons on which it is based shall be stated with a view to justifying its compliance with the principles of subsidiarity and proportionality; the reasons for concluding that a Community objective can be better achieved by the Community must be substantiated by qualitative or, wherever possible, quantitative indicators.

(5) For Community action to be justified, both aspects of the subsidiarity principle shall be met: the objectives of the proposed action cannot be sufficiently achieved by Member States' action in the framework of their national constitutional system and can therefore be better achieved by action on the part of the Community.

The following guidelines should be used in examining whether the above-mentioned condition is fulfilled:

– the issue under consideration has transnational aspects which cannot be satisfactorily regulated by action by Member States;

– actions by Member States alone or lack of Community action would conflict with the requirements of the Treaty (such as the need to correct distortion of competition or avoid disguised restrictions on trade or strengthen economic and social cohesion) or would otherwise significantly damage Member States' interests;

– action at Community level would produce clear benefits by reason of its scale or effects compared with action at the level of the Member States.

(6) The form of Community action shall be as simple as possible, consistent with satisfactory achievement of the objective of the measure and the need for effective enforcement. The Community shall legislate only to the extent necessary. Other things being equal, directives should be preferred to regulations and framework directives to detailed measures. Directives as provided for in Article 249 [189] of the Treaty, while binding upon each Member State to which they are addressed as to the result to be achieved, shall leave to the national authorities the choice of form and methods.

(7) Regarding the nature and the extent of Community action, Community measures should leave as much scope for national decision as possible, consistent with securing the aim of the measure and observing the requirements of the Treaty. While respecting Community law, care should be taken to respect well-established national arrangements and the organisation and working of Member States' legal systems. Where appropriate and subject to the need for proper enforcement, Community measures should provide Member States with alternative ways to achieve the objectives of the measures.

A protocol has been annexed to the EC Treaty to give further details on the application of subsidiarity and proportionality. This is the Protocol on the Application of the Principles of Subsidiarity and Proportionality, extracts from which are set out in Panel 4.6. This makes clear that, where subsidiarity applies, the Community cannot legislate unless *both* limbs of the test in Article 5 [3b] are satisfied: it must be established that the objectives cannot be sufficiently achieved by Member-State action *and* that they can be better achieved by Community action. This means that if they can be sufficiently achieved by Member-State action, it does not matter that they can be better achieved by Community action. Paragraph 5 contains guidelines as to when Community action might be justified.

Despite the fanfare surrounding its introduction, subsidiarity does not seem to have had a very noticeable impact on Community legislation. The onward march of Community jurisdiction continues as before. So far, Article 5 [3b] has not been directly applied by the European Court to strike down legislation. In one case, however, the European Court has struck down legislation in circumstances in which it seems to have been inspired by the *idea* behind subsidiarity, though not its legal expression in Article 5 [3b].

> *European Union*
> **Germany v. European Parliament and Council** (Tobacco Advertising case)
> **COURT OF JUSTICE OF THE EUROPEAN COMMUNITIES**
> Case C-376/98, [2000] ECR I-8419

Background

This was an action brought by Germany to annul Directive 98/43, which had been adopted jointly by the Council and the European Parliament under the co-decision procedure. Subject to limited exceptions, the directive banned all forms of advertising and sponsorship of tobacco products throughout the Community. Article 5 of the directive expressly stated that it did not prevent Member States from imposing more stringent requirements if these were thought necessary to protect people's health. The directive also stated that it would not affect an earlier directive, Directive 89/552, which banned tobacco advertising on television. This earlier directive, which was not subject to challenge, was based on the argument that if tobacco advertising was permitted in one State but not in another, broadcasts could not be made from the former to the latter, thus restricting the free movement of services (television broadcasting being regarded as a service).

Germany put forward various arguments, including subsidiarity, in support of its claim that the directive was void, but the only argument considered by the court was that the measure was outside the powers of the Community (principle of limited powers or *ultra vires* in English legal terminology). The directive was based on three Treaty provisions: Articles 95 [100a], 47(2) [57(2)] and 55 [66] EC. The first grants a power to adopt legislation needed for the establishment of the internal market, and the latter two grant powers to adopt legislation to make it easier to take up an activity as a self-employed person, or to provide and receive a service, in another Member State. Unlike the previous cases, this case did not raise the question whether one of these provisions was more appropriate than another: the Parliament and the Council were fighting side by side to defend the directive, and the Commission was helping them. The sole issue was whether *any* Treaty provision gave the necessary power.

For the enactment of the directive to be justified on the basis of these provisions, it had to be shown that a ban on tobacco advertising was necessary to promote the free movement of goods or services, freedom of establishment, or fair competition. The reason these provisions were chosen as the legal basis of the directive was that there is no Treaty provision giving the Community a general power to legislate in the area of public health. Indeed, Article 152(4)(c) [129(4)(c)] EC, which gives it the power to adopt incentive measures to improve public health, expressly excludes the harmonization of Member State law.

One argument put forward by the defenders of the directive was that it promoted the free movement of periodicals, magazines and newspapers. If tobacco advertising in these media was permitted in one Member State but not in another, the free movement of periodicals, magazines and newspapers from one Member State to another would be impeded. However, the German Government (the applicant in the present case) pointed out that in fact Member States which at present prohibit tobacco advertising in periodicals, magazines and newspapers apply it only to the national press and not to imports.

Another argument was that if tobacco advertising and sponsorship were permitted with regard to sporting activities in one Member State but not in another, major sporting events might be shifted from the latter to the former. This would give an unfair advantage to promoters in Member States which permit tobacco advertising and sponsorship.

Judgment
Elimination of obstacles to the free movement of goods and the freedom to provide services

96. It is clear that, as a result of disparities between national laws on the advertising of tobacco products, obstacles to the free movement of goods or the freedom to provide services exist or may well arise.

97. In the case, for example, of periodicals, magazines and newspapers which contain advertising for tobacco products, it is true, as the applicant has demonstrated, that no obstacle exists at present to their importation into Member States which prohibit such advertising. However, in view of the trend in national legislation towards ever greater restrictions on advertising of tobacco products, reflecting the belief that such advertising gives rise to an appreciable increase in tobacco consumption, it is probable that obstacles to the free movement of press products will arise in the future.

98. In principle, therefore, a Directive prohibiting the advertising of tobacco products in periodicals, magazines and newspapers could be adopted on the basis of Article 95 [100a] of the Treaty with a view to ensuring the free movement of press products, on the lines of Directive 89/552, Article 13 of which prohibits television advertising of tobacco products in order to promote the free broadcasting of television programmes.

99. However, for numerous types of advertising of tobacco products, the prohibition under Article 3(1) of the Directive cannot be justified by the need to eliminate obstacles to the free movement of advertising media or the freedom to provide services in the field of advertising. That applies, in particular, to the prohibition of advertising on posters, parasols,

ashtrays and other articles used in hotels, restaurants and cafes, and the prohibition of advertising spots in cinemas, prohibitions which in no way help to facilitate trade in the products concerned.

[paragraph omitted]

101. Moreover, the Directive does not ensure free movement of products which are in conformity with its provisions.

[paragraph omitted]

103. Under Article 5 of the Directive, Member States retain the right to lay down, in accordance with the Treaty, such stricter requirements concerning the advertising or sponsorship of tobacco products as they deem necessary to guarantee the health protection of individuals.

104. Furthermore, the Directive contains no provision ensuring the free movement of products which conform to its provisions, in contrast to other directives allowing Member States to adopt stricter measures for the protection of a general interest . . .

105. In those circumstances, it must be held that the Community legislature cannot rely on the need to eliminate obstacles to the free movement of advertising media and the freedom to provide services in order to adopt the Directive on the basis of Articles 95 [100a], 47(2) [57(2)] and 55 [66] of the Treaty.

Elimination of distortion of competition

106. In examining the lawfulness of a directive adopted on the basis of Article 95 [100a] of the Treaty, the Court is required to verify whether the distortion of competition which the measure purports to eliminate is appreciable ([*Titanium Dioxide* case], paragraph 23).

[paragraph omitted]

108. It is therefore necessary to verify whether the Directive actually contributes to eliminating appreciable distortions of competition.

109. First, as regards advertising agencies and producers of advertising media, undertakings established in Member States which impose fewer restrictions on tobacco advertising are unquestionably at an advantage in terms of economies of scale and increase in profits. The effects of such advantages on competition are, however, remote and indirect and do not constitute distortions which could be described as appreciable. They are not comparable to the distortions of competition caused by differences in production costs, such as those which, in particular, prompted the Community legislature to adopt [the Titanium Dioxide Directive, in issue in the previous case].

110. It is true that the differences between certain regulations on tobacco advertising may give rise to appreciable distortions of competition. As the Commission and the Finnish and United Kingdom Governments have submitted, the fact that sponsorship is prohibited in some Member States and authorised in others gives rise, in particular, to certain sports events being relocated, with considerable repercussions on the conditions of competition for undertakings associated with such events.

111. However, such distortions, which could be a basis for recourse to Article 95 [100a] of the Treaty in order to prohibit certain forms of sponsorship, are not such as to justify the use of that legal basis for an outright prohibition of advertising of the kind imposed by the Directive.

112. Second, as regards distortions of competition in the market for tobacco products, irrespective of the applicant's contention that such distortions are not covered by the Directive, it is clear that, in that sector, the Directive is likewise not apt to eliminate appreciable distortions of competition.

113. Admittedly, as the Commission has stated, producers and sellers of tobacco products are obliged to resort to price competition to influence their market share in Member States which have restrictive legislation. However, that does not constitute a distortion of competition but rather a restriction of forms of competition which applies to all economic operators in those Member States. By imposing a wide-ranging prohibition on the advertising of tobacco products, the Directive would in the future generalise that restriction of forms of competition by limiting, in all the Member States, the means available for economic operators to enter or remain in the market.

114. In those circumstances, it must be held that the Community legislature cannot rely on the need to eliminate distortions of competition, either in the advertising sector or in the tobacco products sector, in order to adopt the Directive on the basis of Articles 95 [100a], 47(2) [57(2)] and 55 [66] of the Treaty.

115. In view of all the foregoing considerations, a measure such as the directive cannot be adopted on the basis of Articles 95 [100a], 47(2) [57(2)] and 55 [66] of the Treaty.

116. In those circumstances, the pleas alleging that Articles 95 [100a], 47(2) [57(2)] and 55 [66] do not constitute an appropriate legal basis for the Directive must be upheld.

117. As has been observed in paragraphs 98 and 111 of this judgment, a directive prohibiting certain forms of advertising and sponsorship of tobacco products could have been adopted on the basis of Article 95 [100a] of the Treaty. However, given the general nature of the prohibition of advertising and sponsorship of tobacco products laid down by the Directive, partial annulment of the Directive would entail amendment by the Court of provisions of the Directive. Such amendments are a matter for the Community legislature. It is not therefore possible for the Court to annul the Directive partially.

118. Since the Court has upheld the pleas alleging that the choice of Articles 95 [100a], 47(2) [57(2)] and 55 [66] as a legal basis was inappropriate, it is unnecessary to consider the other pleas put forward by the applicant. The Directive must be annulled in its entirety.

QUESTIONS

1. Is the court's reasoning valid?
2. Can you think of any other arguments that might justify a general ban on tobacco advertising being imposed at Community level, rather than at Member-State level?
3. Was the court right to strike down the whole directive, even though it found that a ban would be justified in certain cases (paragraph 117)?

Comment

As we have seen, the court has often struck legislation down on the ground that it was adopted on the wrong legal basis, or that there was some procedural fault. It has also struck it down on the ground that it infringed some legal principle, such as proportionality (discussed above). As far as is known, however, this is the first time that it has struck legislation down simply because the Community was intruding into the sphere of the Member States. What is interesting about the judgment is that much of it is concerned with the question whether there is a good reason why the Community, rather than the Member States, should take action. It is precisely this issue that has to be addressed when questions of subsidiarity are considered.

Further reading

Bermann, "Taking Subsidiarity Seriously: Federalism in the European Community and the United States" (1994) 94 *Columbia Law Review* 331.

Cass, "The Word that Saves Maastricht? The Principle of Subsidiarity and the Division of Powers within the European Community" (1992) 29 CMLRev. 1107.

Commission (EC), *The Principle of Subsidiarity*, Com. Doc. SEC(92) 1990, 27 October 1992, p. 5.

Constantinesco, "Who's Afraid of Subsidiarity?" (1991) 11 YEL 33.

Craig (Paul) and Harlow (Carol), *Lawmaking in the European Union* (Kluwer Law International, London, The Hague and Boston, 1998).

Dashwood, "The Constitution of the European Union after Nice: Law-Making Procedures" (2001) 26 ELRev. 215.

Emiliou, "Subsidiarity: An Effective Barrier against 'the Enterprises of Ambition'?" (1992) 17 ELRev. 383.

Emiliou, "Subsidiarity: Panacea or Fig Leaf?" in David O'Keeffe and Patrick M. Twomey (eds.), *Legal Issues of the Maastricht Treaty* (Wiley Chancery Law, London, 1994), p. 65.

Schilling, "A New Dimension of Subsidiarity: Subsidiarity as a Rule and a Principle" (1994) 14 YEL 203.

Steiner, "Subsidiarity under the Maastricht Treaty" in David O'Keeffe and Patrick M. Twomey (eds.), *Legal Issues of the Maastricht Treaty* (Wiley Chancery Law, London, 1994), p. 49.

Toth, "A Legal Analysis of Subsidiarity" in David O'Keeffe and Patrick M. Twomey (eds.), *Legal Issues of the Maastricht Treaty* (Wiley Chancery Law, London, 1994), p. 37.

Toth, "Is Subsidiarity Justiciable?" (1994) 14 ELRev. 268.

Toth, "The Principle of Subsidiarity in the Maastricht Treaty" (1992) 29 CMLRev. 669.

Van Kersbergen and Verbeek, "The Politics of Subsidiarity in the European Union" (1994) 32 JCMS 215.

PART II
INTERNATIONAL ADJUDICATION

5 Institutions: an overview

Without adjudication, international law would be a poor thing. Disputes would be resolved by political or military means. At best, the law would be merely one factor in the balance.

The concept of adjudication implies a neutral third person, who judges the dispute. He should do so objectively, on the basis of pre-existing rules. His rulings should be binding and there must be some effective way of ensuring compliance. Without these additional elements, the process is more like conciliation, a procedure under which a third person tries to resolve a dispute by finding a compromise acceptable to both parties.

In this Part, we examine international adjudication as a means of resolving disputes and upholding the law. To set the stage, we look first at some international judicial institutions. At this point, we are concerned only with the bare bones – in particular, composition and jurisdiction. We shall flesh this out in Chapters 6 and 7.

The International Court of Justice

The International Court of Justice (ICJ) is in some ways the premier international judicial organ. It operates on a global level and is open to all States that are parties to its Statute.[1]

Structure

There are fifteen judges, and no two judges may be nationals of the same State.[2] Judges are elected by the United Nations for a (renewable) term of nine years, and must normally secure an absolute majority in both the General Assembly and the Security Council.[3] In practice, the permanent members of

---

1 Art. 35(1) of the Statute of the Court: see Panel 5.1. All members of the UN are automatically parties to the Statute. In certain cases, non-members may also become parties: Art. 93 of the UN Charter. Switzerland became a party to the Statute by the latter route.
2 Art. 3 of the Statute.
3 The procedure is laid down in Arts. 4–15 of the Statute.

the Security Council (China, France, Russia, the United Kingdom and the United States) usually have a judge, though there was a period in which China was not represented. There is also an attempt to ensure that every major geographical region and legal system are represented.[4]

The quorum is nine, though the full court normally hears each case. If it happens that a judge of the nationality of one of the parties is sitting on a case, the other party has the right to have an *ad hoc* judge appointed for that case. If neither party has a judge of its nationality sitting on the case, each may appoint an *ad hoc* judge. This appears to be an attempt to obtain balance and to ensure that at least one judge understands the point of view of each party. Dissenting and concurring opinions are permitted; so it is possible to know how individual judges vote. *Ad hoc* judges usually vote for the party that appointed them, but this is also true of judges who happen to be nationals of a State that is a party, though there are exceptions.

Jurisdiction

Only States may be parties to cases before the court.[5] The jurisdiction of the court is laid down in Articles 34–37 of the Statute (Panel 5.1). It is based on the principle that both parties must agree to the court's hearing the case. There are four ways in which this may occur.[6]

1.   After the dispute has arisen, the States in question may agree that the particular case in question will be referred to the court.

2.   The claimant State may bring the proceedings and the defendant may do something regarded as indicating its acceptance of the jurisdiction of the court – for example, appearing and putting its arguments on the merits (substance) of the case.[7]

3.   The dispute may arise out of a treaty between the States in question, and the treaty may contain a clause[8] providing for such disputes to be decided by the court.[9]

4.   The States in question may have previously accepted the so-called "Optional Clause" (Article 36(2) of the Statute of the court), which grants the court jurisdiction over all disputes under international law between two States both of which have accepted the clause.[10]

---

4 Art. 9 of the Statute.
5 Art. 34(1) of the Statute. Certain international organizations may request advisory opinions: Art. 65 of the Statute.
6 The first three come under Art. 36(1) of the Statute; the fourth (the "Optional Clause") comes under Art. 36(2).
7 This is technically known as "submission"; the Latin phrase is *forum prorogatum*.
8 This is called a "compromissory" clause, from the French *clause compromissoire*.
9 Since the ICJ is regarded as the successor to the Permanent Court of International Justice (PCIJ), Art. 37 of the Statute of the ICJ states that, where a treaty concluded previously provided for the submission of disputes to the PCIJ, that clause will be regarded as conferring jurisdiction on the ICJ. This is sometimes called "transferred" jurisdiction.
10 For the exact wording, see Panel 5.1.

Panel 5.1   Jurisdiction of the International Court of Justice

Statute of the International Court of Justice

Article 34

1. Only states may be parties in cases before the Court.

2. The Court, subject to and in conformity with its Rules, may request of public international organizations information relevant to cases before it, and shall receive such information presented by such organizations on their own initiative.

3. Whenever the construction of the constituent instrument of a public international organization or of an international convention adopted thereunder is in question in a case before the Court, the Registrar shall so notify the public international organization concerned and shall communicate to it copies of all the written proceedings.

Article 35

1. The Court shall be open to the states parties to the present Statute.

2. The conditions under which the Court shall be open to other states shall, subject to the special provisions contained in treaties in force, be laid down by the Security Council, but in no case shall such conditions place the parties in a position of inequality before the Court.

3. When a state which is not a Member of the United Nations is a party to a case, the Court shall fix the amount which that party is to contribute towards the expenses of the Court. This provision shall not apply if such state is bearing a share of the expenses of the Court.

Article 36

1. The jurisdiction of the Court comprises all cases which the parties refer to it and all matters specially provided for in the Charter of the United Nations or in treaties and conventions in force.

2. The states parties to the present Statute may at any time declare that they recognize as compulsory ipso facto and without special agreement, in relation to any other state accepting the same obligation, the jurisdiction of the Court in all legal disputes concerning:

a. the interpretation of a treaty;

b. any question of international law;

c. the existence of any fact which, if established, would constitute a breach of an international obligation;

d. the nature or extent of the reparation to be made for the breach of an international obligation.

3. The declarations referred to above may be made unconditionally or on condition of reciprocity on the part of several or certain states, or for a certain time.

4. Such declarations shall be deposited with the Secretary-General of the United Nations, who shall transmit copies thereof to the parties to the Statute and to the Registrar of the Court.

5. Declarations made under Article 36 of the Statute of the Permanent Court of International Justice and which are still in force shall be deemed, as between the parties to the present Statute, to be acceptances of the compulsory jurisdiction of the International Court of Justice for the period which they still have to run and in accordance with their terms.

6. In the event of a dispute as to whether the Court has jurisdiction, the matter shall be settled by the decision of the Court.

Article 37

Whenever a treaty or convention in force provides for reference of a matter to a tribunal to have been instituted by the League of Nations, or to the Permanent Court of International Justice, the matter shall, as between the parties to the present Statute, be referred to the International Court of Justice.

Assessment

In some ways, the International Court of Justice has failed to live up to the promise of its name.[11] When it hears proceedings because the parties have

11 For fuller assessments of the ICJ, see Ian Brownlie, *Principles of Public International Law* (Oxford University Press, Oxford, 5th ed., 1998), pp. 728–730; Malcolm N. Shaw, *International Law* (Cambridge University Press, Cambridge, 4th ed., 1997), p. 776.

agreed to its jurisdiction in the particular case in question, it is little more than an arbitral tribunal. Where it takes jurisdiction on other grounds (under a compromissory clause or the Optional Clause), compliance can be a problem. We shall consider this in the next chapter.

The World Trade Organization

The problem of compliance is less severe (though it still exists) where the litigation takes place in the context of an international organization to which both parties belong. If membership of the organization brings with it valuable benefits, as is the case with the European Union, the WTO and the NAFTA, States will hesitate to break the rules of the organization by refusing to accept rulings against them, since this could undermine the organization as a whole. This is why the dispute-settlement systems of such organizations, though they may seem less ambitious than the ICJ, are in practice more successful.

The dispute-settlement mechanism of the WTO was created by the Dispute Settlement Understanding (DSU).[12] It is based on the procedure previously followed under the GATT, but there are significant improvements. Though the WTO has no organ formally designated a "court", there is nevertheless a compulsory procedure with judicial features. It is administered by an entity called the Dispute Settlement Body (DSB), on which all Member States are represented.[13] The DSB takes decisions by consensus, which means that a single objection can block a decision.[14]

Panel formation and procedure

If a Member State wishes to make a complaint, it must first hold consultations with the other party to try to find a negotiated settlement. If no solution is found within sixty days (twenty in cases of urgency), the complainant may ask the DSB to establish a panel.[15] The DSB must establish it, unless it takes a decision not to do so. Since such a decision is by consensus, the complainant can always block any decision not to establish a panel.

Panel members must be experts in international trade law.[16] The DSB Secretariat maintains an indicative list of suitable persons.[17] Unless both parties agree otherwise, panellists must not be citizens of a State that is a

---

12 It forms Annex 2 to the Agreement Establishing the World Trade Organization, 1994. For it and related materials, see WTO Secretariat, *The WTO Dispute Settlement Procedures* (Cambridge University Press, Cambridge, 2nd ed., 2001). Alternatively, see http://docsonline.wto.org. Click on "Browse" and then on "Legal Texts and Agreements". Under the heading "Understandings" you will find "Understanding on Rules and Procedures Governing the Settlement of Disputes". This is the DSU.
13 WTO Agreement, Art. IV(3).
14 Art. 2(4) DSU provides that a decision is deemed to have been taken if no Member State present at the meeting makes a formal objection.
15 Art. 4 DSU. If both parties agree that the consultations have failed, a panel may be requested earlier.
16 Art. 8(1) DSU.
17 Art. 8(4) DSU.

party to the proceedings.[18] A panel normally consists of three persons.[19] The Secretariat proposes nominations, which the parties may oppose only for compelling reasons. If the composition of the panel is not agreed within twenty days, either party may request the Director-General to name the panel members.[20]

The panel hears submissions and oral argument from the parties. It then sets out its findings and recommendations in a report to the DSB.[21] In the absence of an appeal, the report must be adopted by the DSB unless the DSB decides by consensus not to do so.[22] Since the winning party can block any such decision, adoption is in effect automatic. This is the greatest advance over the procedure used under the old GATT, where the report was adopted only if there was consensus *in favour* of adoption.[23]

Another improvement on the previous system is that there is now provision for an appeal to a new entity called the Appellate Body.[24] Unlike the panels, the Appellate Body is a standing body. It consists of seven persons, three of whom serve (in rotation) on each appeal. They are appointed by the DSB for four-year terms, renewable once. Appeals are limited to points of law. An Appellate Body report must be adopted by the DSB unless the DSB decides by consensus not to do so.

Decisions of panels and of the Appellate Body are available on the Internet.[25] They are also published in the Dispute Settlement Reports.[26] Although there is no formal system of precedent, they are often cited in subsequent cases. It seems clear that an informal body of case law is gradually being established.[27]

Jurisdiction

The DSU procedure is open only to Member States. There is no provision for private parties to bring proceedings. A Member State may bring proceedings only if it considers that benefits accruing to it under one of the agreements covered by the DSU (referred to as "covered agreements")[28] are being impaired by measures taken by another Member State. However, any infringement of an obligation under a covered agreement is presumed to constitute impairment unless the contrary is proved.[29]

---

18 Art. 8(3) DSU.
19 Art. 8(5). The parties may agree to have five panellists.
20 Art. 8(7).
21 The panel first produces an interim report, which is given to the parties for their comments: Art. 15(2).
22 Art. 16(4).
23 On this, see John H. Jackson, *The Jurisprudence of GATT and the WTO* (Cambridge University Press, Cambridge, 2000), p. 123.
24 Art. 17.
25 The website is http://www.wto.org.
26 Co-published by the WTO and Cambridge University Press.
27 See Palmeter and Mavroidis, "The WTO Legal System: Sources of Law" (1998) 92 AJIL 398.
28 They are listed in Appendix 1 to the DSU. The system also applies to disputes under the WTO Agreement and under the DSU itself. In some cases, additional rules and procedures apply. See Art. 1 DSU.
29 Art. 3(8).

How binding are panel reports?

There has been something of a controversy over the exact status of the report of a panel or of the Appellate Body. Let us assume that the report determines that the respondent Member State has violated the law. In such a case, it will normally recommend that the Member State amend its law or change its practice. Is such a ruling legally binding on the respondent? According to one view, it is not binding as such. It merely obliges the respondent *either* to comply *or* to pay compensation. According to this view, to which the European Court appears to adhere,[30] it has a perfectly free choice between these alternatives. The other view is that there is an international legal obligation on the respondent to end the violation. Payment of compensation does not absolve it from doing so: compensation is merely a second-best response that is less reprehensible than total inaction.[31] This seems the better view. Although the text of the DSU is ambiguous, this latter view seems to fit in better with the wording.[32] It also gives effect to the underlying purpose of the dispute-settlement system.

The same problem arises in the case of the NAFTA. As we shall see below, the first view may be justifiable in the case of some procedures under the NAFTA, but is clearly wrong in the case of others.

Assessment

Most commentators agree that the WTO's dispute-settlement system has been remarkably successful.[33] It is widely used, and States have in general been willing to comply with rulings (although an exception will be considered in the next chapter).

The European Union

The European Union has two courts – the Court of Justice of the European Communities (the European Court of Justice, or ECJ), which is its original and main judicial organ, and the Court of First Instance (CFI), which was created

---

30 *Portugal v. Council*, Case C-149/96, [1999] ECR I-8395 (paras. 25–52 of the judgment) (set out in Chap. 13).
31 Jackson, "Editorial Comment: The WTO Dispute Settlement Understanding – Misunderstandings on the Nature of Legal Obligation" (1997) 91 AJIL 60; reprinted in John H. Jackson, *The Jurisprudence of the GATT and the WTO* (Cambridge University Press, Cambridge, 2000), p. 162.
32 See Arts. 3(7), 19(1), 21(1), 22(1) and 22(8). It should also be noted that Art. 26(1)(b) of the DSU states that, where a measure has been found to nullify or impair the benefits of the relevant agreement without violating it, there is no obligation to withdraw the measure. The implication is that where there is a violation, the measure must be withdrawn: see John H. Jackson, *The Jurisprudence of the GATT and the WTO* (Cambridge University Press, Cambridge, 2000), p. 167.
33 For a general assessment, see Jackson, "Dispute Settlement and the WTO: Emerging Problems" (1998) 1 JIEL 329, reprinted in John H. Jackson, *The Jurisprudence of the GATT and the WTO* (Cambridge University Press, Cambridge, 2000), p. 168; Hudec, "The New WTO Dispute Settlement Procedure: An Overview of the First Three Years" (1999) 8 *Minnesota Journal of Global Trade* 1. See also John Collier and Vaughan Lowe, *The Settlement of Disputes in International Law* (Oxford University Press, Oxford, 1999), p. 104.

Panel 5.2 The European Court: structure

EC Treaty

Article 220 [164]

The Court of Justice and the Court of First Instance, each within its jurisdiction, shall ensure that in the interpretation and application of this Treaty the law is observed . . .

Article 221 [165]

The Court of Justice shall consist of one judge per Member State.

   The Court of Justice shall sit in chambers or in a Grand Chamber, in accordance with the rules laid down for that purpose in the Statute of the Court of Justice.

   When provided for in the Statute, the Court of Justice may also sit as a full Court.

Article 222 [166]

The Court of Justice shall be assisted by eight Advocates-General. Should the Court of Justice so request, the Council, acting unanimously, may increase the number of Advocates-General.

   It shall be the duty of the Advocate-General, acting with complete impartiality and independence, to make, in open court, reasoned submissions on cases which, in accordance with the Statute of the Court of Justice, require his involvement.

Article 223 [167]

The Judges and Advocates-General of the Court of Justice shall be chosen from persons whose independence is beyond doubt and who possess the qualifications required for appointment to the highest judicial offices in their respective countries or who are jurisconsults of recognised competence; they shall be appointed by common accord of the governments of the Member States for a term of six years.

   Every three years there shall be a partial replacement of the Judges and Advocates-General, in accordance with the conditions laid down in the Statute of the Court of Justice.

   The Judges shall elect the President of the Court of Justice from among their number for a term of three years. He may be re-elected.

   Retiring Judges and Advocates-General may be reappointed.

   The Court of Justice shall appoint its Registrar and lay down the rules governing his service.

   The Court of Justice shall establish its Rules of Procedure. Those Rules shall require the approval of the Council, acting by a qualified majority.

Article 225 [168a]

1. The Court of First Instance shall have jurisdiction . . .

   Decisions given by the Court of First Instance under this paragraph may be subject to a right of appeal to the Court of Justice on points of law only . . .

subsequently to ease the workload of the ECJ by taking over cases that do not involve major governmental interests.[34] An appeal on points of law lies from the Court of First Instance to the European Court. The following discussion will focus on the European Court, but much of what is said will apply to the Court of First Instance as well.

   Judges on the European Court are appointed by the Member States. In theory, each Member State must agree to every appointment, but in practice they usually agree to each other's nominations. Article 221 EC, as amended by the Treaty of Nice, provides that there is one judge per Member State (Panel 5.2). Before the Treaty of Nice came into force, there was no express rule to this effect, but this was normally what happened in practice. If an attempt had been

---

34 For example, cases in which firms are accused of violating EC competition (antitrust) law. See Art. 225 [168a] EC.

made to deprive one State of "its" judge, it could have retaliated by blocking all the other appointments.

The court usually sits in chambers (panels) of three or five judges. It can also sit in a Grand Chamber of eleven judges. It must sit in a Grand Chamber whenever a Member State or an institution of the Community that is a party to the case so requests. Only in exceptional cases will the full court sit,[35] There is no rule that when a State is a party, one of the judges on the case must be from that State. Even if the State requests a Grand Chamber, it is possible that "its" judge will not be sitting. This is not regarded as a problem.

Judges are appointed for a period of six years. They may be reappointed and this often occurs. This puts them in a weaker position than English judges. They might hesitate to offend a Member State (especially their own) for fear of jeopardizing their chances of reappointment. This is the reason members of the European Court do not give separate judgments – dissenting or concurring – as do the members of, for example, the International Court of Justice or the European Court of Human Rights.[36]

Advocates-general are an unusual feature of the EC system. They are appointed in the same way as judges and have the same tenure. They are regarded as members of the court and sit with the judges when administrative matters concerning the functioning of the court are decided. However, they play no part in the court's deliberations in cases. Their role is to give an Opinion after the hearing is concluded but before the court begins to consider its judgment. Despite their name, they are not advocates for the Community, a Community institution, a Member State or anyone else. They are just as independent as a judge. The idea is that if the advocate-general attempts to decide the case first, his Opinion can serve as a starting point for the court. The court is not bound by his Opinion, but often follows it.

An advocate-general's Opinion is more like an English judgment than the terse and abstract words of the court. It contains a detailed discussion of the facts, and sets out the legal background to the case. It considers the relevant authorities, especially previous judgments of the court. It often deals with more issues: the court normally restricts itself to deciding the minimum necessary to dispose of the case, while the advocate-general considers all the issues. For this reason, his Opinion is useful to lawyers researching the law for later cases. The advocate-general's Opinion sheds light on the court's reasoning and, in so far as the Opinion considers points not discussed by the court, points the way towards future decisions. The Opinions of advocates-general are often cited by counsel in later cases, especially when they consider points never decided by the court. Even if the advocate-general's Opinion is rejected by the court, it may still be cited in later cases in an attempt to induce the court to accept that it was mistaken. Occasionally, this will be successful.

---

35 See Art. 16 of the Protocol on the Statute of the Court of Justice (a protocol to the EC Treaty), as amended by the Treaty of Nice.
36 Another reason is that separate judgments are not found in most civil law countries. The *Bundesverfassungsgericht* (German Constitutional Court) is an exception.

Panel 5.3 Preliminary rulings

EC Treaty

Article 234 [177]

The Court of Justice shall have jurisdiction to give preliminary rulings concerning:

(a) the interpretation of this Treaty;

(b) the validity and interpretation of acts of the institutions of the Community and of the ECB;

(c) the interpretation of the statutes of bodies established by an act of the Council, where those statutes so provide.

Where such a question is raised before any court or tribunal of a Member State, that court or tribunal may, if it considers that a decision on the question is necessary to enable it to give judgment, request the Court of Justice to give a ruling thereon.

Where any such question is raised in a case pending before a court or tribunal of a Member State against whose decisions there is no judicial remedy under national law, that court or tribunal shall bring the matter before the Court of Justice.

Note: "statute" in sub-para. (c) of the first paragraph of this Article does not mean "statute" in the UK sense. It means a legal instrument that sets out the powers of a body – in other words, the act of the Council establishing the body. As far as is known, this provision has never been applied.

The system of advocates-general can, therefore, be regarded as beneficial. However, criticisms are sometimes raised that it is not normally possible for the parties to challenge his views. He gives his Opinion at the end of the oral proceedings, and the parties cannot submit written responses to what he says. It could even be argued that this is contrary to Article 6(1) of the European Convention on Human Rights (right to a fair trial). The European Court has rejected this view, however, on the ground that the advocate-general's Opinion is part of the court's own decision-making process; moreover, if there is a particular need, a party can always ask the court to reopen the oral proceedings.[37]

Jurisdiction

The cases that the European Court can hear fall into two broad categories. The first consists of cases that begin in Member-State courts and are referred to the European Court for a preliminary ruling on a point of Community law. The European Court can never give final judgment in these cases: it decides the point of law and sends the case back to the Member-State court. The second category consists of cases that begin in the European Court. In these cases, known as direct actions, the European Court will give the final judgment.

Preliminary rulings

We shall first consider cases that begin in a Member-State court and are referred to the European Court. This head of jurisdiction is covered by Article 234 [177] EC (Panel 5.3). The European Court has interpreted this to give it jurisdiction to:

---

37 *Emesa Sugar (Free Zone) NV v. Aruba,* Case C-17/89, [2000] ECR I-665 (Order of 4 February 2000). It is not certain that the European Court of Human Rights would take the same view: see *Vermeulen v. Belgium* [1996] I *Reports of Judgments and Decisions* 224.

- interpret the EC Treaty (including any amendment);
- interpret Community acts (legislation and executive decisions);
- determine the validity of Community acts; and
- decide whether a provision in the EC Treaty or a Community act is directly effective (applicable by courts in Member States).[38]

Any court of a Member State *may* refer one of these questions to the European Court. A court from which there is no appeal *must* do so.

The purpose of this procedure is to ensure that Community law is correctly applied by Member-State courts. If the European Court did not have this jurisdiction, the same provision might be interpreted in one way in one Member State and in another way in another Member State. This would mean that the obligations imposed on Member States would not be the same. Although a similar jurisdiction had been previously proposed for other international courts,[39] it had never been put into effect. The European Court was, therefore, breaking new ground when it began to exercise it. Subsequently, similar powers have been conferred on other international courts.[40]

The power to hear references from Member-State courts has been one of the most potent weapons in the hands of the European Court. It has used it to ensure that Community law penetrates into the very heart of the legal systems of the Member States. We shall consider it in further detail in Chapter 11.

Direct actions

The most important forms of direct action[41] are actions against Member States and actions against the Community (or one of its institutions). Actions against Member States are governed by Articles 226 [169] to 228 [171] EC (Panel 5.4). This permits the Commission, or another Member State, to bring proceedings against any Member State that infringes Community law. In practice, virtually all proceedings are brought by the Commission, which fulfils the role of EC law-enforcement agency. If the Commission thinks that a Member State is not obeying Community law, it will first take the matter up privately with the government in question. If this does not yield results, it will formally write to the government telling it what it is alleged to have done wrong and inviting it

---

38 The first three items follow from the text of the Treaty. For the fourth item, see *Van Gend en Loos*, Case 26/62, [1963] ECR 1; [1963] CMLR 105. This question is considered in detail in Chap. 9.

39 In 1907, it was proposed that an International Prize Court be set up with the power to hear appeals from national courts: D. W. Bowett, *The Law of International Institutions* (Sweet and Maxwell, London, 4th ed., 1982), pp. 263–264. In 1929, it was suggested that the Permanent Court of International Justice (the forerunner to the ICJ) might one day be given jurisdiction to hear references from national courts: H. Lauterpacht, "Decisions of Municipal Courts as a Source of International Law" (1929) 10 BYIL 65 at 94–95. See also Plender, "The European Court as an International Tribunal" [1983] CLJ 279 at 284.

40 The Benelux Court, the Andean Court of Justice and the EFTA Court now have it, though the EFTA Court's opinions are only advisory. On the Benelux Court, see Art. 6 of the Treaty Establishing the Benelux Court, 1965 (in force on 1 January 1974); on the Andean Court, see Arts. 28–31 of the Treaty creating the Court of Justice of the Cartagena Agreement, 1979, (1979) 18 ILM 1203; on the EFTA Court, see Art. 34 of the Agreement between the EFTA States on the Establishment of a Surveillance Authority and a Court of Justice, OJ 1994, L344.

41 We shall not discuss some of the less common kinds of proceedings, such as proceedings brought under a clause in a contract conferring jurisdiction on the court (Art. 238 [181] EC). Proceedings to obtain an opinion from the court as to whether a proposed agreement is compatible with the EC Treaty (Art. 300(6) [228(6)] EC) will be discussed in Chap. 12.

Panel 5.4   Enforcement actions

EC Treaty

Article 226 [169]

If the Commission considers that a Member State has failed to fulfil an obligation under this Treaty, it shall deliver a reasoned opinion on the matter after giving the State concerned the opportunity to submit its observations.

   If the State concerned does not comply with the opinion within the period laid down by the Commission, the latter may bring the matter before the Court of Justice.

Article 227 [170]

A Member State which considers that another Member State has failed to fulfil an obligation under this Treaty may bring the matter before the Court of Justice.

   Before a Member State brings an action against another Member State for an alleged infringement of an obligation under this Treaty, it shall bring the matter before the Commission.

   The Commission shall deliver a reasoned opinion after each of the States concerned has been given the opportunity to submit its own case and its observations on the other party's case both orally and in writing.

   If the Commission has not delivered an opinion within three months of the date on which the matter was brought before it, the absence of such opinion shall not prevent the matter from being brought before the Court of Justice.

to explain its position. If the Commission is not convinced, it will issue a formal opinion that the Member State is in default. If the delinquent State does not fall into line, the Commission will bring proceedings before the European Court.

Actions against the Community may be brought to obtain either judicial review or damages. Proceedings for judicial review may be brought either to annul an act of the Commission or Council or to require the Commission or Council to adopt an act.

Annulment proceedings are covered by Articles 230 [173] and 231 [174] EC (Panel 5.5). A Member State may bring annulment proceedings against any legislative or executive act of the Council or Commission. It may also bring proceedings against acts of the European Parliament and the European Central Bank (ECB), though such proceedings are rare.[42] The Council, the Commission and the Parliament may bring proceedings.[43] Private parties[44] may bring proceedings, but only against decisions that are addressed to them or concern them directly and individually. The case law on when a measure concerns a person directly and individually is both complex and inconsistent. It is discussed further in Chapter 18.

Actions for failure to act are governed by Article 232 [175] EC (Panel 5.6). They are less common than annulment actions and the law governing them is less developed. They fulfil the reverse function to that of annulment actions. They apply where the Council, Commission or European Parliament ought to have adopted a legislative or executive act, but failed to do so. Member States (and other Community institutions) can always bring proceedings. Private

---

42 Proceedings against the Parliament and the Council jointly (with regard to joint legislation) take place from time to time.
43 The European Parliament, the Court of Auditors and the European Central Bank may also bring proceedings in certain circumstances.
44 In the Treaty, they are referred to as "natural" or "legal" persons. The former are individuals; the latter, companies.

Panel 5.5   Annulment actions

EC Treaty

Article 230 [173]

The Court of Justice shall review the legality of acts adopted jointly by the European Parliament and the Council, of acts of the Council, of the Commission and of the ECB, other than recommendations and opinions, and of acts of the European Parliament intended to produce legal effects vis-à-vis third parties.

It shall for this purpose have jurisdiction in actions brought by a Member State, the European Parliament, the Council or the Commission on grounds of lack of competence, infringement of an essential procedural requirement, infringement of this Treaty or of any rule of law relating to its application, or misuse of powers.

The Court of Justice shall have jurisdiction under the same conditions in actions brought by the Court of Auditors and by the ECB for the purpose of protecting their prerogatives.

Any natural or legal person may, under the same conditions, institute proceedings against a decision addressed to that person or against a decision which, although in the form of a regulation or a decision addressed to another person, is of direct and individual concern to the former.

The proceedings provided for in this Article shall be instituted within two months of the publication of the measure, or of its notification to the plaintiff, or, in the absence thereof, of the day on which it came to the knowledge of the latter, as the case may be.

Article 231 [174]

If the action is well founded, the Court of Justice shall declare the act concerned to be void.

In the case of a regulation, however, the Court of Justice shall, if it considers this necessary, state which of the effects of the regulation which it has declared void shall be considered as definitive.

Panel 5.6   Failure to act

EC Treaty

Article 232 [175]

Should the European Parliament, the Council or the Commission, in infringement of this Treaty, fail to act, the Member States and the other institutions of the Community may bring an action before the Court of Justice to have the infringement established.

The action shall be admissible only if the institution concerned has first been called upon to act. If, within two months of being so called upon, the institution concerned has not defined its position, the action may be brought within a further period of two months.

Any natural or legal person may, under the conditions laid down in the preceding paragraphs, complain to the Court of Justice that an institution of the Community has failed to address to that person any act other than a recommendation or an opinion.

The Court of Justice shall have jurisdiction, under the same conditions, in actions or proceedings brought by the ECB in the areas falling within the latter's field of competence and in actions or proceedings brought against the latter.

Article 233 [176]

The institution or institutions whose act has been declared void or whose failure to act has been declared contrary to this Treaty shall be required to take the necessary measures to comply with the judgment of the Court of Justice.

This obligation shall not affect any obligation which may result from the application of the second paragraph of Article 288 [215].

This Article shall also apply to the ECB.

Note: Art. 233 [176] also applies to annulment actions under Art. 230[173].

---

parties can do so only where the act should have been addressed to them or, if adopted, would have concerned them directly or individually.[45] Before proceedings may be brought, the applicant must address a formal communication to the institution in question calling on it to act. If it fails to define its

---

[45] This latter possibility is a slight extension of the English text, but finds support in some of the other language versions. It was adopted in *ENU v. Commission*, Case C-107/91, [1993] ECR I-599.

position[46] within two months, the proceedings may be brought within the next two months. These proceedings are discussed further in Chapter 19.

Actions for damages are governed by Article 288 [215]. The relevant part of this reads:

> In the case of non-contractual liability, the Community shall, in accordance with the general principles common to the laws of the Member States, make good any damage caused by its institutions or by its servants in the performance of their duties.

The phrase "non-contractual liability" covers tort. Whether it also covers unjust enrichment (restitution) has not yet been decided. Private parties have the same right to bring proceedings as Member States. In practice, almost all actions are brought by private parties, usually because some legislative or executive action of the Council or Commission has caused them economic loss. Article 288 [215] is interpreted restrictively by the European Court and it is extremely rare for a litigant ever to recover damages from the Community.[47] Nevertheless, it is sometimes useful in order to obtain a ruling on a legal point. Unlike actions for judicial review, which must be brought within a two-month time limit, the applicant has five years within which to commence an action for damages. For further consideration, see Chapter 19.

A diagrammatic representation of all the main heads of jurisdiction is set out in Panel 5.7.

Assessment

It is accepted by all commentators that the European Court has been extremely successful. Its judgments are almost always obeyed – one of the exceptions will be discussed in the next chapter – and it has played a major role in the development of Community law. In the view of some, it has even become so confident of its position that it has begun to abuse it by giving judgments that cannot be justified on normal legal grounds. This contention will be examined in Chapter 7.

The NAFTA

Like the WTO Agreement, the NAFTA (North American Free Trade Agreement)[48] does not establish a body formally designated a "court". It does, however, have dispute-settlement procedures that are similar in many ways to those in the WTO. A body called the Free Trade Commission (FTC), established by Article 2001 of NAFTA, carries out the functions undertaken in the WTO by the DSB.

---

46 A refusal to adopt the act requested constitutes a definition of position and thus blocks an action under Art. 232 [175]; however, the refusal may itself be challenged under Art. 230 [173].

47 In 1995, Advocate-General Tesauro said that only eight awards had ever been made: *Brasserie du Pêcheur v. Germany*, Case C-46/93, [1996] ECR I-1029 at 1101, n. 65, of the Opinion.

48 For the full text of the Agreement, see http://www.nafta-sec-alena.org.

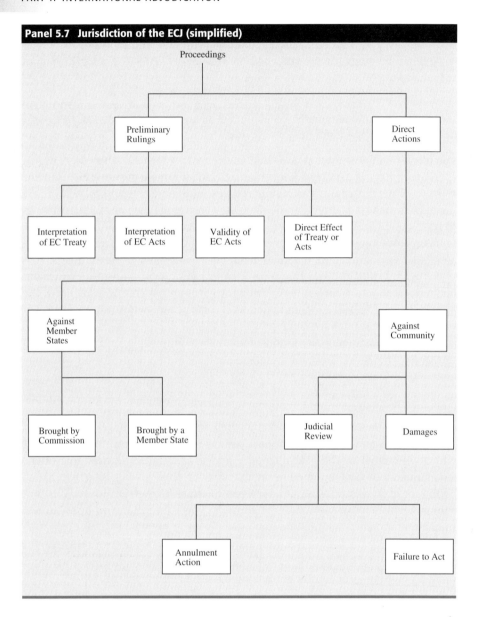

Panel 5.7   Jurisdiction of the ECJ (simplified)

Its functions include resolving disputes regarding the interpretation and application of the Agreement. It takes decisions by consensus.[49] It is assisted by a Secretariat, divided into three national Sections, one for each of the three Member States.

One of the special features of the NAFTA is that, in addition to a general dispute-settlement procedure, there are a number of special procedures applicable in particular cases. These special procedures apply to:

---

49 Art. 2001(4).

- investment disputes (NAFTA Chapter 11);
- financial-services disputes (NAFTA Chapter 14); and
- anti-dumping (AD) and countervailing-duty (CVD) disputes (NAFTA Chapter 19).

We shall first consider the general procedure.

General procedure

The general procedure is laid down in NAFTA Chapter 20. It is open only to States. As under the WTO, the parties to a dispute must first try to resolve it through consultations.[50] If these fail, the complainant can require the FTC to establish a panel.[51] Panels consist of five persons. They are normally drawn from a roster of up to thirty suitably qualified individuals, appointed by consensus for three-year terms. Since each person on the roster must be acceptable to all three Contracting States, one would expect persons of recognised integrity, independence and ability to be appointed.

The first step in establishing a panel is to choose the chairman. He must be selected by mutual agreement, but if the parties fail to agree within fifteen days, one party will be chosen by lot and it will appoint the chairman, who must not be one of its citizens. Each party then chooses two of the remaining panellists. The persons chosen will normally be from the roster – if not, they will be open to peremptory challenge[52] by the other party[53] – and they must be citizens of the other party.[54] Thus if the United States and Canada are in dispute, the US must choose two Canadians, and Canada must choose two Americans.

The panel holds hearings, and issues its report.[55] If the members of the panel are not unanimous, individuals may issue dissenting or concurring reports, but their identity must not be revealed.[56] The report is given to the FTC, which publishes it, unless it agrees (by consensus) not to do so. The NAFTA does not expressly say that the report is binding. The relevant provision, Article 2018, states:

> On receipt of the final report of a panel, the disputing Parties shall agree on the resolution of the dispute, which shall normally conform with the determinations and recommendations of the panel, and shall notify their Sections of the Secretariat of any agreed resolution of the dispute.

If the parties fail to agree on the resolution of the dispute, the complainant may take retaliatory action by suspending the application to the other party of equivalent benefits. If the latter considers that the level of benefits suspended

---

50 Art. 2003.
51 Art. 2008(2).
52 This means that the party may have the panellist removed without having to give any reason.
53 Art. 2011(3).
54 Art. 2011(1).
55 It first issues a draft report on which the parties may comment: Art. 2016.
56 Art. 2017(2).

is "manifestly excessive", it can require the setting up of a panel to decide the question.[57]

Special procedures

Investment disputes

The general procedure applies to investment disputes; so one Member State may bring proceedings under it against another Member State on the ground that the latter has failed to abide by the NAFTA provisions on the protection of investments. In addition, however, NAFTA Chapter 11 allows the investor himself to bring a complaint.[58] If the complaint is not settled by negotiation, the investor can take it to binding arbitration under certain systems for international arbitration that exist independently of the NAFTA.[59] These are:

- the World Bank's International Centre for the Settlement of Investment Disputes (ICSID);[60]
- ICSID's Additional Facility Rules;[61] and
- the rules of the United Nations Commission for International Trade Law (UNCITRAL).

The investor must agree to the arbitration and must waive any remedies available under the internal law of the other party. The other party automatically agrees by virtue of being a party to the NAFTA. The arbitrators can award damages and restitution of property.[62] They may also award costs in accordance with the applicable arbitration rules. Awards are legally binding. An award in favour of the investor may be enforced, at his option, under the ICSID Convention, 1965 (if applicable), the Inter-American Convention on International Commercial Arbitration, 1975 or the New York Convention (UN Convention on the Recognition and Enforcement of Foreign Arbitral Awards, 1958).

There is nothing comparable to this system in the WTO or EU. In both cases, investors must take their complaints to the domestic courts of the Member State in which the investment was made. In the EU, however, investors may

---

57 Art. 2019(3).

58 The complainant must be an "investor of a Party" (Art. 1116). The State against which the complaint is brought must be a different party. Thus a US company cannot bring proceedings against the US. An "investor of a Party" means "a Party or state enterprise thereof, or a national or an enterprise of such Party, that seeks to make, is making or has made an investment" (Art. 1139). An enterprise of a party is an enterprise constituted under the law of a party. It is also a branch located in the territory of a party and carrying out business activities there (*ibid.*). Thus proceedings against the US could be brought by Canada, a Canadian state enterprise, a company incorporated in Canada or the Canadian branch of a foreign company, even, it seems, by the Canadian branch of a US company. In each case, the complainant must be an investor in the US.

59 Art. 1120.

60 This is available only if both the investor's State and the State against which the complaint is brought are parties to the Convention.

61 This is available only if either the investor's State or the State against which the complaint is brought (but not both) is a party to the Convention. The Additional Facility Rules were created so that the ICSID procedure could be used where only one party is a Contracting State to ICSID or is a national of such a State. For further discussion of the ICSID system, see John Collier and Vaughan Lowe, *The Settlement of Disputes in International Law* (Oxford University Press, Oxford, 1999), pp. 59–73.

62 Art. 1135.

ask the court to apply the Community Treaties and, if there is a dispute over their interpretation, ask for a reference to the European Court under Article 234 [177] EC.

Financial-services disputes

The general procedure in NAFTA Chapter 20 also applies to financial-services disputes. However, NAFTA Chapter 14 lays down certain modifications; in particular, there is a special roster of financial-services experts to serve as panellists in such cases.[63] There are also modifications to the procedure for investment disputes under NAFTA Chapter 11 when these concern financial services.[64]

Anti-dumping and countervailing duty disputes

Most countries in the world have anti-dumping (AD) legislation. Dumping is the export of goods at unfairly low prices. Anti-dumping legislation attempts to identify cases of dumping and take appropriate measures, usually in the form of countervailing duties (CVD) (extra customs duties that negate the effect of the dumping). NAFTA Chapter 19 deals with these topics. It permits Member States to retain their AD and CVD legislation and to apply it to goods from the other party.[65] However, it creates special procedures by which disputes regarding such measures may be resolved.

These procedures apply in two situations. The first is where one Member State amends its AD or CVD legislation in a way that another Member State regards as contrary to the GATT or the principles of the NAFTA. The second concerns decisions in individual cases regarding goods imported from another Member State.

In the first situation, the complainant can require the setting up of a panel to adjudicate on the matter. After a hearing, the panel produces a "declaratory opinion",[66] which may recommend modifications to the amending statute. The NAFTA does not say that this is binding. However, if the other party does not put the recommendation into effect within nine months (and no other mutually satisfactory solution is reached), the complainant may take retaliatory action by introducing similar amendments to its AD or CVD legislation; or it may even terminate the NAFTA as regards the offending party.[67]

The second situation concerns final determinations in individual AD or CVD cases. These determinations are made by an administrative authority, which, after an investigation, decides whether dumping has occurred in a particular case and, if it has, adopts counter-measures. In all three Member States, these determinations are subject to judicial review in at least some situations. What NAFTA Chapter 19 does is to provide an international alternative to such review.

---

63 Art. 1414.
64 See Art. 1415.
65 Art. 1902.
66 The procedure, which is laid down in Annex 1903.2, is similar to that under the general procedure.
67 Art. 1903.

Although proceedings under NAFTA Chapter 19 are brought by a Member State, the State is obliged to bring them if requested by a private party that would have been entitled to bring proceedings under the domestic law of the importing State.[68] Thus if, for example, an American company considers that a CVD has been unfairly imposed on its goods in Mexico, it can require the United States to commence proceedings against Mexico under NAFTA Chapter 19 if it would have had a right to bring review proceedings under Mexican law. However, if the company takes advantage of its right to bring review proceedings under Mexican law, proceedings cannot be brought under NAFTA Chapter 19.

The proceedings under NAFTA Chapter 19 are before a panel, which must apply the AD and CVD law of the State of importation. It is assumed that the AD and CVD legislation of the three Member States was consistent with the NAFTA when the Agreement was entered into. The procedure described previously is intended to ensure that it continues to be so. The administrative authority that made the AD or CVD determination is entitled to be represented in the proceedings before the panel, as are any private parties that would have been entitled to participate in review proceedings under the domestic law of the importing State.

In contrast to the first situation covered by NAFTA Chapter 19, a panel decision reviewing a final determination in an individual case is expressly stated to be binding.[69] Member States are required to amend their legislation to ensure that effect is given to a decision for a refund (with interest) of anti-dumping or countervailing duties,[70] and they are expressly prohibited from permitting any appeal under their domestic law from a NAFTA panel decision.[71]

In both the situations covered by NAFTA Chapter 19, there are special rules on the formation of panels. These are similar to those under the general procedure, but there are significant differences.[72] There are special rosters for these cases, and each Member State appoints up to twenty-five persons. Although they consult, they have no veto over each other's appointments. When it comes to forming a panel, each party to the proceedings appoints two panellists, who must "normally" be from the roster. They do not have to be of the nationality of the other party. Each party has four peremptory challenges regarding the other party's nominations. When these are exhausted, however, it seems that it has no option but to accept the other party's choices. The fifth panellist is appointed by mutual agreement. If that fails, one of the parties is chosen by lot and that party chooses the fifth panellist. The five panellists choose the chairman, who must be a lawyer.

Although the NAFTA rules do not normally provide for appeals from panel decisions, there is an exception in the case of AD and CVD determinations in

---

68 Art. 1904(5). The State may also bring proceedings on its own initiative.
69 Art. 1904(9).
70 Art. 1904(15)(a).
71 Art. 1904(11).
72 See Annex 1901.2.

individual cases. This is laid down by Article 1904(13), which provides for an extraordinary challenge procedure where either:[73]

- a panel member is guilty of bias or gross misconduct;
- the panel seriously departed from the fundamental rules of procedure; or
- the panel manifestly exceeded its powers, for example by failing to apply the standard of review applicable under the law of the importing State.

In all these cases, the action complained of must have materially affected the panel's decision and must threaten the integrity of the binational panel review process.

There is a special fifteen-person roster composed of judges or former judges from specified courts in the three Member States.[74] Each Member State names five persons to this roster. When an extraordinary challenge is made, the parties establish an extraordinary challenge committee composed of three persons from this roster. One is selected by each party, and the parties decide by lot which one of them will select the third member. The case is then heard by the committee, which gives its decision after a hearing. It is expressly stated that this decision is binding.[75] If the committee considers that one of the specified grounds has been established, it may either vacate (set aside) the panel's decision (in which case a new panel will be set up), or remand the case to the original panel for action in accordance with the review committee's decision.

None of the other systems considered in this book allows for review of the AD or CVD decisions of Member-State courts in individual cases. In the EU, however, the question does not arise because Member-State legislation in this area has been abolished. The EU itself adopts anti-dumping measures against goods imported from outside the EU. These measures are subject to review by the European Court. Goods imported from one Member State into another may be sold at an unfairly low price due to government subsidies in the State of manufacture. In such a case, the EU will take appropriate measures. These too may be reviewed by the European Court. These differences show that the EU has reached a higher stage of integration than North America.

Assessment

Although the NAFTA dispute-settlement system is generally regarded as a success, it seems unduly complex. It is hard to see why the procedure for panel-formation is different in the various situations considered above. One cannot help wondering whether it would not have been better if, instead of following the GATT/WTO model, it had set up a permanent court with a fixed membership. If the same judges heard each case, they could build up their expertise, which would lead to greater predictability.

---

[73] For the exact wording, see Art. 1904(13) in Annex 3.
[74] The procedure is set out in the Annex to Art. 1904.13.
[75] Annex 1904.13(3).

Conclusions

From a jurisdictional point of view, the International Court of Justice is in the weakest position of all the judicial institutions considered. It can hear a case only if both parties agree. All the other institutions have some measure of compulsory jurisdiction: if a State joins the organization, it must accept the jurisdiction of its dispute-settlement system. Private parties can bring proceedings only in the European Union (where they usually go before the Court of First Instance) and in the NAFTA. As we shall see in Chapter 14, they can also bring cases in the European Court of Human Rights. Indeed, they are the main litigants. Finally, it should be noted that, except in the European Union, it is for the victim to seek legal redress. Only in the EU does the organization itself (the Commission) fulfil a law-enforcement role. Another special feature of the EU is that proceedings before the European Court are often against the Community itself. This is because the EU has significant legislative and executive powers in its own right. The other organizations discussed in this chapter lack such powers.

Further reading

General

Collier (John) and Lowe (Vaughan), *The Settlement of Disputes in International Law* (Oxford University Press, Oxford, 1999), covers all the institutions considered in this chapter. It has references to further sources.

The International Court of Justice

Collier (John) and Lowe (Vaughan), *The Settlement of Disputes in International Law* (Oxford University Press, Oxford, 1999), Chapter 7.
Brownlie (Ian), *Principles of Public International Law* (Oxford University Press, Oxford, 5th ed., 1998), pp. 709–730.

The WTO

Hudec, "The New WTO Dispute Settlement Procedure: An Overview of the First Three Years" (1999) 8 *Minnesota Journal of Global Trade* 1 (available on Lexis).
Jackson, "Dispute Settlement and the WTO: Emerging Problems" (1998) 1 JIEL 329; reprinted in Jackson (John H.), *The Jurisprudence of the GATT and the WTO* (Cambridge University Press, Cambridge, 2000), p. 168.
Petersmann, "The Dispute Settlement System of the World Trade Organization and the Evolution of the GATT Dispute Settlement System since 1948" (1994) 31 CMLRev. 1157.
WTO Secretariat, *The WTO Dispute Settlement Procedures* (Cambridge University Press, Cambridge, 2nd ed., 2001).

The European Union

The best introductory work is Brown (L. Neville) and Kennedy (Tom), *The Court of Justice of the European Communities* (Sweet and Maxwell, London, 5th ed., 2000). More specialized works include: Rasmussen (Hjalte), *European Court of Justice* (GadJura,

Copenhagen, 1998); and Arnull (Anthony), *The European Union and its Court of Justice* (Oxford University Press, Oxford, 1999). See also Dashwood (Alan) and Johnston (Angus) (eds.), *The Future of the European Judicial System* (Hart Publishing, Oxford, 2001).

The NAFTA

Abbott, "The North American Integration Regime and its Implications for the World Trading System" in Weiler (J.H.H.) (ed.), *The EU, the WTO and the NAFTA* (Oxford University Press, Oxford, 2000), p. 169.

Alvarez and Park, "The New Face of Investment Arbitration: NAFTA Chapter 11" (2003) 28 *Yale Journal of International Law* 365.

Huntington, "Settling Disputes under the North American Free Trade Agreement" (1993) 34 *Harvard International Law Journal* 407.

6

The problem of compliance

In the domestic (non-international) arena, enforcing a judgment is not usually a problem. If necessary, the full power of the State (court officials, police, etc.) can be brought to bear. If the State itself is the defendant, this might be more difficult; but in the UK, at least, the government will always comply. On the international level, however, things are not so easy, since there is no international police force to take on this task. Different remedies exist in different courts, but they are not always effective.

The International Court of Justice

Article 94(2) of the UN Charter (Panel 6.1) gives the Security Council the task of ensuring compliance with judgments of the International Court of Justice. However, voting in the Security Council, as in other political bodies, is more strongly influenced by political considerations than by respect for the law. Moreover, if the delinquent State is one of the permanent members,[1] it can use its veto to block any action. Our first case is an example.

> **World**
> **Nicaragua v. United States**
> Military and Paramilitary Activities in and against Nicaragua[2]
> **INTERNATIONAL COURT OF JUSTICE**
> [1984] ICJ Rep. 169 (Order of 10 May 1984: provisional measures); [1984] ICJ Rep. 215 (intervention); [1984] ICJ Rep. 392 (Judgment of 26 November 1984: jurisdiction and admissibility); [1986] ICJ Rep. 14 (Judgment of 27 June 1986: merits). Full text and summaries available on http://www.icj-cij.org.

Background

In recent (and not-so-recent) times, most of the Central American countries have been satellites of the United States. The US has controlled their domestic and foreign policies, which have been operated in the interest of the US, rather than that of the country concerned. This has been the case both when they

---

1 China, France, Russia, the United Kingdom and the United States.
2 For a comment, see Chimni, "The International Court and the Maintenance of Peace and Security: The Nicaragua Decision and the United States Response" (1986) 35 ICLQ 960.

Charter of the United Nations

Article 94

1. Each Member of the United Nations undertakes to comply with the decision of the International Court of Justice in any case to which it is a party.

2. If any party to a case fails to perform the obligations incumbent upon it under a judgment rendered by the Court, the other party may have recourse to the Security Council, which may, if it deems necessary, make recommendations or decide upon measures to be taken to give effect to the judgment.

have been ruled by dictators (the normal state of affairs) and when they have had democratically elected governments. The US has maintained its position by a mixture of rewards (civil and military aid) and sanctions. The latter typically take the form of withdrawal of aid, economic penalties and military intervention. To make the US position more secure, the CIA secretly recruits key figures in the civil service, police and armed forces. These men work directly for the US while pretending to work for their own governments.[3] A similar system was used by the Soviet Union in Eastern Europe during the Cold War. In an earlier period, the UK adopted it in Afro-Asian countries it did not wish to turn into formal colonies.

Nicaragua was a US satellite for a large part of the twentieth century.[4] It was occupied by US Marines from 1912 to 1925 and again from 1926 to 1933. Before leaving, the US established the Nicaraguan National Guard, which they hoped would enable them to maintain control after the Marines were withdrawn. In 1937, the leader of the National Guard, Anastasio Somoza García, became president. The Somoza family then controlled the country more or less continuously until 1979, amassing great wealth in the process.[5]

In 1979, the Sandinistas,[6] a resistance movement that had been fighting the National Guard since 1961, achieved final victory. The Somozas fled and the Sandinistas took over. This was not to the liking of the US, which had supported the Somoza regime until shortly before it fell. In 1981, President Reagan came to power. He was determined to oust the Sandinistas. He armed and supplied the *contras*, a group opposed to the Sandinistas. The *contras*, led by remnants of the former National Guard, waged a terrorist campaign in Nicaragua, attacking

---

3 The career of Manuel Noriega, one-time head of military intelligence in Panama, drug trafficker, CIA agent (whose annual salary is said to have reached US$200,000 a year) and President of Panama, now serving a life-long jail sentence in the United States after being removed from office by US marines, affords a rare public glimpse of the system. For details, see John Dinges, *Our Man in Panama: The Shrewd Rise and Brutal Fall of Manuel Noriega* (Times Books/Random House, New York, rev. ed., 1991); Peter Dale Scott and Jonathan Marshall, *Cocaine Politics: Drugs, Armies and the CIA in Central America* (University of California Press, Berkeley, CA, 1991), Chap. 4.

4 See Richard Fagen, *Forging Peace: The Challenge of Central America* (Basil Blackwell, Oxford, 1987), Chap. 7; Thomas M. Leonard, *Central America and the United States: The Search for Stability* (University of Georgia Press, Athens, GA, and London, 1991).

5 Anastasio Somoza García was president from 1937 to 1947 and again from 1950 until his death in 1956. His eldest son, Luís Somoza Debayle, was president from 1956 to 1963 and a younger son, Anastasio Somoza Debayle, from 1974 to 1979.

6 Its full name was the *Frente Sandinista de Liberación Nacional* (FSLN), named after Augusto Sandino, the leader of a guerrilla movement fighting the US in the 1920s.

agricultural co-operatives, schools and clinics.[7] This is said to have resulted in the deaths of more than 12,000 people.[8]

Proceedings

On 9 April 1984, Nicaragua brought the matter before the International Court of Justice. It began proceedings against the US, claiming that the US had armed the *contras* and instructed them to carry out the attacks. It also claimed that the CIA had mined Nicaraguan harbours.[9] The US denied the Nicaraguan claims and said that Nicaragua was guilty of aggression against its neighbours (where the *contra* bases were situated). Since it was unwilling to have the International Court determine the truth of the matter, however, the US took objection to the jurisdiction of the court.

Nicaragua asserted that the International Court had jurisdiction on two grounds. The first was that both Nicaragua and the United States had accepted the "Optional Clause".[10] In other words, they had both agreed in advance to accept the jurisdiction of the International Court with regard to any dispute under international law if the other party had accepted the same obligation. The second was that the two countries had signed a treaty[11] which conferred jurisdiction on the International Court to hear any dispute arising out of the treaty (compromissory clause). The US raised various objections,[12] but the court held that it had jurisdiction on both grounds.[13]

In addition, the US raised objections as to the admissibility of the proceedings. (Admissibility is also concerned with the question whether the court can hear the case, but it is slightly different from jurisdiction.) The court unanimously dismissed these objections, but some of the objections raise interesting questions. One was that since the case concerned matters of war and peace, only the UN Security Council (where the US has a veto) could decide the matter. The court rejected this on the ground that, although the Security Council has jurisdiction in such matters, this jurisdiction is not exclusive. The Security Council would deal with the political aspects, and the court with the legal aspects. Another objection was that since the case concerned an ongoing armed conflict, the court would not be able to ascertain the facts. This too was

---

7 Rural schools and clinics were regarded as associated with the Sandinistas. Before they came to power, the peasants had little or no access to medicine or education.
8 Fagen, note 4, above, p. 7, n. 5 (figure for the period 1980–1985).
9 It first asked the court for provisional measures. These were granted by an Order dated 10 May 1984. The United States was required to stop laying mines. The court also said that Nicaragua's independence should be respected. See [1984] ICJ Rep. 169.
10 Art. 36(2) of the court's Statute, set out in Panel 5.1, p. 73 above.
11 Treaty of Friendship, Commerce and Navigation, 21 January 1956.
12 The arguments were all rather technical. One example will give the general flavour. When the US originally accepted the Optional Clause, it had stated that it would give six months' notice if it decided to withdraw from it. However, as soon as it discovered that Nicaragua was about to bring the case, it quickly amended the declaration – with immediate effect – to exclude disputes with any Central American State. It then argued that the court had no jurisdiction. The court rejected this on the ground that the US was bound by its undertaking to give six months' notice.
13 Some of the judges dissented on one or other of the two grounds, but only the US judge (Judge Schwebel) dissented on *both* of them.

rejected. It will be seen that if these arguments had been accepted, it would have prevented the court from ever deciding the really important cases.

Having decided that it had jurisdiction and that the proceedings were admissible, the court's next task was to decide the merits (substance). At this point, however, the US walked out. This did not mean that the court could not go on to decide the merits.[14] It could, and did, do this. However, under the Statute of the court, Nicaragua still had to prove its case.[15] It did this and, on 27 June 1986, the court found in Nicaragua's favour.

It held that by arming and financing the *contra* forces the US had violated international law.[16] It also held that it had laid mines in Nicaraguan waters. This too was contrary to international law. Needless to say, the US ignored the ruling. The result was that Nicaragua had obtained a judgment, but could not enforce it. Nicaragua took its case to the Security Council, but the US used its veto to block a decision.[17]

Comment

Though never publicly mentioned, the most important issue in this case was the relation between theory and reality in international law. A major principle of international law is that force is illegal in international relations unless it is used in self-defence or is authorized by the UN Security Council. In practice, major powers regard military action as an option whenever it does not entail serious risk. This is how empires are created and defended. The US has no formal empire, but it nevertheless regards certain States as within its sphere of influence. It defends this "invisible empire" just as tenaciously as the imperial countries of old defended their visible empires. The unspoken question in the *Nicaragua* case was whether the principles of international law – based, as they are, on the premise that all States have equal rights – should give way before the reality of the status of the US as a superpower. The court could not have said this expressly. But it could have "bent" the law to produce a result acceptable to the US. It could have found some technical reason for saying that it lacked jurisdiction. It would then have been spared the embarrassment of seeing its judgment ignored. It is to the court's credit that it did not do this. If there is one thing worse than seeing a court's judgment ignored by a powerful State, it is seeing a court distorting the law so as not to offend such a State.

---

14 Art. 36(6) of the court's Statute (Panel 5.1, p. 73 above) expressly states that it can decide any dispute as to its jurisdiction. Such a decision is binding on the parties. The US could not deprive it of jurisdiction simply by refusing to accept its decision.

15 Art. 53(1) of the Statute provides that if one party fails to defend its case, the other party may call upon the court to decide in its favour. However, Art. 53(2) states that, before doing so, the court must satisfy itself that "the claim is well founded in fact and in law".

16 The US argument that Nicaragua was the aggressor was seriously undermined by a statement made by President Reagan at a press conference that the goal of US policy was to overthrow the Sandinista Government: *New York Times*, 22 February 1985, p. A10, column 1 at column 3.

17 Nicaragua then went to the General Assembly. The General Assembly, by ninety-four votes to three (with forty-seven abstentions), called for full and immediate compliance. (The three opposing votes were the United States, Israel and El Salvador.) The United States ignored this vote.

Panel 6.2 International Court of Justice: provisional measures

Statute of the International Court of Justice

Article 41

1. The Court shall have the power to indicate, if it considers that circumstances so require, any provisional measures which ought to be taken to preserve the respective rights of either party.

2. Pending the final decision, notice of the measures suggested shall forthwith be given to the parties and to the Security Council.

Panel 6.3 Consular rights

Vienna Convention on Consular Relations 1963

Article 36 Communication and contact with nationals of the sending State

1. With a view to facilitating the exercise of consular functions relating to nationals of the sending State:

    (a) consular officers shall be free to communicate with nationals of the sending State and to have access to them. Nationals of the sending State shall have the same freedom with respect to communication with and access to consular officers of the sending State;

    (b) if he so requests, the competent authorities of the receiving State shall, without delay, inform the consular post* of the sending State if, within its consular district, a national of that State is arrested or committed to prison or to custody pending trial or is detained in any other manner . . . The said authorities shall inform the person concerned without delay of his rights under this sub-paragraph;

    (c) consular officers shall have the right to visit a national of the sending State who is in prison, custody or detention, to converse and correspond with him and to arrange for his legal representation . . .

---

* Note: "consular post" means any consulate-general, consulate, vice-consulate or consular agency: see Art. 1(1)(a).

World

Germany v. United States (LaGrand case)

INTERNATIONAL COURT OF JUSTICE

Provisional order, 3 March 1999; final judgment, 27 June 2001 (not yet reported in ICJ Rep.). Full text and summaries available on http://www.icj-cij.org.[18]

Background

The International Court, no less than other courts, needs time to reach a decision. Sometimes, however, time is so vital that delay can deprive the judgment of its purpose. In such circumstances, it is essential for the court to give an interim order freezing the situation until it is able to make a final decision. Most courts have this power. In the case of the International Court it is given by Article 41 of its Statute (see Panel 6.2), though for many years jurists were in dispute as to whether such orders were binding. The issue was finally decided in our next case.

The case arose out of the Vienna Convention on Consular Relations 1963, to which both Germany and the United States were parties. Article 36 (Panel 6.3) gives consular officers the right to communicate with any of their nationals under arrest so as to be able to arrange for their legal representation. It also provides that the foreign national must be immediately informed of his rights under the Convention. An Optional Protocol,[19] to which both Germany and the

---

18 For a comment, see Xiaodong Yang, "Thou Shalt Not Violate Provisional Measures" (2001) 60 CLJ 441.
19 Optional Protocol Concerning the Compulsory Settlement of Disputes.

United States were parties, gave jurisdiction to the International Court over disputes arising out of the Convention.

Facts

Karl and Walter LaGrand were brothers. Both were German nationals, though they had lived in the United States since childhood. In 1982, a bank was robbed in Arizona and the manager murdered. The brothers were arrested and charged with the offence. They were tried before a state court in Arizona, convicted and sentenced to death. Neither was informed of his rights under the Convention. It was only after the trial that they discovered they had rights under the Convention. However, under US law the failure of the authorities to inform them of their rights could not be used as a ground for challenging their conviction.

On 24 February 1999, Karl LaGrand was executed. Late on 2 March 1999, the day before Walter LaGrand was due to be executed, Germany brought proceedings before the International Court. It claimed that the court had jurisdiction by virtue of the Optional Protocol (compromissory clause). It asked the court to grant a provisional order that the United States take all measures at its disposal to ensure that Walter LaGrand was not executed before the court was able to give a final decision. On 3 March 1999, the court made the order. Later that same day, Walter LaGrand was executed.[20]

Despite this setback, the proceedings went ahead. Judgment on the merits was given on 27 June 2001. The court held that the failure of the US to inform the brothers of their rights under the Convention was a violation of international law. The court also held, after careful consideration, that its provisional orders were legally binding (this part of the judgment is set out in the next chapter). The failure of the US to obey the order for a stay of execution was, therefore, a separate violation of international law.

Germany did not seek monetary compensation. The United States admitted that the brothers should have been informed of their rights. It apologized to Germany for this infringement of the Convention. It informed the court that it was carrying out a "vast and detailed" programme to ensure that the same thing did not happen again. The court accepted this. However, it said that if the same thing did happen again, the United States would be legally obliged to allow the accused person to use this fact as a ground for obtaining review of the conviction and sentence.[21]

Comment

Although this is another example of the United States' failing to respect a decision of the International Court, it has a different flavour from the *Nicaragua* case. The US did not walk out. It took sincere steps to prevent a repetition.

---

20 The State Department transmitted the court's order without comment to the Governor of Arizona. He received it in time, but did not stay the execution. Proceedings were also brought before the US Supreme Court. The US Solicitor General informed the court that provisional measures granted by the International Court were not binding. The Supreme Court did not order the execution to be stayed.
21 One interesting aspect of this case is that, though most of the court's findings were subject to one or more dissents, the US judge (Judge Buergenthal) usually voted with the majority.

Moreover, its initial failure could be explained by the shortness of time and uncertainty as to whether provisional measures were binding. The difference in the attitude of the US can be explained by the fact that the case did not touch one of its vital political interests, and that Germany was a respected ally. Moreover, the actual point at issue – consular rights of access – was of just as much concern to the US as to Germany. Next time, it could be an American whose rights were in issue.

The World Trade Organization

The primary objective of the WTO dispute-settlement mechanism is to secure the withdrawal of illegal measures. If immediate withdrawal is impracticable, compensation may be agreed as a temporary measure. As a last resort, the complainant may retaliate by suspending obligations under the covered agreements towards the offending State. However, it cannot do this without authorization from the DSB.

> *World*
> **European Union v. United States** (Helms–Burton Act case, 1997)
> **WTO DISPUTE SETTLEMENT BODY**
> No decision was given in this case, but the relevant facts may be found in Murphy,
> "Contemporary Practice of the United States Relating to International Law" (1999) 93
> AJIL 628, at pp. 660 *et seq.*

Background

The case concerned trade between the European Union and Cuba. Like Nicaragua, Cuba was a satellite of the US during the earlier part of the twentieth century. It was originally a Spanish colony. US troops helped Cuba gain independence from Spain and occupied the country from 1899 to 1901. The Republic of Cuba was proclaimed in 1902, but the country continued to be dominated by the US. It was ruled by a series of corrupt dictators, culminating in Fulengio Batista. His regime was overthrown by a guerrilla movement led by Fidel Castro, who became president in 1959. Castro adopted socialist policies and nationalized assets owned by US companies. This was unacceptable to the US. In 1961, an invasion force of Cuban exiles was organized by the US and landed from US ships in the Bay of Pigs. It was quickly defeated.

The US then turned to economic warfare, banning US companies from trading with Cuba.[22] Castro responded by accepting assistance from the Soviet Union. In 1962, the Soviets began installing nuclear missiles in Cuba, but withdrew them when President Kennedy ordered a naval blockade. Cuba's relationship with Russia came to an end with the collapse of Communism in 1991. By the mid-1990s, Castro was still in power, but the Cuban economy was severely depressed.[23]

---

22 Proclamation 3447 of 3 February 1962, (1962) 27 Fed. Reg. 1085.
23 US sanctions against Cuba have become increasingly unpopular over the years. From 1992 to 1998, the UN General Assembly has adopted annual resolutions calling for their abolition. In 1998, the vote was

Facts

In 1996, Congress passed the Cuban Liberty and Democratic Solidarity (Libertad) Act, widely known as the Helms–Burton Act.[24] One of its provisions was intended to prevent companies outside the US from trading with Cuba. This stated that if any company "trafficked" in property expropriated from a US citizen, the former owner could sue the company in the US for the full value of the property. The precise effect of this provision would depend on the way it was interpreted, but it would seem that if a European company bought sugar grown in Cuba on land once owned by a US company, the latter could sue the European company in the US courts for the value not just of the sugar, but of the land on which the sugar was grown.[25] In certain circumstances, it could obtain three times the value of the land. President Clinton suspended this provision for six months, but the European Union considered that its mere existence was contrary to the GATT.[26] It therefore prepared to bring proceedings against the US under the WTO Dispute Settlement Understanding.[27]

The US made clear that it would not participate in any such proceedings and would ignore any decision against it.[28] The EU could have insisted on the formation of a panel and, if the US refused to accept its decision, the EU could have sought authority to suspend the application of concessions or other obligations towards the US. Instead, it entered into negotiations with the US. In May 1998, a deal was struck: the EU would take steps to discourage investment in property confiscated contrary to international law and the US would permanently suspend the offending provision.[29]

Comment

If Cuba had brought the proceedings, the US would probably have reacted as it did in the *Nicaragua* case. However, the proceedings were brought by the

---

157 in favour, twelve abstentions and two against (the US and Israel): General Assembly Resolution 53/4, 14 October 1998. Cuba is not the only victim. According to one US commentator, in 1998 there were at least forty-two major federal laws and twenty-seven state and local measures imposing economic sanctions on foreigners. They prohibited three billion people in at least twenty-nine countries, comprising almost two-thirds of the world's population, from engaging in commerce with the United States. See Smith, "A High Price to Pay: The Costs of the US Economic Sanctions Policy and the Need for Process Oriented Reform" (2000) 4 *UCLA Journal of International Law and Foreign Affairs* 325.

24 For an analysis, see Lowe, "US Extraterritorial Jurisdiction: The Helms–Burton and D'Amato Acts" (1997) 46 ICLQ 378; Lowenfeld, "Agora: The Cuban Liberty and Democratic Solidarity (Libertad) Act: Congress and Cuba" (1996) 90 AJIL 419.

25 Lowenfeld (above) at 416.

26 For EU legislation intended to counter the effects of the Helms–Burton Act, see Regulation 227/96, OJ 1996, L309/1.

27 On 8 October 1996, the EU requested the formation of a panel under the DSU: see WTO Doc. WT/DS38/2/Corr.1.

28 Art. 21 of the GATT provides that nothing in the agreement prevents any contracting party from "taking any action which it considers necessary for the protection of its essential security interests . . . taken in time of war or other emergency in international relations". It seems that the US considered that this provision justified its action. It was not, however, prepared to allow the panel to decide the point. It took the view that the mere *assertion* by a party that the provision applied was enough to deprive the panel of jurisdiction. It need hardly be pointed out that, if accepted, this argument would totally destroy the WTO Dispute Settlement Understanding. Any party that thought it might lose a case could simply invoke Art. 21 to put a stop to the proceedings. For further analysis, see Schloemann and Ohlhoff, "'Constitutionalization' and Dispute Settlement in the WTO: National Security as an Issue of Competence" (1999) 93 AJIL 424.

29 See Smis and Van der Borght, "The EU–US Compromise of the Helms–Burton and D'Amato Acts" (1999) 93 AJIL 227.

European Union, one of the US's most important economic partners. Thus, though the US was still unwilling to submit to the jurisdiction of an impartial tribunal, it was nevertheless willing to make significant concessions to reach a deal. The EU's willingness to make concessions on its side shows the importance it attaches to the WTO and to its system of judicialized dispute resolution. This could have been seriously undermined if the EU had insisted on its rights. Ironically, the EU was at the same time the unsuccessful defendant in another case before the WTO. This concerned its preferential treatment of imports of bananas grown in territories with links to Europe. The claimant in this case was the United States.[30]

The European Union

Judgments of the European Court have always been binding, but until the Treaty on European Union of 1992 came into force, there was no provision for sanctions. Member States were just expected to obey. Usually they did, but in some cases there were problems.

The European Court has always had the power to grant interim (provisional) measures. This is laid down in Article 243 [186] EC, which states that the court may "in any cases before it prescribe any necessary interim measures". Prior to the case we are about to consider, it had already used this power in enforcement actions against Member States under Article 226 [169] EC. One case was against the United Kingdom.[31] The UK Government had been accused of illegally subsidizing UK pig producers to help them compete against continental imports. An interim order was made against the UK, requiring it to end the subsidy pending a final decision. Another case concerned Ireland, which was accused of introducing fisheries conservation measures that discriminated against the big boats used by fishermen from other Member States.[32] It was ordered to suspend the measures until final judgment. In both cases, the interim orders were obeyed. In view of these cases, the decision below seems hard to understand.

European Union
Commission v. France (Second Lamb and Mutton *case*)
COURT OF JUSTICE OF THE EUROPEAN COMMUNITIES
Cases 24, 97/80 R, [1980] ECR 1319; [1981] 3 CMLR 15

Facts
This particular saga began in January 1978 when the UK complained to the EC Commission that France was using a system of import bans and surcharges to keep UK lamb and mutton out of the French market. The Commission brought

---

30 WTO Appellate Body Report on the Regime for the Importation, Sale and Distribution of Bananas, WT/DS27/AB/R, 9 September 1997.
31 *Commission v. United Kingdom*, Cases 31 and 53/77R, [1977] ECR 921.
32 *Commission v. Ireland*, Case 61/77R, [1977] ECR 937 and 1411; [1978] 2 CMLR 466.

proceedings against France in the European Court under Article 226 [169] EC. In September 1979, the court ruled that France had violated the Treaty. The French, however, refused to comply. They said that unless the other Member States agreed to a support system[33] to protect their farmers, they would continue to exclude UK produce. The UK opposed a support system because it considered that, under the budgetary system then in force, it would have had to bear the brunt of the financial burden.

In November 1979, the Commission brought fresh proceedings against France. This time, it said that France's refusal to obey the judgment was itself a violation of Community law. The relevant provision was Article 228 [171] EC, which says that Member States must comply with the court's judgments. The Commission also asked the court to grant interim measures. It asked it to order France to comply with the earlier judgment until final judgment was given in the new case. This was really all it could do, since at that time there was no provision for sanctions. The case went before the full court.

Judgment

10. Article 228 [171] of the Treaty states that "If the Court of Justice finds that a Member State has failed to fulfil an obligation under this Treaty, the State shall be required to take the necessary measures to comply with the judgment of the Court of Justice".

11. As provided for in Article 211 [155] of the Treaty it is for the Commission to "ensure that the provisions of this Treaty and the measures taken by the institutions pursuant thereto are applied"; the Commission is therefore under a duty to ensure also that Member States comply with the judgments delivered by the Court of Justice.

12. The Commission in the exercise of this power may bring actions pursuant to Article 226 [169] of the Treaty if it considers that a Member State has not taken the necessary steps to ensure compliance with a judgment or that any measures taken for this purpose do not comply with the obligations arising out of the latter. In the context of such an action the possibility cannot be ruled out that the Court be asked to prescribe such interim measures as may be necessary pursuant to Article 243 [186] of the Treaty and Article 36 of the Protocol on the Statute of the Court of Justice of the EEC provided that the conditions laid down by those provisions and by Article 83 of the Rules of Procedure are present. It is for the Court to determine in each individual case the need for such interim measures in accordance with the criteria laid down by the said provisions.

13. In the present case this need must be assessed by taking into account, on the one hand, the legal considerations arising from the above-mentioned judgment of the Court of 25 September 1979 and, on the other hand, the aim of the two actions brought successively by the Commission against the French Republic for failure to fulfil its obligations under Article 228 [171] of the Treaty.

14. In the light of these considerations it is necessary first to recall the terms of the judgment of 25 September 1979. Although it is true that the Court stated that it was aware

---

33 These systems normally involve a Community guarantee of a minimum price. If the farmer cannot get that price on the open market, he can sell the produce to the government intervention board, which may put it into storage or destroy it. The Community taxpayer picks up the bill.

of "the genuine problems which the French authorities have to solve in the sector under consideration and of the desirability of achieving the establishment, in the shortest possible time, of a common organization of the market in mutton and lamb", it nevertheless pointed out that "after the expiration of the transitional period of the EEC Treaty, and, as far as the new Member States are concerned, after the expiration of the time-limits for the transition specifically provided for in the Act of Accession, a national organization of the market must no longer operate in such a way as to prevent the Treaty provisions relating to the elimination of restrictions on intra-Community trade from having full force and effect".

15. Although the Court stressed in its judgment that "it is for the competent institutions and for them alone to adopt within the appropriate periods the requisite measures with a view to finding, in a Community context, a comprehensive solution of the problem of the market in mutton and lamb and of the special difficulties which arise in this connexion in certain areas", it stated that the fact that the work done by the Community institutions with a view to establishing a common organization of the market in the sector under consideration has not yet been successful "is not a sufficient justification for the maintenance by a Member State of a national organization of the market which includes features which are incompatible with the requirements of the Treaty relating to the free movement of goods, such as bans on imports and levying dues on imported products, under any designation whatsoever".

16. As the Court held in its judgment of 13 July 1972 in Case 48/71, *Commission of the European Communities v. Italian Republic* [1972] ECR 527 the finding in a judgment having the force of *res judicata* that the Member State concerned has failed to fulfil its obligations under Community law amounts to "a prohibition having the full force of law on the competent national authorities against applying a national rule recognized as incompatible with the Treaty and, if the circumstances so require, an obligation on them to take all appropriate measures to enable Community law to be fully applied". It follows that by reason solely of the judgment declaring the Member State to be in default, the State concerned is required to take the necessary measures to remedy its default and may not create any impediment whatsoever.

17. The French Republic is therefore required, by virtue of Articles 25 [12] and 28 [30] of the Treaty, as declared in the judgment of 25 September 1979, to desist from applying any restrictive measure of any kind whatsoever to the importation of mutton and lamb from the United Kingdom; as was stated in that judgment, that obligation was effective as from 1 January 1978.

18. It must moreover be borne in mind that the purpose of the applications in Joined Cases 24 and 97/80 is to obtain a declaration that the French Republic, by continuing to apply its restrictive scheme after the judgment of 25 September 1979 has failed to fulfil its obligations under Article 228 [171] of the Treaty.

19. The Commission, by requesting the Court in an application for the adoption of interim measures to order the French Republic to desist forthwith from applying its restrictive scheme, is asking the Court for an order the purpose of which would in substance be the same as that of the judgment of 25 September 1979. It follows that the interim measures which the Commission has asked the Court to order are not in the present circumstances within the meaning of Article 243 [186] of the Treaty.

20. There are therefore no grounds for ordering the interim measures requested by the Commission.

QUESTION

Could it be said that the court's judgment in this case was influenced by the fact that it knew France would not comply with any interim order it might make?

Subsequent developments

After the judgment was given, France continued its policy of defiance. Eventually a deal was struck. A support system for lamb and mutton was established. France then complied with the judgment. (The UK was induced to drop its opposition by concessions on the budgetary system.) France, therefore, won a victory. Its defiance of the court paid dividends.

> *European Union*
> **Commission v. Germany** (road tax on heavy goods vehicles)
> **COURT OF JUSTICE OF THE EUROPEAN COMMUNITIES**
> Case C-195/90R, [1990] ECR I-3351

Facts

Because Germany is in a geographically central position in the EU, trucks from other Member States frequently drive through Germany in order to reach destinations in other countries. German truck drivers resent the fact that these foreign drivers can use German motorways without paying the heavy German road taxes. The environmental impact of motorways also gives rise to concern, and it is argued that taxes on motorways should be increased so as to transfer goods to railways and waterways.

For these reasons, the German Government decided to introduce a new tax on heavy goods vehicles using German motorways.[34] This tax was payable by all users, German and foreign. However, it could be paid at a daily rate, so that a foreign driver who intended to spend only one day in Germany would not have to pay for more than that particular day. The Germans thought this was fair, but foreign drivers complained that they still had to pay taxes in their own countries; moreover, other German taxes that had previously been payable were abolished when the new tax came into force.

Complaints flooded into the EC Commission, which decided to bring proceedings against Germany under Article 226 [169] EC. Belgium, Denmark, France, Luxembourg and the Netherlands all intervened against Germany.

Under normal circumstances, it would have taken the court anything up to two years to reach a decision. Some of the foreign firms claimed that they would go bankrupt if they had to pay the German taxes for as long as that. So the Commission asked the court for an interim order requiring Germany to suspend the tax while the case was being heard. The German Government replied that this would involve their losing a great deal of revenue, since it

---

34 We will refer to it as the "German tax law".

would be virtually impossible, if Germany finally won the case, to recover taxes from the foreign drivers after they had left the country.[35]

The President of the Court granted the Order requested by the Commission, but immediately referred the matter to the full court for a decision.

Judgment

18. Article 242 [185] of the EEC Treaty provides that actions brought before the Court do not have suspensory effect. However, pursuant to Article 243 [186] of the EEC Treaty, the Court may in cases before it prescribe any necessary interim measures.

19. According to Article 83(2) of the Rules of Procedure, a decision ordering an interim measure may be made only where there are circumstances giving rise to urgency and factual and legal grounds establishing a prima-facie case for the interim measure applied for.

[The court then considered the arguments of the parties, and concluded that the Commission had established a prima facie case that the German tax law was contrary to the Treaty. It continued:]

31. As regards the condition of urgency, it is to be borne in mind that the Court has consistently held that the urgency of an application for interim measures, as referred to in Article 83(2) of the Rules of Procedure, must be assessed in relation to the necessity for an order granting interim relief in order to prevent serious and irreparable damage by the immediate application of the measure the subject of the main proceedings.

32. On that issue the Commission, backed by the Member States intervening in its support, alleges that there is a risk of the application of the tax at issue causing irreparable damage at least to certain carriers of the other Member States. The damage to those carriers consists, in the Commission's view, in an increase in transport costs which would force them to increase their tariffs – and risk losing customers – or else reduce their profit margins – and risk having to cease trading. The Commission maintains generally that the unilateral introduction of the road tax by the Federal Republic of Germany constitutes an unacceptable undermining of *ordre public*[36] in the Community. Since there is a danger of the introduction of the tax provoking retaliatory measures on the part of the other Member States, it would render illusory any progress towards achieving the common transport policy.

33. The Federal Republic of Germany denies that there would be any irreparable damage to *ordre public* in the Community and to traders on the transport market as claimed by the Commission.

34. The German tax is neutral as regards competition and brings the German tax system closer into line with those in the majority of Member States and pursues the object of establishing a transport policy based on the principle of territoriality. In those circumstances it cannot be said to jeopardize achievement of the common transport policy.

35. Furthermore, in view of the slight effect it would have on transport costs, the new tax could not affect the competitive position of carriers of other Member States. On the other hand, the danger of deterioration in their competitive position is greater for German carriers who are subject to heavier taxes than their counterparts in other Member States.

---

35 There is a general rule that the courts of one country will not help another country to recover taxes owing to it.
36 Editor's note: the French phrase "*ordre public*" is not the same as "public order" in English. It implies more than the absence of disorder in public places, and includes a certain level of respect for basic values.

36. The Federal Republic of Germany adds that in balancing the interests in question, priority should be given to the requirements of protecting the environment and alleviating congestion on the German road network.

37. It adds that in any event, even if the Court were to uphold the main application and find that the Federal Republic of Germany had failed to fulfil its Community obligations by creating the tax at issue, it would be possible to make good any damage suffered by transport undertakings of other Member States. The damage which the Federal Republic of Germany would suffer as a result of an order suspending the operation of the [German tax law] would, on the other hand, be irreparable.

38. It should be noted that, although, in principle, pecuniary damage is not to be regarded as irreparable, the position may be different in exceptional circumstances where pecuniary compensation cannot restore the injured person to the position prior to the occurrence of the damage.

39. That possibility cannot be ruled out in the present case. In view of the often very slender profit margins of many medium-sized transport undertakings mentioned at the hearing, there is a danger of the effect of the tax in question on the profitability of carriers of other Member States forcing many of them to stop trading. Furthermore, the application of the tax at issue is likely to bring about irremediable changes in the respective market shares of German carriers and of carriers of other Member States. Such an abrupt and substantial change, caused by a unilateral national measure, in the conditions at present existing on the road transport market in the Community, which could not be exactly re-established later if the measures in question are held to be contrary to the Treaty, would also make the development and completion of the common transport policy, required by Article 70 [74] of the EEC Treaty, more difficult.

40. It must therefore be held that the Commission, supported by the interveners, has established the existence of a risk of serious and irreparable damage.

41. The Federal Republic of Germany maintains that the grant of the interim measure applied for would cause it irreparable damage consisting in the loss of revenue from the taxes which are not levied during the main proceedings and the risk to the threat to the economic survival of German carriers.

42. In that respect it should be pointed out that the damage alleged by the Federal Republic of Germany is only the detrimental consequence of a situation existing before the introduction of the new tax. Moreover it has not been shown that the measures which have been introduced were made necessary by a significant change in the factual situation likely to increase substantially the magnitude of the existing damage and to justify a different reaction from the German authorities. Finally there seems little likelihood of any serious risk of the damage increasing to any considerable extent in the time up to the adoption of the decision in the main proceedings.

43. As regards, in particular, the damage arising from uncollected taxes which it will be impossible to recover subsequently, it suffices to observe that no such tax existed in the past and therefore there can be no question of the loss of revenue seriously affecting the public finances of the Federal Republic of Germany.

44. As regards the threat to the economic survival of German carriers as a result of the deterioration in their competitive position, there is, at first sight, nothing to suggest that, in the absence of any substantial change in the market situation in relation to circumstances which have prevailed for a long period, such a risk will materialize in the coming months.

45. Regarding the argument that the environment will be affected, Germany has failed to substantiate its contention that imposition of the contested tax on carriers of other Member States would lead to a transfer of road traffic to the railways and inland waterways rather than the transfer of the market share of carriers of other Member States to German carriers.

46. In those circumstances it must be held that the condition of urgency has been satisfied.

47. It should therefore be ordered, as an interim measure, that the Federal Republic of Germany suspend the charging of the road tax provided for in the [German tax law] in respect of vehicles registered in other Member States pending the delivery of the judgment in the main proceedings brought by the Commission. . . .

Subsequent development

Germany obeyed this order. Subsequently, the court decided definitively that Germany had violated the Treaty.[37]

> *European Union*
> **Commission v. France** (acts of violence by private persons against agricultural imports)
> **COURT OF JUSTICE OF THE EUROPEAN COMMUNITIES**
> Case C-265/95, [1997] ECR I-6959[38]

Facts

For more than a decade, private groups and individuals (mainly farmers) in France had been taking direct action against imported agricultural produce. An organization called *Coordination Rurale* had masterminded this campaign. Lorries (trucks) bringing produce from other Member States were intercepted, their goods destroyed and their drivers subjected to assault. Wholesalers and retailers, including supermarkets, were ordered not to stock foreign produce, and regular checks were made to ensure that these orders were obeyed. If they were not, produce on display was damaged or destroyed. Spanish imports were specially targeted, but goods from other Member States suffered as well. Even when the police were present, they took no effective action to prevent these activities.

Eventually, the Commission complained to the French Government, which said that it strongly condemned these acts and was doing all it could to put a stop to them. Nevertheless, the acts of violence continued. The Commission then brought proceedings against France under Article 226 [169] EC. The United Kingdom and Spain intervened in support of the Commission.

The Commission argued that the free movement of goods, including agricultural produce, is a fundamental principle of the EC Treaty, in particular under Article 28 [30] (set out in Panel 6.4). Under Article 10 [5] (also in Panel 6.4), Member States are required to take all appropriate measures to ensure the fulfilment of obligations arising out of the Treaty. The action against foreign

---

37 *Commission v. Germany*, Case C-195/90, [1992] ECR I-3141.
38 For a comment, see Muylle, "Angry Farmers and Passive Policemen: Private Conduct and the Free Movement of Goods" (1998) 23 ELRev. 467.

Panel 6.4   *Commission v. France* (acts of violence by private persons)

EC Treaty

Article 10 [5]

Member States shall take all appropriate measures, whether general or particular, to ensure fulfilment of the obligations arising out of this Treaty or resulting from action taken by the institutions of the Community. They shall facilitate the achievement of the Community's tasks.

They shall abstain from any measure which could jeopardise the attainment of the objectives of this Treaty.

Article 28 [30]

Quantitative restrictions on imports and all measures having equivalent effect shall be prohibited between Member States.

---

imports was an obstacle to trade, and France was, therefore, obliged to prevent it. It had conspicuously failed to do so.

France replied that it had done all it could, but was faced with difficulties because it was hard to foresee where and when the protesters would strike next. It also claimed that the problem was caused by the unfairly low prices at which Spanish produce was sold. This had led to a substantial fall in the prices received by the French farmers.

Judgment

30. As an indispensable instrument for the realization of a market without internal frontiers, Article 28 [30] therefore does not prohibit solely measures emanating from the State which, in themselves, create restrictions on trade between Member States. It also applies where a Member State abstains from adopting the measures required in order to deal with obstacles to the free movement of goods which are not caused by the State.

31. The fact that a Member State abstains from taking action or, as the case may be, fails to adopt adequate measures to prevent obstacles to the free movement of goods that are created, in particular, by actions by private individuals on its territory aimed at products originating in other Member States is just as likely to obstruct intra-Community trade as is a positive act.

32. Article 28 [30] therefore requires the Member States not merely themselves to abstain from adopting measures or engaging in conduct liable to constitute an obstacle to trade but also, when read with Article 10 [5] of the Treaty, to take all necessary and appropriate measures to ensure that that fundamental freedom is respected on their territory.

33. In the latter context, the Member States, which retain exclusive competence as regards the maintenance of public order and the safeguarding of internal security, unquestionably enjoy a margin of discretion in determining what measures are most appropriate to eliminate barriers to the importation of products in a given situation.

34. It is therefore not for the Community institutions to act in place of the Member States and to prescribe for them the measures which they must adopt and effectively apply in order to safeguard the free movement of goods on their territories.

35. However, it falls to the Court, taking due account of the discretion referred to above, to verify, in cases brought before it, whether the Member State concerned has adopted appropriate measures for ensuring the free movement of goods.

36. It should be added that, by virtue of the combined provisions of Articles 32 [38] to 38 [46] and Article [7(7)] of the EC Treaty, the foregoing considerations apply also to Council regulations on the common organization of the markets for the various agricultural products (see Joined Cases 3/76, 4/76 and 6/76 *Kramer and Others* [1976] ECR 1279, paragraphs 53 and 54, and Case C-228/91 *Commission v Italy* [1993] ECR I-2701, paragraph 11, relating to regulations on the common organization of the markets in fishery products).

37. As regards more specifically the present case, the facts which gave rise to the action brought by the Commission against the French Republic for failure to fulfil obligations are not in dispute.

38. The acts of violence committed in France and directed against agricultural products originating in other Member States, such as the interception of lorries transporting those products, the destruction of their loads and violence towards drivers, as well as threats to wholesalers and retailers and the damaging of goods on display, unquestionably create obstacles to intra-Community trade in those products.

39. It is therefore necessary to consider whether in the present case the French Government complied with its obligations under Article 28 [30], in conjunction with Article 10 [5], of the Treaty, by adopting adequate and appropriate measures to deal with actions by private individuals which create obstacles to the free movement of certain agricultural products.

40. It should be stressed that the Commission's written pleadings show that the incidents to which it objects in the present proceedings have taken place regularly for more than 10 years.

41. It was as long ago as 8 May 1985 that the Commission first sent a formal letter to the French Republic calling on it to adopt the preventive and penal measures necessary to put an end to acts of that kind.

42. Moreover, in the present case the Commission reminded the French Government on numerous occasions that Community law imposes an obligation to ensure *de facto* compliance with the principle of the free movement of goods by eliminating all restrictions on the freedom to trade in agricultural products from other Member States.

43. In the present case the French authorities therefore had ample time to adopt the measures necessary to ensure compliance with their obligations under Community law.

44. Moreover, notwithstanding the explanations given by the French Government, which claims that all possible measures were adopted in order to prevent the continuation of the violence and to prosecute and punish those responsible, it is a fact that, year after year, serious incidents have gravely jeopardized trade in agricultural products in France.

45. According to the summary of the facts submitted by the Commission, which is not contested by the French Government, there are particular periods of the year which are primarily concerned and there are places which are particularly vulnerable where incidents have occurred on several occasions during one and the same year.

46. Since 1993 acts of violence and vandalism have not been directed solely at the means of transport of agricultural products but have extended to the wholesale and retail sector for those products.

47. Further serious incidents of the same type also occurred in 1996 and 1997.

48. Moreover, it is not denied that when such incidents occurred the French police were either not present on the spot, despite the fact that in certain cases the competent authorities had been warned of the imminence of demonstrations by farmers, or did not intervene, even where they far outnumbered the perpetrators of the disturbances. Furthermore, the actions in question were not always rapid, surprise actions by demonstrators who then immediately took flight, since in certain cases the disruption continued for several hours.

49. Furthermore, it is undisputed that a number of acts of vandalism were filmed by television cameras, that the demonstrators' faces were often not covered and that the groups of farmers responsible for the violent demonstrations are known to the police.

50. Notwithstanding this, it is common ground that only a very small number of the persons who participated in those serious breaches of public order has been identified and prosecuted.

51. Thus, as regards the numerous acts of vandalism committed between April and August 1993, the French authorities have been able to cite only a single case of criminal prosecution.

52. In the light of all the foregoing factors, the Court, while not discounting the difficulties faced by the competent authorities in dealing with situations of the type in question in this case, cannot but find that, having regard to the frequency and seriousness of the incidents cited by the Commission, the measures adopted by the French Government were manifestly inadequate to ensure freedom of intra-Community trade in agricultural products on its territory by preventing and effectively dissuading the perpetrators of the offences in question from committing and repeating them.

53. That finding is all the more compelling since the damage and threats to which the Commission refers not only affect the importation into or transit in France of the products directly affected by the violent acts, but are also such as to create a climate of insecurity which has a deterrent effect on trade flows as a whole.

54. The above finding is in no way affected by the French Government's argument that the situation of French farmers was so difficult that there were reasonable grounds for fearing that more determined action by the competent authorities might provoke violent reactions by those concerned, which would lead to still more serious breaches of public order or even to social conflict.

55. Apprehension of internal difficulties cannot justify a failure by a Member State to apply Community law correctly (see, to that effect, Case C-52/95 *Commission* v *France* [1995] ECR I-4443, paragraph 38).

56. It is for the Member State concerned, unless it can show that action on its part would have consequences for public order with which it could not cope by using the means at its disposal, to adopt all appropriate measures to guarantee the full scope and effect of Community law so as to ensure its proper implementation in the interests of all economic operators.

57. In the present case the French Government has adduced no concrete evidence proving the existence of a danger to public order with which it could not cope.

58. Moreover, although it is not impossible that the threat of serious disruption to public order may, in appropriate cases, justify non-intervention by the police, that argument can,

on any view, be put forward only with respect to a specific incident and not, as in this case, in a general way covering all the incidents cited by the Commission.

59. As regards the fact that the French Republic has assumed responsibility for the losses caused to the victims, this cannot be put forward as an argument by the French Government in order to escape its obligations under Community law.

60. Even though compensation can provide reparation for at least part of the loss or damage sustained by the economic operators concerned, the provision of such compensation does not mean that the Member State has fulfilled its obligations.

61. Nor is it possible to accept the arguments based on the very difficult socio-economic context of the French market in fruit and vegetables after the accession of the Kingdom of Spain.

62. It is settled case-law that economic grounds can never serve as justification for barriers prohibited by Article 28 [30] of the Treaty (see, *inter alia*, Case 288/83 *Commission* v *Ireland* [1985] ECR 1761, paragraph 28).

63. As regards the suggestion by the French Government, in support of those arguments, that the destabilization of the French market for fruit and vegetables was brought about by unfair practices, and even infringements of Community law, by Spanish producers, it must be remembered that a Member State may not unilaterally adopt protective measures or conduct itself in such a way as to obviate any breach by another Member State of rules of Community law (see, to that effect, Case C-5/94 *R* v *MAFF, ex parte Hedley Lomas* [1996] ECR I-2553, paragraph 20).

64. This must be so *a fortiori* in the sphere of the common agricultural policy, where it is for the Community alone to adopt, if necessary, the measures required in order to deal with difficulties which some economic operators may be experiencing, in particular following a new accession.

65. Having regard to all the foregoing considerations, it must be concluded that in the present case the French Government has manifestly and persistently abstained from adopting appropriate and adequate measures to put an end to the acts of vandalism which jeopardize the free movement on its territory of certain agricultural products originating in other Member States and to prevent the recurrence of such acts.

66. Consequently, it must be held that, by failing to adopt all necessary and proportionate measures in order to prevent the free movement of fruit and vegetables from being obstructed by actions by private individuals, the French Government has failed to fulfil its obligations under Article 28 [30], in conjunction with Article 10 [5], of the Treaty and under the common organizations of the markets in agricultural products.

Comment

This case illustrates a problem that other international trade organizations have not yet had to face. There is no doubt that private action of this kind can constitute a barrier to trade. It is conceivable that a dishonest government might even instigate it. For these reasons, the judgment is clearly right. However, enforcement could prove difficult. As the court said, the Community cannot tell France what action to take. Nor can it take over policing activities itself. So it has to rely on France.

Panel 6.5 Fines against Member States

EC Treaty

Article 228 [171]
1. If the Court of Justice finds that a Member State has failed to fulfil an obligation under this Treaty, the State shall be required to take the necessary measures to comply with the judgment of the Court of Justice.
2. If the Commission considers that the Member State concerned has not taken such measures it shall, after giving that State the opportunity to submit its observations, issue a reasoned opinion specifying the points on which the Member State concerned has not complied with the judgment of the Court of Justice.
　　If the Member State concerned fails to take the necessary measures to comply with the Court's judgment within the time-limit laid down by the Commission, the latter may bring the case before the Court of Justice. In so doing it shall specify the amount of the lump sum or penalty payment to be paid by the Member State concerned which it considers appropriate in the circumstances.
　　If the Court of Justice finds that the Member State concerned has not complied with its judgment it may impose a lump sum or penalty payment on it.
　　This procedure shall be without prejudice to Article 227 [170].

Note: Art. 227 [170] is the provision which allows the proceedings to be brought by another Member State, instead of by the Commission. It is set out in Panel 5.4, p. 81 above.

In taking action, France enjoys a margin of discretion in determining what measures are appropriate (paragraph 33 of the judgment). It was only because France's inaction so clearly went beyond any possible margin of discretion that the court was able to hold that it had violated the Treaty. The Commission proved this by pointing to a consistent line of conduct stretching over many years. This creates a problem in deciding whether France has complied with the judgment. A single act of violence would be insufficient to show that France had disobeyed it. A series of such acts with no effective counter-measures would have to be proved. This could be difficult, and it would take time to build up a case. For this reason, it is uncertain whether the judgment will have much effect.

Fines for non-compliance

The Treaty on European Union (Maastricht Agreement) of 1992 introduced the possibility of imposing fines on Member States for failure to comply with judgments of the European Court. This was done through an amendment to Article 228 [171] EC (Panel 6.5). Under this provision, the initiative is taken by the Commission, which has the task of ensuring compliance with the court's judgments. If it considers that the respondent Member State has failed to comply, it takes the matter up with the State concerned and asks it to explain its position. The Member State may point to practical difficulties, or it may claim that it has complied (exactly what constitutes compliance could be a difficult question).

If the Commission does not accept the Member State's explanation, it will issue a formal opinion, stating precisely how the Member State has failed to comply, what measures it must take, and the time within which they must be taken. If the Member State does not accept this, the Commission can bring fresh proceedings before the European Court, asking it to impose a fine. The Commission will propose an appropriate amount. Fines may take two forms: a lump sum (fixed amount), or a periodic penalty of so much per day, until the Member State falls into line. The Commission favours the latter, as being more likely to produce results.[39] It has worked out a formula for determining the amount. This varies with the seriousness of the default and the size and wealth of the State concerned.[40] The court is not obliged to follow the Commission's proposal, but may use its judgment to decide what is appropriate.

This system, which is said originally to have been proposed by the United Kingdom,[41] could be of value. Nevertheless, there is a problem. If the Member State is sufficiently defiant to disobey the original judgment, it may also refuse to pay the fine.

There is no way in which it could be forced to pay, except perhaps by deducting the sum in question from money owed to it by the Community. If this were done, however, the Member State might retaliate by deducting the same amount from sums owed by it to the Community. An unseemly game of tit for tat could result, in which the ultimate result might depend on whether or not the State in question was a net contributor to the Community's budget. So far, this has not happened,[42] but the matter has not really been put to the test.

The North–South gradient

Every year the Commission produces a report on its law-enforcement activities, which it presents to the European Parliament. These reports contain figures on the number of times in the year each Member State has, in the Commission's opinion, violated Community law. The figures show that there is a distinct North–South gradient in this regard. The States in the North of the Community have a better record than those in the South. What is remarkable is how consistent the figures are. This is shown by Panel 6.6, which sets out the ranking of each Member State for each year in the period 1990–1997 with regard to the number of formal letters sent to it by the Commission under Article 226 [169] EC. These are the letters in which the Commission states that the Member State appears to have violated the Treaty and invites it to explain its position. They are probably the best indicator of the extent to which each State obeys Community law, though the rankings are not very different if one takes some other indicator, such as a reasoned opinion or a decision to bring proceedings.[43] The figures cover only the twelve States that were members for the whole period.[44]

39 OJ 1996, C242/6.
40 OJ 1997, C63/2.
41 *Financial Times*, 6 February 1991.
42 The first case in which the new power was used was *Commission v. Hellenic Republic*, Case C-387/97, [2000] ECR I-5047. The Commission had received a complaint in 1987 that Greece was violating EC environmental law. It brought proceedings, and a judgment was given in 1992. Greece did not comply with this and, after various discussions, the Commission brought further proceedings for a violation of Art. 228 [171] EC. In 2000, the court imposed a penalty of €20,000 per day. Greece soon fell into line.
43 See Hartley (Trevor C.), *Constitutional Problems of the European Union* (Hart Publishing, Oxford and Portland, OR, 1999), pp. 112–118.
44 Austria, Finland and Sweden joined the Community in 1995.

Panel 6.6   Infringements of Community law, 1990–1997

Formal letters under Article 226 [169]: ranking by State for 1990–1999

	Highest ranking means fewest alleged infringements							
	1990	1991	1992	1993	1994	1995	1996	1997
Denmark	1	1	1	1	1	1	1	2
Netherlands	5 =	5	2	2	4 =	2	2	1
Luxembourg	2	7	4 =	3 =	2	4	3	3
Ireland	4	3	3	3 =	3	3	4	4
UK	3	6	4 =	5 =	4 =	5	5	6
Belgium	7	8	7	5 =	6	6	10	5
Germany	5 =	4	4 =	10	8 =	8	9	10
Spain	10	9	11	8	7	7	8	7
France	8	2	9	7	8 =	9	12	12
Greece	11	11	8	11 =	10 =	10	7	8
Italy	9	12	12	9	12	11	11	11
Portugal	12	10	10	11 =	10 =	12	6	9

Note: The order of the States in the left-hand column reflects their overall ranking for the whole decade.

In Panel 6.6, the ranking is in ascending order of alleged infringements: the country with the lowest ranking has fewest infringements. It will be seen that Denmark had fewest infringements in every year except one. None of the top five States (Denmark, the Netherlands, Luxembourg, Ireland and the UK) ever dropped below sixth place; and, except for France in 1991, none of the bottom four (Portugal, Italy, Greece and France) ever rose above seventh place. It seems that cultural factors are at work here, conditioning the way in which politicians and civil servants view the law.

Panel 6.7 gives figures for the three years 1998–2000. These figures, which show the number of alleged infringements instead of the rankings, include the three new Member States, Austria, Finland and Sweden. These countries are to be found exactly where one would expect them to be: Finland and Sweden at the top and Austria in the middle. Spain and Portugal have however, moved up, while Germany and Belgium have dropped down.

A final word

In this chapter, we have been considering the situation in which proceedings are brought against a State in an international court. In the European Union, however, there is another way in which Community law may be enforced. This is by bringing an action in the courts of the State concerned, a remedy normally pursued only by private persons (individuals or companies). Assume, for example, that a German company considers that the UK Government has infringed its rights under Community law. It could bring proceedings against

Panel 6.7 Infringements of Community law, 1998–2000			
Formal letters under Article 226 [169]: cases pending at end of the year			
	2000	1999	1998	Total
Denmark	41	40	25	106
Finland	52	43	44	139
Sweden	57	46	49	152
Netherlands	98	77	59	234
United Kingdom	90	83	97	270
Luxembourg	84	96	97	277
Ireland	101	98	86	285
Austria	111	109	98	318
Spain	126	112	128	366
Portugal	126	114	142	382
Belgium	133	136	165	434
Germany	155	142	140	437
Greece	166	154	141	461
Italy	190	160	205	555
France	243	236	254	733

the UK Government in the UK courts and invoke Community law before those courts. This is possible because Community law is normally directly effective, which means that it has to be applied by Member-State courts. If there is a dispute as to whether it is directly effective or as to how it should be interpreted, a reference can be made to the European Court. The final judgment, however, will always come from the Member-State court. Enforcement of such a judgment is not usually a problem. The possibility of bringing these proceedings greatly enhances the effectiveness of EU law. They will be discussed further in Chapter 11.

Further reading

Bonnie, "Commission Discretion under Article 171(2) EC" (1998) 23 ELRev. 537.

Bulterman (M. K.) and Kuijer (M.) (eds.), *Compliance with Judgments of International Courts* (Martinus Nijhoff, Dordrecht and London, 1996).

Collier (John) and Lowe (Vaughan), *The Settlement of Disputes in International Law* (Oxford University Press, Oxford, 1999), pp. 263–273.

Hartley (Trevor C.), *Constitutional Problems of the European Union* (Hart Publishing, Oxford and Portland, OR, 1999), Chapter 6.

Rasmussen (Hjalte), *European Court of Justice* (GadJura, Copenhagen, 1998), Chapter 4.

Theodossiou, "An Analysis of the Recent Response of the Community to Non-Compliance with Court of Justice Judgments" (2002) 27 ELRev. 25.

7

Interpretation

In this chapter we consider the ways in which international courts interpret legal texts. This is one of the most controversial aspects of their work, since there is normally no redress if they abuse their power.

Words and meanings

Legal texts – whether treaties, statutes or anything else – are made up of words. Interpretation is the giving of meaning to those words. Since words are notoriously elusive, this is no easy task. However, the whole of civilization is based on the premise that words have meanings. If they did not, language could not operate, and this would mean that modern life would be impossible.

Our starting point must be that words have meanings assigned to them by society. These meanings are, however, subject to uncertainty. There is an inner core of clarity, surrounded by a penumbra of obscurity. Panel 7.1 gives an example. A second problem is that the meanings of words change. They change over time. Some quite common words meant something different in Shakespeare's time from what they do today. Meanings also change as one moves from one social or geographical location to another. Members of a profession, such as doctors, lawyers or scientists, use them in a different way from the general public. A third problem is that the meanings of words depend on the context in which they are spoken. Take the phrase, "Get that man". What does it mean? If spoken when an enemy suddenly appears in the course of a gun-fight, it probably means, "Kill that man". In the context of discussions to select a team, however, it probably means, "Pick that man".

So far we have been looking at the question from only one point of view. We have been trying to find the "objective" meaning of the word. But there is another point of view – the subjective. We can ask ourselves what the speaker meant when he used the word. We might happen to know that he was a foreigner and habitually misused a certain word. From this point of view, the best way to know what a text means is to ask the author. If that is impossible, or if we think we might not get an honest reply, we could look for clues. We might look at the speeches made when the text was adopted. We could look

Panel 7.1 Degrees of clarity

Assume that the word "vehicle" appears in a legal text. What does it mean? Which of the following is covered:

- a motor car;
- a bicycle ridden by a man;
- a sled pulled by a child over snow;
- a horse with a rider;
- a horse without a rider;
- a pedestrian?

You will see that in some cases you can give a clear answer, but in others you cannot.

at earlier drafts in order to see how the provision evolved. We might look at the provision as a whole in order to see its purpose. All of these could help us find the subjective intention of its authors.

In practice, we usually combine these methods. We would think someone was ridiculous if he went by the literal meaning of spoken words, when it was obvious that the speaker meant something else. On the other hand, both in law and in social life, we do not accept that a person can give any meaning he likes to the words he uses. If a person agrees to buy goods for "£1,000", he cannot turn round afterwards and say that, for him, "1,000" meant "500". He is bound by the objective meaning of the words. Likewise, if I agree to meet you at five o'clock and arrive late, you will not accept the excuse that, for me, "five o'clock" means, "half past five", since I always give myself half an hour's grace.[1] Private meanings, even if genuinely held, have no place in public transactions.

The Vienna Convention on the Law of Treaties

Lawyers try to solve these problems by laying down rules on the interpretation of legal texts. In international law, they are found in Articles 31–33 of the Vienna Convention on the Law of Treaties 1969,[2] a convention adopted by a number of States to clarify and develop the rules of international law on treaties between States.[3] At first sight, it might be thought to have a limited scope, since many States have not signed it and, in addition, it says that it is not applicable to treaties concluded before it entered into force.[4] However, it is generally regarded as reflecting customary international law. Consequently, States that have not signed it refer to it as an authoritative source of law,[5] and it is often applied to earlier treaties on this basis, even though it is not

---

1 It would be different if I had told you this in advance.
2 The text may be found on the UN website: http://www.un.org/law/ilc/texts/treatfra.htm.
3 International agreements have various names – for example, "treaty", "convention" or "agreement" – but these names have little significance. The Vienna Convention applies to all international agreements between States in written form and governed by international law, irrespective of their particular designation: Art. 2(1)(a).
4 Art. 4.
5 Anthony Aust, *Modern Treaty Law and Practice* (Cambridge University Press, Cambridge, 2000), pp. 10–11.

Panel 7.2 Interpretation of treaties

Vienna Convention on the Law of Treaties 1969

Article 31 General rule of interpretation

1. A treaty shall be interpreted in good faith in accordance with the ordinary meaning to be given to the terms of the treaty in their context and in the light of its object and purpose.

2. The context for the purpose of the interpretation of a treaty shall comprise, in addition to the text, including its preamble and annexes:

(a) any agreement relating to the treaty which was made between all the parties in connection with the conclusion of the treaty;

(b) any instrument which was made by one or more parties in connection with the conclusion of the treaty and accepted by the other parties as an instrument related to the treaty.

3. There shall be taken into account, together with the context:

(a) any subsequent agreement between the parties regarding the interpretation of the treaty or the application of its provisions;

(b) any subsequent practice in the application of the treaty which establishes the agreement of the parties regarding its interpretation;

(c) any relevant rules of international law applicable in the relations between the parties.

4. A special meaning shall be given to a term if it is established that the parties so intended.

Article 32 Supplementary means of interpretation

Recourse may be had to supplementary means of interpretation, including the preparatory work of the treaty and the circumstances of its conclusion, in order to confirm the meaning resulting from the application of article 31, or to determine the meaning when the interpretation according to article 31:

(a) leaves the meaning ambiguous or obscure; or

(b) leads to a result which is manifestly absurd or unreasonable.

Article 33 Interpretation of treaties authenticated in two or more languages

1. When a treaty has been authenticated in two or more languages, the text is equally authoritative in each language, unless the treaty provides or the parties agree that, in case of divergence, a particular text shall prevail.

2. A version of the treaty in a language other than one of those in which the text was authenticated shall be considered an authentic text only if the treaty so provides or the parties so agree.

3. The terms of the treaty are presumed to have the same meaning in each authentic text.

4. Except where a particular text prevails in accordance with paragraph 1, when a comparison of the authentic texts discloses a difference of meaning which the application of articles 31 and 32 does not remove, the meaning which best reconciles the texts, having regard to the object and purpose of the treaty, shall be adopted.

strictly speaking applicable to them.[6] It can, therefore, be regarded as the best statement of international law on the subject.

Articles 31–33 are set out in Panel 7.2. Article 31 is the key provision. It lays down the general rule. Article 32 is supplementary: it applies only if interpretation on the basis of Article 31 still leaves the provision ambiguous or obscure, or if it leads to a result that is manifestly absurd or unreasonable. Article 33 is concerned with the problem of texts in two or more languages, something that is of particular importance in the case of the European Union. If the texts conflict, the meaning that best reconciles them, having regard to the object and purpose of the treaty, must be adopted.

---

6 Thus, in the case we are about to consider, *Germany v. United States*, the International Court applied it to interpret its Statute, even though the Statute was concluded long before the Vienna Convention entered into force.

Article 31(1) requires a treaty to be interpreted in good faith, something that also applies to the carrying out of a treaty's obligations. An interpretation that was unreasonable, or at variance with the known intention of the parties, would be contrary to good faith. A treaty must be interpreted in accordance with the ordinary meaning of the words. This recognises that words have an objective meaning. However, the words must be interpreted in their context, and in the light of the object and purpose of the treaty, a requirement that harks back to the intention of its framers. Article 31(4) further emphasises the intention of the parties.

Interpretation and legislation

Interpretation is the discovery of the meaning of a text. Legislation is the creation of a new text. They are different things, though in some situations the line between them may be a fine one. A difficulty arises when the procedures discussed above produce no answer. What then? Most lawyers agree that, in such a case, the judge may legitimately decide what, in his opinion, the authors of the text would have intended if they had thought about the question before the court. The judge might do this by deciding what the purpose of the text is, and then giving it the meaning that best fulfils that purpose. This is sometimes called the teleological[7] method, or the principle of effectiveness. This method is much beloved by the European Court. It is a reasonable approach, provided it does not lead to a result that conflicts with the ordinary meaning of the words, or with the known intention of the authors. If used in bad faith, however, it can constitute a disguise for "judicial legislation". This occurs when the court pretends to interpret the text, but in reality changes it to further its own purposes.

In the cases that follow, we will consider whether the court has applied the teleological method legitimately, or whether it has crossed the line and been guilty of judicial legislation.

> ### World
> **Germany v. United States** (LaGrand case)
> **INTERNATIONAL COURT OF JUSTICE**
> Provisional order, 3 March 1999; final judgment 27 June 2001 (not yet reported in ICJ Rep.). Full text available on http://www.icj-cij.org.

Facts

The facts of this case were set out in Chapter 6. It will be remembered that the case arose when two German nationals were charged with murder in Arizona. They were tried and sentenced to death, without being informed of their right to contact the German consulate in order to obtain legal assistance. Germany contended that this was a violation of a convention to which both it and

---

7 From the Greek, *telos*, meaning "purpose".

the US were party, the Convention on Consular Relations 1963. Germany said that the brothers should be allowed to have their convictions and sentences reviewed on this ground. The United States disagreed. So Germany brought proceedings against the US before the International Court of Justice. By the time the action was begun, one brother had already been executed. Germany asked the court for a provisional order requiring the execution of the other brother to be suspended until the court could give final judgment. The court granted the order but, later the same day, the execution took place.

When it came to give final judgment, the court considered whether the failure of the US to obey the provisional order constituted a violation of the law. This raised the question, never before decided, whether such orders are legally binding. The power to grant provisional orders is given by Article 41 of the Statute of the court. In English, this reads as follows (italics added):

1. The Court shall have the power to *indicate*, if it considers that circumstances so require, any provisional measures which *ought* to be taken to preserve the respective rights of either party.
2. Pending the final decision, notice of the measures *suggested* shall forthwith be given to the parties and to the Security Council.

The US argued that the words italicized in the above text show that such orders are not binding. They are mere suggestions.

In its judgment, the court pointed out that the wording of Article 41 was taken from the text of the equivalent provision in the Statute of the Permanent Court of International Justice (PCIJ), the predecessor of the ICJ. The only change was that the reference at the end of the second paragraph to the Security Council was substituted for a reference to the Council of the League of Nations. The Statute of the PCIJ, like that of the ICJ, was in both French and English.

Judgment

99. ... The Court will therefore now proceed to the interpretation of Article 41 of the Statute. It will do so in accordance with customary international law, reflected in Article 31 of the 1969 Vienna Convention on the Law of Treaties. According to paragraph 1 of Article 31, a treaty must be interpreted in good faith in accordance with the ordinary meaning to be given to its terms in their context and in the light of the treaty's object and purpose.

[The court then set out the text of Article 41 in both French and English, italicizing the words italicized above. The French for "indicate" is *"indiquer"*, for "ought to be taken" is *"doivent être prises"* and for "suggested" is the noun, *"l'indication"*. It said that the French terms, *"indiquer"* and *"l'indication"* were neutral as to the mandatory (binding) character of the measure, but the words, *"doivent être prises"* were imperative. The court then continued:]

According to the United States, the use in the English version of "indicate" instead of "order", of "ought" instead of "must" or "shall", and of "suggested" instead of "ordered", is to be understood as implying that decisions under Article 41 lack mandatory effect. It might however be argued, having regard to the fact that in 1920 the French text was the original version, that such terms as "indicate" and "ought" have a meaning equivalent to "order" and "must" or "shall".

101. Finding itself faced with two texts which are not in total harmony, the Court will first of all note that according to Article 92 of the Charter, the Statute "forms an integral part of the present Charter". Under Article 111 of the Charter, the French and English texts of the latter are "equally authentic". The same is equally true of the Statute.

In cases of divergence between the equally authentic versions of the Statute, neither it nor the Charter indicates how to proceed. In the absence of agreement between the parties in this respect, it is appropriate to refer to paragraph 4 of Article 33 of the Vienna Convention on the Law of Treaties, which in the view of the Court again reflects customary international law. This provision reads "when a comparison of the authentic texts discloses a difference of meaning which the application of Articles 31 and 32 does not remove the meaning which best reconciles the texts, having regard to the object and purpose of the treaty, shall be adopted".

The Court will therefore now consider the object and purpose of the Statute together with the context of Article 41.

102. The object and purpose of the Statute is to enable the Court to fulfil the functions provided for therein, and in particular, the basic function of judicial settlement of international disputes by binding decisions in accordance with Article 59 of the Statute. The context in which Article 41 has to be seen within the Statute is to prevent the Court from being hampered in the exercise of its functions because the respective rights of the parties to a dispute before the Court are not preserved. It follows from the object and purpose of the Statute, as well as from the terms of Article 41 when read in their context, that the power to indicate provisional measures entails that such measures should be binding, inasmuch as the power in question is based on the necessity, when the circumstances call for it, to safeguard, and to avoid prejudice to, the rights of the parties as determined by the final judgment of the Court. The contention that provisional measures indicated under Article 41 might not be binding would be contrary to the object and purpose of that Article.

103. A related reason which points to the binding character of orders made under Article 41 and to which the Court attaches importance, is the existence of a principle which has already been recognized by the Permanent Court of International Justice when it spoke of

> "the principle universally accepted by international tribunals and likewise laid down in many conventions . . . to the effect that the parties to a case must abstain from any measure capable of exercising a prejudicial effect in regard to the execution of the decision to be given, and, in general, not allow any step of any kind to be taken which might aggravate or extend the dispute" (*Electricity Company of Sofia and Bulgaria*, Order of 5 December 1939, PCIJ, Series A/B, No. 79, p. 199).

Furthermore measures designed to avoid aggravating or extending disputes have frequently been indicated by the Court. They were indicated with the purpose of being implemented **[citations omitted]**.

104. Given the conclusions reached by the Court above in interpreting the text of Article 41 of the Statute in the light of its object and purpose, it does not consider it necessary to resort to the preparatory work in order to determine the meaning of that Article. The Court would nevertheless point out that the preparatory work of the Statute does not preclude the conclusion that orders under Article 41 have binding force.

[The court then considered the drafting history of the provision in the Statute of the PCIJ equivalent to Article 41. The original draft of this said, "the court may ... order adequate protective measures to be taken". This was changed to "the court shall have the power to suggest". It was subsequently argued that "suggest" should be changed back to "order", but this was rejected on the ground that the court lacked the means to execute its decisions. The court's comment on this was as follows:]

107. ... However, the lack of means of execution and the lack of binding force are two different matters. Hence, the fact that the Court does not itself have the means to ensure the execution of orders made pursuant to Article 41 is not an argument against the binding nature of such orders.

[The court finally considered whether Article 94 of the United Nations Charter precluded attributing binding effect to orders indicating provisional measures. It concluded that it did not. It continued:]

109. In short, it is clear that none of the sources of interpretation referred to in the relevant Articles of the Vienna Convention on the Law of Treaties, including the preparatory work, contradict the conclusions drawn from the terms of Article 41 read in their context and in the light of the object and purpose of the Statute. Thus, the Court has reached the conclusion that orders on provisional measures under Article 41 have binding effect.

QUESTION

Was this a legitimate interpretation of the text?

European Union
Parti Ecologiste ``Les Verts" v. European Parliament (Ecological Party (Greens) case)
COURT OF JUSTICE OF THE EUROPEAN COMMUNITIES
Case 294/43, [1986] ECR 1339

Facts

This case arose because the European Parliament did a rather disreputable thing. Money was available, ostensibly for an information campaign about the European Parliament, but in reality to subsidize political parties in the forth-coming European elections. The Parliament had to decide how it would be divided among the various parties. The formula it chose gave an unfairly large amount to the parties already represented in the Parliament (themselves) and an unfairly small amount to those contesting the elections for the first time. The Ecological Party fell into the latter category. It wanted to challenge the decision. Could it do so? There appears to have been no remedy in the Member-State courts. Did the European Court have jurisdiction? This depended on Article 230 [173] EC. As it then stood, it read: "The Court of Justice shall review the legality of acts of the Council or Commission . . ." Nowhere did Article 230 [173] permit the court to review acts of the Parliament at the suit of an organization such as a political party.[8] The Ecological Party nevertheless brought the action. The court then had to decide whether it had jurisdiction to hear the case.

Judgment

23. It must first be emphasized in this regard that the European Economic Community is a Community based on the rule of law, inasmuch as neither its Member States nor its institutions can avoid a review of the question whether the measures adopted by them are in conformity with the basic constitutional charter, the Treaty. In particular, in Articles 230 [173] and 241 [184], on the one hand, and in Article 234 [177], on the other, the Treaty established a complete system of legal remedies and procedures designed to permit the Court of Justice to review the legality of measures adopted by the institutions. Natural and legal persons are thus protected against the application to them of general measures which they cannot contest directly before the Court by reason of the special conditions of admissibility laid down in the second paragraph of Article 230 [173] of the Treaty. Where the Community institutions are responsible for the administrative implementation of such measures, natural or legal persons may bring a direct action before the Court against implementing measures which are addressed to them or which are of direct and individual concern to them and, in support of such an action, plead the illegality of the general measure on which they are based. Where implementation is a matter for the national authorities, such persons may plead the invalidity of general measures before the national courts and cause the latter to request the Court of Justice for a preliminary ruling.

24. It is true that, unlike Article 234 [177] of the Treaty, which refers to acts of the institutions without further qualification, Article 230 [173] refers only to acts of the Council and the Commission. However, the general scheme of the Treaty is to make a direct action available against "all measures adopted by the institutions . . . which are intended to have legal effects", as the Court has already had occasion to emphasize in its judgment of 31 March 1971 (Case 22/70 *Commission v Council* [1971] ECR 263). The European Parliament is not expressly mentioned among the institutions whose measures may be contested because, in its original version, the EEC Treaty merely granted it powers of consultation and political control rather than the power to adopt measures intended to have legal effects *vis-à-vis* third parties. Article 38 of the ECSC Treaty shows that where the Parliament was given *ab initio* the power to adopt binding measures, as was the case under the last sentence of the fourth paragraph of Article 95 of that Treaty,[9] measures adopted by it were not in principle immune from actions for annulment.

25. Whereas under the ECSC Treaty actions for annulment against measures adopted by the institutions are the subject of two separate provisions, they are governed under the EEC Treaty by Article 230 [173] alone, which is therefore a provision of general application. An interpretation of Article 230 [173] of the Treaty which excluded measures adopted by the European Parliament from those which could be contested would lead to a result contrary both to the spirit of the Treaty as expressed in Article 220 [164] and to its system. Measures adopted by the European Parliament in the context of the EEC Treaty could encroach on the powers of the Member States or of the other institutions, or exceed the

---

8 Art. 38 ECSC permitted the court to review acts of the Parliament at the suit of the Commission or a Member State.
9 Editor's note: the third and fourth paragraphs of Article 95 provided a means of amending the provisions of the ECSC Treaty without having to adopt a new treaty. The procedure was that the amendment had to be proposed jointly by the High Authority (Commission) and the Council (the latter acting by a five-sixths majority) and submitted to the European Court for its scrutiny. The next step was for it to be approved by the European Parliament (also acting by a special majority). It is hard to see on what ground the Parliament's approval could have been challenged before the European Court.

limits which have been set to the Parliament's powers, without its being possible to refer them for review by the Court. It must therefore he concluded that an action for annulment may lie against measures adopted by the European Parliament intended to have legal effects *vis-à-vis* third parties.

[After deciding that it had jurisdiction, the court then went on to consider whether the act was invalid. It held that it was, since the conduct of elections to the European Parliament was a matter for the Member States.]

Comment

In this case, the European Court applied a distortion of the teleological method to come up with an "interpretation" that contradicts the clear words of the text. It did this by purporting to derive a general principle from the terms of the treaty. This is the principle that the treaty establishes a complete system of judicial remedies under which anyone can challenge an act of a Community institution. It then observed that there was a gap in this system, since Article 230 [173] did not apply to the Parliament. The court thought that this was contrary to the "spirit"[10] and "system" of the Treaty; it therefore felt justified in concluding that when Article 230 [173] gave the court jurisdiction to review acts of the Commission and Council, what it really meant was that it could review acts of the Parliament as well.

In order to suggest that this was what the framers of the Treaty really intended, it pointed out that originally the Parliament had no significant powers under the EC Treaty; there was therefore no need to provide for review of its acts. It tried to bolster this argument by saying that when it did have powers, as under the ECSC Treaty, a remedy was given against it. This was under Article 38 ECSC. The flaw in this argument is that Article 38 applied only to actions brought by the Commission or a Member State. None of the Community Treaties had ever given a right of action to organizations such as a political party.[11] So there was no reason to believe that the failure to give such a right under Article 230 [173] was due to an oversight.

Acts of the Parliament ought to be subject to judicial review. However, there is no disguising the fact that this is not what the Treaty said. This highlights a dilemma that often occurs in the law: the conflict between what the law ought to be and what it is. The whole idea of the rule of law, however, is that a court should give judgment on the basis of rules that were already in existence when the facts of the case arose. If the court makes them up after the event, people will never know where they stand.

10 The court supports this assertion by a reference to Art. 220 [164], but, as it stood at the time, all this said was: "The Court of Justice shall ensure that in the interpretation and application of this Treaty, the law is observed."
11 If it had not been for this, the Ecological Party could have relied on Art. 38 in the case before the court, since the decision subject to challenge was adopted under the ECSC Treaty as well as under the EC Treaty. In a previous case, the European Court held that where a measure is adopted under two or more of the Community Treaties, it has jurisdiction to annul it if such jurisdiction exists under *any one* of those Treaties: *Luxembourg v. European Parliament*, Case 230/81, [1983] ECR 255. In this case, a Member State was allowed to use Art. 38 ECSC to challenge an act of the Parliament that applied simultaneously under the ECSC, EC and Euratom Treaties.

Panel 7.3   Article 230 [173] in 1990

EC Treaty (as it stood in 1990)

Article 230 [173]

The Court of Justice shall review the legality of acts of the Council and the Commission other than recommendations or opinions. It shall for this purpose have jurisdiction in actions brought by a Member State, the Council or the Commission on grounds of . . .

Any natural or legal person may, under the same conditions, institute proceedings . . .

A few years after this judgment, the Member States amended Article 230 [173] EC to read, "The Court of Justice shall review the legality . . . of acts of the European Parliament intended to produce legal effects *vis-à-vis* third parties" – almost identical words to those in the judgment.[12] This proves two things: first, that the Member States approved of the court's judgment; and, secondly, that the judgment really did change the text. If it had not done so, there would have been no need to amend it.

> *European Union*
> **European Parliament v. Council** ("Chernobyl" case)
> **COURT OF JUSTICE OF THE EUROPEAN COMMUNITIES**
> Case C-70/88, [1990] ECR I-2041

Facts

In the previous case, the European Court held that actions could be brought against the European Parliament, even though Article 230 [173] EC, as it then stood, permitted actions against only the Council or Commission. The case we are about to consider raises the opposite question: can the European Parliament *bring* actions under Article 230 [173]? As it stood at the time,[13] Article 230 [173] was equally clear on this point. The Parliament could not bring such actions (see Panel 7.3).

In an earlier case, *European Parliament v. Council* ("Comitology" case),[14] the Parliament had argued that since the court had "interpreted" the first paragraph of Article 230 [173] to allow actions to be brought *against* it, it should also interpret it to allow it to *bring* actions. The court rejected this argument.[15] Another argument put forward in the "Comitology" case was that the Parliament needed to be able to bring proceedings under Article 230 [173] in order to defend its prerogatives (special rights and powers). The court rejected this on the ground that the Commission, which did have standing under Article 230 [173], could do this for the Parliament.

The "Chernobyl" case concerned a measure taken by the Community as a result of the nuclear accident in Chernobyl in the Ukraine. The Commission

---

12 Treaty on European Union 1992.
13 The amendment mentioned did not come into force until 1993.
14 Case 302/87, [1988] ECR 5615. It is called the "Comitology" case, because it concerned a measure on the committees that have to be formed when the Commission exercises delegated powers.
15 It also held that the Parliament could not bring actions under the second paragraph of Art. 230 [173]. See Panel 7.3 for the text.

proposed that the measure be adopted under Article 31 Euratom, under which the Parliament had only a right to be consulted. The Commission considered that this was the appropriate provision, since the measure concerned nuclear energy. The Parliament, however, thought that the measure should be adopted under Article 95 [100a] EC, a provision under which the Parliament had wider powers (co-operation procedure). The Parliament argued that, since the Commission had proposed that the measure be adopted under Article 31 Euratom, it could hardly be expected to defend the Parliament's claim that Article 95 [100a] was the appropriate provision.

In its judgment, the court first considered whether there were any alternative legal remedies open to the Parliament. It concluded that there were, but their scope was limited.

Judgment

20. It follows from the foregoing that the existence of those various legal remedies is not sufficient to guarantee, with certainty and in all circumstances, that a measure adopted by the Council or the Commission in disregard of the Parliament's prerogatives will be reviewed.

21. Those prerogatives are one of the elements of the institutional balance created by the Treaties. The Treaties set up a system for distributing powers among the different Community institutions, assigning to each institution its own role in the institutional structure of the Community and the accomplishment of the tasks entrusted to the Community.

22. Observance of the institutional balance means that each of the institutions must exercise its powers with due regard for the powers of the other institutions. It also requires that it should be possible to penalize any breach of that rule which may occur.

23. The Court, which under the Treaties has the task of ensuring that in the interpretation and application of the Treaties the law is observed, must therefore be able to maintain the institutional balance and, consequently, review the observance of the Parliament's prerogatives when called upon to do so by the Parliament, by means of a legal remedy which is suited to the purpose which the Parliament seeks to achieve.

24. In carrying out that task the Court cannot, of course, include the Parliament among the institutions which may bring an action under Article 230 [173] of the EEC Treaty or Article 146 of the Euratom Treaty without being required to demonstrate an interest in bringing an action.

25. However, it is the Court's duty to ensure that the provisions of the Treaties concerning the institutional balance are fully applied and to see to it that the Parliament's prerogatives, like those of the other institutions, cannot be breached without it having available a legal remedy, among those laid down in the Treaties, which may be exercised in a certain and effective manner.

26. The absence in the Treaties of any provision giving the Parliament the right to bring an action for annulment may constitute a procedural gap, but it cannot prevail over the fundamental interest in the maintenance and observance of the institutional balance laid down in the Treaties establishing the European Communities.

27. Consequently, an action for annulment brought by the Parliament against an act of the Council or the Commission is admissible provided that the action seeks only to safeguard its prerogatives and that it is founded only on submissions alleging their infringement. Provided that condition is met, the Parliament's action for annulment is subject to the rules laid down in the Treaties for actions for annulment brought by the other institutions.

28. In accordance with the Treaties, the Parliament's prerogatives include participation in the drafting of legislative measures, in particular participation in the co-operation procedure laid down in the EEC Treaty.

29. In the present case, the Parliament claims that the contested regulation is based on Article 31 of the Euratom Treaty, which provides only that the Parliament is to be consulted, whereas it ought to have been based on Article 95 [100a] of the EEC Treaty, which requires implementation of the procedure for co-operation with the Parliament.

30. The Parliament infers from that that the Council's choice of legal basis for the contested regulation led to a breach of its prerogatives by denying it the possibility, which the co-operation procedure offers, of participating in the drafting of the measure more closely and actively than it could in the consultation procedure.

31. Since the Parliament claims that its prerogatives were breached as a result of the choice of legal basis for the contested measure, it follows from all the foregoing that the present action is admissible. The Council's objection of inadmissibility must therefore be dismissed and the proceedings must be continued with regard to the substance of the case.[16]

Comment

In this case, the court adopts the same tactic as in the last. It declares that the Treaty is based on the principle of "institutional balance". It then finds that full effect is not given to this principle, since the Parliament is not always able to defend its prerogatives. At this point, however, the court does something remarkable. It does not "interpret" the Treaty as meaning that the Parliament can bring proceedings under the first paragraph of Article 230 [173]. It admits (in paragraph 26) that the Treaty does not give it this right. Nevertheless, it still says that the Parliament can bring the action, a clear admission that it is creating a new rule. The new right of action is not under Article 230 [173]. The court says (paragraph 24) that the Parliament cannot be included among the institutions which may bring an action under Article 230 [173] (or under Article 146, the equivalent provision in the Euratom Treaty) without being required to demonstrate an interest. The Parliament's right is more limited. It can bring an action only for the purpose of safeguarding its prerogatives; subject to that, the rules of the first paragraph of Article 230 [173] apply. It was more honest of the court to admit that it was changing the Treaty than to pretend that it was interpreting it.

When the Member States amended the Treaty to give effect to the court's judgment in the *Ecological Party* case, they also gave effect to the judgment in

---

16 When the court came to deal with the substance of the case, it decided that Art. 31 Euratom was after all the correct legal basis: see [1991] ECR I-4529.

this case. This occurred in the Treaty on European Union (Maastricht Agreement) 1992, which amended Article 230 [173] to read:

> The Court shall have jurisdiction under the same conditions in actions brought by the European Parliament and by the ECB for the purpose of protecting their prerogatives.

Again, almost the identical words of the judgment were used.[17]

Conclusions

It might be thought that the European Court's "legislative" rulings do little harm, since the Member States can always reverse them if they do not like them. However, when the judgment concerns a provision in one of the treaties, the only way in which this can be done is by an amendment to the Treaty.[18] To do this, *all* the Member States must agree. If a single Member State supports the court, the ruling will stand. If the provision had originally been changed by means of a Treaty amendment, on the other hand, all the Member States would have had to be in *favour* of it: a single Member State could block the amendment. This is because the Treaty is supposed to be based on the free consent of all the Member States. The effect of a "legislative" ruling by the court is, therefore, to change a system under which all must agree, to one in which it is sufficient for one Member State to want it. Such an amendment is no longer based on the free consent of all the Member States. The court has imposed it on them.

This question did not arise in the two cases we have just considered. The Member States accepted the rulings, and the Treaty was amended to give effect to them. However, these are the only instances in which the Treaty has been amended to bring it into line with the court's rulings, though there have been other cases in which its interpretation of the Treaty has been controversial. One such instance was *Francovich v. Italy*,[19] a case set out in Chapter 11, below. In this case, the court created a new right of action against a Member State, although there was no provision for this in the Treaty. It seems that the European Court suggested to the Member States in the 1970s that the Treaty should be amended to provide for such an action,[20] but this was not done. At least one Member State must have been opposed. The court then effected the change by means of an "interpretation" of the Treaty. Two Member States, the UK and Germany, tried to get this ruling reversed in the negotiations leading to the Treaty of Amsterdam. They were unsuccessful. At least one Member State must have

---

17 In the Treaty of Nice, it was further amended to put the Parliament in the same position as the Council or Commission. See Panel 5.5, p. 82 above.
18 For an instance in which this occurred, see Art. 141 EC, adopted in response to the court's decision in *Kalanke v. Bremen*, Case C-450/93, [1995] ECR I-3051. The court's interpretation of the treaty in that case was actually a reasonable one, though it did not suit certain German politicians. For further details, see Trevor C. Hartley, *Constitutional Problems of the European Union* (Hart Publishing, Oxford and Portland, OR, 1999), pp. 53–56.
19 Cases C-6 and 9/90, [1991] ECR I-5357; [1993] 2 CMLR 66.
20 See *Bulletin of the European Communities*, Supplement 9/75, p. 18 (1975).

supported the court's ruling. The court therefore succeeded in bringing about a change in the Treaty that was not wanted by at least two Member States.

Further reading

International law

Aust (Anthony), *Modern Treaty Law and Practice* (Cambridge University Press, Cambridge, 2000), Chapter 13.

Sinclair (Sir Ian), *The Vienna Convention on the Law of Treaties* (Manchester University Press, Manchester and Dover, NH, 2nd ed. 1984), Chapter V.

The European Court

Arnull, "The European Court and Judicial Objectivity: A Reply to Professor Hartley" (1996) 112 LQR 411.

Hartley (Trevor C.), *Constitutional Problems of the European Union* (Hart Publishing, Oxford and Portland, OR, 1999), Chapters 2 and 3.

Hartley, "The European Court, Judicial Objectivity and the Constitution of the European Union" (1996) 112 LQR 95.

Rasmussen (Hjalte), *European Court of Justice* (GadJura, Copenhagen, 1998).

PART III
RELATIONS BETWEEN LEGAL SYSTEMS: INTERNATIONAL LAW, COMMUNITY LAW AND NATIONAL LAW

8

The role of international law

In this Part, we consider the relations between international law, Community law and national law. This chapter introduces the subject.

International law

International law has two components: customary international law and treaty law. Customary international law consists of legally-binding rules that have evolved in the relations between States. Customary international law is binding on all States. One branch of customary international law is the law of treaties. This contains rules for the making of international agreements, and gives them their binding character. International agreements may be called "treaties", "conventions" or something else, but their name does not affect their legal character. They are binding on the parties to them.

There are two kinds of international agreements, or perhaps it might be more accurate to say that international agreements have two aspects. One aspect is contractual. In a treaty of this kind, State A promises to do something, and in return State B promises to do something. These things are usually different. State A may promise to pay State B some money, and State B may promise to give State A something. Such a treaty is analogous to a contract in English law. Once the parties have carried out their obligations under it, the treaty is at an end. It has fulfilled its purpose.[1]

A treaty can also have a law-making aspect. It may be a means by which States lay down new rules of international law. A treaty of this kind does not become spent (terminated) once it has been obeyed on one occasion. It imposes a continuing obligation – for example, to respect human rights. The obligations under a law-making treaty are usually the same for all the parties.[2]

A good example of a treaty of the law-making kind is the Vienna Convention on the Law of Treaties, 1969. This is an international agreement which codifies the law of treaties. To a large extent it clarifies and sets down the rules of customary international law on the subject, though it may also modify them

---

1 Ian Brownlie, *Principles of Public International Law* (Oxford University Press, Oxford, 6th ed., 2003), pp. 12 *et seq.*
2 *Ibid.*

to some extent. Approximately half the States of the world are parties to it. It is binding on these States. It covers most of the law of treaties, though not all of it.[3] Customary international law continues to apply to the areas not covered.

In principle, customary international law continues to apply to all areas of the law of treaties as far as those States that are not parties to the Vienna Convention are concerned. However, those States generally recognise the Convention as authoritatively expressing the rules of customary international law. In practice, therefore, they accept it too. In fact, if the rules of a multilateral, law-making treaty such as the Vienna Convention are accepted by non-parties as binding on them, whether on this basis or on any other, the treaty could create new rules of customary international law.[4]

A treaty is thus a means by which rules of customary international law may be changed. A law-making treaty might be regarded as the international analogue to a statute. Even if a treaty does not become universalized in this way, it can still create new rules among the parties to it. These new rules may replace the rules of customary international law on a particular topic. Customary international law would continue to apply in general, but the new rules would apply on that topic. The only limit to the extent to which customary international law may be excluded is the doctrine of *ius cogens*,[5] Latin for "mandatory rule" or "peremptory rule". A peremptory rule is a rule of customary international law that cannot be changed by treaty.[6] A treaty that conflicts with such a rule is void.[7]

International organizations

An international organization is created by means of a treaty. The treaty may give it legal personality under international law. It then becomes a subject of international law. It can have rights under international law, and is bound by it. Once created, international organizations can themselves become parties to treaties. The 1969 Vienna Convention applies only to treaties between States, but another convention, the Vienna Convention on the Law of Treaties between States and International Organizations or between International Organizations of 1986 applies similar rules to them. This convention has not yet entered into force, but is generally regarded as expressing the rules of customary international law on the matter.[8]

International organizations have such powers as are conferred on them by their constituent treaties. These powers may include the power to legislate – though any legislation so adopted is binding only on the Member States of the organization. As between the Member States, however, such legislation replaces

---

3 For example, it does not cover unwritten agreements: Art. 2(1)(a). Unwritten treaties, though rare, are possible: Anthony Aust, *Modern Treaty Law and Practice* (Cambridge University Press, Cambridge, 2000), pp. 16–17.
4 *Ibid.*, p. 10; Brownlie, note 1 above, p. 13.
5 Also written "*jus cogens*".
6 See Art. 53 of the 1969 Vienna Convention.
7 *Ibid.*
8 Aust, note 3 above, pp. 7–8.

the rules of customary international law, subject to the doctrine of *ius cogens* and to any conflicting treaty obligations.

Community law

The European Community is an international organization created by treaty, the Treaty Establishing the European Community (EC Treaty), 1957.[9] Euratom was created by the Treaty Establishing the European Atomic Energy Community, 1957. Both these Communities have international legal personality.[10] As we saw in Chapter 1, the European Union is made up of these two (originally, three) Communities plus various policies and forms of co-operation.

As we saw in Chapters 3 and 4, the European Community has legislative powers. It has used these powers to pass a great deal of legislation. This legislation, together with the Treaties themselves, constitutes the Community legal system. To this may be added the legal rules laid down by the European Court. As we saw in Chapter 7, the European Court is prepared to lay down rules of law that are not, on any reasonable interpretation, to be found in the Treaties. When it does this, it is creating new rules of law. (Treaties between the Community and third countries are often said by the European Court to be part of the Community legal system, but, as we shall see in Chapter 13, this is not really so.)

If we define the Community legal system as the sum total of all the legal rules derived from the above sources, we can see that it is a significant body of law. It may not be as massive a body of law as English law, but it is steadily increasing in bulk. A special feature of the Community legal system, however, is that its legal validity is dependent on another legal system – international law. All Community legislation depends on the Community Treaties. They created the Community's legislative institutions, and gave them their powers. The Treaties also created the European Court and gave it its powers. Thus all forms of Community law depend for their validity on the Community Treaties; and the Community Treaties depend for their validity on international law.

The dependent character of Community law is not affected by the fact that the Community Treaties are referred to as the "constitution" of the Community.[11] In international law, the term "constitution" is used to refer to the founding treaty of an international organization.[12] For example, the treaty establishing the International Labour Organization is officially

---

9 It was originally called the "Treaty Establishing the European Economic Community", but its name was changed by the Treaty on European Union, Art. 8 A(1) [G A(1)].
10 Art. 281 [210] EC; Art. 184 Euratom.
11 This usage has been adopted by the European Court. See *Parti Ecologiste "Les Verts" v. European Parliament*, Case 294/83, [1986] ECR 1339 (para. 23 of the judgment). See also *First EEA Case*, Opinion 1/91, [1991] ECR 6079 (para. 21 of the judgment).
12 For example, in one of the best known definitions, that originally proposed by Sir Gerald Fitzmaurice in his report on the law of treaties presented to the International Law Commission in March 1956, an international organization is defined as "a collectivity of States established by treaty, with a *constitution* and common organs, having a personality distinct from that of its member-States, and being a subject of international law with treaty-making capacity" (italics added). See [1956] II *Yearbook of the International Law Commission* 104 at 108.

called the Constitution of the International Labour Organization.[13] The word "constitution" indicates that the treaty establishes a new entity with legal personality in international law. The fact that the Community Treaties are referred to as a constitution does not mean that they are not also treaties under international law. They have not broken free of international law and become independently valid in the way that the constitution of a State has.[14]

One consequence of the dependent character of Community law is that, in the final analysis, international law determines whether the Community treaties have been amended or terminated.[15] The Treaties contain no provision for their termination.[16] This does not, however, mean that they cannot be terminated. Under international law, all that is required is that all the parties should consent.[17] The treaties would then cease to operate. The Community would no longer exist. In practice, of course, it would be desirable to terminate them by means of a new treaty, which would also determine how the Community would be wound up and what would happen to its assets.

The Treaties do make provision for their amendment.[18] Each Member State must agree, and the amending treaty must be adopted by each State according to its constitutional requirements. This is the same as the position under international law.[19] However, if Community law imposed any restrictions on the power of the Member States to amend the Treaties, the Treaties could nevertheless be amended without regard to those restrictions if all the Member States agreed.[20]

The fact that the Community legal system is dependent on international law does not mean that it is identical with international law. We saw above that international law permits a group of States to enter into a treaty that lays down new rules of law. These rules displace customary international law as far as those States are concerned. The only exception is the doctrine of *ius cogens*, but this is unlikely to apply in the case of the Community Treaties.

When they signed the Community Treaties, therefore, the EU Member States had the power under international law to create a self-contained legal system that would apply under the Treaties. Did they exercise this power? According to the European Court, the organ empowered by the Member States to interpret

---

13 It was adopted in April 1919 by the Paris/Versailles Peace Conference convened after the First World War.
14 Hartley, "The Constitutional Foundations of the European Union" (2001) 117 LQR 225 at 226–233.
15 Hartley, "International Law and the Law of the European Union – A Reassessment" (2001) 72 BYIL 1 at 18–22.
16 The only exception was the ECSC Treaty, which provided that it would automatically come to an end after fifty years: Art. 97 ECSC. It terminated on 25 July 2002.
17 It is not even necessary to have a new treaty. Simple agreement is enough: Art. 54(b) of the Vienna Convention on the Law of Treaties 1969. See, further, Anthony Aust, *Modern Treaty Law and Practice* (Cambridge University Press, Cambridge, 2000), p. 232; Sir Ian Sinclair, *The Vienna Convention on the Law of Treaties* (Manchester University Press, Manchester, 2nd ed., 1984), p. 183.
18 Art. 48 [N] TEU.
19 Art. 48 [N] TEU also contains additional requirements. For example, the Parliament must be consulted. These additional requirements are not necessary under international law. Therefore an amendment that was made without complying with them would still be valid. See Hartley, "International Law and the Law of the European Union – A Reassessment" (2001) 72 BYIL 1 at 18–21.
20 *Ibid.*

the Treaties, they did. For example, in *Costa v. ENEL*,[21] the European Court said, "By contrast with [*sic*] ordinary international treaties, the EEC Treaty has created its own legal system . . ."[22] Thus, though the Community Treaties contain no statement that they are intended to establish a separate legal system, Community law is nevertheless regarded as being such a system.

If the Community Treaties had not created a separate legal system, international law would still have applied among the Member States in the area covered by the Treaties. The rules of Community law would simply have been superimposed on it. Where they were different, they would have replaced it (subject to *ius cogens*). Where there was no applicable rule of Community law, international law would have applied. This, however, has been rejected by the European Court in the cases cited above. Instead, customary international law is totally excluded in the area covered by the Community Treaties in so far as relations among the Member States are concerned. If there are any gaps in the law, the European Court fills them by creating new legal rules. This is the consequence of Community law being a separate legal system.

When the European Court creates new rules of Community law, it purports to do so on the basis of "general principles of law".[23] In theory, these are principles found in all, or most, legal systems. The European Court discovers them by a comparative study of the legal systems of the Member States.[24] The reality is slightly different. The principles thus "discovered" by the court are not always found in a majority, or even any, of the legal systems of the Member States. When it wants to create a new legal rule, the European Court certainly looks at the legal systems of the Member States. However, it does not regard itself as bound to adopt the majority view. Once it has informed itself of possible solutions, it considers itself free to fashion the rule it regards as most appropriate to the needs of the Community.

International law and national law

We shall now consider the extent to which international law applies in the legal systems of States. Can international law be invoked in a court in England, the United States or some other country? Unlike Community law, the law of a State

---

21 Case 6/64, [1964] ECR 585 at 593.
22 See also *Van Gend en Loos v. Nederlandse Administratie der Belastingen*, Case 26/62, [1963] ECR 1 at 12 (set out in Chapter 9); *Commission v. Luxembourg and Belgium*, Cases 90 and 91/63, [1964] ECR 625 at 631.
23 "General principles of law" are also one of the sources of international law, recognized in Art. 38(1)(c) of the Statute of the International Court of Justice. The Community Treaties, on the other hand, contain no reference to general principles of law as a general source of Community law (for such a reference in a more limited context, see the second paragraph of Art. 288 [215] EC). Their adoption by the European Court as such a source may have been inspired by the role they play in international law. See, further, Akehurst, "The Application of General Principles of Law by the Court of Justice of the European Communities" (1981) 52 BYIL 29. Since its purposes are different, the European Court would not necessarily derive the same rules from this source as the ICJ.
24 On rare occasions, it also draws inspiration from international law. See, for example, *Fédération Charbonnière de Belgique (Fédéchar) v. High Authority*, Case 8/55, [1956] ECR 292 at 299, in which the European Court justified its adoption of the theory of implied powers by reference to international law as well as to national law.

does not derive its validity from international law. It is independently valid – self-sustaining.[25] International law and national law are thus two independent legal systems. Neither owes its validity to the other. The question whether a provision of one independent legal system is to be applied in another must obviously depend on the latter. For example, the question whether a rule of French law is to be applied in England must depend on English law. The French rule can operate in England only if it is "invited in" by English law. This does indeed happen in some cases. There is a special branch of English law – conflict of laws – that decides when a rule of foreign law will be applied in England. For example, if two people get married in France, an English court will apply French law to determine whether or not the correct formalities were followed.[26]

These principles also govern the relationship between international law and national law. International law decides whether the law of a State can be applied as part of international law.[27] Likewise, the law of a given State decides whether a rule of international law is to be applied as part of that State's legal system.[28] The important issue for our purposes is the application of a treaty in the domestic law of the States that are parties to it. Most States have rules on this question. Some States have a general rule, which might be in their constitution, under which international treaties may in certain circumstances have the force of law in the State concerned, without the need for any national legislation. When this occurs, such treaties are said to be "directly effective" or "directly applicable"[29] in that State.

States that have such a general rule are sometimes called "monist". States that do not have such a rule are sometimes called "dualist". However, the use of these terms is both crude and misleading. It is crude because this is not a simple "either/or" question. There are numerous gradations on either side of the divide.[30] It is misleading because these terms can mean much more than this. The word "monist" comes from the Greek word for "one", and refers

25 The constitutions of States are not normally treaties, nor do they derive their validity from treaties. Their validity flows from political facts, such as a successful revolution or war.

26 Dicey and Morris, *The Conflict of Laws* (Sweet and Maxwell, London, 13th ed. 2000), vol. 2, p. 651, rule 67(1).

27 For example, international law decides whether a State can invoke a rule of its own law in order to invalidate its consent to a treaty to which it is a party. See the Vienna Convention on the Law of Treaties 1969, Art. 46.

28 See Francis G. Jacobs and Shelly Roberts (eds.), *The Effect of Treaties in Domestic Law* (Sweet and Maxwell, London, 1987), p. xxiv (introduction by Jacobs, based on studies of individual countries in later parts of the book). One reason for this is that the courts of a State owe their loyalty to the law and constitution of that State. They cannot apply another system of law unless their own legal system permits them to do so. See Jackson, "United States" in Jacobs and Roberts, above, p. 141 at p. 145.

29 It is not necessary to consider the arguments that raged at one time among European Community lawyers on a possible distinction between direct effect and direct applicability. The differences, if they exist, are of no consequence for our discussion. In any event, the European Court itself uses the two expressions interchangeably: see the cases set out in the next chapter; see also Pescatore, "The Doctrine of 'Direct Effect': An Infant Disease of Community Law" (1983) 8 ELRev. 155, n. 2. Pescatore was for many years a leading judge on the European Court.

30 The issues that may arise include the following: first, whether the treaty must have been duly ratified under the constitution of the State concerned, or whether it is sufficient if it is binding on that State under international law; secondly, whether all treaties are directly effective or only some of them, and, if the latter is the case, what the criterion is and who decides it; thirdly, if at least some treaties can be directly effective, whether they override either prior or subsequent national legislation; fourthly, if they are not directly effective, whether they may nevertheless be taken into account when it comes to interpreting national legislation.

to the theory that national law and international law are ultimately part of one universal legal system. The word "dualist" comes from the Greek word for "two", and refers to the theory that national law and international law are quite separate. However, a State may be willing to give direct application to treaty provisions without accepting that its own law is part of some universal legal system. For our purposes, therefore, the terms "monist" and "dualist" should be understood simply as useful tags to denote two general approaches to the application of treaty provisions in the legal system of a State.

When States sign a treaty, they normally agree to achieve a certain result, but reserve to themselves the right to determine the means by which this will be brought about. If the desired result involves an alteration of their law, their law decides whether this will follow automatically from the treaty (direct effect) or whether legislation will be necessary. The choice is theirs. It is, however, possible that the treaty will say that the parties agree to give direct effect to its provisions. The treaty might also say – and this is more likely – that legislation adopted by an international organization created by the treaty is to be given direct effect. Such a provision is to be found in Article 249 [189] of the EC Treaty, which says that EC regulations are to be directly applicable in all Member States. Since the effect of a rule of international law in the legal system of a State always depends on the law of that State, such a provision does not itself *make* regulations directly applicable in the legal systems of the Member States. It constitutes an undertaking by the parties to the treaty to do what is necessary under their law to bring this result about. How they do this will depend on their own law. In Chapter 9, we shall examine some of the ways in which it might be done.

Having considered the general principles, we shall now look at a few individual countries. We start with the United Kingdom.

United Kingdom

While there is authority for the proposition that certain rules of customary international law have been incorporated into the common law of England, and are thus applicable in the absence of a statute,[31] it is clearly established that a provision in a treaty cannot be applied as a rule of law in a UK court merely because it is binding on the UK under international law. An Act of Parliament (or delegated legislation deriving its authority from an Act of Parliament) is necessary. The reason for this is constitutional. The conclusion of treaties is a matter for the Crown. Legislation is a matter for Parliament. If treaties had direct effect, the Crown could use them to encroach on the prerogatives of Parliament. Consequently, if the government wants to conclude a treaty that requires a change in UK law, it will usually pass the necessary legislation before ratifying the treaty.

---

31 *Triquet v. Bath* (1764) 3 Burr. 1478. For further citations, see Ian Brownlie, *Principles of Public International Law* (Oxford University Press, Oxford, 6th ed., 2003), pp. 41 *et seq.*

Canada (Commonwealth)
Attorney General for Canada v. Attorney General for Ontario (Labour Conventions case)
PRIVY COUNCIL
[1937] AC 326

Background

This was an appeal to the Privy Council from Canada.[32] The Government of Canada had signed certain international conventions, and the question arose as to whether the Parliament of Canada could conclude the legislation necessary to put the conventions into effect, or whether this could be done only by the legislatures of the various provinces of Canada. The following statement by Lord Atkin, who delivered the opinion of the Privy Council, is not directly concerned with this question, but with general questions of principle.

Judgment
Unlike some other countries, the stipulations of a treaty duly ratified do not within the Empire, by virtue of the treaty alone, have the force of law. If the national executive, the government of the day, decide to incur the obligations of a treaty which involve alteration of law they have to run the risk of obtaining the assent of Parliament to the necessary statute or statutes. To make themselves as secure as possible they will often in such cases before final ratification seek to obtain from Parliament an expression of approval. But it has never been suggested, and it is not the law, that such an expression of approval operates as law, or that in law it precludes the assenting Parliament, or any subsequent Parliament, from refusing to give its sanction to any legislative proposals that may subsequently be brought before it.

Giving effect to treaties

Since treaties as such have no effect in the English legal system, it may be necessary to pass legislation in order to give them such effect. There are various ways of doing this. At one end of the spectrum, a statute may simply lay down a rule of law modelled on a provision of the treaty. In doing so, it may not even refer to the treaty. The result will be that UK law will be in conformity with the requirements of the treaty, but one could hardly say that the treaty *applies* in UK law. At the other end of the spectrum, the statute might say that the treaty (which would be set out in a Schedule to the statute) is to have the force of law in the UK.[33] In this situation, it is hard to deny that the treaty applies in the UK, though it does so by virtue of a UK statute.

Treaties and the interpretation of legislation

Although the UK is in the "dualist" camp, this does not mean that treaties as such have no effect in the domestic legal system. There is a well-established rule

---

32 Such appeals were possible at the time, but have now been abolished.
33 For an example of this latter method, see s. 2(1) of the Carriage of Goods by Sea Act 1971, which provides that the Hague–Visby Rules (an international agreement) will have the force of law in the United Kingdom.

of interpretation that if legislation is ambiguous, and one possible meaning is consistent with a treaty and the other is not, the former meaning is – other things being equal – to be preferred.[34]

England
Salomon v. Commissioners of Customs and Excise
COURT OF APPEAL
[1967] 2 QB 116

Background

The UK had become a party to an international convention on customs matters. A statute, the Customs and Excise Act 1952, was passed to give effect to the convention. The convention was not, however, included in a Schedule to the Act, nor was there any mention of it in the Act. The case concerned the interpretation of the Act. What follows is an extract from the judgment.

Judgment

Where by a treaty Her Majesty's Government undertakes either to introduce domestic legislation to achieve a specified result in the United Kingdom or to secure a specified result which can only be achieved by legislation, the treaty, since in English law it is not self-operating, remains irrelevant to any issue in the English courts until Her Majesty's Government has taken steps by way of legislation to fulfil its treaty obligations.[35] Once the Government has legislated, which it may do in anticipation of the coming into effect of the treaty as it did in this case, the court must in the first instance construe the legislation, for that is what the court has to apply. If the terms of the legislation are clear and unambiguous, they must be given effect to whether or not they carry out Her Majesty's treaty obligations, for the sovereign power of the Queen in Parliament extends to breaking treaties (see *Ellerman Lines, Ltd. v. Murray* [1931] AC 126 (HL)), and any remedy for such a breach of an international obligation lies in a forum other than Her Majesty's own courts. If the terms of the legislation are not clear, however, but are reasonably capable of more than one meaning, the treaty itself becomes relevant, for there is a *prima facie* presumption that Parliament does not intend to act in breach of international law, including therein specific treaty obligations; and if one of the meanings which can reasonably be ascribed to the legislation is consonant with the treaty obligations and another or others are not, the meaning which is consonant is to be preferred. Thus, in case of lack of clarity in the words used in the legislation, the terms of the treaty are relevant to enable the court to make its choice between the possible meanings of these words by applying this presumption.

It has been argued that the terms of an international convention cannot be consulted to resolve ambiguities or obscurities in a statute unless the statute itself contains either in the enacting part or in the preamble an express reference to the international convention which it is the purpose of the statute to implement. The learned judge seems to have been persuaded that *Ellerman Lines, Ltd. v. Murray* was authority for this proposition; but, with respect, it is not. The statute with which that case was concerned did refer to the convention. The case is authority only for the proposition for which I have already cited it . . . I can see no reason in comity or common sense for imposing such a limitation on the

---

34 In addition to the case set out below, see *James Buchanan & Co. Ltd v. Babco Forwarding and Shipping (UK) Ltd* [1978] AC 141; and *Fothergill v. Monarch Airlines Ltd* [1981] AC 251.
35 Editor's note: "self-operating" means the same as directly effective.

right and duty of the court to consult an international convention to resolve ambiguities and obscurities in a statutory enactment. If from extrinsic evidence it is plain that the enactment was intended to fulfil Her Majesty's Government's obligations under a particular convention, it matters not that there is no express reference to the convention in the statute. One must not presume that Parliament intends to break an international convention merely because it does not say expressly that it is intending to observe it. Of course, the court must not merely guess that the statute was intended to give effect to a particular international convention. The extrinsic evidence of the connexion must be cogent.

Canada, Australia and New Zealand

The law in these countries is the same as in the United Kingdom. This means that the NAFTA could have no direct effect in Canada, unless Canada passed legislation to provide for this. No such legislation was passed.

United States

US law on this topic is complex. We can deal only with limited aspects.[36]

The conclusion of treaties

Article II, section 2(1) of the United States Constitution states that the President "shall have the power, by and with the advice and consent of the Senate to make treaties, provided two thirds of the senators present concur". As in the case of the United Kingdom, therefore, the Executive has the power to make treaties. Unlike in the case of the United Kingdom, however, this provision requires the Executive to obtain the consent of one branch of the legislature.[37]

Article II of the Constitution does not, however, tell the full story, since an instrument that is a treaty under international law may not be a "treaty" for the purpose of this provision. Since early times, a practice has grown up, which has been confirmed by the courts, for the President to conclude international agreements by other means. These are so-called "executive agreements". Thus, instruments that under international law are treaties may under US law be either treaties or executive agreements. These latter arise in four circumstances:[38]

1. Congress may, by normal legislation, delegate power to the President to conclude a future international agreement.[39]

2. The President may first negotiate an international agreement and Congress may then, by normal legislation, authorize him to conclude it.[40]

---

36 For a full treatment, see the items on US law under "Further reading", p. 144 below.
37 There is no rule of law in the United Kingdom that Parliament must consent to a treaty, though there is a constitutional usage, and possibly a binding convention, that the text of an international agreement must be laid before both Houses of Parliament twenty-one days before ratification. See Stanley de Smith and Rodney Brazier, *Constitutional and Administrative Law* (Penguin, London, 8th ed., 1998), p. 147.
38 Jackson, in Jacobs and Roberts, note 28 above, pp. 143–144; Jackson, *The Jurisprudence of GATT and the WTO* (Cambridge University Press, Cambridge, 2000), pp. 299–300.
39 Known (together with instruments in the next category) as "Congressional-Executive agreements".
40 See previous note.

3.   In certain circumstances (often controversial), the President may claim direct authority under the Constitution to enter into an international agreement without any participation by Congress or the Senate (known as a "sole executive agreement").

4.   In some cases a fully approved and ratified treaty may provide for the parties to settle doubtful points by means of a future agreement.

In all these cases, the President may validly[41] conclude an international agreement without complying with Article II.

Direct effect

It is provided by Article VI, clause (2) of the Constitution that "This Constitution, and the laws of the United States which shall be made in pursuance thereof; and all treaties made, or which shall be made, under the authority of the United States, shall be the supreme law of the land . . .". This provision is the source of the rule that treaties can be directly effective in the United States. Although it might be thought that this would apply only to "treaties" in the sense of Article II of the Constitution (that is, treaties that have been approved by a two-thirds majority in the Senate), it applies to executive agreements as well.[42] Any international agreement validly concluded by the United States[43] can be directly effective if it is "self-executing". The meaning of this phrase is explained in our next case.

> **United States**
> **Foster and Elam v. Neilson**
> **SUPREME COURT OF THE UNITED STATES**
> 27 US (2 Pet.) 253 (1829)

Background

By the Treaty of St Ildefonso, 1800, Spain ceded Louisiana to France, and by the Treaty of Paris, 1803, France ceded it to the United States. In 1819, Spain and the United States signed a treaty in Washington, under which Spain ceded East and West Florida to the United States. Article 8 of this treaty confirmed that all grants of land made by the King of Spain before 24 January 1818 in the ceded territories "shall be ratified and confirmed to the persons in possession of the lands . . .".

The case before the Supreme Court concerned a land dispute, which turned on the effect of a grant by the King of Spain in 1804. The land was in an area which, according to Spain, was not covered by the Treaty of St Ildefonso. In Spain's view, it remained subject to Spanish jurisdiction until the treaty of 1819. The plaintiff in the case argued that this meant that the grant by

---

41 By this is meant that the conclusion is valid under the US Constitution.
42 *United States v. Belmont*, 301 US 324 (1937); *United States v. Pink*, 315 US 203 (1942). See also Louis Henkin, *Foreign Affairs and the US Constitution* (Oxford University Press, Oxford, 2nd ed., 1996), pp. 226 *et seq.*
43 By this is meant that the conclusion is valid under the US Constitution.

the King of Spain was valid and was confirmed by Article 8 of the treaty of 1819. The United States, however, took the view that the area in question *was* covered by the Treaty of St Ildefonso. It ceased to be Spanish territory in 1800, and the King of Spain therefore had no power to make a land grant in 1804.

The Supreme Court held that it could not decide for itself whether or not the area was covered by the Treaty of St Ildefonso. As a US court, it had to follow the US view. It then considered whether Article 8 could be given effect. The following extract is concerned with this question. The opinion of the court was given by Chief Justice Marshall.

Judgment

A treaty is in its nature a contract between two nations, not a Legislative Act. It does not generally effect, of itself, the object to be accomplished, especially so far as its operation is infraterritorial; but is carried into execution by the sovereign power of the respective parties to the instrument.

In the United States a different principle is established. Our Constitution declares a treaty to be the law of the land. It is, consequently, to be regarded in courts of justice as equivalent to an Act of the Legislature, whenever it operates of itself without the aid of any legislative provision. But when the terms of the stipulation import a contract – when either of the parties engages to perform a particular act – the treaty addresses itself to the political, not the judicial department; and the Legislature must execute the contract before it can become a rule for the court.

The article under consideration does not declare that all the grants made by [the King of Spain] before the 24th of January, 1818, shall be valid . . . It does not say that those grants are hereby confirmed. Had such been its language it would have acted directly on the subject, and would have repealed those Acts of Congress which were repugnant to it; but its language is that those grants shall be ratified and confirmed to the persons in possession . . . By whom shall they be ratified and confirmed? This seems to be the language of contract; and if it is, the ratification and confirmation which are promised must be by the Act of the Legislature. Until such Act shall be passed, the court is not at liberty to disregard the existing laws on the subject.

Result: the Spanish land grant was not upheld.

Comment

This case appears to be the origin of the doctrine of the self-executing treaty, though that term does not feature in the judgment. This doctrine is important, not only because it forms the basis of US law on the subject, but also because it has subsequently been taken up by the European Court. The distinction between a treaty in which a party promises to confer a right on a person and a treaty which itself confers that right may seem clear in theory. In practice, however, it is not always easy to distinguish between the two. Everything seems to turn on the intention of the parties. Unless the treaty is clear, which rarely is the case, it is easy for a court to reach whatever conclusion is most convenient for its purposes.

Panel 8.1   The WTO Agreement in US law

Extracts from the Uruguay Round Agreements Act 1994,[1] section 102
Section 102(a)(1)
No provision of any of the Uruguay Round Agreements, nor the application of any such provision to any person or circumstance, that is inconsistent with any law of the United States shall have effect.

Section 102(a)(2)
Nothing in this Act shall be construed –

(A) to amend or modify any law of the United States . . .

Section 102(b)(2)(A)
No State law, or the application of such a State law, may be declared invalid as to any person or circumstance on the ground that the provision or application is inconsistent with any of the Uruguay Round Agreements, except in an action brought by the United States for the purpose of declaring such law or application invalid.

Section 102(c)(1)
No person other than the United States –

(A) shall have any cause of action or defense under any of the Uruguay Round Agreements or by virtue of congressional approval of such an agreement, or

(B) may challenge, in any action brought under any provision of law, any action or inaction by any department, agency, or other instrumentality of the United States, any State, or any political subdivision of a State on the ground that such action or inaction is inconsistent with such agreement.

[1] Pub. L No. 103-465, 108 Stat. 4809 (1994).

Conflicts between a treaty and US law[44]

A treaty cannot prevail against the US Constitution;[45] nor can it prevail against a later federal statute. It can, however, override an earlier federal statute, or any state statute. This also applies to executive agreements, except that it is uncertain whether a sole executive agreement[46] can override any federal statute, even an earlier one.[47]

The WTO and the NAFTA

The WTO Agreement was ratified in the US as a Congressional-Executive agreement. The legislation under which this was done was the Uruguay Round Agreements Act 1994.[48] Section 102 of this Act (extracts in Panel 8.1) precludes any direct effect of the WTO Agreement in the US, except where the federal government brings proceedings to have a state law declared invalid. Section 102 of the NAFTA Implementation Act,[49] which ratified the NAFTA as a Congressional-Executive agreement, contains similar provisions.

---

44 See Jackson, in Jacobs and Roberts, note 28 above, pp. 159–164; Jackson, *The Jurisprudence of GATT and the WTO* (Cambridge University Press, Cambridge, 2000), pp. 316–321.
45 Henkin, note 42 above, pp. 185 *et seq.*
46 In other words, an international agreement entered into by the President without any participation by Congress or the Senate.
47 See *United States v. Guy W. Capps, Inc.*, 204 F 2d 655 (4th Cir., 1953), *affirmed on other grounds*, 348 US 296 (1955); see, further, Henkin, note 42 above, pp. 226–228.
48 Pub. L No. 103-465, 108 Stat. 4809 (1994).
49 Pub. L No. 103-182, 107 Stat. 2057 (1993).

The Netherlands

To conclude our survey, it should be mentioned that in the Netherlands a treaty, if self-executing, has direct effect and prevails over all legislation, both earlier and later.[50] It even prevails over the Constitution.[51] It does all this, how-ever, because this is what the Constitution provides. Presumably, this could be changed through a constitutional amendment.

Conclusions

It will be seen from this brief survey that there is a wide range of possibilities as to the effect of treaties in national law. In the next chapter, we shall see how this has affected the position of the Community Treaties in the Member States.

Further reading

Akehurst, "The Application of General Principles of Law by the Court of Justice of the European Communities" (1981) 52 BYIL 29.

Aust (Anthony), *Modern Treaty Law and Practice* (Cambridge University Press, Cambridge, 2000).

Brownlie (Ian), *Principles of Public International Law* (Oxford University Press, Oxford, 5th ed., 1998), Chapters 1 and 2.

Evans, "Self-Executing Treaties in the United States of America" (1953) 30 BYIL 178.

Hartley, "International Law and the Law of the European Union – A Reassessment" (2001) 72 BYIL 1.

Henkin (Louis), *Foreign Affairs and the US Constitution* (Oxford University Press, Oxford, 2nd ed., 1996), especially Chapter VII.

Iwasawa, "The Doctrine of Self-Executing Treaties in the United States: A Critical Analysis" (1986) 26 *Virginia Journal of International Law* 627.

Jackson (John H.), *The Jurisprudence of GATT and the WTO* (Cambridge University Press, Cambridge, 2000), Chapter 17 (this is a revised version of Chapter 8 of Jacobs and Roberts, below).

Jacobs (Francis G.) and Roberts (Shelly) (eds.), *The Effect of Treaties in Domestic Law* (Sweet and Maxwell, London, 1987), especially the Introduction and Chapters 6, 7 and 8.

Sinclair (Sir Ian), *The Vienna Convention on the Law of Treaties* (Manchester University Press, Manchester, 2nd ed., 1984).

---

50 Schermers, "The Netherlands" in Jacobs and Roberts, note 28 above, at pp. 112–114.
51 Under the Dutch Constitution, courts cannot consider the constitutionality of either a statute or a treaty. Treaties that conflict with the Constitution must, however, be approved by a two-thirds majority in the Dutch Parliament. On both these points, see Schermers, note 50 above, p. 111.

9

The Community Treaties in the legal systems of the Member States

Community law

The EC Treaty contains only one provision on direct effect, Article 249 [189] EC, which provides that EC regulations are "directly applicable in all Member States". There is no provision indicating that the Treaty itself is directly applicable. This should have meant that each Member State could decide for itself what effect the Treaty had, provided that the Member State carried out the Treaty's provisions. The European Court, however, has taken a different view.

The first case in which the matter came before the European Court was a case from the Netherlands. As we saw in the previous chapter, the Netherlands is a country which adopts a very "monist" position towards treaties. A self-executing treaty has direct effect and prevails over all Dutch legislation, both earlier and later.

> *European Union*
> **Van Gend en Loos v. Nederlandse Administratie der Belastingen**
> **COURT OF JUSTICE OF THE EUROPEAN COMMUNITIES**
> **Case 26/62, [1963] ECR 1; [1963]** CMLR 105

Background

This was a reference under Article 234 [177] EC to the European Court from the *Tariefcommissie*, a Dutch administrative court dealing with customs duties. The issue before the court was the duty payable on a product imported from Germany into the Netherlands. At the time in question, customs duties were still payable on goods from other Member States, but Article 25 [12] EC, as it then existed,[1] provided:

> Member States shall refrain from introducing between themselves any new customs duties on imports or exports or any charges having equivalent effect, and from increasing those which they already apply in their trade with each other.

The product in question had been reclassified, which meant that a higher rate of duty was payable. Was this contrary to Article 25 [12] and, if so, could Article 25 [12] be applied by the Dutch court in order to rule in favour of the

---

1 It has since been substantially amended. See Chap. 20.

importer? The Dutch court referred two questions to the European Court. The first was whether Article 25 [12] was directly applicable. The second was whether Article 25 [12] covered the situation in which the product was reclassified.

When the case came before the European Court, the Dutch and Belgian Governments challenged the jurisdiction of the European Court. They said that the question whether a provision of a treaty was directly applicable in the Netherlands was a question for Dutch law to decide. The European Court had no power to rule on it.

Judgment
The first question
A – Jurisdiction of the Court

The Government of the Netherlands and the Belgian Government challenge the jurisdiction of the Court on the ground that the reference relates not to the interpretation but to the application of the Treaty in the context of the constitutional law of the Netherlands, and that in particular the Court has no jurisdiction to decide, should the occasion arise, whether the provisions of the EEC Treaty prevail over Netherlands legislation or over other agreements entered into by the Netherlands and incorporated into Dutch national law. The solution of such a problem, it is claimed, falls within the exclusive jurisdiction of the national courts, subject to an application in accordance with the provisions laid down by Articles 226 [169] and 227 [170] of the Treaty.

However in this case the Court is not asked to adjudicate upon the application of the Treaty according to the principles of the national law of the Netherlands, which remains the concern of the national courts, but is asked, in conformity with subparagraph (a) of the first paragraph of Article 234 [177] of the Treaty, only to interpret the scope of Article 25 [12] of the said Treaty within the context of Community law and with reference to its effect on individuals. This argument has therefore no legal foundation.

The Belgian Government further argues that the Court has no jurisdiction on the ground that no answer which the Court could give to the first question of the *Tariefcommissie* would have any bearing on the result of the proceedings brought in that court.

However, in order to confer jurisdiction on the Court in the present case it is necessary only that the question raised should clearly be concerned with the interpretation of the Treaty. The considerations which may have led a national court or tribunal to its choice of questions as well as the relevance which it attributes to such questions in the context of a case before it are excluded from review by the Court of Justice.

It appears from the wording of the questions referred that they relate to the interpretation of the Treaty. The Court therefore has the jurisdiction to answer them.

This argument, too, is therefore unfounded.

B – On the substance of the case

The first question of the *Tariefcommissie* is whether Article 25 [12] of the Treaty has direct application in national law in the sense that nationals of Member States may on the basis of this Article lay claim to rights which the national court must protect.

To ascertain whether the provisions of an international treaty extend so far in their effects it is necessary to consider the spirit, the general scheme and the wording of those provisions.

The objective of the EEC Treaty, which is to establish a Common Market, the functioning of which is of direct concern to interested parties in the Community, implies that this Treaty is more than an agreement which merely creates mutual obligations between the contracting states. This view is confirmed by the preamble to the Treaty which refers not only to governments but to peoples. It is also confirmed more specifically by the establishment of institutions endowed with sovereign rights, the exercise of which affects Member States and also their citizens. Furthermore, it must be noted that the nationals of the states brought together in the Community are called upon to co-operate in the functioning of this Community through the intermediary of the European Parliament and the Economic and Social Committee.

In addition the task assigned to the Court of Justice under Article 234 [177], the object of which is to secure uniform interpretation of the Treaty by national courts and tribunals, confirms that the states have acknowledged that Community law has an authority which can be invoked by their nationals before those courts and tribunals.

The conclusion to be drawn from this is that the Community constitutes a new legal order of international law for the benefit of which the states have limited their sovereign rights, albeit within limited fields, and the subjects of which comprise not only Member States but also their nationals. Independently of the legislation of Member States, Community law therefore not only imposes obligations on individuals but is also intended to confer upon them rights which become part of their legal heritage. These rights arise not only where they are expressly granted by the Treaty, but also by reason of obligations which the Treaty imposes in a clearly defined way upon individuals as well as upon the Member States and upon the institutions of the Community.

With regard to the general scheme of the Treaty as it relates to customs duties and charges having equivalent effect it must be emphasized that Article 23 [9], which bases the Community upon a customs union, includes as an essential provision the prohibition of these customs duties and charges. This provision is found at the beginning of the part of the Treaty which defines the "Foundations of the Community". It is applied and explained by Article 25 [12].

The wording of Article 25 [12] contains a clear and unconditional prohibition which is not a positive but a negative obligation. This obligation, moreover, is not qualified by any reservation on the part of states which would make its implementation conditional upon a positive legislative measure enacted under national law. The very nature of this prohibition makes it ideally adapted to produce direct effects in the legal relationship between Member States and their subjects.

The implementation of Article 25 [12] does not require any legislative intervention on the part of the states. The fact that under this Article it is the Member States who are made the subject of the negative obligation does not imply that their nationals cannot benefit from this obligation.

In addition the argument based on Articles 226 [169] and 227 [170] of the Treaty put forward by the three Governments which have submitted observations to the Court in their statements of case is misconceived. The fact that these Articles of the Treaty enable the Commission and the Member States to bring before the Court a State which has not fulfilled its obligations does not mean that individuals cannot plead these obligations, should the occasion arise, before a national court, any more than the fact that the Treaty places at the disposal of the Commission ways of ensuring that obligations imposed upon those subject to the Treaty are observed, precludes the possibility, in actions between individuals before a national court, of pleading infringements of these obligations.

A restriction of the guarantees against an infringement of Article 25 [12] by Member States to the procedures under Article 226 [169] and 227 [170] would remove all direct legal protection of the individual rights of their nationals. There is the risk that recourse to the procedure under these Articles would be ineffective if it were to occur after the implementation of a national decision taken contrary to the provisions of the Treaty.

The vigilance of individuals concerned to protect their rights amounts to an effective supervision in addition to the supervision entrusted by Articles 226 [169] and 227 [170] to the diligence of the Commission and of the Member States.

It follows from the foregoing considerations that, according to the spirit, the general scheme and the wording of the Treaty, Article 25 [12] must be interpreted as producing direct effects and creating individual rights which national courts must protect.

[The court then went on to interpret Article 25 [12]. It concluded that it prohibited any increase in the customs duties actually applied, even if this resulted from a reclassification of the product.]

Comment

Jurisdiction

If the European Court had not only been able to interpret Community law, but had also had the final say as to whether it was directly effective, the Member States would have lost their sovereignty. A foreign institution would have had the power to decide what the law of the land was in their countries. As we saw previously, however, Community law is valid only because the Community Treaties say so. The European Court has its powers only because the Community Treaties say so. And the Community Treaties are valid only because international law says so. The whole Community system is, therefore, dependent on international law, and the effect of international law in a State must depend on the law of that State. Thus the Dutch and Belgian Governments were quite right to say that the direct effect of Treaty provisions fell within the exclusive jurisdiction of the national courts.

However, as we saw in the previous chapter, Dutch law gives primacy to international treaties, provided they are self-executing. In deciding whether a provision of a treaty is self-executing, the terms of the provision, correctly interpreted, are of great – probably, decisive – importance. Since the Member States had agreed in the EC Treaty that the European Court was to have the power to give authoritative interpretations of the Treaty, it was reasonable for the Dutch court to ask the European Court to interpret the relevant provision. The Belgian Government was therefore wrong in saying that no answer that the European Court might give could have any bearing on the proceedings before the Dutch court.

Substance

In this part of the judgment there is a lack of clarity as to exactly what the European Court is deciding. Is it deciding whether the Member States intended to impose on themselves a *legal obligation* to give direct effect to at least some provisions of the treaty? Or is it deciding simply whether Article 25 [12] is suitable for direct application in those States (such as the Netherlands) that wish to apply it? It seems that it is doing the former, though once it decides that there is a legal obligation on the Member States to give direct effect to suitable provisions in the Treaty, it then goes on to consider whether Article 25 [12] is such a provision.

We shall first consider the arguments in favour of the proposition that the Member States intended to impose a legal obligation on themselves to give direct effect to suitable provisions of the Treaty. The court gives three arguments:

1. The EC Treaty is more than a contract between States because its objectives are of concern to interested parties in the Community.
2. The fact that the European Court is given power to interpret the treaty on a reference from a Member-State court implies that it is intended to have direct effect.
3. Community law is a separate legal system ("a new legal order of international law").

The first of these arguments seems to hark back to the distinction drawn by the US Supreme Court in *Foster and Elam v. Neilson* (see Chapter 8 above) between a treaty in which the parties agree to take the necessary steps to create rights for individuals and a treaty which itself creates such rights. However, this distinction is relevant only to those States that adopt the US approach to international treaties. It is not relevant to the question whether the parties intended to impose an *obligation* to give it direct effect. The fact that the objective of the treaty is of direct concern to interested parties is also irrelevant. Human rights conventions are of even more direct concern to individuals. Yet, as we shall see in Chapter 14, the European Convention on Human Rights and other human rights conventions do *not* impose an obligation to give direct effect to their provisions. All they require is that Contracting States ensure, by whatever means, that the rights concerned are respected.

At first sight, the second argument seems more convincing. If the Treaty's provisions were not intended to be directly effective, why did the Treaty create a procedure under which Member-State courts could refer questions concerning their interpretation to the European Court? There is, however, an answer to this. As we know, some Member States are "monist". They would want to give direct effect to suitable Treaty provisions. Courts in such States would need to know the correct interpretation. In "dualist" States, this would not arise. However, such States would pass their own legislation to give effect to the Treaty. That legislation would have to be interpreted by the national courts. In doing so, they would want, wherever possible, to interpret that legislation in conformity with the Treaty. Even in "arch-dualist" States like the United Kingdom this is the case. So they too would need to know the correct interpretation of Treaty provisions. In other words, the existence of the preliminary reference procedure is equally consistent with an intention that direct effect would depend on the law of the Member States. It is not, therefore, an argument in favour of the proposition that the Treaty lays down an obligation to give direct effect to its provisions.

The argument that the Treaties create a new legal system – something that is by no means obvious from the terms of the Treaties themselves – is also irrelevant. As we saw in the previous chapter, international law permits the parties to a treaty to create an independent legal system, provided they do not go against any peremptory norms of international law (*ius cogens*). This has consequences concerning the rules to be applied. However, it has nothing to do with direct effect.

The strongest argument in favour of the court's position is one that was not clearly made in this case.[2] This is the argument of efficiency. A common market works better if the rules on which it is based are directly effective. If each Member State could decide for itself, the Treaty would be directly effective in some, but not in others. In the latter, it would have to be transposed into national law before it could be applied. Inevitably, there would be delays. Some States might even make subtle changes when they transposed it. Community law would then apply in an uneven way in different Member States.

This is a strong argument for saying that Community law *should* be directly effective in all Member States. However, it does not prove that this is what the parties to the EC Treaty intended. A common market can work perfectly well without direct effect. The NAFTA is not directly effective. Yet it works satisfactorily. It is not as effective as it would be if it were directly effective, but it still works.

The strongest argument against the court's position is that the Treaty does not say that it is to be directly effective. It expressly states that regulations are to be directly effective. Since it would be unusual for an international treaty to impose an obligation on the parties to it to make its provisions directly effective, it is hardly credible that the Member States would not have said so expressly if that had been what they intended.

However, the question whether the Treaty imposes an obligation on the Member States to give direct effect to its provisions is a question of interpretation. It therefore falls within the jurisdiction of the European Court. Even a wrong decision is binding. So we must conclude that the Treaty imposes such an obligation.

Was Article 25 [12] directly effective?

Having decided that the Treaty imposed an obligation on the Member States to make appropriate provisions directly effective, the court then had to consider whether Article 25 [12] was such a provision. It held that it was. It gave four reasons:

1.   It is clear.
2.   It is unconditional.
3.   It is a prohibition (an obligation not to do something).
4.   It is not qualified by any reservation that would make its implementation conditional upon positive legislative measures enacted under national law.

These requirements, especially the last, seem based on the idea of a self-executing treaty, as set out in the decision of the US Supreme Court in *Foster*

---

2 It was deployed in a later case, *Costa v. ENEL*, Case 6/64, [1964] ECR 585.

and Elam v. Neilson (see chapter 8 above). However, Article 25 [12] said: "Member States shall refrain from introducing . . . any new customs duties . . ." It did not say: "Any new customs duties shall be invalid . . ." It is by no means certain, therefore, that the test in *Foster and Elam v. Neilson* was satisfied.

As we shall see, the European Court moved rapidly in later cases to cut down these requirements. This is a tactic often used by the court when it introduces a new concept. The first case lays down stringent conditions for the application of the concept. This gives the idea that it will apply only in rare instances. Once the concept is accepted, however, the conditions are stripped away and it is seen that it is only in rare instances that the concept will *not* be applied. This is what happened in the case of direct effect.

Costa v. ENEL

The above arguments were repeated, with even greater emphasis, in a case decided the following year, *Costa v. ENEL*,[3] a case in which the European Court said that the EC Treaty obliged Member States to give directly effective Treaty provisions supremacy over national legislation, both prior and subsequent. Some of the language in this case could be interpreted as going further than this. It could be interpreted as claiming that Treaty provisions automatically *have* direct effect, whatever national law may say. The passage which most lends itself to this interpretation is the following:[4]

> The transfer by the States from their domestic legal system to the Community legal system of the rights and obligations arising under the Treaty carries with it a permanent limitation of their sovereign rights, against which a subsequent unilateral act incompatible with the concept of the Community cannot prevail. Consequently Article 234 [177] is to be applied regardless of any domestic law, whenever questions relating to the interpretation of the Treaty arise.

However, if this was what the European Court was saying, it would have been going beyond its jurisdiction. As Advocate-General Lagrange said in the same case:[5]

> What must be avoided – and this is a danger which becomes apparent as cases under Article 234 [177] multiply – is that this Court, under the guise of interpretation, might more or less substitute itself for the national court which, let us not forget, retains jurisdiction to apply the Treaty and the regulations of the Community which have been incorporated into national law by ratification.

If the European Court gave a ruling that went beyond its jurisdiction, that ruling would not be binding on national courts. We must assume, therefore, that this is not what it intended to do.

---

3 Case 6/64, [1964] ECR 585.
4 [1964] ECR 585 at 594.
5 [1964] ECR 585 at 601.

European Union
Amministrazione delle Finanze dello Stato v. Simmenthal (Simmenthal case)
COURT OF JUSTICE OF THE EUROPEAN COMMUNITIES
Case 106/77, [1978] ECR 629; [1978] 3 CMLR 263

Background

When this case was decided, the position under Italian law was that Italian legislation that conflicted with EC law could not be declared invalid by the court hearing the case. Only the Constitutional Court (*Corte Costituzionale*) could do that. This meant that the court hearing the case had to refer the matter to the Constitutional Court, something that would result in a significant delay. The issue in the *Simmenthal* case was whether this was consistent with Community law. The following extract deals with the point.

Judgment

13 The main purpose of the *first question* is to ascertain what consequences flow from the direct applicability of a provision of Community law in the event of incompatibility with a subsequent legislative provision of a Member State.

14 Direct applicability in such circumstances means that rules of Community law must be fully and uniformly applied in all the Member States from the date of their entry into force and for so long as they continue in force.

15 These provisions are therefore a direct source of rights and duties for all those affected thereby, whether Member States or individuals, who are parties to legal relationships under Community law.

16 This consequence also concerns any national court whose task it is as an organ of a Member State to protect, in a case within its jurisdiction, the rights conferred upon individuals by Community law.

17 Furthermore, in accordance with the principle of the precedence of Community law, the relationship between provisions of the Treaty and directly applicable measures of the institutions on the one hand and the national law of the Member States on the other is such that those provisions and measures not only by their entry into force render automatically inapplicable any conflicting provision of current national law but – in so far as they are an integral part of, and take precedence in, the legal order applicable in the territory of each of the Member States – also preclude the valid adoption of new national legislative measures to the extent to which they would be incompatible with Community provisions.

18 Indeed any recognition that national legislative measures which encroach upon the field within which the Community exercises its legislative power or which are otherwise incompatible with the provisions of Community law had any legal effect would amount to a corresponding denial of the effectiveness of obligations undertaken unconditionally and irrevocably by Member States pursuant to the Treaty and would thus imperil the very foundations of the Community.

19 The same conclusion emerges from the structure of Article 234 [177] of the Treaty which provides that any court or tribunal of a Member State is entitled to make a reference

to the Court whenever it considers that a preliminary ruling on a question of interpretation or validity relating to Community law is necessary to enable it to give judgment.

20 The effectiveness of that provision would be impaired if the national court were prevented from forthwith applying Community law in accordance with the decision or the case-law of the Court.

21 It follows from the foregoing that every national court must, in a case within its jurisdiction, apply Community law in its entirety and protect rights which the latter confers on individuals and must accordingly set aside any provision of national law which may conflict with it, whether prior or subsequent to the Community rule.

22 Accordingly any provision of a national legal system and any legislative, administrative or judicial practice which might impair the effectiveness of Community law by withholding from the national court having jurisdiction to apply such law the power to do everything necessary at the moment of its application to set aside national legislative provisions which might prevent Community rules from having full force and effect are incompatible with those requirements which are the very essence of Community law.

23 This would be the case in the event of a conflict between a provision of Community law and a subsequent national law if the solution of the conflict were to be reserved for an authority with a discretion of its own, other than the court called upon to apply Community law, even if such an impediment to the full effectiveness of Community law were only temporary.

24 The first question should therefore be answered to the effect that a national court which is called upon, within the limits of its jurisdiction, to apply provisions of Community law is under a duty to give full effect to those provisions, if necessary refusing of its own motion to apply any conflicting provision of national legislation, even if adopted subsequently, and it is not necessary for the court to request or await the prior setting aside of such provision by legislative or other constitutional means.

Comment

In this case, the European Court demanded that the supremacy of Community law take precedence over the procedures laid down by the Italian Constitution. Subsequently, it has made clear that it must also prevail even over substantive provisions of national constitutions.[6]

> *European Union*
> **Defrenne v. Sabena**
> **COURT OF JUSTICE OF THE EUROPEAN COMMUNITIES**
> Case 43/75, [1976] ECR 455

Background

With this case, we return to the issue of when a Treaty provision is suitable for direct application. In *Van Gend en Loos*, it will be remembered, the European Court said that the provision must meet four requirements:
1. It must be clear.
2. It must be unconditional.
3. It must be a prohibition (an obligation not to do something).

---

6 *Internationale Handelsgesellschaft* case, Case 11/70, [1970] ECR 1125, para. 3 of the judgment.

4.   It must not be qualified by any reservation that would make its implementation conditional upon positive legislative measures enacted under national law.

We said previously that these conditions had been whittled down. The *Defrenne* case illustrates this.

Ms Defrenne worked for Sabena, the Belgian national airline, as an air hostess. At that time, Sabena paid female cabin crew less than male cabin crew, even though they did the same work. Article 141 [119] EC prohibited sex discrimination as regards pay. As it stood at the time, the first paragraph of Article 141 [119] provided:

> Each Member State shall during the first stage ensure and subsequently maintain the application of the principle that men and women should receive equal pay for equal work.

The second paragraph of Article 141 [119] defined "pay", and the third paragraph indicated that the provision applied both where pay is calculated on the basis of items produced (piece rates) and where it is based on the hours worked (time rates).

This provision imposes an obligation on the Member States to take action by the end of the first stage (i.e. the first stage of the implementation of the Treaty) to adopt the principle of equal pay as part of their national law. Many Member States, including Belgium, did not do so. Moreover, the Commission and Council showed little inclination to take effective measures to bring the defaulting Member States into line.

Ms Defrenne brought proceedings against Sabena in the Belgian courts. A reference was made to the European Court. One question was whether Article 141 [119] was directly effective. On the basis of the criteria in *Van Gend en Loos*, it could not have been. It did not contain a prohibition, but laid down a positive requirement. It did not itself grant rights, but called on the Member States to do so. Its implementation thus seems to have been conditional on national measures. The following extract from the judgment shows how the European Court dealt with these arguments.

Judgment

30 It is also impossible to put forward arguments based on the fact that Article 141 [119] only refers expressly to "Member States".

31 Indeed, as the Court has already found in other contexts, the fact that certain provisions of the Treaty are formally addressed to the Member States does not prevent rights from being conferred at the same time on any individual who has an interest in the performance of the duties thus laid down.

32 The very wording of Article 141 [119] shows that it imposes on States a duty to bring about a specific result to be mandatorily achieved within a fixed period.

33 The effectiveness of this provision cannot be affected by the fact that the duty imposed by the Treaty has not been discharged by certain Member States and that the joint institutions have not reacted sufficiently energetically against this failure to act.

Comment

Both in this case and in other cases, the European Court has made clear that if Member States are required to do something, that does not prevent the provision from being directly effective if there is a deadline. Once the deadline has passed, the provision can be directly effective. Since almost all such requirements in the EC Treaty contain a deadline, they are all potentially directly effective.

However, a provision cannot be applied directly if it lacks sufficient detail to make this feasible. The European Court therefore held that Article 141 [119] was directly effective only with regard to "direct and overt" discrimination.[7] Its application to indirect and disguised discrimination would have to await implementing measures at the national or Community level. Thus, for example, it could not apply directly where the woman did different work, but claimed that the work was of equal value.

The cumulative result of the European Court's case law on this subject is that most provisions of the EC Treaty are directly effective. Although the court uses words like "clear and unconditional", it seems that provisions will be directly effective in practice unless there is a good reason why they should not be. The following are examples of provisions that are not directly effective:

- those that require Member States to achieve some result, but give them the choice of two or more ways of doing so: such provisions cannot be directly effective until the Member State has made its choice;[8]
- those that require Member States to create a new criminal offence: the offence cannot come into existence until Member-State law so provides;
- those that require Member States to set up institutions against which workers may bring proceedings to obtain pay owing to them if their employer becomes bankrupt: if the institutions do not exist, there can be no directly effective right;[9]
- those that empower the Commission or the Council to prohibit certain actions by Member States: if the Commission or Council does not take the necessary decision, the provision can have no direct effect.[10]

This list is not exhaustive.

---

7 This was sufficient for Ms Defrenne to win her case.

8 *Von Colson and Kamann v. Land Nordrhein-Westfalen,* Case 14/83, [1984] ECR 1891; [1986] 2 CMLR 430. In this case, Community law required Member States to give a legal remedy to persons who had been refused a job on account of their sex. Germany had not implemented it. A woman who had been refused a job as a warder in a men's prison in Germany brought proceedings, and argued that she had a directly effective right to be given the job. The European Court, however, ruled that the provision was not directly effective to this extent, since Germany had the choice whether to provide such a right or to provide other effective rights – for example, the right to sue for damages, or the right to initiate criminal proceedings.

9 *Francovich v. Italy,* Cases C-6 and 9/90, [1991] ECR I-5357; [1993] 2 CMLR 66. As we shall see in Chap. 11, a different remedy may be available.

10 Thus, subsidies to industry by Member States are not illegal in Member-State law until the Commission has taken a decision to this effect: *Capolongo,* Case 77/72, [1973] ECR 611; [1974] 1 CMLR 230.

Conclusions

A number of conclusions may be drawn from the cases we have considered.

- The EC Treaty (and the other Community Treaties) impose a legal obligation on the Member States to give direct effect to provisions that are suitable for direct effect.
- The question whether a particular provision is suitable is a question of Community law on which the European Court has the final say.
- Treaty provisions will normally be held directly effective if it is reasonably feasible for a court to apply them to decide a case.
- Member States are obliged to ensure that directly effective provisions of Community law prevail over national legislation, both earlier and later, and even over their own constitutions.
- Every court in a Member State must be required to declare Member-State law inapplicable when it conflicts with Community law.

In a nutshell, the European Court requires the total and unconditional supremacy of Community law.

The result of all this is that Treaty provisions are now in the same position as regulations with regard to direct effect. Moreover, the other rulings of the European Court set out above also apply to regulations.

- Regulations are directly effective only if they are suitable for direct effect.[11]
- The same test applies as for Treaty provisions.
- If regulations are directly effective, they must be given automatic and immediate supremacy over Member-State law, both prior and subsequent.

It has been argued elsewhere that some of the rulings discussed above go beyond what may reasonably be regarded as interpretation.[12] They are not what the Member States intended when they drew up the Treaties. These rulings may, therefore, be regarded as demands by the European Court that the Member States change their law. How far have the Member States complied?

We shall focus on three countries.

Denmark

In general, Denmark has been perfectly willing to give direct effect to Community law. The Danish Constitution contains a provision, Article 20, which permits Denmark to delegate powers to an international organization "to the extent specified by statute". It is by virtue of this provision that Community law has effect in Denmark. The leading case is *Carlsen v. Rasmussen*.

---

11 See *per* Advocate-General Warner in *Galli*, Case 31/74, [1975] ECR 47 at 70, and in *Steinike und Weinlig v. Germany*, Case 78/76, [1977] ECR 595, 557 at 583; and *per* Advocate-General Reischl in *Ratti*, Case 148/78, [1979] ECR 1629 *passim*.
12 Hartley, "The European Court, Judicial Objectivity and the Constitution of the European Union" (1996) 112 LQR 95 at 96 *et seq.*; Trevor C. Hartley, *Constitutional Problems of the European Union* (Hart Publishing, Oxford, 1999), pp. 24 *et seq.*

Denmark
Carlsen v. Rasmussen (Danish Maastricht case)
SUPREME COURT OF DENMARK (HØJESTERET)
Judgment of 6 April 1998, [1999] 3 CMLR 854 (English translation)

This case concerns the constitutionality of Denmark's ratification of the Treaty on European Union (Maastricht Agreement). The appellants argued that the powers delegated to the Community under the Maastricht Agreement were too ill-defined to satisfy the requirements of Article 20 of the Constitution. The Supreme Court rejected this argument and upheld the treaty. However, in the course of its judgment it clarified a number of issues concerning the operation of Community law in Denmark.

- The Danish Constitution does not permit power to be given to an international organization such as the Community to make decisions that are contrary to the Constitution.[13]
- The European Community cannot determine for itself what its powers are.[14]
- The Danish courts have the right to judge for themselves whether EC acts go beyond the powers conferred on the Community.[15]
- A Community act that went beyond the powers conferred on the Community would be inapplicable in Denmark.[16]
- The same applies to legal rules laid down by the European Court.[17]

This makes clear that the application of Community law in Denmark depends on Danish law. It can apply only to the extent permitted by the Constitution. As the Supreme Court made clear, Denmark remains an independent State.[18] So far, however, the Danish courts have never held that the Community has gone beyond the powers transferred to it.

Germany

The German Constitution (*Grundgesetz*) has created a special court, the Federal Constitutional Court (*Bundesverfassungsgericht*), to decide constitutional questions. It can declare invalid any German law that infringes the Constitution. As we shall see in Part V of this book, the protection of fundamental rights (human rights) is one of the most important aims of the Constitution.

The Constitution contains a provision, Article 24 (see Panel 9.1), which allows Germany to transfer sovereign powers to international organizations, and it was on the basis of this provision that Germany originally joined the Community. In 1992, the Constitution was amended to provide specifically for Germany's membership of the European Union. The result is Article 23 (also in Panel 9.1).

---

13 Section 9.2 of the judgment (para. [13] of the CMLR translation).
14 *Ibid.* (para. [15] of the CMLR translation).
15 Section 9.6 of the judgment (para. [33] of the CMLR translation).
16 *Ibid.*
17 *Ibid.*
18 Section 9.8 of the judgment (para. [35] of the CMLR translation).

Panel 9.1   Constitution of the Federal Republic of Germany (Grundgesetz)

Article 1

(1) Human dignity shall be inviolable. To respect and protect it shall be the duty of all state authority.

(2) The German people therefore acknowledge inviolable and inalienable human rights as the basis of every community, of peace and of justice in the world.

(3) The following basic rights shall bind the legislature, the executive, and the judiciary as directly applicable law.

Article 20

(1) The Federal Republic of Germany is a democratic and social federal state.

(2) All state authority is derived from the people. It shall be exercised by the people through elections and other votes and through specific legislative, executive, and judicial bodies.

Article 23 (1992 amendment)

(1) With a view to establishing a united Europe, the Federal Republic of Germany shall participate in the development of the European Union that is committed to democratic, social, and federal principles, to the rule of law, and to the principle of subsidiarity, and that guarantees a level of protection of basic rights essentially comparable to that afforded by this Basic Law. To this end the Federation may transfer sovereign powers by a law with the consent of the *Bundesrat*. The establishment of the European Union, as well as changes in its treaty foundations and comparable regulations that amend or supplement this Basic Law, or make such amendments or supplements possible, shall be subject to paragraphs (2) and (3) of Article 79.

Article 24

(1) The Federation may by a law transfer sovereign powers to international organizations.

Article 25

The general rules of international law shall be an integral part of federal law. They shall take precedence over the laws and directly create rights and duties for the inhabitants of the federal territory.

Article 79

(2) Any such law [law amending the Constitution] shall be carried by two thirds of the Members of the *Bundestag* [Lower House of the German Parliament] and two thirds of the votes of the *Bundesrat* [Upper House of the German Parliament, representing the States (*Länder*)].

(3) Amendments to this Basic Law [*Grundgesetz*, the German Constitution] affecting the division of the Federation into *Länder* [States], their participation on principle in the legislative process, or the principles laid down in Articles 1 and 20 shall be inadmissible.

Under these provisions, the German courts have had no problem giving direct effect to Community law and allowing for the supremacy of Community law over German legislation, both earlier and later. Prior to the coming into effect of Article 23, the German courts had been prepared to accept, in principle, that Community law could prevail over the German Constitution. However, they made clear that this did not apply to the core provisions of the Constitution – in particular, those concerning human rights (the cases will be considered in Chapter 15). This position is confirmed by Article 23. The last sentence of Article 23(1) envisages the supremacy of Community law over the Constitution, but provides that this is subject to paragraphs (2) and (3) of Article 79. Article 79(3) states that the following cannot be changed by constitutional amendment:

1. the division of Germany into States (*Länder*) and their participation in the legislative process;

2. human rights (Article 1); and

3. the democratic nature of Germany (Article 20).

The operation of Community law is, therefore, subject to these principles. It cannot apply in Germany if it infringes them.

The most authoritative statement of the effect of Community law in Germany is the decision of the Federal Constitutional Court in the *Brunner* case.

Germany
Brunner v. European Union Treaty (German Maastricht case)
GERMAN FEDERAL CONSTITUTIONAL COURT (BUNDESVERFASSUNGSGERICHT)
89 BVerfGE 155; 20 EuGRZ 429; [1993] NJW 3047; English translations in: [1994]
1 CMLR 57; (1994) 33 ILM 388; Andrew Oppenheimer, *The Relationship between European Community Law and National Law: The Cases* (1994), p. 526.[19]

This case concerns the constitutionality of Germany's ratification of the Treaty on European Union. The Constitutional Court held that this was permissible, but some important points emerge from its judgment.[20]

- Community law applies in Germany only because German law says it does.[21]

- The Constitutional Court guarantees the effective protection of fundamental rights (human rights) in Germany, even against the powers of the Community, though it does so in co-operation with the European Court.[22]

- No power to extend its powers (*Kompetenz-Kompetenz*)[23] is conferred on the European Union.[24]

- An interpretation of the Treaty on European Union that was equivalent to its extension would not be binding on Germany.[25]

- If the Community adopts laws that go beyond the powers conferred on it, those laws will not be binding in Germany, and the Constitutional Court can review them to decide whether this is so.[26]

It will be seen from this that, though Germany has carried out the obligations of membership of the Community, the German courts have not surrendered German sovereignty. Community law applies only to the extent permitted by the Constitution. In practice, the only problem is human rights. As we shall see in Chapter 15, the European Court has moved to accommodate Germany on this issue. It has decided that human rights, a subject in which it had previously shown little interest, are an integral part of Community law, and it has undertaken to ensure that Community law complies with them. By

---

19 For a full discussion and analysis, see Everling, "The Maastricht Judgment of the German Federal Constitutional Court and its Significance for the Development of the European Union" (1994) 14 YEL 1; Foster, "The German Constitution and EC Membership" [1994] PL 392; Herdegen, "Maastricht and the German Constitutional Court: Constitutional Restraints for an 'Ever Closer Union'" (1994) 31 CMLRev. 233; Kokott, "Report on Germany" in Anne-Marie Slaughter, Alec Stone Sweet and Joseph H. H. Weiler, *The European Courts and National Courts – Doctrine and Jurisprudence* (Hart Publishing, Oxford, 1998), p. 77; MacCormick, "The Maastricht-Urteil: Sovereignty Now" (1995) 1 ELJ 259.
20 References in the following footnotes are to the paragraphs of the judgment as numbered in the *Common Market Law Reports*.
21 Para. [55] CMLR.
22 Para. [13] CMLR.
23 On *Kompetenz-Kompetenz*, see Trevor C. Hartley, *Constitutional Problems of the European Union* (Hart Publishing, Oxford, 1999), Chap. 8.
24 Para. [33] CMLR.
25 Para. [99] CMLR.
26 Para. [49] CMLR.

thus changing Community law to meet the requirements of the German Constitution, the European Court has ensured that no provision of Community
law has so far been refused application in Germany by the Constitutional
Court.

United Kingdom

The basic principle of the UK constitution is the sovereignty of Parliament.
There are no legal limits to the power of Parliament to pass any laws it wants,
except that it cannot validly restrict its own future powers. From a practical point of view, there are all sorts of limits to Parliament's powers. That is
accepted. But there are no *legal* limits. There are no limits that a UK court
would recognize. As we saw in *Salomon v. Commissioners of Customs and Excise* (see
Chapter 8 above), the power of Parliament "extends to breaking treaties". Therefore the existence of the Community Treaties does not limit the sovereignty of
Parliament.

We have already seen that Community law, as interpreted by the European
Court, requires the Member States to give direct effect to all Community provisions that, in the opinion of the European Court, are suitable for direct
effect. Such directly effective provisions must be given a status in the legal
systems of the Member States that allows them to override all national legislation, both prior and subsequent. How was the United Kingdom to achieve
this? The sovereignty of Parliament cannot be abolished. The one limit on the
power of Parliament is that it cannot limit its own powers. So all that could
be done was to pass an Act of Parliament, the European Communities Act
1972.

Extracts from the European Communities Act are set out in Panel 9.2. The
key provision is section 2(1). This provides that all Community provisions that
Community law requires to be directly effective are directly effective. This applies both to provisions that existed when the European Communities Act was
passed and to future provisions. If this meaning is not immediately apparent,
the following might help to unlock the draftsman's code:

- "all such rights, powers, liabilities, obligations and restrictions" = provisions of (Community) law
- "from time to time" = past, present and future
- "created or arising by or under the Treaties" = provisions in the Treaties
  or provisions of legislation enacted under the Treaties
- "all such remedies and procedures" = provisions of a procedural nature
- "in accordance with the Treaties" = under Community law
- "without further enactment to be given legal effect or used" = directly
  effective
- "shall be recognised and available in law, and be enforced, allowed and
  followed accordingly" = directly effective (in the United Kingdom).

This meets the requirements of the European Court as regards direct effect.

Panel 9.2 The European Communities Act 1972

Section 1(2)
[defines "the Treaties"].

Section 2

(1) All such rights, powers, liabilities, obligations and restrictions from time to time created or arising by or under the Treaties, and all such remedies and procedures from time to time provided for by or under the Treaties, as in accordance with the Treaties are without further enactment to be given legal effect or used in the United Kingdom shall be recognised and available in law, and be enforced, allowed and followed accordingly; and the expression "enforceable Community right" and similar expressions shall be read as referring to one to which this subsection applies.

(2) Subject to Schedule 2 of this Act, at any time after its passing Her Majesty may by Order in Council, and any designated minister or department may by regulations, make provision:

   (a) for the purpose of implementing any Community obligation of the United Kingdom, or of enabling any such obligation to be implemented, or of enabling any rights enjoyed or to be enjoyed by the United Kingdom under or by virtue of the Treaties to be exercised; or

   (b) for the purpose of dealing with matters arising out of or related to any such obligation or rights or the coming into force, or the operation from time to time, of subsection (1) above;

   and in the exercise of any statutory power or duty, including any power to give directions or to legislate by means of orders, rules, regulations or other subordinate instrument, the person entrusted with the power or duty may have regard to the objects of the Communities and to any such obligation or rights as aforesaid.

(3) . . .

(4) The provision that may be made under subsection (2) above includes, subject to Schedule 2 to this Act, any such provision (of any such extent) as might be made by Act of Parliament, and any enactment passed or to be passed, other than one contained in this Part of this Act, shall be construed and have effect subject to the foregoing provisions of this section; but, except as may be provided by any Act passed after this Act, Schedule 2 shall have effect in connection with the powers conferred by this and the following sections of this Act to make Orders in Council and regulations.

Section 3

(1) For the purposes of all legal proceedings any question as to the meaning or effect of any of the Treaties, or as to the validity, meaning or effect of any Community instrument, shall be treated as a question of law (and, if not referred to the European Court, be for determination as such in accordance with the principles laid down by and any relevant decision of the European Court or any court attached thereto).

Note
Schedule 2 states that the power to enact subordinate legislation under section 2(2) may not be used:
1 to impose taxes;
2 to enact retroactive legislation;
3 to sub-delegate legislative power (except for the rules of procedure of a court or tribunal); or
4 to create a criminal offence with punishment greater than two years' imprisonment . . .

What about the supremacy of Community law? Provision for this is made, somewhat obliquely, by a sentence in the middle of section 2(4). The sentence reads:

> [A]ny enactment passed or to be passed, other than one contained in this Part of this Act, shall be construed and have effect subject to the foregoing provisions of this section.

Again, this is in code. The words "any enactment" mean any United Kingdom legislation. The phrase "passed or to be passed" means past or future. Therefore any past or future United Kingdom legislation (including, in particular, Acts of Parliament) must be "construed" (interpreted) subject to the earlier provisions of section 2. One such provision is section 2(1), which, as we have seen, provides that any Community provision that according to Community law (as interpreted by the European Court) is to be given direct effect must be directly effective. All past and future United Kingdom legislation must be interpreted and have effect subject to this requirement. In other words, it must give way to directly effective Community law. This way of putting it does not exactly jump out of the text and shout at you, but its meaning is clear, at least to a lawyer.

Thus the statute says that all past or future UK legislation is to be subordinate to directly effective Community law. But what about the sovereignty of Parliament? There is no problem about Acts of Parliament passed prior to the European Communities Act. Parliament can easily make them subject to Community law, including future provisions of Community law. It has the power to repeal any existing Act of Parliament. Therefore it can make existing Acts of Parliament subject to Community law. But if it says that *future* Acts of Parliament are subordinate to Community law, it is trying to restrict its own powers. This is something it cannot do. Of course, it can *say* that. But it will have no effect. Its future powers will be as full as before.

When Parliament passed the European Communities Act, it knew what the constitutional position was. It knew it could not limit its own future powers. Nor did it want to. So what does the sentence quoted above mean? What it means – all it can mean – is that Parliament is saying that it has no intention of exercising its powers in the future in a way that conflicts with Community law. It is announcing this intention, and asking the courts to take note of it. In other words, it is laying down a rule of interpretation. Future Acts of Parliament are not to be interpreted in a way that conflicts with the supremacy of directly effective Community law.

As we saw in Chapter 8, there is a general rule of English law that Acts of Parliament are, if possible, to be interpreted in a way consistent with international treaties binding the United Kingdom. However, the rule in the European Communities Act goes much further than this. It applies not only to legislation passed to give effect to Community law, but to *any* legislation. It is also not limited to cases where the Act of Parliament is reasonably capable of two or more meanings. It applies even if the words are clear. This is because Parliament has said in the European Communities Act that it does not intend to use its powers in such a way as to conflict with Community law.

What is the effect of this rule of interpretation? There are three situations in which the question may arise.

1.   The first is a conflict between Community law (of any date) and a United Kingdom statute passed before the European Communities Act. Such a statute would simply be repealed by the European Communities Act to the extent to which it conflicted with Community law. This is within the power of Parliament.

2.   The second situation is a conflict between a UK statute passed after the European Communities Act and a Community provision that came into existence before the UK statute. In such a case, the courts would be entitled to assume that Parliament had not been aware of the Community

provision. If it had known about it, it would not have passed the statute. The courts would therefore be carrying out the intention of Parliament if they made the Community provision prevail over the statute.

3. The third case is where the Act of Parliament is passed after the European Communities Act and the Community provision comes into existence after the Act of Parliament. When it passed the Act, Parliament would not have known that one day a conflicting provision of Community law would come into existence. However, the courts would be justified in assuming that if it had known, it would not have passed the Act. So they would be carrying out the will of Parliament by making the Community provision prevail.

Does this destroy the sovereignty of Parliament? It does not, because all the courts are doing is giving effect to what might genuinely and realistically be regarded as the will of Parliament. Of course, if there was reason to believe that Parliament really did want to legislate against Community law, the position would be different. Then the courts would have to give supremacy to the Act of Parliament. This was made clear many years ago by Lord Denning in *Macarthys Ltd v. Smith*,[27] where he said:

> If the time should come when our Parliament deliberately passes an Act with the intention of repudiating the Treaty or any provision in it or intentionally of acting inconsistently with it and says so in express terms then I should have thought that it would be the duty of our courts to follow the statute of our Parliament . . . Unless there is such an intentional and express repudiation of the Treaty, it is our duty to give priority to the Treaty.

So, unless Parliament expresses a contrary intention, directly effective Community law prevails over United Kingdom law. But if Parliament does express such an intention, and does so clearly, then the Act of Parliament will prevail. Moreover, Parliament could always repeal the European Communities Act, in which case Community law would have no direct effect at all in the United Kingdom.

The leading authority is *Thoburn v. Sunderland City Council*.

England
Thoburn v. Sunderland City Council ("Metric Martyrs" case)
DIVISIONAL COURT
[2002] 3 WLR 247; [2002] 1 CMLR 50; [2002] EWHC 195 (Admin)[28]

Mr Thoburn was a trader, who sold goods by the pound, instead of by the kilogram. This was contrary to UK legislation enacted to give effect to an EC directive. He was prosecuted by Sunderland City Council and convicted. He appealed. Since the case concerned UK legislation passed to give effect to a Community directive, the question of direct effect was not in issue. Nevertheless,

---

27 [1979] 3 All ER 325 at 329 (CA).
28 See Marshall, "Metric Measures and Martyrdom by Henry VIII Clause" (2002) 118 LQR 493; Boyron "In the Name of European Law: The Metric Martyrs Case" (2002) 27 ELRev. 771.

the court had some interesting things to say about the relationship between Community law and UK law.

The prosecuting authorities argued that Community law is supreme in the United Kingdom. They said that this is by virtue of a rule of Community law, not a rule of United Kingdom law. The court rejected this contention. The following extract from Lord Justice Laws' judgment explains why.

Judgment
Thus there is nothing in the [European Communities Act] which allows the [European Court], or any other institutions of the EU, to touch or qualify the conditions of Parliament's legislative supremacy in the United Kingdom. Not because the legislature chose not to allow it; because by our law it could not allow it. That being so, the legislative and judicial institutions of the EU cannot intrude upon those conditions. The British Parliament has not the authority to authorise any such thing. Being sovereign, it cannot abandon its sovereignty. Accordingly there are no circumstances in which the jurisprudence of the [European Court] can elevate Community law to a status within the corpus of English domestic law to which it could not aspire by any route of English law itself. This is, of course, the traditional doctrine of sovereignty. If it is to be modified, it certainly cannot be done by the incorporation of external texts. The conditions of Parliament's legislative supremacy in the United Kingdom necessarily remain in the United Kingdom's hands.

He went on to make clear that the relationship between the United Kingdom and the European Union depends on United Kingdom law, not European Union law.[29]

Conclusions

It is clear from the above discussion, as well as from an analysis of the position in other Member States,[30] that the effect of Community law in the legal systems of the Member States ultimately depends on Member-State law, not Community law. Member-State law might say that a provision of Community law will be granted direct effect if it has direct effect under Community law. Nevertheless, that effect is given to Community law by national law: Community law has direct effect because national law says so. The sovereignty (ultimate authority) of the Member States remains intact. This is why the Community is still an

---

29 Para. 69, proposition 4.
30 See the decisions of the French *Conseil Constitutionnel* in *Maastricht* I, Decision 92-308 DC, 9 April 1992, *Recueil*, p. 55; [1993] 3 CMLR 345 (English translation); and *Amsterdam*, Decision 97-394 DC, 31 December 1997, JORF No. 2 of 3 January 1998; the decisions of the Italian Constitutional Court (*Corte Costituzionale*) in *Frontini*, Decision No. 183 of 27 December 1973, [1974] RDI 154; [1974] 2 CMLR 372 (English translation) and *Fragd*, Corte Costituzionale, Decision No. 168 of 21 April 1989, [1990] I *Foro Italiano* 1855 (English translation in Andrew Oppenheimer, *The Relationship between European Community Law and National Law – The Cases* (Cambridge University Press, Cambridge, 1994), p. 653); and the decisions of the Greek Council of State in *Vagias v. DI KATSA*, Decision No. 2808/1997 of 8 July 1997, discussed in Maganaris, "The Principle of Supremacy of Community Law – The Greek Challenge" (1998) 23 ELRev. 179 and "The Principle of Supremacy of Community Law in Greece – From Direct Challenge to Non-Application" (1999) 24 ELRev. 426.

international organization (albeit with supranational powers), not a federal State.

National legal systems normally accept direct effect, and give directly effective Community law supremacy over national legislation, both prior and subsequent. Some Member States (for example, Germany) give it supremacy over certain provisions of their constitutions. However, it is doubtful whether any Member State (except possibly the Netherlands) gives it supremacy over all provisions of its constitution. Denmark, Germany and the United Kingdom do not. The same is almost certainly true of France and Italy. The national response to the European Court is, therefore, one of qualified acceptance: "Thus far and no further."

Further reading

Alter (Karen J.), *Establishing the Supremacy of European Law* (Oxford University Press, Oxford, 2001).

Hartley (Trevor C.), *Constitutional Problems of the European Union* (Hart Publishing, Oxford, 1999), Chapters 7–9.

Hartley, "The Constitutional Foundations of the European Union" (2001) 117 LQR 225.

Oppenheimer (Andrew), *The Relationship between European Community Law and National Law: The Cases* (Cambridge University Press, Cambridge, 1994). This book contains many of the leading cases, both from the European Court and from national courts.

Slaughter (Anne-Marie), Alec Stone Sweet and Joseph H. H. Weiler (eds.), *The European Courts and National Courts* (Hart Publishing, Oxford, 1998).

The direct effect
of directives

As we saw in the previous chapter, Article 249 [189] EC expressly says that regulations have direct effect. With regard to directives, on the other hand, the Article says:

> A directive shall be binding, as to the result to be achieved, upon each Member State to which it is addressed, but shall leave to the national authorities the choice of form and methods.

This makes clear that directives were not intended to be directly effective. They are not binding in their entirety, as are regulations, but only as to the result to be achieved. Clearly, something has to be done to achieve that result. And that something has to be done by the national authorities. The latter are given the choice of form and methods.

The European Court makes its move

The European Court, however, had other ideas. The problem is that the national authorities do not always take the necessary action. The Commission could respond by bringing proceedings under Article 226 [169] EC (see Chapter 5 above). However, this would involve a lot of work for the Commission. It could also be several years before judgment was obtained. Then there would be the problem of enforcing the judgment. So the European Court thought that things would be simpler and more efficient if directives were directly effective. The case in which it first established this principle was *Van Duyn v. Home Office*.

European Union
Van Duyn v. Home Office
COURT OF JUSTICE OF THE EUROPEAN COMMUNITIES
Case 41/74, [1974] ECR 1337; [1975] 1 CMLR 1

Facts

Ms van Duyn was a Dutch citizen, who wanted to come to the UK to work. Article 39 [48] EC gave her that right, but it permitted Member States to make exceptions on grounds of public policy. The UK Home Office invoked this proviso in order to exclude her from the country. Article 3(1) of Directive 64/221[1] provided that the public policy proviso could be invoked only on the basis of the personal conduct of the would-be immigrant. This particular provision had not been transposed into United Kingdom law. Ms van Duyn brought proceedings in an English court and claimed that she could nevertheless rely on Article 3(1), a claim which raised the question whether directives could be directly effective. The English court referred the matter to the European Court. The following extract sets out the European Court's reasons for holding that directives are capable of being directly effective.

Judgment

11. The United Kingdom observes that, since Article 249 [189] of the Treaty distinguishes between the effects ascribed to regulations, directives and decisions, it must therefore be presumed that the Council, in issuing a directive rather than making a regulation, must have intended that the directive should have an effect other than that of a regulation and accordingly that the former should not be directly applicable.

12. If, however, by virtue of the provisions of Article 249 [189] regulations are directly applicable and, consequently, may by their very nature have direct effects, it does not follow from this that other categories of acts mentioned in that Article can never have similar effects. It would be incompatible with the binding effect attributed to a directive by Article 249 [189] to exclude, in principle, the possibility that the obligation which it imposes may be invoked by those concerned. In particular, where the Community authorities have, by directive, imposed on Member States the obligation to pursue a particular course of conduct, the useful effect of such an act would be weakened if individuals were prevented from relying on it before their national courts and if the latter were prevented from taking it into consideration as an element of Community law. Article 234 [177], which empowers national courts to refer to the Court questions concerning the validity and interpretation of all acts of the Community institutions, without distinction, implies furthermore that these acts may be invoked by individuals in the national courts. It is necessary to examine, in every case, whether the nature, general scheme and wording of the provision in question are capable of having direct effects on the relations between Member States and individuals.

[Having decided, as a general question, that directives are capable of being directly effective, the court then went on to consider whether Article 3(1) was directly effective. It held that it was, applying a test similar to that applied in earlier cases to Treaty provisions.]

Comment

In the above judgment, the European Court put forward three arguments to justify its ruling. The first was that it would be incompatible with its binding effect if a directive was not capable of being directly effective. This, however, ignores the fact that an obligation can be legally binding on the international level without being directly effective. Under the "dualist" approach to international law, no provision of international law is directly effective. Yet "dualist"

---

1 OJ 1963/64 (Special Ed.) 117.

countries do not deny the binding effect of international law. Indeed, their record of respect for international law is in general no worse than that of "monist" countries.

The second argument was that the practical effectiveness (*effet utile*, in French) of directives would be greater if they were directly effective. This is true. If directives were directly effective, individuals could claim rights under them even if they were not implemented. This, therefore, is an argument for saying that directives *ought* to be directly effective. It is not, however, an argument for saying that they *are* directly effective. The Community system could function if directives were not directly effective. It just would not function so well.

The third argument was based on Article 234 [177] EC. This permits national courts to ask the European Court to give preliminary rulings on the validity and effect of acts of the institutions of the Community. The European Court argued that since this covers directives, it must mean that the authors of the treaty intended them to be directly effective. However, national courts might need a ruling on the validity or interpretation of a directive even if it was not directly effective. If a national court was called upon to interpret the national measure giving effect to the directive, it might well want to know the correct interpretation of the directive so it could interpret the national measure in harmony with it. The European Court itself has said that national courts must do this.[2] A ruling on the validity of a directive might be needed in order to determine the validity of the national measure transposing it into the national legal system. For these reasons, no inferences can be drawn from the terms of Article 234 [177] EC.

None of the arguments, therefore, justifies the court's position.

France rebels

The judgment in *Van Duyn* and the cases that followed it provoked considerable criticism. The French courts were the first to react.

France
Minister of the Interior v. Cohn-Bendit
COUNCIL OF STATE (CONSEIL D'ETAT)
Decision of 22 December 1978, [1979] *Dalloz* 155; [1979] *Revue Générale de Droit International Public* 832; English translations in [1980] 1 CMLR 543 and in Andrew Oppenheimer, *The Relationship between European Community Law and National Law: The Cases*, p. 317.

Facts
This was another immigration case. Daniel Cohn-Bendit was one of the leaders of the student rebellion in France in May 1968. Although permanently resident in France, he was a German citizen. After the rebellion was over, the French Government deported him to Germany. Some years later, he wanted to

---

2 *Von Colson and Kamann v. Land Nordrhein-Westfalen*, Case 14/83, [1984] ECR 1891.

return to France to work. Permission was refused. He challenged this decision in the French administrative courts in much the same way that Ms van Duyn challenged the decision against her in the English courts. Mr Cohn-Bendit also wanted to rely on Directive 64/221. Another provision, Article 6, said that when the immigration authorities invoke public policy as a ground for refusing permission to enter the country, they must give their reasons. This provision had not been transposed into French law. Mr Cohn-Bendit had not been given the reasons for the government's decision, and he wanted to invoke Article 6 in the French court.

The French court before which the proceedings had been brought, the Paris administrative court (*tribunal administratif de Paris*), made a reference to the European Court on the interpretation of the directive. The Minister of the Interior (the defendant in the proceedings) appealed against the order for reference. The appeal was decided by the French Council of State (*Conseil d'Etat*), the highest administrative court in France[3] and one of the most prestigious courts in continental Europe.

> **Judgment**[4]
> According to Article 46 [56] EC (no provision of which entitles any organ of the EC to issue regulations – measures which are directly applicable in the Member States – with regard to action taken on the basis of public policy) the harmonization of legislation "providing for special treatment for foreign nationals on grounds of public policy, public security or public health" is to be attained by means of directives, adopted on a proposal from the Commission and after consulting the European Parliament. It follows clearly from Article 249 [189] EC that while directives bind the Member States "as to the result to be achieved" and while, to achieve that result, the national authorities are obliged to adapt Member-State law and administrative practice to comply with directives addressed to them, those authorities retain the exclusive power to decide the form of the implementing measures, and to determine for themselves, subject to review by the national courts, the appropriate means to give them effect in the national legal system. Consequently, whatever significance they may have for Member States, directives cannot be invoked by nationals of Member States in the course of proceedings against an individual administrative act.
>
> **[The court then ruled that Mr Cohn-Bendit could not invoke the directive in support of his action in the Paris administrative court. Therefore, the outcome of the case could not depend on the interpretation of the directive. Consequently, the Paris administrative court was wrong to ask the European Court to interpret the directive. The order for reference was set aside.]**

Comment

While the Council of State's interpretation of Article 249 [189] EC was perfectly reasonable, its failure itself to make a reference to the European Court could be

---

3 France has two entirely separate and independent court systems – the judicial courts and the administrative courts. Public-law proceedings may be brought only in the latter.
4 Translation by Trevor Hartley. No attempt has been made to reproduce the characteristic style of the *Conseil d'Etat*, or to translate literally each word of the judgment. Instead, I have tried to make the reasoning as clear as possible for the English-speaking reader.

regarded as a violation of Article 234 [177], the last paragraph of which states that where a question on the interpretation of the Treaties is raised before a court from whose decisions there is no judicial remedy (appeal), that court *must* refer the matter to the European Court. Of course, if it had done so, it would have been told that directives *can* be directly effective. If it wanted to avoid being forced to follow what it regarded as a wrong interpretation of the Treaty, it could not afford to make a reference.[5]

The *Cohn-Bendit* case was followed in Germany by the Federal Tax Court (*Bundesfinanzhof*, the highest German court in fiscal matters) in two cases decided in 1981[6] and 1985.[7] They both concerned an EC directive on VAT, which had not been implemented by Germany. Could the provisions of the directive be relied on by a taxpayer in order to claim an exemption? In the second of the two cases, *Kloppenburg,* the lower court had made a reference to the European Court and had been told that the relevant provision was directly effective.[8] On the basis of this, the lower tax court had found for the taxpayer. However, the tax authorities appealed to the Federal Tax Court, which reversed this decision on the ground that, under the EC Treaty, directives can never be directly effective. It refused to accept the ruling by the European Court on the ground that the European Court's jurisdiction under Article 234 [177] could not be used to extend the legislative powers of the Community.

The European Court offers a compromise

Clearly, the European Court felt that something had to be done. It offered a compromise.[9] It so happened that all the cases it had decided previously involved claims by individuals against the State. The State had failed to implement a directive, and the individual claimed that he was entitled to invoke

---

5 If pressed, the *Conseil d'Etat* would probably have justified its failure to refer on the basis of the *acte clair* doctrine. On this, see Chap. 11.
6 *Bundesfinanzhof,* decision of 16 July 1981, [1982] 1 CMLR 527.
7 *Bundesfinanzhof,* decision of 25 April 1985 (VR 123/84), *Kloppenburg, Entscheidungen des Bundesfinanzhofes* 143, p. 383 (noted by Crossland, (1986) 11 ELRev. 473 at 476–479).
8 *Kloppenburg,* Case 70/83, [1984] ECR 1075.
9 Judges on the European Court hold regular consultations with judges on the most important national courts. Since these are held in private, it is not known whether the matter was discussed. However, it would be surprising if it was not. It is interesting to note that, shortly after the decision in the *Marshall* case, the Federal Tax Court's judgment in the *Kloppenburg* case was overturned by the Federal Constitutional Court (*Bundesverfassungsgericht*) on the ground that it violated a provision in the German Constitution (Art. 101), guaranteeing the right to bring legal proceedings and obtain a ruling from the appropriate court: *Bundesverfassungsgericht,* decision of 8 April 1987 (2 BvR 687/85), [1987] RIW 878; [1988] 3 CMLR 1. In later years, the French *Conseil d'Etat* seems to have modified its position on directives: see *Conseil d'Etat,* 7 December 1984, [1985] RTDE 187; *Conseil d'Etat,* 28 September 1984, *Confédération Nationale des Sociétés de Protection des Animaux,* [1984] RTDE 759; *Conseil d'Etat,* 6 March 1987, *Fédération Française des Sociétés de Protection de la Nature,* [1985] *Revue Française de Droit Administratif* 303; *Conseil d'Etat,* 3 February 1989, *Compagnie Alitalia,* [1990] 1 CMLR 248; *Conseil d'Etat,* 28 February 1992, *Rothmans* and *Arizona Tobacco* cases, [1993] 1 CMLR 253. See, further, Tatham, "Effect of European Community Directives in France: The Development of the Cohn-Bendit Jurisprudence" (1991) 40 ICLQ 907; Simon, "Le Conseil d'Etat et les directives communautaires: Du gallicanisme à l'orthodoxie" [1992] RTDE 265. Thus, the Member-State courts seem to have accepted the compromise.

the right that would have been conferred on him if the directive had been implemented. Thus the *Van Duyn* case concerned immigration; the *Kloppenburg* and *Becker*[10] cases concerned tax; and the *Ratti*[11] case concerned a criminal prosecution. Thanks to this fortuitous circumstance, the European Court was able, without going back on its previous case law, to say in the case we are about to consider that this was the maximum extent to which directives could be directly effective. It could thus ask the Member-State courts to accept direct effect to this extent, and promise in return not to extend it to cases where a directive is invoked *against* an individual. (In this context, the word "individual" means anyone other than the State.)

European Union
Marshall v. Southampton and South West Hampshire Area Health Authority
COURT OF JUSTICE OF THE EUROPEAN COMMUNITIES
Case 152/84, [1986] ECR 723; [1986] 1 CMLR 688; [1986] 2 WLR 780; [1986] 2 All ER 584

Background
Ms Marshall worked as a dietitian for the National Health Service, her employer being the Southampton and South West Hampshire Area Health Authority. Under its policy at the time, women were able, and obliged, to retire at the age of 60, while men were able, and obliged, to work until 65.[12] Ms Marshall wanted to continue working, but was forced to retire.[13] She sued her employer for sex discrimination before an employment tribunal in England and wanted to rely on an EC directive, Directive 76/207,[14] which made it illegal to dismiss an employee on the ground of her sex. This directive had been implemented in the United Kingdom, but not as regards retirement matters. One question in the case was whether the directive applied to compulsory retirement. The European Court held that it did. The next question was whether it was directly effective. The English Court of Appeal, which had made the reference to the European Court, had held that the Southampton and South West Hampshire Area Health Authority was part of the State.[15] So, in a way, the question whether a directive could be directly effective against an "individual" did not arise. However, the United Kingdom argued that even a public body should count as an "individual" if it was not acting in its capacity as the State. In entering into a contract of employment with Ms Marshall, the Health Authority was acting just like any private employer. It was not relying on any special governmental powers. So the United Kingdom maintained that the directive could not be invoked against it.

---

10 *Becker v. Finanzamt Münster-Innenstadt*, Case 8/81, [1982] ECR 53; [1982] CMLR 499.
11 *Ratti*, Case 148/78, [1979] ECR 1629; [1980] 1 CMLR 96.
12 These were the ages at which the State pension was payable.
13 As a special favour, she was actually allowed to continue working until she was sixty-two.
14 OJ 1976, L39/40.
15 It said it was an "emanation" of the State.

Judgment

[After referring to the previous decisions in which it had held that directives can be directly effective, the court continued:]

47. That view is based on the consideration that it would be incompatible with the binding nature which Article 249 [189] confers on the directive to hold as a matter of principle that the obligation imposed thereby cannot be relied on by those concerned. From that the Court deduced that a Member State which has not adopted the implementing measures required by the directive within the prescribed period may not plead, as against individuals, its own failure to perform the obligations which the directive entails.

48. With regard to the argument that a directive may not be relied upon against an individual, it must be emphasized that according to Article 249 [189] of the EEC Treaty the binding nature of a directive, which constitutes the basis for the possibility of relying on the directive before a national court, exists only in relation to "each Member State to which it is addressed." It follows that a directive may not of itself impose obligations on an individual and that a provision of a directive may not be relied upon as such against such a person. It must therefore be examined whether, in this case, the respondent must be regarded as having acted as an individual.

49. In that respect it must be pointed out that where a person involved in legal proceedings is able to rely on a directive as against the State he may do so regardless of the capacity in which the latter is acting, whether employer or public authority. In either case it is necessary to prevent the State from taking advantage of its own failure to comply with Community law.

Comment

The European Court's reasoning in this case, based as it is on the wording of the Treaty, is perfectly logical. The Treaty says that directives are binding on the Member States to which they are addressed, while regulations are binding in their entirety. So it follows that directives were not intended to be binding on persons other than the State. However, as we have seen, the European Court does not usually pay much attention to the wording of the Treaty; nor does it normally consider what the authors of the Treaty must have intended. If it had done so, it would not have made directives directly effective at all. Therefore its sudden conversion to a text-based method of interpretation must not be taken at face value.

Once it decided that directives could be directly effective only as regards rights claimed against the State (usually called "vertical" direct effect), the court then had to face the problem of defining what is meant by the "State". In *Marshall*, it was easy to say that the NHS was part of the State, since the English court had already said so. All it had to do in that case was to rule that it did not matter in what capacity the State was acting. In later cases, however, it has had to give its attention to the problem.

European Union
Foster v. British Gas
COURT OF JUSTICE OF THE EUROPEAN COMMUNITIES
Case C-188/89, [1990] ECR I-3313; [1990] 2 CMLR 833

Background

This case also concerned a woman who had been forced to retire early. Ms Foster worked for British Gas in the days when it was a publicly owned corporation (nationalized industry). Did it count as the "State"?

Judgment

18. . . . the Court has held in a series of cases that unconditional and sufficiently precise provisions of a directive could be relied on against organizations or bodies which were subject to the authority or control of the State or had special powers beyond those which result from the normal rules applicable to relations between individuals.

19. The Court has accordingly held that provisions of a directive could be relied on against tax authorities [citations omitted], local or regional authorities [citations omitted], constitutionally independent authorities responsible for the maintenance of public order and safety [the Chief Constable of the RUC: *Johnston v. Chief Constable of the RUC*, Case 222/84, [1986] ECR 1651; [1986] 3 CMLR 240], and public authorities providing public health services [*Marshall*].

20. It follows from the foregoing that a body, whatever its legal form, which has been made responsible, pursuant to a measure adopted by the State, for providing a public service under the control of the State and has for that purpose special powers beyond those which result from the normal rules applicable in relations between individuals is included in any event among the bodies against which the provisions of a directive capable of having direct effect may be relied upon.

Comment

Once the European Court had put the new doctrine into effect, it then tried to lessen its impact by giving a wide meaning to the "State". As it pointed out in *Foster*, local authorities are included, as well as the chief constable of a United Kingdom police force, both of which are constitutionally independent of the central government.

Part of the rationale for direct effect (not mentioned in the *Van Duyn* case, but much emphasized in later cases)[16] is that it would be wrong to allow a State to use its own failure to transpose a directive as a ground for preventing individuals from invoking against it rights contained in the directive. That would allow the State to benefit from its own wrongdoing. However, this rationale breaks down when applied to independent entities like a local authority or a chief constable. *They* are not responsible for the failure to transpose the directive.

---

16 See, for example, the judgment in *Marshall*, para. 49, last sentence.

When the *Foster* case came back to the English court (the House of Lords), it had to apply the European Court's ruling.[17] The European Court laid down a four-point test.

1. The body must be responsible for providing a public service.
2. It must be responsible pursuant to a measure adopted by the State.
3. It must be under the control of the State.
4. It must have special powers beyond those which result from the normal rules applicable in relations between individuals.

The House of Lords held that this test was satisfied in the case of British Gas as it then existed.

1. British Gas had been given the duty of maintaining an efficient system of gas supply in Britain.
2. This duty had been imposed by a statute, the Gas Act 1972.
3. The government could give British Gas general directions.
4. British Gas had special powers: no one else could supply gas without the permission of British Gas.

So Ms Foster was also able to invoke the directive, although no one could say that British Gas was to blame for the failure to transpose its provisions.

A later case raised the question whether Rolls Royce PLC was part of the State.[18] This was a normal commercial company, but all the shares in it were held by nominees of the State. The court held that it was not part of the State. Even if it was under the control of the State, it did not provide a public service, and it had no special powers. So the claimant could not invoke the directive.

Indirect effect

Another part of the European Court's strategy of minimizing the consequences of its decision to give directives only "vertical" direct effect was to develop the doctrine of "indirect effect".[19] According to this, provisions of Community law that are not directly effective in the circumstances of the case nevertheless have an "indirect" effect in that they must be taken into account when interpreting national law.[20] We saw in Chapter 8 that the United Kingdom has a rule to this effect with regard to all treaties. However, the EC rule goes much further in that it applies even if the national provision was not adopted to transpose the Community provision. It also applies to national provisions irrespective of whether they were passed before or after the Community provision. However, it applies only if the national provision is reasonably capable of being interpreted in the way required by Community law.

17 [1991] 2 WLR 1075.
18 *Doughty v. Rolls Royce* [1992] *Industrial Relations Law Reports* 126 (CA). No reference was made to the European Court in this case.
19 Like "vertical" and "horizontal" direct effect, this phrase is not used by the court itself. The doctrine of indirect effect was originally laid down in *Von Colson and Kamann v. Land Nordrhein-Westfalen*, Case 14/83, [1984] ECR 1891; [1986] 2 CMLR 430.
20 It applies to all provisions of Community law that are not directly effective, including a directive in a case in which rights are claimed against an individual.

In a case decided by a three-judge Chamber of the European Court in 1990, *Marleasing*,[21] there is a hint that indirect effect applies even if the national provision is *not* capable of bearing the meaning required by Community law. This interpretation was rejected by the House of Lords in *Webb v. Emo Air Cargo*,[22] where it was stressed that the national provision must be open to an interpretation consistent with the directive. In later cases, the European Court has always used the words "as far as possible" when referring to indirect effect.[23]

A reconsideration?

In the early 1990s, there seems to have been a campaign by a number of advocates-general at the European Court to reverse the *Marshall* compromise. We give one example.

European Union
Vaneetveld
COURT OF JUSTICE OF THE EUROPEAN COMMUNITIES
Case C-316/93, [1994] ECR I-763

The issue of "horizontal" direct effect (direct effect against an individual) did not actually arise in this case, since the deadline for implementation of the directive had not expired. Nevertheless, Advocate-General Jacobs went to great lengths to put the case for extending the direct effect of directives.

Opinion of Advocate-General Jacobs[24]

19. It was in the *Marshall* case in 1986 (which may now be referred to as *Marshall I*) that the Court finally took a position on the horizontal direct effect of directives, holding that "a directive may not of itself impose obligations on an individual and . . . a provision of a directive may not be relied upon as such against such a person". There however the Court indicated that Miss Marshall could rely on the directive in question against the defendant, the Southampton and South-West Hampshire Area Health Authority (Teaching), which could be regarded as an organ of the State, and that it was immaterial whether that body was acting as employer or as public authority. Curiously, therefore, the Court decided the issue in a case in which it was not necessary to do so: the Court could simply have found that the defendant was an organ of the State, leaving open the question whether directives could ever be invoked against private bodies.

20. In deciding the issue, the Court relied – and relied exclusively – on the wording of Article 249 [189] of the Treaty. As is well known, and for good reasons, such reliance on the wording of the Treaty has not generally been decisive in the Court' s interpretation of it. Moreover the argument based on the wording, although it carries some weight, is not wholly convincing. Article 249 [189] says that a directive "shall be binding, as to the result to be achieved, upon each Member State to which it is addressed . . .". Quite apart from

---

21 Case C-106/89, [1990] ECR I-4135; [1992] 1 CMLR 305.
22 [1993] 1 WLR 49 (HL).
23 See, for example, para. 26 of its judgment in *Faccini Dori*, below.
24 Footnotes omitted.

the fact that Article 249 [189] does not expressly exclude the possibility of derived obligations arising for persons other than Member States, it may be noted that, on the basis of such an argument from the text, it would have been wholly impossible to maintain that Article 141 [119] of the Treaty, for example, imposed obligations on private employers as the Court had held as long ago as 1976. Moreover, if a directive can impose obligations only on Member States, it is by no means easy to justify imposing obligations on a body such as the Southampton and South-West Hampshire Area Health Authority (Teaching). The well-known attempt at a rationale for assigning direct effect to a directive as against a Member State, namely that a Member State ought not to be allowed to rely upon its own failure to implement a directive, is singularly inapposite in relation to such a body, which has no responsibility for that failure.

21. In any event, once the Court had accepted that directives did have such a reach, it became difficult to justify distinctions between, for example, employers in the public sector and employers in the private sector. Moreover, once direct effect, although limited, had been recognized, some of the general arguments of principle against assigning horizontal direct effect to directives – for example, the argument that, under Article 249 [189] of the Treaty, directives leave to the national authorities the choice of form and methods – could no longer be sustained.

22. It becomes difficult, also, in my view, to sustain a distinction in this respect between directives – which are, after all, the main, and often the only, form of Community legislation provided for under many areas of the Treaty – and other binding provisions of Community law, namely treaties, regulations and decisions, all of which, it is accepted, may impose obligations on individuals . . .

25. The above considerations do not in my view obviate the important differences which still remain between directives and regulations. In *Marshall I* the Court rightly, in my view, refrained from relying on the argument (mentioned in the Opinion of Advocate General Slynn) that to make directives directly enforceable against individuals would obliterate the distinction between directives and regulations. To recognize that even the provisions of a directive may be directly enforceable, in the exceptional case where they have not been correctly transposed, in no way affects the obligation of Member States to take all measures necessary to implement them; while regulations, being directly applicable, do not normally require implementation. Moreover, a directive, as we have seen, will produce legal effects only after the period which it lays down for its implementation has expired. Regulations and directives will remain different instruments, appropriate in different situations and achieving their aims by different means, even if it is recognized that in certain circumstances a directive which has not been correctly implemented may impose obligations on certain private entities.

26. More than 30 years ago in *Van Gend en Loos* the Court recognized the specific character of Community law as a system of law which could not be reduced to an arrangement between States, as was often the case in traditional international law. After the developments in the Community legal system which have taken place since then, it may be necessary to recognize that in certain circumstances directives which have not been properly implemented may confer rights on individuals even as against private bodies. Perhaps a particular contrast could be drawn in this respect between the Community legal order and the international legal order.

27. It is a notorious weakness of international law that a treaty may not be enforceable in the courts of a State party to it, even if the treaty provisions themselves are apt to be

applied by the courts. This regrettable result is especially likely to occur in so-called "dualist" States which do not recognize any constitutional principle giving internal legal effect to treaties binding on them under international law. Thus it may often arise, in an international transaction between private parties, that a party to the transaction, intending that the transaction should be governed by a particular treaty, takes care to ascertain that the treaty has been ratified by the State of the other party, but finds when a dispute occurs that the treaty does not form part of that State's domestic law and will not be applied by that State's courts.

28. It is unacceptable that the weakness of international law should be reproduced in the Community legal order. As is often the case with a treaty, a directive is binding upon the State as to the result to be achieved, but leaves to the national authorities the choice of form and methods. But the role of directives in the EC Treaty has developed, as a result of the legislative practice of the Council, in a way which makes the language of Article 249 [189] of the Treaty no longer appropriate. Notwithstanding the wording of the third paragraph of that article, it is no longer accurate to say that directives are binding only "as to the result to be achieved". The "choice of form and methods" left to the Member States is often illusory because the discretion of the Member States in implementing directives is severely limited by the detailed, exhaustive nature of much of the legislation now emanating from the Council in the form of directives. Many of the provisions contained in directives are in consequence ideally suited to have direct effect . . .

31. It cannot, I think, be objected that imposing obligations on individuals will prejudice legal certainty. On the contrary, perhaps the most significant feature of the existing case-law on this point is that it has generated uncertainty. It has led, first, to a very broad interpretation of the notion of Member State so that directives can be enforced even against commercial enterprises in which there is a particular element of State participation or control, notwithstanding that those enterprises have no responsibility for the default of the Member States, and notwithstanding that they might be in direct competition with private sector undertakings against which the same directives are not enforceable. And it has led to great uncertainty on the scope of national legislation, in view of the duty imposed on national courts to stretch to their limits the terms of national legislation so as to give effect to directives which have not been properly implemented. Moreover, where national legislation is interpreted extensively so as to give effect to a directive, the result may well be to impose on individuals obligations which they would not have in the absence of the directive. Thus directives which have not been correctly implemented may already give rise to obligations for individuals. Against that background, it does not seem a valid criticism that enforcing directives directly against individuals would endanger legal certainty. On the contrary, it might well be conducive to greater legal certainty, and to a more coherent system, if the provisions of a directive were held in appropriate circumstances to be directly enforceable against individuals.

32. Because the existing case-law already requires national courts in effect to enforce directives against individuals, by construing all provisions of national law, whether or not adopted for the purpose of implementing a directive and whether prior or subsequent to the directive, so as to give effect to the provisions of directives, it would not be a radical departure from the existing state of the law, in terms of its practical consequences, to assign horizontal direct effect to directives; such direct effect will arise only when it is impossible so to construe any provision of national law. . . .

[The court did not comment on this.]

QUESTION

Are you convinced by the Advocate-General's reasoning?

European Union
Faccini Dori v. Recreb
COURT OF JUSTICE OF THE EUROPEAN COMMUNITIES
Case C-91/92, [1994] ECR I-3325

Background

Shortly after Advocate-General Jacobs gave his Opinion in the *Vaneetveld* case, the European Court gave judgment in the *Faccini Dori* case. In this case, the question of horizontal direct effect *did* arise. Ms Faccini Dori had been approached by a salesman on Milan railway station who induced her to sign up for a correspondence course to learn English. Afterwards, she regretted this. An EC consumer-protection directive, Directive 85/577,[25] would have given her the right to cancel the contract, but this directive, the deadline of which had expired, had not been transposed by Italy. Could she nevertheless rely on its provisions against an "individual", Recreb Srl, the company to which the contract had been assigned?

Judgment

19. The second issue raised by the national court relates more particularly to the question whether, in the absence of measures transposing the directive within the prescribed time-limit, consumers may derive from the directive itself a right of cancellation against traders with whom they have concluded contracts and enforce that right before a national court.

20. As the Court has consistently held since its judgment in [*Marshall*], a directive cannot of itself impose obligations on an individual and cannot therefore be relied upon as such against an individual.

21. The national court observes that if the effects of unconditional and sufficiently precise but untransposed directives were to be limited to relations between State entities and individuals, this would mean that a legislative measure would operate as such only as between certain legal subjects, whereas, under Italian law as under the laws of all modern States founded on the rule of law, the State is subject to the law like any other person. If the directive could be relied on only as against the State, that would be tantamount to a penalty for failure to adopt legislative measures of transposition as if the relationship were a purely private one.

22. It need merely be noted here that, as is clear from the judgment in *Marshall*, cited above (paragraphs 48 and 49), the case-law on the possibility of relying on directives against State entities is based on the fact that under Article 249 [189] a directive is binding only in relation to "each Member State to which it is addressed". That case-law seeks to prevent "the State from taking advantage of its own failure to comply with Community law".

25 OJ 1985, L372, p. 31.

23. It would be unacceptable if a State, when required by the Community legislature to adopt certain rules intended to govern the State's relations – or those of State entities – with individuals and to confer certain rights on individuals, were able to rely on its own failure to discharge its obligations so as to deprive individuals of the benefits of those rights. Thus the Court has recognized that certain provisions of directives on conclusion of public works contracts and of directives on harmonization of turnover taxes may be relied on against the State (or State entities) [citations omitted].

24. The effect of extending that case-law to the sphere of relations between individuals would be to recognize a power in the Community to enact obligations for individuals with immediate effect, whereas it has competence to do so only where it is empowered to adopt regulations.

25. It follows that, in the absence of measures transposing the directive within the prescribed time-limit, consumers cannot derive from the directive itself a right of cancellation as against traders with whom they have concluded a contract or enforce such a right in a national court.

26. It must also be borne in mind that, as the Court has consistently held . . . , the Member States' obligation arising from a directive to achieve the result envisaged by the directive and their duty under Article 10 [5] of the Treaty to take all appropriate measures, whether general or particular, is binding on all the authorities of Member States, including, for matters within their jurisdiction, the courts. The judgments of the Court [citations omitted] make it clear that, when applying national law, whether adopted before or after the directive, the national court that has to interpret that law must do so, as far as possible, in the light of the wording and the purpose of the directive so as to achieve the result it has in view and thereby comply with the third paragraph of Article 249 [189] of the Treaty.

Comment

This seems to have disposed of the matter. However, in the years that followed, there have been a number of cases that raised issues as to the exact borderline between vertical and horizontal direct effect. We shall look at three of them.

> *European Union*
> **CIA Security v. Signalson and Securitel**
> **COURT OF JUSTICE OF THE EUROPEAN COMMUNITIES**
> Case C-194/94, [1996] ECR I-2201.

Facts

A Belgian law passed in 1990 said that all "security firms" (defined as firms supplying alarm systems designed to prevent or record crimes) had to obtain authorization from the government before they could operate. A decree passed in 1991 said that alarm systems could not be sold in Belgium unless they had been approved by a government-appointed committee. An EC directive, Directive 83/189,[26] said that all "technical regulations" had to be notified to the Commission. In certain circumstances, they could not come into force for specified periods. Neither the law of 1990 nor the decree of 1991 had been notified.

26 OJ 1983, L109, p. 8.

CIA Security, Signalson and Securitel were all security firms. The latter two had claimed that one of CIA Security's alarm systems did not fulfil Belgian requirements. CIA Security brought proceedings in Belgium for a court order to prevent them from making such statements. The other two firms counterclaimed for an order that CIA Security be ordered to cease trading because it had not been authorized under the law of 1990 and was selling an alarm system that had not been approved under the decree of 1991. This raised the question whether the law and the decree should have been notified under the directive and, if so, whether the directive could be invoked in the proceedings before the Belgian court. The Belgian court referred these questions to the European Court.

Judgment
[The court held that the 1990 law was not a "technical regulation" and consequently did not have to be notified. The 1991 decree, on the other hand, was a "technical regulation" and should have been notified.[27] It then continued:]

45. It remains to examine the legal consequences to be drawn from a breach by Member States of their obligation to notify and, more precisely, whether Directive 83/189 is to be interpreted as meaning that a breach of the obligation to notify, constituting a procedural defect in the adoption of the technical regulations concerned, renders such technical regulations inapplicable so that they may not be enforced against individuals.

46. The German and Netherlands Governments and the United Kingdom consider that Directive 83/189 is solely concerned with relations between the Member States and the Commission, that it merely creates procedural obligations which the Member States must observe when adopting technical regulations, their competence to adopt the regulations in question after expiry of the suspension period being, however, unaffected, and, finally, that it contains no express provision relating to any effects attaching to non-compliance with those procedural obligations.

47. The Court observes first of all in this context that none of those factors prevents non-compliance with Directive 83/189 from rendering the technical regulations in question inapplicable.

48. For such a consequence to arise from a breach of the obligations laid down by Directive 83/189, an express provision to this effect is not required. As pointed out above, it is undisputed that the aim of the directive is to protect freedom of movement for goods by means of preventive control and that the obligation to notify is essential for achieving such Community control. The effectiveness of Community control will be that much greater if the directive is interpreted as meaning that breach of the obligation to notify constitutes a substantial procedural defect such as to render the technical regulations in question inapplicable to individuals.

---

27 The Belgian Government said in court that the 1991 decree had actually been replaced by a later decree which *had* been notified and that the later decree was the one that should have been applied by the Belgian court. The European Court, however, refused to listen to this argument. It said it had to answer the questions put to it by the Belgian court.

[After considering various other points, the court concluded:]

54. In view of the foregoing considerations, it must be concluded that Directive 83/189 is to be interpreted as meaning that breach of the obligation to notify renders the technical regulations concerned inapplicable, so that they are unenforceable against individuals.

Comment

In this judgment, the court fails to deal squarely with the real issue. Its argument leads logically (in terms of its previous case law) to the conclusion that an "individual" could invoke the directive against the State if the latter tried to enforce against it a national provision that should have, but had not, been notified. However, this was only the first step in answering the Belgian court's questions. The next step was to determine whether the same applied in proceedings between two "individuals". Plausible arguments could be advanced for saying that it did, but the court did not advance them. Instead, it merely ruled that the relevant provisions of the directive "are to be interpreted as meaning that individuals may rely on them before the national court which must decline to apply a national technical regulation which has not been notified in accordance with the directive",[28] which seems to mean that the directive could be invoked in the proceedings in the Belgian court.

In view of the court's failure to give any reasons, which may have been due to disagreement among the judges themselves, it is useful to set out an extract from the Opinion of Advocate-General Elmer. This was of course given before the judgment.

Opinion of Advocate-General Elmer

67. In summary, I consider that the [relevant provisions] of the Directive confer rights on individuals and are unconditional and sufficiently precise so that they may be relied upon by an individual before a national court; accordingly technical regulations which have not been notified will not be enforceable in relation to individuals. A non-notified regulation will consequently not furnish a basis for imposing a penalty on a trader or prevent him from marketing a product which does not comply with the regulations.

68. Consideration must, however, be given to the question whether the direct effect of the notification procedure in the Directive can be relied upon in a case such as that in the main proceedings, where the action is between two individuals. Under the Court's case-law a directive cannot, as stated, of itself impose obligations on an individual. A provision in a directive cannot therefore be relied upon as such against an individual, in the same way as the Community may not issue rules in the form of a directive which impose obligations on an individual. On the other hand, when applying national law, national courts must interpret national legal provisions, as far as possible, in the light of the wording and purpose of the directive so as to achieve the result it has in view. That obligation applies both to provisions in a law which has been specifically introduced in order to implement the directive and to provisions in other legislation, and it applies regardless whether the legislation preceded the directive or vice versa.

28 These are the words of the formal ruling given by the court.

69. In the main proceedings Signalson and Securitel have claimed that CIA should cease marketing [the alarm system in question] since it has not received type approval under the provisions contained in the Law and 1991 Decree. They have further claimed that CIA should be ordered to pay a periodic penalty payment as a result. Those claims are based on national regulations which have not been notified in accordance with the Directive, namely the Law and the 1991 Decree.[29] On the basis of the Belgian Law on Commercial Practices it is claimed that those regulations should be enforced in relation to a trader by way of an order that he cease marketing and pay a periodic penalty. Such enforcement must, in my view, be contrary to the direct effect of the notification procedure set out in Articles 8(1) and 9 of the Directive. That would, under the Court's case-law hitherto, be clear without more if it was the State which, as prosecutor, consumer ombudsman or similar had brought proceedings against CIA. The fact that the question in this case has been raised in the context of a private action, however, in my view can make no difference whatsoever. It is the State which lays down rules on penalties, prohibitions on marketing, etc. and it is the courts which must impose such sanctions regardless of who, under the national rules on procedure, might have brought the case.

70. In the main proceedings CIA claimed that Signalson and Securitel should be fined for having acted in breach of good commercial practice by stating that [the alarm system in question] was not approved in accordance with regulations contained in the Law and the 1991 Decree. That claim is based on the fact that CIA was not obliged to seek type approval since the Belgian regulations had not been notified in accordance with the Directive. The question might be raised whether it can be said that if CIA's claim is upheld that would amount to allowing the Directive to impose obligations on individuals (in this case Signalson and Securitel).

71. The notification procedure in the Directive imposes a number of obligations on the Member States. The Directive does not, however, on its wording, aim to impose duties on individuals and therefore no question arises as to whether the Directive should have direct effect as far as individuals' obligations are concerned. The Directive is thus essentially different from Directive 85/577/EEC which was at issue in [*Faccini Dori*, above].

72. CIA's claim is itself based on national law. The purpose of the reference to the Court would appear, in the light of CIA's claims, [to be] to obtain the necessary basis for the national court's interpretation of the Belgian Law on Commercial Practices. I would refer to what was stated above concerning the national court's duty, as far as possible, to interpret national law in the light of Community law. Such interpretation of national law in the light of Community law can naturally indirectly be of significance for the claims relating to Signalson and Securitel, but that is no different from the situation in other cases, whether the Court has indicated the rule of interpretation to be applied [citation omitted].

73. If it were held that CIA was not able to point to the incompatibility of the Belgian regulations with Community law in its claims against Signalson and Securitel that would, in my view, create an unsatisfactory and incomprehensible situation where Community law would on the one hand be seeking to prevent a Member State from prosecuting an individual who had not complied with a non-notified technical provision, but on the other hand would debar the same individual from relying on the same circumstance in a case against a competitor who had stated that the individual in question had conducted himself unlawfully by not complying with the (unlawful) national regulation . . .

---

29 Editor's note: the court actually held that the law of 1990 did not have to be notified, but the Advocate-General's comments still apply to the decree, which should have been notified.

Comment

Advocate-General Elmer's arguments point to the conclusion that a directive can be directly effective when it is used to block proceedings brought to enforce a national provision of a public nature, even if those proceedings are brought by a private citizen. This would cover the counterclaims by Signalson and Securitel. CIA Security's original action raises more difficult issues, but perhaps it could be said that it would be misleading for the defendants to say that it was violating a national provision if that provision was inapplicable because it was contrary to a directive. These arguments therefore provide a justification for the court's decision. They are not, however, the arguments put forward by the court. The court seems to be saying that the failure to notify the Commission vitiated the adoption of the national measure, so that it was automatically inapplicable.

European Union
Lemmens
COURT OF JUSTICE OF THE EUROPEAN COMMUNITIES
Case C-226/97, [1998] ECR I-3711

Facts

This was a reference from a criminal court in the Netherlands. The accused was Mr Lemmens, who had been convicted of drunken driving. Under a Dutch statute, it was an offence to drive a motor vehicle if a breathalyser[30] test produced a reading above a prescribed limit. A Dutch regulation laid down the technical specifications for breathalyser equipment. Mr Lemmens appealed against his conviction on the ground that the regulation was a "technical regulation" in terms of Directive 83/189 (the same directive as was in issue in the *CIA Security* case) and should have been notified to the Commission. Lemmens argued that, since it had not been notified, his conviction was contrary to Community law.

The first question before the European Court was whether the Dutch regulation was indeed a "technical regulation" in terms of the directive. It held that it was. It then considered the consequences of this ruling.

Judgment
27. In its first question, the national court essentially asks whether the Directive is to be interpreted as meaning that, if the obligation imposed by Article 8 thereof to notify a technical regulation on breath-analysis apparatus has been infringed, the effect is that evidence obtained by means of such apparatus, authorised in accordance with that regulation, cannot be relied upon against an individual charged with driving while under the influence of alcohol.

[The court then considered the arguments put forward.]

---

30 A device for measuring alcohol in the breath.

32. In that regard, it should be noted that, in paragraph 40 of its judgment in *CIA Security International*, cited above, the Court emphasised that the Directive is designed to protect, by means of preventive control, freedom of movement for goods, which is one of the foundations of the Community. This control serves a useful purpose in that technical regulations covered by the Directive may constitute obstacles to trade in goods between Member States, such obstacles being permissible only if they are necessary to satisfy compelling requirements relating to the public interest.

33. In paragraphs 48 and 54 of that judgment, the Court pointed out that the obligation to notify is essential for achieving such Community control and went on to state that the effectiveness of such control will be that much greater if the Directive is interpreted as meaning that breach of the obligation to notify constitutes a substantial procedural defect such as to render the technical regulations in question inapplicable, and thus unenforceable against individuals.

34. In criminal proceedings such as those in the main action, the regulations applied to the accused are those which, on the one hand, prohibit and penalise driving while under the influence of alcohol and, on the other, require a driver to exhale his breath into an apparatus designed to measure the alcohol content, the result of that test constituting evidence in criminal proceedings. Such regulations differ from those which, not having been notified to the Commission in accordance with the Directive, are unenforceable against individuals.

35. While failure to notify technical regulations, which constitutes a procedural defect in their adoption, renders such regulations inapplicable inasmuch as they hinder the use or marketing of a product which is not in conformity therewith, it does not have the effect of rendering unlawful any use of a product which is in conformity with regulations which have not been notified.

36. The use of the product by the public authorities, in a case such as this, is not liable to create an obstacle to trade which could have been avoided if the notification procedure had been followed.

37. The answer to the first question must therefore be that the Directive is to be interpreted as meaning that breach of the obligation imposed by Article 8 thereof to notify a technical regulation on breath-analysis apparatus does not have the effect of making it impossible for evidence obtained by means of such apparatus, authorised in accordance with regulations which have not been notified, to be relied upon against an individual charged with driving while under the influence of alcohol.

Comment

We are now told that a measure adopted contrary to the directive is inapplicable only if it hinders the use or marketing of the product. Otherwise, it still applies.

European Union
Unilever Italia v. Central Food
COURT OF JUSTICE OF THE EUROPEAN COMMUNITIES
Case C-443/98, [2000] ECR I-7535[31]

---

31 For a comment, see Weatherill, "Breach of Directives and Breach of Contract" (2001) 26 ELRev. 177.

Facts

Unilever Italia and Central Food were two Italian companies. Unilever sold Central Food a consignment of olive oil. Central Food refused to accept it on the ground that the labels did not comply with Italian legislation. Unilever replied that the legislation was contrary to Directive 83/189 and therefore inapplicable. (The legislation had been notified as required by Article 8 of the directive, but it had been brought into force contrary to Article 9.) Unilever insisted that Central Food accept the consignment and, when it refused, sued it for damages. The Italian court made a reference to the European Court.

The European Court first considered whether the Italian legislation was inapplicable by reason of Directive 83/189. It held that it was. The next question was whether this inapplicability could be invoked in civil proceedings between private individuals concerning contractual rights and obligations.

Judgment

46. First, in civil proceedings of that nature, application of technical regulations adopted in breach of Article 9 of Directive 83/189 may have the effect of hindering the use or marketing of a product which does not conform to those regulations.

47. That is the case in the main proceedings, since application of the Italian rules is liable to hinder Unilever in marketing the extra virgin olive oil which it offers for sale.

48. Next, it must be borne in mind that, in *CIA Security*, the finding of inapplicability as a legal consequence of breach of the obligation of notification was made in response to a request for a preliminary ruling arising from proceedings between competing undertakings based on national provisions prohibiting unfair trading.

49. Thus, it follows from the case-law of the Court that the inapplicability of a technical regulation which has not been notified in accordance with Article 8 of Directive 83/189 can be invoked in proceedings between individuals for the reasons set out in paragraphs 40 to 43 of this judgment.[32] The same applies to non-compliance with the obligations laid down by Article 9 of the same directive, and there is no reason, in that connection, to treat disputes between individuals relating to unfair competition, as in the *CIA Security* case, differently from disputes between individuals concerning contractual rights and obligations, as in the main proceedings.

50. Whilst it is true, as observed by the Italian and Danish Governments, that a directive cannot of itself impose obligations on an individual and cannot therefore be relied on as such against an individual (see *Faccini Dori* [above] paragraph 20), that case-law does not apply where non-compliance with Article 8 or Article 9 of Directive 83/189, which constitutes a substantial procedural defect, renders a technical regulation adopted in breach of either of those articles inapplicable.

51. In such circumstances, and unlike the case of non-transposition of directives with which the case-law cited by those two Governments is concerned, Directive 83/189 does not in any way define the substantive scope of the legal rule on the basis of which the national court must decide the case before it. It creates neither rights nor obligations for individuals.

---

32 Editor's note: in these paragraphs, the court said that Arts. 8 and 9 of Directive 83/189 were necessary to ensure free movement of goods.

52. In view of all the foregoing considerations, the answer to the question submitted must be that a national court is required, in civil proceedings between individuals concerning contractual rights and obligations, to refuse to apply a national technical regulation which was adopted during a period of postponement of adoption prescribed in Article 9 of Directive 83/189.

Comment

In this case, the court imposes a limit on the rule that directives cannot impose obligations on individuals. The rule now applies only where the directive requires the Member State to take positive action, normally the adoption of legislation. The position is different where the directive has a purely negative effect by prohibiting the adoption of legislation. If that legislation is nevertheless adopted, it will be inapplicable even in proceedings between two private parties – though only, it seems, if it has the effect of hindering the use or marketing of the product.

This new position of the court has been subject to strong criticism on the ground that it creates intolerable uncertainty in legal relations between individuals. It seems that Central Food had no way of knowing whether the Italian legislation had been promulgated contrary to the directive. As far as it knew, it could have been prosecuted if it sold the oil. These considerations were made clear in the Opinion of Advocate-General Jacobs, which, though delivered before the judgment, foresaw the possibility that the court might take the position it did.

Opinion of Advocate-General Jacobs

111. In my view, a failure to notify (which may happen very frequently, given the vast range of measures potentially within the scope of the directive, and which may of course be inadvertent) cannot be treated as having far-reaching effects on contractual relations between individuals. In substance the effect would be that, solely on the basis of such failures by Member States, courts would be obliged to find a breach of contract.

112. Such consequences would be contrary to principles fundamental to our legal systems, and contrary in particular to fundamental requirements of legal certainty. There may be uncertainty as to whether the measure is a technical regulation and whether it required notification; uncertainty, in the absence of any provisions laying down a transparent procedure, as to whether it has in fact been notified; uncertainty, where a national regulation or parts of it are disapplied, as to what legal regime is to replace the disapplied measures; uncertainty as to the appropriate remedies for the breach of contract, in the absence of fault in either party. Moreover, such consequences would follow whether or not the technical regulation was an obstacle to the free movement of goods, and even where it facilitated such freedom of movement. I can see no basis for giving such consequences to a failure to notify.

113. If, as I have argued, the failure of a Member State to notify a technical regulation should not be treated as affecting contractual relations between individuals and as founding a breach of contract, then it is clear that infringement of the standstill

requirements should not be so treated either. There are several arguments common to both. In particular, the arguments based on legal certainty, on injustice, and on the absence of transparency apply, in different ways, to all the consequences of procedural irregularities on the part of Member States.

114. The truth is that the code of procedure laid down by the directive is a code designed to regulate relations between the Commission and the Member States. It was not designed to confer substantive rights on individuals, still less to have adverse effects on them. Nor does it seem necessary that it should be given such effects. The Community's overriding interest in ensuring the free movement of goods does not arise until it is established that the technical regulation does obstruct such freedom of movement. In cases such as the present the Community's interest can be fully secured by reliance on Article 30 [36] of the Treaty.

115. Accordingly the question referred by the Pretura Circondariale di Milano should in my opinion be answered as follows:

Where a Member State fails to comply with the procedural requirements laid down by Articles 8 and 9 of Council Directive 83/189/EEC of 28 March 1983 laying down a procedure for the provision of information in the field of technical standards and regulations, such a failure cannot be relied upon in national courts in proceedings between individuals arising from a contract.

Comment

A further issue is that the court could be accused of ignoring the boundary between Community law and Member-State law. In the *Lemmens* case, it could be argued that it was for Dutch law to decide whether the inapplicability of the Dutch regulation laying down specifications for breathalysers entailed the inadmissibility of evidence obtained through the use of such equipment. Perhaps the European Court was just trying to be helpful by making clear that the demands of Community law did not extend this far.

In the *Unilever Italia* case, the inapplicability of the Italian legislation presumably meant that it could not be invoked by Central Food, even though the oil might have been difficult to sell in practice, since a lengthy law-suit would have been necessary to establish the legal position. In future cases, supermarkets might try to protect themselves by specifying in their contracts that the product must comply with particular pieces of national legislation, even if the latter are inapplicable. They could even copy out the relevant provisions into the contract. Such a contract would be perfectly valid in most legal systems. In such a case, would the European Court say that the buyer could be forced to accept a product that did not conform?

Further reading

Craig, "Directives: Direct Effect, Indirect Effect and the Construction of National Legislation" (1997) 22 ELRev. 519.

Curtin, "Directives: The Effectiveness of Judicial Protection of Individual Rights" (1990) 27 CMLRev. 709.

Curtin, "The Province of Government: Delimiting the Direct Effect of Directives in the Common Law Context" (1990) 15 ELRev. 195.

Dougan, "The 'Disguised' Vertical Direct Effect of Directives?" [2000] CLJ 586.

Maltby, "Marleasing: What is All the Fuss About?" (1993) 109 LQR 301.

Plaza Martin, "Furthering the Effectiveness of EC Directives and the Judicial Protection of Individual Rights Thereunder" (1994) 43 ICLQ 26.

Steiner, "Coming to Terms with EEC Directives" (1990) 106 LQR 144.

Tridimas, "Black, White and Shades of Grey: Horizontality of Directives Revisited" (2001–2002) 21 YEL 327.

Weatherill, "Breach of Directives and Breach of Contract" (2001) 26 ELRev. 177.

11

Enforcement of EU law in Member-State courts

General principles

In principle, the normal rules of procedure apply in Member-State courts when proceedings are brought to enforce rights under Community law. This means that though the substantive right is based on Community law, questions of procedure – for example, time limits, evidence and remedies – are governed by national law. This principle is subject to two general conditions.

1. The remedies and procedures available to enforce Community rights must be no less favourable than those available to enforce comparable national rights (rule of non-discrimination).[1]
2. It must not be impossible in practice (or excessively difficult) to enforce the Community right (rule of effectiveness).[2]

Both these rules must be satisfied. Even if the Community right is given the same treatment as comparable national rights, it must still not be impossible in practice to enforce it. If it is, new remedies must be created by the national courts just for Community rights.[3]

In addition to these general principles, there are a number of specific remedies, either created by the European Court or laid down in the Treaties.

Preliminary rulings

The most important remedy is one expressly laid down in the EC Treaty. This is the procedure for a reference to the European Court for a preliminary ruling. This enables the European Court to oversee the way in which Member-State courts apply Community law. The system was outlined in Chapter 5, where the text of Article 234 [177] is set out in Panel 5.3. It will be remembered that

---

1 See, for example, *Rewe-Handelsgesellschaft Nord v. Hauptzollamt Kiel*, Case 158/80, [1981] ECR 1805; [1982] CMLR 440 (para. 44 of the judgment).
2 See, for example, *Von Colson and Kamann v. Land Nordrhein-Westfalen*, Case 14/83, [1984] ECR 1891; [1986] 2 CMLR 430 (para. 23 of the judgment).
3 Although these rules are clear in theory, some decisions of the European Court are hard to reconcile with them, or indeed with each other. For example, compare *Peterbroeck v. Belgium*, Case C-312/93, [1995] ECR I-4599 with *Van Schijndel*, Cases C-430 and 431/93, [1995] ECR I-4705.

Panel 11.1 References to the European Court

Civil Procedure Rules 1998, Part 68

68.1 Interpretation

In this Part –

(a) "the court" means the court making the order;

(b) "the European Court" means the Court of Justice of the European Communities;

(c) "order" means an order referring a question to the European Court for a preliminary ruling under

   (i) article 234 of the Treaty establishing the European Community;

   (ii) article 150 of the Euratom Treaty;

   (iii) article 41 of the ECSC Treaty;

   (iv) the Protocol of 3 June 1971 on the interpretation by the European Court of the Convention of 27 September 1968 on Jurisdiction and the Enforcement of Judgments in Civil and Commercial Matters; or

   (v) the Protocol of 19 December 1988 on the interpretation by the European Court of the Convention of 19 June 1980 on the Law applicable to Contractual Obligations.

68.2 Making of order of reference

(1) An order may be made at any stage of the proceedings –

   (a) by the court of its own initiative; or

   (b) on an application by a party in accordance with Part 23.

(2) An order may not be made –

   (a) in the High Court, by a Master or district judge;

   (b) in a county court, by a district judge.

(3) The request to the European Court for a preliminary ruling must be set out in a schedule to the order, and the court may give directions on the preparation of the schedule.

68.3 Transmission to the European Court

(1) The Senior Master will send a copy of the order to the Registrar of the European Court.

(2) Where an order is made by a county court, the proper officer will send a copy of it to the Senior Master for onward transmission to the European Court.

(3) Unless the court orders otherwise, the Senior Master will not send a copy of the order to the European Court until –

   (a) the time for appealing against the order has expired; or

   (b) any application for permission to appeal has been refused, or any appeal has been determined.

68.4 Stay of proceedings

Where an order is made, unless the court orders otherwise the proceedings will be stayed until the European Court has given a preliminary ruling on the question referred to it.

---

the Member-State court stays the proceedings before it and refers questions to the European Court. The European Court in due course holds a hearing at which the parties (as well as national governments and Community institutions) may present their views. It then rules on the questions submitted to it. If it thinks that the wrong questions were submitted, it may modify them. If it thinks that it is not necessary to answer certain questions, it will not do so. The answers are then returned to the national court, which lifts the stay and carries on from where it left off. Under the Civil Procedure Rules, the procedure is governed by Part 68. This is set out in Panel 11.1.

Preliminary rulings differ from appeals in several important ways.

- The decision to make the reference rests with the Member-State court, not with the parties.[4]
- The Member-State court makes the reference *before* it gives final judgment.
- The European Court decides only the questions referred; it does not decide the case.
- The case always comes back to the national court, which gives the final judgment.

The jurisdiction of the European Court under this procedure is limited to deciding the following:

- the interpretation of the EC Treaty (and any treaties amending or supplementing it);
- the interpretation or validity of any act[5] of the institutions of the Community; and
- whether the provision is directly effective (regarded as a question of interpretation by the European Court).

The European Court has no jurisdiction to give binding rulings on:

- questions of fact;[6] or
- questions of national law.

These are for the Member-State court to decide.

In its eagerness to lay down the law, the European Court sometimes forgets the limits to its jurisdiction. This can cause trouble. Our next case is an example.

European Union
Maïseries de Beauce v. ONIC
COURT OF JUSTICE OF THE EUROPEAN COMMUNITIES
Case 109/79, [1980] ECR 2883

Facts

Maïseries de Beauce was a French company, which exported agricultural products. ONIC was a French governmental agency which had the task of collecting "monetary compensatory amounts" (MCAs). These were payments made on the export of agricultural produce. They were intended to counteract the effect of currency fluctuations on the Common Agricultural Policy in the days before the advent of the euro. When the export was made from a Member State with a soft (depreciating) currency, the MCA was a kind of tax paid by the exporter.

---

4 If a party goes directly to the European Court, the court will not hear him. It has jurisdiction only if a Member-State court makes a reference.
5 Such acts need not be directly effective or even binding. The national court may want a ruling on their validity or interpretation if it is argued that they should be taken into account when interpreting Member-State law.
6 In certain rare cases, the validity of a Community act will depend on a question of fact – for example, where the Treaty permits the Commission to adopt an act only if certain facts exist. In such cases, the European Court will have to decide the question of fact in order to determine the validity of the act. It is entitled to do this. Its decision on the validity of the Community act will be binding on the Member-State court, but its decision on the question of fact will not, as such, be binding. If that same question was relevant for a different purpose, the Member-State court would be entitled to decide it for itself.

Where the export was made from a Member State with a hard (appreciating) currency, it took the form of a subsidy paid to the exporter. In both cases, the money was collected, or paid, by national agencies, which acted on behalf of the Community. The basic regulation setting up the whole system was Council Regulation 974/71. The actual amounts payable were laid down by a series of Commission regulations. The regulation which fixed the amount that Maïseries de Beauce had to pay was Commission Regulation 938/77.

Maïseries de Beauce claimed that Regulation 938/77 was invalid, and that the MCAs it had paid should be returned to it. ONIC refused to return them. Maïseries de Beauce then brought proceedings in the *Tribunal Administratif d'Orléans* (the Orleans Administrative Court), which made a reference to the European Court under Article 234 [177] EEC, asking for a ruling on the validity of Regulation 938/77. The European Court ruled that it (and certain other regulations) were invalid because they infringed the basic regulation, Regulation 974/71. However, it continued:

Judgment

44. Although the Treaty does not expressly lay down the consequences which flow from a declaration of invalidity within the framework of a reference to the Court for a preliminary ruling, Articles 231 [174] and 233 [176] contain clear rules as to the effects of the annulment of a regulation within the framework of a direct action.[7] Thus Article 233 [176] provides that the institution whose act has been declared void shall be required to take the necessary measures to comply with the judgment of the Court of Justice. . . .

45. In this case it is necessary to apply by analogy the second paragraph of Article 231 [174] of the Treaty, whereby the Court of Justice may state which of the effects of the regulation which it has declared void shall be considered as definitive, for the same reasons of legal certainty as those which form the basis of that provision. On the one hand the invalidity of the regulation in this case might give rise to the recovery of sums paid but not owed by the undertakings concerned in countries with depreciated currencies and by the national authorities in question in countries with hard currencies which, in view of the lack of uniformity of the relevant national legislation, would be capable of causing considerable differences in treatment, thereby causing further distortion in competition. On the other hand, it is impossible to appraise the economic disadvantages resulting from the invalidity of the fixing of the monetary compensatory amounts under the system of calculation adopted by the Commission without making assessments which that institution alone is required to make under Regulation No 974/71, having regard to other relevant factors, for example the allocation of the maximum permissible amount amongst the various derived or dependent products.

46. For these reasons it must he held that the fact that the fixing of the monetary compensatory amounts which result from the system of calculating those compensatory amounts on products processed from maize contained in Regulation No 938/77 has been found invalid does not enable the charging or payment of monetary compensatory amounts by the national authorities on the basis of that regulation to be challenged as regards the period prior to the date of this judgment.

---

7 Editor's note: a direct action is one which is commenced in the European Court. See Chap. 5.

Comment

In this case, the European Court ignored the letter of the law in order to reach the solution it thought desirable. It did this in two ways. The first was that it took a treaty provision (Article 231 [174]) that applied to actions brought in the European Court, and applied it to references from a national court. Admittedly, these two kinds of proceedings have something in common. They are both a means of determining the validity of a Community act, but procedurally they are quite different. In any event, the Treaty is clear. Article 231 [174] applies only in the context of an annulment action. That is why the European Court said that it had to be applied "by analogy".

The second way in which the European Court ignored the letter of the law was that the French court had asked it to rule only on the validity of the regulation. The European Court went beyond this and also ruled on whether the French agency, ONIC, should repay the money which it had – wrongly, as it turned out – collected from Maïseries de Beauce.

After the European Court had given its judgment, the case returned to the Orleans Administrative Court. The latter accepted the ruling that Regulation 938/77 was invalid, but did not accept the ruling that ONIC should not refund the money. It said that it had not asked the European Court whether the money should be refunded. It therefore gave judgment for Maïseries de Beauce. ONIC appealed to the Council of State (*Conseil d'Etat*), the highest administrative court in France.

France
Maïseries de Beauce v. ONIC
COUNCIL OF STATE (CONSEIL D'ETAT)
Conseil d'Etat, 26 July 1985, [1985] *Recueil des Decisions du Conseil d'Etat* 233;
[1986] RTDE 158

Judgment[8]
By an order of 22 June 1979, the Orleans Administrative Court stayed the proceedings before it so that the European Court could give a ruling on the validity of the regulations under which ONIC had collected MCAs on the export of maize grits by Maïseries de Beauce. The European Court, by its judgment of 15 October 1980, ruled in response to the reference that the regulations imposing MCAs on maize exports were invalid. In ordering ONIC to refund the payments, the Orleans Administrative Court was doing no more than drawing the necessary consequences from the ruling of the European Court on the question referred to it.

If the European Court added an additional ruling to the answer to the question which had been submitted to it, namely a ruling that the invalidity of the regulations could not have any effect on payments made prior to the judgment of the European Court, this additional ruling, which did not come within the scope of the question asked by the Orleans Administrative Court, was not binding on the latter.

---

8 Translation by Trevor Hartley.

It follows from the above that, in the absence of a new regulation imposing MCAs for the period in question, the Orleans Administrative Court was quite correct in ordering ONIC to refund the money . . .

Final ruling: appeal dismissed.

Comment

As always, the judgment of the *Conseil d'Etat* was perfectly logical. It could, however, be objected that under the EC Treaty the European Court had the right to give definitive interpretations of Treaty provisions. Since Article 234 [177] is itself a Treaty provision, any ruling by the European Court as to what it means is binding on all Member-State courts. Thus if the European Court thinks that a request to rule on the validity of a regulation also gives it the right to rule on the consequences of invalidity, that ruling, it might be argued, is also an interpretation of Article 234 [177], and is therefore binding on national courts.

This argument raises what the Germans call the question of *Kompetenz-Kompetenz*. In German, *Kompetenz* means "jurisdiction".[9] In legal terminology, "jurisdiction" is the power to give a binding ruling. If a judicial authority has jurisdiction to decide a given question, its ruling on that question has to be accepted. No one can question it (unless an appeal lies to some higher authority). *Kompetenz-Kompetenz*, therefore, means jurisdiction to give a binding ruling on the extent of one's own jurisdiction.

Most decision-makers have limited jurisdiction. They can give a binding ruling only on particular questions. A ruling outside their jurisdiction is not binding. Individuals or courts do not have to accept it. An English lawyer would say that it was *ultra vires*. To give an illustration from the world of sport, a referee in a football match has jurisdiction to give rulings on whether a player has broken a rule of the game in the course of the match. All the players must accept his ruling even if it is wrong. However, if the referee were to rule on whether a player owed another player a sum of money as a result of a business transaction, the ruling would be outside his jurisdiction. It would not be binding.

The next question is who decides whether a decision on a particular question is within the jurisdiction of the decision-maker. Is this a matter which can be decided by the person to whom the decision was addressed? Or should it be decided by some other body, perhaps a court? Or should it be decided by the decision-maker himself? This depends (in the terminology we are using) on whether the decision-maker has *Kompetenz-Kompetenz*. If he has, he can first decide whether the question before him is within his jurisdiction. If he decides that it is, he can then proceed to decide it. Then, both the jurisdictional decision and the substantive decision will be binding on all concerned. No one can challenge the substantive decision on the ground that it is outside his

---

9 From the French, *compétence* (jurisdiction).

jurisdiction (*ultra vires*), since his decision that it is within his jurisdiction is itself binding. If, on the other hand, he not does have *Kompetenz-Kompetenz*, it will be open to an appropriate court to decide whether the substantive ruling was within his jurisdiction. If it was not, it will not be binding.

It follows from this that if the European Court has *Kompetenz-Kompetenz*, any ruling it gives on the extent of its own jurisdiction – for example, a ruling that a question on the validity of a regulation also entitles it to rule on the consequences of the invalidity of that regulation – is itself binding on national courts. As applied to the *Maïseries de Beauce* case, this would mean that the French courts could not refuse to follow the ruling that Maïseries de Beauce had no right to a refund. They could not argue that that ruling was outside the European Court's jurisdiction. If, on the other hand, the European Court does not have *Kompetenz-Kompetenz*, national courts can decide for themselves whether the European Court was acting outside its jurisdiction. If it was, the national court can refuse to follow the European Court's ruling.

Does the European Court have *Kompetenz-Kompetenz*? As we saw in Chapter 9, the highest courts of Denmark[10] and Germany[11] have expressly said that it does not. This is probably also the view of the *Conseil d'Etat*. If so, it would explain why it refused to follow the European Court's ruling.

If the highest court in a Member State refuses to request a ruling or if, having requested it, refuses to follow the ruling, there is little that the Community can do. In theory, it might be possible for the Commission to bring proceedings under Article 226 [169] EC (see Chapter 5). But this would raise serious issues. If the European Court ordered the French Government to make the *Conseil d'Etat* obey it, how would the French Government go about doing that? After all, the courts of a State are supposed to be independent. It is hardly surprising, therefore, that no such attempt has ever been made.

Which courts may make a reference?

The Treaty says that *any* court or tribunal of a Member State may make a reference. The European Court gives a wide interpretation to this provision and considers that any judicial body in a Member State may make a reference if it enjoys some measure of official recognition.[12] An arbitrator,[13] on the other hand, may not make a reference.[14] This makes sense. Not only is an arbitrator

---

10 *Carlsen v. Rasmussen* (Danish Maastricht case).
11 *Brunner v. European Union Treaty* (German Maastricht case).
12 For example, in *Broekmeulen*, Case 246/80, [1981] ECR 2311; [1982] 1 CMLR 91, the European Court held that an Appeals Committee established by the Royal Netherlands Society for the Promotion of Medicine could make a reference. The Society was a private body, but under Dutch legislation fees charged by doctors could not be reclaimed under State social security schemes unless the doctor was registered with the Society. The Appeals Committee (some of whose members were appointed by the government) decided appeals against a refusal of registration.
13 It is assumed that the arbitrator is acting under an arbitration clause in a contract between private parties. The position may be different if the government is involved.
14 *Nordsee v. Reederei Mond*, Case 102/81, [1982] ECR 1095. On the duty of national courts to review arbitral awards where questions of Community law are involved, see *Eco Swiss v. Benetton International*, Case C-126/97, [1999] ECR I-3055.

not a "court or tribunal of a Member State", but the whole purpose of arbitration is to get the dispute resolved as speedily as possible without going to court. A reference to the European Court, with its inevitable delays, would defeat this.

When may a court make a reference?

According to the Treaty, a court may make a reference when an issue of Community law arises which it has to decide in order to give judgment.[15] This of course assumes that there is a claim before it that it has jurisdiction to decide. This was the issue in our next case.

European Union
Borker
COURT OF JUSTICE OF THE EUROPEAN COMMUNITIES
Case 138/80, [1980] ECR 1975; [1980] 3 CMLR 638

Facts

Mr Borker was a member of the Paris Bar. He wanted to appear before a German court. He considered that Community law gave him the right to do so. The German court refused. Instead of bringing legal proceedings in Germany, he complained to the Paris Bar Council. The latter made a reference to the European Court, asking them to rule on the matter.

Judgment

4. It is apparent from [Article 234 [177]] that the Court[16] can only be requested to give a preliminary ruling . . . by a court or tribunal which is called upon to give judgment in proceedings intended to lead to a decision of a judicial nature. That is not the position in this case since the [Paris Bar Council] does not have before it a case which it is under a legal duty to try but a request for a declaration relating to a dispute between a member of the Bar and the courts or tribunals of another Member State.

5. It is therefore clear that the Court has no jurisdiction to give a ruling in connexion with the decision sent to it by the [Paris Bar Council].

6. In these circumstances there are grounds for the Court to . . . declare of its own motion that it has no jurisdiction.

---

15 In *Foglia v. Novello*, Case 104/79, [1980] ECR 745; [1981] 1 CMLR 45 and *Foglia v. Novello (No. 2)*, Case 244/80, [1981] ECR 3045; [1982] 1 CMLR 585 the European Court held that a reference cannot be made where there is no genuine dispute between the parties and the case was contrived simply in order to obtain a ruling. In that case, the parties had set up an elaborate transaction in order to get the Italian courts to rule on whether a French tax was consistent with Community law. The Italian court made a reference to the European Court, which the latter refused to accept. A second reference was also rejected. There is reason to believe, however, that the European Court was less concerned with the lack of a genuine dispute than with not offending France by permitting Italian courts to question the validity of a French tax. In two subsequent cases, *Vinal v. Orbat*, Case 46/80, [1981] ECR 77; [1981] 3 CMLR 524 and *Chemial v. DAF*, Case 140/79, [1981] ECR 1; [1981] 3 CMLR 350, in which the validity of an *Italian* tax was raised in the Italian courts by equally contrived transactions, the European Court happily accepted the reference.
16 Editor's note: the European Court uses a capital "C" for "Court" when referring to itself and a small "c" when referring to other courts.

Comment

Under French law, the Paris Bar Council may well have had jurisdiction to decide who could appear before the Paris courts. If it did, and if it had been hearing such a case, it would almost certainly have had the right to make a reference to the European Court.[17] But in this case, Mr Borker asked it to decide whether he had the right to appear before the *German* courts. Clearly, the Paris Bar Council had no jurisdiction to decide that. That is why the European Court refused to entertain the reference.

Which courts must make a reference?

The Treaty says that a court "from whose decisions there is no judicial remedy under national law" *must* make a reference. There is a controversy as to what this means. Does it refer to a court from the decision of which there is no appeal *in the case at hand* (concrete theory)? Or does it refer to a court from the decisions of which there is *never* any appeal (abstract theory)? The question arises because in some countries the right to appeal to the highest court is limited to what are regarded as important cases. If the case is not regarded as important, because the sum of money involved is small or the issue at stake is unlikely to arise again, an intermediate court of appeal may be as far as the case can go. In such cases, preventing the litigation from dragging out for too long is regarded as more important than exhausting every avenue of appeal.

In civil cases in England, for example, an appeal from the Court of Appeal to the House of Lords may not be made as of right. Either the Court of Appeal or the House of Lords must give permission to appeal. If the case turns on a point of Community law and the Court of Appeal refuses permission to appeal to the House of Lords, is it then *obliged* to make a reference to the European Court?

The argument in favour of the concrete theory is that if a case can run its course without any court being obliged to make a reference, the European Court will never have the opportunity to decide whether Community law is being correctly applied. The argument in favour of the abstract theory is that if the issue is not sufficiently important to warrant an appeal to the highest court in the land, there should be no obligation to send it to the European Court, with the additional delay that would inevitably result.

The text of the Treaty favours the abstract theory, since the word "decisions" is in the plural, but there is an early *dictum* by the European Court in favour of the concrete theory.[18] The leading case today is the *Lyckeskog* case.

European Union
Lyckeskog
COURT OF JUSTICE OF THE EUROPEAN COMMUNITIES
Case C-99/00, [2002] ECR I-4839; [2003] 1 WLR 9

17 Compare the *Broekmeulen* case, note 12 above.
18 *Costa v. ENEL*, Case 6/64, [1964] ECR 585 at 592.

Facts

This was a reference made by the Court of Appeal for Western Sweden (*Hovrätten för Västra Sverige*). In Sweden, appeals from a Court of Appeal lie to the Supreme Court (*Högsta Domstolen*), the highest court in the country. However, such appeals are not as of right. If an appeal is made, the Supreme Court must first decide whether the appeal is admissible. Under Swedish law, an appeal is always admissible when made by the public prosecutor in cases involving the exercise of public authority. When made by a private party, however, an appeal is admissible only if the point at issue is likely to be of importance for the application of the law in future cases, or if there are certain special grounds of appeal – for example, if the Court of Appeal's decision is clearly the result of error. If the appeal is not admissible, it will not be heard.

In its reference, the Court of Appeal for Western Sweden asked the European Court whether, in view of these rules, it should be regarded as a court "against whose decisions there is no judicial remedy under national law" in terms of Article 234 [177] EC.

Judgment

14. The obligation on national courts against whose decisions there is no judicial remedy to refer a question to the Court[19] for a preliminary ruling has its basis in the co-operation established, in order to ensure the proper application and uniform interpretation of Community law in all the Member States, between national courts, as courts responsible for applying Community law, and the Court. That obligation is in particular designed to prevent a body of national case-law that is not in accordance with the rules of Community law from coming into existence in any Member State [citations omitted].

15. That objective is secured when, subject to the limits accepted by the Court of Justice (*CILFIT*), supreme courts are bound by this obligation to refer [citation omitted] as is any other national court or tribunal against whose decisions there is no judicial remedy under national law [citation omitted].

16. Decisions of a national appellate court which can be challenged by the parties before a supreme court are not decisions of a "court or tribunal of a Member State against whose decisions there is no judicial remedy under national law" within the meaning of Article 234 [177] EC. The fact that examination of the merits of such appeals is subject to a prior declaration of admissibility by the supreme court does not have the effect of depriving the parties of a judicial remedy.

17. That is so under the Swedish system. The parties always have the right to appeal to the [Supreme Court] against the judgment of a [Court of Appeal], which cannot therefore be classified as a court delivering a decision against which there is no judicial remedy. Under [the relevant Swedish legislation], the [Supreme Court] may issue a declaration of admissibility if it is important for guidance as to the application of the law that the appeal be examined by that court. Thus, uncertainty as to the interpretation of the law applicable, including Community law, may give rise to review, at last instance, by the supreme court.

18. If a question arises as to the interpretation or validity of a rule of Community law, the supreme court will be under an obligation, pursuant to the third paragraph of Article 234

19 Editor's note: see note 16 above.

[177] EC, to refer a question to the Court of Justice for a preliminary ruling either at the stage of the examination of admissibility or at a later stage.

19. The answer to the first question must therefore be that, where the decisions of a national court or tribunal can be appealed to the supreme court under conditions such as those that apply to decisions of the referring court in the present case, that court or tribunal is not under the obligation referred to in the third paragraph of Article 234 [177] EC.

Comment

This case does not definitively decide between the abstract and concrete theories. However, if one reads between the lines, it seems that the court prefers the latter. The desirability that a body of case law contrary to Community law should not come into existence seems to take precedence over the desirability of deciding cases within a reasonable time – the rationale for rules limiting appeals.

The Swedish system is similar to that applicable in England when a party wishes to appeal from the Court of Appeal to the House of Lords, and the Court of Appeal has refused permission to appeal. The appellant must then apply to the House of Lords for permission to appeal. The effect of the *Lyckeskog* case seems to be that, in such circumstances, the Court of Appeal is not obliged to make a reference, but the House of Lords must do so, either when application is made for permission to appeal or, if permission is granted, when the appeal is heard.[20] This is subject to the exceptions laid down in the *CILFIT* case, to which we shall now turn.

When is a court obliged to make a reference?

Even if the court is the highest court in the land, it could be argued that it is still not obliged to make a reference if the point is clear. This is the *acte clair* theory (in French, *acte clair* means "clear provision"). In many ways this is an attractive theory. It has common sense on its side and it prevents the European Court from being flooded with more cases than it can decide. However, it is open to abuse. The following case shows how the European Court has tried to balance these considerations.

> *European Union*
> **CILFIT v. Ministry of Health**
> **COURT OF JUSTICE OF THE EUROPEAN COMMUNITIES**
> Case 283/81, [1982] ECR 3415; [1983] 1 CMLR 472.

Background

In this case, the Italian Supreme Court of Cassation (*Corte Suprema di Cassazione*), the highest civil court in Italy, used the procedure under Article 234 [177] to request a ruling on the interpretation of Article 234 [177] itself. The question

---

20 On the effect of a right to have questions referred to the Benelux Court from the supreme courts of the three Benelux States, see *Parfums Christian Dior v. Evora*, Case C-337/95, [1997] ECR I-6013.

was whether the third paragraph of Article 234 [177] requires a court from whose decisions there is no judicial remedy to make a reference even if there is no reasonable doubt as to the meaning of the provision in question.

Judgment

7. That obligation to refer a matter to the Court of Justice is based on co-operation, established with a view to ensuring the proper application and uniform interpretation of Community law in all the Member States, between national courts, in their capacity as courts responsible for the application of Community law, and the Court of Justice. More particularly, the third paragraph of Article 234 [177] seeks to prevent the occurrence within the Community of divergences in judicial decisions on questions of Community law. The scope of that obligation must therefore be assessed, in view of those objectives, by reference to the powers of the national courts, on the one hand, and those of the Court of Justice, on the other, where such a question of interpretation is raised within the meaning of Article 234 [177].

8. In this connection, it is necessary to define the meaning for the purposes of Community law of the expression "where any such question is raised" in order to determine the circumstances in which a national court or tribunal against whose decisions there is no judicial remedy under national law is obliged to bring a matter before the Court of Justice.

9. In this regard, it must in the first place be pointed out that Article 234 [177] does not constitute a means of redress available to the parties to a case pending before a national court or tribunal. Therefore the mere fact that a party contends that the dispute gives rise to a question concerning the interpretation of Community law does not mean that the court or tribunal concerned is compelled to consider that a question has been raised within the meaning of Article 234 [177]. On the other hand, a national court or tribunal may, in an appropriate case, refer a matter to the Court of Justice of its own motion.

10. Secondly, it follows from the relationship between the second and third paragraphs of Article 234 [177] that the courts or tribunals referred to in the third paragraph have the same discretion as any other national court or tribunal to ascertain whether a decision on a question of Community law is necessary to enable them to give judgment. Accordingly, those courts or tribunals are not obliged to refer to the Court of Justice a question concerning the interpretation of Community law raised before them if that question is not relevant, that is to say, if the answer to that question, regardless of what it may be, can in no way affect the outcome of the case.

11. If, however, those courts or tribunals consider that recourse to Community law is necessary to enable them to decide a case, Article 234 [177] imposes an obligation on them to refer to the Court of Justice any question of interpretation which may arise.

12. The question submitted by the Corte di Cassazione seeks to ascertain whether, in certain circumstances, the obligation laid down by the third paragraph of Article 234 [177] might none the less be subject to certain restrictions.

13. It must be remembered in this connection that in [Da Costa v Nederlandse Belastingadministratie, Cases 28–30/62, [1963] ECR 31] the Court ruled that: "Although the third paragraph of Article 234 [177] unreservedly requires courts or tribunals of a Member State against whose decisions there is no judicial remedy under national law . . . to refer to the Court every question of interpretation raised before them, the authority of an interpretation under Article 234 [177] already given by the Court may deprive the

obligation of its purpose and thus empty it of its substance. Such is the case especially when the question raised is materially identical with a question which has already been the subject of a preliminary ruling in a similar case."

14. The same effect, as regards the limits set to the obligation laid down by the third paragraph of Article 234 [177], may be produced where previous decisions of the Court have already dealt with the point of law in question, irrespective of the nature of the proceedings which led to those decisions, even though the questions at issue are not strictly identical.

15. However, it must not be forgotten that In all such circumstances national courts and tribunals, including those referred to in the third paragraph of Article 234 [177], remain entirely at liberty to bring a matter before the Court of Justice if they consider it appropriate to do so.

16. Finally, the correct application of Community law may be so obvious as to leave no scope for any reasonable doubt as to the manner in which the question raised is to be resolved. Before it comes to the conclusion that such is the case, the national court or tribunal must be convinced that the matter is equally obvious to the courts of the other Member States and to the Court of Justice. Only if those conditions are satisfied, may the national court or tribunal refrain from submitting the question to the Court of Justice and take upon itself the responsibility for resolving it.

17. However, the existence of such a possibility must be assessed on the basis of the characteristic features of Community law and the particular difficulties to which its interpretation gives rise.

18. To begin with, it must be borne in mind that Community legislation is drafted in several languages and that the different language versions are all equally authentic. An interpretation of a provision of Community law thus involves a comparison of the different language versions.

19. It must also be borne in mind, even where the different language versions are entirely in accord with one another, that Community law uses terminology which is peculiar to It. Furthermore, it must be emphasized that legal concepts do not necessarily have the same meaning in Community law and in the law of the various Member States.

20. Finally, every provision of Community law must be placed in its context and interpreted in the light of the provisions of Community law as a whole, regard being had to the objectives thereof and to its state of evolution at the date on which the provision in question is to be applied.

21. In the light of all those considerations, the answer to the question submitted by the Corte Suprema di Cassazione must be that the third paragraph of Article 234 [177] of the EEC Treaty is to be interpreted as meaning that a court or tribunal against whose decisions there is no judicial remedy under national law is required, where a question of Community law is raised before it, to comply with its obligation to bring the matter before the Court of Justice, unless it has established that the question raised is irrelevant or that the Community provision in question has already been interpreted by the Court or that the correct application of Community law is so obvious as to leave no scope for any reasonable doubt. The existence of such a possibility must be assessed in the light of the specific characteristics of Community law, the particular difficulties to which its interpretation gives rise and the risk of divergences in judicial decisions within the Community.

QUESTIONS

1. When may a final court of appeal refrain from making a reference?
2. It has been said that although the European Court purported to accept the *acte clair* doctrine in this case, it hedged it about with so many qualifications that it can never apply in practice.[21] Do you agree?

Interim measures

In view of the long time it takes the European Court to answer questions referred to it by Member-State courts, the question of interim measures assumes great importance. We shall consider two cases.

European Union
R v. Secretary of State for Transport, ex parte Factortame (No. 2)
COURT OF JUSTICE OF THE EUROPEAN COMMUNITIES
Case C-213/89, [1990] ECR I-2433; [1990] 3 WLR 818; [1990] 3 CMLR 1[22]

Facts

In order to conserve fish stocks, the Community adopted a system of quotas for different species of fish. These quotas were divided out among the various Member States. Some Spanish fishermen tried to increase the quantity of fish they could catch by registering companies in England and transferring their boats to those companies. They then claimed their boats were British and tried to obtain a share of the UK quota. The UK Government stopped this by passing legislation, the Merchant Shipping Act 1988, Part II, which said that boats could not fly the British flag unless there was a genuine link (defined in the Act) with the United Kingdom. The Spaniards challenged this legislation in the English courts on the ground that it was contrary to EC law. The Divisional Court referred the question to the European Court. However, the European Court can easily take two years to decide a case. The Spaniards did not want to wait this long before they could resume fishing. So they asked the English courts to issue an interim (temporary) injunction against the Crown forbidding it to enforce the Act until the European Court had given its ruling. Under English law this was not possible. Therefore a second reference was made, this time by the House of Lords, as to whether Community law required the granting of the injunction. This second reference was actually decided first by the European Court.

---

21 See Rasmussen, "The European Court's Acte Clair Strategy in CILFIT" (1984) 9 ELRev. 242.
22 See Noirfalisse, "The Community System of Fisheries Management and the Factortame Case" (1992) 12 YEL 325.

Judgment

17. [T]he preliminary question raised by the House of Lords seeks essentially to ascertain whether a national court which, in a case before it concerning Community law, considers that the sole obstacle which precludes it from granting interim relief is a rule of national law, must disapply that rule . . .

19. In accordance with the case-law of the Court, it is for the national courts, in application of the principle of co-operation laid down in Article 10 [5] of the EEC Treaty, to ensure the legal protection which persons derive from the direct effect of provisions of Community law [citations omitted].

20. The Court has also held that any provision of a national legal system and any legislative, administrative or judicial practice which might impair the effectiveness of Community law by withholding from the national court having jurisdiction to apply such law the power to do everything necessary at the moment of its application to set aside national legislative provisions which might prevent, even temporarily, Community rules from having full force and effect are incompatible with those requirements, which are the very essence of Community law ([*Simmenthal* case, set out in Chapter 9, above], paragraphs 22 and 23).

21. It must be added that the full effectiveness of Community law would be just as much impaired if a rule of national law could prevent a court seised of a dispute governed by Community law from granting interim relief in order to ensure the full effectiveness of the judgment to be given on the existence of the rights claimed under Community law. It follows that a court which in those circumstances would grant interim relief, if it were not for a rule of national law, is obliged to set aside that rule.

22. That interpretation is reinforced by the system established by Article 234 [177] of the EEC Treaty whose effectiveness would be impaired if a national court, having stayed proceedings pending the reply by the Court of Justice to the question referred to it for a preliminary ruling, were not able to grant interim relief until it delivered its judgment following the reply given by the Court of Justice.

23. Consequently, the reply to the question raised should be that Community law must be interpreted as meaning that a national court which, in a case before it concerning Community law, considers that the sole obstacle which precludes it from granting interim relief is a rule of national law must set aside that rule.

Comment

This judgment does not mean that national legislation must be temporarily suspended every time it is argued that it is contrary to Community law. What it means is that the normal rules for the granting of interim injunctions must be applied. When the case came back to the House of Lords, they gave the matter careful consideration and finally decided that the injunction should be granted.[23] They applied the normal English test, but not the rule that injunctions cannot be granted against the Crown. These rules are in fact similar to those that the European Court says must be applied where the question arises of suspending a national measure implementing a Community provision, when it is argued that the Community provision is invalid. This is the subject of our next case.

23 [1990] 3 WLR 856 (HL).

European Union
Zuckerfabrik Süderdithmarschen
COURT OF JUSTICE OF THE EUROPEAN COMMUNITIES
Cases C-143/88 and 92/89, [1991] ECR I-415

Background

In this case, a German sugar producer challenged the validity of a Community regulation imposing a special levy on sugar production. It also challenged a decision of the relevant national authority assessing the sum it had to pay. It asked the Hamburg Tax Court (*Finanzgericht Hamburg*) to make a reference to the European Court to determine the validity of the regulation. It also asked the German court to suspend the assessment decision while the reference was pending. The German court acceded to both requests. However, it also asked the European Court whether the second paragraph of Article 249 [189] EC, the provision which states that regulations have binding effect, precluded it from suspending the assessment decision. We shall consider only that part of the judgment dealing with this question.

Judgment

18. [R]equests for preliminary rulings which seek to ascertain the validity of a measure, like actions for annulment, constitute means for reviewing the legality of acts of the Community institutions. In the context of actions for annulment, Article 242 [185] of the EEC Treaty enables applicants to request suspension of the enforcement of the contested act and empowers the Court to order such suspension. The coherence of the system of interim legal protection therefore requires that national courts should also be able to order suspension of enforcement of a national administrative measure based on a Community regulation, the legality of which is contested.

19. Furthermore, in its judgment in [*Factortame*, above], delivered in a case concerning the compatibility of national legislation with Community law, the Court, referring to the effectiveness of Article 234 [177], took the view that the national court which had referred to it questions of interpretation for a preliminary ruling in order to enable it to decide that issue of compatibility, had to be able to grant interim relief and to suspend the application of the disputed national legislation until such time as it could deliver its judgment on the basis of the interpretation given in accordance with Article 234 [177].

20. The interim legal protection which Community law ensures for individuals before national courts must remain the same, irrespective of whether they contest the compatibility of national legal provisions with Community law or the validity of secondary Community law, in view of the fact that the dispute in both cases is based on Community law itself. . . .

Conditions for suspension . . .

23. It must first of all be noted that interim measures suspending enforcement of a contested measure may be adopted only if the factual and legal circumstances relied on by the applicants are such as to persuade the national court that serious doubts exist as to the validity of the Community regulation on which the contested administrative measure is based. Only the possibility of a finding of invalidity, a matter which is reserved to the Court,[24] can justify the granting of suspensory measures.

---

24 Editor's note: remember that "Court" with a capital "C" means the European Court.

24. It should next be pointed out that suspension of enforcement must retain the character of an interim measure. The national court to which the application for interim relief is made may therefore grant a suspension only until such time as the Court has delivered its ruling on the question of validity. Consequently, it is for the national court, should the question not yet have been referred to the Court of Justice, to refer that question itself, setting out the reasons for which it believes that the regulation must be held to be invalid.

25. As regards the other conditions concerning the suspension of enforcement of administrative measures, it must be observed that the rules of procedure of the courts are determined by national law and that those conditions differ according to the national law governing them, which may jeopardize the uniform application of Community law.

26. Such uniform application is a fundamental requirement of the Community legal order. It therefore follows that the suspension of enforcement of administrative measures based on a Community regulation, whilst it is governed by national procedural law, in particular as regards the making and examination of the application, must in all the Member States be subject, at the very least, to conditions which are uniform so far as the granting of such relief is concerned.

27. Since the power of national courts to grant such a suspension corresponds to the jurisdiction reserved to the Court of Justice by Article 242 [185] in the context of actions brought under Article 230 [173], those courts may grant such relief only on the conditions which must be satisfied for the Court of Justice to allow an application to it for interim measures.

28. In this regard, the Court has consistently held that measures suspending the operation of a contested act may be granted only in the event of urgency, in other words, if it is necessary for them to be adopted and to take effect before the decision on the substance of a case, in order to avoid serious and irreparable damage to the party seeking them.

29. With regard to the question of urgency, it should be pointed out that damage invoked by the applicant must be liable to materialize before the Court of Justice has been able to rule on the validity of the contested Community measure. With regard to the nature of the damage, purely financial damage cannot, as the Court has held on numerous occasions, be regarded in principle as irreparable. However, it is for the national court hearing the application for interim relief to examine the circumstances particular to the case before it. It must in this connection consider whether immediate enforcement of the measure which is the subject of the application for interim relief would be likely to result in irreversible damage to the applicant which could not be made good if the Community act were to be declared invalid.

30. It should also be added that a national court called upon to apply, within the limits of its jurisdiction, the provisions of Community law is under an obligation to ensure that full effect is given to Community law and, consequently, where there is doubt as to the validity of Community regulations, to take account of the interest of the Community, namely that such regulations should not be set aside without proper guarantees.

31. In order to comply with that obligation, a national court seised of an application for suspension must first examine whether the Community measure in question would be deprived of all effectiveness if not immediately implemented.

32. If suspension of enforcement is liable to involve a financial risk for the Community, the national court must also be in a position to require the applicant to provide adequate guarantees, such as the deposit of money or other security.

33. It follows from the foregoing that the reply to the second part of the first question put to the Court by the Finanzgericht Hamburg must be that suspension of enforcement of a national measure adopted in implementation of a Community regulation may be granted by a national court only:

(i) if that court entertains serious doubts as to the validity of the Community measure and, should the question of the validity of the contested measure not already have been brought before the Court, itself refers that question to the Court;

(ii) if there is urgency and a threat of serious and irreparable damage to the applicant;

(iii) and if the national court takes due account of the Community's interests.

Comment

This is another example of law-creation disguised as Treaty interpretation. The European Court was supposed to be interpreting Article 249 [189] EC.[25] Nowhere in that Article is there any mention of suspending national measures. It then resorted to Article 242 [185], a provision which, according to the Treaty, applies only to actions begun in the European Court (see Panel 11.2). The European Court considered that the "coherence of the system" required it to be applied to national courts as well.[26] The reason was that, by suspending the national measure giving effect to it, the German court was suspending the operation of the regulation in Germany. The European Court considered that, though this should be possible, it should be based on Community law rather than national law. That is not unreasonable. Nevertheless, in order to reach that position, the European Court had to cut right across the wording of the Treaty.

Government liability in tort

If a government takes action which turns out to have been unlawful, it is possible in most countries for individuals who were harmed by the action to sue the State for damages. In most countries, however, the conditions that must be fulfilled are so restrictive that such proceedings are rarely successful. This is justified on the ground that public authorities would be unduly fettered in their activities if they could be sued for acts done in good faith in the public interest.

As far as the Community is concerned, the second paragraph of Article 288 [215] EC provides for Community liability "in accordance with the general principles common to the laws of the Member States". Acting under this provision, the European Court has built up a body of rules (discussed in Chapter 19) on the liability of the Community for harm caused by action contrary to Community law. The most striking feature of these rules is that it is extremely difficult in practice for claimants to obtain damages against the Community. Indeed,

---

25 Set out in Panel 4.1, p. 45 above.
26 See para. 18 of the judgment.

Advocate-General Tesauro, speaking in 1995, said that only eight awards had ever been made.[27]

Prior to the *Francovich* case, the liability of Member States for violations of Community law was determined by national law. Consequently, the same rules applied where it was alleged that action by a national government was contrary to Community law as where it was alleged that it was contrary to national law. This seems reasonable in principle. From the Community point of view, it would be wrong if it was more difficult to obtain damages where Community law was violated, while, from the national point of view, it would be wrong if it was more difficult to obtain damages where national law was violated.

Originally, the European Court itself seems to have taken the view that the Treaty makes no provision for the liability of Member States. In the early 1970s, it was asked for its views on the changes in the Treaty that would be needed to create a European Union. One suggestion it made was that "in the event of a failure by a State to fulfil an obligation, persons adversely affected thereby [should be able to] obtain redress before their national courts".[28] This suggests that the Treaty should be amended to give a right of action for damages against Member States under Community law. The Member States did not act on this suggestion. So the European Court decided to take matters into its own hands.

> **Panel 11.2 Suspension of Community acts challenged in the European Court**
>
> **EC Treaty**
>
> **Article 242 [185]**
>
> Actions brought before the Court of Justice shall not have suspensory effect. The Court of Justice may, however, if it considers that circumstances so require, order that application of the contested act be suspended.

European Union
Francovich v. Italy
COURT OF JUSTICE OF THE EUROPEAN COMMUNITIES
Cases C-6 and 9/90, [1991] ECR I-5357; [1993] 2 CMLR 66

Background

A Community directive, Directive 80/987,[29] required Member States to set up "guarantee institutions" to ensure that when an employer goes bankrupt, the employees will be paid any wages owing to them. These institutions have to be independent of employers and not subject to claims by their creditors. Italy failed to implement the directive by the deadline. Proceedings were brought against Italy under Article 226 [169] EC, and judgment was obtained against it. Still no action was taken by Italy to implement the directive.

Mr Francovich was an Italian whose employer became bankrupt. He was unable to obtain the wages owing to him. Since no guarantee institutions had been established in Italy, he could not claim his wages from them. So he sued the Italian Government. He put forward two arguments. He first argued that the directive was directly effective so that he could claim from the government the rights which, under the directive, he could have claimed from the

---

27 *Brasserie du Pêcheur v. Germany*, Cases C-46/93 and C-48/93, [1996] ECR I-1029 at 1101, n. 65, of his Opinion.
28 *Bulletin of the European Communities*, Supplement 9/75, p. 18 (1975).
29 OJ 1980, L283, p. 23.

guarantee institution. This argument was rejected by the European Court. His second argument was that the Italian Government was liable in tort under Community law.

Judgment

(a) The existence of State liability as a matter of principle

33. The full effectiveness of Community rules would be impaired and the protection of the rights which they grant would be weakened if individuals were unable to obtain redress when their rights are infringed by a breach of Community law for which a Member State can be held responsible.

34. The possibility of obtaining redress from the Member State is particularly indispensable where, as in this case, the full effectiveness of Community rules is subject to prior action on the part of the State and where, consequently, in the absence of such action, individuals cannot enforce before the national courts the rights conferred upon them by Community law.

35. It follows that the principle whereby a State must be liable for loss and damage caused to individuals as a result of breaches of Community law for which the State can be held responsible is inherent in the system of the Treaty.

36. A further basis for the obligation of Member States to make good such loss and damage is to be found in Article 10 [5] of the Treaty, under which the Member States are required to take all appropriate measures, whether general or particular, to ensure fulfilment of their obligations under Community law. Among these is the obligation to nullify the unlawful consequences of a breach of Community law . . .

37. It follows from all the foregoing that it is a principle of Community law that the Member States are obliged to make good loss and damage caused to individuals by breaches of Community law for which they can be held responsible.

(b) The conditions for State liability

38. Although State liability is thus required by Community law, the conditions under which that liability gives rise to a right to reparation depend on the nature of the breach of Community law giving rise to the loss and damage.

39. Where, as in this case, a Member State fails to fulfil its obligation under the third paragraph of Article 249 [189] of the Treaty to take all the measures necessary to achieve the result prescribed by a directive, the full effectiveness of that rule of Community law requires that there should be a right to reparation provided that three conditions are fulfilled.

40. The first of those conditions is that the result prescribed by the directive should entail the grant of rights to individuals. The second condition is that it should be possible to identify the content of those rights on the basis of the provisions of the directive. Finally, the third condition is the existence of a causal link between the breach of the State's obligation and the loss and damage suffered by the injured parties.

41. Those conditions are sufficient to give rise to a right on the part of individuals to obtain reparation, a right founded directly on Community law.

42. Subject to that reservation, it is on the basis of the rules of national law on liability that the State must make reparation for the consequences of the loss and damage caused. In

the absence of Community legislation, it is for the internal legal order of each Member State to designate the competent courts and lay down the detailed procedural rules for legal proceedings intended fully to safeguard the rights which individuals derive from Community law [citations omitted].

43. Further, the substantive and procedural conditions for reparation of loss and damage laid down by the national law of the Member States must not be less favourable than those relating to similar domestic claims and must not be so framed as to make it virtually impossible or excessively difficult to obtain reparation [citations omitted].

44. In this case, the breach of Community law by a Member State by virtue of its failure to transpose Directive 80/987 within the prescribed period has been confirmed by a judgment of the Court. The result required by that directive entails the grant to employees of a right to a guarantee of payment of their unpaid wage claims. As is clear from the examination of the first part of the first question, the content of that right can be identified on the basis of the provisions of the directive.

45. Consequently, the national court must, in accordance with the national rules on liability, uphold the right of employees to obtain reparation of loss and damage caused to them as a result of failure to transpose the directive.

46. The answer to be given to the national court must therefore be that a Member State is required to make good loss and damage caused to individuals by failure to transpose Directive 80/987.

Comment

The method of reasoning employed by the European Court repays careful analysis. It starts with the general proposition that Community law would be more effective if individuals could claim damages from national governments that infringed their rights by a breach of Community law (paragraph 33 of the judgment). This is hard to dispute. It then says that the possibility of claiming damages is especially important where the Community provision is not directly effective. Again, few would disagree. From these two propositions as to what the law ought to be, it then derives a proposition as to what it is. The statement that "It follows that the principle whereby a State must be liable . . . is inherent in the system of the Treaty" (paragraph 35) is breathtaking in the violence it does to legal logic. It totally ignores the distinction between what the law ought to be and what it is, a distinction basic to the Western understanding of law. It also totally ignores the basic issue in the case, which was whether liability should be based on national law or Community law. Moreover, the statement that the principle is inherent in the "system of the Treaty" is a tacit admission that it is not to be found in any particular provision of the Treaty.

In paragraph 36, the Court comes up with Article 10 [5] EC, which it refers to as "a further basis" for its ruling. Article 10 [5] states:

> Member States shall take all appropriate measures, whether general or particular, to ensure fulfilment of the obligations arising out of this Treaty or resulting from action taken by the institutions of the Community. They shall facilitate the achievement of the Community's tasks.

They shall abstain from any measure which could jeopardize the attainment of the objectives of this Treaty.

At most, this vague provision might require Member States to enact legislation to provide for liability. By no stretch of the imagination can it be regarded as directly creating liability. Since the authors of the Treaty made express provision for the liability of the Community, they would hardly have failed to make express provision for the liability of the Member States if they had intended it to be regulated by Community law.

European Union
Brasserie du Pêcheur v. Germany; R v. Secretary of State for Transport, ex parte Factortame (No. 4)
COURT OF JUSTICE OF THE EUROPEAN COMMUNITIES
Cases C-46 and 48/93, [1996] ECR I-1029; [1996] 2 WLR 506

Background

Once it had created this new cause of action, the European Court had to fill in the details. It had already begun to do this in *Francovich*. In that case, it made clear that the new tort was based on an amalgam of Community law and national law. The basic principle of liability is a matter for Community law. The procedural details are to be decided by national law.[30] Since *Francovich* concerned a failure to transpose a directive, the judgment in that case concentrates on this issue. To obtain compensation for loss caused by the failure of a Member State to transpose a directive, the claimant must establish three things:

1. The directive must require the granting of rights to individuals.[31]
2. It must be possible to identify the content of those rights from the terms of the directive.
3. The breach of the obligation to transpose the directive within the time limit must have caused the damage suffered by the claimant.

This was enough to decide that the Italian Government was liable. In later cases, however, the court had to develop the law further.

In *Brasserie du Pêcheur v. Germany*, a French beer company was suing the German Government because it had excluded its beer from the German market under German legislation prohibiting additives. *R v. Secretary of State for Transport, ex parte Factortame* was discussed above. After the Spaniards had won the right to continue fishing, they demanded compensation for the profits they had lost during the period when their boats were idle. These two cases were heard together. The result was a wide-ranging judgment that sought to lay down the basic rules for the new cause of action. We shall content ourselves with a summary.

---

30 Para. 42 in *Francovich*.
31 "Individual" must have the same meaning here as in the rules on the direct effect of directives. In other words, an "individual" can be a company or anyone other than a public authority.

Basic points

The court expressly rejected certain limitations on liability.

- Liability does not arise only when the Community provision is not directly effective (paragraphs 22–23 of the judgment).
- There does not have to be a prior ruling on the point in an enforcement action under Article 226 [169] EC (paragraph 95 of the judgment).
- Liability is not excluded when the violation of Community law was committed by the national legislature (paragraph 36 of the judgment).

What law determines liability?

As the European Court made clear in *Francovich*,[32] the two general conditions for the application of national law concerning remedies (the rule of non-discrimination and the rule of effectiveness)[33] continue to apply. The new principle is superimposed. Under this principle, Member States are liable in tort for harm resulting from a violation of Community law whenever the conditions are such that, if the harm had been caused by the Community, the latter would have been liable under Article 288 [215] (second paragraph) EC.[34] If these conditions are fulfilled, the Member State will be liable. However, this does not preclude the imposition of liability in other circumstances on the basis of national law if the latter lays down less strict requirements (paragraph 66 of the judgment). This means that Community law gets the best of both worlds. If a Member State violates Community law, it can be sued if it is liable under Community tort law, and it can be sued if it is liable under national tort law.

Once the question of liability has been decided, other aspects of the proceedings are governed by national law, subject always to the rules of non-discrimination and effectiveness (paragraph 67 of the judgment). The court expressly held that the rule of effectiveness would preclude "any condition that may be imposed by English law on State liability requiring proof of misfeasance in public office, such an abuse of power being inconceivable in the case of the legislature" (paragraph 73 of the judgment).

Conditions for liability

Since the rules on the liability of the Community now apply also to the Member States, we must consider briefly what these are.[35] Under the court's previous case law on the subject, special rules apply where the Community is exercising legislative powers in a field in which it has a wide discretion. These special rules are encapsulated in what is sometimes known as the "*Schöppenstedt* formula" (so-called because it was first enunciated in *Zuckerfabrik Schöppenstedt v. Council*).[36] There are three requirements.

---

32 Para. 43 of the judgment.
33 See the discussion at the beginning of this chapter.
34 This states that the Community must, in accordance with the general principles common to the laws of the Member States, make good any damage caused by its institutions (or by its servants in the performance of their duties).
35 They are discussed more fully in Chap. 19.
36 Case 5/71, [1971] ECR 975. It has been slightly modified since. The version in the text is the up-to-date one.

1.   The rule of Community law infringed must be one intended to confer rights on individuals.

2.   The breach must be sufficiently serious.

3.   There must be a causal link between the breach and the damage.

Before this formula becomes applicable, however, it must be established that the Member State was acting in a field in which it enjoyed a wide margin of discretion. The European Court has not laid down any general rule as to when this would be the case. However, the margin of discretion would be reduced, "sometimes to a considerable degree", when a Member State is implementing a directive (paragraph 46 of the judgment).

Where a wide discretion exists, the *Schöppenstedt* formula will apply. As regards the first requirement, it is not necessary for the rule to be directly effective. This was made clear in *Francovich*. The third requirement, which is basic to any system of tort liability, is to be determined by the national courts (paragraph 65 of the judgment). The second requirement is the most problematic. In 1978, in *HNL v. Council and Commission*,[37] the European Court held that for this to be satisfied it must be shown that the violation was "manifest" and "grave". Where the *Schöppenstedt* formula is applicable, therefore, the Member State must have "manifestly and gravely disregarded the limits on its discretion" (paragraph 55 of the judgment). In determining whether this is the case, there are a number of factors which the national court may take into consideration (paragraph 56 of the judgment):

1.   the clarity and precision of the rule breached;

2.   the measure of discretion left by that rule to the national or Community authorities;

3.   whether the infringement and the damage were intentional;

4.   whether any error of law was excusable;

5.   whether the position taken by a Community institution contributed towards the omission; and

6.   whether national measures or practices contrary to Community law were adopted or retained.[38]

Factors 1 and 4 are linked. If the Community rule is unclear, the breach is likely to be excusable.

There are three situations, however, in which the violation will be regarded as sufficiently serious irrespective of these factors (paragraph 57 of the judgment). These are:

1.   where the breach of Community law is persisted in despite a judgment (presumably under Article 226 [169]) by the European Court finding it to be established;

2.   where the European Court has given a preliminary ruling from which it is clear that the conduct in question constitutes an infringement of Community law; and

---

37 Cases 83 and 94/76 and 4, 15 and 40/77, [1978] ECR 1209. Set out in Chap. 19.
38 It is not clear exactly what the European Court meant by this.

3.   where it is clear from the settled case law of the European Court that this is so.

A fourth situation would appear to be where a Member State does not "immediately" give effect to interim measures ordered by the court (or its President) (paragraph 64 of the judgment).

Although the principles of liability under the *Schöppenstedt* formula depend on Community law, the finding of facts in national proceedings and the characterisation of those facts as establishing a sufficiently serious violation are within the sole jurisdiction of the national courts (paragraph 58 of the judgment). However, after saying that it could not "substitute its assessment for that of the national courts", the European Court in *Factortame* nevertheless implied that the UK Government was liable (paragraphs 61–64 of the judgment).

Fault

The requirement of a sufficiently serious violation takes the place of any idea of fault. National courts are not permitted to add any such requirement to those laid down by Community law (paragraph 79 of the judgment).

Damages

Subject to the rules of non-discrimination and effectiveness, the assessment of damages is a matter for national law. Damages must, however, be commensurate with the loss sustained (paragraph 82 of the judgment). The national court may consider whether the plaintiff took all reasonable steps to mitigate his loss and, in particular, whether he availed himself in time of all legal remedies open to him (paragraph 84 of the judgment). Loss of profit cannot be excluded in principle as a head of damage (paragraph 87 of the judgment). Exemplary damages may be awarded if they would have been awarded under the principles normally applicable in national law (paragraph 89 of the judgment).

Comment

This judgment was supposed to put the Member States in the same position as the Community. However, though the same principles apply, they seem to be interpreted very differently. It was said above that it is rare for the Community to be held liable. Where a Member State is the defendant, on the other hand, liability seems to be the norm. In five of the first six cases to come before it, the European Court's judgment suggested that the Member State was liable.[39]

---

[39] Since the cases all began in the national courts, the final outcome depended on those courts. The five cases in which the European Court gave rulings that seemed to imply liability were: *Francovich v. Italy*, Cases C-6 and 9/90, [1991] ECR I-5357; *Brasserie du Pêcheur v. Germany*; *R v. Secretary for Transport, ex parte Factortame*, Joined Cases C-46 and 48/93, [1996] ECR I-1029; [1996] 2 WLR 506; *R v. Ministry of Agriculture, Fisheries and Food, ex parte Hedley Lomas*, Case C-5/94, [1996] ECR I-2553; [1996] 3 WLR 787; and *Dillenkofer v. Germany*, Cases C-178, 179 and 188–190/94, [1996] ECR 4845. In *Brasserie du Pêcheur v. Germany*, the *Bundesgerichtshof* (German Supreme Court) decided in the end that Germany was not liable: BGH, EuZW 1996, 761. The case in which the European Court indicated that there should be no liability was *R v. HM Treasury, ex parte British Telecommunications*, Case C-392/93, [1996] ECR I-1631; [1996] 3 WLR 203.

The European Court created this remedy because Member States often fail to comply with Community law. However, since the remedy is administered by the national courts, its effectiveness depends on the willingness of those courts to apply it in good faith. There is no reason to believe that courts that generally fail to respect Community law will be any more willing to do so in the context of tort actions. It is significant that most of the cases to have reached the European Court so far have come from the UK, Germany, Austria, Denmark or Sweden – countries with fairly good records for compliance. The countries with the worst records – the Mediterranean countries – have sent almost no cases. The *Francovich* case came from Italy. Four years after that case was decided, however, Mr Francovich was back in the European Court.[40] Italy had passed a law which was supposed to solve the problem, but it was drafted in such a way that Mr Francovich got nothing.

Further reading

Anderson (David) and Demetriou (Marie), *References to the European Court* (Sweet and Maxwell, London, 2nd ed., 2002).

Anderson, "The Admissibility of Preliminary References" (1994) 14 YEL 179.

Arnull, "The Evolution of the Court's Jurisdiction under Article 177 EEC" (1993) 18 ELRev. 129.

Barnard and Sharpston, "The Changing Face of Article 177 References" (1997) 34 CMLRev. 1113.

Collins (Lawrence), *European Community Law in the United Kingdom* (Butterworths, London, 5th ed., 1999), Chapter 3.

O'Keeffe, "Is the Spirit of Article 177 under Attack? Preliminary References and Admissibility" (1998) 23 ELRev. 509.

Strasser, "Evolution and Effort: Docket Control and Preliminary References in the European Court of Justice" (1995–1996) 2 Columbia JEL 49.

Tridimas, "Enforcing Community Rights in National Courts: Some Recent Developments", in David O'Keeffe and Antonio Bavasso (eds.), *Judicial Review in European Union Law: Liber Amicorum Gordon Slynn* (Kluwer Law International, The Hague and Boston, 2000), p. 465.

Tridimas, "Liability for Breach of Community Law: Growing Up and Mellowing Down?" (2001) 38 CMLRev. 301.

---

40 *Francovich v. Italy*, Case C-479/93, [1995] ECR I-3843.

PART IV
THE COMMUNITY AND THE
WORLD SYSTEM

12

The conclusion of treaties

In this Part of the book, we consider the Community as an actor on the world stage. We start with its power to enter into treaties.

Since the general rule is that the Community has only such powers as are conferred on it (Article 5 [3b] EC), the power to enter into treaties must come from some provision in one of the Community Treaties. As usual, we shall focus on the EC Treaty, but we shall also look at the Euratom Treaty, since it provides an interesting contrast.

Legal personality

If an entity has legal personality, it is recognized by the law as a person. It can have rights and obligations. It can enter into agreements, incur liability and perform other acts that result in a change in its legal position. If it has international legal personality, it is recognized by international law as a person. International legal personality is therefore an essential precondition for concluding a treaty.

The EC and Euratom are separate entities for international purposes. Each has expressly been given legal personality by the treaty which created it.[1] There is no treaty provision expressly giving legal personality to the European Union, which, as we have seen, consists of the two Communities plus certain "policies and forms of co-operation".[2] Nevertheless, in 2001 it concluded an international agreement with the Federal Republic of Yugoslavia.[3] It did this under Article 24 [J.14] TEU (set out in Panel 12.2, below), a provision which lays down the procedure for the conclusion of agreements in connection with the common foreign and security policy (CFSP). The CFSP is one of the "policies and forms of co-operation" covered by the EU but not by either of the Communities. Article 24 [J.14] does not expressly confer legal personality on the Union, but the Council and the Member States must have thought that it did so by implication.

---

1 For the EC, see Art. 281 [210] EC. For Euratom, see Art. 184 Euratom.
2 Art. 1 [A] TEU.
3 Council Decision 2001/352/CFSP of 9 April 2001, OJ 2001, L125, p. 1.

Panel 12.1 Treaty-making procedure under the EC Treaty

Article 300 [228] EC

1. Where this Treaty provides for the conclusion of agreements between the Community and one or more States or international organizations, the Commission shall make recommendations to the Council, which shall authorize the Commission to open the necessary negotiations. The Commission shall conduct these negotiations in consultation with special committees appointed by the Council to assist it in this task and within the framework of such directives as the Council may issue to it.

In exercising the powers conferred upon it by this paragraph, the Council shall act by a qualified majority, except in the cases where the first subparagraph of paragraph 2 provides that the Council shall act unanimously.

2. Subject to the powers vested in the Commission in this field, the signing, which may be accompanied by a decision on provisional application before entry into force, and the conclusion of the agreements shall be decided on by the Council, acting by a qualified majority on a proposal from the Commission. The Council shall act unanimously when the agreement covers a field for which unanimity is required for the adoption of internal rules and for the agreements referred to in Article 310 [238].

By way of derogation from the rules laid down in paragraph 3, the same procedures shall apply for a decision to suspend the application of an agreement, and for the purpose of establishing the positions to be adopted on behalf of the Community in a body set up by an agreement, when that body is called upon to adopt decisions having legal effects, with the exception of decisions supplementing or amending the institutional framework of the agreement.

The European Parliament shall be immediately and fully informed of any decision under this paragraph concerning the provisional application or the suspension of agreements, or the establishment of the Community position in a body set up by an agreement.

3. The Council shall conclude agreements after consulting the European Parliament, except for the agreements referred to in Article 133(3) [113(3)], including cases where the agreement covers a field for which the procedure referred to in Article 251 [189b] or that referred to in Article 252 [189c] is required for the adoption of internal rules. The European Parliament shall deliver its opinion within a time-limit which the Council may lay down according to the urgency of the matter. In the absence of an opinion within that time-limit, the Council may act.

By way of derogation from the previous subparagraph, agreements referred to in Article 310 [238], other agreements establishing a specific institutional framework by organising co-operation procedures, agreements having important budgetary implications for the Community and agreements entailing amendment of an act adopted under the procedure referred to in Article 251 [189b] shall be concluded after the assent of the European Parliament has been obtained.

The Council and the European Parliament may, in an urgent situation, agree upon a time-limit for the assent.

4. When concluding an agreement, the Council may, by way of derogation from paragraph 2, authorize the Commission to approve modifications on behalf of the Community where the agreement provides for them to be adopted by a simplified procedure or by a body set up by the agreement; it may attach specific conditions to such authorization.

5. When the Council envisages concluding an agreement which calls for amendments to this Treaty, the amendments must first be adopted in accordance with the procedure laid down in Article 48 [N] of the Treaty on European Union.

6. The European Parliament, the Council, the Commission or a Member State may obtain the opinion of the Court of Justice as to whether an agreement envisaged is compatible with the provisions of this Treaty. Where the opinion of the Court of Justice is adverse, the agreement may enter into force only in accordance with Article 48 [N] of the Treaty on European Union.

7. Agreements concluded under the conditions set out in this Article shall be binding on the institutions of the Community and on Member States.

Although legal personality is necessary for the conclusion of international agreements, it is not enough. The power to make treaties must also exist. A number of provisions in the EC Treaty expressly give such a power. For example, Article 133 [113] gives the EC power to conclude tariff and trade agreements. A noteworthy feature of the EC Treaty, however, is that the external (treaty-making) powers of the EC are considerably narrower than its internal (legislative and executive) powers. There are many topics on which the EC is expressly empowered to adopt legislation, but with regard to which no treaty-making power is given. This disparity between internal and external competence is something we shall investigate below.

Panel 12.2   Treaty making procedure under the Treaty on European Union

Article 24 [J.14] TEU

1. When it is necessary to conclude an agreement with one or more States or international organizations in implementation of this Title, the Council may authorize the Presidency, assisted by the Commission as appropriate, to open negotiations to that effect. Such agreements shall be concluded by the Council on a recommendation from the Presidency.

2. The Council shall act unanimously when the agreement covers an issue for which unanimity is required for the adoption of internal decisions.

3. When the agreement is envisaged in order to implement a joint action or common position, the Council shall act by a qualified majority in accordance with Article 23(2) [J.13(2)].

4. The provisions of this Article shall also apply to matters falling under Title VI. When the agreement covers an issue for which a qualified majority is required for the adoption of internal decisions or measures, the Council shall act by a qualified majority in accordance with Article 34(3) [K.6(3)].

5. No agreement shall be binding on a Member State whose representative in the Council states that it has to comply with the requirements of its own constitutional procedure; the other members of the Council may agree that the agreement shall nevertheless apply provisionally.

6. Agreements concluded under the conditions set out by this Article shall be binding on the institutions of the Union.

Procedure

Article 300 [228] EC (set out in Panel 12.1) lays down the procedure to be followed when the European Community enters into treaties. The decision to commence negotiations is taken by the Council on a proposal from the Commission. If the Council decides to go ahead, the Commission will conduct the negotiations. However, the Council lays down the negotiating mandate, which instructs the Commission on what it must try to achieve. The Council may also appoint a committee to keep an eye on the Commission.

If the negotiations are successful, the Council takes the decision to sign the agreement and to conclude it.[4] The Parliament must be consulted (except for agreements under Article 133 [113] EC). In certain cases, the Parliament must give its assent.

These rules apply only when the European Community (EC) is concluding the treaty. There are separate rules in Article 101 Euratom, which apply where Euratom is the contracting party. We shall consider them below. As we saw above, Article 24 [J.14] TEU contains special rules on the conclusion of treaties to carry out the Common Foreign and Security Policy (Title V TEU) and the provisions on Police and Judicial Co-operation in Criminal Matters (Title VI TEU). These rules are set out in Panel 12.2. Under them the negotiations are conducted by the Member State holding the Presidency of the Community

---

4 The first paragraph of Art. 300(2) [228(2)] EC refers to "signing" and "conclusion" as if they were two separate things. However, Anthony Aust, *Modern Treaty Law and Practice* (Cambridge University Press, Cambridge, 2000), p. 74, says that the meaning of "conclusion" is unclear. For most purposes, a bilateral treaty (a treaty between two States only) is concluded when it is signed. A multilateral treaty is usually regarded as concluded when the Final Act is signed or when the treaty is opened for signature. He rejects the suggestion that "conclusion" means "entry into force". In international law, a treaty may become binding either on signature or on ratification, depending on the intention of the parties as expressed in the treaty or otherwise (see Arts. 11–18 of the 1969 Vienna Convention on the Law of Treaties). It is not clear what the authors of the EC Treaty meant by "conclusion". It may mean ratification. What is clear, however, is that the Community cannot become bound by an international agreement unless the Council so decides.

at the time in question. The Commission assists "as appropriate". The role of the Council remains the same. Article 24 [J.14] TEU does not state explicitly that the agreement will be concluded by the European Union, but, as we saw above, it appears to be thought that this was implicit.

Legal proceedings

Article 300(6) [228(6)] EC lays down a procedure under which the European Court can give a ruling on whether a proposed agreement is compatible with the EC Treaty. Prior to the Treaty of Nice, only the Council, the Commission or a Member State could bring such proceedings. Under the Treaty of Nice, the European Parliament may also bring them. The procedure is unusual in that the hearings are held in private. All the advocates-general give opinions, but none is published. (This is probably because it was felt that it would be embarrassing if it was seen that the advocates-general had given conflicting opinions.) The court's judgment *is* published. If the court decides that the proposed agreement is incompatible with the EC Treaty, the agreement cannot enter into force unless the EC Treaty is first amended. In practice, it will usually be the agreement that is amended. If this is not possible, it will be abandoned.

Although Article 300 [228] seems to have been intended to provide a check on the Community's treaty-making powers, the European Court has allowed it to be used for a quite different purpose – to prevent the Member States from becoming joint parties to the proposed agreement.[5] Treaties to which both the Community and the Member States are parties, usually called "mixed agreements", are common. This way of proceeding is adopted when the proposed agreement falls partly within the jurisdiction of the Community and partly within that of the Member States. Sometimes, the Commission and the Member States cannot agree which of them has the power to conclude the agreement. The Commission may then allow the Member States to participate as joint signatories, but subsequently challenge their participation before the European Court.

Judgments by the European Court under Article 300 [228] EC are referred to as "opinions". Such cases are separately numbered, for example, as "Opinion 1/78", not "Case 1/78". They are, however, just as binding.

Binding the Community and the Member States

Article 300(7) [228(7)] EC expressly says that agreements concluded under its provisions are binding on the institutions of the Community and on the Member States.[6]

---

5 See, for example, the *International Agreement on Natural Rubber* case, Opinion 1/78, [1979] ECR 2871; [1979] 3 CMLR 639.
6 Note the somewhat different formulation in Art. 24(5) and (6) [J.14] TEU, as amended by the Treaty of Nice (Panel 12.2).

Treaty-making powers

Many international organizations have the power to enter into treaties and this power is frequently used. There is nothing unusual in the fact that the Community has it. What is unusual is the breadth and scope of the Community's power. It is the only international organization that has significant jurisdictional conflicts with its Member States in this respect. There is little to be gained, therefore, by comparing the Community's treaty-making powers with those of other international organizations. Instead, we shall draw comparisons with the position in federal States.

The most interesting question is the relationship between the division of power between the centre and the units on the internal (domestic) level and on the external (international) level. In the Community, competence (jurisdiction) is divided between the centre (the Community) and the units (the Member States). On the internal (non-international) level, there is the power to pass legislation (legislative jurisdiction) and the power to take administrative action (executive jurisdiction). On some matters, the Community has jurisdiction, which may be shared with the Member States or exclusive, and on other matters jurisdiction remains with the Member States. On the external level, there is the power to enter into treaties and to take other steps. This too is divided between the Community and the Member States. On some matters, the Community has exclusive or non-exclusive jurisdiction. On other matters, the Member States have it. However, the way in which the EC Treaty divides competence is not the same on the two levels. As was said above, the Treaty gives the Community much wider powers on the internal level than on the international level. Thus there are some matters with regard to which the Treaty gives competence to the Community internally and to the Member States internationally. Does it matter if the Community's external jurisdiction is narrower than its internal jurisdiction?

In most federations, things are the other way round. The federal government normally has full treaty-making power on all matters. If the units have any power at all in this regard, it is extremely limited. Internally, on the other hand, significant areas fall within the jurisdiction of the units. Thus in most cases the external jurisdiction of the federal authorities is considerably wider than their internal jurisdiction. In order to see whether this causes any problems, we shall consider two examples, the United States and Canada.

The United States

Article II of the US Constitution gives the treaty-making power to the President.[7] Article 1, Section 10, prohibits the states from entering into treaties. It goes on to provide, however, that the states may not, *without the consent of Congress,*

---

7 It must be exercised by and with the advice and consent of the Senate. The role of the Senate was considered in Chap. 8.

enter into any "agreement or compact" with a foreign power. This means that states are absolutely prohibited from concluding "treaties" with foreign countries, but they are permitted to enter into "agreements" or "compacts" if they have the consent of Congress. The difference between "treaties", on the one hand, and "agreements" or "compacts", on the other hand, has never been satisfactorily explained.[8]

Whether the protection of the interests of the states results in any restrictions on the treaty-making power of the federal government is uncertain.[9] What is clear, however, is that federal treaty-making power is considerably wider than (internal) federal legislative power. The President (and the Senate) can do things by treaty that Congress cannot, in the absence of a treaty, do by legislation. Our next case is an example.

> *United States*
> **Missouri v. Holland**
> **SUPREME COURT OF THE UNITED STATES**
> 252 US 416 (1920)

Background

In 1913, Congress passed a statute to protect migrating birds. It was struck down by two federal courts of first instance on the ground that this was a matter for the states. It was feared that the Supreme Court would take the same view. So the United States instead entered into a treaty with the United Kingdom (acting on behalf of Canada) to protect migrating birds in Canada and the US. Congress then enacted a statute, the Migratory Bird Treaty Act 1918, that was similar to the one previously declared unconstitutional.

Mr Holland was a federal game warden, whose job it was to enforce the Act. The state of Missouri brought proceedings against him to prevent him from enforcing it. Missouri claimed that it was unconstitutional. The Supreme Court thus had to decide whether legislation which Congress could not pass without a treaty could be passed if it was necessary to give effect to a treaty.

Judgment
Mr Justice Holmes delivered the opinion of the court. . . .
To answer this question it is not enough to refer to the Tenth Amendment, reserving the powers not delegated to the United States,[10] because by Article 2, Section 2, the power to make treaties is delegated expressly, and by Article 6 treaties made under the authority of the United States, along with the Constitution and laws of the United States made in pursuance thereof, are declared the supreme law of the land. If the treaty is valid there can be no dispute about the validity of the statute under Article 1, Section 8, as a necessary and proper means to execute the powers of the Government.[11] The language of the

---

8 For discussion and examples, see Louis Henkin, *Foreign Affairs and the US Constitution* (Oxford University Press, Oxford, 2nd ed., 1996), pp. 151–156.
9 Henkin, *ibid.*, p. 193, thinks there may be some restrictions.
10 Editor's note: the Tenth Amendment says: "All powers not delegated to the United States by the Constitution, nor prohibited by it to the States, are reserved to the States respectively, or to the people."
11 Editor's note: Art. 1, Section 8 (set out in Panel 12.3), gives Congress the power to make all laws which are "necessary and proper for carrying into execution" the powers given to the government of the United States by the Constitution. The power to make treaties is of course one such power.

Constitution as to the supremacy of treaties being general, the question before us is narrowed to an inquiry into the ground upon which the present supposed exception is placed.

It is said that a treaty cannot be valid if it infringes the Constitution, that there are limits, therefore, to the treaty-making power, and that one such limit is that what an act of Congress could not do unaided, in derogation of the powers reserved to the States, a treaty cannot do. An earlier act of Congress that attempted by itself and not in pursuance of a treaty to regulate the killing of migratory birds within the States had been held bad in the District Court [citation omitted]. Those decisions were supported by arguments that migratory birds were owned by the States in their sovereign capacity for the benefit of their people, and that [citation omitted] this control was one that Congress had no power to displace. The same argument is supposed to apply now with equal force.

Whether the two cases cited were decided rightly or not they cannot be accepted as a test of the treaty power. Acts of Congress are the supreme law of the land only when made in pursuance of the Constitution, while treaties are declared to be so when made under the authority of the United States. It is open to question whether the authority of the United States means more than the formal acts prescribed to make the convention. We do not mean to imply that there are no qualifications to the treaty-making power; but they must be ascertained in a different way. It is obvious that there may be matters of the sharpest exigency for the national well being that an act of Congress could not deal with but that a treaty followed by such an act could . . .

Here a national interest of very nearly the first magnitude is involved. It can be protected only by national action in concert with that of another power. The subject matter is only transitorily within the State and has no permanent habitat therein. But for the treaty and the statute there soon might be no birds for any powers to deal with. We see nothing in the Constitution that compels the Government to sit by while a food supply is cut off and the protectors of our forests and our crops are destroyed. It is not sufficient to rely upon the States. The reliance is vain, and were it otherwise, the question is whether the United States is forbidden to act. We are of opinion that the treaty and statute must be upheld.

Comment

This case establishes that if the federal government has power to conclude a treaty, the federal legislature (Congress) is entitled to enact legislation needed to carry it out, even if the subject matter would otherwise fall within the jurisdiction of the states. The Supreme Court regarded this as resulting from Article 1, Section 8, of the Constitution (see Panel 12.3). To a certain extent, such an outcome was inevitable in view of the fact that, as we saw in Chapter 8, treaties can have direct effect in the United States. If they are self-executing, they apply as the law of the land and override inconsistent state law. The question of implementing legislation only arises when the treaty is not self-executing. It would be anomalous if a self-executing treaty could apply automatically just because the federal government had concluded it, but the federal legislature could not pass a statute to give effect to a treaty that was not self-executing. The Supreme Court could of course have said that the federal government had no power to conclude a treaty in an area within the jurisdiction of the states, but this would have created a serious gap in its treaty-making powers, a gap that does not exist in the case of other federations.

Panel 12.3 Powers of Congress under the United States Constitution

Article 1 Section 8

[1] The Congress shall have power to lay and collect taxes, duties, imposts and excises, to pay the debts and provide for the common defence and general welfare of the United States . . .

. . .

[18] To make all laws which shall be necessary and proper for carrying into execution the foregoing powers, and all other powers vested by this Constitution in the Government of the United States, or in any Department or officer thereof.

Note: Paragraphs 2–17 (omitted) list a number of specific matters with regard to which Congress has legislative competence. Paragraph 18 may be regarded as a kind of residuary provision.

Canada

In Canada, the position is different. This is partly because its Constitution was adopted before it became an independent State, and partly because treaties can never have direct effect in Canada. The leading case is a decision of the Privy Council on appeal from the Supreme Court of Canada.

> **Commonwealth**
> **Attorney General for Canada v. Attorney General for Ontario** (Labour Conventions case)
> **PRIVY COUNCIL**
> [1937] AC 326

Background

Canada had concluded a number of conventions under the auspices of the International Labour Organization (ILO). In 1934 and 1935, the federal legislature, the Parliament of Canada, adopted legislation to give effect to them. The relevant statutes were the Weekly Rest in Industrial Undertakings Act, the Minimum Wages Act and the Limitation of Hours of Work Act. In the absence of a treaty, the Canadian Parliament could not have passed these statutes, since their subject matter fell within the jurisdiction of the provinces. Did the fact that they were necessary to give effect to a treaty make any difference?

In considering this question, it is necessary to say something about the constitutional position of Canada. At the time of the case, the Constitution of Canada was contained in a UK statute, the British North America Act 1867. This statute created Canada from a number of provinces and territories, the most important being Lower Canada (now called Quebec) and Upper Canada (now called Ontario). Canada is a federation. Legislative jurisdiction is divided between the centre (the Parliament of Canada) and the units (the provincial Parliaments). The main provisions on the division of power are sections 91 and 92 of the British North America Act. Section 92 lists a number of specific topics which fall within provincial jurisdiction, one of which is "property and civil rights in the province",[12] an area of jurisdiction which covered the

---

12 The phrase "civil rights" does not here refer to civil liberties in the modern sense, but to the matters usually covered by private law – for example, contract and torts. This is why legislation dealing with

subject-matter of the ILO conventions. Section 91 lists a number of specific topics which fall within the jurisdiction of the Parliament of Canada. It also states that all matters not specifically assigned to the provinces fall within the jurisdiction of the Parliament of Canada. As we saw above, the opposite rule applies in the United States. Under the Tenth Amendment, powers not given to the United States by the Constitution (or prohibited to the states) are reserved to the states (or the people).

When the British North America Act was adopted, Canada was not an independent country. It had no power to enter into treaties. The UK Government could, however, enter into treaties on its behalf. We saw an example of this in our previous case. There, the United Kingdom had acted on behalf of Canada in concluding the treaty with the United States on migrating birds. In such cases, the British North America Act expressly gave jurisdiction to the Parliament of Canada to enact the legislation necessary to give effect to the treaty. The relevant provision was section 132, which gave the Parliament of Canada the power to adopt legislation "necessary or proper for performing the obligations of Canada, or of any Province thereof, as part of the British Empire, towards foreign countries, arising under treaties between the Empire and such foreign countries". Under this provision, which is analogous to Article 1, Section 8, of the US Constitution, the Parliament of Canada could enact legislation that it could not enact in the absence of a treaty.

Section 132 applied only to treaties between the British Empire and foreign countries. When the British North America Act was adopted, these were the only treaties that could apply to Canada. Subsequently, Canada gained independence and international legal personality, an event usually regarded as dating from the Statute of Westminster 1931. However, no change was made in the British North America Act to allow the Parliament of Canada to enact legislation to give effect to international agreements concluded by Canada on its own behalf.

The ILO was created by the Treaty of Versailles. This was the Treaty of Peace, signed in 1919, between the Allied Powers and Germany. It formally put an end to World War I. Since, at that time, Canada had no treaty-making power of its own, Canada was not a party in its own right. Canada was represented at the Peace Conference, but it was the King of England, acting on behalf of the British Empire, who actually concluded the treaty. This treaty was therefore covered by section 132 of the British North America Act.

However, though it set up the ILO, the Treaty of Versailles did not create any legal obligation on ILO members to ratify conventions. Consequently, Canada's decision in 1935 to ratify the ILO conventions was not required by the Treaty of Versailles. It was an exercise of Canada's newly acquired power to enter into treaties on its own behalf. Consequently, legislation needed to give effect to the conventions could not be adopted under section 132 of the British North America Act.

employment contracts fell within the area of civil rights. The provision was included in s. 92 because Quebec has a distinctive system of civil law based on the French tradition.

Judgment
Lord Atkin [after pointing out that section 132 was inapplicable, continued:]

For the purposes of sections 91 and 92, i.e., the distribution of legislative powers between the Dominion and the Provinces, there is no such thing as treaty legislation as such. The distribution is based on classes of subjects; and as a treaty deals with a particular class of subjects so will the legislative power of performing it be ascertained. No one can doubt that this distribution is one of the most essential conditions, probably the most essential condition, in the inter-provincial compact to which the British North America Act gives effect. If the position of Lower Canada, now Quebec, alone were considered, the existence of her separate jurisprudence as to both property and civil rights might be said to depend upon loyal adherence to her constitutional right to the exclusive competence of her own Legislature in these matters. Nor is it of less importance for the other Provinces, though their law may be based on English jurisprudence, to preserve their own right to legislate for themselves in respect of local conditions which may vary by as great a distance as separates the Atlantic from the Pacific. It would be remarkable that while the Dominion could not initiate legislation, however desirable, which affected civil rights in the Provinces, yet its Government not responsible to the Provinces nor controlled by Provincial Parliaments need only agree with a foreign country to enact such legislation, and its Parliament would be forthwith clothed with authority to affect Provincial rights to the full extent of such agreement. Such a result would appear to undermine the constitutional safeguards of Provincial constitutional autonomy.

It follows from what has been said that no further legislative competence is obtained by the Dominion from its accession to international status, and the consequent increase in the scope of its executive functions. It is true, as pointed out in the judgment of the Chief Justice, that as the executive is now clothed with the powers of making treaties so the Parliament of Canada, to which the executive is responsible, has imposed upon it responsibilities in connection with such treaties, for if it were to disapprove of them they would either not be made or the Ministers would meet their constitutional fate. But this is true of all executive functions in their relation to Parliament. There is no existing constitutional ground for stretching the competence of the Dominion Parliament so that it becomes enlarged to keep pace with enlarged functions of the Dominion executive. If the new functions affect the classes of subjects enumerated in section 92 legislation to support the new functions is in the competence of the Provincial Legislatures only. If they do not, the competence of the Dominion Legislature is declared by section 91 and existed *ab origine*. In other words, the Dominion cannot, merely by making promises to foreign countries, clothe itself with legislative authority inconsistent with the constitution which gave it birth . . .

It must not be thought that the result of this decision is that Canada is incompetent to legislate in performance of treaty obligations. In totality of legislative powers, Dominion and Provincial together, she is fully equipped. But the legislative powers remain distributed, and if in the exercise of her new functions derived from her new international status Canada incurs obligations they must, so far as legislation be concerned, when they deal with Provincial classes of subjects, be dealt with by the totality of powers, in other words by co-operation between the Dominion and the Provinces. While the ship of state now sails on larger ventures and into foreign waters she still retains the watertight compartments which are an essential part of her original structure. The Supreme Court was equally divided and therefore the formal judgment could only state the opinions of the three judges on either side. Their Lordships are of opinion that the answer to the three questions should be that the Act in each case is *ultra vires* of the Parliament of Canada, and they will humbly advise His Majesty accordingly.

Comment

In this decision, the Privy Council came to the opposite conclusion from that of the US Supreme Court. If the Parliament of Canada has no power to adopt legislation without a treaty, it cannot adopt it with a treaty. The only exception is section 132, but this has become inoperative since Canada gained independence. The Privy Council could have adapted section 132 to take account of the change in Canada's status, but it declined to do so. Lord Atkin said: "No further legislative competence is obtained by the Dominion [Canada] from its accession to international status." The Privy Council thought it was more important to protect the rights of the provinces than to protect the treaty-making power of Canada.

The rule laid down in this case still applies today. The Government of Canada has full treaty-making powers, but the Parliament of Canada cannot adopt the legislation necessary to give effect to the treaty unless it could have adopted such legislation in the absence of a treaty.[13] This means that if Canada wants to conclude a treaty on a subject with regard to which internal jurisdiction belongs to the provinces, it has to insist on a special clause in the proposed treaty allowing it to ratify the treaty province by province.[14] It then has to ask the provinces to pass the necessary legislation, and will ratify the treaty only with regard to those provinces that do so. To make provincial acceptance more likely, provincial representatives are often included in the Canadian delegation.[15] The result is a little awkward, but other countries understand. Canada is not the only State that asks for such a clause. Other counties request it too, even if it is not constitutionally necessary for them.

QUESTIONS

1. Which approach do you think is correct – that of the US Supreme Court or that of the Privy Council?
2. Was Lord Atkin right to say that an approach such as that adopted by the US Supreme Court would "undermine the constitutional safeguards of Provincial constitutional autonomy"?
3. Was he right to say that there was no ground for "stretching the competence of the Dominion Parliament so that it becomes enlarged to keep pace with enlarged functions of the Dominion executive"?

The European Community

We have seen that in most federations the treaty-making power of the federal government is wider than its internal legislative jurisdiction. In the United

---

13 It must be remembered that in Canada a treaty can never have direct effect.
14 Sometimes called a "federal clause". This terminology is misleading since other federations – for example, the United States and Australia – do not require it.
15 Even countries that do not have Canada's constitutional structure may do this when the subject matter of the negotiations falls within the internal jurisdiction of a separate governmental unit – for example, China (Hong Kong), Australia and the United Kingdom (Scotland).

States, federal legislative jurisdiction automatically increases to enable the federal legislature to adopt legislation needed to give effect to a treaty. In Canada, this is not the case. The European Community is in a different position. The treaty-making power of the Community under the EC Treaty is *narrower* than its internal legislative power. There are some matters with regard to which the treaty gives internal legislative power to the Community but with regard to which the Member States enjoy external competence.

If effect had been given to this, the Community would, in some ways, have been in a similar position to Canada. The Member States would have negotiated the agreement, but the Community would have adopted the implementing legislation. Of course, in the case of the Community there would have been fifteen (or more) negotiators and one legislature, while in the case of Canada there are ten provincial legislatures but only one negotiator. However, the example of Canada proves that this would have been feasible, though cumbersome. The Member States could have agreed to act in concert, with the State holding the Presidency acting as spokesman, as happens today under Article 24 [J.14] TEU (see Panel 12.2, above).

In fact, this did not happen. The reason is that the European Court took it upon itself radically to change the EC Treaty through judicial "interpretation". What it did was to enlarge the treaty-making power of the EC to coincide (to a large extent) with its internal legislative power, a development sometimes referred to as "parallelism". Our next case shows how it did this.

European Union
Commission v. Council (European Road Transport Agreement (ERTA/AETR) case)
Case 22/70, [1971] ECR 263; [1971] CMLR 335

Background

The case concerned an international agreement called the European Road Transport Agreement (ERTA or, in French, AETR), an agreement with certain non-Community countries in Europe on the social aspects of road transport. Negotiations, conducted by the Member States, began in 1967.[16] In 1969, the Council adopted a regulation, Regulation 543/69,[17] which covered much the same ground, but applied only within the Community. In 1970, the Council decided that the parties to the final agreement would be the Member States. The Commission objected to this, and brought legal proceedings under Article 230 [173] EC to annul the decision.[18]

Road transport is covered in the EC Treaty by a series of provisions of which the most important are Articles 70 [74] and 71 [75]. They are set out

---

16 They were actually a continuation of earlier negotiations. These resulted in an agreement, signed in 1962, that never came into force.
17 OJ 1969, L77, p. 49.
18 This gave rise to major jurisdictional problems, since the legal nature of the Council's decision was in dispute. The European Court ruled that it was not a decision in terms of Art. 249 [189], but that it nevertheless fell within the scope of Art. 230 [173], a ruling dictated mainly by policy. If Art. 230 [173] had not been broadened to cover so-called acts *sui generis*, the court would not have been able to rule on the EC's treaty-making power. If it had held that the Council's decision was a "decision" in terms of Art. 249 [189], it would have been obliged to annul it for lack of reasons, something that would have been politically unacceptable.

Panel 12.4 Transport (EC Treaty at the time of the *ERTA* case)

Article 70 [74]

The objectives of this Treaty shall, in matters governed by this Title, be pursued by Member States within the framework of a common transport policy.

Article 71 [75]

1. For the purpose of implementing Article 70 [74], and taking into account the distinctive features of transport, the Council shall, acting unanimously until the end of the second stage and by a qualified majority thereafter, lay down, on a proposal from the Commission and after consulting the Economic and Social Committee and the Assembly:

(a) common rules applicable to international transport to or from the territory of a Member State or passing across the territory of one or more Member States;

(b) the conditions under which non-resident carriers may operate transport services within a Member State;

(c) any other appropriate provisions.

2. The provisions referred to in (a) and (b) of paragraph 1 shall be laid down during the transitional period.

3. . . .

---

in Panel 12.4, in the form in which they existed at the time of the case. It will be seen that, though the Member States were obliged to adopt a common policy, there was no provision conferring on the Community the power to conclude international agreements.

Judgment

6. The Commission takes the view that Article 71 [75] of the Treaty, which conferred on the Community powers defined in wide terms with a view to implementing the common transport policy, must apply to external relations just as much as to domestic measures in the sphere envisaged.

7. It believes that the full effect of this provision would be jeopardized if the powers which it confers, particularly that of laying down "any appropriate provisions", within the meaning of subparagraph (1)(c) of the Article cited, did not extend to the conclusion of agreements with third countries.

8. Even if, it is argued, this power did not originally embrace the whole sphere of transport, it would tend to become general and exclusive as and where the common policy in this field came to be implemented.

9. The Council, on the other hand, contends that since the Community only has such powers as have been conferred on it, authority to enter into agreements with third countries cannot be assumed in the absence of an express provision in the Treaty.

10. More particularly, Article 71 [75] relates only to measures internal to the Community, and cannot be interpreted as authorizing the conclusion of international agreements.

11. Even if it were otherwise, such authority could not be general and exclusive, but at the most concurrent with that of the Member States.

12. In the absence of specific provisions of the Treaty relating to the negotiation and conclusion of international agreements in the sphere of transport policy – a category into which, essentially, the AETR falls – one must turn to the general system of Community law in the sphere of relations with third countries.

13. Article 281 [210] provides that "The Community shall have legal personality."

14. This provision, placed at the head of Part Six of the Treaty, devoted to "General and Final Provisions", means that in its external relations the Community enjoys the capacity to establish contractual links with third countries over the whole field of objectives defined in Part One of the Treaty, which Part Six supplements.[19]

15. To determine in a particular case the Community's authority to enter into international agreements, regard must be had to the whole scheme of the Treaty no less than to its substantive provisions.

16. Such authority arises not only from an express conferment by the Treaty – as is the case with Articles 133 [113] and [114] for tariff and trade agreements and with Article 310 [238] for association agreements – but may equally flow from other provisions of the Treaty and from measures adopted, within the framework of those provisions, by the Community institutions.

17. In particular, each time the Community, with a view to implementing a common policy envisaged by the Treaty, adopts provisions laying down common rules, whatever form these may take, the Member States no longer have the right, acting individually or even collectively, to undertake obligations with third countries which affect those rules.

18. As and when such common rules come into being, the Community alone is in a position to assume and carry out contractual obligations towards third countries affecting the whole sphere of application of the Community legal system.

19. With regard to the implementation of the provisions of the Treaty the system of internal Community measures may not therefore be separated from that of external relations.

20. Under Article 3(f) [3(e)], the adoption of a common policy in the sphere of transport is specially mentioned amongst the objectives of the Community.

21. Under Article 10 [5], the Member States are required on the one hand to take all appropriate measures to ensure fulfilment of the obligations arising out of the Treaty or resulting from action taken by the institutions and, on the other hand, to abstain from any measure which might jeopardize the attainment of the objectives of the Treaty.

22. If these two provisions are read in conjunction, it follows that to the extent to which Community rules are promulgated for the attainment of the objectives of the Treaty, the Member States cannot, outside the framework of the Community institutions, assume obligations which might affect those rules or alter their scope.

[The court then applied these principles to the facts of the case, and held that the Community gained exclusive treaty-making power on 25 March 1969, the date on which Regulation 543/69 (the regulation which dealt with the same matter internally) came into force. One might have thought that this would have meant that the agreement was invalid. However, to avoid this, the court held that since negotiations had been started before the Community gained exclusive competence, the Commission and the Member States should have reached agreement on the smooth transition of representation. Since this did not occur, the agreement was valid.]

19 Editor's note: in this judgment the court distinguishes between capacity to conclude treaties (para. 14) and authority to do so (para. 15). What is meant by these two terms is unclear, but "capacity" may refer to the question whether the treaty is valid under international law and "authority" to the question whether the Community acted contrary to Community law by concluding it.

Comment

In this judgment, the court tries to establish that internal competence and external competence are necessarily linked. In paragraph 18, it says that the Community alone is in a position to carry out the obligations under the agreement, and, in paragraph 22, it says that the Member States cannot assume international obligations that might affect internal Community law. However, this ignores Canadian experience, which shows that such a split is feasible. The Member States could enter into the agreement, provided ratification was made conditional upon the Community's adopting the necessary measures. Since the main element in the Community legislature is the Council, this would not have raised serious problems.

It is possible to demonstrate that not only does this decision run counter to the words of the Treaty, but it is also contrary to the intention of its framers. This can be done by comparing the EC Treaty with the Euratom Treaty. While Article 300 [228] EC starts off with the words, "Where this Treaty provides for the conclusion of agreements between the Community and one or more States or international organizations . . .", thus making clear that it applies only where other provisions of the Treaty grant treaty-making powers to the Community, the equivalent provision in the Euratom Treaty, Article 101, begins:

> The Community may, within the limits of its powers and jurisdiction, enter into obligations by concluding agreements or contracts with a third State, an international organization or a national of a third State.[20]

This establishes that Euratom's treaty-making power extends over the full area of its internal jurisdiction. What the European Court did in the *ERTA* case was to put the European Community in the same position. However, as we shall see in *France v. Commission* (below), the EC and Euratom Treaties were negotiated in parallel and concluded together. In many Articles, the words are identical. Consequently, if the framers of the two Treaties had intended the European Community to have the same wide powers as Euratom, they would have said so.[21] The different wording in Article 300 [228] was intentional. The EC was not meant to have such powers.

The final outcome of the case (upholding the agreement despite the general tenor of the judgment) is an instructive example of the court's policy of not actually applying a new rule in the case in which it was originally developed. Once adopted, however, it is applied in future cases.

The *ERTA* case appears to lay down the rule that a new treaty-making power, which is exclusive, arises whenever internal measures are adopted. This power applies to the extent that international agreements entered into by the Member States might affect the operation of those measures. Later cases,[22] however, show that an external power may flow from an internal power even in the

---

[20] For the full text, see Panel 12.5, below.
[21] See *France v. Commission* (below), at para. 39 of the judgment.
[22] This principle is actually foreshadowed in the *ERTA* case itself in paras. 23–27 of the judgment (not reproduced above).

absence of measures under it. This is sometimes called the "complementarity" principle.[23] It arises where the objective of the internal power cannot be fully attained without its being complemented by an external power.

The first decision on the "complementarity" principle was the *Kramer* case,[24] which concerned a convention to restrict fishing in the North-East Atlantic. The EC had internal competence, but it had never been exercised. It had no express treaty-making power. The parties to the convention were seven of the Member States and several non-member States. It was argued that the convention was invalid because the Community was not a party. The European Court rejected this. It held that the Community had the power to enter into such an agreement, but this power was concurrent with that of the Member States. Until such time as the Community exercised its competence in the area, either by adopting internal measures or by concluding a convention, the Member States retained the power to enter into such agreements.

In the *Kramer* case there was some suggestion that the special problems of fisheries agreements made it an exception. In our next case, however, it is clear that the court is laying down a general rule.

> *European Union*
> **Laying-Up Fund for Inland Waterway Vessels**
> **COURT OF JUSTICE OF THE EUROPEAN COMMUNITIES**
> Opinion 1/76, [1977] ECR 741[25]

Background

This case concerned transport on inland waterways. On the continent, there are extensive waterways on which goods are carried by barge. At the time in question, there was an oversupply of carriers on the Rhine-Moselle system, and rates had fallen to uneconomic levels. Instead of leaving the matter to the market, the Community authorities decided that the solution was to establish a special authority, the Laying-Up Fund, which would pay barge-owners to take their boats out of the water, thus reducing the supply of boats. It was thought this would lead to an increase in rates. The scheme was to be financed by a levy on all vessels. Since Switzerland was part of the waterway system, it was essential that Swiss barge-owners should be covered. So it was decided that the Fund would be established as an international organization with a structure not dissimilar to that of the Community itself. There was thus an organ analogous to the Council and another analogous to the Commission. There was also a court. All this was done by means of an international agreement to which the parties were the European Community, six of its Member States and Switzerland. The six Member States were all parties to earlier agreements on the same subject and their participation was necessary in order to ensure that

---

23 See Dashwood, in Alan Dashwood and Christophe Hillion (eds.), *The General Law of EC External Relations* (Sweet and Maxwell, London, 2000), pp. 127 *et seq*. See also pp. 9 *et seq*.
24 Cases 3–4 and 6/76, [1976] ECR 1279; [1976] 2 CMLR 440 (North-East Atlantic Fisheries Convention).
25 For a comment, see Hartley, (1977) 2 ELRev. 275.

the new agreement prevailed.[26] Inland waterways are covered by the provisions of the EC Treaty on transport, but at the time there had been no Community legislation on the matter.

The Commission brought proceedings before the European Court under Article 300 [228] EC for an opinion as to whether the agreement was compatible with the EC Treaty.

Judgment

3. The power of the Community to conclude such an agreement is not expressly laid down in the Treaty. However, the Court has already had occasion to state, most recently in [the *Kramer* case], that authority to enter into international commitments may not only arise from an express attribution by the Treaty, but equally may flow implicitly from its provisions. The Court has concluded *inter alia* that whenever Community law has created for the institutions of the Community powers within its internal system for the purpose of attaining a specific objective, the Community has authority to enter into the international commitments necessary for the attainment of that objective even in the absence of an express provision in that connexion.

4. This is particularly so in all cases in which internal power has already been used in order to adopt measures which come within the attainment of common policies. It is, however, not limited to that eventuality. Although the internal Community measures are only adopted when the international agreement is concluded and made enforceable, as is envisaged in the present case by the proposal for a regulation to be submitted to the Council by the Commission, the power to bind the Community *vis-à-vis* third countries nevertheless flows by implication from the provisions of the Treaty creating the internal power and in so far as the participation of the Community in the international agreement is, as here, necessary for the attainment of one of the objectives of the Community.

5. In order to attain the common transport policy, the contents of which are defined in Articles 70 [74] and 71 [75] of the Treaty, the Council is empowered to lay down "any other appropriate provisions", as expressly provided in Article 71(1)(c) [75(1)(c)]. The Community is therefore not only entitled to enter into contractual relations with a third country in this connexion but also has the power, while observing the provisions of the Treaty, to co-operate with that country in setting up an appropriate organism such as the public international institution which it is proposed to establish under the name of the "European Laying-up Fund for Inland Waterway Vessels". The Community may also, in this connexion, co-operate with a third country for the purpose of giving the organs of such an institution appropriate powers of decision and for the purpose of defining, in a manner appropriate to the objectives pursued, the nature, elaboration, implementation and effects of the provisions to be adopted within such a framework.

Comment

This case firmly establishes the "complementarity" principle. It also establishes that the Community can become a member of another international organization. In the end, however, the court struck the agreement down. This was not because the Community had no power to enter into such an agreement,

---

26 Under Art. 30(3) of the 1969 Vienna Convention on the Law of Treaties, if there is a conflict between two treaties and all the parties to the earlier treaty are also parties to the later one, the latter will prevail.

but because the court did not like the structure of the proposed organization. In particular, it did not approve of the fact that the Fund's court would have been composed largely of judges from the European Court.[27] As our next case shows, the European Court has no objection in principle to the Community's participation in other international organizations.

European Union
WTO case
COURT OF JUSTICE OF THE EUROPEAN COMMUNITIES
Opinion 1/94, [1994] ECR I-5267

The original GATT was concluded prior to the EC Treaty. All the EC Member States were parties to it. The Community was not a party to it and never became one. However, the European Court has held, as we shall see in the next chapter, that the GATT became binding on the Community. The position was different under the WTO Agreement, which created a new GATT. The Community was a formal party to the Agreement. The Member States were also parties. In the *WTO* case the Commission brought proceedings under Article 300 [228] EC in an attempt to have the court declare that the participation of the Member States was contrary to Community law.

The European Court rejected this claim. It accepted that the new GATT fell within the scope of Article 133 [113] EC, and was thus within exclusive Community jurisdiction, but held that the participation of the Member States was justified by reason of the fact that they enjoyed joint competence with regard to certain other agreements annexed to the WTO Agreement, namely, GATS (General Agreement on Trade in Services) and TRIPS (Trade-Related Aspects of Intellectual Property Rights).

Summary

At this point it is appropriate to summarize the rules resulting from these (and other) cases as to the treaty-making power of the European Community (EC) outside the areas covered by express provisions in the EC Treaty.

- Where the Community has adopted common rules in a given area,[28] it has the exclusive power to enter into international agreements that might affect those rules or alter their scope. The Member States are precluded from entering into such agreements (paragraphs 17 and 22 of *ERTA*).
- In later cases, the court has said that in an area "already largely covered by such rules" the Member States may not enter into international agreements even if there is no contradiction between such agreements and the common rules.[29]

---

27 The court thought that intolerable conflicts would arise if the same issue came before both it and the Fund court.
28 This might be by internal legislation – for example, a regulation – or even by means of an international agreement with one or more non-member States.
29 *ILO* case, Opinion 2/91, [1993] ECR I-1061 (paragraphs 25 and 26 of the judgment); *Commission v. Denmark*, Case C-467/98, 5 November 2002 (paragraphs 81 and 82 of the judgment).

Panel 12.5 Treaties concluded by Euratom

Euratom Treaty

Article 101

The Community may, within the limits of its powers and jurisdiction, enter into obligations by concluding agreements or contracts with a third State, an international organization or a national of a third State.

Such agreements or contracts shall be negotiated by the Commission in accordance with the directives of the Council; they shall be concluded by the Commission with the approval of the Council, which shall act by a qualified majority.

Agreements or contracts whose implementation does not require action by the Council and can be effected within the limits of the relevant budget shall, however, be negotiated and concluded solely by the Commission; the Commission shall keep the Council informed.

- Even in the absence of common measures, there is a treaty-making power where the objective of an internal power cannot be fully attained unless it is complemented by an external power (*Laying-Up Fund* case, paragraph 3). In the *Kramer* and *Laying-Up Fund* cases, it was non-exclusive, but it may be exclusive in some situations.

These rules apply only as regards the European Community. There are different rules for Euratom and the EU.

The Commission goes too far

The last case in this chapter constitutes an attempt by the Commission to take the European Court's case law one step further. It was pointed out above that what the court did in the *ERTA* case was to expand the treaty-making powers of the European Community so that it enjoyed something approaching the extensive competence of Euratom. However, the Euratom Treaty has another feature that distinguishes it from the EC Treaty. Under the EC Treaty, it will be remembered, the agreement is negotiated by the Commission, but concluded by the Council. Under the Euratom Treaty, in contrast, the agreement is both negotiated *and* concluded by the Commission. The Commission normally has to obtain the consent of the Council, but this does not apply where it can put the treaty into effect without the assistance of the Council. See Panel 12.5.

European Union
France v. Commission (Competition (Antitrust) Agreement case)
COURT OF JUSTICE OF THE EUROPEAN COMMUNITIES
Case C-327/91, [1994] ECR I-3641

Background

Under the EC Treaty, competition (antitrust) is a matter of Community competence. Legislation has to be adopted by the Council, but enforcement is a matter for the Commission. In the United States, the federal government also has enforcement jurisdiction in certain circumstances. The case concerned an agreement concluded between the Commission (on behalf of the Community) and the US Government (on behalf of the United States) concerning the enforcement of competition/antitrust law. It mainly required the parties to consult with each other, and expressly said that it did not change the law in either the United States or the Community. France brought proceedings to have the agreement struck down.[30] The Commission argued that since it had internal competence to enforce competition law, it should have external competence in this area. It said that it could carry out the agreement without the assistance of the Council.

Judgment
[After ruling that the agreement had legal effects and that the Commission's decision to conclude it was subject to review under Article 230 [173] EC, the court continued:]

19. Article 300(1) [228(1)] of the EEC Treaty, in the version in force at the time of the events material to this case, provided as follows:

"Where this Treaty provides for the conclusion of agreements between the Community and one or more States or an international organization, such agreements shall be negotiated by the Commission. Subject to the powers vested in the Commission in this field, such agreements shall be concluded by the Council, after consulting the European Parliament where required by this Treaty."

20. The French Republic argues that that provision expressly reserves to the Council the power to conclude international agreements. Consequently, by concluding the Agreement, the Commission, which is empowered merely to conduct negotiations in that field, exceeded its powers.

21. The Commission contends that the Agreement in fact constitutes an administrative agreement which it is competent to conclude. In view of the nature of the obligations which it lays down, failure to perform the Agreement would result, not in an international claim capable of giving rise to liability on the part of the Community, but merely in termination of the Agreement.

22. The Commission further points out that, in any event, Article IX of the Agreement, cited above, precludes the parties from interpreting its provisions in a manner inconsistent with their own laws (and, moreover, as regards the European Communities, with the laws of the Member States) or as requiring any change in their own laws.

23. As the Court has already found, the Agreement produces legal effects.

24. Next, it is the Community alone, having legal personality pursuant to Article 281 [210] of the Treaty, which has the capacity to bind itself by concluding agreements with a non-member country or an international organization.

25. There is no doubt, therefore, that the Agreement is binding on the European Communities. It falls squarely within the definition of an international agreement concluded between an international organization and a State, within the meaning of Article 2(1)(a)(i) of the Vienna Convention of 21 March 1986 on the Law of Treaties

---

30 The action was brought under Article 230 [173] EC. There was some disagreement as to whether it was directed against the Commission decision to conclude the agreement or against the agreement itself. It was argued that the word "acts" in the first paragraph of Art. 230 [173] did not cover bilateral acts such as an international agreement. The court held that the action should be regarded as being directed against the Commission decision.

between States and International Organizations or between International Organizations.[31] In the event of non-performance of the Agreement by the Commission, therefore, the Community could incur liability at international level.

26. That being so, the question is whether the Commission was competent under Community law to conclude such an agreement.

27. As the Court explained in Opinion 1/75 of 11 November 1975 ([1975] ECR 1355), Article 300 [228] uses the expression "agreement" in a general sense to indicate any undertaking entered into by entities subject to international law which has binding force, whatever its formal designation.

[The court then considered, and rejected, various arguments of a rather technical nature put forward by the Commission. It continued:]

37. It follows from the foregoing that the Commission cannot claim to derive from Article 300 [228] of the Treaty powers analogous to those which it enjoys by virtue of the third paragraph of Article 101 of the Euratom Treaty.

38. First, as the Advocate General has pointed out in paragraph 26 of his Opinion, Article 101 provides for a procedure which is quite different from that referred to in Article 300 [228] of the EEC Treaty.

39. Second, the EEC and the Euratom Treaties were negotiated simultaneously and signed on the same day; accordingly, if those negotiating the two treaties had intended to grant the Commission the same powers, they would have done so expressly.

40. The Commission's final argument against the French Government's plea is that its power to conclude international agreements is all the more clear-cut in the present case, since the EEC Treaty has conferred on it specific powers in the field of competition. Under Article 85 [89] of the Treaty and Regulation No 17 of the Council of 6 February 1962, the first regulation implementing Articles 81 [85] and 82 [86] of the EEC Treaty (OJ, English Special Edition 1959–1962, p. 87), the Commission is entrusted with the task of ensuring the application of the principles laid down in Articles 81 [85] and 82 [86] of the EEC Treaty and the application of Council Regulation (EEC) No 4064/89 of 21 December 1989 on the control of concentrations between undertakings (OJ 1990 L 257, p. 14).

41. That argument cannot be accepted either. Even though the Commission has the power, internally, to take individual decisions applying the rules of competition, a field covered by the Agreement, that internal power is not such as to alter the allocation of powers between the Community institutions with regard to the conclusion of international agreements, which is determined by Article 300 [228] of the Treaty.

42. The plea alleging lack of competence on the part of the Commission to conclude the Agreement at issue must therefore be upheld.

43. It follows, without there being any need to examine the other pleas relied on by the French Republic, that the act whereby the Commission sought to conclude the Agreement with the United States regarding the application of the competition laws of the European Communities and the United States must be declared void.

---

31 Editor's note: unlike the 1969 Vienna Convention on the Law of Treaties (which covers treaties between States), this Convention is not in force. However, it is generally regarded as setting out customary international law on the subject.

Comment

The court's reasoning in this case is convincing. However, it appears blissfully unaware of the fact that it could equally well be applied to its previous decisions.

Assessment

The main effect of the European Court's initiative in expanding the treaty-making power of the EC has been to increase the power of the Commission. In particular, where the power is exclusive, the Community replaces the Member States in the negotiations. Although beneficial in some respects,[32] this has its disadvantages. Compared with the larger Member States, such as the UK, France or Germany, the Commission lacks expertise in international affairs. This might be no problem if it was willing to work closely with the national governments, but it is not always willing to do so. Sometimes one gets the impression that the Commission is more concerned with safeguarding its powers and prerogatives than with ensuring that the negotiations are successful. Consequently, the effect of a transfer of competence can be to bog down negotiations, thus making international co-operation more difficult.

Further reading

Bourgeois, "The EC in the WTO and Advisory Opinion 1/94: An Echternacht Procession" (1995) 32 CMLRev. 763.

Dashwood (Alan) and Hillion (Christophe) (eds.), *The General Law of EC External Relations* (Sweet and Maxwell, London, 2000).

Lenaerts and De Smijter, "The European Union as an Actor under International Law" (1999) 19 YEL 95.

MacLeod (I.), Hendry (I. D.) and Hyett (Stephen), *The External Relations of the European Communities* (Clarendon Press, Oxford, 1996).

McGoldrick (Dominic), *International Relations Law of the European Union* (Longman, London and New York, 1997).

Neuwahl, "Shared Powers or Shared Incompetence? More on Mixity" (1996) 33 CMLRev. 667.

O'Keeffe (David) and Schermers (Henry, G.) (eds.), *Mixed Agreements* (Kluwer, Deventer, The Netherlands, 1983).

Sack, "The European Community's Membership of International Organizations" (1995) 32 CMLRev. 1227.

Tridimas and Eeckhout, "The External Competence of the Community and the Case-Law of the Court of Justice: Principle versus Pragmatism" (1994) 14 YEL 143.

---

32 If the alternative is for the Member States to act on their own without any co-ordination, it has the advantage that the Community will speak with one voice. If the alternative is for negotiations to be conducted by the Member State holding the Presidency, the advantages are, first, that the Commission will be more neutral as between the Member States and, secondly, that the negotiators will not keep changing (the Presidency rotates every six months). These problems are not, of course, insuperable.

13 International law in the Community legal system

The main question to be considered in this chapter is whether international agreements concluded by the Community can have direct effect and, if so, what the consequences are. The two most important situations in which this question arises are, first, where such an agreement conflicts with Member-State legislation, and, secondly, where it conflicts with Community legislation. We shall consider the second situation first.

International agreements and Community legislation

What happens when a Community measure conflicts with an international agreement? This question can arise both in a Member-State court and in the European Court. We shall first consider the position in a Member-State court. The most important issue has been the effect of the GATT and the WTO Agreement.

The GATT in Member-State courts

European Union
International Fruit Company v. Produktschap voor Groenten en Fruit
(Third International Fruit case)
COURT OF JUSTICE OF THE EUROPEAN COMMUNITIES
Cases 21–23/72, [1972] ECR 1219; [1975] 2 CMLR 1

Facts
In this case, a Dutch tribunal asked the European Court whether three Commission regulations could be challenged on the ground that they were contrary to Article XI of the old GATT. This raised the question whether references under Article 234 [177] EC can be used to decide whether a Community measure is valid under international law.

Judgment

4. According to the first paragraph of Article 234 [177] of the EEC Treaty "the Court of Justice shall have jurisdiction to give preliminary rulings concerning . . . the validity . . . of acts of the institutions of the Community".

5. Under that formulation, the jurisdiction of the Court cannot be limited by the grounds on which the validity of those measures may be contested.

6. Since such jurisdiction extends to all grounds capable of invalidating those measures, the Court is obliged to examine whether their validity may be affected by reason of the fact that they are contrary to a rule of international law.

7. Before the incompatibility of a Community measure with a provision of international law can affect the validity of that measure, the Community must first of all be bound by that provision.

8. Before invalidity can be relied upon before a national court, that provision of international law must also be capable of conferring rights on citizens of the Community which they can invoke before the courts.

9. It is therefore necessary to examine whether the General Agreement satisfies these two conditions.

10. It is clear that at the time when they concluded the Treaty establishing the European Economic Community the Member States were bound by the obligations of the General Agreement.

11. By concluding a Treaty between them they could not withdraw from their obligations to third countries.

12. On the contrary, their desire to observe the undertakings of the General Agreement follows as much from the very provisions of the EEC Treaty as from the declarations made by Member States on the presentation of the Treaty to the Contracting Parties of the General Agreement in accordance with the obligation under Article XXIV thereof.

13. That intention was made clear in particular by Article 131 [110] of the EEC Treaty, which seeks the adherence of the Community to the same aims as those sought by the General Agreement, as well as by the first paragraph of Article 307 [234] which provides that the rights and obligations arising from agreements concluded before the entry into force of the Treaty, and in particular multilateral agreements concluded with the participation of Member States, are not affected by the provisions of the Treaty.

14. The Community has assumed the functions inherent in the tariff and trade policy, progressively during the transitional period and in their entirety on the expiry of that period, by virtue of Articles [111] and 133 [113] of the Treaty.

15. By conferring those powers on the Community, the Member States showed their wish to bind it by the obligations entered into under the General Agreement.

16. Since the entry into force of the EEC Treaty and more particularly, since the setting up of the common external tariff, the transfer of powers which has occurred in the relations between Member States and the Community has been put into concrete form in different ways within the framework of the General Agreement and has been recognized by the other Contracting Parties.

17. In particular, since that time, the Community, acting through its own institutions, has appeared as a partner in the tariff negotiations and as a party to the agreements of all types concluded within the framework of the General Agreement, in accordance with the

provisions of Article [114] of the EEC Treaty which provides that the tariff and trade agreements "shall be concluded . . . on behalf of the Community".

18. It therefore appears that, in so far as under the EEC Treaty the Community has assumed the powers previously exercised by Member States in the area governed by the General Agreement, the provisions of that Agreement have the effect of binding the Community.

19. It is also necessary to examine whether the provisions of the General Agreement confer rights on citizens of the Community on which they can rely before the courts in contesting the validity of a Community measure.

20. For this purpose, the spirit, the general scheme and the terms of the General Agreement must be considered.

21. This Agreement which, according to its preamble, is based on the principle of negotiations undertaken on the basis of "reciprocal and mutually advantageous arrangements" is characterized by the great flexibility of its provisions, in particular those conferring the possibility of derogation, the measures to be taken when confronted with exceptional difficulties and the settlement of conflicts between the Contracting Parties.

22. Consequently, according to the first paragraph of Article XXII "each Contracting Party shall accord sympathetic consideration to, and shall afford adequate opportunity for consultation regarding, such representations as may be made by any other Contracting Party with respect to . . . all matters affecting the operation of this Agreement".

23. According to the second paragraph of the same Article, "the Contracting Parties" – this name designating "the Contracting Parties acting jointly" as is stated in the first paragraph of Article XXV – "may consult with one or more Contracting Parties on any question to which a satisfactory solution cannot be found through the consultations provided under paragraph (1)".

24. If any Contracting Party should consider "that any benefit accruing to it directly or indirectly under this Agreement is being nullified or impaired or that the attainment of any objective of the Agreement is being impeded as a result of", *inter alia*, "the failure of another Contracting Party to carry out its obligations under this Agreement", Article XXIII lays down in detail the measures which the Parties concerned, or the Contracting Parties acting jointly, may or must take in regard to such a situation.

25. Those measures include, for the settlement of conflicts, written recommendations or proposals which are to be "given sympathetic consideration", investigations possibly followed by recommendations, consultations between or decisions of the Contracting Parties, including that of authorizing certain Contracting Parties to suspend the application to any others of any obligations or concessions under the General Agreement and, finally, in the event of such suspension, the power of the party concerned to withdraw from that Agreement.

26. Finally, where by reason of an obligation assumed under the General Agreement or of a concession relating to a benefit, some producers suffer or are threatened with serious damage, Article XIX gives a Contracting Party power unilaterally to suspend the obligation and to withdraw or modify the concession, either after consulting the Contracting Parties jointly and failing agreement between the Contracting Parties concerned, or even, if the matter is urgent and on a temporary basis, without prior consultation.

27. Those factors are sufficient to show that, when examined in such a context, Article XI of the General Agreement is not capable of conferring on citizens of the Community rights which they can invoke before the courts.

Result: the Community regulations were valid.

Comment

In this case, the European Court decided three important points.

- A Community measure is invalid if it is contrary to a directly effective provision of a treaty binding on the Community.
- The GATT is binding on the Community, even though it was not signed by the Community.
- Article XI of the GATT (and probably the whole Agreement) is not directly effective.

Monism

The first of these propositions establishes that the Community adopts a "monist" approach to international treaties. Appropriate provisions are directly effective in the Community legal system. Such provisions override Community legislation. It seems to make no difference whether the Community measure was adopted before or after the treaty. This is a highly internationalist approach. However, it is hardly surprising, since the European Court is itself an international court, though of a rather special kind.

The reason the old GATT was not directly effective seems to have been because it was too flexible. Article XXIII specified the measures that could be taken by a party if another party failed to carry out its obligations. These included the right of the injured party to take countervailing action and even to withdraw from the GATT. As we saw in Chapter 5, there was no right to the formation of a panel to resolve disputes, since this could always be blocked by the other party. Whether the court was right to rule that the old GATT was unsuitable for direct effect is a question on which views may differ, but few, if any, countries in the world have ever given it such effect.

Binding the Community

International agreements concluded by the Community (either with or without the participation of the Member States) are obviously binding on the Community,[1] but what about agreements concluded by the Member States alone? The GATT was concluded prior to the EC Treaty. All the Member States were parties to it, but it was never signed by the Community.

Article 307 [234] EC[2] provides that the rights of non-member States under international agreements concluded with one or more Member States prior to the EC Treaty will not be affected by the EC Treaty. The old GATT was such an agreement. However, Article 307 [234] does not mean that the Community is bound by such an agreement. The Community is not responsible to the non-member States for the carrying-out of the agreement. Article 307 [234] simply means that Community law does not prevent a Member State from carrying out its obligations. That is all.

---

1 See Art. 300(7) [228(7)] EC.
2 Set out in Panel 17.3, p. 334 below.

So there is nothing in the EC Treaty providing for the Community to be bound by agreements concluded by the Member States alone. However, as the court pointed out, the field covered by the GATT – tariffs and trade – was brought within the exclusive jurisdiction of the Community by Article 133 [113] of the EC Treaty. This covers external, as well as internal, jurisdiction. In fact, Article 133 [113] is one of the few Treaty provisions which expressly gives treaty-making power to the Community. Moreover, the Community had taken part in negotiations and concluded agreements within the GATT framework, which suggests that the other parties were willing to accept the Community as a partner. From these facts, the court concluded that the GATT had become binding on the Community. This seems to be by succession, though that term is not used in the judgment.[3] When the old GATT was replaced by the WTO Agreement, the Community was a party, alongside the Member States.

The GATT in the European Court

Does the rule that an international agreement must be directly effective before it can be used to challenge Community legislation apply if the proceedings are brought directly in the European Court? It could be argued that it should not. Since the European Court is itself an international court, it might be thought that the concept of direct effect is inapplicable. It should give effect to all treaties, as does the International Court of Justice. This view is supported by the fact that, in two cases decided in 1989 and 1991 respectively, the European Court appeared willing to apply provisions of the GATT. These are our next cases.

> **European Union**
> **Fediol v. Commission**
> **COURT OF JUSTICE OF THE EUROPEAN COMMUNITIES**
> Case 70/87, [1989] ECR 1781

Background

Council Regulation 2641/84 enabled the Commission to take action regarding imports from outside the Community in the case of an "illicit commercial practice". This was defined as an international trade practice attributable to a non-member State that is incompatible with international law or with the generally accepted rules. Fediol, an association of seed-oil producers, asked the Commission to take action regarding imports of soya from Argentina. They claimed that Argentina was guilty of a violation of the GATT by charging differential rates of duty on raw soya beans and soya cake.

---

3 In *Nederlandse Spoorwegen*, Case 38/75, [1975] ECR 1439 (at paras. 16 and 21 of the judgment), the European Court said that the Community had "replaced" the Member States. It is not entirely clear in what circumstances this will occur, but see *per* Advocate-General Capotorti in *Procureur Général v. Arbelaiz-Emazabel*, Case 181/80, [1981] ECR 2961 at 2987, and in *Attorney General v. Burgoa*, Case 812/79, [1980] ECR 2787 at 2815–2816.

After examining the facts, the Commission took a decision rejecting the request. It considered that what Argentina had done was not contrary to the GATT. Fediol then brought proceedings in the European Court under Article 230 [173] EC to annul this decision. The Commission advanced certain objections to the admissibility of the proceedings. We shall consider one of them.

Judgment

18. The Commission further maintains that when, as in this case, its decision deals with the interpretation of GATT provisions, the complainant cannot be permitted to put forward submissions calling that interpretation in question, because the interpretation which the Commission, pursuant to Regulation No 2641/84, places on the term "illicit commercial practice" and on the rules of international law, in particular those of GATT, is subject to review by the Court only in so far as the disregard or misapplication of those rules amounts to an infringement of the provisions of Community law which vest rights in individuals, directly and specifically; however, the GATT rules themselves are not sufficiently precise to give rise to such rights on the part of individuals.

19. It should be recalled that the Court has certainly held, on several occasions, that various GATT provisions were not capable of conferring on citizens of the Community rights which they can invoke before the courts[4] [citations omitted]. Nevertheless, it cannot be inferred from those judgments that citizens may not, in proceedings before the Court,[5] rely on the provisions of GATT in order to obtain a ruling on whether conduct criticized in a complaint lodged under Article 3 of Regulation No 2641/84 constitutes an illicit commercial practice within the meaning of that regulation. The GATT provisions form part of the rules of international law to which Article 2(1) of that regulation refers, as is borne out by the second and fourth recitals in its preamble, read together.

20. It is also appropriate to note that the Court did indeed hold in the above-mentioned judgments [citations omitted], that a particular feature of GATT is the broad flexibility of its provisions, especially those concerning deviations from general rules, measures which may be taken in cases of exceptional difficulty, and the settling of differences between the contracting parties. That view does not, however, prevent the Court from interpreting and applying the rules of GATT with reference to a given case, in order to establish whether certain specific commercial practices should be considered incompatible with those rules. The GATT provisions have an independent meaning which, for the purposes of their application in specific cases, is to be determined by way of interpretation.

21. Lastly, the fact that Article XXIII of GATT provides a special procedure for the settlement of disputes between contracting parties is not such as to preclude its interpretation by the Court . . .

[The court, therefore, rejected the objection of admissibility raised by the Commission. It then went on to consider whether Argentina was indeed guilty of violating the GATT. It decided that it was not. It therefore held the Commission decision valid.]

---

4 Editor's note: "court" with a small "c", means a Member-State court.
5 Editor's note: "Court" with a capital "C" means the European Court.

European Union
Nakajima v. Council
COURT OF JUSTICE OF THE EUROPEAN COMMUNITIES
Case C-69/89, [1991] ECR I-2069

Facts

Acting under Council Regulation 2423/88 ("the new basic regulation"), the
Council imposed an anti-dumping duty on dot-matrix printers from Japan.
Nakajima, a major Japanese producer, brought proceedings in the European
Court under Article 230 [173] EC to annul the regulation laying down the duty.
One of its arguments was that certain provisions of the new basic regulation
were contrary to the GATT Anti-Dumping Code.

Judgment
27. The Council takes the view that, as is the case with the General Agreement, the
Anti-Dumping Code does not confer on individuals rights which may be relied on before
the Court and that the provisions of that Code are not directly applicable within the
Community. From this the Council concludes that Nakajima cannot place in question the
validity of the new basic regulation on the ground that it may be in breach of certain
provisions in the Anti-Dumping Code.

28. It should, however, be pointed out that Nakajima is not relying on the direct effect of
those provisions in the present case. In making this plea in law, the applicant is in fact
questioning, in an incidental manner under Article 241 [184] of the Treaty,[6] the
applicability of the new basic regulation by invoking one of the grounds for review of
legality referred to in Article 230 [173] of the Treaty, namely that of infringement of the
Treaty or of any rule of law relating to its application.[7]

29. It ought to be noted in this regard that, in its judgment in [the *International Fruit* case],
the Court ruled (at paragraph 18) that the provisions of the General Agreement had the
effect of binding the Community. The same conclusion must be reached in the case of the
Anti-Dumping Code, which was adopted for the purpose of implementing Article VI of the

---

6 Editor's note: Art. 241 [184] provides: "Notwithstanding the expiry of the period laid down in the fifth
paragraph of Article 230 [173], any party may, in proceedings in which the validity of a regulation . . . is
at issue, plead the grounds specified in the second paragraph of Article 230 [173] in order to invoke
before the Court of Justice the inapplicability of that regulation."
7 Editor's note: Art. 230 [173] is set out in Panel 5.5, p. 82 above. The grounds of review specified in it are
"lack of competence, infringement of an essential procedural requirement, infringement of this Treaty or
of any rule of law relating to its application, or misuse of powers".

General Agreement and the recitals in the preamble to which specify that it is designed to "interpret the provisions of . . . the General Agreement" and to "elaborate rules for their application in order to provide greater uniformity and certainty in their implementation".

30. According to the second and third recitals in the preamble to the new basic regulation, it was adopted in accordance with existing international obligations, in particular those arising from Article VI of the General Agreement and from the Anti-Dumping Code.

31. It follows that the new basic regulation, which the applicant has called in question, was adopted in order to comply with the international obligations of the Community, which, as the Court has consistently held, is therefore under an obligation to ensure compliance with the General Agreement and its implementing measures [citations omitted].

32. In those circumstances, it is necessary to examine whether the Council went beyond the legal framework thus laid down, as Nakajima claims, and whether, by adopting the disputed provision, it acted in breach of Article 2(4) and (6) of the Anti-Dumping Code.

[The court considered this question and concluded that the new basic regulation was not unlawful for being in breach of the Anti-Dumping Code.]

QUESTION

If Nakajima could ask the court to declare certain provisions of the new basic regulation inapplicable on the ground that they conflicted with the GATT Anti-Dumping Code, why could International Fruit not have done the same with regard to the regulations in issue in that case?

Comment

These two cases suggest that the European Court was moving in the direction of allowing Community measures to be challenged on the basis that they were contrary to the GATT. However, out next case shows that it then changed direction.

European Union
Germany v. Council (Bananas case)
COURT OF JUSTICE OF THE EUROPEAN COMMUNITIES
Case C-280/93, [1994] ECR I-4973

Facts

In this case, Germany challenged the validity of a Council regulation on the ground that it was contrary to the GATT. It claimed that the regulation infringed certain basic provisions of the old GATT, and argued that this made it invalid, irrespective of whether or not the GATT was directly effective. The Council, on the other hand, maintained that, in view of its special features, the GATT could not be used to attack a Community measure unless the latter was adopted in order to give effect to obligations arising under the GATT.

Judgment
[After repeating the reasoning in the *International Fruit* case (above) which led it to conclude that the GATT was not directly effective, the European Court continued:]

109. Those features of GATT, from which the Court concluded that an individual within the Community cannot invoke it in a court[8] to challenge the lawfulness of a Community act, also preclude the Court[9] from taking provisions of GATT into consideration to assess the lawfulness of a regulation in an action brought by a Member State under the first paragraph of Article 230 [173] of the Treaty.

110. The special features noted above show that the GATT rules are not unconditional and that an obligation to recognize them as rules of international law which are directly applicable in the domestic legal systems of the contracting parties cannot be based on the spirit, general scheme or terms of GATT.

111. In the absence of such an obligation following from GATT itself, it is only if the Community intended to implement a particular obligation entered into within the framework of GATT, or if the Community act expressly refers to specific provisions of GATT, that the Court can review the lawfulness of the Community act in question from the point of view of the GATT rules (see [*Fediol v. Commission*] and [*Nakajima v. Council*]).

112. Accordingly, the Federal Republic of Germany cannot invoke the provisions of GATT to challenge the lawfulness of certain provisions of the Regulation.

Comment

If the *Fediol* and *Nakajima* cases show a softening of the court's position towards the GATT, this case constitutes a return to a hard-line approach. Fortunately for the court, the earlier cases could be distinguished on the grounds set out in paragraph 111. In all other cases, the treaty provision must be directly effective.

This case reveals the hollowness of the court's often-asserted statement that treaties binding the Community are part of the Community legal system.[10] If that were true, the concept of direct effect would have no place in proceedings brought in the European Court. Direct effect is concerned with the application of a rule in a legal system other than that to which it belongs. It constitutes a "gate" allowing such a rule to enter the system. For example, it allows rules of Community law to apply in the systems of the Member States. However, if the GATT were part of the Community legal system, there would be no need for a "gate". It would be inside the system anyway.

By invoking the concept of direct effect with regard to proceedings brought directly in it, the court shows that the GATT is not really part of the Community legal system. It is part of international law. Community law derives its validity from international law. However, as we saw in Chapter 8, the European Court has declared it a separate system of law. It is only by reason of this fact that

---

8 Editor's note: remember that "court" with a small "c" means a court other than the European Court, here a Member-State court.
9 Editor's note: "Court" with a capital "C" refers to the European Court.
10 See, for example, *Sevince* (below), para. 8 of the judgment and *Racke v. Hauptzollamt Mainz* (below), para. 41 of the judgment.

the concept of direct effect has any application with regard to treaties such as the GATT.

The WTO Agreement

It will be remembered from the discussion in Chapter 5 that the new GATT is significantly different from the old GATT. In particular, if one party infringes it, another party has a right to the formation of a panel. The decisions of such a panel are binding.[11] In Chapter 5, the question was discussed whether a panel decision that a party has infringed the Agreement requires that party to change its law or merely to pay compensation. It was concluded that the better view is that it is obliged to change its law.[12] In view of these differences, it might have been thought that the new GATT would have been given direct effect. On the other hand, it must not be forgotten that, in the United States, Congress has specifically provided that the new GATT will not be directly effective.[13] There is a similar provision in the preamble to the Council decision concluding the new GATT on behalf of the Community.[14]

The point arose for decision in our next case.

European Union
Portugal v. Council
COURT OF JUSTICE OF THE EUROPEAN COMMUNITIES
Case C-149/96, [1999] ECR I-8395

Facts

This was an action brought by Portugal in the European Court under Article 230 [173] EC to annul the Council decision (the "contested decision") which concluded an international agreement (Memorandum of Understanding) between the Community and Pakistan and between the Community and India. One of the grounds on which Portugal wished to attack the contested decision was that it was contrary to certain fundamental principles of the WTO, in particular those of the new GATT (GATT 1994) and certain other WTO agreements.

Judgment

27. Although the Court held in [*Germany v. Council* (banana case)], paragraphs 103 to 112, that the GATT rules do not have direct effect and that individuals cannot rely on them before the courts, it held in the same judgment that that does not apply where the adoption of the measures implementing obligations assumed within the context of the GATT is in issue or where a Community measure refers expressly to specific provisions of the general agreement. In such cases, as the Court held in paragraph 111 of that judgment, the Court must review the legality of the Community measure in the light of the GATT rules.

---

11 Under the old GATT, a panel decision was binding only if it was unanimously agreed that it would be. The losing party could thus block agreement. Under the WTO Agreement, on the other hand, a panel decision is binding unless it is unanimously agreed that it will *not* be binding. The winning party can always block such agreement.
12 See Chap. 5, note 31, p. 76 above, and text thereto.
13 See the Uruguay Round Agreements Act 1994, s. 102, set out in Chap. 8, Panel 8.1, p. 143 above.
14 See para. 48 of the judgment in *Portugal v. Council*.

28. The Portuguese Government claims that that is precisely the position in this case, which concerns the adoption of a measure – the contested decision – approving the Memoranda of Understanding negotiated with India and Pakistan following the conclusion of the Uruguay Round for the specific purpose of applying the rules in GATT 1994 and the ATC.[15]

29. The Council, supported by the French Government and by the Commission, relies rather on the special characteristics of the WTO agreements, which in their view provide grounds for applying to those agreements the decisions in which the Court held that the provisions of GATT 1947 do not have direct effect and cannot be relied upon.

30. They claim that the contested decision is of a special kind and is thus not comparable to the regulations at issue in [*Fediol v. Commission*] and [*Nakajima v. Council*]. The decision is not a Community measure intended to "transpose" certain provisions of the ATC into Community law.

31. The Portuguese Government replies that it is not GATT 1947 that is in issue in the present case but the WTO agreements, which include GATT 1994, the ATC and the Agreement on Import Licensing Procedures. The WTO agreements are significantly different from GATT 1947, in particular in so far as they radically alter the dispute settlement procedure.

32. Nor, according to the Portuguese Government, does the case raise the problem of direct effect: it concerns the circumstances in which a Member State may rely on the WTO agreements before the Court for the purpose of reviewing the legality of a Council measure.

33. The Portuguese Government maintains that such a review is justified in the case of measures such as the contested decision which approve bilateral agreements governing, in relations between the Community and non-member countries, matters to which the WTO rules apply.

34. It should be noted at the outset that in conformity with the principles of public international law Community institutions which have power to negotiate and conclude an agreement with a non-member country are free to agree with that country what effect the provisions of the agreement are to have in the internal legal order of the contracting parties. Only if that question has not been settled by the agreement does it fall to be decided by the courts having jurisdiction in the matter, and in particular by the Court of Justice within the framework of its jurisdiction under the EC Treaty, in the same manner as any question of interpretation relating to the application of the agreement in the Community (see Case 104/81 *Hauptzollamt Mainz v. Kupferberg* [1982] ECR 3641, paragraph 17).

35. It should also be remembered that according to the general rules of international law there must be *bona fide* performance of every agreement. Although each contracting party is responsible for executing fully the commitments which it has undertaken it is nevertheless free to determine the legal means appropriate for attaining that end in its legal system, unless the agreement, interpreted in the light of its subject-matter and purpose, itself specifies those means (*Kupferberg*, paragraph 18).

36. While it is true that the WTO agreements, as the Portuguese Government observes, differ significantly from the provisions of GATT 1947, in particular by reason of the

---

15 Editor's note: ATC means "Agreement on Textiles and Clothing", an agreement annexed to the WTO Agreement.

strengthening of the system of safeguards and the mechanism for resolving disputes, the system resulting from those agreements nevertheless accords considerable importance to negotiation between the parties.

37. Although the main purpose of the mechanism for resolving disputes is in principle, according to Article 3(7) of the Understanding on Rules and Procedures Governing the Settlement of Disputes (Annex 2 to the WTO), to secure the withdrawal of the measures in question if they are found to be inconsistent with the WTO rules, that understanding provides that where the immediate withdrawal of the measures is impracticable compensation may be granted on an interim basis pending the withdrawal of the inconsistent measure.

38. According to Article 22(1) of that Understanding, compensation is a temporary measure available in the event that the recommendations and rulings of the dispute settlement body provided for in Article 2(1) of that Understanding are not implemented within a reasonable period of time, and Article 22(1) shows a preference for full implementation of a recommendation to bring a measure into conformity with the WTO agreements in question.

39. However, Article 22(2) provides that if the member concerned fails to fulfil its obligation to implement the said recommendations and rulings within a reasonable period of time, it is, if so requested, and on the expiry of a reasonable period at the latest, to enter into negotiations with any party having invoked the dispute settlement procedures, with a view to finding mutually acceptable compensation.

40. Consequently, to require the judicial organs to refrain from applying the rules of domestic law which are inconsistent with the WTO agreements would have the consequence of depriving the legislative or executive organs of the contracting parties of the possibility afforded by Article 22 of that memorandum of entering into negotiated arrangements even on a temporary basis.

41. It follows that the WTO agreements, interpreted in the light of their subject-matter and purpose, do not determine the appropriate legal means of ensuring that they are applied in good faith in the legal order of the contracting parties.

42. As regards, more particularly, the application of the WTO agreements in the Community legal order, it must be noted that, according to its preamble, the agreement establishing the WTO, including the annexes, is still founded, like GATT 1947, on the principle of negotiations with a view to "entering into reciprocal and mutually advantageous arrangements" and is thus distinguished, from the viewpoint of the Community, from the agreements concluded between the Community and non-member countries which introduce a certain asymmetry of obligations, or create special relations of integration with the Community, such as the agreement which the Court was required to interpret in *Kupferberg*.[16]

43. It is common ground, moreover, that some of the contracting parties, which are among the most important commercial partners of the Community, have concluded from

---

16 Editor's note: at one time it was argued that agreements between the Community and other countries could not be directly effective where they imposed greater burdens on the Community than on the non-member States. See *Bresciani*, Case 87/75, [1976] ECR 129 at 148–149 (*per* Advocate-General Trabucchi) and para. 22 of the judgment; and *Polydor*, Case 270/80, [1982] ECR 329 at 355 (*per* Advocate-General Rozès). This was, however, rejected by the European Court in the *Kupferberg* case, Case 104/81, [1982] ECR 3641; [1983] 1 CMLR 1, with regard to agreements that were intended to have an "aid" element or to lead to a certain level of integration with the Community, as occurs in the case of association agreements. (Such agreements are usually regarded as either a prelude to full membership of the Community or as a substitute for it.)

the subject-matter and purpose of the WTO agreements that they are not among the rules applicable by their judicial organs when reviewing the legality of their rules of domestic law.

44. Admittedly, the fact that the courts of one of the parties consider that some of the provisions of the agreement concluded by the Community are of direct application whereas the courts of the other party do not recognise such direct application is not in itself such as to constitute a lack of reciprocity in the implementation of the agreement (*Kupferberg*, paragraph 18).

45. However, the lack of reciprocity in that regard on the part of the Community's trading partners, in relation to the WTO agreements which are based on "reciprocal and mutually advantageous arrangements" and which must *ipso facto* be distinguished from agreements concluded by the Community, referred to in paragraph 42 of the present judgment, may lead to disuniform application of the WTO rules.

46. To accept that the role of ensuring that those rules comply with Community law[17] devolves directly on the Community judicature would deprive the legislative or executive organs of the Community of the scope for manoeuvre enjoyed by their counterparts in the Community's trading partners.

47. It follows from all those considerations that, having regard to their nature and structure, the WTO agreements are not in principle among the rules in the light of which the Court is to review the legality of measures adopted by the Community institutions.

48. That interpretation corresponds, moreover, to what is stated in the final recital in the preamble to Decision 94/800, according to which "by its nature, the Agreement establishing the World Trade Organisation, including the Annexes thereto, is not susceptible to being directly invoked in Community or Member State courts".

49. It is only where the Community intended to implement a particular obligation assumed in the context of the WTO, or where the Community measure refers expressly to the precise provisions of the WTO agreements, that it is for the Court to review the legality of the Community measure in question in the light of the WTO rules (see, as regards GATT 1947, *Fediol*, paragraphs 19 to 22, and *Nakajima*, paragraph 31).

Result: Portugal could not invoke the alleged infringement of the WTO rules as a ground for challenging the validity of the contested decision.

Comment

It is hard to avoid the feeling that the real reason the court concluded that the WTO Agreement is not directly effective is that expressed in paragraph 46 of the judgment, namely, that it would prevent the Community from breaking the Agreement when it thought this would be advantageous. This rather cynical argument is more persuasive than the arguments that purport to be based on the nature of the Agreement itself.[18]

---

17 Editor's note: this is a strange way of putting it. The question is not whether WTO rules comply with Community law, but whether Community law complies with the WTO rules.
18 It is interesting to note that the Advocate-General took the view that Portugal *should* be allowed to invoke the WTO Agreement. This was on the ground that direct effect has no role to play when the proceedings are brought in the European Court, since the WTO Agreement is part of the Community legal system. See paras. 14–24 of his Opinion.

Panel 13.1   Article 234 [177] EC

The Court of Justice shall have jurisdiction to give preliminary rulings concerning:

(a) the interpretation of this Treaty;

(b) the validity and interpretation of acts of the institutions of the Community and of the ECB;

(c) the interpretation of the statutes of bodies established by an act of the Council, where those statutes so provide.

International agreements and Member-State legislation

Do international agreements concluded by the Community have direct effect in the legal systems of the Member States? If so, do they prevail over Member-State legislation? These are the questions we must now consider.

From a policy point of view, there are solid reasons why the European Court would want to say they do. When the Community concludes an agreement, it is responsible towards the other parties to the agreement for ensuring that its provisions are obeyed not only by the Community institutions but also by the Member States. This latter task is much easier if the agreement is directly effective in the Member States and prevails over their legislation. The Commission does not then have to resort to the cumbersome machinery of an action under Article 226 [169] EC.

References for interpretation

In giving effect to this policy, the European Court is faced with a problem, since it seems to lack a suitable instrument for imposing its views on the courts of the Member States. When an international agreement conflicts with a Community measure, Article 234 [177] provides a means by which the question can be brought to the European Court for a decision. This provision (set out in Panel 13.1) gives the European Court jurisdiction to rule on the validity of Community acts. If it is argued in a Member-State court that a Community measure is invalid because it conflicts with an international agreement, the validity of the measure can be referred to the European Court under Article 234 [177]. Where, on the other hand, the conflict is between an international agreement and a Member-State measure, it would seem that Article 234 [177] cannot be invoked, since it does not give the European Court jurisdiction to rule on the validity of Member-State legislation.

The European Court has solved this problem in characteristic fashion by "bending" the provisions of Article 234 [177] to give it jurisdiction to interpret international treaties with non-member States. The following cases show how it did this.

> *European Union*
> **Haegeman v. Belgium**
> **COURT OF JUSTICE OF THE EUROPEAN COMMUNITIES**
> Case 181/73, [1974] ECR 449; [1975] 1 CMLR 515

Facts

Before Greece became a Member State, the Community concluded an association agreement with it. In proceedings before a Belgian court, it was argued that this agreement, known as the Athens Agreement, was relevant to the matters before the court. The court therefore asked the European Court to give a ruling on its interpretation. The first question the European Court had to decide was whether it had jurisdiction to do so.

It will be remembered from the discussion in the previous chapter, that Community agreements are negotiated by the Commission and concluded by the Council. The way the Council gives formal assent on behalf of the Community is to adopt a decision to this effect. In the case of the Athens Agreement, this was a decision dated 25 September 1961.

Judgment

2. Under the first paragraph of Article 234 [177] of the EEC Treaty "the Court of Justice shall have jurisdiction to give preliminary rulings concerning . . . the interpretation of acts of the institutions of the Community".

3. The Athens Agreement was concluded by the Council under Articles 300 [228] and 310 [238] of the Treaty as appears from the terms of the Decision dated 25 September 1961.

4. This agreement is, therefore, in so far as concerns the Community, an act of one of the institutions of the Community within the meaning of subparagraph (b) of the first paragraph of Article 234 [177].

5. The provisions of the agreement, from the coming into force thereof, form an integral part of Community law.

6. Within the framework of this law, the Court accordingly has jurisdiction to give preliminary rulings concerning the interpretation of this agreement.

Comment

The court's argument is that because the Athens Agreement was concluded by a decision of the Council, it is therefore an act of the Council in terms of Article 234 [177]. The flaw in this argument is that it was not the Council decision that the court was asked to interpret, but the Agreement. The Agreement was not an act of the Council, but an act of the Community. It was the Community that was the party to it.[19] Moreover, it was a bilateral act (agreement), not a unilateral act (legislative or executive measure).[20] The court's reasoning might have made sense if the Agreement took effect in the Community simply as a provision in Community legislation ("dualist" standpoint). However, as we have seen, the court adopts a clear "monist" stance.[21]

---

19 See paras. 24 and 25 of the court's judgment in *France v. Commission (Competition (Antitrust) Agreement* case), Case C-327/91, [1994] ECR I-3641, set out at p. 236 above.
20 It is generally thought that the word "act" in Art. 234 [177] refers only to unilateral acts: see *per* Advocate-General Trabucchi in *Bresciani*, Case 87/75, [1976] ECR 129 at 147.
21 If the agreement falls partly within the jurisdiction of the Community and partly within that of the Member States, it will be concluded as a "mixed" agreement. The Community *and* the Member States will be parties. (The Association Agreement with Greece was a "mixed" agreement.) In such a case, the

European Union
Amministrazione delle Finanze dello Stato v. SPI (SPI case)
COURT OF JUSTICE OF THE EUROPEAN COMMUNITIES
Cases 267–269/81, [1983] ECR 801

Facts

In this case, an Italian court asked the European Court to interpret the old GATT. Since the Community never formally became a party to the old GATT, the argument used in the previous case was inapplicable. There was no decision of the Council concluding it. This did not, however, deter the court, which solved the problem by ignoring it. Instead of setting out the words of Article 234 [177] and interpreting them, it resorted to a policy argument.

Judgment

14. [I]t is important that the provisions of GATT should, like the provisions of all other agreements binding the Community, receive uniform application throughout the Community. Any difference in the interpretation and application of provisions binding the Community as regards non-member countries would not only jeopardize the unity of the commercial policy, which according to Article 133 [113] of the Treaty must be based on uniform principles, but also create distortions in trade within the Community, as a result of differences in the manner in which the agreements in force between the Community and non-member countries were applied in the various Member States.

15. It follows that the jurisdiction conferred upon the Court in order to ensure the uniform interpretation of Community law must include a determination of the scope and effect of the rules of GATT within the Community and also of the effect of the Tariff Protocols concluded in the framework of GATT. In that regard it does not matter whether the national court is required to assess the validity of Community measures or the compatibility of national legislative provisions with the commitments binding the Community.

Comment

It will be noticed that the court was careful not to say whether the GATT was covered by subparagraph (a) of Article 234 [177] ("this Treaty") or subparagraph (b) ("acts of the institutions of the Community"). Looking too closely at the words would have spoilt the argument. The case also concerned another agreement (the Tariff Protocols), which *had* been concluded by the Community. The court had no hesitation in saying that that agreement was covered by subparagraph (b).

The court went on to say that its self-granted power to interpret the old GATT came into existence on 1 July 1968, the date on which, according to the court, the Community was substituted for the Member States as a party to the GATT.[22]

European Court's jurisdiction under Art. 234 [177] will extend only to interpreting those parts of the agreement that fall within the (exclusive or concurrent) jurisdiction of the Community. In the absence of special circumstances, it will have no jurisdiction to interpret those parts falling outside the jurisdiction of the Community. See *Hermès v. FHT*, Case C-53/96, [1998] ECR I-3603; and *Dior v. Tuk Consultancy*, Cases C-300 and 392/98, [2000] ECR I-11307.

22 This was the date on which the Community's Common Customs Tariff came into force.

Prior to that date, the Member-State courts alone had jurisdiction to interpret the GATT.

The court went on the hold, as it had done in previous cases, that the GATT was not directly effective. This meant that it could not be used to challenge the validity of the Italian legislation said to be in conflict with it.

> **European Union**
> **Sevince**
> **COURT OF JUSTICE OF THE EUROPEAN COMMUNITIES**
> Case C-192/89, [1990] ECR I-3461

Facts

Turkey is not a Member State. However, the Community has entered into an association agreement with it under Article 310 [238] EC. This agreement made provision for the setting up of a Council of Association, which had power to adopt decisions. The case concerned two such decisions, Decisions 2/76 and 1/80, which gave Turkish citizens the right to work in EC States.

Mr Sevince was a Turkish citizen, who brought proceedings in the Dutch courts against the refusal of the Dutch authorities to grant him a residence permit. He claimed that the decision was contrary to the two decisions of the Council of Association. This raised the question whether the decisions were directly effective and overrode Dutch legislation. The Dutch court made a reference to the European Court.

The European Court first had to decide whether it had jurisdiction to interpret the Decisions.

Judgment

7. The national court's first question is essentially whether an interpretation of Decisions Nos 2/76 and 1/80 may be given under Article [234] 177 of the EEC Treaty.

8. By way of a preliminary observation, it should be borne in mind that, as the Court has consistently held, the provisions of an agreement concluded by the Council under Articles 300 [228] and 310 [238] of the EEC Treaty form an integral part of the Community legal system as from the entry into force of that agreement [citations omitted].

9. The Court has also held that, since they are directly connected with the Agreement to which they give effect, the decisions of the Council of Association, in the same way as the Agreement itself, form an integral part, as from their entry into force, of the Community legal system [citation omitted].

10. Since the Court has jurisdiction to give preliminary rulings on the Agreement, in so far as it is an act adopted by one of the institutions of the Community (see [*Haegeman*]), it also has jurisdiction to give rulings on the interpretation of the decisions adopted by the authority established by the Agreement and entrusted with responsibility for its implementation.

11. That finding is reinforced by the fact that the function of Article 234 [177] of the EEC Treaty is to ensure the uniform application throughout the Community of all provisions forming part of the Community legal system and to ensure that the interpretation thereof

does not vary according to the interpretation accorded to them by the various Member States [citations omitted].

12. It must therefore be stated in reply to the first question submitted by the Raad van State that the interpretation of Decisions Nos 2/76 and 1/80 falls within the scope of Article 234 [177] of the EEC Treaty.

Comment

In this case, the European Court made no serious attempt to justify its ruling. The Association Agreement with Turkey was supposed to be an act of the Council in terms of the second subparagraph of Article 234 [177] ("acts of the institutions of the Community"). Can it seriously be contended that the decisions of the Council of Association were acts of institutions of the Community under this provision?

Direct effect

After having furnished itself with the procedural instrument for deciding the matter, the European Court has had no hesitation in ruling that international agreements binding the Community, as well as decisions of bodies such as the Council of Association under the Association Agreement with Turkey, can be directly effective in the Member States.[23] The test seems to be the same as for the Community Treaties.[24] When directly effective, they override national legislation.

Customary international law

We finally consider whether customary international law may be applied in order to challenge the validity of a Community measure.

European Union
Racke v. Hauptzollamt Mainz
COURT OF JUSTICE OF THE EUROPEAN COMMUNITIES
Case C-162/96, [1998] ECR I-3655

Background

In 1980, the Community signed a co-operation agreement with Yugoslavia. Article 22 of the Agreement provided for a reduced rate of duty on wine imported from Yugoslavia into the Community. The Community adopted a regulation to give effect to this, though (as we shall see in the judgment) this was not strictly necessary. Article 60 of the Agreement provided that the Agreement was concluded for an indefinite period, but either party could terminate it on

---

23 See, for example, *Kupferberg*, Case 104/81, [1982] ECR 3641; [1983] 1 CMLR 1.
24 See, for example, paras. 13–26 of the judgment in *Sevince* (not reproduced above).

six months' notice. However, in 1991, when the crisis in Yugoslavia erupted, the EU suspended the Agreement with immediate effect. This was done by Council Decision 91/586 of 11 November 1991. Regulation 3300/91 was then passed to suspend the trade concession.

The justification given by the Council for suspending the Agreement without notice was that there had been a fundamental change of circumstances (the doctrine of *rebus sic stantibus*). This is an exception to the general rule of *pacta sunt servanda* (agreements must be carried out). The rules of international law on the doctrine of *rebus sic stantibus* are to be found in Article 62 of the Vienna Convention on the Law of Treaties, 1969.[25] Extracts are set out in Panel 13.2. It will be seen from this that the doctrine is recognized, but only in restricted circumstances. The Community is not a party to the Vienna Convention, but Article 62 is generally recognized as expressing customary international law.

Racke was a German firm that had imported wine from Serbia. It had been required by the German authorities to pay a higher rate of duty by reason of the suspension. It challenged that decision in the German courts. It argued that the suspension of the trade agreement was contrary to international law and, therefore, of no effect. The German court made a reference to the European Court under Article 234 [177] on the validity of Regulation 3300/91 (the "disputed regulation"). This raised the question whether it is open to a private person to challenge a Community measure on the ground that it is contrary to customary international law.

Panel 13.2 Doctrine of rebus sic stantibus

Vienna Convention on the Law of Treaties 1969

Article 62

1. A fundamental change of circumstances which has occurred with regard to those existing at the time of the conclusion of a treaty, and which was not foreseen by the parties, may not be invoked as a ground for terminating or withdrawing from the treaty unless:

   (a) the existence of those circumstances constituted an essential basis of the consent of the parties to be bound by the treaty; and
   (b) the effect of the change is radically to transform the extent of obligations still to be performed under the treaty.

2. . . .

3. If, under the foregoing paragraphs, a party may invoke a fundamental change of circumstances as a ground for terminating or withdrawing from a treaty it may also invoke the change as a ground for suspending the operation of the treaty.

Judgment

24. By way of a preliminary observation, it should be noted that even though the Vienna Convention does not bind either the Community or all its Member States, a series of its provisions, including Article 62, reflect the rules of international law which lay down, subject to certain conditions, the principle that a change of circumstances may entail the lapse or suspension of a treaty. Thus the International Court of Justice held that "[t]his principle, and the conditions and exceptions to which it is subject, have been embodied in Article 62 of the Vienna Convention on the Law of Treaties, which may in many respects be considered as a codification of existing customary law on the subject of the termination of a treaty relationship on account of change of circumstances" (judgment of 2 February 1973, *Fisheries Jurisdiction (United Kingdom v. Iceland)*, ICJ Reports 1973, p. 3, paragraph 36).

---

25 There are two Vienna conventions on the law of treaties. The 1969 Convention applies to treaties between two or more States. The 1986 Convention applies to treaties between international organizations and states, or between two or more international organizations. The 1986 Convention is not in force. Both conventions are similar. Sometimes the European Court refers to the one and sometimes to the other.

The jurisdiction of the Court

25. The Commission has expressed doubts as to the jurisdiction of the Court to rule on the first question because it relates to the validity of the disputed regulation under rules of customary international law. Even though the regulation constitutes an act of the Community within the meaning of subparagraph (b) of the first paragraph of Article 234 [177] of the Treaty, the preliminary rulings procedure does not permit the development of an argument based on international law alone, and in particular on the principles governing the termination of treaties and the suspension of their operation.

26. As the Court has already held in [the *International Fruit* case], paragraph 5, the jurisdiction of the Court to give preliminary rulings under Article 234 [177] of the Treaty concerning the validity of acts of the Community institutions cannot be limited by the grounds on which the validity of those measures may be contested.

27. Since such jurisdiction extends to all grounds capable of invalidating those measures, the Court is obliged to examine whether their validity may be affected by reason of the fact that they are contrary to a rule of international law (*International Fruit Company*, paragraph 6).

28. The Court therefore has jurisdiction to rule on the first question.

The validity of the disputed regulation

[The court then considered whether Article 22(4) of the Co-operation Agreement was directly effective. It held that it was.]

37. It next needs to be examined whether, when invoking in legal proceedings the preferential customs treatment granted to him by Article 22(4) of the Co-operation Agreement, an individual may challenge the validity under customary international law rules of the disputed regulation, suspending the trade concessions granted under that Agreement as from 15 November 1991.

38. In that respect, the Council maintains that the adoption of the disputed regulation was preceded, logically and legally, by the adoption of Decision 91/586, suspending the application of the Co-operation Agreement on the international level. Adoption of the disputed regulation became necessary in its turn, since the trade concessions provided for in the Agreement had been implemented in the past by an internal Community regulation.

39. The Council submits that, since international law does not prescribe the remedies for breach of its rules, the possible breach of those rules by Decision 91/586 does not necessarily lead to the restoration in force of the Co-operation Agreement and hence, at the Community level, to the invalidity of the disputed regulation by reason of its being contrary to the restored Agreement. Breach of international law might for instance also be penalised by means of damages, leaving the Co-operation Agreement suspended. The Council therefore argues that, in assessing the validity of the disputed regulation, the Court does not need to examine whether suspension of the Co-operation Agreement by Decision 91/586 infringed rules of international law.

40. It is important to note at the outset that the question referred by the national court concerns only the validity of the disputed regulation under rules of customary international law.

41. As far as the Community is concerned, an agreement concluded by the Council with a non-member country in accordance with the provisions of the EC Treaty is an act of a

Community institution, and the provisions of such an agreement form an integral part of Community law [citation omitted].

42. If, therefore, the disputed regulation had to be declared invalid, the trade concessions granted by the Co-operation Agreement would remain applicable in Community law until the Community brought that Agreement to an end in accordance with the relevant rules of international law.

43. It follows that a declaration of the invalidity of the disputed regulation by reason of its being contrary to rules of customary international law would allow individuals to rely directly on the rights to preferential treatment granted to them by the Co-operation Agreement.

44. For its part, the Commission doubts whether, in the absence of an express clause in the EC Treaty, the international law rules referred to in the order for reference may be regarded as forming part of the Community legal order. Thus, in order to challenge the validity of a regulation, an individual might rely on grounds based on the relationship between him and the Community, but does not, the Commission argues, have the right to rely on grounds deriving from the legal relationship between the Community and a non-member country, which fall within the scope of international law.

45. It should be noted in that respect that, as is demonstrated by the Court's judgment in Case C-286/90 *Poulsen and Diva Navigation* [1992] ECR I-6019, paragraph 9, the European Community must respect international law in the exercise of its powers. It is therefore required to comply with the rules of customary international law when adopting a regulation suspending the trade concessions granted by, or by virtue of, an agreement which it has concluded with a non-member country.

46. It follows that the rules of customary international law concerning the termination and the suspension of treaty relations by reason of a fundamental change of circumstances are binding upon the Community institutions and form part of the Community legal order.

47. In this case, however, the plaintiff is incidentally challenging the validity of a Community regulation under those rules in order to rely upon rights which it derives directly from an agreement of the Community with a non-member country. This case does not therefore concern the direct effect of those rules.

48. Racke is invoking fundamental rules of customary international law against the disputed regulation, which was taken pursuant to those rules and deprives Racke of the rights to preferential treatment granted to it by the Co-operation Agreement (for a comparable situation in relation to basic rules of a contractual nature, see [*Nakajima v. Council*].

49. The rules invoked by Racke form an exception to the *pacta sunt servanda* principle, which constitutes a fundamental principle of any legal order and, in particular, the international legal order. Applied to international law, that principle requires that every treaty be binding upon the parties to it and be performed by them in good faith (see Article 26 of the Vienna Convention).

50. The importance of that principle has been further underlined by the International Court of Justice, which has held that "the stability of treaty relations requires that the plea of fundamental change of circumstances be applied only in exceptional cases" (judgment of 25 September 1997, *Gabcíkovo-Nagymaros Project* (*Hungary* v *Slovakia*), at paragraph 104, not yet published in the ICJ Reports).

51. In those circumstances, an individual relying in legal proceedings on rights which he derives directly from an agreement with a non-member country may not be denied the possibility of challenging the validity of a regulation which, by suspending the trade concessions granted by that agreement, prevents him from relying on it, and of invoking, in order to challenge the validity of the suspending regulation, obligations deriving from rules of customary international law which govern the termination and suspension of treaty relations.

52. However, because of the complexity of the rules in question and the imprecision of some of the concepts to which they refer, judicial review must necessarily, and in particular in the context of a preliminary reference for an assessment of validity, be limited to the question whether, by adopting the suspending regulation, the Council made manifest errors of assessment concerning the conditions for applying those rules.

53. For it to be possible to contemplate the termination or suspension of an agreement by reason of a fundamental change of circumstances, customary international law, as codified in Article 62(1) of the Vienna Convention, lays down two conditions. First, the existence of those circumstances must have constituted an essential basis of the consent of the parties to be bound by the treaty; secondly, that change must have had the effect of radically transforming the extent of the obligations still to be performed under the treaty.

54. Concerning the first condition, the preamble to the Co-operation Agreement states that the contracting parties are resolved "to promote the development and diversification of economic, financial and trade co-operation in order to foster a better balance and an improvement in the structure of their trade and expand its volume and to improve the welfare of their populations" and that they are conscious "of the need to take into account the significance of the new situation created by the enlargement of the Community for the organisation of more harmonious economic and trade relations between the Community and the Socialist Federal Republic of Yugoslavia". Pursuant to those considerations, Article 1 of the Agreement provides that its object "is to promote overall co-operation between the contracting parties with a view to contributing to the economic and social development of the Socialist Federal Republic of Yugoslavia and helping to strengthen relations between the parties".

55. In view of such a wide-ranging objective, the maintenance of a situation of peace in Yugoslavia, indispensable for neighbourly relations, and the existence of institutions capable of ensuring implementation of the co-operation envisaged by the Agreement throughout the territory of Yugoslavia constituted an essential condition for initiating and pursuing that co-operation.

56. Regarding the second condition, it does not appear that, by holding in the second recital in the preamble to the disputed regulation that "the pursuit of hostilities and their consequences on economic and trade relations, both between the Republics of Yugoslavia and with the Community, constitute a radical change in the conditions under which the Co-operation Agreement between the European Economic Community and the Socialist Federal Republic of Yugoslavia and its Protocols . . . were concluded" and that "they call into question the application of such Agreements and Protocols", the Council made a manifest error of assessment.

57. Whilst it is true, as Racke argues, that a certain volume of trade had to continue with Yugoslavia and that the Community could have continued to grant tariff concessions, the fact remains, as the Advocate General has pointed out in paragraph 93 of his Opinion, that application of the customary international law rules in question does not require an

impossibility to perform obligations, and that there was no point in continuing to grant preferences, with a view to stimulating trade, in circumstances where Yugoslavia was breaking up.

58. As for the question raised in the order for reference whether, having regard to Article 65 of the Vienna Convention, it was permissible to proceed with the suspension of the Co-operation Agreement with no prior notification or waiting period, this Court observes that, in the joint statements of 5, 6 and 28 October 1991, the Community and the Member States announced that they would adopt restrictive measures against those parties which did not observe the cease-fire agreement of 4 October 1991 which they had signed in the presence of the President of the Council and the President of the Conference on Yugoslavia; moreover, the Community had made known during the conclusion of that agreement that it would bring the Co-operation Agreement to an end in the event of the cease-fire not being observed (*Bull. EC* 10-1991, paragraphs 1.4.6, 1.4.7 and 1.4.16).

59. Even if such declarations do not satisfy the formal requirements laid down by Article 65 of the Vienna Convention, it should be noted that the specific procedural requirements there laid down do not form part of customary international law.

Result: the regulation suspending the tariff concessions is valid.

Comment

By allowing parties to invoke rules of customary international law in order to challenge Community measures the European Court adopted an internationalist approach. However, it took back most of what it gave by ruling that it would hold the measure invalid only if it was shown that the Council had made manifest errors of assessment (paragraph 52 of the judgment).

Conclusions

The following principles may be derived from the cases considered in this chapter.

1.   It is possible, as a matter of Community law, for international agreements binding the Community to be directly effective, both in the Community legal system and in the legal systems of the Member States.
2.   The same is true for decisions of bodies established by such agreements.
3.   In principle, the test for direct effect is the same as that for the Community Treaties.
4.   In certain circumstances, the Community will be bound by international agreements concluded by the Member States before the Community came into existence. In theory, such agreements may also have direct effect.
5.   Neither the old GATT nor the WTO Agreement is directly effective.
6.   International agreements (and decisions of bodies established by such agreements) that have direct effect may be invoked in both Member-State courts and the European Court in order to challenge the validity of a Community measure. Such measures are invalid if contrary to such an

agreement. It seems to make no difference whether the measure was adopted prior, or subsequent, to the agreement.

7.   Such agreements (and decisions) may also be invoked to challenge the validity of Member-State measures. It seems that the same principles apply.

8.   Rules of customary international law may be invoked in Member-State courts and (no doubt) in the European Court in order to challenge the validity of Community measures. However, such a challenge will be successful only if the violation of international law is manifest.

9.   The European Court has jurisdiction under Article 234 [177] EC to interpret international agreements binding on the Community and decisions of bodies established by such agreements.

Further reading

Búrca (Gráinne de) and Scott (Joanna) (eds.), *The EU and the WTO* (Hart Publishing, Oxford and Portland, OR, 2001), especially Chapters 4, 5 and 6.

Cheyne, "International Agreements and the European Community Legal System" (1994) 19 ELRev. 581.

Dashwood (Alan) and Hillion (Christophe) (eds.), *The General Law of EC External Relations* (Sweet and Maxwell, London, 2000).

Klabbers, "International Law in Community Law: The Law and Politics of Direct Effect" (2001–2002) 21 YEL 263.

MacLeod (I.), Hendry (I. D.) and Hyett (Stephen), *The External Relations of the European Communities* (Clarendon Press, Oxford, 1996).

Weiss, "Succession of States in Respect of Treaties Concluded by the European Communities" (1994) 10 SEW 661.

PART V
FUNDAMENTAL RIGHTS

14

The human-rights revolution

The modern human-rights[1] revolution took place through the combination of two powerful ideas – that of a "higher law" and that of judicial review of legislation. Most legal systems have the concept of a legal hierarchy – statutes are superior to common law or to measures passed by local councils – but the idea that there can be legal norms superior to statutes is another matter. The concept of higher law has little significance, however, unless it is coupled with judicial review. Unless the ordinary courts, or a special constitutional court, have power to strike down legislation that infringes higher law, the concept remains an empty slogan without practical significance.

In combination, these two ideas have the effect of shifting ultimate power from the legislature to the judiciary. The supremacy of parliament is replaced by the supremacy of the constitutional court. This shift of power is apparent if we compare the UK (which, domestically, has largely retained the traditional system) with Germany (which has adopted the new one). In both countries, the constitution is supreme. However, while the British Constitution gives supreme power to Parliament – the only limit to its legislative power is that it cannot limit its powers – the German Constitution gives ultimate power to the *Bundesverfassungsgericht*, the German Constitutional Court. This is because the German Constitution (*Grundgesetz*) imposes limits on the power of the German legislature (on human-rights grounds, amongst others) and the *Bundesverfassungsgericht* has the power to strike down legislation that goes beyond those limits. Moreover, since the *Bundesverfassungsgericht* has the power to interpret the Constitution and thus to determine what those limits are, it has the ultimate say on what the powers of the legislature are. Thus, while the UK system may be summed up in the phrase "sovereignty of Parliament", the German one is based on the sovereignty of the *Bundesverfassungsgericht*.

The twin ideas on which this revolution is based were not, however, invented in Europe. At least as far as the modern Western political tradition is concerned, they were first established in the United States. Ever since the famous decision of *Marbury v. Madison* in 1803,[2] the United States Supreme Court

---

1 In this book, the terms "human rights" and "fundamental rights" will be used interchangeably, as they are in legal texts. Compare, for example, "European Convention on Human Rights" with "Charter of Fundamental Rights of the European Union". In the United States, the terms "civil rights" and "civil liberties" are often used.
2 5 US 137 (1803).

has exercised the power of reviewing legislation passed by Congress (and by the state legislatures) to ensure its conformity with the higher law of the US Constitution, and has struck it down if it infringed the Constitution. It was under US influence (and under the influence of pre-war European theorists such as Hans Kelsen) that Germany and other European States such as Austria, Italy and Spain decided to adopt the new system.

We shall therefore examine the US system, before turning to that of Germany, the most influential exemplar of the system in Europe. The adoption of a somewhat similar system at the international level (under the European Convention on Human Rights) will form a later part of the chapter. This is the background against which we will consider the development of a doctrine of human rights in the European Union.

Characteristics of human rights

The concept of "higher law" is an ancient one. It may even be older than that of enacted law. In the past, it was often regarded as laid down by God. Christianity, Islam and Judaism all recognize the idea of divine law. However, ancient codes of divine law were often based on prohibitions – for example, "Thou shalt not kill" – that were regarded as addressed by God to man. The modern concept of human rights, on the other hand, emphasizes rights.

At least in their original conception, these rights were directed against the State. The human-rights equivalent of "Thou shalt not kill" is a formula such as "Everyone has the right to life".[3] What this means (at least, primarily) is that the State must not kill the citizen. The old religious codes, on the other hand, were directed primarily at the people. They were told not to kill each other. The modern concept of human rights is, therefore, distinguished by the fact that it grants rights to the citizen against the State.

These rights have another characteristic feature. At least as originally conceived, they were negative. They meant that the State should refrain from killing, not that it should take positive steps to protect life – for example, by providing medical care. Likewise, the right to free speech means that the State must not punish persons because of words spoken or written. It does not mean that the State must provide free printing presses and paper for citizens who want to publicize their ideas.

It is of course true that, like all successful ideas, the idea of human rights has been extended beyond its original meaning. First, the requirement that the State should not kill the citizen is extended to include the requirement that it should impose an obligation on citizens not to kill each other. Some people would go further and say that human rights can apply "horizontally" as well as "vertically". In other words, that they *can* impose obligations directly on the citizen. Once one has reached this point, however, there is little to distinguish the modern concept of the right to life from the ancient commandment that you must not kill.

---

3 See, for example, Art. 2(1) of the Charter of Fundamental Rights of the European Union.

The view has also been advanced that there should be a positive obligation on the State to provide, if not printing presses, at least medical services.[4] If this is accepted, as it is by many, human rights become more like a political programme, though – where embodied in a justiciable bill of rights – one directed more at the judges than the electorate.[5]

Where do human rights come from?

Where do human rights come from? Why were *these* rights, rather than other rights, chosen for special protection in legal documents such as constitutions and treaties? Is there anything that distinguishes a human right from any other kind of right – besides the fact that it is enshrined in a human-rights text?

Some philosophers have sought to maintain that human rights are objective – that they are not simply a matter of opinion. These philosophers also claim that human rights are universal – that they are the same for all times, all places and all peoples.[6] It is not difficult to see, however, that this is not true – at least with regard to the rights actually recognized and enforced.

Rights *do* change over time. Even within the lifetime of one person, there have been changes in what are considered human rights. Fifty years ago, capital punishment was not generally regarded as contrary to human rights. Today, there is a growing consensus in Europe that it is. This shift of opinion is reflected in the relevant texts. The European Convention on Human Rights was signed in 1950 and came into force in 1953. Article 2, which recognizes the right to life, expressly makes an exception for capital punishment. However, Protocol No. 6, which was opened for signature in 1983, outlaws it, except in time of war. The Protocol entered into force in 1985, when five States had ratified it.[7] Today, it is in force in forty-one States.[8] In 2002, another protocol, Protocol No. 13, was opened for signature in Vilnius, Lithuania. This bans capital punishment in all circumstances, even in time of war.[9] Article 2 of the EU Charter of Human Rights (proclaimed in 2000, but so far having no legal force) also outlaws capital punishment in all circumstances.

Homosexuality is another example. In the past, it was generally considered compatible with human rights for homosexual activity to be a criminal offence. Today, it is not. Indeed, many now consider that the law should not discriminate between heterosexual and homosexual activities. There has been a similar change in attitudes towards transsexuals, which has been recognized by the

4 See, for example, Art. 35 of the Charter of Fundamental Rights of the EU.
5 This is apparent in the case of the EU Charter (proclaimed in 2000, but so far without legal force), which includes consumer protection (Art. 38), health care (Art. 35), social security (Art. 34) and free placement (job-finding) services (Art. 29) among the rights it protects.
6 They may claim that they are derived from the law of nature, human nature or the law of God. For an overview, see Michael Freeman, *Human Rights* (Polity Press (in association with Blackwell Publishers), Cambridge, 2002), Chaps. 2–4.
7 Austria, Denmark, Luxembourg, Spain and Sweden. It came into force in the United Kingdom in 1999, though no executions had taken place since the death penalty was abolished for murder in 1969.
8 In practice, executions do not take place in any Member State of the Council of Europe.
9 It is not yet in force.

European Court of Human Rights with regard to such matters as a post-operative transsexual's right to marry someone of the same biological sex.[10]

Not only do concepts of human rights change over time; they also vary from one country to another. Attitudes towards capital punishment in the United States, Japan or the West Indies are different from those in Europe. As we shall see in Chapter 16, attitudes towards abortion are different in the United States compared with Ireland.

Even greater differences are to be found if one compares attitudes towards fundamental rights in Islamic countries with those in Europe. The rules enforced in Taleban-controlled Afghanistan (before the US attack) were deeply shocking to Westerners. On the other hand, many aspects of Western society – for example, the all-pervasive emphasis on sex and the wide availability of pornography – are equally shocking to devout Muslims. Nor is there any reason to believe that an Afghan mullah is less sincerely attached to the values he derives from Islam than a Western liberal is to the secular-humanist concept of human rights enshrined in the European Convention.[11] Each believes that his values should prevail.

Even within the same country, there are significant differences between social groups. In the UK, the intellectual elite – the educated, professional class that controls the political process, the media and the judicial system – has a significantly different attitude towards capital punishment from the broad mass of the population. For many years now, the elite has been opposed to capital punishment, while the general population has favoured it. As one might expect, it has been the values of the elite that have influenced legal developments.

In view of these considerations, there can be little doubt that concepts of fundamental rights are neither universal nor objective. They just express the values held most strongly by the dominant groups in the countries in question at the time in question. Strongly held opinion, and nothing more, is the foundation of fundamental rights in the West.

Fundamental rights in the United States

As originally drafted, the United States Constitution contained little that pertained to fundamental rights.[12] However, the first ten (more accurately, eight) Amendments, all adopted in 1791 and collectively referred to as "the Bill of Rights", made good this omission (Panel 14.1). They were drafted by James Madison, and the states would probably not have adopted the Constitution if

---

10 Compare the judgments in *Rees v. United Kingdom* (1987) 9 EHRR 56 and *Cassey v. United Kingdom* (1991) 13 EHRR 622 (decided in 1986 and 1990 respectively) with *Goodwin v. United Kingdom* and *I v. United Kingdom*, both decided on 11 July 2002 (available on www.coe.int). In *Goodwin v. United Kingdom*, the court referred to the continuing international trend in favour not only of increased social acceptance of transsexuals but of legal recognition of the new sexual identity of post-operative transsexuals.
11 There is even a gulf between the latter and traditional Christian values. The Vatican, for example, has condemned the EU Charter on Human Rights as a godless document, partly because of its attitude towards homosexuality: *The Times* (London), 2 December 2000.
12 There are exceptions – for example, the limitations imposed on the legislative power of Congress by Art. I, Section 9(2) (*habeas corpus*) and Section 9(3) (*ex post facto* laws).

Panel 14.1 US Bill of Rights

United States Constitution

Amendment I

Congress shall make no law respecting an establishment of religion, or prohibiting the free exercise thereof; or abridging the freedom of speech, or of the press; or the right of the people peaceably to assemble, and to petition the government for a redress of grievances.

Amendment II

A well regulated militia, being necessary to the security of a free state, the right of the people to keep and bear arms, shall not be infringed.

Amendment III

No soldier shall, in time of peace be quartered in any house, without the consent of the owner, nor in time of war, but in a manner to be prescribed by law.

Amendment IV

The right of the people to be secure in their persons, houses, papers, and effects, against unreasonable searches and seizures, shall not be violated, and no warrants shall issue, but upon probable cause, supported by oath or affirmation, and particularly describing the place to be searched, and the persons or things to be seized.

Amendment V

No person shall be held to answer for a capital, or otherwise infamous crime, unless on a presentment or indictment of a grand jury, except in cases arising in the land or naval forces, or in the militia, when in actual service in time of war or public danger; nor shall any person be subject for the same offense to be twice put in jeopardy of life or limb; nor shall be compelled in any criminal case to be a witness against himself, nor be deprived of life, liberty, or property, without due process of law; nor shall private property be taken for public use, without just compensation.

Amendment VI

In all criminal prosecutions, the accused shall enjoy the right to a speedy and public trial, by an impartial jury of the state and district wherein the crime shall have been committed, which district shall have been previously ascertained by law, and to be informed of the nature and cause of the accusation; to be confronted with the witnesses against him; to have compulsory process for obtaining witnesses in his favor, and to have the assistance of counsel for his defense.

Amendment VII

In suits at common law, where the value in controversy shall exceed twenty dollars, the right of trial by jury shall be preserved, and no fact tried by a jury, shall be otherwise reexamined in any court of the United States, than according to the rules of the common law.

Amendment VIII

Excessive bail shall not be required, nor excessive fines imposed, nor cruel and unusual punishments inflicted.

Amendment IX

The enumeration in the Constitution, of certain rights, shall not be construed to deny or disparage others retained by the people.

Amendment X

The powers not delegated to the United States by the Constitution, nor prohibited by it to the states, are reserved to the states respectively, or to the people.

they had not been promised. They were intended to protect the citizen against federal power, and applied only against the federal authorities.[13] It was thought at the time that the various state bills of rights gave ample protection against the state authorities.

13 *Barron v. Mayor of Baltimore*, 32 US (7 Pet.) 243 (1833).

Panel 14.2   Second US Bill of Rights

United States Constitution

Amendment XIII

Section 1.   Neither slavery nor involuntary servitude, except as a punishment for crime whereof the party shall have been duly convicted, shall exist within the United States, or any place subject to their jurisdiction.

Section 2.   Congress shall have power to enforce this article by appropriate legislation.

Amendment XIV

Section 1.   All persons born or naturalized in the United States, and subject to the jurisdiction thereof, are citizens of the United States and of the state wherein they reside. No state shall make or enforce any law which shall abridge the privileges or immunities of citizens of the United States; nor shall any state deprive any person of life, liberty, or property, without due process of law; nor deny to any person within its jurisdiction the equal protection of the laws.

Section 2.   [omitted]

Section 3.   [omitted]

Section 4.   [omitted]

Section 5.   The Congress shall have power to enforce, by appropriate legislation, the provisions of this article.

Amendment XV

Section 1.   The right of citizens of the United States to vote shall not be denied or abridged by the United States or by any state on account of race, color, or previous condition of servitude.

Section 2.   The Congress shall have power to enforce this article by appropriate legislation.

The US Bill of Rights was the fruit of the first great wave of enthusiasm for fundamental rights, a wave generated, or at least articulated, by the philosophers of natural law and natural rights. In the English-speaking world, John Locke and Thomas Paine were two of the most important. The US Bill of Rights was their greatest legacy.[14] A similar wave in France produced the Declaration of the Rights of Man and the Citizen of 1789. Enthusiasm for fundamental rights subsequently waned, to be revived after World War II in a second wave. This second wave is still continuing.

Viewed through modern eyes, the US Bill of Rights seems unsystematic and incomplete. This is apparent if one compares it with the European Convention on Human Rights, adopted over 150 years later. The most notable gap in the US Bill of Rights is that it does not prohibit slavery.[15] It was only after the American Civil War that this omission was made good with the Thirteenth (1865), Fourteenth (1868) and Fifteenth (1870) Amendments. Sometimes called "the Second Bill of Rights", these amendments were designed to outlaw slavery, give equal protection of the law and ensure that racial minorities had the right to vote. Unlike the first Bill of Rights, they bind the states. They are set out in Panel 14.2.

---

14 Its ancestry may be traced back through the various state Bills of Rights to the English Bill of Rights of 1689, though the latter was concerned with protecting the rights of Parliament (against the King), not those of the people.

15 Nor did it prohibit sex discrimination. Equal voting rights for women were given constitutional protection only in 1920, with the Nineteenth Amendment.

There is controversy among scholars over whether the privileges and immunities that Section 1 of the Fourteenth Amendment requires the states to respect were intended to include the rights set out in the (first) Bill of Rights. In 1873, however, the Supreme Court held that they did not.[16] Nevertheless, subsequent cases gradually read most of these rights into the Due Process clause of the Fourteenth Amendment, thus making them applicable against the states.[17] The reverse process has also occurred. The Supreme Court has held the Equal Protection clause of the Fourteenth Amendment applicable to the federal authorities by virtue of the federal Due Process clause in the Fifth Amendment.[18] The result is that the constitutional protection of fundamental rights is now largely the same as against both state and federal authorities.

It would be a mistake to think that a bill of rights coupled with judicial review is sufficient in itself to prevent major human-rights abuses. For almost a century after the Fifteenth Amendment was passed, Blacks were in practice denied the right to vote in the American South. Despite the Equal Protection clause, a similar period was to elapse before legally mandated racial segregation was ended. In the notorious case of *Plessy v. Ferguson*,[19] the Supreme Court held in 1896 that a Louisiana law requiring separate but (supposedly) equal accommodation on railway trains was constitutional. It was only in 1954, in *Brown v. Board of Education*,[20] a case concerning segregated schools, that the "separate but equal" doctrine was repudiated. Although both the Supreme Court and Congress[21] played a role, it was the civil rights movement, a political campaign by ordinary citizens, that brought about this change.

The maltreatment of the American Indians, at times amounting to genocide, is another example.[22] Persecution began with the first European settlers and continued until the earlier part of the twentieth century. Small-scale massacres were common – and almost always unpunished.[23] Many tribes were entirely eliminated. At times, the US Government joined the persecution. For example, the Cherokees and other tribes were ethnically cleansed from their homeland in the southern Appalachians and forced to go to what is now Oklahoma, a

---

16 *Slaughter-House* cases, 83 US (16 Wall.) 36 (1873).
17 Key cases include *Gitlow v. New York*, 268 US 652 (1925) (freedom of speech) and *Cantwell v. Connecticut*, 310 US 296 (1940) (freedom of religion). To the casual reader, the Due Process clause seems a much less suitable vehicle for this process than the Privileges and Immunities clause.
18 *Bolling v. Sharpe*, 347 US 497 (1954). This process is sometimes referred to as "reverse incorporation".
19 63 US 537 (1896).
20 347 US 483 (1954).
21 Most notably by passing the Civil Rights Act of 1964.
22 For general histories of the American Indians, see Dee Brown, *Bury My Heart at Wounded Knee: An Indian History of the American West* (Vintage, London, 1991); Angie Debo, *History of the Indians of the United States* (Pimlico, London, 1995); William T. Hagan, *American Indians* (University of Chicago Press, Chicago and London, 1992); and James Wilson, *The Earth Shall Weep: A History of Native America* (Picador, London and Basingstoke, 1998).
23 For massacres by settlers in California in the middle years of the nineteenth century, see Robert F. Heizer, *The Destruction of California Indians* (University of Nebraska Press, Lincoln, NE, and London, 1993), Chap. 7; and Wilson, note 22 above, Chap. 8. For massacres of Apaches in the American Southwest in the period 1850–1870 (General Carleton frequently ordered his men to kill all adult males), see Paul I. Wellman, *Death in the Desert* (University of Nebraska Press, Lincoln, NE, and London, 1987), especially at pp. 85–86; and Donald E. Worcester, *The Apaches* (University of Oklahoma Press, Norman, OK, and London, 1992), Chaps. 5 and 6.

distance of a thousand miles. Many died on the way.[24] This happened because Whites wanted their land.[25]

There are several reasons – apart from the shortcomings of the constitutional provisions – why judicial review failed to prevent these abuses:

- In 1830, the Supreme Court, under Chief Justice Marshall, gave a judgment favourable to the Cherokee Indians, who were being harassed by the state of Georgia.[26] It is a matter of dispute whether President Andrew Jackson actually said of this case "John Marshall has made his law; now let him enforce it." Nevertheless, in the early years, the judges must have been alive to the danger of non-enforcement.[27] This could have influenced their judgments.

- If a Black or Indian had wanted to challenge oppressive laws or governmental action, he would have had to find a lawyer. Since few of them had any money in the early days, he could have brought proceedings only if a well-disposed White had been willing to pay the bill. On some occasions this occurred, but there must have been many occasions when it did not.

- Politics has always played – and probably must play – a role in Supreme Court decisions. The understandable desire not to alienate the southern states and to reintegrate them into the nation after the Civil War may well have made the court cautious about upholding the rights of Blacks.

- Just because a person puts on judicial robes, he does not cease to be a member of the society in which he lives. Although judges try to be impartial, they are subject to the same beliefs and prejudices as other members of society. This is bound to influence them. For example, if most Whites believe that Blacks and Indians are untrustworthy and incapable of improving themselves, judges might feel disinclined to give them equal rights.[28]

These factors could also apply to international human-rights courts both in Europe and world-wide. It is still true that it is easier for rich people to vindicate

---

24 This was done under a federal statute, the Indian Removal Act 1830, Ch. 148, 4 Stat. 411. The statute contemplated voluntary removal, but in fact the Cherokees were forced to move by the US Army. See Felix S. Cohen, *Handbook of Federal Indian Law* (Michie Bobbs-Merrill, Charlottesville, VA, 1982), pp. 91–92; and Wilson, note 22 above, Chap. 6, especially pp. 163–172.

25 It should be said at this point that the human-rights record of the United States is no worse than that of other countries. For example, racism and even genocide were a feature of British colonial rule during the same period.

26 *Worcester v. Georgia*, 31 US (6 Pet.) 515 (1832).

27 See, further, Cohen, note 24 above, pp. 82–83; and Burke, "The Cherokee Cases: A Study in Law, Politics and Morality" (1969) 21 *Stanford Law Review* 500.

28 An example is to be found in the decisions of the Supreme Court on Japanese-Americans in the early 1940s. After Pearl Harbor, a wave of anti-Japanese hysteria swept America. The Army was afraid that Japanese-Americans were preparing a campaign of sabotage. They demanded that all persons of Japanese race be removed from militarily sensitive areas. Congress passed legislation and the President gave orders. Japanese-Americans, many of whom were US citizens, were rounded up and put into concentration camps. Their homes and businesses had to be sold at knock-down prices. In *Korematsu v. United States*, 323 US 241 (1944), the Supreme Court held that this was constitutionally justified on grounds of military security. Some Japanese-Americans were disloyal: it was impossible to know which; so it was justified to intern them all. German-Americans were not treated in the same way. General John L. DeWitt, commanding the West Coast area, justified this difference on racial grounds. For the background to this case, including the role played by racial prejudice, see Walter F. Murphy, James E. Fleming and Sotirios A. Barber, *American Constitutional Interpretation* (Foundation Press, Westbury, NY, 2nd ed., 1995), pp. 87–89. For further material, see *ibid.*, p. 89, n. 24. Many years later, compensation was paid to the survivors.

their rights than for poor people. Enforcement is still a problem. Politics still plays a role; so does prejudice.

Fundamental rights in Germany

After Germany's defeat in World War II, sovereignty passed to the four Occupying Powers. The three Western Powers subsequently decided to establish a constitution in their part of Germany (West Germany). The country was first divided up into states (in German, *Länder*; singular, *Land*), since it was agreed that Germany would be a federation, not a unitary State. After the *Länder* had been established, the *Land* Parliaments elected the members of a Parliamentary Council, which adopted the new Constitution (known in German as the *Grundgesetz*, or Basic Law) in 1949. After the military governors of the three Occupying Powers had approved the new Constitution, it was accepted by the *Land* Parliaments and promulgated on 23 May 1949. East Germany became part of the Federal Republic in 1990.

The provisions on fundamental rights come right at the beginning of the Constitution and are to be found in Articles 1–19. They are too long to be reproduced in full, but extracts are set out in Panel 14.3. While the influence of the US Constitution is clear, the German Constitution is more thorough and systematic. At least in English, however, it lacks the elegant simplicity of the US Bill of Rights. In parts (omitted from Panel 14.3), it seems excessively detailed, prompting the question whether it is right that the views of a group of politicians in 1949 should bind future generations. It should be noted that Article 79(3) of the *Grundgesetz* provides that amendments affecting the principles laid down in the Articles concerning fundamental rights are inadmissible. It seems, therefore, that there is no way (other than judicial interpretation) in which these principles may lawfully be changed.

Article 93 of the *Grundgesetz* sets up a special court, the *Bundesverfassungsgericht* (Federal Constitutional Court) to interpret the Constitution. It has the power to strike down legislation that is unconstitutional. Half the judges are elected by the *Bundestag* (Lower House of the German Parliament) and half by the *Bundesrat* (Upper House).[29] Unlike other German courts (and most continental courts), its members can give concurring and dissenting judgments. Some of its judgments will be examined in the next chapter.

The European Convention on Human Rights

Officially entitled the "Convention for the Protection of Human Rights and Fundamental Freedoms", the European Convention was opened for signature

---

29 The *Bundesrat* represents the *Länder* (states).

Panel 14.3 Fundamental Rights in Germany

Grundgesetz (German Constitution)[1]

Article 1 [Human dignity]

(1) Human dignity shall be inviolable. To respect and protect it shall be the duty of all state authority.

(2) The German people therefore acknowledge inviolable and inalienable human rights as the basis of every community, of peace and of justice in the world.

(3) The following basic rights shall bind the legislature, the executive, and the judiciary as directly applicable law.

Article 2 [Personal freedoms]

(1) Every person shall have the right to free development of his personality insofar as he does not violate the rights of others or offend against the constitutional order or the moral law.

(2) Every person shall have the right to life and physical integrity. Freedom of the person shall be inviolable. These rights may be interfered with only pursuant to a law.

Article 3 [Equality before the law]

(1) All persons shall be equal before the law.

(2) Men and women shall have equal rights. The state shall promote the actual implementation of equal rights for women and men and take steps to eliminate disadvantages that now exist.

(3) No person shall be favoured or disfavoured because of sex, parentage, race, language, homeland and origin, faith, or religious or political opinions. No person shall be disfavoured because of disability.

Article 4 [Freedom of faith, conscience, and creed]

(1) Freedom of faith and of conscience, and freedom to profess a religious or philosophical creed, shall be inviolable.

(2) The undisturbed practice of religion shall be guaranteed.

(3) No person shall be compelled against his conscience to render military service involving the use of arms. Details shall be regulated by a federal law.

Article 5 [Freedom of expression]

(1) Every person shall have the right freely to express and disseminate his opinions in speech, writing, and pictures and to inform himself without hindrance from generally accessible sources. Freedom of the press and freedom of reporting by means of broadcasts and films shall be guaranteed. There shall be no censorship.

(2) These rights shall find their limits in the provisions of general laws, in provisions for the protection of young persons, and in the right to personal honour.

(3) Art and scholarship, research, and teaching shall be free. The freedom of teaching shall not release any person from allegiance to the constitution.

Article 6 [Marriage and the family; children born outside of marriage]

(1) Marriage and the family shall enjoy the special protection of the state.

(2) The care and upbringing of children is the natural right of parents and a duty primarily incumbent upon them. The state shall watch over them in the performance of this duty.

(3) Children may be separated from their families against the will of their parents or guardians only pursuant to a law, and only if the parents or guardians fail in their duties or the children are otherwise in danger of serious neglect.

(4) Every mother shall be entitled to the protection and care of the community.

(5) Children born outside of marriage shall be provided by legislation with the same opportunities for physical and mental development and for their position in society as are enjoyed by those born within marriage.

---

[1] English translation: Press and Information Office of the Federal German Government.

⟫➔

Article 8 [Freedom of assembly]

(1) All Germans shall have the right to assemble peacefully and unarmed without prior notification or permission.

(2) In the case of outdoor assemblies, this right may be restricted by or pursuant to a law.

Article 9 [Freedom of association]

(1) All Germans shall have the right to form corporations and other associations.

(2) Associations whose aims or activities contravene the criminal laws, or that are directed against the constitutional order or the concept of international understanding, shall be prohibited.

(3) The right to form associations to safeguard and improve working and economic conditions shall be guaranteed to every individual and to every occupation or profession. Agreements that restrict or seek to impair this right shall be null and void; measures directed to this end shall be unlawful. Measures taken pursuant to Article 12a, to paragraphs (2) and (3) of Article 35, to paragraph (4) of Article 87a, or to Article 91 may not be directed against industrial disputes engaged in by associations within the meaning of the first sentence of this paragraph in order to safeguard and improve working and economic conditions.

Article 12 [Occupational freedom; prohibition of forced labour]

(1) All Germans shall have the right freely to choose their occupation or profession, their place of work, and their place of training. The practice of an occupation or profession may be regulated by or pursuant to a law.

(2) No person may be required to perform work of a particular kind except within the framework of a traditional duty of community service that applies generally and equally to all.

(3) Forced labour may be imposed only on persons deprived of their liberty by the judgment of a court.

Article 13 [Inviolability of the home]

(1)The home is inviolable.

(2) Searches may be authorized only by a judge or, when time is of the essence, by other authorities designated by the laws, and may be carried out only in the manner therein prescribed.

[Remainder omitted.]

Article 14 [Property, inheritance, expropriation]

(1) Property and the right of inheritance shall be guaranteed. Their content and limits shall be defined by the laws.

(2) Property entails obligations. Its use shall also serve the public good.

(3) Expropriation shall only be permissible for the public good. It may only be ordered by or pursuant to a law that determines the nature and extent of compensation. Such compensation shall be determined by establishing an equitable balance between the public interest and the interests of those affected. In case of dispute respecting the amount of compensation, recourse may be had to the ordinary courts.

Article 18 [Forfeiture of basic rights]

Whoever abuses the freedom of expression, in particular the freedom of the press (paragraph (1) of Article 5), the freedom of teaching (paragraph (3) of Article 5), the freedom of assembly (Article 8), the freedom of association (Article 9), the privacy of correspondence, posts and telecommunications (Article 10), the rights of property (Article 14), or the right of asylum (Article 16a) in order to combat the free democratic basic order shall forfeit these basic rights. This forfeiture and its extent shall be declared by the Federal Constitutional Court.

Article 19 [Restriction of basic rights]

(1) Insofar as, under this Basic Law, a basic right may be restricted by or pursuant to a law, such law must apply generally and not merely to a single case. In addition, the law must specify the basic right affected and the Article in which it appears.

(2) In no case may the essence of a basic right be affected.

(3) The basic rights shall also apply to domestic artificial persons to the extent that the nature of such rights permits.

(4) Should any person's rights be violated by public authority, he may have recourse to the courts. If no other jurisdiction has been established, recourse shall be to the ordinary courts. The second sentence of paragraph (2) of Article 10 shall not be affected by this paragraph.

in Rome in 1950 and entered into force on 3 September 1953.[30] It is the most notable achievement of the Council of Europe, a body described in Chapter 1 of this book. Since the end of the Cold War, most European States (including Russia) have joined the Council of Europe and become parties to the Convention.[31] In all, there were forty-four parties to the Convention at the end of 2002. The rights protected are set out in Articles 2–18 of the Convention (Panel 14.4). Under Article 1, the Contracting States must "secure" these rights and freedoms "to everyone within their jurisdiction", a matter to which we shall return in due course. Additional rights are to be found in Protocol No. 1. This was opened for signature in Paris in 1952 and entered into force on 18 May 1954 (Panel 14.5). Protocols No. 4,[32] 6[33] and 7[34] grant yet further rights. They are summarized in Panel 14.6.

The most innovative aspect of the Convention is the enforcement mechanism. There is a court of compulsory jurisdiction, the European Court of Human Rights, and individuals have the right to bring cases before it. Originally, both the jurisdiction of the court and the right of individual petition were applicable only with regard to those States that specifically accepted them, though in time they all did. Since the coming into force of Protocol No. 11 on 1 November 1998, however, the right of individual petition and the compulsory jurisdiction of the court have applied automatically to all parties to the Convention.

Originally, another body, the European Commission of Human Rights, received complaints in the first instance. It had the task of establishing the facts and deciding whether the complaint was admissible. If the complaint was admissible, the Commission would consider the issues raised and produce a report giving its ruling. This report was then sent to the Council of Ministers, a political body on which the Contracting States were represented. In certain circumstances, the case would then go to the court. All this has now been changed by Protocol No. 11, which abolished the Commission and the old court, which consisted of part-time judges. There is now a new court with full-time judges. The present system will be outlined in the following paragraphs.

The European Court of Human Rights

The European Court of Human Rights is entirely distinct from the Court of Justice of the European Communities. However, since the latter is usually known as the "European Court", the two are often mixed up – at least by the media. In this Part of the book, we shall refer to the Court of Justice of the European Communities as the "European Court (EC)" where any possibility of confusion

---

30 The full text of the Convention and other relevant documents, including judgments, are available on the Council of Europe website, http://www.coe.int.
31 In recent times, joining the Convention has come to be regarded as a condition of membership of the Council of Europe.
32 In force in 1968.
33 In force in 1985.
34 In force in 1988.

Panel 14.4 Substantive provisions of the European Convention on Human Rights

Article 2 Right to life

1 Everyone's right to life shall be protected by law. No one shall be deprived of his life intentionally save in the execution of a sentence of a court following his conviction of a crime for which this penalty is provided by law.

2 Deprivation of life shall not be regarded as inflicted in contravention of this article when it results from the use of force which is no more than absolutely necessary:

 a in defence of any person from unlawful violence;

 b in order to effect a lawful arrest or to prevent the escape of a person lawfully detained;

 c in action lawfully taken for the purpose of quelling a riot or insurrection.

Article 3 Prohibition of torture

No one shall be subjected to torture or to inhuman or degrading treatment or punishment.

Article 4 Prohibition of slavery and forced labour

1 No one shall be held in slavery or servitude.

2 No one shall be required to perform forced or compulsory labour.

3 For the purpose of this article the term "forced or compulsory labour" shall not include:

 a any work required to be done in the ordinary course of detention imposed according to the provisions of Article 5 of this Convention or during conditional release from such detention;

 b any service of a military character or, in the case of conscientious objectors in countries where they are recognised, service exacted instead of compulsory military service;

 c any service exacted in case of an emergency or calamity threatening the life or well-being of the community;

 d any work or service which forms part of normal civic obligations.

Article 5 Right to liberty and security

1 Everyone has the right to liberty and security of the person. No one shall be deprived of his liberty save in the following cases and in accordance with a procedure prescribed by law:

 a the lawful detention of a person after conviction by a competent court;

 b the lawful arrest or detention of a person for non-compliance with the lawful order of a court or in order to secure the fulfilment of any obligation prescribed by law;

 c the lawful arrest or detention of a person effected for the purpose of bringing him before the competent legal authority on reasonable suspicion of having committed an offence or when it is reasonably considered necessary to prevent his committing an offence or fleeing after having done so;

 d the detention of a minor by lawful order for the purpose of educational supervision or his lawful detention for the purpose of bringing him before the competent legal authority;

 e the lawful detention of persons for the prevention of the spreading of infectious diseases, of persons of unsound mind, alcoholics or drug addicts or vagrants;

 f the lawful arrest or detention of a person to prevent his effecting an unauthorised entry into the country or of a person against whom action is being taken with a view to deportation or extradition.

2 Everyone who is arrested shall be informed promptly, in a language which he understands, of the reasons for his arrest and of any charge against him.

3 Everyone arrested or detained in accordance with the provisions of paragraph 1(c) of this article shall be brought promptly before a judge or other officer authorised by law to exercise judicial power and shall be entitled to trial within a reasonable time or to release pending trial. Release may be conditioned by guarantees to appear for trial.

4 Everyone who is deprived of his liberty by arrest or detention shall be entitled to take proceedings by which the lawfulness of his detention shall be decided speedily by a court and his release ordered if the detention is not lawful.

5 Everyone who has been the victim of arrest or detention in contravention of the provisions of this article shall have an enforceable right to compensation.

⋙➤

Article 6   Right to a fair trial

1 In the determination of his civil rights and obligations or of any criminal charge against him, everyone is entitled to a fair and public hearing within a reasonable time by an independent and impartial tribunal established by law. Judgment shall be pronounced publicly but the press and public may be excluded from all or part of the trial in the interests of morals, public order or national security in a democratic society, where the interests of juveniles or the protection of the private life of the parties so require, or to the extent strictly necessary in the opinion of the court in special circumstances where publicity would prejudice the interests of justice.

2 Everyone charged with a criminal offence shall be presumed innocent until proved guilty according to law.

3 Everyone charged with a criminal offence has the following minimum rights:

a to be informed promptly, in a language which he understands and in detail, of the nature and cause of the accusation against him;

b to have adequate time and facilities for the preparation of his defence;

c to defend himself in person or through legal assistance of his own choosing or, if he has not sufficient means to pay for legal assistance, to be given it free when the interests of justice so require;

d to examine or have examined witnesses against him and to obtain the attendance and examination of witnesses on his behalf under the same conditions as witnesses against him;

e to have the free assistance of an interpreter if he cannot understand or speak the language used in court.

Article 7   No punishment without law

1 No one shall be held guilty of any criminal offence on account of any act or omission which did not constitute a criminal offence under national or international law at the time when it was committed. Nor shall a heavier penalty be imposed than the one that was applicable at the time the criminal offence was committed.

2 This article shall not prejudice the trial and punishment of any person for any act or omission which, at the time when it was committed, was criminal according to the general principles of law recognised by civilised nations.

Article 8   Right to respect for private and family life

1 Everyone has the right to respect for his private and family life, his home and his correspondence.

2 There shall be no interference by a public authority with the exercise of this right except such as is in accordance with the law and is necessary in a democratic society in the interests of national security, public safety or the economic well-being of the country, for the prevention of disorder or crime, for the protection of health or morals, or for the protection of the rights and freedoms of others.

Article 9   Freedom of thought, conscience and religion

1 Everyone has the right to freedom of thought, conscience and religion; this right includes freedom to change his religion or belief and freedom, either alone or in community with others and in public or private, to manifest his religion or belief, in worship, teaching, practice and observance.

2 Freedom to manifest one's religion or beliefs shall be subject only to such limitations as are prescribed by law and are necessary in a democratic society in the interests of public safety, for the protection of public order, health or morals, or for the protection of the rights and freedoms of others.

Article 10   Freedom of expression

1 Everyone has the right to freedom of expression. This right shall include freedom to hold opinions and to receive and impart information and ideas without interference by public authority and regardless of frontiers. This article shall not prevent States from requiring the licensing of broadcasting, television or cinema enterprises.

2 The exercise of these freedoms, since it carries with it duties and responsibilities, may be subject to such formalities, conditions, restrictions or penalties as are prescribed by law and are necessary in a democratic society, in the interests of national security, territorial integrity or public safety, for the prevention of disorder or crime, for the protection of health or morals, for the protection of the reputation or rights of others, for preventing the disclosure of information received in confidence, or for maintaining the authority and impartiality of the judiciary.

Article 11   Freedom of assembly and association

1 Everyone has the right to freedom of peaceful assembly and to freedom of association with others, including the right to form and to join trade unions for the protection of his interests.

2 No restrictions shall be placed on the exercise of these rights other than such as are prescribed by law and are necessary in a democratic society in the interests of national security or public safety, for the prevention of disorder or crime, for the protection of health or morals or for the protection of the rights and freedoms of others. This article shall not prevent the imposition of lawful restrictions on the exercise of these rights by members of the armed forces, of the police or of the administration of the State.

Article 12   Right to marry

Men and women of marriageable age have the right to marry and to found a family, according to the national laws governing the exercise of this right.

Article 13   Right to an effective remedy

Everyone whose rights and freedoms as set forth in this Convention are violated shall have an effective remedy before a national authority notwithstanding that the violation has been committed by persons acting in an official capacity.

Article 14   Prohibition of discrimination

The enjoyment of the rights and freedoms set forth in this Convention shall be secured without discrimination on any ground such as sex, race, colour, language, religion, political or other opinion, national or social origin, association with a national minority, property, birth or other status.

Article 15   Derogation in time of emergency

1 In time of war or other public emergency threatening the life of the nation any High Contracting Party may take measures derogating from its obligations under this Convention to the extent strictly required by the exigencies of the situation, provided that such measures are not inconsistent with its other obligations under international law.

2 No derogation from Article 2, except in respect of deaths resulting from lawful acts of war, or from Articles 3, 4 (paragraph 1) and 7 shall be made under this provision.

3 Any High Contracting Party availing itself of this right of derogation shall keep the Secretary General of the Council of Europe fully informed of the measures which it has taken and the reasons therefor. It shall also inform the Secretary General of the Council of Europe when such measures have ceased to operate and the provisions of the Convention are again being fully executed.

Article 16   Restrictions on political activity of aliens

Nothing in Articles 10, 11 and 14 shall be regarded as preventing the High Contracting Parties from imposing restrictions on the political activity of aliens.

Article 17   Prohibition of abuse of rights

Nothing in this Convention may be interpreted as implying for any State, group or person any right to engage in any activity or perform any act aimed at the destruction of any of the rights and freedoms set forth herein or at their limitation to a greater extent than is provided for in the Convention.

Article 18   Limitation on use of restrictions on rights

The restrictions permitted under this Convention to the said rights and freedoms shall not be applied for any purpose other than those for which they have been prescribed.

might arise. Unlike the European Court (EC), which sits in Luxembourg, the Human Rights Court sits in Strasbourg, the headquarters of the Council of Europe. It has two official languages – English and French, the official languages of the Council of Europe.

There are as many judges are there are parties to the Convention. There is no requirement regarding the nationality of judges; therefore it is possible to have two judges from one State and none from another. The Parliamentary Assembly

Panel 14.5 Protocol No. 1 to the European Convention on Human Rights

Article 1 Protection of property

Every natural or legal person is entitled to the peaceful enjoyment of his possessions. No one shall be deprived of his possessions except in the public interest and subject to the conditions provided for by law and by the general principles of international law.

The preceding provisions shall not, however, in any way impair the right of a State to enforce such laws as it deems necessary to control the use of property in accordance with the general interest or to secure the payment of taxes or other contributions or penalties.

Article 2 Right to education

No person shall be denied the right to education. In the exercise of any functions which it assumes in relation to education and to teaching, the State shall respect the right of parents to ensure such education and teaching in conformity with their own religious and philosophical convictions.

Article 3 Right to free elections

The High Contracting Parties undertake to hold free elections at reasonable intervals by secret ballot, under conditions which will ensure the free expression of the opinion of the people in the choice of the legislature.

Article 4[1] Territorial application

Any High Contracting Party may at the time of signature or ratification or at any time thereafter communicate to the Secretary General of the Council of Europe a declaration stating the extent to which it undertakes that the provisions of the present Protocol shall apply to such of the territories for the international relations of which it is responsible as are named therein.

Any High Contracting Party which has communicated a declaration in virtue of the preceding paragraph may from time to time communicate a further declaration modifying the terms of any former declaration or terminating the application of the provisions of this Protocol in respect of any territory.

A declaration made in accordance with this article shall be deemed to have been made in accordance with paragraph 1 of Article 56 of the Convention.

Article 5 Relationship to the Convention

As between the High Contracting Parties the provisions of Articles 1, 2, 3 and 4 of this Protocol shall be regarded as additional articles to the Convention and all the provisions of the Convention shall apply accordingly.

[1] Text amended according to the provisions of Protocol No. 11 (ETS No. 155).

of the Council of Europe[35] elects the judges, who must possess the qualifications required for high judicial office or be jurisconsults (legal scholars) of recognized competence. Each Contracting State presents the Assembly with three names (usually with an indication of its preferred candidate), and the Assembly must choose one of them.[36] Judges hold office for six years. They may be re-elected.

Judges are not supposed to represent their countries.[37] Some of the individuals selected have been practising lawyers, academics and other persons likely to be independent. Unfortunately, a number of government officials have also been appointed. In the 1998 elections, both Turkey and Slovakia nominated their permanent representatives to the Council of Europe. Both were elected. The Russians nominated their permanent representative, but he was killed in a car crash before the elections took place.

35 The Parliamentary Assembly, originally called the "Consultative Assembly", consists of representatives of the Member States, the size of each national contingent depending on the population of the State concerned. The representatives are elected by the national parliaments from among their own members.
36 Previously, it was possible for the Assembly to reject all three.
37 Art. 21(2).

Since judges are appointed for a term of only six years, a judge who fails to support his government in a case may find that he is not nominated for re-election. Judges in the European Court (EC) are also appointed for only six years. However, there is an important difference. In the European Court (EC) there is only one judgment of the court and it is never revealed how individual judges voted. The Human Rights Court, on the other hand, is more open. Concurring and dissenting judgments are allowed; therefore it is apparent if a judge voted against his country. The case of *Lukanov v. Bulgaria*[38] is an example. There, the Bulgarian judge voted against his own country. When his term of office expired, the Government of Bulgaria did not propose him for re-election. Instead, they nominated an ambassador as their preferred candidate. He was duly elected.[39]

> **Panel 14.6 Summary of Protocols No. 4, 6 and 7 to the European Convention on Human Rights**
>
> **Protocol No. 4**
> 1. Prohibition of imprisonment for debt.
> 2. Freedom of movement within a State and freedom to leave it.
> 3. Prohibition of expulsion of nationals of a State.
> 4. Prohibition of collective expulsion of aliens.
>
> **Protocol No. 6**
> Abolition of death penalty, except in time of war.
>
> **Protocol No. 7**
> 1. Procedural safeguards relating to expulsion of aliens.
> 2. Right of appeal in criminal matters.
> 3. Compensation for wrongful conviction.
> 4. Right not to be tried or punished twice.
> 5. Equality between spouses.

Procedure

Any person[40] may bring proceedings before the court.[41] It is not necessary for that person to be a national of the State concerned, or indeed of any Contracting State.[42] Applications may, however, be brought only against States, and only against States that are parties to the Convention. There is therefore no remedy against non-contracting States, international organizations (such as the European Union or NATO)[43] or private bodies (such as multinational companies), even if the infringement occurred within the territory of a Contracting State.[44] The application must relate to a right guaranteed by the Convention, and the applicant must be a victim of its breach. The applicant must first exhaust all domestic remedies, and then bring the complaint within the next six months. If any of these requirements is not fulfilled, the application will be declared inadmissible. The application may also be declared inadmissible if it is manifestly ill-founded – a rule that allows the court to filter out obviously unmeritorious

---

38 20 March 1997, available on http://www.coe.int.
39 For further information, see Schermers, "Election of Judges to the European Court of Human Rights" (1998) 23 ELRev. 568.
40 Non-governmental organizations and groups of individuals (including companies) may also bring proceedings.
41 It is also possible for one Contracting State to bring proceedings against another Contracting State. The vast bulk of cases are, however, brought by non-state applicants, and our description will focus on them.
42 A significant number of applicants are in fact nationals of non-contracting States or stateless persons.
43 This does not necessarily mean that a Contracting State can avoid liability by conferring powers on an international organization. See the discussion in Chap. 17 below.
44 If it took place with the assistance or permission of the Contracting State within the territory of which it occurred, proceedings could be brought against that State.

cases – or if the same complaint has already been submitted for a remedy to some other international body.[45] It seems that the framers of the Convention felt that applicants should not be allowed more than one remedy.

Proceedings are normally heard by a seven-judge Chamber,[46] which must include a judge from the respondent State. The Chamber first decides on admissibility. If the application is admissible, the Chamber will determine the facts and give judgment.[47] Instead of deciding the case itself, however, a Chamber may (in certain circumstances) relinquish the case to a Grand Chamber of seventeen judges.[48] If this is done, the judgment of the Grand Chamber is final.

If judgment is given by a Chamber, either party may request that the case be referred to a Grand Chamber by way of appeal. A five-judge panel of the Grand Chamber will then decide whether the circumstances justify the reference.[49] If the reference is granted, the Grand Chamber holds a hearing and gives judgment.[50] Such a judgment is final. If the reference is not granted (or if it is not requested within a period of three months), the judgment of the Chamber is final.[51]

The judgment takes the form of a declaration that the Convention has, or has not, been infringed. Like the European Court (EC), the Human Rights Court has no power to order the respondent State to take any particular action. Nevertheless, judgments are binding and Contracting States are expected to comply.[52] This almost always occurs. The Human Rights Court can grant monetary compensation, known as "just satisfaction".[53] This may include the costs of bringing the action.

The court can "indicate" interim measures.[54] In 1991, it held that measures "indicated" by the Commission (under the old system) were not binding.[55] In 2003, however, it reversed this decision by ruling that failure to obey measures "indicated" by the court constitutes a violation of Article 34 of the Convention, which requires Contracting States not to hinder the effective exercise of the right to bring proceedings.[56]

---

45 Art. 35(2)(b).
46 It may be sent to a three-judge committee to decide whether it is admissible. If the committee is unanimous, it may declare it inadmissible or strike it out.
47 Before doing so, it will help the parties reach a settlement, if this is possible.
48 A case cannot be relinquished if one of the parties objects: Art. 30.
49 A reference will be granted only in exceptional cases when a serious issue is involved: Art. 43.
50 In principle, the Grand Chamber consists of different judges from those who heard the original proceedings. However, there are two exceptions: the President of the Chamber that heard the case and the judge from the respondent State (Art. 27(3)). These two judges will thus sit on the appeal from their own judgments, something that the Human Rights Court regards as contrary to human rights when done by a court in a Contracting State.
51 Art. 44.
52 Art. 46. The Committee of Ministers has the task of supervising the execution of judgments.
53 Art. 41.
54 Rule 39 of the Rules of Court.
55 *Cruz Varas v. Sweden*, 20 March 1991, (1992) 14 EHRR 1. This judgment, which was given before that of the International Court of Justice in the *LaGrand* case (see Chap. 6), was reached by ten votes to nine.
56 *Mamatkulov and Abdurasulovic v. Turkey*, 6 February 2001. This was a judgment of a seven-judge chamber. Turkey objected to the proposal that the case be sent to a Grand Chamber.

Direct effect

We saw in Chapter 9 that the European Court (EC) insists that EU Member States give direct effect to the Community Treaties. The Human Rights Court, on the other hand, has never required Contracting States to give direct effect to the Convention. In fact, it has said that the Convention does not lay down for Contracting States "any given manner for ensuring within their internal law the effective implementation of any of the provisions of the Convention".[57] Contracting States must ensure that the rights set out in the Convention are respected, but how they do this is up to them. In the Netherlands, for example, the Convention has been held to be directly effective. In the United Kingdom, on the other hand, it was not directly effective until the Human Rights Act 1998 came into force.[58]

The purpose of the Human Rights Act is to give direct effect to the rights set out in the Convention and in certain Protocols thereto.[59] These rights do not, however, prevail against United Kingdom legislation, whether prior or subsequent. As far as possible, however, legislation must be interpreted in a way compatible with Convention rights.[60] Where it is impossible to do this, a court may make a declaration of incompatibility. Such a declaration does not affect the outcome of the case in which it was made, nor does it affect the validity of the legislation.[61] However, it opens the way for a special procedure under which the legislation may be amended to bring it into line with the requirements of the Convention.[62]

Except where legislation gives them no choice, public authorities must not act in a way that is incompatible with a Convention right.[63] If they do so, the victim may bring proceedings before the United Kingdom courts for an appropriate remedy, including damages.[64]

It is a matter of controversy whether the Act makes Convention rights horizontally directly effective – that is, whether they may be invoked against private persons as well as public authorities.[65] As we saw above, proceedings in the European Court of Human Rights can be brought only against States. However, the position may be different within the United Kingdom. Some writers

---

57 *Swedish Engine Drivers' Union v. Sweden*, Case A-20, (1979–1980) 1 EHRR 617, para. 50.
58 *R v. Chief Immigration Officer, ex parte Bibi* [1976] 1 WLR 979 (CA); and *R v. Home Secretary, ex parte Brind* [1991] 1 AC 696; [1991] 2 WLR 588. For Scotland, see *Kaur v. Lord Advocate*, 1981 SLT 322; and *Moore v. Secretary of State for Scotland*, 1985 SLT 38. The Human Rights Act came into force on 2 October 2000. In Scotland, it has been binding on the Scottish Executive and the Scottish Parliament since the Scotland Act 1998 came into force in 1999. The text may be found on www.hmso.gov.uk/acts.htm.
59 Arts. 2–12 and 14 of the Convention, Arts. 1–3 of Protocol No. 1 and Arts. 1 and 2 of Protocol No. 6, all read with Arts. 16–18 of the Convention: see s. 1(1) of the Act. In interpreting these provisions, United Kingdom courts must have regard to any relevant judgments of the Human Rights Court (and reports of the Commission, before it was abolished): see s. 2 of the Act.
60 S. 3. For a discussion of this requirement, see Gearty, "Reconciling Parliamentary Democracy and Human Rights" (2002) 118 LQR 248.
61 S. 5.
62 S. 10 and Sched. 2.
63 S. 6.
64 Ss. 7 and 8. Awards of damages are based on the principles applicable to just satisfaction under Art. 41 of the Convention.
65 For a discussion of the concept of horizontal direct effect in the context of EC directives, see Chap. 10 above.

point to the statement in section 6(1) of the Act that it is unlawful for a public authority to act in a way that is incompatible with a Convention right. This, they argue, requires the United Kingdom courts, themselves public authorities according to the Act,[66] to give effect to Convention rights even in proceedings between two private persons.[67] So far the matter has not arisen for decision.[68]

Territorial scope

We now return to the question mentioned earlier: the territorial scope of the Convention. Article 1 of the Convention provides:

> The High Contracting Parties shall secure to everyone within their jurisdiction the rights and freedoms defined in Section I of this Convention.

Section I consists of Articles 2–18, set out in Panel 14.4, above. These contain the substantive rights laid down by the Convention. It has already been noted that these rights apply irrespective of the nationality of the person concerned. But what is meant by "within their jurisdiction"? This is the question that arose in our next case.

Council of Europe
Bankovic v. Belgium, Czech Republic, Denmark, France, Germany, Greece, Hungary, Iceland, Italy, Luxembourg, Netherlands, Norway, Poland, Portugal, Spain, Turkey and United Kingdom (Bombing of Serbian TV station case)
EUROPEAN COURT OF HUMAN RIGHTS
Grand Chamber decision on admissibility
12 December 2001[69]

Background

Though historically part of Serbia, Kosovo has in recent times come to be populated mainly by ethnic Albanians. However, the province was controlled by the Serbian minority, who discriminated against the Albanians in various ways and committed serious infringements of their human rights. Demonstrations and protests were savagely repressed.[70] The Albanians wanted independence, or at least autonomy, from Serbia. They created a fighting force, the Kosovo Liberation Army (KLA), to achieve this. On their own, however, the Albanians stood little chance of attaining their objectives.

In 1999, NATO decided to intervene in support of the Kosovar Albanians. They demanded that Serbia withdraw its forces from Kosovo and, when it

---

66 S. 6(3)(a).
67 In support of this view, see Wade, "Horizons of Horizontality" (2000) 116 LQR 217. For the opposite view, see Buxton, "The Human Rights Act and Private Law" (2000) 116 LQR 48. See also Beyleveld and Pattinson, "Horizontal Applicability and Direct Effect" (2002) 118 LQR 623, where much of the literature is discussed.
68 If horizontal direct effect is possible, there are various situations in which it might apply. For example, Art. 10 (freedom of expression) could apply in defamation proceedings and Art. 8 (respect for private and family life) might even give rise to a new tort (invasion of privacy).
69 Available on www.coe.int.
70 Massacres of Albanians also occurred, though it is not clear whether these took place before or after the beginning of the NATO bombing campaign.

refused, launched a massive bombing campaign.[71] Initially, this was directed against military targets in Kosovo. This had limited effect, since NATO planes were reluctant to attack at low-level for fear of anti-aircraft fire. NATO then turned its attention to Serbia proper. Its strategy was to attack economic targets, such as power stations and bridges. The plan was to devastate the economy to such an extent that life would become unbearable and Serbia would give in.[72] This is what happened. Serbia withdrew its forces from Kosovo and NATO troops moved in unopposed. The Albanians then drove out many of the remaining Serbs.

The *Bankovic* case concerned one small episode in this story. At 2 a.m. on 23 April 1999, a NATO missile hit a TV studio in Belgrade operated by the Serbian radio and television network, RTS. The attack was deliberate.[73] According to NATO, RTS was broadcasting propaganda on behalf of the Serbian Government. Various people were killed, including the daughter of Mr and Mrs Bankovic. Mr and Mrs Bankovic, together with the parents and wives of other victims, brought proceedings against those parties to the Human Rights Convention that were members of NATO, a total of seventeen States.[74] The respondent States argued that the applications were inadmissible because the attack had occurred outside their territories. The case went to a Grand Chamber for decision.

Our first extract from the judgment shows how the court defined the issue.[75]

Judgment: extract one

54. The Court notes that the real connection between the applicants and the respondent States is the impugned act which, wherever decided, was performed, or had effects, outside of the territory of those States ("the extra-territorial act"). It considers that the essential question to be examined therefore is whether the applicants and their deceased relatives were, as a result of that extra-territorial act, capable of falling within the jurisdiction of the respondent States . . .

To decide this question, the court had to interpret the phrase "within their jurisdiction" in Article 1 of the Convention. Unlike the European Court (EC), the Human Rights Court is conscious of the fact that it is an international court, applying international law.[76] So, to interpret the Convention, it applied Articles 31 and 32 of the Vienna Convention on the Law of Treaties, 1969. These were set out in Panel 7.2, in Chapter 7. Article 31 lays down the general rule.

---

71 This was probably illegal under international law: see the Report on Kosovo by the Foreign Affairs Committee of the House of Commons, HC Paper 28-I of 1999–2000, paras. 128–138. This report was based on expert evidence by leading international lawyers. The memoranda of four of them are published in (2000) 49 ICLQ 876.
72 This also was the strategy pursued by the IRA in their bombing campaign in Britain in the 1980s and 1990s, the objective of which was to secure the withdrawal of British troops from Northern Ireland. They failed to achieve this objective but did obtain a power-sharing agreement under which members of the Catholic minority were allowed to participate in the government of the province.
73 NATO claimed that it gave a warning.
74 For reasons explained above, proceedings could not be brought against NATO itself.
75 In the following extracts, citations of authority and footnotes are omitted.
76 For further discussion of the international-law context in which the Human Rights Court operates, see J. G. Merrills, *The Development of International Law by the European Court of Human Rights* (Manchester University Press, Manchester and New York, 2nd ed., 1993).

Under this, the terms of a treaty must be given their ordinary meaning in the context in which they appear. Article 32 is concerned with supplementary means of interpretation. It states that preparatory work on the treaty may be considered, though only for limited purposes.

Our next extract shows how the court set about applying these rules.

Judgment: extract two

55. The Court recalls that the Convention must be interpreted in the light of the rules set out in the Vienna Convention 1969 . . .

56. It will, therefore, seek to ascertain the ordinary meaning to be given to the phrase "within their jurisdiction" in its context and in the light of the object and purpose of the Convention (Article 31 §1 of the Vienna Convention 1969 . . .). The Court will also consider "any subsequent practice in the application of the treaty which establishes the agreement of the parties regarding its interpretation" (Article 31 §3 (b) of the Vienna Convention 1969 . . .).

57. Moreover, Article 31 §3 (c) indicates that account is to be taken of "any relevant rules of international law applicable in the relations between the parties". More generally, the Court recalls that the principles underlying the Convention cannot be interpreted and applied in a vacuum. The Court must also take into account any relevant rules of international law when examining questions concerning its jurisdiction and, consequently, determine State responsibility in conformity with the governing principles of international law, although it must remain mindful of the Convention's special character as a human rights treaty . . . The Convention should be interpreted as far as possible in harmony with other principles of international law of which it forms part . . .

58. It is further recalled that the *travaux préparatoires* can also be consulted with a view to confirming any meaning resulting from the application of Article 31 of the Vienna Convention 1969 or to determining the meaning when the interpretation under Article 31 of the Vienna Convention 1969 leaves the meaning "ambiguous or obscure" or leads to a result which is "manifestly absurd or unreasonable" (Article 32). . . .

(a) The meaning of the words "within their jurisdiction"

59. As to the "ordinary meaning" of the relevant term in Article 1 of the Convention, the Court is satisfied that, from the standpoint of public international law, the jurisdictional competence of a State is primarily territorial. While international law does not exclude a State's exercise of jurisdiction extra-territorially, the suggested bases of such jurisdiction (including nationality, flag, diplomatic and consular relations, effect, protection, passive personality and universality) are, as a general rule, defined and limited by the sovereign territorial rights of the other relevant States . . .

60. Accordingly, for example, a State's competence to exercise jurisdiction over its own nationals abroad is subordinate to that State's and other States' territorial competence . . . In addition, a State may not actually exercise jurisdiction on the territory of another without the latter's consent, invitation or acquiescence, unless the former is an occupying State in which case it can be found to exercise jurisdiction in that territory, at least in certain respects . . .

61. The Court is of the view, therefore, that Article 1 of the Convention must be considered to reflect this ordinary and essentially territorial notion of jurisdiction, other bases of jurisdiction being exceptional and requiring special justification in the particular circumstances of each case . . .

The court then confirmed this conclusion by referring to the preliminary work on the Convention. The relevant points are best summarized by quoting an earlier part of the judgment.

Judgment: extract three

19. The text prepared by the Committee of the Consultative Assembly of the Council of Europe on legal and administrative questions provided, in what became Article 1 of the Convention, that the "Member States shall undertake to ensure to all persons residing within their territories the rights . . .". The Expert Intergovernmental Committee, which considered the Consultative Assembly's draft, decided to replace the reference to "all persons residing within their territories" with a reference to persons "within their jurisdiction". The reasons were noted in the following extract from the *Collected Edition of the* Travaux Préparatoires *of the European Convention on Human Rights* (Vol. III, p. 260):

> "The Assembly draft had extended the benefits of the Convention to 'all persons residing within the territories of the signatory States'. It seemed to the Committee that the term 'residing' might be considered too restrictive. It was felt that there were good grounds for extending the benefits of the Convention to all persons in the territories of the signatory States, even those who could not be considered as residing there in the legal sense of the word. The Committee therefore replaced the term 'residing' by the words 'within their jurisdiction' which are also contained in Article 2 of the Draft Covenant of the United Nations Commission."

20. The next relevant comment prior to the adoption of Article 1 of the Convention, made by the Belgian representative on 25 August 1950 during the plenary sitting of the Consultative Assembly, was to the effect that

> "henceforth the right of protection by our States, by virtue of a formal clause of the Convention, may be exercised with full force, and without any differentiation or distinction, in favour of individuals of whatever nationality, who on the territory of any one of our States, may have had reason to complain that [their] rights have been violated".

21. The *travaux préparatoires* go on to note that the wording of Article 1 including "within their jurisdiction", did not give rise to any further discussion and the text as it was (and is now) was adopted by the Consultative Assembly on 25 August 1950 without further amendment (the above-cited Collected Edition (Vol. VI, p. 132).

The court next turned to its own case law. There have been a number of decisions on Article 1, of which the most important is the first *Loizidou* case (preliminary objections),[77] a decision which concerned northern Cyprus. Originally a British colony, Cyprus was granted independence under a Constitution guaranteeing extensive rights to the Turkish minority. When the Constitution was overthrown by a Greek-Cypriot coup in 1974, Turkish forces invaded the island and occupied northern Cyprus. They claimed they had the right to do this as one of the three guarantor powers of the Republic of Cyprus.[78] Greek Cypriots were expelled from the territory under Turkish control, and Turkish Cypriots moved in from other parts of the island. The Turkish Cypriots formed

---

77 Judgment of 23 March 1995, available on www.coe.int.
78 The other two were Greece and the United Kingdom.

their own administration, though Turkish troops remained in the territory. In 1983, the Turkish Cypriots proclaimed the Turkish Republic of Northern Cyprus (TRNC). Though purporting to be an independent State, it was recognized only by Turkey. Other countries considered the territory to be part of the Republic of Cyprus.

Ms Loizidou owned land in the territory of the TRNC, which she was prevented from using by the TRNC authorities. She claimed this constituted a violation of various rights guaranteed under the Convention, in particular Article 1 of Protocol 1 (Panel 14.5, above). She brought proceedings against Turkey, claiming it was responsible.[79] Turkey claimed the proceedings were inadmissible, but a Grand Chamber held otherwise. Its reasons are summarized in the next extract from the *Bankovic* case.

Judgment: extract four

70. Moreover, in that first *Loizidou* judgment (*preliminary objections*), the Court found that, bearing in mind the object and purpose of the Convention, the responsibility of a Contracting Party was capable of being engaged when as a consequence of military action (lawful or unlawful) it exercised effective control of an area outside its national territory. The obligation to secure, in such an area, the Convention rights and freedoms was found to derive from the fact of such control whether it was exercised directly, through the respondent State's armed forces, or through a subordinate local administration. The Court concluded that the acts of which the applicant complained were capable of falling within Turkish jurisdiction within the meaning of Article 1 of the Convention.[80]

On the merits, the Court found that it was not necessary to determine whether Turkey actually exercised detailed control over the policies and actions of the authorities of the "Turkish Republic of Northern Cyprus" ("TRNC"). It was obvious from the large number of troops engaged in active duties in northern Cyprus that Turkey's army exercised "effective overall control over that part of the island". Such control, according to the relevant test and in the circumstances of the case, was found to entail the responsibility of Turkey for the policies and actions of the "TRNC". The Court concluded that those affected by such policies or actions therefore came within the "jurisdiction" of Turkey for the purposes of Article 1 of the Convention. Turkey's obligation to secure the rights and freedoms set out in the Convention was found therefore to extend to northern Cyprus. In its subsequent *Cyprus v. Turkey* judgment [judgment of 10 May 2001], the Court added that since Turkey had such "effective control", its responsibility could not be confined to the acts of its own agents therein but was engaged by the acts of the local administration which survived by virtue of Turkish support. Turkey's "jurisdiction" under Article 1 was therefore considered to extend to securing the entire range of substantive Convention rights in northern Cyprus.

71. In sum, the case-law of the Court demonstrates that its recognition of the exercise of extra-territorial jurisdiction by a Contracting State is exceptional: it has done so when the respondent State, through the effective control of the relevant territory and its inhabitants

---

79 The TRNC was not a party to the Convention.
80 Editor's note: see para. 62 of the *Loizidou* judgment.

abroad as a consequence of military occupation or through the consent, invitation or acquiescence of the Government of that territory, exercises all or some of the public powers normally to be exercised by that Government.

In our final extract, we show how the court reached its conclusion.

Judgment: extract five
Were the present applicants therefore capable of coming within the "jurisdiction" of the respondent States?

74. The applicants maintain that the bombing of RTS by the respondent States constitutes yet a further example of an extra-territorial act which can be accommodated by the notion of "jurisdiction" in Article 1 of the Convention, and are thereby proposing a further specification of the ordinary meaning of the term "jurisdiction" in Article 1 of the Convention. The Court must be satisfied that equally exceptional circumstances exist in the present case which could amount to the extra-territorial exercise of jurisdiction by a Contracting State.

75. In the first place, the applicants suggest a specific application of the "effective control" criteria developed in the northern Cyprus cases. They claim that the positive obligation under Article 1 extends to securing the Convention rights in a manner proportionate to the level of control exercised in any given extra-territorial situation. The Governments contend that this amounts to a "cause-and-effect" notion of jurisdiction not contemplated by or appropriate to Article 1 of the Convention. The Court considers that the applicants' submission is tantamount to arguing that anyone adversely affected by an act imputable to a Contracting State, wherever in the world that act may have been committed or its consequences felt, is thereby brought within the jurisdiction of that State for the purpose of Article 1 of the Convention.

The Court is inclined to agree with the Governments' submission that the text of Article 1 does not accommodate such an approach to "jurisdiction". Admittedly, the applicants accept that jurisdiction, and any consequent State Convention responsibility, would be limited in the circumstances to the commission and consequences of that particular act. However, the Court is of the view that the wording of Article 1 does not provide any support for the applicants' suggestion that the positive obligation in Article 1 to secure "the rights and freedoms defined in Section I of this Convention" can be divided and tailored in accordance with the particular circumstances of the extra-territorial act in question and it considers its view in this respect supported by the text of Article 19 of the Convention.[81] Indeed the applicants' approach does not explain the application of the words "within their jurisdiction" in Article 1 and it even goes so far as to render those words superfluous and devoid of any purpose. Had the drafters of the Convention wished to ensure jurisdiction as extensive as that advocated by the applicants, they could have adopted a text the same as or similar to the contemporaneous Articles 1 of the four Geneva Conventions of 1949 . . .

Furthermore, the applicants' notion of jurisdiction equates the determination of whether an individual falls within the jurisdiction of a Contracting State with the question of whether that person can be considered to be a victim of a violation of rights guaranteed by the Convention. These are separate and distinct admissibility conditions, each of which

---

81 Editor's note: Art. 19 indicates that the function of the court is to ensure the observance of the engagements undertaken by the Contracting States in the Convention and Protocols.

has to be satisfied in the afore-mentioned order, before an individual can invoke the Convention provisions against a Contracting State.

76. Secondly, the applicants' alternative suggestion is that the limited scope of the airspace control only circumscribed the scope of the respondent States' positive obligation to protect the applicants and did not exclude it. The Court finds this to be essentially the same argument as their principal proposition and rejects it for the same reasons.

[Paragraphs omitted.]

The Court's conclusion

82. The Court is not therefore persuaded that there was any jurisdictional link between the persons who were victims of the act complained of and the respondent States. Accordingly, it is not satisfied that the applicants and their deceased relatives were capable of coming within the jurisdiction of the respondent States on account of the extra-territorial act in question.

Result: application declared inadmissible.

Comment

The court was surely correct is rejecting the view expressed in the preparatory documents[82] that the Convention applies only within the territories of the Contracting States. If this had been the intention of the framers of the Convention, they would have said that the Contracting States had to secure the rights in question to everyone "within their *territories*", rather than "within their jurisdiction". On the other hand, it might be argued that if there was no territorial limit to the Convention, they would have said simply "secure to everyone". By saying that the Convention applies beyond the territory of a Contracting State, but only to the extent that it exercises governmental authority (whether lawful or unlawful), the court could be regarded as giving effect to the words of the Convention.

There is, however, another view. This was put forward, before the *Bankovic* judgment, in one of the leading textbooks on the Convention.[83] According to this view, we must ask ourselves what the word "secure" means. The Contracting Parties must *secure* to everyone within their jurisdiction the rights in the Convention. This means more than that the Contracting States must not violate those rights. Of course they must not violate them. But, in addition, they must secure them to everyone within their jurisdiction. This means that governments must take the steps necessary to ensure that the rights are actually enjoyed by everyone within their jurisdiction. In other words, Article 1 imposes a double obligation on Contracting States. First, they must not themselves violate the rights. Secondly, they must ensure that one person's rights are not violated by another person. This can be done by passing the necessary legislation and enforcing it.

82 See para. 20 of the judgment (in extract three, above).
83 Francis G. Jacobs and Robin C. A. White, *The European Convention on Human Rights* (Clarendon Press, Oxford, 2nd ed., 1996), pp. 17 *et seq.*

If we keep this double obligation in mind, the meaning of Article 1 becomes clear. The second obligation can apply only with regard to territory over which the State in question exercises governmental authority. It cannot be expected to secure rights beyond its jurisdiction. However, there is no reason to limit the first obligation in this way. A government should be responsible for its own actions anywhere in the world.[84]

From the point of view of human rights, it is unfortunate that the court did not accept this view.[85] By its very nature, a human right is a right accorded to everyone who is human. It is no less culpable for a State to infringe human rights outside its territory than inside it. States are in fact more likely to infringe human rights outside their territories, especially in wartime. An effective remedy is therefore even more important.[86] However, the court was probably right in saying that the Contracting States did not intend to assume such an obligation when they concluded the Convention.[87]

Assessment

How effective is the Convention? Most cases before the court are concerned with rights which, if fundamental at all, lie at the very edge of that area. Does this mean that core human rights, like freedom from torture, are well protected in Europe? Such a view would be misleading. Despite the inspiring words of the Convention, violations of the most fundamental human rights do occur.

The position is worst in countries like Russia and Turkey. Let us take what is probably the most extreme example: Chechnya. Since that country is part of Russia (a Contracting State), it is fully covered by the Convention. There have been persistent reports of massive human-rights violations there.[88] Details are scanty, since it is difficult and dangerous for Western reporters to visit the country. In order to get an idea of how the Convention would apply in such

84 For this reason Jacobs and White say, with reference to the words "within their jurisdiction": "Clearly these words do not mean that States are not liable for violations committed by them outside their territory; such an interpretation would be manifestly unreasonable, and would misconstrue the function of Article 1. A State must be responsible for its own violations of the Convention, wherever they are committed, but it can be responsible for securing human rights, in the sense of implementing them by the necessary legislation, only within its jurisdiction." *Ibid.*, p. 17.
85 If the Convention were to be applied to military operations, Art. 2 would have to be adapted so as to apply only to killing that is contrary to international law – for example, killing of civilians.
86 Even the court accepts that the Convention applies to human-rights violations committed by a Contracting State in an area outside its territory occupied by its forces. This was the situation in the *Loizidou* case. What is not clear, however, is whether the area must be within the territory of *some* Contracting State. Northern Cyprus is regarded by all States (except Turkey) as being part of the Republic of Cyprus, a Contracting State. Serbia, on the other hand, is not a Contracting State. So it remains to be seen whether, for example, the United Kingdom would be liable under the Convention for human rights violations committed in the part of Kosovo under its control.
87 If the court had decided to hear the application and had found against the NATO countries, the political repercussions would have been enormous.
88 For Russia in general and Chechnya in particular, see Amnesty International, *Denial of Justice – The Russian Federation* (Amnesty International, 2002), www.amnesty.org; Human Rights Watch, "*Welcome to Hell*"– *Arbitrary Detention, Torture and Extortion in Chechnya* (Human Rights Watch, New York, Washington, London and Brussels, 2000), www.hrw.org; and Human Rights Watch, *Confessions at Any Cost – Torture in Russia* (1999).

a situation, let us take an imaginary case of a Chechen who was arrested and tortured by Russian forces. Would the Convention be of any use to him?

First of all, he would face immense practical difficulties in bringing proceedings. There are probably no lawyers in Chechnya who know about the Convention. So he would have to find a lawyer outside the country. Communications would be difficult. Unless the lawyer was prepared to work without payment, money would have to be found. The Russians would no doubt deny that torture had occurred. The word of the victim would not be enough. So medical evidence would be needed. Whether this could be obtained would depend on the method of torture used and the length of time that had elapsed before the victim was released. In many instances, he would be kept in jail indefinitely or even killed. In such circumstances, proof would be almost impossible.

Even if the victim was released and able to find a doctor, the latter might be unwilling to testify for fear of reprisals. If an application were made to the Human Rights Court, the applicant and his witnesses, if they remained in Chechnya, would risk imprisonment or assassination. The only practical solution would be for them all to leave the country before bringing proceedings. However, Russia might then object that domestic remedies had not been exhausted.

For these reasons, proceedings could be brought only in rare instances. Even then, the victim might not think them worthwhile. Because the court moves slowly, it would be a long time before any remedy could be expected. Even if the applicant were able to prove his case, he might feel that the result was of little value. No doubt monetary compensation would be awarded. Russia would be under an obligation to stop using torture, but how would this be enforced? The Committee of Ministers, a political body, is supposed to secure enforcement. But many States might be unwilling to press Russia too hard for fear of evoking antagonism. They might want Russia's help in other matters – in Afghanistan, for example. Even if they were willing to take a strong line, what could they actually do? In view of all this, it is unlikely that the Russian Government would feel significantly constrained by the Convention if it were considering whether to use torture as a general policy.[89]

The above example is hypothetical, but similar cases have actually occurred in Turkey. In one, *Aksoy v. Turkey*,[90] the victim was subjected to horrendous torture. After his release, he made an application to the European Court of Human Rights. According to his legal representative, he was then subjected to death threats. Subsequently, his body was found. He had been shot. His father took over the proceedings and eventually the court found that torture had been proved. It awarded substantial compensation. It is doubtful, however, whether

---

89 If the worst came to the worst, Russia might simply leave the Council of Europe and denounce the Convention. This is what Greece did when it was found guilty of torture (and other violations of the Convention) during the regime of the Colonels. (After democracy was restored, it rejoined the Council and again became a party to the Convention.)
90 18 December 1996 (available on www.coe.int).

Turkey has changed its ways.[91] This case suggests that the Convention works least well where its protection is most needed.

The position is better in Western Europe. Nevertheless, there have been cases of torture. In *Ireland v. United Kingdom*,[92] the Commission found the United Kingdom guilty of torturing IRA suspects. When the case went to the court, however, it decided that the method used (sensory deprivation) amounted only to inhuman and degrading treatment – also a violation of Article 3, though a less serious one.[93] The Commission's view was surely the right one. More recently, the court has found France guilty of torture.[94] There have been subsequent allegations that torture is still used in France, especially against Muslims.[95]

The worst human-rights infringements committed by West European States take place abroad. Estimates vary of the number of civilians killed in the bombing of Serbia. There can be no doubt, however, that hundreds died. As we have seen, the Convention provides no remedy.

Another limitation is that proceedings under the Convention can be brought only against States. Racist crimes committed by individuals and political groups probably constitute the most serious violation of human rights within the territories of the Western European countries. They take many forms, including the killing of members of racial minorities. Unless the State in question deliberately allows such violations to happen, there is no remedy under the Convention.

In European cities, there are women, usually illegal immigrants, who are forced by gangsters to work as prostitutes. If they escape and seek protection from the police, they are usually deported. The Convention does nothing for them.

These examples show that a human rights convention, valuable though it may be, is not enough in itself to ensure that human rights are respected.

International adjudication or democracy?

The basic premise of the modern human-rights movement is that human-rights instruments, as interpreted by courts, should prevail over laws enacted by legislative bodies. The will of the judges overrides that of the legislature. Is it right that democracy should be downgraded in this way?

It can easily be justified on a formal basis. If a State agrees to a treaty under which it is obliged to obey human rights, and if it agrees to establish a court to determine what those rights are, it is obliged by international law to abide by the result. It makes no difference if its legislature takes a different view. Treaty obligations prevail over democracy. If this were not so, treaties would mean nothing.

91 See also *Aydin v. Turkey*, 25 September 1997 (available on www.coe.int).
92 18 January 1978, (1979–1980) 2 EHRR 25.
93 The use of these techniques had in fact been abandoned some years before the Commission issued its report.
94 *Selmouni v. France*, 28 July 1999 (available on www.coe.int).
95 See "Torture Claim Angers French Police", *The Times* (London), 9 January 2003, p. 10.

On a more fundamental level, however, the problem persists. Should States enter into international agreements on human rights that allow a group of judges to decide matters that would otherwise fall within the jurisdiction of democratically elected legislatures?

There are, however, two factors that must be taken into account. The first is that the victims of the violation may be members of groups excluded from the national democratic process. Where this is the case, there is no reason why they should be required to look to that process for the vindication of their rights. The groups in question are the following:

- **Persons resident outside the territory of the State in question.** They will have no right to vote in that State and no voice in its democratic process. Unfortunately, they are (normally) outside the scope of the European Convention on Human Rights as well. So they have no prospect of a remedy.

- **Aliens within the territory of the State in question.**[96] They have no voting rights, but they are covered by the European Convention. A significant number of applications before the European Court of Human Rights come from such persons.

- **Ethnic minorities struggling for independence.** Chechens in Russia, Kurds in Turkey and Republicans in Northern Ireland are examples. Since they do not want to be part of the political system in the State in question, it is unreasonable to expect them to look to it for redress.

- **Ethnic minorities that are not integrated into normal society.** Groups such as Gypsies who, by choice or by compulsion, live separately from the rest of society may be so marginalized that, even if they have the vote, they cannot make their voice heard through the normal political process.

In the case of these groups, the democratic process is not a suitable vehicle for solving grievances. So, it may be argued, where an alleged human-rights violation is directed at them, it is right that international adjudication should replace democracy

The other factor is that there may be little room for dispute that the act in question is a violation of human rights. Few would claim, for example, that torture or assassination can be justified. Such acts will normally be contrary to the law of the State concerned. Cases will come to the European Court of Human Rights only if for some reason the domestic courts are unable to provide a remedy or if the national government or legislature is so overcome by panic or prejudice that a remedy is blocked. Here too it might be thought that international adjudication is justified.

Where both these factors apply – for example, where minority groups are subjected to systematic torture – the case is particularly strong. At the

---

96 Aliens are significantly more likely than citizens to suffer infringements of their human rights. In the United Kingdom, for example, the Anti-Terrorism, Crime and Security Act 2001 allows the government to imprison foreign nationals indefinitely without trial if they are suspected of having links with terrorist activities. This does not apply to United Kingdom citizens.

other end of the spectrum, however, there are cases (not concerning ethnic minorities) where genuine disagreement exists as to whether human rights are involved at all. Examples include:

- the right of homosexuals to serve in the armed forces;
- the right of homosexuals to marry other homosexuals;
- the right of transsexuals to be given new birth certificates;
- the right of pregnant women to have an abortion;
- the right of criminals not to suffer capital punishment;
- the right of prostitutes to carry on their profession in safe, hygienic conditions in state-regulated establishments;
- the right of sado-masochists to inflict pain on each other; and
- the right of terminally ill patients to assisted suicide.

Here the argument is strongest in favour of allowing democratically elected legislatures to decide. It is true that, when it deals with such cases, the Human Rights Court takes account of public opinion. However, the opinion it takes account of is almost exclusively that of the intellectual elite, not that of ordinary people. Moreover, if it finds a European trend in favour of a particular policy, it feels justified in imposing that policy on the minority of States that are against it. In matters of this kind, however, each country should be entitled to decide for itself.

Further reading

General

Campbell (Tom), Ewing (K. D.) and Tomkins (Adam) (eds.), *Sceptical Essays on Human Rights* (Oxford University Press, Oxford, 2001).

Ekins, "Judicial Supremacy and the Rule of Law" (2003) 119 LQR 127.

Freeman (Michael), *Human Rights* (Polity Press (in association with Blackwell Publishers), Cambridge, 2002) (this book contains an introductory survey from an interdisciplinary perspective).

Robertson (Geoffrey), *Crimes against Humanity* (Allen Lane: The Penguin Press, London, 1999).

Simpson (A. W. Brian), *Human Rights and the End of Empire* (Oxford University Press, Oxford, 2001) (Britain and the genesis of the European Convention on Human Rights).

Sweet (Alec Stone), *Governing with Judges* (Oxford University Press, Oxford, 2000) (this deals with constitutional review in Europe).

United States

The literature on constitutionally protected rights in the US is enormous. Introductory works include:

Morrison (Alan B.) (general editor), *Fundamentals of American Law* (Oxford University Press, Oxford, 1996), Chapter 5 by Burt Neuborne.

Williams (Jerre S.), *Constitutional Analysis* ("Nutshell" Series, West Publishing Co., St Paul, MN, 1979).

Germany

Kommers (Donald P.), *The Constitutional Jurisprudence of the Federal Republic of Germany* (Duke University Press, Durham, NC, and London, 2nd ed., 1997).

European Convention on Human Rights

Harris (D. J.), O'Boyle (M.) and Warbrick (C.), *Law of the European Convention on Human Rights* (Butterworths, London, 1995).

Jacobs (Francis G.) and White (Robin C. A.), *The European Convention on Human Rights* (Clarendon Press, Oxford, 3rd ed., 2002).

Lawson (R. A.) and Schermers (H. G.), *Leading Cases of the European Court of Human Rights* (Ars Aequi Libri, Nijmegen, Netherlands, 2nd ed., 1999).

Merrills (J. G.) and Robertson (A. H.), *Human Rights in Europe* (Manchester University Press, Manchester, 4th ed., 2001).

Schermers, "Election of Judges to the European Court of Human Rights" (1998) 23 ELRev. 568.

15

The European Court and the Bundesverfassungsgericht

The origin of the EC fundamental-rights doctrine

Human rights were not mentioned in the original Community Treaties, possibly because it was thought they would not be relevant to an organization whose immediate aims were economic. However, it soon became apparent that there could be a conflict between Community measures and the fundamental-rights provisions of the German *Grundgesetz* (Constitution), especially those with an economic slant.[1] Some German lawyers said that Community law could not apply in Germany if it infringed these provisions. At first, the European Court was not interested in such arguments.[2] However, when it became apparent that the *Bundesverfassungsgericht* (Constitutional Court) would take such arguments seriously, the European Court changed its tune. The case in which this occurred was *Stauder v. Ulm*.

> **European Union**
> **Stauder v. Ulm**
> **COURT OF JUSTICE OF THE EUROPEAN COMMUNITIES**
> Case 29/69, [1969] ECR 419

Facts
EC Decision 69/71 established a scheme to provide cheap butter for recipients of welfare benefits. Mr Stauder received war victims' welfare benefits in Germany (he had been disabled in the war) and was therefore entitled to the butter. However, he objected to being obliged to present a coupon bearing his name and address. He thought it was a humiliation to have to reveal his identity. He argued that this constituted a violation of his fundamental rights under Articles 1 and 3 of the *Grundgesetz* (see Panel 14.3 in the previous chapter). He argued that Decision 69/71 was invalid in so far as it contained this requirement. The action was originally brought before the *Verwaltungsgericht* (administrative court) in Stuttgart, Germany. A reference was made to the European Court.

---

1 For example, Art. 12 (freedom to pursue a trade or profession) and Art. 14 (property rights).
2 *Stork v. High Authority*, Case 1/58, [1959] ECR 17 at 26 (rights under *Grundgesetz*, Arts. 2 and 12); *Geitling v. High Authority*, Cases 36–38 and 40/59, [1960] ECR 423 at 438 (rights under *Grundgesetz*, Art. 14).

Judgment

2. . . . Article 4 of Decision No. 69/71 stipulates in two of its versions, one being the German version, that the States must take all necessary measures to ensure that beneficiaries can only purchase the product in question on presentation of a "coupon indicating their names", whilst in the other versions, however, it is only stated that a "coupon referring to the person concerned" must be shown, thus making it possible to employ other methods of checking in addition to naming the beneficiary. It is therefore necessary in the first place to ascertain exactly what methods the provision at issue prescribes.

3. When a single decision is addressed to all the Member States the necessity for uniform application and accordingly for uniform interpretation makes it impossible to consider one version of the text in isolation but requires that it be interpreted on the basis of both the real intention of its author and the aim he seeks to achieve, in the light in particular of the versions in all four languages.

4. In a case like the present one, the most liberal interpretation must prevail, provided that it is sufficient to achieve the objectives pursued by the decision in question. It cannot, moreover, be accepted that the authors of the decision intended to impose stricter obligations in some Member States than in others.

5. This interpretation is, moreover, confirmed by the Commission's declaration that an amendment designed to remove the requirement that a name shall appear on the coupon was proposed by the Management Committee to which the draft of Decision No. 69/71 was submitted for its opinion. The last recital of the preamble to this decision shows that the Commission intended to adopt the proposed amendment.

6. It follows that the provision in question must be interpreted as not requiring – although it does not prohibit – the identification of beneficiaries by name. The Commission was thus able to publish on 29 July 1969 an amending decision to this effect. Each of the Member States is accordingly now able to choose from a number of methods by which the coupons may refer to the person concerned.

7. Interpreted in this way the Provision at issue contains nothing capable of prejudicing the fundamental human rights enshrined in the general principles of Community law and protected by the Court.

Comment

The court reached its conclusion by interpreting the Dutch and German versions of the provision to give them the same meaning as the versions in the other languages, a result which was almost inevitable in view of the fact that, after the reference had been made but before the court gave judgment, the Dutch and German versions were retrospectively amended by the Commission to bring this about.[3] For the purpose of this chapter, however, the interesting statement is that in the final paragraph, which announces the European Court's conversion to the doctrine of human rights. The vehicle it used for incorporating human rights into Community law was the concept of "general principles of law". There was no other way in which it could have done this,

---

3 Decision 69/244 of 29 July 1969, OJ 1969, L200, p. 29. In the German text, the words "*auf ihren Namen ausgestellten*" were replaced by "*individualisierten*". The change was retroactive to 17 February 1969.

since there was at the time no provision in the Treaties that could serve as a foundation for the new doctrine.

General principles of law were discussed in Chapter 8. It will be remembered that, though they are not stated in the Treaties to be a source of Community law (as is the case in the Statute of the International Court of Justice),[4] they have nevertheless been treated as such by the European Court. In theory, they are derived from the legal systems of the Member States (and international law). In practice, they are a device to allow the European Court to create new rules of law as it sees fit.

Development of the new doctrine

The *Stauder* case served simply to announce the new doctrine. It was developed in subsequent cases. In particular, the European Court had to make clear how it proposed to go about deciding what actual rights were covered. Moreover, since its purpose was to deter the *Bundesverfassungsgericht* from rebellion, it was essential that it should be sufficiently far-reaching to convince the Germans that Community law would pose no threat to fundamental rights in Germany.

The ideal way of satisfying the Germans would have been to say that anything that was a fundamental right under the constitution of any Member State would automatically qualify as such under Community law. Such a conclusion could be justified by the following argument:

> The Community obtained its powers from the Member States: they conferred legislative and other powers on the Community when they concluded the Community Treaties. However, countries like Germany that were subject to constitutional limitations derived from fundamental rights were constitutionally unable to adopt legislation, or take administrative action, that contravened fundamental rights. Consequently, they were unable to confer such powers on the Community.[5]

If one accepts this argument, it follows that the Community has no power to act contrary to human rights as understood under the constitution of any Member State.

Though attractive, this argument has never been expressly adopted by the European Court. Perhaps it considers that it would imply that Community law was subordinate to Member-State law. There are, however, some cases in which it has come fairly close to it, though in others it has stressed the independence of Community law and emphasized that the standards of Member-State law can never be used to judge it. This is illustrated by the next two cases, which also show how the European Court has applied the new doctrine.

---

4 Art. 38(1)(c).
5 See *per* Advocate-General Warner, *IRCA*, Case 7/76, [1976] ECR 1213, at 1237; see also Schermers, "The European Communities Bound by Fundamental Human Rights" (1990) 27 CMLRev. 249 at 253–255.

European Union
Internationale Handelsgesellschaft case
COURT OF JUSTICE OF THE EUROPEAN COMMUNITIES
Case 11/70, [1970] ECR 1125

Facts

In order to control the market in certain agricultural products, the Community had introduced a system under which exports were permitted only if the exporter first obtained an export licence. When application was made for the licence, the exporter had to deposit a sum of money which would be forfeit if he failed to make the export during the period of validity of the licence.

The applicants in this case claimed that the whole system was invalid as being contrary to fundamental human rights. One principle invoked was that of proportionality. This is a doctrine of German constitutional law, which is regarded as underpinning Articles 2(1) and 14 of the *Grundgesetz* (see Panel 14.3, above). Under this doctrine, public authorities may impose on the citizen only such obligations as are necessary for attaining the public objective in question. It was argued in the German *Verwaltungsgericht* (administrative court), where the proceedings commenced, that the relevant Community measure was invalid for violating the *Grundgesetz*. The question of the validity of the measure was referred to the European Court.

Judgment

3. Recourse to the legal rules or concepts of national law in order to judge the validity of measures adopted by the institutions of the Community would have an adverse effect on the uniformity and efficacy of Community law. The validity of such measures can only be judged in the light of Community law. In fact, the law stemming from the treaty, an independent source of law, cannot because of its very nature be overridden by rules of national law, however framed, without being deprived of its character as Community law and without the legal basis of the Community itself being called in question. Therefore the validity of a Community measure or its effect within a Member State cannot be affected by allegations that it runs counter to either fundamental rights as formulated by the Constitution of that State or the principles of a national constitutional structure.

4. However, an examination should be made as to whether or not any analogous guarantee inherent in Community law has been disregarded. In fact, respect for fundamental rights forms an integral part of the general principles of law protected by the Court of Justice. The protection of such rights, whilst inspired by the constitutional traditions common to the Member States, must be ensured within the framework of the structure and objectives of the Community. It must therefore be ascertained, in the light of the doubts expressed by the *Verwaltungsgericht*, whether the system of deposits has infringed rights of a fundamental nature, respect for which must be ensured in the Community legal system.

[The European Court then went on to examine the details of the system and concluded that, since the costs involved in the deposit were not disproportionate to the total value of the goods and the burdens of the system were not excessive (i.e. that the system was not contrary to the principle of proportionality), it did not infringe any fundamental right under Community law. It therefore declared the measure valid.]

European Union
Nold v. Commission
COURT OF JUSTICE OF THE EUROPEAN COMMUNITIES
Case 4/73, [1974] ECR 491

Facts

This case concerned a Commission decision under the ECSC Treaty, which provided that coal wholesalers could not buy Ruhr coal direct from the selling
agency unless they agreed to purchase a certain minimum quantity. Nold was
a Ruhr wholesaler who was not in a position to meet this requirement and consequently had to deal with an intermediary. He claimed that the decision was
a violation of his fundamental human rights, partly because it deprived him of
a property right (Article 14 of the *Grundgesetz*) and partly because it infringed
his freedom to pursue a trade or profession (Article 12). He therefore brought
proceedings before the European Court under Article 33 ECSC (equivalent to
Article 230 [173] EC) for annulment of the decision.

Judgment

12. The applicant asserts finally that certain of its fundamental rights have been violated, in
that the restrictions introduced by the new trading rules authorized by the Commission
have the effect, by depriving it of direct supplies, of jeopardizing both the profitability of
the undertaking and the free development of its business activity, to the point of
endangering its very existence. In this way, the decision is said to violate, in respect of the
applicant, a right akin to a proprietary right, as well as its right to the free pursuit of
business activity, as protected by the *Grundgesetz* of the Federal Republic of Germany and
by the constitutions of other Member States and various international treaties, including in
particular the Convention for the Protection of Human Rights and Fundamental Freedoms
of 4 November 1950 and the Protocol to that Convention of 20 March 1952.

13. As the Court has already stated, fundamental rights form an integral part of the general
principles of law, the observance of which it ensures. In safeguarding these rights, the
Court is bound to draw inspiration from constitutional traditions common to the Member
States, and it cannot therefore uphold measures which are incompatible with fundamental
rights recognized and protected by the Constitutions of those States. Similarly,
international treaties for the protection of human rights on which the Member States have
collaborated or of which they are signatories, can supply guidelines which should be
followed within the framework of Community law. The submissions of the applicant must
be examined in the light of these principles.

14. If rights of ownership are protected by the constitutional laws of all the Member States
and if similar guarantees are given in respect of their right freely to choose and practise
their trade or profession, the rights thereby guaranteed, far from constituting unfettered
prerogatives, must be viewed in the light of the social function of the property and
activities protected thereunder. For this reason, rights of this nature are protected by law
subject always to limitations laid down in accordance with the public interest. Within the
Community legal order it likewise seems legitimate that these rights should, if necessary,
be subject to certain limits justified by the overall objectives pursued by the Community,
on condition that the substance of these rights is left untouched. As regards the

guarantees accorded to a particular undertaking, they can in no respect be extended to protect mere commercial interests or opportunities, the uncertainties of which are part of the very essence of economic activity.

15. The disadvantages claimed by the applicant are in fact the result of economic change and not of the contested Decision. It was for the applicant, confronted by the economic changes brought about by the recession in coal production, to acknowledge the situation and itself carry out the necessary adaptations.

[Result: action dismissed.]

European Union
Hauer v. Land Rheinland-Pfalz
COURT OF JUSTICE OF THE EUROPEAN COMMUNITIES
Case 44/79, [1979] ECR 3727

Facts

Ms Hauer owned land in Germany, which she wanted to plant as a vineyard. Under German law, she was required to obtain authorization from the competent administrative authority. This was refused on the ground that the land was not suitable. She appealed to a higher administrative authority. While this appeal was pending, the Community adopted Regulation 1162/76 imposing a temporary ban on all new planting of vines. Her appeal was then dismissed on two grounds: that the land was unsuitable and that all new planting was forbidden by the Community regulation. She then appealed to the local administrative court. This decided that the land *was* suitable for wine production. As far as German law was concerned, therefore, there was no longer any impediment to her planting her vineyard.

She was still prevented from doing so, however, by Community law. She then argued, first, that the regulation did not apply to her case (because she had made her original application before it was adopted); and, secondly, that, if it did apply, it was invalid because it infringed her human rights, in particular her right to property (Article 14 of the *Grundgesetz*) and her right to pursue a trade or profession (Article 12 of the *Grundgesetz*) (both set out in Panel 14.3, above). The *Verwaltungsgericht* referred the matter to the European Court.

Judgment
[On the question whether the regulation applied in her case, the European Court ruled as follows:]

6. In this regard, the plaintiff in the main action claims that her application, submitted to the competent administrative authority on 6 June 1975, should in the normal course of events have led to a decision in her favour before the entry into force of the Community regulation if the administrative procedure had taken its usual course and if the administration had recognized without delay the fact that her plot of land is suitable for wine-growing in accordance with the requirements of national law. It is, she argues, necessary to take account of that situation in deciding the time from which the

Community regulation is applicable, the more so as the production of the vineyard in question would not have had any appreciable influence on market conditions, in view of the time which elapses between the planting of a vineyard and its first production.

7. The arguments advanced by the plaintiff in the main action cannot be upheld. Indeed the second subparagraph of Article 2 (1) of [the regulation in question] expressly provides that Member States shall no longer grant authorizations for new planting "as from the date on which this Regulation enters into force". By referring to the act of granting authorization, that provision rules out the possibility of taking into consideration the time at which an application was submitted. It indicates the intention to give immediate effect to the regulation, to such an extent that even the exercise of rights to plant or re-plant acquired prior to the entry into force of the regulation is suspended during the period of the prohibition as a result of Article 4 of the same regulation.

8. As is stated in the sixth recital of the preamble, with regard to the last-mentioned provision, the prohibition on new plantings is required by an "undeniable public interest", making it necessary to put a brake on the overproduction of wine in the Community, to re-establish the balance of the market and to prevent the formation of structural surpluses. Thus it appears that the object of [the regulation in question] is the immediate prevention of any extension in the area covered by vineyards. Therefore no exception may be made in favour of an application submitted before its entry into force.

[On the question of human rights, the European Court ruled as follows:]

The Protection of Fundamental Rights in the Community Legal Order

13. In its order making the reference, the *Verwaltungsgericht* states that if [the regulation in question] must be interpreted as meaning that it lays down a prohibition of general application, so as to include even land appropriate for wine growing, that provision might have to be considered inapplicable in the Federal Republic of Germany owing to doubts existing with regard to its compatibility with the fundamental rights guaranteed by Articles 14 and 12 of the *Grundgesetz* concerning, respectively, the right to property and the right freely to pursue trade and professional activities.

14. As the Court declared in [*Internationale Handelsgesellschaft*, above], the question of a possible infringement of fundamental rights by a measure of the Community institutions can only be judged in the light of Community law itself. The introduction of special criteria for assessment stemming from the legislation or constitutional law of a particular Member State would, by damaging the substantive unity and efficacy of Community law, lead inevitably to the destruction of the unity of the Common Market and the jeopardizing of the cohesion of the Community.

15. The Court also emphasized in the judgment cited, and later in [*Nold*, above], that fundamental rights form an integral part of the general principles of the law, the observance of which it ensures; that in safeguarding those rights, the Court is bound to draw inspiration from constitutional traditions common to the Member States, so that measures which are incompatible with the fundamental rights recognized by the constitutions of those States are unacceptable in the Community; and that similarly, international treaties for the protection of human rights on which the Member States have collaborated or of which they are signatories, can supply guidelines which should be followed within the framework of Community law. That conception was later recognized by the joint declaration of the European Parliament, the Council and the Commission of 5 April 1977, which, after recalling the case-law of the Court, refers on the one hand to the rights guaranteed by the constitutions of the Member States and on the other hand to the

European Convention for the Protection of Human Rights and Fundamental Freedoms of 4 November 1950 . . .

16. In these circumstances, the doubts evinced by the *Verwaltungsgericht* as to the compatibility of the provisions of [the regulation in question] with the rules concerning the protection of fundamental rights must be understood as questioning the validity of the regulation in the light of Community law. In this regard, it is necessary to distinguish between, on the one hand, a possible infringement of the right to property and, on the other hand, a possible limitation upon the freedom to pursue a trade or profession.

The Question of the Right to Property

17. The right to property is guaranteed in the Community legal order in accordance with the ideas common to the constitutions of the Member States, which are also reflected in the first Protocol to the European Convention for the Protection of Human Rights.

[Paragraph 18, which sets out Article 1 of Protocol No. 1 (Panel 14.4, in the previous chapter) is omitted.]

19. Having declared that persons are entitled to the peaceful enjoyment of their property, that provision envisages two ways in which the rights of a property owner may be impaired, according as the impairment is intended to deprive the owner of his right or to restrict the exercise thereof. In this case it is incontestable that the prohibition on new planting cannot be considered to be an act depriving the owner of his property, since he remains free to dispose of it or to put it to other uses which are not prohibited. On the other hand, there is no doubt that that prohibition restricts the use of the property. In this regard, the second paragraph of Article 1 of the Protocol provides an important indication in so far as it recognizes the right of a State "to enforce such laws as it deems necessary to control the use of property in accordance with the general interest". Thus the Protocol accepts in principle the legality of restrictions upon the use of property, whilst at the same time limiting those restrictions to the extent to which they are deemed "necessary" by a State for the protection of the "general interest". However, that provision does not enable a sufficiently precise answer to be given to the question submitted by the *Verwaltungsgericht*.

20. Therefore, in order to be able to answer that question, it is necessary to consider also the indications provided by the constitutional rules and practices of the nine Member States. One of the first points to emerge in this regard is that those rules and practices permit the legislature to control the use of private property in accordance with the general interest. Thus some constitutions refer to the obligations arising out of the ownership of property (German *Grundgesetz*, Article 14 (2), first sentence), to its social function (Italian Constitution, Article 42 (2)), to the subordination of its use to the requirements of the common good (German *Grundgesetz*, Article 14 (2), second sentence, and the Irish Constitution, Article 43.2.2), or of social justice (Irish Constitution, Article 43.2.1). In all the Member States, numerous legislative measures have given concrete expression to that social function of the right to property. Thus in all the Member States there is legislation on agriculture and forestry, the water supply, the protection of the environment and town and country planning, which imposes restrictions, sometimes appreciable, on the use of real property.

21. More particularly, all the wine-producing countries of the Community have restrictive legislation, albeit of differing severity, concerning the planting of vines, the selection of varieties and the methods of cultivation. In none of the countries concerned are those provisions considered to be incompatible in principle with the regard due to the right to property.

22. Thus it may be stated, taking into account the constitutional precepts common to the Member States and consistent legislative practices, in widely varying spheres, that the fact that [the regulation in question] imposed restrictions on the new planting of vines cannot be challenged in principle. It is a type of restriction which is known and accepted as lawful, in identical or similar forms, in the constitutional structure of all the Member States.

23. However, that finding does not deal completely with the problem raised by the *Verwaltungsgericht*. Even if it is not possible to dispute in principle the Community's ability to restrict the exercise of the right to property in the context of a common organization of the market and for the purposes of a structural policy, it is still necessary to examine whether the restrictions introduced by the provisions in dispute in fact correspond to objectives of general interest pursued by the Community or whether, with regard to the aim pursued, they constitute a disproportionate and intolerable interference with the rights of the owner, impinging upon the very substance of the right to property. Such in fact is the plea submitted by the plaintiff in the main action, who considers that only the pursuit of a qualitative policy would permit the legislature to restrict the use of wine-growing property, with the result that she possesses an unassailable right from the moment that it is recognized that her land is suitable for wine growing. It is therefore necessary to identify the aim pursued by the disputed regulation and to determine whether there exists a reasonable relationship between the measures provided for by the regulation and the aim pursued by the Community in this case.

[The court considered Community policy as contained in various measures. It continued:]

27. . . . It is apparent from the preamble to [the regulation in question] and from the economic circumstances in which it was adopted, a feature of which was the formation as from the 1974 harvest of permanent production surpluses, that that regulation fulfils a double function: on the one hand, it must enable an immediate brake to be put on the continued increase in the surpluses; on the other hand, it must win for the Community institutions the time necessary for the implementation of a structural policy designed to encourage high-quality production, whilst respecting the individual characteristics and needs of the different wine-producing regions of the Community, through the selection of land for grape growing and the selection of grape varieties, and through the regulation of production methods.

28. It was in order to fulfil that twofold purpose that the Council introduced by [the regulation in question] a general prohibition on new plantings, without making any distinction, apart from certain narrowly defined exceptions, according to the quality of the land. It should be noted that, as regards its sweeping scope, the measure introduced by the Council is of a temporary nature. It is designed to deal immediately with a conjunctural situation characterized by surpluses, whilst at the same time preparing permanent structural measures.

29. Seen in this light, the measure criticized does not entail any undue limitation upon the exercise of the right to property. Indeed, the cultivation of new vineyards in a situation of continuous over-production would not have any effect, from the economic point of view, apart from increasing the volume of the surpluses; further, such an extension at that stage would entail the risk of making more difficult the implementation of a structural policy at the Community level in the event of such a policy resting on the application of criteria more stringent than the current provisions of national legislation concerning the selection of land accepted for wine-growing.

30. Therefore it is necessary to conclude that the restriction imposed upon the use of property by the prohibition on the new planting of vines introduced for a limited period by [the regulation in question] is justified by the objectives of general interest pursued by the Community and does not infringe the substance of the right to property in the form in which it is recognized and protected in the Community legal order.

The Question of the Freedom to Pursue Trade or Professional Activities

[The court considered that any restriction placed on Ms Hauer's freedom to pursue a trade or profession was justified on similar grounds. Result: the regulation was held valid.]

Comment

As is well known, the EC does not believe in giving free play to market forces in agriculture. It strives to control the market to ensure that farmers obtain what is regarded as a reasonable price for their produce. This requires the Community taxpayer to provide the subsidies that seem an inevitable part of the common agricultural policy.

This is not, however, the only policy the Community could adopt. The alternative would be to allow the market to operate without interference. If there was over-production, prices would fall. The least efficient farmers would go bankrupt and have to leave the land. Equilibrium would then be restored. The question of quality could also be left to market forces. If consumers cared enough to pay more for wine of good quality, farmers would be rewarded for the extra work entailed. All that would be required would be a system to ensure that the consumer knew what he was buying.

The problem with an interventionist policy is that it requires restrictions on property rights and economic freedoms. The essence of Ms Hauer's challenge was that such restrictions are contrary to fundamental rights. From a strictly legal point of view, such a contention is far from indefensible. From a political point of view, however, it is unacceptable. Whether the Community should pursue free-market or market-management policies is a question that should be decided through the political system. It should not be decided by judges.

In the United States, the Supreme Court has in the past used the Constitution to strike down legislation that conflicted with free-market principles. This policy reached its high point during the early years of the New Deal, when President Roosevelt resorted to state regulation to combat the effects of the Great Depression. In the years 1934 to 1936, the court gave twelve decisions declaring New Deal measures invalid. In essence, its argument was that restrictions on freedom of contract or property were contrary to the Due Process Clause of the Fifth and Fourteenth Amendments.[6] In 1937, however, there occurred a

---

6 Thus, legislation on minimum wages and maximum hours of work was regarded as restricting contractual rights. For an early example of this approach, see *Lochner v. New York*, 198 US 45 (1905), in which a New York statute forbidding employment in a bakery for more than sixty hours a week was struck down on the ground that "the right to purchase or sell labor is part of the liberty protected by [the Fourteenth Amendment]". Justice Holmes dissented: "This case is decided upon an economic theory which a large part of the country does not entertain." *Lochner* was overruled in *Bunting v. Oregon*, 243

remarkable turnabout, perhaps the most remarkable in the whole history of the court. Beginning in April 1937, it upheld every New Deal law presented to it, including many that were basically similar to those previously rejected.[7]

The reasons for the turnabout were complex. In part, it may have been because certain judges began to see things differently. However, Roosevelt's plan to pack the court with new judges sympathetic to his point of view, though ultimately defeated in the Senate Judiciary Committee, may have had its effect.

It is likely that the European Court (which likes to compare itself to the US Supreme Court) was aware of these events when it decided *Hauer*. If it had had any inclination to strike down the Community legislation (which it almost certainly did not), it would have been dissuaded from doing so by the example from across the Atlantic.

QUESTIONS

1. What exactly is the effect of national constitutional provisions on human rights in Community law? Could a Community measure be consistent with Community human rights if it was contrary to fundamental rights as protected by the constitution of a Member State?

2. Is there any inconsistency between the statement in *Nold* (above, at paragraph 13) that "the Court is bound to draw inspiration from the constitutional traditions common to the Member States and it cannot therefore uphold measures which are incompatible with fundamental rights recognized and protected by the constitutions of those States" and its statement in the *Internationale Handelsgesellschaft* case (above, at paragraph 3), repeated in *Hauer* (above, at paragraph 14), that the introduction of special criteria stemming from the constitutional law of a particular Member State is not permissible?

3. Would a Community measure necessarily be invalid in Community eyes if it was contrary to the European Convention on Human Rights?

Germany
Internationale Handelsgesellschaft case
BUNDESVERFASSUNGSGERICHT (GERMAN CONSTITUTIONAL COURT)
Judgment of 29 May 1974, 37 BVerfGE 271; English translation in [1974] 2 CMLR 540

US 426 (1917), when the court was presented with social statistics in a so-called "Brandeis brief". However, similar arguments were used by the court to strike down minimum-wage legislation in *Adkins v. Children's Hospital*, 261 US 525 (1923) (Fifth Amendment) and *Morehead v. People of New York, ex rel. Tipaldo*, 298 US 587 (1936) (Fourteenth Amendment). After the "turnabout" these decisions were overruled in *West Coast Hotel Co. v. Parrish*, 300 US 379 (1937). For further details, see William B. Lockhart, Yale Kamisar, Jesse H. Choper, Steven H. Shiffrin and Richard H. Fallon Jr, *Constitutional Rights and Liberties* (West Publishing Co., St Paul, MN, 8th ed., 1996), pp. 57–69.

7 For the full story, see Bernard Schwartz, *A History of the Supreme Court* (Oxford University Press, New York and London, 1993), pp. 231–238.

Panel 15.1 *Grundgesetz*, **Articles 24(1) and 25**

Article 24

(1) The Federation may by a law transfer sovereign powers to international organizations.

Article 25

The general rules of international law shall be an integral part of federal law. They shall take precedence over the laws and directly create rights and duties for the inhabitants of the federal territory.

Background

After the European Court gave its ruling in the *Internationale Handelsgesellschaft* case (above), the case was sent back to the German administrative court that made the reference. The latter then referred the case to the *Bundesverfassungsgericht* for a ruling on the question whether the Community measure was contrary to the *Grundgesetz* and, if so, whether that meant that it could not be applied in Germany. The first question considered by the *Bundesverfassungsgericht* was whether it had jurisdiction. This depended on whether Community measures are subject to the *Grundgesetz*. The court limited its inquiry to the relationship between Community legislation (as distinct from the Treaties themselves) and the fundamental-rights provisions of the *Grundgesetz*.

Judgment

[19.] 2. This Court – in this respect in agreement with the law developed by the European Court of Justice – adheres to its settled view that Community law is neither a component part of the national legal system nor international law, but forms an independent system of law flowing from an autonomous legal source;[8] for the Community is not a State, in particular not a federal State, but "a *sui generis* community in the process of progressive integration", an "inter-State institution" within the meaning of Article 24(1) of the Constitution.[9]

[20.] It follows from this that, in principle, the two legal spheres stand independent of and side by side one another in their validity, and that, in particular, the competent Community organs, including the European Court of Justice, have to rule on the binding force, construction and observance of Community law, and the competent national organs on the binding force, construction and observance of the constitutional law of the Federal Republic of Germany. The European Court of Justice cannot with binding effect rule on whether a rule of Community law is compatible with the Constitution, nor can the *Bundesverfassungsgericht* rule on whether, and with what implications, a rule of secondary Community law is compatible with primary Community law. This does not lead to any difficulties as long as the two systems of law do not come into conflict with one another in their substance. There therefore grows forth from the special relationship which has arisen between the Community and its members by the establishment of the Community first and foremost the duty for the competent organs, in particular for the two courts charged with reviewing law – the European Court of Justice and the *Bundesverfassungsgericht* – to concern themselves in their decisions with the concordance of the two systems of law. Only in so far as this is unsuccessful can there

8 22 BVerfGE 293 at 296; 31 BverfGE 145 at 173–174.
9 Editor's note: see Panel 15.1.

arise the conflict which demands the drawing of conclusions from the relationship of principle between the two legal spheres set out above.

[21.] For, in this case, it is not enough simply to speak of the "precedence" of Community law over national constitutional law, in order to justify the conclusion that Community law must always prevail over national constitutional law because, otherwise, the Community would be put in question. Community law is just as little put in question when, exceptionally, Community law is not permitted to prevail over entrenched (*zwingende*) constitutional law, as international law is put in question by Article 25 of the Constitution[10] when it provides that the general rules of international law only take precedence over simple federal law, and as another (foreign) system of law is put in question when it is ousted by the public policy of the Federal Republic of Germany. The binding of the Federal Republic of Germany (and of all Member States) by the Treaty is not, according to the meaning and spirit of the Treaties, one-sided, but also binds the Community which they establish to carry out its part in order to resolve the conflict here assumed, that is, to seek a system which is compatible with an entrenched precept of the constitutional law of the Federal Republic of Germany. Invoking such a conflict is therefore not in itself a violation of the Treaty, but sets in motion inside the European organs the Treaty mechanism which resolves the conflict on a political level.

[22.] 3. Article 24 of the Constitution deals with the transfer of sovereign rights to inter-State institutions. This cannot be taken literally. Like every constitutional provision of a similar fundamental nature, Article 24 of the Constitution must be understood and construed in the overall context of the whole Constitution. That is, it does not open the way to amending the basic structure of the Constitution, which forms the basis of its identity, without a formal amendment to the Constitution, that is, it does not open any such way through the legislation of the inter-State institution. Certainly, the competent Community organs can make law which the competent German constitutional organs could not make under the law of the Constitution and which is nonetheless valid and is to be applied directly in the Federal Republic of Germany. But Article 24 of the Constitution limits this possibility in that it nullifies any amendment of the Treaty which would destroy the identity of the valid constitution of the Federal Republic of Germany by encroaching on the structures which go to make it up. And the same would apply to rules of secondary Community law made on the basis of a corresponding interpretation of the valid Treaty and in the same way affecting the structures essential to the Constitution. Article 24 does not actually give authority to transfer sovereign rights, but opens up the national legal system (within the limitations indicated) in such a way that the Federal Republic of Germany's exclusive claim to rule is taken back in the sphere of validity of the Constitution and room is given, within the State's sphere of rule, to the direct effect and applicability of law from another source.

[23.] 4. The part of the Constitution dealing with fundamental rights is an inalienable essential feature of the valid Constitution of the Federal Republic of Germany and one which forms part of the constitutional structure of the Constitution. Article 24 of the Constitution does not without reservation allow it to be subjected to qualifications. In this, the present state of integration of the Community is of crucial importance. The Community still lacks a democratically legitimated parliament directly elected by general suffrage which possesses legislative powers and to which the Community organs empowered to legislate are fully responsible on a political level; it still lacks in particular a codified catalogue of

---

10 Editor's note: see Panel 15.1.

fundamental rights, the substance of which is reliably and unambiguously fixed for the future in the same way as the substance of the Constitution and therefore allows a comparison and a decision as to whether, at the time in question, the Community law standard with regard to fundamental rights generally binding in the Community is adequate in the long term measured by the standard of the Constitution with regard to fundamental rights (without prejudice to possible amendments) in such a way that there is no exceeding the limitation indicated, set by Article 24 of the Constitution. As long as this legal certainty, which is not guaranteed merely by the decisions of the European Court of Justice, favourable though these have been to fundamental rights, is not achieved in the course of the further integration of the Community, the reservation derived from Article 24 of the Constitution applies. What is involved is, therefore, a legal difficulty arising exclusively from the Community's continuing integration process, which is still in flux and which will end with the present transitional phase.

[24.] Provisionally, therefore, in the hypothetical case of a conflict between Community law and a part of national constitutional law or, more precisely, of the guarantees of fundamental rights in the Constitution, there arises the question of which system of law takes precedence, that is, ousts the other. In this conflict of norms, the guarantee of fundamental rights in the Constitution prevails as long as the competent organs of the Community have not removed the conflict of norms in accordance with the Treaty mechanism.

[25.] 5. From the relationship between Constitution and Community law outlined above, the following conclusions emerge with regard to the jurisdiction of the European Court of Justice and of the *Bundesverfassungsgericht*.

[26.] (a) In accordance with the Treaty rules on jurisdiction, the European Court of Justice has jurisdiction to rule on the legal validity of the norms of Community law (including the unwritten norms of Community law which it considers exist) and on their construction. It does not, however, decide incidental questions of national law of the Federal Republic of Germany (or in any other Member State) with binding force for this State. Statements in the reasoning of its judgments that a particular aspect of a Community norm accords or is compatible in its substance with a constitutional rule of national law – here, with a guarantee of fundamental rights in the Constitution – constitute non-binding *obiter dicta*.

[27.] In the framework of this jurisdiction, the European Court determines the content of Community law with binding effect for all the Member States. Accordingly, under the terms of Article 234 [177] of the Treaty, the courts of the Federal Republic of Germany have to obtain the ruling of the European Court before they raise the question of the compatibility of the norm of Community law which is relevant to their decision with guarantees of fundamental rights in the Constitution.

[After considering various other matters, the court concluded:]

[35.] The result is: as long as the integration process has not progressed so far that Community law also receives a catalogue of fundamental rights decided on by a parliament and of settled validity, which is adequate in comparison with the catalogue of fundamental rights contained in the Constitution, a reference by a court in the Federal Republic of Germany to the *Bundesverfassungsgericht* in judicial review proceedings, following the obtaining of a ruling of the European Court under Article 234 [177] of the Treaty, is admissible and necessary, if the German court regards the rule of Community law which is relevant to its decision as inapplicable in the interpretation given by the European Court, because and in so far as it conflicts with one of the fundamental rights in the Constitution.

Comment

When they read the above, the judges on the European Court must have thought that their strategy had failed. Despite their efforts, the *Bundesverfassungsgericht* had insisted that Community provisions could not apply in Germany if they conflicted with the fundamental-rights provisions of the *Grundgesetz*. However, in the *Internationale Handelsgesellschaft* case, the *Bundesverfassungsgericht* held in the end that the Community measure in issue did not contravene the *Grundgesetz*. In fact, it has never found any Community measure to be contrary to the *Grundgesetz*. Moreover, as paragraph [23] of the judgment makes clear, it has always been willing to reconsider its position if the level of protection of fundamental rights under Community law was raised.

The *Internationale Handelsgesellschaft* case was not, therefore, a rejection of the European Court's strategy. The *Bundesverfassungsgericht* was simply saying that what the European Court had done was not enough. It was hardly surprising, therefore, that, after hinting at a new approach in 1979,[11] the *Bundesverfassungsgericht* finally ruled in 1986 that the protection of human rights in the Community had developed sufficiently to meet the requirements of the *Grundgesetz*. This occurred in the *Wünsche Handelsgesellschaft* case.

Germany
Wünsche Handelsgesellschaft case
BUNDESVERFASSUNGSGERICHT (GERMAN CONSTITUTIONAL COURT)
Judgment of 22 October 1986; English translation in [1987] 3 CMLR 225

It will be remembered that the requirements laid down in the *Internationale Handelsgesellschaft* case were:
- a "catalogue" of fundamental rights,
- decided on by a parliament,
- which is of settled validity, and
- which is adequate in comparison with that in the *Grundgesetz*.

A number of developments had taken place since the *Internationale Handelsgesellschaft* case. These were:
- The Parliament, the Council and the Commission had made a declaration in April 1977 in which they stressed "the importance they attach to the protection of fundamental rights, as derived in particular from the constitutions of the Member States and the [European Convention on Human Rights]". They undertook to respect those rights in the exercise of their powers.
- In the *Nold* case, the European Court had said that it would not uphold measures "incompatible with fundamental rights recognized and protected by the constitutions of [the Member States]".[12]
- The European Court had accepted various specific rights and principles (such as proportionality).

---

11 *Steinike and Weinlig*, 25 July 1979, [1980] 2 CMLR 531 at 537 (para. 12).
12 Para. 13 of the judgment. The *Bundesverfassungsgericht* omitted to mention the contradictory statements in other cases.

- The European Court had accepted that it should have regard to the European Convention on Human Rights in determining what rights were to be protected.

The *Bundesverfassungsgericht* recognized that the Declaration of April 1977 was not legally binding, and that the Community was not a party to the European Convention on Human Rights. Nevertheless, it considered the requirements satisfied because:

- all the Member States were parties to the European Convention on Human Rights;
- the Declaration of April 1977 was sufficient recognition by the Parliament of a "catalogue" of fundamental rights; and
- although the European Parliament did not possess the powers of a proper parliament, there was no intention in the *Internationale Handelsgesellschaft* case to make this an essential requirement.

For these reasons, the *Bundesverfassungsgericht* concluded that as long as the EC and, in particular, the European Court ensured effective protection of fundamental rights that were substantially similar to those protected by the *Grundgesetz*, it would no longer review Community legislation to ensure that it complied with the requirements of the *Grundgesetz*.

Comment

It is important to appreciate, as is apparent from the above, that the *Bundesverfassungsgericht* still takes the view that the fundamental rights provisions of the *Grundgesetz* prevail over the Community Treaties in Germany. However, it is prepared to leave to the European Court the task of ensuring that Community law is consistent with fundamental rights. If the European Court were to fall down on this task, the *Bundesverfassungsgericht* would take it over again.[13] This position is reinforced by Article 23 of the *Grundgesetz*, as amended in 1992 to make express provision for German membership of the EU. Article 23(1) now reads:

> With a view to establishing a united Europe, the Federal Republic of Germany shall participate in the development of the European Union that is committed to democratic, social and federal principles, to the rule of law, and to the principle of subsidiarity and that guarantees a level of protection of basic rights essentially comparable to that afforded by this Basic Law. To this end the Federation may transfer sovereign powers by a law with the consent of the *Bundesrat*. The establishment of the European Union, as well as changes in its treaty foundations and comparable regulations that amend or supplement this Basic Law, or make such amendments or supplements possible, shall be subject to paragraphs (2) and (3) of Article 79.

---

13 See, for example, its decision of 12 May 1989 in the *Tobacco Advertising* case, Case 2 BvQ 3/89, [1990] 1 CMLR 570. In this case, the *Bundesverfassungsgericht* pointed out that a directive infringing fundamental human rights as understood in Community law could be brought before the European Court. It added, however, that if this proved inadequate to protect the constitutional standards required by the *Grundgesetz*, proceedings could be brought before it. It also said that German legislation to implement a directive would be subject to constitutional review.

Article 79 is the provision dealing with amendments to the Constitution. Paragraph (2) requires a two-thirds vote in both the *Bundestag* (the lower house of the German Parliament) and in the *Bundesrat* (the upper house, representing the *Länder* (states)). Paragraph (3) states, among other things, that the principles laid down in Articles 1 to 20 (the provisions on basic rights) cannot be amended. This makes clear that Community law cannot prevail over them.

Panel 15.2   Human rights in the EU Treaties

Treaty on European Union

Article 6 [F]

1. The Union is founded on the principles of liberty, democracy, respect for human rights and fundamental freedoms, and the rule of law, principles which are common to the Member States.

2. The Union shall respect fundamental rights, as guaranteed by the European Convention for the Protection of Human Rights and Fundamental Freedoms signed in Rome on 4 November 1950 and as they result from the constitutional traditions common to the Member States, as general principles of Community law.

QUESTION

Was the *Bundesverfassungsgericht* being quite honest when it found that the requirements set down in the *Internationale Handelsgesellschaft* case had been satisfied, or do you think it scaled down the level of protection needed?

Later developments

The Member States and Community institutions have since taken steps to strengthen human rights in the Community. The Treaty on European Union states that the EU is founded on respect for human rights. It requires it to respect human rights, as guaranteed by the European Convention on Human Rights, as general principles of law (Article 6(1) and 6(2) [F(1) and F(2)], set out in Panel 15.2). This merely confirms what the European Court has already laid down, but it is of value to have it expressly stated that the Convention is binding on the Community, even if it is only as a general principle of law. (The significance of this is that general principles prevail over Community legislation, but not over the Community Treaties.)

On 7 December 2000, the European Parliament, the Council and the Commission "proclaimed" the Charter of Fundamental Rights of the European Union.[14] At present, the Charter has no binding force. The rights it contains are similar to those in the European Convention, though in some ways it goes further. It is addressed to the institutions of the Community, and it binds the Member States only when implementing EU law. Article 52(3) of the Charter provides that, in so far as it contains rights which correspond to those in the European Convention, the meaning and scope of those rights is the same as that in the Convention. Extracts from certain general provisions are set out in Panel 15.3.

---

14 OJ 2000, C364, p. 1. It has been slightly amended in the proposed Constitution for Europe.

Panel 15.3   Charter of Fundamental Rights of the European Union

Article 51   Scope

1. The provisions of this Charter are addressed to the institutions and bodies of the Union with due regard for the principle of subsidiarity and to the Member States only when they are implementing Union law. They shall therefore respect the rights, observe the principles and promote the application thereof in accordance with their respective powers.

2. This Charter does not establish any new power or task for the Community or the Union, or modify powers and tasks defined by the Treaties.

Article 52   Scope of guaranteed rights

1. Any limitation on the exercise of the rights and freedoms recognized by this Charter must be provided for by law and respect the essence of those rights and freedoms. Subject to the principle of proportionality, limitations may be made only if they are necessary and genuinely meet objectives of general interest recognised by the Union or the need to protect the rights and freedoms of others.

2. Rights recognised by this Charter which are based on the Community Treaties or the Treaty on European Union shall be exercised under the conditions and within the limits defined by those Treaties.

3. In so far as this Charter contains rights which correspond to rights guaranteed by the Convention for the Protection of Human Rights and Fundamental Freedoms, the meaning and scope of those rights shall be the same as those laid down by the said Convention. This provision shall not prevent Union law providing more extensive protection.

Article 53   Level of protection

Nothing in this Charter shall be interpreted as restricting or adversely affecting human rights and fundamental freedoms as recognised, in their respective fields of application, by Union law and international law and by international agreements to which the Union, the Community or all the Member States are party, including the European Convention for the Protection of Human Rights and Fundamental Freedoms, and by the Member States' constitutions.

Article 54   Prohibition of abuse of rights

Nothing in this Charter shall be interpreted as implying any right to engage in any activity or to perform any act aimed at the destruction of any of the rights and freedoms recognised in this Charter or at their limitation to a greater extent than is provided for herein.

These changes have only limited significance. In the future, however, the Community may become a party to the European Convention, thus allowing the European Court of Human Rights to rule on whether the Community has violated the provisions of the Convention.[15] It is also possible that the Charter will be given binding force. Either course would provide the "codified catalogue of fundamental rights" desired by the *Bundesverfassungsgericht*.

Further reading

Alston (Philip) (ed.), *The EU and Human Rights* (Oxford University Press, Oxford, 1999).

Kommers (Donald P.), *The Constitutional Jurisprudence of the Federal Republic of Germany* (Duke University Press, Durham, NC, and London, 2nd ed., 1997).

Lenaerts and de Smijter, "A 'Bill of Rights' for the European Union" (2001) 38 CMLRev. 273.

Oppenheimer (Andrew) (ed.), *The Relationship between European Community Law and National Law: The Cases* (Cambridge University Press, Cambridge, 1994), pp. 410–575.

---

15 This would require an amendment to the Community Treaties: Opinion 2/94, [1996] ECR I-1759.

16

Special topic: abortion

Abortion is chosen as a topic for more detailed examination because of the difficulties it poses for human-rights theory. It is regarded as sinful by many religious authorities (especially the Catholic Church) and could be regarded as contrary to the "right to life" provisions found in some bills of rights. On the other hand, provisions concerning dignity and privacy could be regarded as giving the mother-to-be the right to decide for herself whether to continue with her pregnancy. Abortion bans also give rise to social problems. "Back-street" abortionists flourish and often cause serious injury – sometimes death – to the woman, while unwanted births can ruin the life of both mother and child. In view of these contradictions, it is hardly surprising that different jurisdictions have adopted radically different approaches.

> *United States*
> **Roe v. Wade**
> **SUPREME COURT OF THE UNITED STATES**
> 410 US 113 (1973)

Facts

Under Texas law, it was a criminal offence to procure an abortion, except on medical advice to save the life of the mother.[1] Jane Roe,[2] a single woman, who was residing in Dallas County, Texas, instituted a federal action against the District Attorney of the county. She sought a declaratory judgment that the Texas criminal abortion statutes were unconstitutional on their face, and an injunction restraining the defendant from enforcing the statutes. She was un-married and pregnant. She wished to terminate her pregnancy by an abortion performed by a competent, licensed physician, under safe, clinical conditions. She could not get a legal abortion in Texas because her life was not threat-ened, and she could not afford to travel to another state. She claimed that the Texas statutes were unconstitutionally vague and that they abridged her right of personal privacy, protected by the First, Fourth, Fifth, Ninth and Fourteenth Amendments, all of which are set out in Chapter 14, Panels 14.1 and 14.2. By an amendment to her complaint she purported to sue "on behalf of herself and all other women" similarly situated.

---

1 Similar statutes existed in most states.
2 This was not her real name.

Judgment

Blackmun J delivered the opinion of the court, in which Burger CJ and Douglas, Brennan, Stewart, Marshall and Powell JJ joined. Burger CJ, Douglas J and Stewart J filed concurring opinions. White J filed a dissenting opinion, in which Rehnquist J joined. Rehnquist J filed a dissenting opinion.

Blackmun J[3]

V

The principal thrust of appellant's attack on the Texas statutes is that they improperly invade a right, said to be possessed by the pregnant woman, to choose to terminate her pregnancy. Appellant would discover this right in the concept of personal "liberty" embodied in the Fourteenth Amendment's Due Process Clause; or in personal, marital, familial, and sexual privacy said to be protected by the Bill of Rights or its penumbras . . . ; or among those rights reserved to the people by the Ninth Amendment. . . . Before addressing this claim, we feel it desirable briefly to survey, in several aspects, the history of abortion, for such insight as that history may afford us, and then to examine the state purposes and interests behind the criminal abortion laws.

VI

It perhaps is not generally appreciated that the restrictive criminal abortion laws in effect in a majority of States today are of relatively recent vintage. Those laws, generally proscribing abortion or its attempt at any time during pregnancy except when necessary to preserve the pregnant woman's life, are not of ancient or even of common-law origin. Instead, they derive from statutory changes effected, for the most part, in the latter half of the 19th century.

1. Ancient attitudes. These are not capable of precise determination. We are told that at the time of the Persian Empire abortifacients were known and that criminal abortions were severely punished. We are also told, however, that abortion was practiced in Greek times as well as in the Roman Era, and that "it was resorted to without scruple." The Ephesian, Soranos, often described as the greatest of the ancient gynecologists, appears to have been generally opposed to Rome's prevailing free-abortion practices. He found it necessary to think first of the life of the mother, and he resorted to abortion when, upon this standard, he felt the procedure advisable. Greek and Roman law afforded little protection to the unborn. If abortion was prosecuted in some places, it seems to have been based on a concept of a violation of the father's right to his offspring. Ancient religion did not bar abortion.

2. The Hippocratic Oath. What then of the famous Oath that has stood so long as the ethical guide of the medical profession and that bears the name of the great Greek (460(?)–377(?) B. C.), who has been described as the Father of Medicine, the "wisest and the greatest practitioner of his art," and the "most important and most complete medical personality of antiquity," who dominated the medical schools of his time, and who typified the sum of the medical knowledge of the past? The Oath varies somewhat according to the particular translation, but in any translation the content is clear: "I will give no deadly medicine to anyone if asked, nor suggest any such counsel; and in like manner I will not give to a woman a pessary to produce abortion," or "I will neither give a deadly drug to anybody if asked for it, nor will I make a suggestion to this effect. Similarly, I will not give to a woman an abortive remedy."

---

3 Footnotes and citations are omitted.

Although the Oath is not mentioned in any of the principal briefs in this case . . . , it represents the apex of the development of strict ethical concepts in medicine, and its influence endures to this day. Why did not the authority of Hippocrates dissuade abortion practice in his time and that of Rome? The late Dr. Edelstein provides us with a theory: The Oath was not uncontested even in Hippocrates' day; only the Pythagorean school of philosophers frowned upon the related act of suicide. Most Greek thinkers, on the other hand, commended abortion, at least prior to viability. See Plato, Republic, V, 461; Aristotle, Politics, VII, 1335b 25. For the Pythagoreans, however, it was a matter of dogma. For them the embryo was animate from the moment of conception, and abortion meant destruction of a living being. The abortion clause of the Oath, therefore, "echoes Pythagorean doctrines," and "[i]n no other stratum of Greek opinion were such views held or proposed in the same spirit of uncompromising austerity."

Dr. Edelstein then concludes that the Oath originated in a group representing only a small segment of Greek opinion and that it certainly was not accepted by all ancient physicians. He points out that medical writings down to Galen (A. D. 130–200) "give evidence of the violation of almost every one of its injunctions." But with the end of antiquity a decided change took place. Resistance against suicide and against abortion became common. The Oath came to be popular. The emerging teachings of Christianity were in agreement with the Pythagorean ethic. The Oath "became the nucleus of all medical ethics" and "was applauded as the embodiment of truth." Thus, suggests Dr. Edelstein, it is "a Pythagorean manifesto and not the expression of an absolute standard of medical conduct."

This, it seems to us, is a satisfactory and acceptable explanation of the Hippocratic Oath's apparent rigidity. It enables us to understand, in historical context, a long-accepted and revered statement of medical ethics.

3. The common law. It is undisputed that at common law, abortion performed before "quickening"[4]– the first recognizable movement of the fetus in utero, appearing usually from the 16th to the 18th week of pregnancy – was not an indictable offense. The absence of a common-law crime for pre-quickening abortion appears to have developed from a confluence of earlier philosophical, theological, and civil and canon law concepts of when life begins. These disciplines variously approached the question in terms of the point at which the embryo or fetus became "formed" or recognizably human, or in terms of when a "person" came into being, that is, infused with a "soul" or "animated." A loose consensus evolved in early English law that these events occurred at some point between conception and live birth. This was "mediate animation." Although Christian theology and the canon law came to fix the point of animation at 40 days for a male and 80 days for a female, a view that persisted until the 19th century, there was otherwise little agreement about the precise time of formation or animation. There was agreement, however, that prior to this point the fetus was to be regarded as part of the mother, and its destruction, therefore, was not homicide. Due to continued uncertainty about the precise time when animation occurred, to the lack of any empirical basis for the 40-80-day view, and perhaps to Aquinas' definition of movement as one of the two first principles of life, Bracton focused upon quickening as the critical point. The significance of quickening was echoed by later common-law scholars and found its way into the received common law in this country.

Whether abortion of a quick fetus was a felony at common law, or even a lesser crime, is still disputed. Bracton, writing early in the 13th century, thought it homicide. But the later and predominant view, following the great common-law scholars, has been that it was, at

---

4 Editor's note: in the past, "quick" meant "alive"; so "quickening" meant "coming alive".

most, a lesser offense. In a frequently cited passage, Coke took the position that abortion of a woman "quick with childe" is "a great misprision, and no murder." Blackstone followed, saying that while abortion after quickening had once been considered manslaughter (though not murder), "modern law" took a less severe view. A recent review of the common-law precedents argues, however, that those precedents contradict Coke and that even post-quickening abortion was never established as a common-law crime. This is of some importance because while most American courts ruled, in holding or dictum, that abortion of an unquickened fetus was not criminal under their received common law, others followed Coke in stating that abortion of a quick fetus was a "misprision," a term they translated to mean "misdemeanor." That their reliance on Coke on this aspect of the law was uncritical and, apparently in all the reported cases, dictum (due probably to the paucity of common-law prosecutions for post-quickening abortion), makes it now appear doubtful that abortion was ever firmly established as a common-law crime even with respect to the destruction of a quick fetus.

[Blackmun J then considered English statutory law, which was originally very harsh – Lord Ellenborough's Act in 1803 made abortion of a "quick" foetus a capital offence – but subsequently became more lenient. In the US, legislation was passed in some states in the early nineteenth century to make abortion a criminal offence. Towards the end of the nineteenth century and in the twentieth century, these too became more lenient. Blackmun J summed up the history of the matter in the paragraph that follows.]

It is thus apparent that at common law, at the time of the adoption of our Constitution, and throughout the major portion of the 19th century, abortion was viewed with less disfavor than under most American statutes currently in effect. Phrasing it another way, a woman enjoyed a substantially broader right to terminate a pregnancy than she does in most States today. At least with respect to the early stage of pregnancy, and very possibly without such a limitation, the opportunity to make this choice was present in this country well into the 19th century. Even later, the law continued for some time to treat less punitively an abortion procured in early pregnancy.

[Blackmun J next considered the position of the American Medical Association. In the nineteenth century, they were in the forefront of opponents of abortion, but their position subsequently became less condemnatory and also more divided.]

VII

Three reasons have been advanced to explain historically the enactment of criminal abortion laws in the 19th century and to justify their continued existence.

It has been argued occasionally that these laws were the product of a Victorian social concern to discourage illicit sexual conduct. Texas, however, does not advance this justification in the present case, and it appears that no court or commentator has taken the argument seriously. The appellants and amici[5] contend, moreover, that this is not a proper state purpose at all and suggest that, if it were, the Texas statutes are overbroad in protecting it since the law fails to distinguish between married and unwed mothers.

A second reason is concerned with abortion as a medical procedure. When most criminal abortion laws were first enacted, the procedure was a hazardous one for the woman. This was particularly true prior to the development of antisepsis. Antiseptic techniques, of course, were based on discoveries by Lister, Pasteur, and others first announced in 1867, but were not generally accepted and employed until about the turn of

---

5 Editor's note: "amici" means *amici curiae*, Latin for "friends of the court", that is, lawyers who are not briefed by a party, but who appear before the court to help it. The singular is "amicus".

the century. Abortion mortality was high. Even after 1900, and perhaps until as late as the development of antibiotics in the 1940s, standard modern techniques such as dilation and curettage were not nearly so safe as they are today. Thus, it has been argued that a State's real concern in enacting a criminal abortion law was to protect the pregnant woman, that is, to restrain her from submitting to a procedure that placed her life in serious jeopardy.

Modern medical techniques have altered this situation. Appellants and various amici refer to medical data indicating that abortion in early pregnancy, that is, prior to the end of the first trimester, although not without its risk, is now relatively safe. Mortality rates for women undergoing early abortions, where the procedure is legal, appear to be as low as or lower than the rates for normal childbirth. Consequently, any interest of the State in protecting the woman from an inherently hazardous procedure, except when it would be equally dangerous for her to forgo it, has largely disappeared. Of course, important state interests in the areas of health and medical standards do remain. The State has a legitimate interest in seeing to it that abortion, like any other medical procedure, is performed under circumstances that insure maximum safety for the patient. This interest obviously extends at least to the performing physician and his staff, to the facilities involved, to the availability of after-care, and to adequate provision for any complication or emergency that might arise. The prevalence of high mortality rates at illegal "abortion mills" strengthens, rather than weakens, the State's interest in regulating the conditions under which abortions are performed. Moreover, the risk to the woman increases as her pregnancy continues. Thus, the State retains a definite interest in protecting the woman's own health and safety when an abortion is proposed at a late stage of pregnancy.

The third reason is the State's interest – some phrase it in terms of duty – in protecting prenatal life. Some of the argument for this justification rests on the theory that a new human life is present from the moment of conception. The State's interest and general obligation to protect life then extends, it is argued, to prenatal life. Only when the life of the pregnant mother herself is at stake, balanced against the life she carries within her, should the interest of the embryo or fetus not prevail. Logically, of course, a legitimate state interest in this area need not stand or fall on acceptance of the belief that life begins at conception or at some other point prior to live birth. In assessing the State's interest, recognition may be given to the less rigid claim that as long as at least potential life is involved, the State may assert interests beyond the protection of the pregnant woman alone.

Parties challenging state abortion laws have sharply disputed in some courts the contention that a purpose of these laws, when enacted, was to protect prenatal life. Pointing to the absence of legislative history to support the contention, they claim that most state laws were designed solely to protect the woman. Because medical advances have lessened this concern, at least with respect to abortion in early pregnancy, they argue that with respect to such abortions the laws can no longer be justified by any state interest. There is some scholarly support for this view of original purpose. The few state courts called upon to interpret their laws in the late 19th and early 20th centuries did focus on the State's interest in protecting the woman's health rather than in preserving the embryo and fetus. Proponents of this view point out that in many States, including Texas, by statute or judicial interpretation, the pregnant woman herself could not be prosecuted for self-abortion or for cooperating in an abortion performed upon her by another. They claim that adoption of the "quickening" distinction through received common law and state statutes tacitly recognizes the greater health hazards inherent in late abortion and impliedly repudiates the theory that life begins at conception.

It is with these interests, and the weight to be attached to them, that this case is concerned.

VIII

The Constitution does not explicitly mention any right of privacy. In a line of decisions, however, going back perhaps as far as . . . [1891], the Court has recognized that a right of personal privacy, or a guarantee of certain areas or zones of privacy, does exist under the Constitution. In varying contexts, the Court or individual Justices have, indeed, found at least the roots of that right in the First Amendment . . . ; in the Fourth and Fifth Amendments . . . ; in the penumbras of the Bill of Rights . . . ; in the Ninth Amendment . . . ; or in the concept of liberty guaranteed by the first section of the Fourteenth Amendment. . . . These decisions make it clear that only personal rights that can be deemed "fundamental" or "implicit in the concept of ordered liberty" . . . are included in this guarantee of personal privacy. They also make it clear that the right has some extension to activities relating to marriage . . . ; procreation . . . ; contraception . . . ; family relationships . . . ; and child rearing and education. . . .

This right of privacy, whether it be founded in the Fourteenth Amendment's concept of personal liberty and restrictions upon state action, as we feel it is, or, as the District Court determined, in the Ninth Amendment's reservation of rights to the people, is broad enough to encompass a woman's decision whether or not to terminate her pregnancy. The detriment that the State would impose upon the pregnant woman by denying this choice altogether is apparent. Specific and direct harm medically diagnosable even in early pregnancy may be involved. Maternity, or additional offspring, may force upon the woman a distressful life and future. Psychological harm may be imminent. Mental and physical health may be taxed by child care. There is also the distress, for all concerned, associated with the unwanted child, and there is the problem of bringing a child into a family already unable, psychologically and otherwise, to care for it. In other cases, as in this one, the additional difficulties and continuing stigma of unwed motherhood may be involved. All these are factors the woman and her responsible physician necessarily will consider in consultation.

On the basis of elements such as these, appellant and some amici argue that the woman's right is absolute and that she is entitled to terminate her pregnancy at whatever time, in whatever way, and for whatever reason she alone chooses. With this we do not agree. Appellant's arguments that Texas either has no valid interest at all in regulating the abortion decision, or no interest strong enough to support any limitation upon the woman's sole determination, are unpersuasive. The Court's decisions recognizing a right of privacy also acknowledge that some state regulation in areas protected by that right is appropriate. As noted above, a State may properly assert important interests in safeguarding health, in maintaining medical standards, and in protecting potential life. At some point in pregnancy, these respective interests become sufficiently compelling to sustain regulation of the factors that govern the abortion decision. The privacy right involved, therefore, cannot be said to be absolute. In fact, it is not clear to us that the claim asserted by some amici that one has an unlimited right to do with one's body as one pleases bears a close relationship to the right of privacy previously articulated in the Court's decisions. The Court has refused to recognize an unlimited right of this kind in the past. . . .

We, therefore, conclude that the right of personal privacy includes the abortion decision, but that this right is not unqualified and must be considered against important state interests in regulation.

We note that those federal and state courts that have recently considered abortion law challenges have reached the same conclusion. A majority, in addition to the District Court in the present case, have held state laws unconstitutional, at least in part, because of vagueness or because of overbreadth and abridgment of rights . . .

Others have sustained state statutes. . . .

Although the results are divided, most of these courts have agreed that the right of privacy, however based, is broad enough to cover the abortion decision; that the right, nonetheless, is not absolute and is subject to some limitations; and that at some point the state interests as to protection of health, medical standards, and prenatal life, become dominant. We agree with this approach.

Where certain "fundamental rights" are involved, the Court has held that regulation limiting these rights may be justified only by a "compelling state interest," . . . , and that legislative enactments must be narrowly drawn to express only the legitimate state interests at stake . . .

In the recent abortion cases, cited above, courts have recognized these principles. Those striking down state laws have generally scrutinized the State's interests in protecting health and potential life, and have concluded that neither interest justified broad limitations on the reasons for which a physician and his pregnant patient might decide that she should have an abortion in the early stages of pregnancy. Courts sustaining state laws have held that the State's determinations to protect health or prenatal life are dominant and constitutionally justifiable.

IX

The District Court held that the appellee failed to meet his burden of demonstrating that the Texas statute's infringement upon Roe's rights was necessary to support a compelling state interest, and that, although the appellee presented "several compelling justifications for state presence in the area of abortions," the statutes outstripped these justifications and swept "far beyond any areas of compelling state interest." . . . Appellant and appellee both contest that holding. Appellant, as has been indicated, claims an absolute right that bars any state imposition of criminal penalties in the area. Appellee argues that the State's determination to recognize and protect prenatal life from and after conception constitutes a compelling state interest. As noted above, we do not agree fully with either formulation.

A. The appellee and certain amici argue that the fetus is a "person" within the language and meaning of the Fourteenth Amendment. In support of this, they outline at length and in detail the well-known facts of fetal development. If this suggestion of personhood is established, the appellant's case, of course, collapses, for the fetus' right to life would then be guaranteed specifically by the Amendment. The appellant conceded as much on reargument. On the other hand, the appellee conceded on reargument that no case could be cited that holds that a fetus is a person within the meaning of the Fourteenth Amendment.

The Constitution does not define "person" in so many words. Section 1 of the Fourteenth Amendment contains three references to "person." . . . The word also appears both in the Due Process Clause and in the Equal Protection Clause. "Person" is used in other places in the Constitution . . . But in nearly all these instances, the use of the word is such that it has application only postnatally. None indicates, with any assurance, that it has any possible pre-natal application.

All this, together with our observation, supra, that throughout the major portion of the 19th century prevailing legal abortion practices were far freer than they are today, persuades us that the word "person," as used in the Fourteenth Amendment, does not include the unborn. This is in accord with the results reached in those few cases where the issue has been squarely presented. . . .

This conclusion, however, does not of itself fully answer the contentions raised by Texas, and we pass on to other considerations.

B. The pregnant woman cannot be isolated in her privacy. She carries an embryo and, later, a fetus, if one accepts the medical definitions of the developing young in the human uterus. . . . The situation therefore is inherently different from marital intimacy, or bedroom possession of obscene material, or marriage, or procreation, or education, with which [some previous decisions of the Supreme Court] were respectively concerned. As we have intimated above, it is reasonable and appropriate for a State to decide that at some point in time another interest, that of health of the mother or that of potential human life, becomes significantly involved. The woman's privacy is no longer sole and any right of privacy she possesses must be measured accordingly.

Texas urges that, apart from the Fourteenth Amendment, life begins at conception and is present throughout pregnancy, and that, therefore, the State has a compelling interest in protecting that life from and after conception. We need not resolve the difficult question of when life begins. When those trained in the respective disciplines of medicine, philosophy, and theology are unable to arrive at any consensus, the judiciary, at this point in the development of man's knowledge, is not in a position to speculate as to the answer.

It should be sufficient to note briefly the wide divergence of thinking on this most sensitive and difficult question. There has always been strong support for the view that life does not begin until live birth. This was the belief of the Stoics. It appears to be the predominant, though not the unanimous, attitude of the Jewish faith. It may be taken to represent also the position of a large segment of the Protestant community, insofar as that can be ascertained; organized groups that have taken a formal position on the abortion issue have generally regarded abortion as a matter for the conscience of the individual and her family. As we have noted, the common law found greater significance in quickening. Physicians and their scientific colleagues have regarded that event with less interest and have tended to focus either upon conception, upon live birth, or upon the interim point at which the fetus becomes "viable," that is, potentially able to live outside the mother's womb, albeit with artificial aid. Viability is usually placed at about seven months (28 weeks) but may occur earlier, even at 24 weeks. The Aristotelian theory of "mediate animation," that held sway throughout the Middle Ages and the Renaissance in Europe, continued to be official Roman Catholic dogma until the 19th century, despite opposition to this "ensoulment" theory from those in the Church who would recognize the existence of life from the moment of conception. The latter is now, of course, the official belief of the Catholic Church. As one brief amicus discloses, this is a view strongly held by many non-Catholics as well, and by many physicians. Substantial problems for precise definition of this view are posed, however, by new embryological data that purport to indicate that conception is a "process" over time, rather than an event, and by new medical techniques such as menstrual extraction, the "morning-after" pill, implantation of embryos, artificial insemination, and even artificial wombs.

[The court then considered areas of the law other than criminal law and concluded that there was no recognition that life began at conception.]

X

In view of all this, we do not agree that, by adopting one theory of life, Texas may override the rights of the pregnant woman that are at stake. We repeat, however, that the State does have an important and legitimate interest in preserving and protecting the health of the pregnant woman, whether she be a resident of the State or a nonresident who seeks medical consultation and treatment there, and that it has still another important and legitimate interest in protecting the potentiality of human life. These interests are separate and distinct. Each grows in substantiality as the woman approaches term and, at a point during pregnancy, each becomes "compelling."

With respect to the State's important and legitimate interest in the health of the mother, the "compelling" point, in the light of present medical knowledge, is at approximately the end of the first trimester. This is so because of the now-established medical fact . . . that until the end of the first trimester mortality in abortion may be less than mortality in normal childbirth. It follows that, from and after this point, a State may regulate the abortion procedure to the extent that the regulation reasonably relates to the preservation and protection of maternal health. Examples of permissible state regulation in this area are requirements as to the qualifications of the person who is to perform the abortion; as to the licensure of that person; as to the facility in which the procedure is to be performed, that is, whether it must be a hospital or may be a clinic or some other place of less-than-hospital status; as to the licensing of the facility; and the like.

This means, on the other hand, that, for the period of pregnancy prior to this "compelling" point, the attending physician, in consultation with his patient, is free to determine, without regulation by the State, that, in his medical judgment, the patient's pregnancy should be terminated. If that decision is reached, the judgment may be effectuated by an abortion free of interference by the State.

With respect to the State's important and legitimate interest in potential life, the "compelling" point is at viability. This is so because the fetus then presumably has the capability of meaningful life outside the mother's womb. State regulation protective of fetal life after viability thus has both logical and biological justifications. If the State is interested in protecting fetal life after viability, it may go so far as to proscribe abortion during that period, except when it is necessary to preserve the life or health of the mother.

Measured against these standards, Art. 1196 of the Texas Penal Code, in restricting legal abortions to those "procured or attempted by medical advice for the purpose of saving the life of the mother," sweeps too broadly. The statute makes no distinction between abortions performed early in pregnancy and those performed later, and it limits to a single reason, "saving" the mother's life, the legal justification for the procedure. The statute, therefore, cannot survive the constitutional attack made upon it here.

This conclusion makes it unnecessary for us to consider the additional challenge to the Texas statute asserted on grounds of vagueness. . . .

XI

To summarize and to repeat:

1. A state criminal abortion statute of the current Texas type, that excepts from criminality only a life-saving procedure on behalf of the mother, without regard to pregnancy stage and without recognition of the other interests involved, is violative of the Due Process Clause of the Fourteenth Amendment.
   (a) For the stage prior to approximately the end of the first trimester, the abortion decision and its effectuation must be left to the medical judgment of the pregnant woman's attending physician.
   (b) For the stage subsequent to approximately the end of the first trimester, the State, in promoting its interest in the health of the mother, may, if it chooses, regulate the abortion procedure in ways that are reasonably related to maternal health.
   (c) For the stage subsequent to viability, the State in promoting its interest in the potentiality of human life may, if it chooses, regulate, and even proscribe, abortion except where it is necessary, in appropriate medical judgment, for the preservation of the life or health of the mother. . .

[Concurring and dissenting opinions omitted.].

Comment

This opinion has been set out at length because its discussion of the historical, medical, ethical and social aspects of abortion is so good. However, it contains little in the way of legal analysis. It reads more like a report recommending legislation than a judicial opinion.

The constitutional provision on which it rested was the Fourteenth Amendment. It will be seen from Panel 14.2 in Chapter 14 that there is nothing about abortion, or even privacy,[6] in this. Nor has it ever been suggested that the amendment was intended to deal with these matters. The district court held that abortion rights flowed from the Ninth Amendment (Panel 14.1). This simply says that the enumeration of certain rights in the Constitution does not deny or disparage other rights, hardly an adequate basis for saying that the Constitution grants the right to an abortion. The truth of the matter is that – however desirable they may be – abortion rights are not covered by the words of the Constitution.

Germany
First German Abortion case
BUNDESVERFASSUNGSGERICHT (FEDERAL CONSTITUTIONAL COURT)
Judgment of 25 February 1975, (1975) 39 BVerfGE 1[7]

This case was a constitutional challenge brought by certain German *Länder* (states) and Christian Democrat members of the *Bundestag* against an abortion law passed by a coalition of Social Democrats and Free Democrats in 1974 (Law of 26 April 1974). Previously, abortion had been a criminal offence except in certain specified circumstances (for example, when the life or health of the mother was at stake). The new law provided that abortion would no longer be criminal if carried out by a qualified doctor within the first twelve weeks of pregnancy.

The judgment is too long to set out. We will simply summarize a few salient points. The provisions of the *Grundgesetz* (German Constitution) referred to are set out in Chapter 14, Panel 14.3.

Judgment
The court first laid down some general principles.

●   Article 2(2) of the *Grundgesetz* (which was adopted in reaction to Nazi ideas) protects the life developing within the mother's womb.

●   According to medical research, life begins on the fourteenth day after conception.

---

6 In an earlier case, *Griswold v. Connecticut*, 381 US 479 (1965), the court had established a right of privacy and used it to strike down a Connecticut statute prohibiting the use of contraceptives. In his concurring judgment in *Roe v. Wade*, Douglas J spoke of customary, traditional and time-honoured rights retained by the people, many of which come within the meaning of "liberty" as used in the Fourteenth Amendment. These fall into three categories. First, there is the autonomous control over the development and expression of one's intellect, interests, tastes and personality. He considered that these rights are protected by the First Amendment and are absolute. Secondly, there is freedom of choice in the basic decisions of one's life respecting marriage, divorce, procreation, contraception and the education and upbringing of children. These rights are subject to some control, but a compelling state interest must be shown. Thirdly, there is the freedom to care for one's health and person, freedom from bodily restraint or compulsion, freedom to walk, stroll or loaf. These rights are also subject to regulation, but only on the showing of a compelling state interest.

7 An English translation may be found in Donald P. Kommers, *The Constitutional Jurisprudence of the Federal Republic of Germany* (Duke University Press, Durham, NC, and London, 2nd ed., 1997), pp. 336 *et seq.*

- The process of development is a continuous one, the stages of which cannot be precisely defined.
- The protection granted by Article 2(2) cannot be limited to a person who has been born, nor to an independently viable foetus.
- Failure to protect unborn life from its inception (the fourteenth day after conception) would place the security of human existence in jeopardy.
- The framers of the *Grundgesetz* intended Article 2(2) to cover unborn life.

The court then noted that the State is also obliged to protect the life of the mother. Pregnancy, it said, belongs to the private life of the mother, a sphere that is protected by Article 2(1) read in conjunction with Article 1(1). If a foetus were not an independent form of life, abortion would be entirely covered by the right to privacy. However, because the foetus is itself entitled to protection, abortion has a social dimension and is amenable to State regulation. It is not possible to balance the rights of the woman against those of the foetus, since abortion necessarily results in the destruction of the latter. Consequently, the protection of the foetus must prevail over the right of the woman to privacy. This applies to the entire duration of the pregnancy. The woman has a duty to carry the foetus to term. A termination of pregnancy should not be regarded as equivalent to a visit to the doctor to cure an illness.

The court then considered whether it was right for the *Bundestag* to decriminalize abortion. It said it would have been constitutional to do this only if some other sanction had been imposed which would have clearly stigmatized abortion as wrong and which would have been just as effective in preventing its occurrence. It accepted that there were special cases in which giving birth would cause unusual hardship. In these cases, the court said, the woman's rights might prevail over those of the unborn child. Examples include not only a threat to the woman's life or health, but also serious social problems. The court's final conclusion was, however, that the new statute did not go far enough in protecting the unborn. It was therefore unconstitutional and had to be struck down.[8]

QUESTIONS
1. What does the reasoning of this case have in common with that in *Roe v. Wade*, and what are the most important differences?
2. Why did the *Bundesverfassungsgericht* reach such a different result from the US Supreme Court?

Council of Europe
Brüggemann and Scheuten v. Germany
EUROPEAN COMMISSION OF HUMAN RIGHTS
(1977) 3 EHRR 244

---

8 Many years later, in 1993, the *Bundesverfassungsgericht* delivered a second judgment, in which it softened its stance by accepting that abortion during the first twelve weeks of pregnancy could be decriminalized if the woman had undergone counselling designed to make her change her mind: 88 BverfGE 203.

As a result of the decision of the *Bundesverfassungsgericht* set out above, the abortion law of 26 April 1974, in so far as it permitted abortion within the first twelve weeks of pregnancy, never entered into force. A new law was then passed, based on the reasoning of the *Bundesverfassungsgericht*. Under this, abortion remained a criminal offence, but it provided that, in certain specified cases in which the woman was suffering particular hardship, an abortion performed by a doctor would not be punishable.

The applicants were two German women from Hamburg. One was unmarried and the other divorced. They claimed that both the judgment of the *Bundesverfassungsgericht* and the abortion law passed to meet its requirements infringed their right to respect for their private and family life under Article 8 of the European Convention on Human Rights (set out in Panel 14.4, Chapter 14, above).[9] The application never came before the European Court of Human Rights, but it was considered by the European Commission of Human Rights, and an extract from the report of the latter is set out below.

Report

54. According to Article 8 of the Convention, "Everyone has the right to respect for his private . . . life . . .". In its decision on admissibility, the Commission has already found that legislation regulating the interruption of pregnancy touches upon the sphere of private life. The first question which must be answered is whether the legal rules governing abortion in the Federal Republic of Germany since the judgment of the Constitutional Court of 25 February 1975 constitute an interference with the right to respect for private life of the applicants.

55. The right to respect for private life is of such a scope as to secure to the individual a sphere within which he can freely pursue the development and fulfilment of his personality. To this effect, he must also have the possibility of establishing relationships of various kinds, including sexual, with other persons. In principle, therefore, whenever the State sets up rules for the behaviour of the individual within this sphere, it interferes with the respect for private life and such interference must be justified in the light of Article 8 (2).

56. However, there are limits to the personal sphere. While a large proportion of the law existing in a given State has some immediate or remote effect on the individual's possibility of developing his personality by doing what he wants to do, not all of these can be considered to constitute an interference with private life in the sense of Article 8 of the Convention. In fact, as the earlier jurisprudence of the Commission has already shown, the claim to respect for private life is automatically reduced to the extent that the individual himself brings his private life into contact with public life or into close connection with other protected interests.

57. Thus, the Commission has held that the concept of private life in Article 8 was broader than the definition given by numerous Anglo-Saxon and French authors, namely, the "right to live as far as one wishes, protected from publicity", in that it also comprises, "to a certain degree, the right to establish and to develop relationships with other human beings,

---

9 They also claimed that certain other provisions were infringed – for example, they said that the judgment infringed Art. 9 because it was based on religious grounds – but these claims were summarily rejected by the Commission.

especially in the emotional field for the development and fulfilment of one's own personality". But it denied "that the protection afforded by Article 8 of the Convention extends to relationships of the individual with his entire immediate surroundings". It thus found that the right to keep a dog did not pertain to the sphere of private life of the owner because "the keeping of dogs is by the very nature of that animal necessarily associated with certain interferences with the life of others and even with public life".[10]

58. In two further cases, the Commission has taken account of the element of public life in connection with Article 8 of the Convention. It held that subsequent communication of statements made in the course of public proceedings[11] or the taking of photographs of a person participating in a public incident[12] did not amount to interference with private life.

59. The termination of an unwanted pregnancy is not comparable with the situation in any of the above cases. However, pregnancy cannot be said to pertain uniquely to the sphere of private life. Whenever a woman is pregnant, her private life becomes closely connected with the developing foetus.

60. The Commission does not find it necessary to decide, in this context, whether the unborn child is to be considered as "life" in the sense of Article 2 of the Convention, or whether it could be regarded as an entity which under Article 8 (2) could justify an interference "for the protection of others". There can be no doubt that certain interests relating to pregnancy are legally protected, e.g. as shown by a survey of the legal order in 13 High Contracting Parties.[13] This survey reveals that, without exception, certain rights are attributed to the conceived but unborn child, in particular the right to inherit. The Commission also notes that Article 6 (5) of the United Nations Covenant on Civil and Political Rights prohibits the execution of death sentences on pregnant women.

61. The Commission therefore finds that not every regulation of the termination of unwanted pregnancies constitutes an interference with the right to respect for the private life of the mother. Article 8 (1) cannot be interpreted as meaning that pregnancy and its termination are, as a principle, solely a matter of the private life of the mother. In this respect the Commission notes that there is not one Member State of the Convention which does not, in one way or another, set up legal rules in this matter. The applicants complain about the fact that the Constitutional Court declared null and void the Fifth Criminal Law Reform Act, but even this Act was not based on the assumption that abortion is entirely a matter of the private life of the pregnant woman. It only provided that an abortion performed by a physician with the pregnant woman's consent should not be punishable if no more than 12 weeks had elapsed after conception.

62. The legal solutions following the Fifth Criminal Law Reform Act cannot be said to disregard the private-life aspect connected with the problem of abortion. The judgment of the Federal Constitutional Court of 25 February 1975 not only recognised the medical, eugenic and ethical indications but also stated that, where the pregnancy was terminated by a doctor with the pregnant woman's consent within the first 12 weeks after conception "in order to avert from the pregnant woman the risk of serious distress that cannot be averted in any other way she might reasonably be expected to bear, the Court may abstain from imposing punishment".

---

10 App. No. 6825/75, *X v. Iceland* (1976) 5 D&R 87.
11 App. No. 3868/68, *X v. UK* (1970) 34 CD 10, 18.
12 App. No. 5877/72, *X v. UK* (1974) 45 CD 90, 93.
13 See the Commission's Report, App. VII.

According to Article 218a of the Criminal Code in the version of the Fifteenth Criminal Law Reform Act of 18 May 1976,[14] an abortion performed by a physician is not punishable if the termination of pregnancy is advisable for any reason in order to avert from the pregnant woman the danger of a distress which is so serious that the pregnant woman cannot be required to continue the pregnancy and which cannot be averted in any other way the pregnant woman might reasonably be expected to bear. In particular, the abortion is admitted if continuation of the pregnancy would create a danger to the life or health of the woman, if it has to be feared that the child might suffer from an incurable injury to its health or if the pregnancy is the result of a crime. The woman is required also to seek advice on medically significant aspects of abortion as well as on the public and private assistance available for pregnant women, mothers and children.

In the absence of any of the above indications, the pregnant woman herself is nevertheless exempt from any punishment if the abortion was performed by a doctor within the first 22 weeks of pregnancy and if she made use of the medical and social counselling.

63. In view of this situation, the Commission does not find that the legal rules complained about by the applicants interfere with their right to respect for their private life.

64. Furthermore, the Commission has had regard to the fact that, when the European Convention of Human Rights entered into force, the law on abortion in all member States was at least as restrictive as the one now complained of by the applicants. In many European countries the problem of abortion is or has been the subject of heated debates on legal reform since. There is no evidence that it was the intention of the Parties to the Convention to bind themselves in favour of any particular solution under discussion – e.g. a solution of the kind set out in the [the abortion law declared unconstitutional by the *Bundesverfassungsgericht*]) which was not yet under public discussion at the time the Convention was drafted and adopted . . .

Conclusion

66. The Commission unanimously concludes that the present case does not disclose a breach of Article 8 of the Convention.[15]

QUESTIONS

1. Is abortion covered by Article 8(1)? If so, does it come within one of the exceptions in Article 8(2)? If not, did the Commission create a new exception?

2. If the European Convention on Human Rights had been interpreted as giving women the right to choose, it would have required what the *Bundesverfassungsgericht* had forbidden, thus creating a direct conflict between the Convention and the German

---

14 Editor's note: this was the abortion law passed to give effect to the judgment of the *Bundesverfassungsgericht*.

15 The Committee of Ministers, agreeing with the Commission's opinion, decided that there had been no violation of the Convention: Res. DH (78) 1 (17 March 1978). The case did not, therefore, go to the court. One member of the Commission, Mr Fawcett, was not present when the vote was taken. He was permitted to give a separate opinion in which he dissented on the ground that abortion was covered by the right to privacy in Article 8(1). He considered that the German legislation did not come within any of the exceptions in Art. 8(2). There was also a separate opinion by Mr Opsahl.

Constitution. Would it have been legally possible for Germany to accept such a ruling? Might the danger of non-acceptance by Germany have influenced the Commission in its interpretation?

European Union
Society for the Protection of Unborn Children v. Grogan
COURT OF JUSTICE OF THE EUROPEAN COMMUNITIES
Case C-159/90, [1991] ECR I-4685

Facts and background

The Society for the Protection of Unborn Children (SPUC) was an anti-abortion organization in Ireland. Grogan and the other defendants were officers of students unions in Ireland that helped pregnant students by giving them the names and addresses of abortion clinics in England. Abortion was illegal in Ireland. It was prohibited by the Constitution and was a criminal offence under a statute, the Offences against the Person Act 1861. The relevant constitutional provision was Article 40, section 3, which provided: "The State acknowledges the right to life of the unborn and, with due regard to the equal right to life of the mother, guarantees in its laws to respect, and, as far as practicable, by its laws to defend and vindicate that right." SPUC had brought civil proceedings in the Irish courts against the defendants for a declaration that their activities were unlawful and for an injunction. The students claimed that Community law gave them a defence. They said that abortion constituted a "service" within the terms of Article 50 [60] EC. This provision is found in the part of the Treaty providing for the free movement of services in the Community, a concept which requires residents of one Member State to be free to travel to another Member State in order to receive a service there. The students claimed, on the basis of certain decisions of the European Court, that the provider of a service must be entitled to advertise his services in other Member States. This, they argued, gave them the right under Community law to publicize the names and addresses of English clinics. SPUC, on the other hand, claimed that abortion was inherently immoral and against human rights; therefore, it could not constitute a "service" for the purpose of Community law. The Irish court referred these matters to the European Court.

Judgment
16. In its first question, the national court essentially seeks to establish whether medical termination of pregnancy, performed in accordance with the law of the State where it is carried out, constitutes a service within the meaning of Article 50 [60] of the EEC Treaty.

17. According to the first paragraph of that provision, services are to be considered to be "services" within the meaning of the Treaty where they are normally provided for remuneration . . . Indent (d) of the second paragraph of Article 50 [60] expressly states that activities of the professions fall within the definition of services.

18. It must be held that termination of pregnancy, as lawfully practised in several Member States, is a medical activity which is normally provided for remuneration and may be carried out as part of a professional activity. In any event, the Court has already held [citation omitted] that medical activities fall within the scope of Article 50 [60] of the Treaty.

19. SPUC, however, maintains that the provision of abortion cannot be regarded as being a service, on the grounds that it is grossly immoral and involves the destruction of the life of a human being, namely the unborn child.

20. Whatever the merits of those arguments on the moral plane, they cannot influence the answer to the national court's first question. It is not for the Court to substitute its assessment for that of the legislature in those Member States where the activities in question are practised legally.

21. Consequently, the answer to the national court's first question must be that medical termination of pregnancy, performed in accordance with the law of the State in which it is carried out, constitutes a service within the meaning of Article 50 [60] of the Treaty.

[The court went on, however, to hold that because Grogan and the other students were not acting on behalf of the abortion clinics but were acting on their own initiative, their activities were not covered by the relevant provisions on free movement of services, namely, Articles 49 [59] and [62]. The court then considered the final argument of the students. This was that the case raised an issue of free speech.]

30. [The students] maintain that a prohibition such as the one at issue is in breach of fundamental rights, especially of freedom of expression and the freedom to receive and impart information, enshrined in particular in Article 10(1) of the European Convention on Human Rights.

31. According to, *inter alia*, [*Elliniki Radiophonia Tileorasi*, Case C-260/89, [1991] ECR I-2951, paragraph 42], where national legislation falls within the field of application of Community law the Court, when requested to give a preliminary ruling, must provide the national court with all the elements of interpretation which are necessary in order to enable it to assess the compatibility of that legislation with the fundamental rights – as laid down in particular in the European Convention on Human Rights – the observance of which the Court ensures. However, the Court has no such jurisdiction with regard to national legislation lying outside the scope of Community law. In view of the facts of the case and of the conclusions which the Court has reached above with regard to the scope of Articles 49 [59] and [62] of the Treaty, that would appear to be true of the prohibition at issue before the national court.

32. The reply to the national court's second and third questions must therefore be that it is not contrary to Community law for a Member State in which medical termination of pregnancy is forbidden to prohibit students associations from distributing information about the identity and location of clinics in another Member State where voluntary termination of pregnancy is lawfully carried out and the means of communicating with those clinics, where the clinics in question have no involvement in the distribution of the said information.

QUESTIONS

1. Some people have said that this case shows that the European Court does not take human rights seriously.[16] Do you agree?
2. If the court had held that abortion is not a "service" within the meaning of the Treaty, this would have meant that abortion clinics in Member States where abortion was lawful would not have been able to benefit from the Treaty provisions on services: would this not have meant that Ireland's anti-abortion views would have been imposed on other Member States which held different views?
3. What legal and political considerations might have influenced the court in reaching the conclusion it did?

After this case was decided, the Constitution of Ireland was amended by referendum. Article 40.3.3 now makes clear that it does not limit the freedom to travel to another State to receive a service (abortion) there, nor does it limit the freedom to obtain or make available information on such services (subject to conditions laid down by law).

The European Court's ruling in paragraphs 30–32 of its judgment that the Community concept of human rights does not apply to Member States when acting outside the scope of Community law is in accordance with its previous case law. The main situations in which the Community concept would apply to Member States are where they are implementing Community law,[17] or where they impose restrictions on Community rights (assuming Community law permits such restrictions).[18] Article 51(1) of the Charter of Fundamental Rights of the European Union[19] (which at present has no binding force) provides that its provisions apply to the Member States only when they are implementing EU law (see Panel 15.3, above).

Further reading

Forder, "Abortion: A Constitutional Problem in European Perspective" (1994) 1 *Maastricht Journal of European and Comparative Law* 56.

Kommers (Donald P.), *The Constitutional Jurisprudence of the Federal Republic of Germany* (Duke University Press, Durham, NC, and London, 2nd ed., 1997), pp. 335–359.

Phelan, "Right to Life of the Unborn v. Promotion of Trade in Services" (1992) 55 MLR 670.

Schwartz (Bernard), *A History of the Supreme Court* (Oxford University Press, New York and Oxford, 1993), Chapter 15.

---

16 See Phelan, "Right to Life of the Unborn v. Promotion of Trade in Services" (1992) 55 MLR 670.
17 *Wachauf*, Case 5/88, [1989] ECR 2609 (para. 19 of the judgment).
18 *ERT*, Case C-260/89, [1991] ECR I-2925 (para. 43 of the judgment); *Rutili v. Minister of the Interior*, Case 36/75, [1975] ECR 1219 (paras. 31 and 32 of the judgment).
19 OJ 2000, C364, p. 1.

17

The Human Rights Convention and the EU: a clash of two systems?

What happens if there is a conflict between the European Convention on Human Rights and one of the Community Treaties? To answer this question, we shall first consider the general problem of conflicting treaties, and then apply the relevant principles to the specific question of conflicts between the Community Treaties and the Human Rights Convention.

Conflicting treaties in international law

The problem of conflicting treaties has long exercised international lawyers, and the most authoritative statement of the law is that contained in Article 30 of the 1969 Vienna Convention on the Law of Treaties (Panel 17.1). The ECSC, EEC and Euratom Treaties were all concluded before the Vienna Convention entered into force.[1] Since Article 4 of the Vienna Convention provides that it applies only to treaties concluded after it entered into force, it cannot as such apply to the original Community Treaties. Moreover, Article 5 of the Vienna Convention states that the Convention applies to a treaty which is the constituent instrument of an international organization, and to any treaty adopted within an international organization, "without prejudice to any relevant rules of the organization". This means that a principle laid down in the Vienna Convention cannot apply if it conflicts with such a rule, unless that principle would have applied under customary international law if the Vienna Convention had not been adopted. Since the Communities are international organizations, this provision applies to them. For these reasons, it might be thought that the Vienna Convention was irrelevant. However, it may, to a considerable extent, be regarded as stating the customary international law previously applicable,[2] and it is for this reason that it will form the basis of our analysis.

---

1 The Vienna Convention entered into force (for the original parties) on 27 January 1980.
2 Sir Ian Sinclair, *The Vienna Convention on the Law of Treaties* (Manchester University Press, Manchester and Dover, NH, 2nd ed., 1984), pp. 10–21; Anthony Aust, *Modern Treaty Law and Practice* (Cambridge University Press, Cambridge, 2000), pp. 10–11. On the question whether the Vienna Convention may itself have created new rules of customary international law, see Sinclair, above, pp. 22–24; and Aust, above, pp. 11–12. As we have seen in previous chapters, the International Court of Justice, the European Court of Human Rights and the European Court (EC) all cite the Vienna Convention even when it is not, strictly speaking, applicable.

Panel 17.1   Conflicting treaties: international law

Vienna Convention on the Law of Treaties, 1969

Article 30   Application of successive treaties relating to the same subject-matter

1. Subject to Article 103 of the Charter of the United Nations, the rights and obligations of States parties to successive treaties relating to the same subject-matter shall be determined in accordance with the following paragraphs.

2. When a treaty specifies that it is subject to, or that it is not to be considered as incompatible with, an earlier or later treaty, the provisions of that other treaty prevail.

3. When all the parties to the earlier treaty are parties also to the later treaty but the earlier treaty is not terminated or suspended in operation under article 59, the earlier treaty applies only to the extent that its provisions are compatible with those of the latter treaty.

4. When the parties to the later treaty do not include all the parties to the earlier one:

   (a) as between States parties to both treaties the same rule applies as in paragraph 3

   (b) as between a State party to both treaties and a State party to only one of the treaties, the treaty to which both States are parties governs their mutual rights and obligations.

5. Paragraph 4 is without prejudice to article 41, or to any question of the termination or suspension of the operation of a treaty under article 60 or to any question of responsibility which may arise for a State from the conclusion or application of a treaty, the provisions of which are incompatible with its obligations towards another State under another treaty.

The first rule laid down by the Vienna Convention is that if two treaties conflict but one says that the other prevails, that one will prevail.

If neither treaty contains such a provision, the position is more complicated. The relevant rules may be summarized as follows.

1. If the parties to the two treaties are the same, the second one prevails.

2. Even if the parties are not the same, the second one prevails if all the parties to the first treaty are also parties to the second.

3. If only some of the parties to the first treaty are also parties to the second treaty, the second treaty prevails as between those States that are parties to both.

This is really as far as the Vienna Convention goes. Article 30(4)(b) states that as between a State that is a party to both treaties and a State that is a party to only one, the treaty to which they are both parties governs their mutual rights and obligations. This, however, is to state the obvious. It simply means that if the United Kingdom and Germany conclude a treaty, the United Kingdom's rights under that treaty cannot be affected by another treaty to which Germany is a party but to which the United Kingdom is not.

The really difficult problem is what happens if the United Kingdom enters into one treaty with Germany and another with France. If there is a conflict between the two – if the former requires the United Kingdom to do something and the latter forbids it to do that same thing – what is the United Kingdom to do? The Vienna Convention provides no answer. All it says is that a breach of the treaty with one country cannot be excused on the basis of a treaty with another country. So, in our example, whatever the United Kingdom does, or does not do, it will be breaking international law in one way or another.

Panel 17.2   Conflicts between Community Treaties

EC Treaty

Article 305 [232]

1 The provisions of this Treaty shall not affect the provisions of the [ECSC Treaty], in particular as regards the rights and obligations of Member States, the powers of the institutions of that Community and the rules laid down by that Treaty for the functioning of the common market in coal and steel.

2 The provisions of this Treaty shall not derogate from those of the [Euratom Treaty].

Panel 17.3   Conflicting treaties: EC Treaty

EC Treaty

Article 307 [234] (first paragraph)

The rights and obligations arising from agreements concluded before 1 January 1958 or, for acceding States, before the date of their accession, between one or more Member States on the one hand, and one or more third countries on the other, shall not be affected by the provisions of this treaty.

Conflicts between two Community Treaties

We can now apply these rules to the Community Treaties. We shall first consider the problem of a conflict between two of the Community Treaties. Since the parties to these treaties are all the same, the later treaty will always prevail unless it contains a provision to the contrary. The EC Treaty does in fact contain such a provision. This is Article 305 [232] EC (Panel 17.2), which states that it is subject to both the ECSC Treaty (now expired) and the Euratom Treaty. The Euratom Treaty would, therefore, prevail over the EC Treaty if there was any incompatibility. This does not of course preclude the application of provisions of the EC Treaty in the fields covered by the Euratom Treaty to the extent to which there is no contrary provision in the latter.[3]

Treaties with non-member States

What happens if the EC Member States conclude a treaty with one or more non-member States and that treaty conflicts with one of the Community Treaties? If the treaty with the non-member States was subsequent to the Community Treaty, and if all the Member States were parties to it, it would prevail, unless it provided to the contrary. This follows from Article 30(3) of the Vienna Convention. It is possible that the Member States would be guilty of a violation of Community law if they entered into such a treaty. Nevertheless, it would prevail under international law.

What happens if the treaty with the non-member States is prior to the relevant Community Treaty? Under international law, the Community Treaty cannot affect the rights of the non-member States.[4] There is an express provision to this effect in Article 307 [234] EC, the first paragraph of which is set out in Panel 17.3. In one sense, this does no more than confirm the rule of international law. However, it seems that it was intended to go further and

---

3 *WTO* case, Opinion 1/94, [1994] ECR I-5267 (paras. 22 *et seq.* of the Opinion).
4 Art. 30(4)(b) of the Vienna Convention.

provide that an EC Member State does not violate EC law by carrying out its obligations under the other treaty. Thus, something that would otherwise be a violation of EC law is excused if it is required under the other treaty. However, the second paragraph of Article 307 [234] requires the Member State in question to take all appropriate steps to eliminate the incompatibilities. This would normally require it to attempt to renegotiate the agreement.

Article 307 [234] was probably adopted because some States might have been reluctant to conclude the EC Treaty if it could have given rise to obligations inconsistent with those arising out of earlier treaties. There is no equivalent provision in the ECSC[5] or Euratom Treaties, probably because it was thought unlikely that those treaties would ever conflict with other treaties.

It is important to be clear as to what Article 307 [234] does. It does not say that the Community is bound by the agreement, though (as we saw in Chapter 13) in certain special cases the Community *is* bound by such agreements.[6] The Community is not, therefore, responsible to the non-member States if the relevant Member State violates the agreement. All that Article 307 [234] says is that Community law will not prevent the Member State from fulfilling its obligations under the earlier agreement.

It is also important to consider what agreements are covered. According to Article 307 [234], they must be "concluded" before 1 January 1958 or, for acceding States, before the date of their accession. What is meant by "concluded"? The original text of the EC Treaty spoke of "agreements concluded before the entry into force of this Treaty". The Treaty of Amsterdam 1997 amended this by deleting the words "before the entry into force of this Treaty" and replacing them with the present wording.[7] Since the relevant date for the EC Treaty is when it entered into force, not when the text was adopted,[8] it might be argued that the relevant date for the other agreement (the date on which it was "concluded") should also be when it entered into force. Under Article 30 of the 1969 Vienna Convention, however, the relevant date for deciding which treaty is earlier appears to be that on which the text is adopted, not that on which the treaty enters into force.[9] According to the European Court, Article 307 [234] was intended to reflect the principles of international law.[10] In view of this, it would make sense to interpret it (in this respect) in the same way as Article 30 of the Vienna Convention. Moreover, if the purpose of Article 307 [234] is to protect Member States from the embarrassment of conflicting obligations, the relevant date should be that on which the text of the other agreement was adopted, rather than that on which it entered into force.

---

5 But see Part Two of the Convention on Transitional Provisions, a convention annexed to the ECSC Treaty (see Art. 85 ECSC). This recognized that the ECSC Treaty could not affect the rights of third countries, but its scope was narrow.
6 The old GATT is an example.
7 Art. 6 (heading I, point 78).
8 For acceding Member States it is when the EC Treaty enters into force as regards them, in other words when the treaty of accession enters into force.
9 Sinclair, note 2 above, p. 98; Aust, note 2 above, p. 183; Mus, "Conflicts Between Treaties in International Law" (1998) 45 NILR 208 at 220–222. A different view is advanced in Vierdag, "The Time of the 'Conclusion' of a Multilateral Treaty: Article 30 of the Vienna Convention on the Law of Treaties and Related Provisions" (1988) 59 BYIL 75, but this seems to be incorrect for the reasons given in Mus, above.
10 *Commission v. Italy* (below). See also *Levy* (below) at para. 12 of the judgment.

If this is correct, "concluded" in Article 307 [234] should be interpreted to mean the date on which the text was established.[11] This appears to be its normal meaning in international law.[12] The result is that an agreement is covered by Article 307 [234] if the text was established (for example, by signature) before the EC Treaty entered into force or, in the case of acceding Member States, before the treaty of accession entered into force.

We shall now consider some cases in which the European Court has applied these principles.

European Union
Commission v. Italy
COURT OF JUSTICE OF THE EUROPEAN COMMUNITIES
Case 10/61, [1962] ECR 1

Facts

Italy was a party to a GATT agreement adopted in Geneva in 1956 under which Italy had the right to impose a duty of 30 per cent, plus a minimum levy of 150 lire per article, on a certain category of goods. The Geneva agreement was prior to the EC Treaty, and Italy claimed that, under Article 307 [234], its terms prevailed over the EC Treaty even as regards imports from other Member States.

Judgment

The defendant [Italy] raises an objection based on the first paragraph of Article 307 [234] relating to the maintenance of rights and obligations arising from prior agreements concluded with third countries. The defendant maintains that this text permits and even obliges it to impose in every case the duty of 30% subject to the fixed minimum established under the Geneva Agreements of 1956 . . .

The applicant [Commission] replies that the terms "rights and obligations" in Article 307 [234] refer, as regards the "rights", to the rights of third countries and, as regards the "obligations", to the obligations of Member States and that, by virtue of the principles of international law, by assuming a new obligation which is incompatible with rights held under a prior treaty a State *ipso facto* gives up the exercise of these rights to the extent necessary for the performance of its new obligations.

The applicant's interpretation is well founded and the objections raised by the defence must be dismissed.

In fact, in matters governed by the EEC Treaty, that Treaty takes precedence over agreements concluded between Member States before its entry into force, including agreements made within the framework of GATT . . .

Moreover, the correct application of [the relevant provision of the EEC Treaty] does not adversely affect the rights and obligations of Member States in relation to third countries which arise from agreements concluded before the entry into force of the EEC Treaty.

As a result of Article 307 [234] different tariffs are applied to Member States and third countries, even though they are parties to the same Geneva Agreement of 1956. This is the normal effect of the Treaty establishing the EEC. The manner in which Member States

---

11 In the case of a bilateral treaty, this would normally be when it is signed.
12 Aust, note 2 above, p. 74.

proceed to reduce customs duties amongst themselves cannot be criticized by third countries since this abolition of customs duties is accomplished according to the provisions of the Treaty and does not interfere with the rights held by third countries under agreements still in force.

The application is therefore well founded.

Comment

This decision is entirely in accordance with international law. The European Court did not refer to the 1969 Vienna Convention because the case was decided before the Convention was adopted. Nevertheless, it is consistent with it. The EC Treaty was concluded after the GATT agreement. Under Article 30(4)(a) of the Vienna Convention, the EC Treaty prevailed as between two or more of the EC Member States. Consequently, the EC Treaty, not the GATT agreement, applied to imports from other Member States into Italy. Imports from non-Community States would of course have been governed by the GATT agreement.

> **European Union**
> **Levy**
> **COURT OF JUSTICE OF THE EUROPEAN COMMUNITIES**
> Case C-158/91, [1993] ECR I-4287

Facts and background

Prior to the conclusion of the EC Treaty, France had concluded an ILO agreement which provided that women would not be permitted to work at night.[13] France gave effect to this agreement by passing legislation prohibiting women from doing such work. Subsequently, the EC adopted a directive on sex equality in employment,[14] which the European Court interpreted as giving women the same rights as men to work at night.[15] There was thus a conflict between, on the one hand, the ILO agreement and the French legislation and, on the other hand, the directive. Levy, an employer who had infringed the French legislation, was prosecuted before the French courts. He claimed that the directive gave him a defence. Normally, this would have been the case.[16] The question before the European Court was whether the position was any different in view of the fact that the French legislation had been adopted to give effect to the ILO agreement.

> **Judgment**
> 12. According to the judgment in [*Commission v. Italy* (above)], the purpose of the first paragraph of Article 307 [234] of the Treaty is to make clear, in accordance with the principles of international law, that application of the Treaty does not affect the commitment of the Member State concerned to respect the rights of non-member countries under an earlier agreement and to comply with its corresponding obligations.

---

13 Convention 89 of 9 July 1948.
14 Equal Treatment Directive 76/207, OJ 1976, L39, p. 40.
15 *Stoeckel*, Case C-345/89, [1991] ECR I-4047.
16 The directive would have been vertically directly effective.

It follows that, in that provision, the terms "rights and obligations" refer, as regards "rights", to the rights of non-member countries and, as regards "obligations", to the obligations of Member States.

13. Consequently, in order to determine whether a Community rule may be deprived of effect by an earlier international agreement, it is necessary to examine whether that agreement imposes on the Member State concerned obligations whose performance may still be required by non-member countries which are parties to it.

14. In that respect, the Commission maintains that, since the Court ruled in [*Stoeckel,* Case C-345/89, [1991] ECR I-4047] that the concern for protection which originally inspired the principle of the prohibition on night work for women is no longer well founded, the Member States are required, by virtue of Article 5(2)(c) of the directive, to take the measures necessary to revise those laws, regulations and administrative provisions which are contrary to the principle of equal treatment. Where the laws which are to be revised result from the conclusion of earlier international agreements, such as the ILO Convention, the measures to be taken by the Member States are the same as the "appropriate steps" to which they must resort, pursuant to the second paragraph of Article 307 [234] of the Treaty, in order to eliminate the incompatibilities established between those international agreements and Community law, namely the extension of the prohibition on night work to workers of the opposite sex or the abrogation of the earlier international agreement.

15. The Commission adds that, in any event, the obligation arising from the ILO Convention not to have women working at night cannot allow a Member State not to observe the principle of equal treatment of men and women, a fundamental human right respect for which forms an integral part of the general principles of law protected by the Court of Justice (see [*Internationale Handelsgesellschaft,* above]). It argues that, according to the case-law of the European Court of Human Rights [citation omitted], a difference of treatment between men and women must be justified on objective and reasonable grounds and there must be a reasonable relationship of proportionality between the means employed and the aim sought to be realised. In view of the similarity of the risks to which both men and women who work at night are exposed, a difference of treatment between men and women may only be justified by the need to protect the biological condition of women.

16. In reply to that argument, it should he pointed out that, while it is true that equal treatment of men and women constitutes a fundamental right recognized by the Community legal order, its implementation, even at Community level, has been gradual, requiring the Council to take action by means of directives, and that those directives allow, temporarily, certain derogations from the principle of equal treatment.

17. In those circumstances, it is not sufficient to rely on the principle of equal treatment in order to evade performance of the obligations which are incumbent on a Member State in that field under an earlier international agreement and observance of which is safeguarded by the first paragraph of Article 307 [234] of the Treaty.

18. The Commission also bases its argument on the development of international law in that field and, in particular, on the Convention for the Elimination of all Forms of Discrimination against Women, concluded in New York on 18 December 1979 (hereinafter "the New York Convention"), ratified by France on 14 December 1983, and on developments within the International Labour Organization itself. As regards the latter, the Commission makes special mention of the 1990 Protocol on the 1948 ILO Convention,

ILO Convention No 171 of 1990 on night work and ILO Recommendation No 178 of 1990 on night work, all of which were adopted on 26 June 1990.

19. It is true that the provisions of an international agreement may be deprived of their binding force if it appears that all the parties to the agreement have concluded a subsequent agreement whose provisions are so far incompatible with those of the earlier one that the two agreements are not capable of being applied at the same time (see Article 59(1)(b) of the Vienna Convention on the Law of Treaties of 21 March 1986).[17]

20. In the present case, if it were apparent from the development of international law, as recalled by the Commission, that the prohibition on night work for women, provided for in the ILO Convention, had been annulled by virtue of subsequent agreements binding on the same parties, the first paragraph of Article 307 [234] of the Treaty would not he applicable. There would then be nothing to prevent the national court from applying Article 5 of the directive as interpreted by the Court in *Stoeckel*, cited above, and disapplying any national provisions conflicting therewith.

21. However, in proceedings for a preliminary ruling, it is not for this Court but for the national court to determine which obligations are imposed by an earlier international agreement on the Member State concerned and to ascertain their ambit so as to be able to determine the extent to which they constitute an obstacle to the application of Article 5 of the directive.

22. In view of the foregoing considerations, the answer to the question submitted for a preliminary ruling must be that the national court is under an obligation to ensure that Article 5 of Directive 76/207 is fully complied with by refraining from applying any conflicting provision of national legislation, unless the application of such a provision is necessary in order to ensure the performance by the Member State concerned of obligations arising under an agreement concluded with non-member countries prior to the entry into force of the EEC Treaty.

Comment

This case shows that Article 307 [234] permits a Member State to act contrary to Community law where this is necessary to comply with an obligation under an earlier treaty which is still binding.

The Community Treaties and the Human Rights Convention

Having considered the general rules applying to conflicting treaties, we are now in a position to focus on the specific question of conflicts between the Community Treaties and the Human Rights Convention. There are two issues: the position of the Community (which is not a party to the Human Rights

---

17 Editor's note: there are two Vienna Conventions on the Law of Treaties. The one usually cited is the 1969 Convention, which applies to treaties between two or more States. The other is the 1986 Convention, which applies to treaties between international organizations and States, or between two or more international organizations. The 1986 Convention is not in force. It is not clear why the European Court cited the 1986 Convention here. In *Racke v. Hauptzollamt Mainz*, set out in Chap. 13, pp. 257–261, above, it cited the 1969 Vienna Convention. Since both Conventions are very similar and are usually regarded as setting out the relevant principles of customary international law, it does not matter much which one is cited. Art. 59(1)(b) is identical in the two texts.

Convention) and that of the Member States. We first consider the views of the Human Rights Commission.[18]

Council of Europe
CFDT case
EUROPEAN COMMISSION OF HUMAN RIGHTS
Application 8030/77, Decision of 10 July 1978, 13 Decisions and Reports 213

Facts

This case concerned appointments to the ECSC Consultative Committee, a body which advised the Commission (originally called the "High Authority") under the ECSC Treaty. The Committee was made up of the following three groups, each entitled to equal representation: (a) producers of coal and steel; (b) workers in those industries; and (c) consumers and dealers in those industries. The case concerned workers' representatives. According to Article 18 ECSC, they were appointed by the following procedure. The EC Council designated "representative organizations" (trade unions) and allocated a given number of seats to each of them. Each organization then drew up a list containing twice as many names as there were seats allocated to it, and the Council made appointments from the lists. In practice, each Member State was allowed to nominate the organizations that would be designated for its territory.

The CFDT (*Confédération Française Démocratique du Travail*) was the second-largest federation of labour unions in France. Over a number of years, the French Government had consistently excluded the CFDT from the organizations nominated by it. In addition to the largest labour organization, the French Government also nominated three others that were smaller than the CFDT. Although not mentioned in the case, the reason was obvious. The CFDT was Communist-dominated. After attempts to secure a remedy in the European Court and in the French courts were dismissed on jurisdictional grounds, the CFDT turned to the European Commission of Human Rights. Its action was against (a) the European Communities; (b) the Member States collectively (jointly); and (c) the Member States individually (severally).

Report

1. The applicant complains that it was not designated by the Council of the European Communities as a representative organisation entitled to submit lists of candidates for the Consultative Committee of the ECSC (Article 18 of the ECSC Treaty) although it is the second largest among the five representative organisations in France. This appointment was made on the proposal of the Governments of the Member States and in the present case France had not included the CFDT on its list. In simply confirming the French Government's proposals the Council had not properly exercised the power conferred on it by Article 18 (2) of the ECSC Treaty.

Being thus excluded from consultation and having no available appeal to remedy this situation – its appeal to the Court of Justice of the European Communities and to the

---

18 The powers and functions of the Human Rights Commission were discussed in Chap. 14 above. It has now been abolished.

French Conseil d'Etat having been declared inadmissible on 17 February 1977 and 10 February 1978 respectively – the applicant considers that the Council's decision makes the European Communities itself, the Member States of the European Communities jointly and severally responsible under the European Convention on Human Rights.

In this connection it alleges a violation of Articles 11, 13 and 14 of the Convention.[19]

2. The Commission would first like to point out that the applicant is complaining of the act of an organ of the Communities, i.e. the Council of the European Communities, relating to the composition of another organ of the Communities, i.e. the Consultative Committee to the High Authority. This is an act whose effects concern the internal organisation of the European Communities who under Article 6 of the ECSC Treaty, Article 281 [210] of the EEC Treaty and Article 184 of the EAEC treaty have their own legal personality and are represented by their own institutions, each acting within the ambit of their powers.

On the alleged responsibility of the European Communities itself

3. In so far as the application is directed against the European Communities as such the Commission points out that the European Communities are not a Contracting Party to the European Convention on Human Rights (Article 66 of the Convention). To this extent the consideration of the applicant's complaint lies outside the Commission's jurisdiction *ratione personae*.[20]

On the alleged responsibility of the Member States of the European Communities jointly

4. In so far as the application is directed against "the Member States jointly", the Commission finds that the applicant has not defined what it means by this. On this point the Commission considers that the application is in fact directed against the Council of the European Communities. It follows that a consideration of the applicant's complaints, in this case also, lies outside the Commission's jurisdiction *ratione personae*.

On the alleged responsibility of the Member States of the European Communities severally

5. In so far as the application is directed against each of the Member States of the European Communities who are at the same time Contracting Parties to the Convention the question might be raised whether the act complained of, which was carried out by an organ of the European Communities, can involve the responsibility of the nine Member States of the European Communities under the Convention.

6. Whatever the answer to this question the Commission points out that as far as France is concerned a consideration of the application lies outside its jurisdiction *ratione personae* as France has not so far recognised the right of individual petition under Article 25 of the Convention.

7. As regards the eight other Member States of the European Communities, the Commission considers that an examination of the applicant's complaints is also outside its jurisdiction *ratione personae* since these States by taking part in the decision of the Council of the European Communities had not in the circumstances of the instant case exercised their "jurisdiction" within the meaning of Article 1 of the Convention.

Result: application inadmissible.

---

19 Editor's note: these are set out in Panel 14.4, p. 279 above.
20 Editor's note: *ratione personae* is Latin for "by reason of the person", in other words the person against whom the complaint was brought.

QUESTION

Why were the Member States other than France not liable for voting in the Council in favour of the proposals put forward by France to designate organizations other than the CFDT? Were they bound under Community law to act as they did?

Council of Europe
M & Co. v. Germany
EUROPEAN COMMISSION OF HUMAN RIGHTS
Application 13258/87, Decision of 9 February 1990, 64 *Decisions and Reports* 138

Facts and background

M & Co. was a German partnership which had been accused of violating EC competition (antitrust) law. Proceedings were brought before the EC Commission, and these resulted in a fine of approximately DM3.5 million. M & Co. appealed to the European Court, claiming, among other things, that its human rights had not been respected. It was successful in part, but the Commission's decision was otherwise upheld. The fine was reduced to just under DM1 million. M & Co. refused to pay, and enforcement proceedings were brought in Germany. M & Co. challenged these in the German courts, claiming that its constitutional rights had been infringed in the proceedings before the Commission. This claim was rejected, and M & Co. was forced to pay. It then turned to the Human Rights Commission, arguing that Germany had violated the Convention by enforcing the fine.

Report

The applicant company complains that the German authorities issued a writ for the execution of a judgment of the European Court of Justice according to which it has to pay a heavy fine for having violated Article 81 [85] of the EC Treaty. The applicant company mainly submits that in its case the Court of Justice violated the principle of presumption of innocence as guaranteed by Article 6 para. 2 of the Convention by fining its associates for a wrong committed without their knowledge by an employee. Furthermore the applicant company considers the right of every accused to defend himself in person as guaranteed by Article 6 para. 3 (c) of the Convention as being violated.

According to the applicant company the respondent State's obligation to secure the rights guaranteed by the Convention has absolute priority over any other treaty obligations. Therefore the competent Minister, before issuing a writ of execution, should examine whether or not the judgment of the European Court of Justice had been given in proceedings respecting the guarantees set out in Article 6 of the Convention. As this was not the case the granting of the writ of execution, so the applicant company argues, gave effect to the violations complained of and therefore violated the provisions invoked.

The respondent Government argue that the Federal Republic of Germany is not responsible under the Convention for acts and decisions of the European Communities. The Federal Minister of Justice, in granting a writ of execution for a judgment of the European Court of Justice, did not have to examine whether the judgment in question had been reached in proceedings compatible with fundamental rights guaranteed by the European Convention on Human Rights or the German Basic Law. He only had to examine whether the judgment was authentic. Therefore, he neither had to determine a civil right, nor a criminal charge within the meaning of Article 6 of the Convention.

Furthermore, the Federal Republic's responsibility under the Convention could not be derived from the fact that it transferred part of its powers to the European Communities. Otherwise all Community acts would indirectly be subject to control by the Convention organs. However, such a result would not be compatible with the generally accepted principle that the Convention did not apply to the European Communities and would become binding for them only if they formally adhered to it. In this context the respondent Government also point out that, in any event, observance of fundamental rights is secured by the European Court of Justice. Even if it should be found that national authorities nevertheless also remained bound to control Community acts as to manifest and flagrant violations of fundamental rights, such a control had, in the present case, been effected by the German civil courts which had found no appearance of such a violation.

The Commission first recalls that it is in fact not competent *ratione personae* to examine proceedings before or decisions of organs of the European Communities, the latter not being a Party to the European Convention on Human Rights [*CFDT* and another case cited]. This does not mean, however, that by granting executory power to a judgment of the European Court of Justice the competent German authorities acted quasi as Community organs and are to that extent beyond the scope of control exercised by the Convention organs. Under Article 1 of the Convention the Member States are responsible for all acts and omissions of their domestic organs allegedly violating the Convention regardless of whether the act or omission in question is a consequence of domestic law or regulations or of the necessity to comply with international obligations . . .

The question therefore is whether by giving effect to a judgment reached in proceedings that allegedly violated Article 6 the Federal Republic of Germany incurred responsibility under the Convention on account of the fact that these proceedings against a German company were possible only because the Federal Republic has transferred its powers in this sphere to the European Communities.

For the purpose of the examination of this question it can be assumed that the anti-trust proceedings in question would fall under Article 6 had they been conducted by German and not by European judicial authorities . . .

It has next to be observed that the Convention does not prohibit a Member State from transferring powers to international organisations. Nonetheless, the Commission recalls that "if a State contracts treaty obligations and subsequently concludes another international agreement which disables it from performing its obligations under the first treaty it will be answerable for any resulting breach of its obligations under the earlier treaty" (cf., No. 235/56, Dec. 10.6.58, Yearbook 2 p. 256 (300)). The Commission considers that a transfer of powers does not necessarily exclude a State's responsibility under the Convention with regard to the exercise of the transferred powers. Otherwise the guarantees of the Convention could wantonly be limited or excluded and thus be deprived of their peremptory character. The object and purpose of the Convention as an instrument for the protection of individual human beings requires that its provisions be interpreted and applied so as to make its safeguards practical and effective . . . Therefore the transfer of powers to an international organisation is not incompatible with the Convention provided that within that organisation fundamental rights will receive an equivalent protection.

The Commission notes that the legal system of the European Communities not only secures fundamental rights but also provides for control of their observance. It is true that the constituent treaties of the European Communities did not contain a catalogue of such rights. However, the Parliament, the Council and the Commission of the European Communities have stressed in a joint declaration of 5 April 1977 that they attach prime importance to the protection of fundamental rights, as derived in particular from the Constitutions of the Member States and the European Convention for the Protection of Human Rights and Fundamental Freedoms. They pledged that, in the exercise of their powers and in pursuance of the aims of the European Communities, they would respect and continue to respect these human rights (Official Journal of the European Communities, XX, 1977, Information and Notices, No. C 103/1). In addition the Court of Justice of the European Communities has developed a case-law according to which it is called upon to control Community acts on the basis of fundamental rights, including those enshrined in the European Convention on Human Rights. In accordance with this reasoning the Court of Justice underlined in the present case that the right to a fair hearing is a fundamental principle of Community law. It stated that Community law contained all criteria which are prerequisites not only to examine but, if necessary, to remedy the applicant company's complaint that its right to a fair hearing was violated . . . However, it came to the conclusion that this complaint was unfounded.

The Commission has also taken into consideration that it would be contrary to the very idea of transferring powers to an international organisation to hold the Member States responsible for examining, in each individual case before issuing a writ of execution for a judgment of the European Court of Justice, whether Article 6 of the Convention was respected in the underlying proceedings.

It follows that the application is incompatible with the provisions of the Convention *ratione materiae*[21] and must be rejected in accordance with Article 27 para. 2 of the Convention.

Result: application inadmissible.

Council of Europe
Matthews v. United Kingdom
EUROPEAN COURT OF HUMAN RIGHTS
18 February 1999, (1999) 28 EHRR 361

Facts and background

The issue in this case was whether persons resident in Gibraltar could vote in elections to the European Parliament. Originally, the Community Treaties provided that the Parliament (then called the "Assembly") would consist of delegates designated by Member-State parliaments from among their own number.[22] The Treaties went on to state, however, that the European Parliament would draw up proposals for direct elections. These had to be agreed by the Council and adopted by the Member States "in accordance with their respective constitutional requirements".[23] After a long delay, the Council adopted a decision to which was annexed an "Act" providing for direct elections.[24] The Act was ratified as a treaty by the Member States, and, though there is some controversy surrounding its legal status, it is best regarded as a treaty amending

---

21 Editor's note: *ratione materiae* is Latin for "by reason of the subject-matter".
22 Arts. 21(1) ECSC; [138(1)] EC; and 108(1) Euratom.
23 Arts. 21(3) ECSC; 190(4) [138(3)] EC; and 108(3) Euratom.
24 Decision 76/787, OJ 1976, L278, p. 1.

the relevant Community Treaties.[25] The Act specifies how many representatives will be elected in each Member State; it also states in Annex II that the United Kingdom will apply the provisions of the Act only in respect of the United Kingdom itself. Article 15 of the Act states that the Annexes form an integral part of the Act. Since Gibraltar, though a British dependency, is not constitutionally part of the United Kingdom, this had the effect of excluding Gibraltarians from participating in elections to the European Parliament, even though the Community Treaties apply, in part, to Gibraltar and, to that extent, the European Parliament has jurisdiction over Gibraltar.[26]

Ms Matthews, a resident of Gibraltar, brought proceedings before the Human Rights Commission, claiming that the denial of her right to vote in European elections constituted a violation of Article 3 of Protocol No. 1 to the Convention (set out in Panel 14.5, Chapter 14, above), a provision which guarantees the right to free elections.[27] The Commission found the complaint admissible, but considered that no violation had taken place.[28] The case then came before the European Court of Human Rights.

Judgment
I. ALLEGED VIOLATION OF ARTICLE 3 OF PROTOCOL No. 1

1. The applicant alleged a breach of Article 3 of Protocol No. 1, which provides:
"The High Contracting Parties undertake to hold free elections at reasonable intervals by secret ballot, under conditions which will ensure the free expression of the opinion of the people in the choice of the legislature."

2. The Government maintained that, for three main reasons, Article 3 of Protocol No. 1 was not applicable to the facts of the present case or, in the alternative, that there had been no violation of that provision.

A. Whether the United Kingdom can be held responsible under the Convention for the lack of elections to the European Parliament in Gibraltar

3. According to the Government, the applicant's real objection was to Council Decision 76/787 and to the 1976 Act concerning elections to the European Parliament . . . That Act, which had the status of a treaty, was adopted in the Community framework and

---

25 René Joliet, *Le droit institutionnel des Communautés européennes: Les Institutions; Les sources; Les rapports entre ordres juridiques* (Faculté de Droit, d'Economie et de Sciences Sociales, Université de Liège, Liège, Belgium, 1983), pp. 75–77; T. C. Hartley, *The Foundations of European Community Law* (Oxford University Press, Oxford, 5th ed., 2003), pp. 29–30. If this is correct, the Act forms part of the EC Treaty for the purpose of Art. 307 [234] EC.
26 The Treaties apply by virtue of Art. 299(4) [227(4)] EC. However, the Treaty of Accession (by which the United Kingdom joined the Community) provides that many parts of the Community Treaties, including such important matters as the free movement of goods and the Common Agricultural Policy, will not apply.
27 She also invoked Art. 14 of the Convention, which provides that the enjoyment of the rights laid down in the Convention must be secured without discrimination. The Convention applies to Gibraltar by virtue of a declaration made by the United Kingdom on 23 October 1953 under what was then Art. 63 of the Convention; Protocol No. 1 applies by virtue of a declaration made on 25 February 1988 under Art. 4 of Protocol No. 1.
28 Application No. 24833/94 (report reproduced as an annex to the judgment). The Human Rights Commission considered that Art. 3 of Protocol No. 1 is not applicable to supranational representative organs, such as the European Parliament.

could not be revoked or varied unilaterally by the United Kingdom. The Government underlined that the European Commission of Human Rights had refused on a number of occasions to subject measures falling within the Community legal order to scrutiny under the Convention. Whilst they accepted that there might be circumstances in which a Contracting Party might infringe its obligations under the Convention by entering into treaty obligations which were incompatible with the Convention, they considered that in the present case, which concerned texts adopted in the framework of the European Community, the position was not the same. Thus, acts adopted by the Community or consequent to its requirements could not be imputed to the Member States, together or individually, particularly when those acts concerned elections to a constitutional organ of the Community itself. At the hearing, the Government suggested that to engage the responsibility of any State under the Convention, that State must have a power of effective control over the act complained of. In the case of the provisions relating to the elections to the European Parliament, the United Kingdom Government had no such control.

4. The applicant disagreed. For her, the Council Decision and 1976 Act constituted an international treaty, rather than an act of an institution whose decisions were not subject to Convention review. She thus considered that the Government remained responsible under the Convention for the effects of the Council Decision and 1976 Act. In the alternative – that is, if the Council Decision and 1976 Act were to be interpreted as involving a transfer of powers to the Community organs – the applicant argued, by reference to Commission case-law, that in the absence of any equivalent protection of her rights under Article 3 of Protocol No. 1, the Government in any event retained responsibility under the Convention.

5. The majority of the Commission took no stand on the point, although it was referred to in concurring and dissenting opinions.

6. Article 1 of the Convention requires the High Contracting Parties to "secure to everyone within their jurisdiction the rights and freedoms defined in . . . [the] Convention". Article 1 makes no distinction as to the type of rule or measure concerned, and does not exclude any part of the Member States' "jurisdiction" from scrutiny under the Convention . . .

7. The Court notes that the parties do not dispute that Article 3 of Protocol No. 1 applies in Gibraltar. It recalls that the Convention was extended to the territory of Gibraltar by the United Kingdom's declaration of 23 October 1953 . . . and Protocol No. 1 has been applicable in Gibraltar since 25 February 1988. There is therefore clearly territorial "jurisdiction" within the meaning of Article 1 of the Convention.

8. The Court must nevertheless consider whether, notwithstanding the nature of the elections to the European Parliament as an organ of the EC, the United Kingdom can be held responsible under Article 1 of the Convention for the absence of elections to the European Parliament in Gibraltar, that is, whether the United Kingdom is required to "secure" elections to the European Parliament notwithstanding the Community character of those elections.

9. The Court observes that acts of the EC as such cannot be challenged before the Court because the EC is not a Contracting Party. The Convention does not exclude the transfer of competences to international organisations provided that Convention rights continue to be "secured". Member States' responsibility therefore continues even after such a transfer.

10. In the present case, the alleged violation of the Convention flows from an annex to the 1976 Act, entered into by the United Kingdom, together with the extension to the European Parliament's competences brought about by the Maastricht Treaty. The Council Decision and the 1976 Act . . . and the Maastricht Treaty, with its changes to the EEC Treaty,

all constituted international instruments which were freely entered into by the United Kingdom. Indeed, the 1976 Act cannot be challenged before the European Court of Justice for the very reason that it is not a "normal" act of the Community, but is a treaty within the Community legal order. The Maastricht Treaty, too, is not an act of the Community, but a treaty by which a revision of the EEC Treaty was brought about. The United Kingdom, together with all the other parties to the Maastricht Treaty, is responsible *ratione materiae* under Article 1 of the Convention and, in particular, under Article 3 of Protocol No. 1, for the consequences of that Treaty.

11. In determining to what extent the United Kingdom is responsible for "securing" the rights in Article 3 of Protocol No. 1 in respect of elections to the European Parliament in Gibraltar, the Court recalls that the Convention is intended to guarantee rights that are not theoretical or illusory, but practical and effective . . . It is uncontested that legislation emanating from the legislative process of the European Community affects the population of Gibraltar in the same way as legislation which enters the domestic legal order exclusively via the House of Assembly. To this extent, there is no difference between European and domestic legislation, and no reason why the United Kingdom should not be required to "secure" the rights in Article 3 of Protocol No. 1 in respect of European legislation, in the same way as those rights are required to be "secured" in respect of purely domestic legislation. In particular, the suggestion that the United Kingdom may not have effective control over the state of affairs complained of cannot affect the position, as the United Kingdom's responsibility derives from its having entered into treaty commitments subsequent to the applicability of Article 3 of Protocol No. 1 to Gibraltar, namely the Maastricht Treaty taken together with its obligations under the Council Decision and the 1976 Act. Further, the Court notes that on acceding to the EC Treaty, the United Kingdom chose, by virtue of Article 299(4) [227(4)] of the Treaty, to have substantial areas of EC legislation applied to Gibraltar . . .

12. It follows that the United Kingdom is responsible under Article 1 of the Convention for securing the rights guaranteed by Article 3 of Protocol No. 1 in Gibraltar regardless of whether the elections were purely domestic or European.

B. Whether Article 3 of Protocol No. 1 is applicable to an organ such as the European Parliament

13. The Government claimed that the undertaking in Article 3 of Protocol No. 1 was necessarily limited to matters falling within the power of the parties to the Convention, that is, sovereign States. They submitted that the "legislature" in Gibraltar was the House of Assembly, and that it was to that body that Article 3 of Protocol No. 1 applied in the context of Gibraltar. For the Government, there was no basis upon which the Convention could place obligations on Contracting Parties in relation to elections for the parliament of a distinct, supranational organisation, and they contended that this was particularly so when the Member States of the European Community had limited their own sovereignty in respect of it and when both the European Parliament itself and its basic electoral procedures were provided for under its own legal system, rather than the legal systems of its Member States.

14. The applicant referred to previous decisions of the European Commission of Human Rights in which complaints concerning the European Parliament were dealt with on the merits, so that the Commission in effect assumed that Article 3 of Protocol No. 1 applied to elections to the European Parliament . . . She agreed with the dissenting members of the Commission who did not accept that because the European Parliament did not exist when Protocol No. 1 was drafted, it necessarily fell outside the ambit of Article 3 of that Protocol.

15. The majority of the Commission based its reasoning on this jurisdictional point. It considered that "to hold Article 3 of Protocol No. 1 to be applicable to supranational representative organs would be to extend the scope of Article 3 beyond what was intended by the drafters of the Convention and beyond the object and purpose of the provision. . . . [T]he role of Article 3 is to ensure that elections take place at regular intervals to the national or local legislative assembly, that is, in the case of Gibraltar, to the House of Assembly" (see paragraph 63 of the Commission's report).

16. That the Convention is a living instrument which must be interpreted in the light of present-day conditions is firmly rooted in the Court's case-law . . . The mere fact that a body was not envisaged by the drafters of the Convention cannot prevent that body from falling within the scope of the Convention. To the extent that Contracting States organise common constitutional or parliamentary structures by international treaties, the Court must take these mutually agreed structural changes into account in interpreting the Convention and its Protocols.

The question remains whether an organ such as the European Parliament nevertheless falls outside the ambit of Article 3 of Protocol No. 1.

17. The Court recalls that the word "legislature" in Article 3 of Protocol No. 1 does not necessarily mean the national parliament: the word has to be interpreted in the light of the constitutional structure of the State in question. In the case of *Mathieu-Mohin and Clerfayt v. Belgium* [judgment of 2 March 1987, Series A no. 113, p. 23, § 53], the 1980 constitutional reform had vested in the Flemish Council sufficient competence and powers to make it, alongside the French Community Council and the Walloon Regional Council, a constituent part of the Belgian "legislature", in addition to the House of Representatives and the Senate . . .

18. According to the case-law of the European Court of Justice, it is an inherent aspect of EC law that such law sits alongside, and indeed has precedence over, domestic law . . . In this regard, Gibraltar is in the same position as other parts of the European Union.

19. The Court reiterates that Article 3 of Protocol No. 1 enshrines a characteristic of an effective political democracy . . . In the present case, there has been no submission that there exist alternative means of providing for electoral representation of the population of Gibraltar in the European Parliament, and the Court finds no indication of any.

20. The Court thus considers that to accept the Government's contention that the sphere of activities of the European Parliament falls outside the scope of Article 3 of Protocol No. 1 would risk undermining one of the fundamental tools by which "effective political democracy" can be maintained.

21. It follows that no reason has been made out which could justify excluding the European Parliament from the ambit of the elections referred to in Article 3 of Protocol No. 1 on the ground that it is a supranational, rather than a purely domestic, representative organ.

C. Whether the European Parliament, at the relevant time, had the characteristics of a "legislature" in Gibraltar

[The court considered whether the European Parliament had sufficient powers to constitute a "legislature" within the meaning of the Convention. The United Kingdom argued that it continued to lack both of the most fundamental attributes of a legislature: the power to initiate legislation and the power to adopt it. Ms Matthews, on the other hand, argued that the Maastricht Agreement (Treaty on

European Union) had increased the Parliament's powers to such an extent that it
had been transformed from a mere advisory and supervisory organ to a body
which assumed, or assumed at least in part, the powers and functions of legislative
bodies within the meaning of Article 3 of Protocol No. 1.

The court examined the powers of the European Parliament. These included the
following: its powers under the procedure laid down by Article 252 [189c] (where it
could be overruled by the Council, provided the latter was unanimous); its powers
under the procedure laid down by Article 251 [189b] (where it could not be
overruled at all); its veto rights with regard to matters such as the accession of new
Member States and the conclusion of certain types of international agreements; its
powers in relation to the appointment and removal of the Commission; and its
powers in relation to the budget. It then continued as follows.]

25. As to the context in which the European Parliament operates, the Court is of the view
that the European Parliament represents the principal form of democratic, political
accountability in the Community system. The Court considers that, whatever its limitations,
the European Parliament, which derives democratic legitimation from the direct elections
by universal suffrage, must be seen as that part of the European Community structure
which best reflects concerns as to "effective political democracy".

26. Even when due allowance is made for the fact that Gibraltar is excluded from certain
areas of Community activity . . . there remain significant areas where Community activity
has a direct impact in Gibraltar. Further, as the applicant points out, measures taken under
Article 251 [189b] of the EC Treaty and which affect Gibraltar relate to important matters
such as road safety, unfair contract terms and air pollution by emissions from motor
vehicles and to all measures in relation to the completion of the internal market.

27. The Court thus finds that the European Parliament is sufficiently involved in the specific
legislative processes leading to the passage of legislation under Articles 251 [189b] and
252 [189c] of the EC Treaty, and is sufficiently involved in the general democratic
supervision of the activities of the European Community, to constitute part of the
"legislature" of Gibraltar for the purposes of Article 3 of Protocol No. 1 . . .

[After considering various other arguments, the court concluded as follows.]

33. In the circumstances of the present case, the very essence of the applicant's right to
vote, as guaranteed by Article 3 of Protocol No. 1, was denied.

It follows that there has been a violation of that provision . . .

Dissenting opinion of Judges Freeland and Jungwiert omitted.

QUESTIONS
1. The 1976 Act had the status of a treaty. Did this mean that the
   United Kingdom was not responsible for any violations of human
   rights that resulted from it?
2. Can Article 3 of Protocol No. 1 apply to the legislative body of an
   international organization or does it apply only to that of a State?
3. Do you agree that the European Parliament has sufficient powers
   to be regarded as a "legislature" within the meaning of Article 3 of
   Protocol No. 1?

Comment

Since the Act providing for direct elections is a treaty, it is not subject to annulment by the European Court (EC) on human rights grounds. Therefore, it could be said that the Community system for the protection of human rights does not apply to it. To this extent, the judgment could be reconciled with the decision of the Human Rights Commission in *M & Co.* However, the court did not attempt to reconcile it on this ground, or indeed on any ground, and there seems little doubt that it represents a new approach towards the Community. One possible explanation is that, after the decision in *M & Co.* but before that in *Matthews v. United Kingdom*, the European Court (EC) ruled that the Community could not accede to the Human Rights Convention without an amendment to the Community Treaties,[29] a ruling that is said to have been felt as a rebuff by the Human Rights Court. Perhaps this made them reassess their attitude towards the Community.

The obvious way to resolve the clash between EC law and the Human Rights Convention would have been to amend the Annex so as to allow Gibraltarians to vote as part of the United Kingdom electorate. However, Spain, which has a claim to Gibraltar, refused to agree. The United Kingdom therefore decided to go ahead on its own. So the European Parliament (Representation) Act 2003 was enacted. Part 2 of this Act gives Gibraltarians the right to vote in elections to the European Parliament as part of one of the electoral regions in England and Wales. This means that MEPs from the United Kingdom will be elected in a way that is contrary to the provisions of the Act of 1976. Does this mean that such elections are invalid?

To answer this question, we must be clear as to exactly what the conflicting provisions are. One could say that they are, on the one hand, the Act of 1976 providing for direct elections to the European Parliament, an instrument which amended the EC and Euratom Treaties, and, on the other hand, the Protocol to the Human Rights Convention. However, the failure to grant voting rights to Gibraltarians only became an infringement of the Protocol when the European Parliament gained sufficient powers to constitute a "legislature" for the purpose of the Protocol. This occurred as a result of the Treaty on European Union (Maastricht Agreement). It would, therefore, be more accurate to say that the conflict is between, on the one hand, the Act and the Maastricht Agreement and, on the other hand, the Protocol.

All the parties to the Community Treaties are also parties to the Protocol; but not all the parties to the Protocol are parties to the Community Treaties. Various non-Community countries such as Norway and Iceland have been parties to the Protocol from the very beginning.[30] In these circumstances, could one apply Article 30(3) of the Vienna Convention? Under this,

---

29 Opinion 2/94, [1996] ECR I-1759. Its decision is thought by some to have been due to its unwillingness to subordinate itself, even within a limited area, to another court.

30 The Protocol was opened for signature on 20 March 1952 and came into force for the original parties on 18 June 1954. Iceland and Norway, like the United Kingdom, signed the Protocol on the first of these dates and it came into force for all three States on the second of them.

the Protocol would prevail if it was later than the Act and the Maastricht Agreement.

Was the Protocol later than the Act and the Agreement? The Vienna Convention does not specify how to determine which treaty is later; nevertheless, as we saw above, it seems that the date of adoption, rather than that of entry into force, is the criterion.[31] The Protocol was adopted on 20 March 1952, the Act on 20 September 1976 and the Maastricht Agreement on 7 February 1992. Clearly, the Protocol was *not* later. It must be admitted that the conflict arose only because the Protocol was extended to Gibraltar under a Declaration made by the United Kingdom on 28 February 1988.[32] However, it is doubtful whether this is of any relevance, since the crucial time is when the Protocol was adopted, not when it came into force.[33] It follows that Article 30(3) of the Vienna Convention does not apply.

Could the answer be found in the Community Treaties themselves? As we saw earlier, Article 307 [234] EC provides that where a new Member State joins the Community, its obligations towards non-member States under treaties concluded before the date of its accession will not be affected by the EC Treaty. If we accept that the relevant date is that on which the Protocol was adopted, rather than that on which it was extended to Gibraltar, it was clearly concluded before the United Kingdom acceded to the Community treaties.[34] It is suggested, therefore, that by virtue of Article 307 [234], the EC Treaty is subject to the Protocol.

Unfortunately, this is not sufficient to solve the problem because the Act providing for direct elections amends the Euratom Treaty as well as the EC Treaty, and the former contains no equivalent provision. Does this mean that the Protocol does not prevail over the Euratom Treaty? This cannot be the case, since there is, and always has been, a single Parliament for both Communities, and it often acts under both Treaties simultaneously. It would be impossible for Gibraltarians to vote under the EC Treaty but not under the Euratom Treaty. It has to be both or neither. Since the Member States cannot have intended to produce an impossible situation, they must have intended that the Act providing for direct elections would be subject to the Protocol, not only in so far as it amended the EC Treaty, but also in so far as it amended the Euratom

---

31 See note 9 above.

32 The power to make such a Declaration was granted by Article 4 of the Protocol.

33 Once the United Kingdom was a party to the Protocol, it could have extended it to Gibraltar at any time it chose. The Protocol was *potentially* applicable to Gibraltar from the moment it was adopted. The question of priority should not depend on something within the discretion of one of the parties.

34 As we saw above, there is some doubt whether, in Art. 307 [234], "concluded" refers to the date of adoption or the date of entry into force. However, this makes no difference for present purposes, as long as "entry into force" means entry into force for the United Kingdom, as distinct from entry into force for Gibraltar: the United Kingdom signed the Protocol in 1952 and it entered into force for the United Kingdom in 1954, many years before the United Kingdom joined the Community (the instruments of accession to the Community were signed in 1972 and came into force in 1973). It should also be mentioned that the Protocol was adopted and entered into force some time before the EC Treaty itself (the EC Treaty came into force on 1 January 1958); consequently, it has priority under Art. 307 [234] even with regard to the original Member States.

Treaty.[35] It seems, therefore, that the United Kingdom was entitled to act as it did.

Further reading

Mus, "Conflicts Between Treaties in International Law" (1998) 45 NILR 208.
Schermers, Comment on the *Matthews* case, (1999) 36 CMLRev. 673.

35 This would be in accord with Article 30(2) of the Vienna Convention, since the reference in the Vienna Convention to a treaty that "specifies" that it is subject to another treaty includes an implied provision as well as an express one: Mus, "Conflicts Between Treaties in International Law" (1998) 45 NILR 208 at 217–219. This interpretation is supported by the fact that the Member States and the Community institutions have always emphasized their attachment to human rights: see the joint declaration of the European Parliament, the Council and the Commission of 5 April 1977, OJ 1977, C103, p. 1, as well as Art. 6(2) [F(2)] TEU.

PART VI
DIRECT ACTIONS IN THE
EUROPEAN COURT

18

Remedies available to private litigants – I

In this Part of the book, we look at actions begun in the European Court. We shall focus on the remedies available to private litigants – ordinary people, as distinct from governments and Community institutions.

The availability of a legal remedy to vindicate one's rights is generally regarded as a human right.[1] To what extent is this requirement satisfied with regard to rights against the European Union? This is the question we shall consider in this Part of the book.

There are two main avenues by which rights may be vindicated against the Community. The first is by direct actions – that is, actions begun in the European Court. The second is by actions begun in the Member-State courts and referred for a ruling to the European Court. The second avenue of redress was considered in Part III, especially Chapter 11. Here, we shall focus on the first avenue of redress, though we shall also consider the relationship between them.

The most important direct action available to private litigants is the so-called action for annulment under Article 230 [173] EC. It constitutes the subject matter of this chapter. Other remedies will be considered in Chapter 19.

Article 230 [173] (Panel 18.1) contains five paragraphs. The first specifies the parties against whom the action may be brought. These are:

- the Parliament;
- the Council;
- the Commission; and
- the European Central Bank (ECB).

It also makes clear that the measure to be annulled must be an act of one of these bodies other than a recommendation or opinion. The European Court has said that this means an act having legal effects, a concept to which we shall return in a moment. Where the measure is adopted by the European Parliament acting alone, it must be an act intended to produce legal effects as regards third parties. Thus, in the case of the other defendants, it is enough if the measure is intended to produce legal effects as regards anyone. In the case of the Parliament, however, measures that affect only the members of

---

1 See Arts. 6 and 13 of the European Convention on Human Rights and Art. 47 of the Charter of Fundamental Rights of the European Union.

Panel 18.1 Actions for annulment

EC Treaty

Article 230 [173]

The Court of Justice shall review the legality of acts adopted jointly by the European Parliament and the Council, of acts of the Council, of the Commission and of the ECB, other than recommendations and opinions, and of acts of the European Parliament intended to produce legal effects vis-à-vis third parties.

It shall for this purpose have jurisdiction in actions brought by a Member State, the European Parliament, the Council or the Commission on grounds of lack of competence, infringement of an essential procedural requirement, infringement of this Treaty or of any rule of law relating to its application, or misuse of powers.

The Court of Justice shall have jurisdiction under the same conditions in actions brought by the Court of Auditors and by the ECB for the purpose of protecting their prerogatives.

Any natural or legal person may, under the same conditions, institute proceedings against a decision addressed to that person or against a decision which, although in the form of a regulation or a decision addressed to another person, is of direct and individual concern to the former.

The proceedings provided for in this Article shall be instituted within two months of the publication of the measure, or of its notification to the plaintiff, or, in the absence thereof, of the day on which it came to the knowledge of the latter, as the case may be.

the Parliament are not subject to review by the court. This is because the Parliament has exclusive jurisdiction over internal matters.

The next three paragraphs of Article 230 [173] are concerned with the persons who may bring proceedings. The second paragraph deals with the Member States, the Parliament, the Council and the Commission. These so-called "privileged applicants" have unlimited standing, as long as the requirements of the first paragraph are met. Other applicants are not so fortunate.

The third paragraph deals with proceedings brought by the Court of Auditors and the ECB. They are "semi-privileged". They may bring proceedings only to protect their prerogatives (special powers).

The fourth paragraph is concerned with private litigants – natural or legal persons (individuals or corporations). They constitute the subject of our chapter.

The fifth paragraph lays down the time limit within which proceedings must be brought. The time limit is short – only two months.

Reviewable acts

We shall first consider the requirement in the first paragraph of Article 230 [173] that the act challenged must have legal effects. It is important to note that in Community law there is no such thing as an action for a declaration. A litigant cannot get into court unless he can produce a "reviewable act" – a measure that meets the requirements of the first paragraph of Article 230 [173].

The first paragraph of the Article refers to acts "other than recommendations or opinions". It will be remembered that Article 249 [189] (Panel 4.1) lists five measures that the Community institutions can adopt. They are:

- regulations;
- directives;
- decisions;
- recommendations; and
- opinions.

Article 249 [189] makes clear that the first three have binding effect, but that recommendations and opinions do not. It is probable that the framers of the Treaty intended Article 249 [189] to be an exhaustive list of the acts that the institutions can adopt. The wording of Article 230 [173] was probably a shorthand way of saying that review proceedings may be brought against regulations, directives and decisions. However in the *ERTA* case[2] (set out in Chapter 12 above), the court decided that the list in Article 249 [189] is not exhaustive. It is possible to have binding acts that are neither regulations, directives nor decisions.[3] Moreover, the court has ruled in many cases that the right to bring proceedings does not depend on the form of the act but on its real nature. For these reasons, the court has decided that a reviewable act under Article 230 [173] is any act that produces legal effects. Its form does not matter.

The meaning of this is explored in our next case.

European Union
Cimenteries v. Commission (Noordwijks Cement Accoord case)
COURT OF JUSTICE OF THE EUROPEAN COMMUNITIES
Cases 8–11/66, [1967] ECR 75; [1967] CMLR 77

Facts

Under EC competition (antitrust) law, firms that enter into agreements that restrict competition face the prospect of being fined by the Commission. However, it is not always certain whether a particular agreement has this effect. Moreover, the Commission can grant exemptions in certain cases. Firms are, therefore, required to notify their agreements to the Commission for scrutiny and possible exemption. Unfortunately, it takes the Commission quite a long time to give a ruling. What are the firms to do in the meantime? If they operate the agreement, they might be fined. If they do not, they might lose its benefits.

Article 15(5) of the relevant provision, Regulation 17, therefore grants them an immunity once the agreement is notified. However, to prevent abuse, Article 15(6) states that if, after a preliminary examination, the Commission forms the opinion that the agreement appears to violate Community law and there appear to be no grounds to justify an exemption, the immunity ceases to apply. The Commission will continue with its examination and may in the end take a different view. However, once the firms receive notification of the Commission's opinion under Article 15(6), they lose their immunity. If they continue to operate the agreement, they do so at their own risk.

This is what happened in the *Noordwijks Cement Accoord* case. The cement producers that were parties to the agreement communicated it to the Commission. They thus obtained an immunity. However, they subsequently received a communication under Article 15(6) (the "measure of 14 December 1965 and 3 January 1966"). This meant that they lost their immunity. They wanted to challenge the Commission determination under Article 15(6). The Commission

---

2 *Commission v. Council*, Case 22/70, [1971] ECR 263.
3 The reasons for this are explained in note 18 in Chap. 12.

said that it was not a reviewable act. It argued that it was a mere opinion, with no legal effect. The firms, however, said it *did* have a legal effect. It took away their immunity.

Judgment

The effect of the measure of 14 December 1965 and 3 January 1966 was that the undertakings ceased to be protected by Article 15(5) which exempted them from fines, and came under the contrary rules of Article 15(2) which thenceforth exposed them to the risk of fines. This measure deprived them of the advantages of a legal situation which Article 15(5) attached to the notification of the agreement, and exposed them to a grave financial risk. Thus the said measure affected the interests of the undertakings by bringing about a distinct change in their legal position. It is unequivocally a measure which produces legal effects touching the interests of the undertakings concerned and which is binding on them. It thus constitutes not a mere opinion but a decision. Any doubt which might be raised by the question whether the notification of the said decision was made in proper form in no way alters the nature of that decision and cannot affect the admissibility of the application.

Result: the measure was quashed for failure to give reasons.

Comment

If, in the end, it had turned out that there was no violation of Community law, the firms would not have needed the immunity. However, at the time they did not know whether this would happen. The immunity was like an insurance policy. It would be needed only if things went wrong. This case shows, therefore, that even a contingent (conditional) legal effect – an effect that applies only if there is a violation – is sufficient for the purposes of Article 230 [173].

European Union
IBM v. Commission
COURT OF JUSTICE OF THE EUROPEAN COMMUNITIES
Case 60/81, [1981] ECR 2639

Facts

IBM received a communication from the Commission informing it that the Commission was opening proceedings against it for a violation of EC competition law. A statement of objections was enclosed. This was a statement of what IBM was alleged to have done wrong. It was an essential preliminary to any proceedings. IBM wished to challenge the decision on the following grounds:

- The decision had been taken by an official, not by the Commission.
- The statement of objections did not give IBM a clear idea of what it was accused of doing.
- The proceedings were contrary to international law because they involved the application of EC law to acts done outside the territory of the EC.

Since these objections did not relate to the substance of the case, IBM wanted them decided as a preliminary matter. It therefore brought proceedings under

Article 230 [173] to annul the decision taken by the Commission to commence proceedings.

The Commission claimed that the action was inadmissible because the decision was not a reviewable act. It said it was just a procedural step by which the Commission expressed an opinion, an opinion which it might change at a later stage. It said that such procedural steps could not be challenged. IBM would have to wait for the final decision and challenge that.

Judgment

8. According to Article 230 [173] of the Treaty proceedings may be brought for a declaration that acts of the Council and the Commission other than recommendations or opinions are void. That remedy is available in order to ensure, as required by Article 220 [164], that in the interpretation and application of the Treaty the law is observed, and it would be inconsistent with that objective to interpret restrictively the conditions under which the action is admissible by limiting its scope merely to the categories of measures referred to in Article 249 [189].

9. In order to ascertain whether the measures in question are acts within the meaning of Article 230 [173] it is necessary, therefore, to look to their substance. According to the consistent case-law of the Court any measure the legal effects of which are binding on, and capable of affecting the interests of, the applicant by bringing about a distinct change in his legal position is an act or decision which may be the subject of an action under Article 230 [173] for a declaration that it is void. However, the form in which such acts or decisions are cast is, in principle, immaterial as regards the question whether they are open to challenge under that Article.

10. In the case of acts or decisions adopted by a procedure involving several stages, in particular where they are the culmination of an internal procedure, it is clear from the case-law that in principle an act is open to review only if it is a measure definitively laying down the position of the Commission or the Council on the conclusion of that procedure, and not a provisional measure intended to pave the way for the final decision.

11. It would be otherwise only if acts or decisions adopted in the course of the preparatory proceedings not only bore all the legal characteristics referred to above but in addition were themselves the culmination of a special procedure distinct from that intended to permit the Commission or the Council to take a decision on the substance of the case.

12. Furthermore, it must be noted that whilst measures of a purely preparatory character may not themselves be the subject of an application for a declaration that they are void, any legal defects therein may be relied upon in an action directed against the definitive act for which they represent a preparatory step.

[After considering, and rejecting, various arguments put forward by IBM, the court continued:]

19. A statement of objections does not compel the undertaking concerned to alter or reconsider its marketing practices and it does not have the effect of depriving it of the protection hitherto available to it against the application of a fine, as is the case when the Commission informs an undertaking, pursuant to Article 15(6) of Regulation No. 17, of the results of the preliminary examination of an agreement which has been notified by the undertaking. Whilst a statement of objections may have the effect of showing the

undertaking in question it is incurring a real risk of being fined by the Commission, that is merely a consequence of fact, and not a legal consequence which the statement of objections is intended to produce.

20. An application for a declaration that the initiation of a procedure and a statement of objections are void might make it necessary for the Court to arrive at a decision on questions on which the Commission has not yet had an opportunity to state its position and would as a result anticipate the arguments on the substance of the case, confusing different procedural stages both administrative and judicial. It would thus be incompatible with the system of the division of powers between the Commission and the Court and of the remedies laid down by the Treaty, as well as the requirements of the sound administration of justice and the proper course of the administrative procedure to be followed in the Commission.

21. It follows from the foregoing that neither the initiation of a procedure nor a statement of objections may be considered, on the basis of their nature and the legal effects they produce, as being decisions within the meaning of Article 230 [173] of the EEC Treaty which may be challenged in an action for a declaration that they are void. In the context of the administrative procedure as laid down by Regulations No. 17 and No. 99/63, they are procedural measures adopted preparatory to the decision which represents their culmination.

22. In support of its submission that the application is admissible IBM relies further on the special circumstances of the case and on the nature and implications of the submission which it puts forward on the substance of its case, claiming that a judicial review ought to be made available at an early stage in this case both in accordance with the principles of international law in such matters and pursuant to general principles flowing from the laws of the Member States. The present application is intended to establish that the administrative procedure was wholly unlawful from the beginning under the rules of Community law and international law, particularly those concerning the power to initiate such procedures. Any continuation of that administrative procedure is unlawful, it claims, and the fact that IBM may subsequently have the final decision declared void is not sufficient to give it effective legal protection.

23. It is not necessary for the purposes of this case to decide whether, in exceptional circumstances, where the measures concerned lack even the appearance of legality, a judicial review at an early stage such as that envisaged by IBM may be considered compatible with the system of remedies provided for in the Treaty, because the circumstances referred to by the applicant in this case are in any event not such as would make it possible to regard the action as admissible.

24. Moreover, in this instance adequate legal protection for IBM does not require that the measures in question be subject to immediate review. If, on the conclusion of the administrative procedure and after any observations which IBM may submit in the course of it have been examined, the Commission were to adopt a decision which affects IBM's interests, that decision will, in accordance with Article 230 [173] of the EEC Treaty, be subject to judicial review in the course of which it will be permissible for IBM to advance all the appropriate arguments. It will then be for the Court to decide whether anything unlawful has been done in the course of the administrative procedure and if so whether it is such as to affect the legality of the decision taken by the Commission on the conclusion of the administrative procedure.

25. The application must therefore be dismissed as inadmissible.

Comment

The consequences of this ruling were awkward for IBM. The decision meant that IBM would have to go to the considerable expense of defending the case on the substance before it could obtain a ruling on its preliminary objections.[4]

Standing for private applicants

The requirement of a reviewable act applies to all applicants, both privileged and non-privileged. In addition, however, private applicants must surmount the hurdle of standing. Standing (*locus standi*) is probably a requirement in all systems of administrative law. A private applicant cannot bring review proceedings unless he has sufficient interest. In Community law, the matter is covered by the fourth paragraph of Article 230 [173]. Under this, a private litigant may bring proceedings against:

- a decision addressed to him;
- a decision in the form of a regulation; or
- a decision addressed to another person.

In the latter two cases, the applicant must also show that the decision is of "direct and individual concern" to him.

It is clear from this that, in all cases, the challenged act must be a decision. However, it need not take the form of a decision. It is enough if in reality it is one. This is apparent from the words of the Treaty. It has also been the consistent position of the European Court. There are thus three requirements to be met by the private applicant (in addition to that of a reviewable act):

- The act must be (in substance) a decision.
- It must be of direct concern to him.
- It must be of individual concern to him.

We shall consider each of these.

Direct concern relates to the chain of cause and effect between the decision and its impact on the applicant. The impact must not be too remote or doubtful. Thus in one case Belgium asked the Commission to give it the power to allow the importation of a product at a reduced tariff during a particular period. The Commission refused. An importer who had imported the product during the period in question brought proceedings to annul the Commission's refusal. The court held that the importer was not directly concerned because, even if the Belgian Government had been granted the power, it might not in fact have exercised it.[5] In another case, however, the Member State first exercised the power and then sought approval from the Commission. In that case, the court held that the applicant *was* directly concerned.[6] It is hard to understand

---

4 For a case applying the same principle to an action to annul a decision by the Commission to bring proceedings against a company in the United States, see *Philip Morris International v. Commission*, Cases T-377/00, etc., 15 January 2003; [2003] 1 CMLR 21 (Court of First Instance).
5 *Alcan Aluminium v. Commission*, Case 69/69, [1970] ECR 385.
6 *Toepfer v. Commission*, Cases 106 and 107/63, [1965] ECR 405.

why the right to bring proceedings should depend on such fine distinctions as these.

When is a measure a decision? Although it is not very clear, Article 249 [189] (Panel 4.1, Chapter 4, above) suggests that, while a regulation lays down general rules, a decision is concerned with individual cases. Thus, if a regulation requires everyone to pay a tax, a decision would decide how much a particular individual had to pay.

A major difficulty arises at this point. If an applicant is individually concerned by a measure, as he must be if he is to bring proceedings, does that not automatically mean that it is a decision? Surely, the essence of a decision is that it individually concerns a particular person? This is a problem that has caused the court some difficulty over the years. We shall see below how it has dealt with it.

The cases we shall now consider deal both with the nature of a decision and the meaning of individual concern.

> *European Union*
> **Plaumann v. Commission**
> **COURT OF JUSTICE OF THE EUROPEAN COMMUNITIES**
> Case 25/62, [1963] ECR 95

Facts

The German Government asked the Commission to lower the import duty on clementines. It refused. The refusal took the form of a decision addressed to Germany. Plaumann, a fruit importer, challenged this decision under Article 230 [173]. The Commission claimed that the application was inadmissible because Plaumann was not individually concerned.

Judgment

Persons other than those to whom a decision is addressed may only claim to be individually concerned if that decision affects them by reason of certain attributes which are peculiar to them or by reason of circumstances in which they are differentiated from all other persons and by virtue of these factors distinguishes them individually just as in the case of the person addressed. In the present case the applicant is affected by the disputed Decision as an importer of clementines, that is to say, by reason of a commercial activity which may at any time be practised by any person and is not therefore such as to distinguish the applicant in relation to the contested Decision as in the case of the addressee.

For these reasons the present action for annulment must be declared inadmissible.

Comment

Since Plaumann was affected by the decision solely in his capacity as a fruit importer – something that anyone could do – it is easy to see why he was not individually concerned. Other cases, however, are more difficult.

European Union
Binderer v. Commission
COURT OF JUSTICE OF THE EUROPEAN COMMUNITIES
Case 147/83, [1985] ECR 257

Facts

Binderer was a German company that specialized in importing wine from Hungary and Yugoslavia. The wines in question were of a kind that could be described in German by the words *Spätlese* (late harvest) and *Auslese* (selected grapes). However, EC law prohibited the use of those words unless the wine was produced in the Community.[7] So Binderer proposed to the Commission and the German authorities that he should use the words *spätgelesen* and *ausgelesen*. The Commission approved that proposal by a letter dated 14 August 1981. Binderer then took the decision to import the wines, using labels with the words in question. In May 1983, however, a Commission measure, Regulation 1224/83, prohibited *spätgelesen* and *ausgelesen* as well. The alleged reason was to protect the consumer.

Binderer then brought proceedings to annul the relevant provision of Regulation 1224/83, Article 1(3)(g). The Commission, supported by Germany, argued that the application was inadmissible. Binderer replied that there were only three importers of Hungarian or Yugoslav wines – itself and two other companies. Moreover, the fact that it had previously obtained the approval of the Commission showed that the measure was directed against it.

Judgment

11. The second paragraph[8] of Article 230 [173] of the EEC Treaty provides that even though the contested decision is in the form of a regulation, an individual may institute proceedings for a declaration that it is void, provided that it is in fact of direct and individual concern to him. The purpose of that provision is, in particular, to prevent the Community institutions from being able to deny an individual the right to institute proceedings against a decision which is of direct and individual concern to him simply by choosing to issue that decision in the form of a regulation and, hence, to make it clear that the choice of form cannot alter the nature of a measure.

12. However, as the Court held [citation omitted], an action brought by an individual is not admissible in so far as it is directed against a regulation having general application, within the meaning of the second paragraph of Article 249 [189] of the Treaty, the test for distinguishing between a regulation and a decision, according to the settled case-law of the Court, being whether or not the measure in question has general application. It is therefore necessary to appraise the nature of the contested measure and in particular the legal effects which it is intended to produce or in fact produces.

13. In that connection it should be noted that the purpose of the contested provision is to prohibit the use of certain translations by any undertakings which at present or in the

---

7 Though ostensibly to protect consumers, one assumes that the real reason was to protect Community producers.
8 Editor's note: it is now the fourth paragraph.

future import wines of the relevant type into the Community from non-member countries. Consequently, *vis-à-vis* importers, that measure is of general application within the meaning of the second paragraph of Article 249 [189] of the Treaty, since it applies to objectively determined situations and entails legal effects for categories of persons regarded generally and in the abstract. Moreover, as the Court has already held, a measure does not cease to be a regulation because it is possible to determine the number or even the identity of the persons to whom it applies at any given time.

14. Finally, as the Court has already held, the distinction between a regulation and a decision may be based only on the nature of the measure itself and the legal effects which it produces and not on the procedures for its adoption.

15. For the reasons stated above it must be concluded that Article 1(3)(g) of Regulation No. 1224/83 is not of individual concern to the applicant and hence the latter may not challenge it under the second paragraph[9] of Article 230 [173] of the Treaty. Consequently, the claim for a declaration that it is void must be dismissed as inadmissible.

QUESTION

Could it not be said that the fact that Binderer had obtained Commission approval for the words in question before the regulation was adopted meant that he was "differentiated" from all other persons in terms of the *Plaumann* test?

Comment

In this case, the court seems to treat the question whether the measure is a decision, and the question whether it is of individual concern to the applicant, as being essentially the same thing. Thus, in paragraphs 12–14, it considers whether it is a decision and decides that it is not. From this, it concludes (in paragraph 15) that it is not of individual concern to the applicant.

European Union
Sofrimport v. Commission
COURT OF JUSTICE OF THE EUROPEAN COMMUNITIES
Case C-152/88, [1990] ECR I-2477

Facts

Sofrimport was a fruit importer. It bought a consignment of apples from Chile and had them shipped to France. While the apples were on the high seas, the Commission banned imports of Chilean apples. This was done by a number of Commission regulations. The Commission had the power to do this, but it was required by a Council measure, Regulation 2707/72, to take account of the interests of importers whose goods were in transit.

Sofrimport brought proceedings to annul the Commission regulations, claiming that they were in fact a series of decisions which concerned it both

---

9 Editor's note: it is now the fourth paragraph.

directly and individually. The Commission denied that Sofrimport was individually concerned. It said that the ban applied to all importers of Chilean apples.

Judgment

10. With regard to the question whether the applicant is individually concerned, it must be determined whether the contested measures affect it by reason of certain attributes which are peculiar to it or by reason of circumstances in which it is differentiated from all other persons . . .

11. It should be observed first of all that the applicant is in the position referred to in Article 3(3) of [Regulation No 2707/72] which requires the Commission, in adopting such measures, to take account of the special position of products in transit to the Community. Only importers of Chilean apples whose goods were in transit when Regulation No 962/88 was adopted are in that position. Those importers thus constitute a restricted group which is sufficiently well defined in relation to any other importer of Chilean apples and cannot be extended after the suspensory measures in question take effect.

12. Secondly, since Article 3 of Regulation No 2707/72 gives specific protection to those importers, they must therefore be able to enforce observance of that protection and bring legal proceedings for that purpose.

13. Importers whose goods were in transit when the contested regulations came into force must therefore be considered to be individually concerned by those regulations in so far as they concern those goods. The application for annulment is therefore admissible only in so far as it challenges the application of protective measures to products in transit.

[The court went on to annul the regulations in so far as they applied to goods in transit.]

Comment

It will be noticed that in this case the court skipped over the question whether the measures were true regulations and instead focused on the matter of individual concern. Once it found this requirement satisfied, it seemed to assume that the measures were disguised decisions.

QUESTION

How would you distinguish this case from (a) *Plaumann* and (b) *Binderer*?

European Union
Codorniu v. Council
COURT OF JUSTICE OF THE EUROPEAN COMMUNITIES
Case C-309/89, [1994] ECR I-1853

Facts

The Council passed a regulation which prohibited the use of the French word *crémant*, or its translations into other languages, with reference to "sparkling wine psr",[10] unless the wine was produced in France or Luxembourg. Codorniu was a Spanish firm that had registered the Spanish phrase *Gran Cremant de Codorniu* as a graphic trademark in 1924 and had used it ever since on wines produced in Spain. It brought proceedings under Article 230 [173] to annul the regulation in so far as it prohibited it from using the word *cremant*. The Council argued that the application was inadmissible.

The case was heard by a Full Court (nine judges). It was in fact the last case of its kind to come before the European Court before jurisdiction to hear actions brought by private persons under Article 230 [173] was transferred to the Court of First Instance.[11] It could therefore be regarded as the European Court's final word to the Court of First Instance.

Judgment

14. In support of its objection of inadmissibility the Council states that it did not adopt the contested provision on the basis of the circumstances peculiar to certain producers but on the basis of a choice of wine-marketing policy in relation to a particular product. The contested provision reserves the use of the term *"crémant"* to quality sparkling wines psr manufactured under specific conditions in certain Member States. It thus constitutes a measure applicable to an objectively determined situation which has legal effects in respect of categories of persons considered in a general and abstract manner.

15. According to the Council, Codorniu is concerned by the contested provision only in its capacity as a producer of quality sparkling wines psr using the term *"crémant"*, like any other producer in an identical situation. Even if when that provision was adopted the number or identity of producers of sparkling wines using the term *"crémant"* could theoretically be determined, the measure in question remains essentially a regulation inasmuch as it applies on the basis of an objective situation of law or fact defined by the measure in relation to its objective.

16. Codorniu alleges that the contested provision is in reality a decision adopted in the guise of a regulation. It has no general scope but affects a well-determined class of producers which cannot be altered. Such producers are those who on 1 September 1989 traditionally designated their sparkling wines with the term *"crémant"*. For that class the contested provision has no general scope. Furthermore, the direct result of the contested provision will be to prevent Codorniu from using the term *"Gran Cremant"* which will involve a loss of 38% of its turnover. The effect of that damage is to distinguish it, within the meaning of the second paragraph of Article 230 [173] of the Treaty, from any other trader. Codorniu alleges that the Court has already recognized the admissibility of an action for annulment brought by a natural or legal person against a regulation in such circumstances (see the judgment in Case C-358/89 *Extramet Industrie v. Council* [1991] ECR I-2501).

17. Under the second paragraph of Article 230 [173] of the Treaty the institution of proceedings by a natural or legal person for a declaration that a regulation is void is subject to the condition that the provisions of the regulation at issue in the proceedings constitute in reality a decision of direct and individual concern to that person.

---

10 The letters "psr" mean "produced in a specified region". Sparkling wine psr is quality sparking wine.
11 There is an appeal on points of law to the European Court.

18. As the Court has already held, the general applicability, and thus the legislative nature, of a measure is not called in question by the fact that it is possible to determine more or less exactly the number or even the identity of the persons to whom it applies at any given time, as long as it is established that it applies to them by virtue of an objective legal or factual situation defined by the measure in question in relation to its purpose [citation omitted].

19. Although it is true that according to the criteria in the second paragraph of Article 230 [173] of the Treaty the contested provision is, by nature and by virtue of its sphere of application, of a legislative nature in that it applies to the traders concerned in general, that does not prevent it from being of individual concern to some of them.

20. Natural or legal persons may claim that a contested provision is of individual concern to them only if it affects them by reason of certain attributes which are peculiar to them or by reason of circumstances in which they are differentiated from all other persons (see the judgment in Case 25/62 *Plaumann v. Commission* [1963] ECR 95).

21. Codorniu registered the graphic trade mark "*Gran Cremant de Codorniu*" in Spain in 1924 and traditionally used that mark both before and after registration. By reserving the right to use the term "*crémant*" to French and Luxembourg producers, the contested provision prevents Codorniu from using its graphic trade mark.

22. It follows that Codorniu has established the existence of a situation which from the point of view of the contested provision differentiates it from all other traders.

23. It follows that the objection of inadmissibility put forward by the Council must be dismissed.

[The court went on to annul the relevant provision on the ground that there was no reason for treating Spanish wines less favourably than those from France and Luxembourg.]

Comment

If this decision was intended to provide guidance to the Court of First Instance, it was remarkably short on legal reasoning. The laconic statement in paragraph 19 that the contested measure was "of a legislative nature" was, however, widely taken to mean that private litigants *could* challenge a true regulation, provided they were individually concerned by it. In subsequent cases, therefore, the Court of First Instance did not normally concern itself with the nature of the act challenged, but focused its attention on the question of individual concern.

An interesting question of a factual nature is why the Spanish Government did not itself bring the proceedings. As a "privileged" applicant, it would have had no problem of standing. It is also hard to understand why the Council adopted a measure that discriminated so blatantly against producers outside France and Luxembourg. Perhaps there was some kind of deal. It is possible that the court decided to "bend" the standing rules a little to allow it to strike down the measure. It is also of interest that, though the court obtained jurisdiction on the basis of the particular circumstances of Codorniu, its annulment of the relevant provision benefited all producers.

European Union
Unión de Pequeños Agricultores (UPA) v. Council
COURT OF JUSTICE OF THE EUROPEAN COMMUNITIES
Case C-50/00 P, [2002] ECR I-6677; [2002] 3 CMLR 1

Facts

UPA was an organization that represented small agricultural producers in Spain. It brought proceedings before the Court of First Instance to challenge a Council regulation that withdrew subsidies from olive oil producers. The Court of First Instance declared the proceedings inadmissible on the ground that UPA was not individually concerned by the regulation. UPA appealed to the European Court.

UPA accepted that the measure was a true regulation. It also accepted that it was not individually concerned within the terms of the *Plaumann* test. It argued, however, that its fundamental right to an effective judicial remedy was in issue. It said there was no way in which it could bring the matter before the Spanish courts. Since the regulation merely abolished what had previously been a right, there was no need for the Spanish authorities to adopt implementing measures. Nor was it possible for it to get the matter before a court by deliberately breaking the law. There was no law to break. It claimed, therefore, that the Court of First Instance had infringed its fundamental right by not inquiring whether there was an alternative remedy.

The Commission, which intervened in the proceedings, argued that there *was* a remedy before the Spanish courts. It said that a person entitled to a grant under the previous law could demand the grant from the relevant Spanish authority. If it was not forthcoming, it could commence proceedings in the Spanish courts. The authority would have to invoke the new regulation to justify its failure to provide the grant. The applicant could then claim that the regulation was invalid, and request a reference to the European Court under Article 234 [177] EC to decide the matter.

The Commission and Council both argued that there was in any event no justification under the Treaty for considering the availability of alternative remedies.[12]

The case was heard by a Full Court, thus indicating the court's willingness to reconsider its previous case law.

---

12 UPA said that the court had considered the question of alternative remedies in *Greenpeace v. Commission*, Case C-321/95 P [1998] ECR I-1651 (paras. 32 and 33 of the judgment). For earlier cases in which the court alluded to the question, see *Alusuisse v. Council and Commission*, Case 307/81, [1982] ECR 3463 (para. 13 of the judgment); *Spijker v. Commission*, Case 231/82, [1983] ECR 2559 (para. 11 of the judgment); *Allied Corporation v. Commission*, Cases 239 and 275/82, [1984] ECR 1005 (para. 15 of the judgment); and *Union Deutsche Lebensmittelwerke v. Commission*, Case 97/85, [1987] ECR 2265 (para. 12 of the judgment).

Judgment

35. [U]nder Article 230 [173] of the Treaty, a regulation, as a measure of general application, cannot be challenged by natural or legal persons other than the institutions, the European Central Bank and the Member States ...

36. However, a measure of general application such as a regulation can, in certain circumstances, be of individual concern to certain natural or legal persons and is thus in the nature of a decision in their regard [*Codorniu* and various other cases cited]. That is so where the measure in question affects specific natural or legal persons by reason of certain attributes peculiar to them, or by reason of a factual situation which differentiates them from all other persons and distinguishes them individually in the same way as the addressee [*Plaumann* and another case cited].

37. If that condition is not fulfilled, a natural or legal person does not, under any circumstances, have standing to bring an action for annulment of a regulation ...

38. The European Community is, however, a community based on the rule of law in which its institutions are subject to judicial review of the compatibility of their acts with the Treaty and with the general principles of law which include fundamental rights.

39. Individuals are therefore entitled to effective judicial protection of the rights they derive from the Community legal order, and the right to such protection is one of the general principles of law stemming from the constitutional traditions common to the Member States. That right has also been enshrined in Articles 6 and 13 of the European Convention for the Protection of Human Rights and Fundamental Freedoms ...

40. By Article 230 [173] and Article 241 [184], on the one hand, and by Article 234 [177], on the other, the Treaty has established a complete system of legal remedies and procedures designed to ensure judicial review of the legality of acts of the institutions, and has entrusted such review to the Community Courts ... Under that system, where natural or legal persons cannot, by reason of the conditions for admissibility laid down in the fourth paragraph of Article 230 [173] of the Treaty, directly challenge Community measures of general application, they are able, depending on the case, either indirectly to plead the invalidity of such acts before the Community Courts under Article 241 [184] of the Treaty or to do so before the national courts and ask them, since they have no jurisdiction themselves to declare those measures invalid [citation omitted], to make a reference to the Court of Justice for a preliminary ruling on validity.

41. Thus it is for the Member States to establish a system of legal remedies and procedures which ensure respect for the right to effective judicial protection.

42. In that context, in accordance with the principle of sincere co-operation laid down in Article 10 [5] of the Treaty, national courts are required, so far as possible, to interpret and apply national procedural rules governing the exercise of rights of action in a way that enables natural and legal persons to challenge before the courts the legality of any decision or other national measure relative to the application to them of a Community act of general application, by pleading the invalidity of such an act.

43. As the Advocate General has pointed out in paragraphs 50 to 53 of his Opinion, it is not acceptable to adopt an interpretation of the system of remedies, such as that favoured by the appellant, to the effect that a direct action for annulment before the Community Court will be available where it can be shown, following an examination by that Court of the particular national procedural rules, that those rules do not allow the individual to bring proceedings to contest the validity of the Community measure at issue. Such an

interpretation would require the Community Court, in each individual case, to examine and interpret national procedural law. That would go beyond its jurisdiction when reviewing the legality of Community measures.

44. Finally, it should be added that, according to the system for judicial review of legality established by the Treaty, a natural or legal person can bring an action challenging a regulation only if it is concerned both directly and individually. Although this last condition must be interpreted in the light of the principle of effective judicial protection by taking account of the various circumstances that may distinguish an applicant individually [examples omitted], such an interpretation cannot have the effect of setting aside the condition in question, expressly laid down in the Treaty, without going beyond the jurisdiction conferred by the Treaty on the Community Courts.

45. While it is, admittedly, possible to envisage a system of judicial review of the legality of Community measures of general application different from that established by the founding Treaty and never amended as to its principles, it is for the Member States, if necessary, in accordance with Article 48 [N] TEU,[13] to reform the system currently in force.

46. In the light of the foregoing, the Court finds that the Court of First Instance did not err in law when it declared the appellant's application inadmissible without examining whether, in the particular case, there was a remedy before a national court enabling the validity of the contested regulation to be examined.

47. The appeal must therefore be dismissed.

Comment

In a forcefully argued Opinion, Advocate-General Jacobs had proposed that the previous case law should be cast aside and a new test introduced. The test he put forward was that a private applicant should be regarded as individually concerned whenever, by reason of his particular circumstances, the measure has, or is liable to have, a substantial adverse effect on his interests. In support of this, he put forward three propositions:

- A direct action under Article 230 [173] would be a more efficient way to determine the validity of Community measures than an action brought in the national courts and referred to the European Court.
- The restrictive nature of the *Plaumann* test means that an applicant's fundamental right to an effective remedy could be infringed.
- The test he proposed would not conflict with the words of the treaty.

It is suggested that the first of these propositions is correct. The second is doubtful. The third cannot be accepted. The Treaty says that the measure challenged must be of "individual concern" to the applicant. His proposal would have the effect of reading this to mean "substantial concern". That is something different.[14] Individual concern has a comparative element. The applicant must be concerned in a different way from others. Substantial concern has no such element. It simply looks to the degree of concern.

---

13 Editor's note: this is the provision dealing with amendments to the Community Treaties.
14 He tried to justify his position by pointing out that in other contexts the court had adopted "a generous and dynamic interpretation of the Treaty, or even a position contrary to the text" (para. 71 of his Opinion).

The court was right, therefore, to follow the words of the Treaty. It had previously suggested to the Member States that standing under Article 230 [173] should be liberalized, but the Member States took no action. This is why it said in its judgment that, if change is needed, it is up to the Member States to amend the Treaty.[15]

The court also made clear that the requirement in Article 230 [173] that a private applicant cannot challenge a true regulation is still good law. It explained *Codorniu* by saying that a provision can, at the same time, constitute a decision as regards one or more specific persons and a regulation as regards everyone else. This is perfectly logical. Measures can affect different persons in different ways. They can affect one person individually and others as members of a general category. In *Codorniu*, the regulation affected Codorniu individually by reason of the fact that it had previously registered the word *cremant* as a trademark. Other producers were affected, if at all, only as producers of sparkling wine, something anyone could do. The measure was therefore a regulation with regard to most people, but "in the nature of a decision" with regard to Codorniu.[16] It seems, therefore, that satisfying the *Plaumann* test automatically establishes that the measure is a decision – but only with regard to those persons who do satisfy it.

Further reading

Arnull, "Private Applicants and the Action for Annulment since Codorniu" (2001) 38 CMLRev. 7.

Arnull, "Private Applicants and the Action for Annulment under Article 173 of the EC Treaty" (1995) 32 CMLRev. 7.

Schermers (Henry G.) and Waelbroeck (Denis F.), *Judicial Protection in the European Union* (Kluwer Law International, The Hague and London, 6th ed., 2001), Chapter 2.

Ward (Angela), *Judicial Review and the Rights of Private Parties in EC Law* (Oxford University Press, Oxford, 2000).

---

15 Para. 45 of the judgment.
16 Para. 36 of the judgment in *UPA*.

Remedies available to private litigants – II

Indirect challenge

We saw in the last chapter that the European Court is not prepared to make the availability of a remedy in a direct action under Article 230 [173] EC dependent on whether or not there is an alternative remedy in the courts of the relevant Member State. The issues of Member-State law would be too difficult for it to decide. The first question we shall consider in this chapter is in some ways the reverse: does the availability of a remedy in the European Court under Article 230 [173] have any effect on the right to challenge the validity of a Community measure in the courts of a Member State?

It will be remembered from the discussion in Chapter 11 that if a Member-State court has to determine the validity of a Community measure in order to decide a case, it can refer that question to the European Court under Article 234 [177] EC.[1] What we must consider, therefore, is whether the existence of this right is affected by the fact that the party claiming that the measure is invalid could have brought a challenge directly in the European Court.

European Union
Universität Hamburg
COURT OF JUSTICE OF THE EUROPEAN COMMUNITIES
Case 216/82, [1983] ECR 2771

Facts
An international agreement adopted under the auspices of UNESCO provided that scientific equipment intended exclusively for educational or scientific purposes could be imported free of duty provided no comparable equipment was manufactured in the importing country. Under the Community legislation giving effect to this, the importer addressed his request to the national customs authority. The latter had to decide in the first instance whether the relevant requirements were met. If it was not able to do this, it would refer the matter to the Commission, which would take a decision. This decision would be addressed to the Member States and would be binding on them.

---

1 It cannot itself rule that the Community measure is invalid. The treaty does not say this, but the European Court laid it down in *Foto-Frost*, Case 314/85, [1987] ECR 4199.

The customs authority to which the original request had been made would then take a decision addressed to the importer either granting or denying the request.

In the *Universität Hamburg* case, the University had asked the German Customs for permission to import some equipment free of duty. The German Customs had referred the matter to the Commission. The latter had taken a decision addressed to the Member States refusing the request. The German Customs had then informed the University that its request was rejected.

The University wished to challenge this rejection. It brought proceedings against the German Customs in the relevant German court, the Hamburg *Finanzgericht*. The German Customs said that they were bound by the Commission decision. So the University challenged that. It asked the German court to refer the validity of that decision to the European Court under Article 234 [177]. However, an earlier case[2] showed that the University would probably have had standing to bring a direct challenge to the Commission decision under Article 230 [173]. The German court therefore asked the European Court whether this fact precluded a reference under Article 234 [177].

Judgment

7. The decision adopted by the Commission is addressed to all the Member States. By virtue of Article 254 [191] of the Treaty it must therefore be notified to the Member States and it takes effect upon such notification. However, it does not have to be notified to the person applying for exemption from customs duty and it is not one of the measures which the Treaty requires to be published. Even if in practice the decision is in fact published in the *Official Journal of the European Communities*, its wording does not necessarily enable the applicant to ascertain whether it was adopted in relation to the procedure which he initiated.

8. Since the decision is binding on the Member States, the national authority must reject the application for duty-free admission in the event of a negative decision on the part of the Commission; however, Community law does not require it to refer to the Commission's decision in its own decision rejecting the application. Furthermore, as this case demonstrates, the national authority's decision may be adopted some time after the notification of the Commission's decision.

9. Finally, as the Finanzgericht rightly points out, for the purpose of bringing an action under the second paragraph [now the fourth] of Article 230 [173] of the Treaty against the Commission's decision, the scientific establishment in question[3] must demonstrate that the decision is of direct and individual concern to it.

10. In those circumstances the rejection by the national authority of the scientific establishment's application is the only measure which is directly addressed to it, of which it has necessarily been informed in good time and which the establishment may challenge in the courts without encountering any difficulty in demonstrating its interest in bringing proceedings. According to a general principle of law which finds its expression in Article 241 [184] of the EEC Treaty, in proceedings brought under national law against the

2 *Control Data Belgium v. Commission*, Case 294/81, [1983] ECR 911. In this case, however, the local subsidiary of the manufacturer joined with the university in making the application.
3 Editor's note: in this case, the "scientific establishment" was the University of Hamburg.

rejection of his application the applicant must be able to plead the illegality of the Commission's decision on which the national decision adopted in his regard is based.

Result: its failure to challenge the Commission decision in a direct action did not prevent the University from challenging it before the German courts and obtaining a reference to the European Court under Article 234 [177].

Comment

In this case, the European Court based its ruling on the fact that in practice the University might have found it difficult to make a direct challenge. However, a *dictum* in a later case, *Rau v. BALM*,[4] seems to put the matter more broadly:[5]

It must be emphasized that there is nothing in Community law to prevent an action from being brought before a national court against a measure implementing a decision adopted by a Community institution where the conditions laid down by national law are satisfied. When such an action is brought, if the outcome of the dispute depends on the validity of that decision the national court may submit questions to the Court of Justice by way of a reference for a preliminary ruling, without there being any need to ascertain whether or not the plaintiff in the main proceedings has the possibility of challenging the decision directly before the Court.

In 1994, however, the European Court changed direction.

European Union
TWD
COURT OF JUSTICE OF THE EUROPEAN COMMUNITIES
Case C-188/92, [1994] ECR I-833

Facts

The German Government had given aid to the TWD company. Subsequently, the Commission decided that the aid was contrary to Community law and took a decision addressed to the German Government requiring it to reclaim the aid. The German Government informed TWD of this decision and said that TWD could challenge it in a direct action in the European Court under Article 230 [173]. However, TWD allowed the two-month time limit to expire without doing so. The German Government then ordered TWD to repay the aid. TWD challenged that order in the German courts and asked them to refer the validity of the Commission decision to the European Court under Article 234 [177].

Judgment
10. The issue before the national court is whether or not, in the factual and legal circumstances of the main proceedings, the applicant is time-barred from pleading the unlawfulness of the Commission's decision in support of an action brought against the administrative act by which the national authority, in implementation of the Commission's decision, revoked the certificates which formed the legal basis for the aid which it had received.

---

4 Cases 133–136/85, [1987] ECR 2289.
5 Para. 11 of the judgment.

11. The national court emphasizes that the Commission's decision was not challenged by the applicant in the main proceedings, the recipient of the aid with which the decision was concerned, although a copy of that decision had been sent to it by the Federal Ministry of Economic Affairs and that Ministry had explicitly informed it that it could bring an action against that decision before the Court of Justice.

12. The question submitted to the Court must be answered in the light of those circumstances.

13. It is settled law that a decision which has not been challenged by the addressee within the time-limit laid down by Article 230 [173] of the Treaty becomes definitive as against him . . .

14. The undertaking in receipt of individual aid which is the subject-matter of a Commission decision adopted on the basis of Article 88 [93] of the Treaty has the right to bring an action for annulment under the second paragraph [now the fourth] of Article 230 [173] of the Treaty even if the decision is addressed to a Member State . . . By virtue of the third paragraph [now the fifth] of that article, the expiry of the time-limit laid down in that provision has the same time-barring effect *vis-à-vis* such an undertaking as it does *vis-à-vis* the Member State which is the addressee of the decision.

15. It is settled law that a Member State may no longer call in question the validity of a decision addressed to it on the basis of Article 88(2) [93(2)] of the Treaty once the time-limit laid down in the third paragraph of Article 230 [173] of the Treaty has expired . . .

16. That case-law, according to which it is impossible for a Member State which is the addressee of a decision taken under the first paragraph of Article 88(2) [93(2)] of the Treaty to call in question the validity of the decision in the proceedings for non-compliance provided for in the second paragraph of that provision, is based in particular on the consideration that the periods within which applications must be lodged are intended to safeguard legal certainty by preventing Community measures which involve legal effects from being called in question indefinitely.

17. It follows from the same requirements of legal certainty that it is not possible for a recipient of aid, forming the subject-matter of a Commission decision adopted on the basis of Article 88 [93] of the Treaty, who could have challenged that decision and who allowed the mandatory time-limit laid down in this regard by the third paragraph of Article 230 [173] of the Treaty to expire, to call in question the lawfulness of that decision before the national courts in an action brought against the measures taken by the national authorities for implementing that decision.

18. To accept that in such circumstances the person concerned could challenge the implementation of the decision in proceedings before the national court on the ground that the decision was unlawful would in effect enable the person concerned to overcome the definitive nature which the decision assumes as against that person once the time-limit for bringing an action has expired.

19. It is true that in its judgment in [*Rau v. BALM*], on which the French Government relies in its observations, the Court held that the possibility of bringing a direct action under the second paragraph of Article 230 [173] of the EEC Treaty against a decision adopted by a Community institution did not preclude the possibility of bringing an action in a national court against a measure adopted by a national authority for the implementation of that decision, on the ground that the latter decision was unlawful.

20. However, as is clear from the Report for the Hearing in those cases, each of the plaintiffs in the main proceedings had brought an action before the Court of Justice for the

annulment of the decision in question. The Court did not therefore rule, and did not have to rule, in that judgment on the time-barring effects of the expiry of time-limits. It is precisely that issue with which the question referred by the national court in this case is concerned.

21. This case is also distinguishable from [the *Universität Hamburg* case].

22. In the judgment in that case the Court held that a plaintiff whose application for duty-free admission had been rejected by a decision of a national authority taken on the basis of a decision of the Commission addressed to all the Member States had to be able to plead, in proceedings brought under national law against the rejection of his application, the illegality of the Commission's decision on which the national decision adopted in his regard was based.

23. In that judgment the Court took into account the fact that the rejection of the application by the national authority was the only measure directly addressed to the person concerned of which it had necessarily been informed in good time and which it could challenge in the courts without encountering any difficulty in demonstrating its interest in bringing proceedings. It held that in those circumstances the possibility of pleading the unlawfulness of the Commission's decision derived from a general principle of law which found its expression in Article 241 [184] of the EEC Treaty, namely the principle which confers upon any party to proceedings the right to challenge, for the purpose of obtaining the annulment of a decision of direct and individual concern to that party, the validity of previous acts of the institutions which form the legal basis of the decision which is being attacked, if that party was not entitled under Article 230 [173] of the Treaty to bring a direct action challenging those acts by which it was thus affected without having been in a position to ask that they be declared void . . .

24. In the present case, it is common ground that the applicant in the main proceedings was fully aware of the Commission's decision and of the fact that it could without any doubt have challenged it under Article 230 [173] of the Treaty.

25. It follows from the foregoing that, in factual and legal circumstances such as those of the main proceedings in this case, the definitive nature of the decision taken by the Commission pursuant to Article 88 [93] of the Treaty *vis-à-vis* the undertaking in receipt of the aid binds the national court by virtue of the principle of legal certainty.

26. The reply to be given to the first question must therefore be that the national court is bound by a Commission decision adopted under Article 88(2) [93(2)] of the Treaty where, in view of the implementation of that decision by the national authorities, the recipient of the aid to which the implementation measures are addressed brings before it an action in which it pleads the unlawfulness of the Commission's decision and where that recipient of aid, although informed in writing by the Member State of the Commission's decision, did not bring an action against that decision under the second paragraph of Article 230 [173] of the Treaty, or did not do so within the period prescribed.

Comment

In this case, the European Court took the two-month time limit in Article 230 [173] and applied it to proceedings under Article 234 [177], even though the latter contains no time limit. The result is that a party now loses his right to challenge a Community measure in a Member-State court if he failed to challenge it within the time limit in the European Court. However, this

---

Panel 19.1 Remedy for failure to act

EC Treaty

Article 232 [175]

Should the European Parliament, the Council or the Commission, in infringement of this Treaty, fail to act, the Member States and the other institutions of the Community may bring an action before the Court of Justice to have the infringement established.

The action shall be admissible only if the institution concerned has first been called upon to act. If, within two months of being so called upon, the institution concerned has not defined its position, the action may be brought within a further period of two months.

Any natural or legal person may, under the conditions laid down in the preceding paragraphs, complain to the Court of Justice that an institution of the Community has failed to address to that person any act other than a recommendation or an opinion.

The Court of Justice shall have jurisdiction, under the same conditions, in actions or proceedings brought by the ECB in the areas falling within the latter's field of competence and in actions or proceedings brought against the latter.

---

applies only if his right to do so was clear. The *Universität Hamburg* case, which appears still to be good law, shows that in doubtful cases a challenge in the Member-State courts is still possible. However, it will not always be easy to tell whether the right to bring a direct challenge is so doubtful that the applicant can safely let the time limit go by. He might feel that he ought to try. If it is declared inadmissible, he will have to pay costs. But at least he will know that he can then challenge it in the Member-State courts.

Failure to act

Next we must consider the remedies available to the private litigant who wishes to challenge a failure by the Community to adopt a measure having legal effects. This is the reverse of the question we considered in the previous chapter, or perhaps it would be more accurate to say that it is the negative aspect of the same question. The European Court has recognized this in a case decided many years ago in which it said that the two procedures are different aspects of the same remedy.[6] This means that it is legitimate to draw analogies from the one to the other, usually from annulment proceedings to proceedings for a remedy for failure to act.

The relevant provision is Article 232 [175] EC, set out in Panel 19.1. It will be seen from this that there is again a distinction between a privileged applicant (a Member State or Community institution)[7] and a private applicant. The latter comes under the third paragraph of Article 232 [175], which states that he may complain to the European Court that the European Parliament, the Council, the Commission or the European Central Bank[8] has "failed to address [to him] any act other than a recommendation or opinion". This makes clear that the requirement of a reviewable act, discussed in the previous chapter, applies here too. The procedure can, therefore, be brought only against one of the

---

6 *Chevalley v. Commission*, Case 15/70, [1970] ECR 975.
7 Under the fourth paragraph of Art. 232 [175], the ECB is again in a "semi-privileged" position.
8 The fourth paragraph allows actions to be brought against the ECB.

four defendants mentioned above, and only on the ground that the defendant failed to adopt a reviewable act which Community law required it to adopt.

This is all pretty much the same as under Article 230 [173]. However, in one respect, Article 232 [175] appears stricter. It limits the private applicant to complaints that the defendant failed to address the act to him. However, some of the other language versions are more liberal,[9] and the European Court has held that the position is in fact the same as under Article 230 [173]. Even if the act requested would not have been addressed to the applicant, it is enough if it would have been of direct and individual concern to him.[10] In other words, a private litigant can use Article 232 [175] to challenge a failure to adopt any act which, if it had been adopted, he could have challenged under Article 230 [173].

The procedure is laid down in the second paragraph of Article 232 [175]. Under this, the applicant must first call upon the defendant to act. He must specify clearly what act he wants the defendant to adopt and demand that it adopt it. Having done this, he must wait two months to allow it to consider its position. If, during this period, it has not "defined its position", the applicant may bring the proceedings within the following two months – in other words, within the third or fourth month following the request for action. If proceedings are brought too soon or too late, they will be inadmissible.

What happens if the defendant defines its position within the first two months? This will block the action under Article 232 [175], but will usually – possibly always – open up an action under Article 230 [173]. This is because a decision refusing to adopt an act is itself regarded as a reviewable act if it is clear and definite and if the act the defendant refused to adopt would have been reviewable. It can then be challenged under Article 230 [173], provided the applicant can prove direct and individual concern. It must, however, be stressed that in applying this test (and in applying the test for a reviewable act), one must look at the act which the defendant was asked to adopt, not at its decision of refusal. The latter will be addressed to the applicant, but that will not help him if he cannot show that the act that the defendant refused to adopt would have been of direct and individual concern to him.

Our next cases illustrate these points.

European Union
Lütticke v. Commission
COURT OF JUSTICE OF THE EUROPEAN COMMUNITIES
Case 48/65, [1966] ECR 19; [1966] CMLR 378

Facts

Lütticke was a German company. It considered that Germany had violated Community law and asked the Commission to take action against Germany under

---

9 The Dutch and the Italian versions say that the defendant must have failed to adopt an act "with respect to him".
10 *ENU v. Commission*, Case C-107/91, [1993] ECR I-599. This was decided under the Euratom Treaty. For the EC Treaty, see *Port*, Case C-68/95, [1996] ECR I-6065 at paras. 58–59 of the judgment; *Gestevisión Telecinco v. Commission*, Case T-95/96, [1998] ECR II-3407 at paras. 58. *et seq.* of the judgment.

Article 226 [169]. The Commission refused. It considered that no violation had occurred. Lütticke then brought two actions against the Commission in the European Court. The first was an action under Article 230 [173] to annul the decision of refusal. The second was under Article 232 [175].

Judgment

[Article 226 [169]] empowers the Commission to set in motion a procedure which may lead to an action before the Court of Justice to determine the existence of such a failure by a Member State; under the terms of Article 228 [171] of the Treaty the State concerned would then be required to take the necessary measures to comply with the judgment of the Court.

The part of the procedure which precedes reference of the matter to the Court constitutes an administrative stage intended to give the Member State concerned the opportunity of conforming with the Treaty. During this stage, the Commission makes known its view by way of an opinion only after giving the Member State concerned the opportunity to submit its observations.

No measure taken by the Commission during this stage has any binding force. Consequently, an application for the annulment of the measure by which the Commission arrived at a decision on the application is inadmissible.

In their alternative conclusions the applicants complain of failure to act under Article 232 [175].

The defendant claims that the alternative application is also inadmissible.

Under the terms of the second paragraph of Article 232 [175], proceedings for failure to act may only be brought if at the end of a period of two months from being called upon to act the institution has not defined its position.

It is established that the Commission has defined its position and has notified this position to the applicants within the prescribed period.

The plea of inadmissibility is therefore well founded.

QUESTION

What would have happened if the Commission had not replied to Lütticke during the two-month period?

European Union
Nordgetreide v. Commission
COURT OF JUSTICE OF THE EUROPEAN COMMUNITIES
Case 42/71, [1972] ECR 105

Facts

Nordgetreide, a German firm, requested the Commission to amend two regulations by including certain products in an annex to the regulations. This would have involved passing another regulation. The Commission refused. Nordgetreide brought an action under Article 230 [173] to annul the refusal. It also brought an action under Article 232 [175].

Judgment

4. . . . Since the Commission, within the time-limit fixed by Article 232 [175], defined its position . . . the conditions for application of that Article are not satisfied; the admissibility of the action must, in consequence, be considered in the light of Article 230 [173] alone.

5. Since the definition by the Commission of its position amounts to a rejection it must be appraised in the light of the object of the request to which it constituted a reply. The object of the request was the inclusion in the annex to [the regulations in question] of the products of concern to the applicant; it accordingly sought amendment of a regulation by an act which would itself have taken the form of a regulation. In fact, inclusion in the annex to the regulations concerned of the products referred to by the applicant would have had the effect of applying the system of compensatory amounts to all exports and, furthermore, to all imports of the products involved to the advantage or the disadvantage, as the case may be, of any and every exporter or importer. Such a provision would have affected the applicant only in so far as it belongs to a category viewed in the abstract and in its entirety and not as the person to whom an act of direct and individual concern to him was addressed. In consequence there is a want of the conditions to which under Article 230(2) [173(2)] proceedings by individuals against the acts of the institutions are subject.

6. The application must therefore be dismissed as inadmissible.

Comment

Here, the application failed because the act requested would not, if adopted, have been of direct and individual concern to the applicant. It therefore lacked standing.

QUESTION

What would have happened if the Commission had not replied to the applicant within the two-month period?

European Union
Lord Bethell v. Commission
COURT OF JUSTICE OF THE EUROPEAN COMMUNITIES
Case 246/81, [1982] ECR 2277; [1982] 3 CMLR 300

Facts

Lord Bethell was an MEP, a member of the British House of Lords and chairman of the Freedom of the Skies Campaign. He wanted to put an end to the cartel which at that time kept air tickets expensive in Europe. In a letter of 13 May 1981, he asked the Commission to take action under Community competition law against the airlines. When it refused (in a communication of 17 July 1981), he brought proceedings against it under Articles 230 [173] and 232 [175] EC.

Judgment
[After referring to the words of Articles 230 [173] and 232 [175], the court continued:]

13. It appears from the provisions quoted that the applicant, for his application to be admissible, must be in a position to establish either that he is the addressee of a measure of the Commission having specific legal effects with regard to him, which is, as such, capable of being declared void, or that the Commission, having been duly called upon to act in pursuance of the second paragraph of Article 232 [175], has failed to adopt in relation to him a measure which he was legally entitled to claim by virtue of the rules of Community law.

14. In reply to a question from the Court the applicant stated that the measure to which he believed himself to be entitled was "a response, an adequate answer to his complaint saying either that the Commission was going to act upon it or saying that it was not and, if not, giving reasons." Alternatively the applicant took the view that the letter addressed to him on 17 July 1981 by the Director-General for Competition was to be described as an act against which proceedings may be instituted under the second paragraph [now the fourth] of Article 230 [173].

15. The principal question to be resolved in this case is whether the Commission had, under the rules of Community law, the right and the duty to adopt in respect of the applicant a decision in the sense of the request made by the applicant to the Commission in his letter of 13 May 1981. It is apparent from the content of that letter and from the explanations given during the proceedings that the applicant is asking the Commission to undertake an investigation with regard to the airlines in the matter of the fixing of air fares with a view to a possible application to them of the provisions of the Treaty with regard to competition.

16. It is clear therefore that the applicant is asking the Commission, not to take a decision in respect of him, but to open an inquiry with regard to third parties and to take decisions in respect of them. No doubt the applicant, in his double capacity as a user of the airlines and a leading member of an organization of users of air passenger services, has an indirect interest, as other users may have, in such proceedings and their possible outcome, but he is nevertheless not in the precise legal position of the actual addressee of a decision which may be declared void under the second paragraph of Article 230 [173] or in that of the potential addressee of a legal measure which the Commission has a duty to adopt with regard to him, as is [the] position under the third paragraph of Article 232 [175].

17. It follows that the application is inadmissible from the point of view of both Article 232 [175] and Article 230 [173].

QUESTION
Would it have made any difference if the Commission had not replied to Lord Bethell's request?

Comment
One important respect in which actions for failure to act are different from annulment actions is that there can never be an equivalent remedy in the

Member-State courts. This is because Article 234 [177] makes no provision for a Member-State court to ask the European Court to decide whether a failure by the Community to adopt an act was contrary to Community law. There was, therefore, no other way in which any of the three applicants in the above cases could have challenged the Commission's failure to act.[11] However, there must be limits to the extent to which a private person can seek to control Community policy through legal proceedings. There must be an area within which the political process can operate. It could be argued that in all three cases the issue in question fell within that area. If this was so, the outcome of the cases would not constitute an infringement of the fundamental right to a legal remedy.

Actions in tort

Actions in tort against the Community are governed by the second paragraph of Article 288 [215] EC. This provides that, in the case of non-contractual liability, "the Community shall, in accordance with the general principles common to the laws of the Member States, make good any damage caused by its institutions or by its servants in the performance of their duties". The third paragraph extends this to cover the ECB.

The European Court does not take this provision literally by finding liability only when it exists under the law of every Member State. Rather, it has tried to build up a Community law of tort, using the general principles of Member-State law as a starting point. Harm (actual or threatened) and causation are two basic principles found in all systems of tort law. They are also part of Community law. It must therefore be possible to show that some act (or omission) imputable to the Community has caused loss to the applicant. An act is imputable to the Community if it is an act of a Community institution (or the ECB) or if it is an act of a Community official in the performance of his duties. Unlike annulment actions, there are no problems of standing. Moreover, the time limit is fairly long: five years.

Although liability may flow from a physical act, such as negligent driving[12] or the negligent release of confidential information,[13] most claims normally concern legislative or administrative acts – acts intended to have legal effects. Many years ago, the European Court laid down the rule that, in the case of legislative measures involving choices of economic policy, there are three additional requirements.[14]

---

11 It might, however, have been possible for Lütticke to bring proceedings against Germany in the German courts.
12 Cf. *Sayag v. Leduc (No. 1)*, Case 5/68, [1968] ECR 395; [1969] CMLR 12; *Sayag v. Leduc (No. 2)*, Case 9/69, [1969] ECR 329.
13 See *Adams v. Commission*, Case 145/83, [1985] ECR 3539; [1986] 1 CMLR 506; [1986] 2 WLR 367.
14 *Zuckerfabrik Schöppenstedt v. Council*, Case 5/71, [1971] ECR 975.

- There must be a breach of a superior rule of law.
- The breach must be sufficiently serious.
- The superior rule of law must be one for the protection of the individual.

More recently, this formula has been held to apply to all measures involving a significant degree of discretion (policy choices) on the part of the author. It was also reworded to cover the requirements of damage and causation.[15] Its present form is as follows.

- There must be a breach of a rule of law intended to confer rights on individuals.
- The breach must be sufficiently serious.
- There must be a direct causal link between the breach and the damage sustained by the injured party.

The remaining cases in this chapter show how the European Court has applied this formula.

European Union
HNL v. Council and Commission (Second Skimmed Milk Powder case)
COURT OF JUSTICE OF THE EUROPEAN COMMUNITIES
Cases 83 and 94/76 and 4, 15 and 40/77, [1978] ECR 1209; [1978] 3 CMLR 566

Facts

In order to find a use for the skimmed-milk powder "mountain" that had built up in the Community, the Council adopted a regulation (Regulation 563/76) requiring producers of animal feeding-stuffs to buy skimmed-milk powder to replace soya as the protein element in their product. Since skimmed-milk powder was more expensive, this pushed up the price of the feeding-stuffs. Livestock farmers were the ones who had to absorb this increase. In previous proceedings, the European Court had already declared Regulation 563/76 void because it infringed the principle of equality by making all livestock farmers suffer in order to benefit one sub-category of such farmers – dairy farmers. This solved the problem for the future, but it did not undo the past effects of the regulation. So a number of farmers sued for compensation for the losses they had suffered during the period when the regulation was in force.

Judgment
4. The finding that a legislative measure such as the regulation in question is null and void is however insufficient by itself for the Community to incur non-contractual liability[16] for damage caused to individuals under the second paragraph of Article 288 [215] of the EEC Treaty. The Court of Justice has consistently stated that the Community does not incur liability on account of a legislative measure which involves choices of economic policy unless a sufficiently serious breach of a superior rule of law for the protection of the individual has occurred.

---

15 *Bergaderm v. Commission*, Case C-352/98 P, [2000] ECR I-5291. The *Bergaderm* version of the formula was originally devised for the purpose of determining the liability of Member States for a breach of Community law, but it has now been applied to Community liability as well.
16 Editor's note: here "non-contractual" means tortious.

5. In the present case there is no doubt that the prohibition on discrimination laid down in the second subparagraph of the third paragraph of Article 34 [40] of the Treaty and infringed by Regulation No 563/76 is in fact designed for the protection of the individual, and that it is impossible to disregard the importance of this prohibition in the system of the Treaty. To determine what conditions must be present in addition to such breach for the Community to incur liability in accordance with the criterion laid down in the case-law of the Court of Justice it is necessary to take into consideration the principles in the legal systems of the Member States governing the liability of public authorities for damage caused to individuals by legislative measures. Although these principles vary considerably from one Member State to another, it is however possible to state that the public authorities can only exceptionally and in special circumstances incur liability for legislative measures which are the result of choices of economic policy. This restrictive view is explained by the consideration that the legislative authority, even where the validity of its measures is subject to judicial review, cannot always be hindered in making its decisions by the prospect of applications for damages whenever it has occasion to adopt legislative measures in the public interest which may adversely affect the interests of individuals.

6. It follows from these considerations that individuals may be required, in the sectors coming within the economic policy of the Community, to accept within reasonable limits certain harmful effects on their economic interests as a result of a legislative measure without being able to obtain compensation from public funds even if that measure has been declared null and void. In a legislative field such as the one in question, in which one of the chief features is the exercise of a wide discretion essential for the implementation of the common agricultural policy, the Community does not therefore incur liability unless the institution concerned has manifestly and gravely disregarded the limits on the exercise of its powers.

7. This is not so in the case of a measure of economic policy such as that in the present case, in view of its special features. In this connexion it is necessary to observe first that this measure affected very wide categories of traders, in other words all buyers of compound feeding-stuffs containing protein, so that its effects on individual undertakings were considerably lessened. Moreover, the effects of the regulation on the price of feeding-stuffs as a factor in the production costs of those buyers were only limited since that price rose by little more than 2%. This price increase was particularly small in comparison with the price increases resulting, during the period of application of the regulation, from the variations in the world market prices of feeding-stuffs containing protein, which were three or four times higher than the increase resulting from the obligation to purchase skimmed-milk powder introduced by the regulation. The effects of the regulation on the profit-earning capacity of the undertakings did not ultimately exceed the bounds of the economic risks inherent in the activities of the agricultural sectors concerned.

8. In these circumstances the fact that the regulation is null and void is insufficient for the Community to incur liability under the second paragraph of Article 288 [215] of the Treaty. The application must therefore be dismissed as unfounded.

Comment

In this case, the European Court expanded the requirement of a breach of a superior rule of law. It must now be shown that the defendant has manifestly and gravely disregarded the limits on the exercise of its powers. It also seems that the impact on the applicant is relevant. If the harm is spread over a large number of individuals and each one suffers only slightly, none will be awarded damages.

> **European Union**
> **Ireks-Arkady v. Council and Commission** (Quellmehl and Gritz case)
> **COURT OF JUSTICE OF THE EUROPEAN COMMUNITIES**
> Case 238/78, [1979] ECR 2955[17]

Facts

The Council had subsidized starch in order to help it compete with artificial products. This meant that starch could undercut two other products, quellmehl and gritz. So they too were given a subsidy. Later, however, the subsidy was removed from quellmehl and gritz, but not from starch. In proceedings brought originally in the Member-State courts, the European Court had held that the Council had been guilty of discrimination in treating quellmehl and gritz less favourably than starch. The Council then restored the subsidy, but only from the date of the judgment. The quellmehl and gritz producers, who were few in number, brought proceedings in tort to recover the loss they had suffered during the period when they were without a subsidy.

Judgment
[After referring to the previous case on quellmehl and gritz, the court continued:]
8. ... In so far as it is thus established that the abolition of the refunds was unlawful, the first problem which arises in this case is whether the unlawfulness thus established is of such a nature as to render the Community liable under the second paragraph of Article 288 [215] of the EEC Treaty.

9. The finding that a legal situation resulting from the legislative measures of the Community is unlawful is not sufficient in itself to give rise to such liability. The Court has already expressed that view in [the second *Skimmed-Milk* case]. In this regard, the Court recalled its settled case-law, according to which the Community does not incur liability on account of a legislative measure which involves choices of economic policy unless a sufficiently serious breach of a superior rule of law for the protection of the individual has occurred. Taking into consideration the principles in the legal systems of the Member States governing the liability of public authorities for damage caused to individuals by legislative measures, the Court said that in the context of Community provisions in which one of the chief features was the exercise of a wide discretion essential for the implementation of the common agricultural policy, the Community did not incur liability unless the institution concerned manifestly and gravely disregarded the limits on the exercise of its powers.

10. In the circumstances of this case, the Court is led to the conclusion that there was on the part of the Council such a grave and manifest disregard of the limits on the exercise of its discretionary powers in matters of the common agricultural policy. In this regard the Court notes the following findings in particular.

---

17 This was one of a group of cases all concerned with the same issue. The others were *Dumortier v. Council*, Cases 64 and 113/76, 167 and 239/78 and 27, 28 and 45/79, [1979] ECR 3091; *DGV v. Council and Commission*, Cases 241, 242 and 245–250/78, [1979] ECR 3017; and *Interquell v. Council and Commission*, Cases 261–262/78, [1979] ECR 3045.

11. In the first place it is necessary to take into consideration that the principle of equality, embodied in particular in the second subparagraph of Article 34(2) [40(3)] of the EEC Treaty, which prohibits any discrimination in the common organization of the agricultural markets, occupies a particularly important place among the rules of Community law intended to protect the interests of the individual. Secondly, the disregard of that principle in this case affected a limited and clearly defined group of commercial operators. It seems, in fact, that the number of quellmehl producers in the Community is very limited. Further, the damage alleged by the applicants goes beyond the bounds of the economic risks inherent in the activities in the sector concerned. Finally, equality of treatment with the producers of maize starch, which had been observed from the beginning of the common organization of the market in cereals, was ended by the Council in 1974 without sufficient justification.

12. For those reasons the Court arrives at the conclusion that the Community incurs liability for the abolition of the refunds for quellmehl under Regulation No. 1125/74 of the Council.

[The court went on to hold that, since the applicants had been unable to pass on the increased prices, the damages should be based on the subsidy they would have received if it had not been abolished.]

QUESTIONS

1. In this case, the Community was guilty of subsidizing one product and not another. In the *Skimmed Milk Powder* case, it forced farmers to buy more expensive feeding-stuffs. Was the former really a more serious violation of the law?
2. Why should it make a difference that in this case the claimants were few in number?

European Union
Amylum and Tunnel Refineries v. Council and Commission (Second Isoglucose case[18])
COURT OF JUSTICE OF THE EUROPEAN COMMUNITIES
Cases 116 and 124/77, [1979] ECR 3497

Facts

Isoglucose is a kind of manufactured sugar, which can replace natural sugar in certain products. The manufacturing process was originally developed in the United States. When production began in Europe, the Community imposed a levy (tax) on it that was so high that production was largely uneconomic. It was thought by some that this was done deliberately to protect sugar-beet producers. In an earlier case, the European Court had ruled that the regulation imposing the levy (Regulation 1111/77) was invalid because the treatment of isoglucose was grossly unequal compared with natural sugar. The regulation

18 See also *KSH v. Council and Commission*, Case 143/77, [1979] ECR 3583.

was then repealed. Even though the repeal had retroactive effect, this did not entirely solve the problem for the producers. Because the levy had been so large, their factories had been operating below capacity for much of the time. In some cases, they had been forced to switch to alternative products. This had resulted in financial losses. They now sued for compensation. Their losses had been large. One firm had even gone bankrupt. Moreover, there were only a small number of firms. On the basis of the *Quellmehl and Gritz* cases, one would have thought that they would have been successful.

Judgment

13. A finding that a legal situation resulting from legislative measures by the Community is illegal is insufficient by itself to involve it in liability. The Court has already stated this in [the *Second Skimmed-Milk Powder case*]. In this connexion the Court referred to its consistent case-law in accordance with which the Community does not incur liability on account of a legislative measure which involves choices of economic policy unless a sufficiently serious breach of a superior rule of law for the protection of the individual has occurred. Having regard to the principles in the legal systems of the Member States, governing the liability of public authorities for damage caused to individuals by legislative measures, the Court has stated that in the context of Community legislation in which one of the chief features is the exercise of a wide discretion essential for the implementation of the common agricultural policy, the liability of the Community can arise only exceptionally in cases in which the institution concerned has manifestly and gravely disregarded the limits on the exercise of its powers.

14. This is confirmed in particular by the fact that, even though an action for damages under Articles 235 [178] and 288 [215] of the Treaty constitutes an independent action, it must nevertheless be assessed having regard to the whole of the system of legal protection of individuals set up by the Treaty. If an individual takes the view that he is injured by a Community legislative measure which he regards as illegal he has the opportunity, when the implementation of the measure is entrusted to national authorities, to contest the validity of the measure, at the time of its implementation, before a national court in an action against the national authority. Such a court may, or even must, in pursuance of Article 234 [177], refer to the Court of Justice a question on the validity of the Community measure in question. The existence of such an action is by itself of such a nature as to ensure the efficient protection of the individuals concerned.

15. These considerations are of importance where, as in these cases, the Court, within the framework of a reference for a preliminary ruling, has declared a production levy to be illegal and where the competent institution, following that finding, has abolished the levy concerned with retroactive effect.

16. It is appropriate to inquire in the light of these considerations whether, in the circumstances of these cases, there has been, on the part of the Council and the Commission, a grave and manifest disregard of the limits which they are required to observe in exercising their discretion within the framework of the common agricultural policy.

17. In this respect it must be recalled that the Court did not declare invalid any isoglucose production levy but only the method of calculation adopted and the fact that the levy applied to the whole of the isoglucose production. Having regard to the fact that the production of isoglucose was playing a part in increasing sugar surpluses it was permissible for the Council to impose restrictive measures on such production.

18. Although, in its judgment [in which it held that Regulation 1111/77 was invalid], the Court found that the charges borne in pursuance of that regulation by isoglucose producers by way of production levy were manifestly unequal as compared with those imposed on sugar producers, it does not follow that, for the purposes of an assessment of the illegality of the measure in connexion with Article 288 [215] of the Treaty, the Council has manifestly and gravely disregarded the limits on the exercise of its discretion.

19. In fact, even though the fixing of the isoglucose production levy at five units of account[19] per 100 kg of dry matter was vitiated by errors, it must nevertheless be pointed out that, having regard to the fact that an appropriate levy was fully justified, these were not errors of such gravity that it may be said that the conduct of the defendant institutions in this respect was verging on the arbitrary and was thus of such a kind as to involve the Community in non-contractual liability.

20. It must also be recalled that Regulation No. 1111/77 was adopted in particular to deal with an emergency situation characterized by growing surpluses of sugar and in circumstances which, in accordance with the principles set out in Article 33 [39] of the Treaty, permitted a certain preference in favour of sugar beet, Community production of which was in surplus, whilst Community production of maize was to a considerable extent deficient.[20]

21. It follows from these considerations that the Council and the Commission did not disregard the limits which they were required to observe in the exercise of their discretion in the context of the common agricultural policy in such a serious manner as to incur the non-contractual liability of the Community.

22. The applications must be dismissed as unfounded.

Comment

In this judgment, the court made recovery even more difficult by saying that the defendant's conduct must verge on the arbitrary. However, the court has subsequently gone back on this,[21] and it no longer applies.

QUESTION

Was the conduct of the Community really less bad in this case than in the *Quellmehl and Gritz* case?

Conclusion

The most striking feature of Community tort law is that, whatever reasons the European Court or the Court of First Instance[22] may give, they usually end

---

19 Editor's note: the "unit of account" was the forerunner of the euro.
20 Editor's note: isoglucose was made from starch, usually obtained from maize.
21 *Stahlwerke Peine-Salzgitter v. Commission*, Case C-220/91 P, [1993] ECR I-2393 (para. 51 of the judgment).
22 The Court of First Instance now has jurisdiction in tort actions brought by private litigants. There is a right of appeal on points of law to the European Court.

up denying recovery.[23] In the few cases in which they do find liability, they often discover some reason for reducing the amount of the award, possibly by saying that the applicant was partly to blame.[24] In most Member States, it is also difficult to win a tort action against a public authority. However, public authorities in the Member States are usually subject to democratic control. The relative lack of democracy at the Community level makes judicial remedies more important.

Further reading

Hartley (T. C.), *The Foundations of European Community Law* (Oxford University Press, Oxford, 5th ed., 2003), Chapters 13, 14 and 17.
Heukels (Ton) and McDonnell (Alison) (eds.), *The Action for Damages in Community Law* (Kluwer Law International, The Hague and Boston, 1997).
Tridimas, "Liability for Breach of Community Law: Growing Up and Mellowing Down?" (2001) 38 CMLRev. 301 at 321–332.

---

23 See *per* Advocate-General Tesauro in *Brasserie du Pêcheur v. Germany*, Case C-46/93, [1996] ECR I-1029 at 1101 (para. 63, last sentence, of the Opinion).
24 See, for example, *Adams v. Commission*, Case 145/83, [1985] ECR 3539; [1986] 1 CMLR 506; [1986] 2 WLR 367; and *Fresh Marine v. Commission*, Case T-178/98, [2000] ECR II-3331 affirmed in Case C-472/00 P, 10 July 2003.

PART VII
SUBSTANTIVE LAW – A TASTE

20

The common market – I

In the previous chapters of this book we have examined the legal structure of the Community – its institutions, its legal system and the relationship between that system and other systems of law, both national and international. We have created a picture of the Community from the legal point of view. It will be seen that the Community is a complex and carefully tuned machine. You may have wondered what this is all for. What is its purpose and what does it do?

The answer is that it does a great number of things. The Community has a wide range of policies, including:
* the free movement of goods;
* the free movement of persons;
* the freedom for providers of services to work for clients from other Member States;
* the freedom for companies and businessmen to do business in other Member States;
* a common agricultural policy;
* common rules on competition (antitrust) law;
* common rules on State aid (subsidies) to industry;
* a common economic and monetary policy;
* a common currency (the euro) for some Member States;
* a common commercial policy towards non-Community countries;
* a social policy;
* education;
* culture;
* public health;
* consumer protection; and
* the environment.

There are sections of the EC Treaty devoted to all of these.

In a book of this kind, it is impossible to cover all these topics. So, in this Part we shall offer just a small taste of substantive Community law. The subject we have chosen is the most basic – the common market, the original objective of the Community. The first four freedoms listed above are the most important for this. We shall look at the free movement of goods in this chapter. In the next chapter we shall consider the free movement of persons, the free movement of services and freedom of establishment.

Panel 20.1   The customs union

EC Treaty

Article 23 [9]

1 The Community shall be based upon a customs union which shall cover all trade in goods and which shall involve the prohibition between Member States of customs duties on imports and exports and of all charges having equivalent effect, and the adoption of a common customs tariff in their relations with third countries.

2 The provisions of Article 25 [12] and of Chapter 2 of this Title¹ shall apply to products originating in Member States and to products coming from third countries which are in free circulation in Member States.

Article 25 [12]

Customs duties on imports and exports and charges having equivalent effect shall be prohibited between Member States. This prohibition shall also apply to customs duties of a fiscal nature.

¹ Chap. 2 consists of Arts. 28–31 [30–37]. It covers quantitative restrictions on trade between Member States. Arts. 28–30 [30–36] are set out in Panel 20.3. Art. 31 [37] deals with State monopolies.

The customs union

A customs union is an area in which goods can move freely without any barriers. The difference between a customs union and a free trade area is that in the latter the free trade rules apply only to goods produced within the area. In the case of a customs union, on the other hand, they apply also to goods imported from the outside. Goods imported from outside the union into Member State X can move into Member State Y on the same basis as goods produced in Member State X. A customs union makes sense only if all the Member States agree to a common external tariff. Imports from the outside must receive the same treatment irrespective of the State through which they enter the union.

The European Community is a customs union. The free trade rules apply not only to goods produced in another Member State, but also to imports from non-member States. The Community has a common customs tariff, which ensures that no advantage can be gained by routing imports from outside the Community through one Member State rather than another. On all this, see Panel 20.1.

Customs duties

Article 25 [12] EC (Panel 20.1) prohibits all customs duties (and charges having equivalent effect) on imports and exports between Member States. It is directly effective,¹ and covers any payment that has to be made by virtue of the fact

---

1 It was this very same provision (though at the time in a different form) that was in issue in the first case on direct effect, *Van Gend en Loos*, Case 26/62, discussed in Chap. 9. When the Community was originally formed, the first step was to prohibit any increases in customs duties between Member States. The second step was to abolish them entirely.

that goods have crossed a frontier.[2] It is strictly applied, as is shown by our next case.

European Union
Sociaal Fonds voor de Diamantarbeiders (Diamond Workers case)
COURT OF JUSTICE OF THE EUROPEAN COMMUNITIES
Cases 2 and 3/69, [1969] ECR 211; [1969] CMLR 335

Facts

Belgium imposed a levy of 0.33 per cent of the value of imported diamonds. The money was paid into a fund for welfare benefits for workers in the diamond-cutting industry, of which Antwerp is a major centre. The levy was challenged in a Belgian court as contrary to Article 25 [12] and a reference was made to the European Court. Since no diamonds were produced in Belgium, the Belgian Government argued that the levy had no protectionist effect.

Judgment
It follows from the system as a whole and from the general and absolute nature of the prohibition of any customs duty applicable to goods moving between Member States that customs duties are prohibited independently of any consideration of the purpose for which they were introduced and the destination of the revenue obtained therefrom. The justification for this prohibition is based on the fact that any pecuniary charge – however small – imposed on goods by reason of the fact that they cross a frontier constitutes an obstacle to the free movement of such goods.

Result: the levy was illegal.

QUESTION
What was gained by striking down this method of financing the diamond workers' welfare scheme?

Taxes on imports

There would be no point in banning customs duties if the same result could be achieved through the tax system. For this reason, the EC Treaty contains a provision (Article 90 [95] EC, set out in Panel 20.2) on the taxation of imported products. It is directly effective. The first paragraph prohibits any greater taxation of imports than is applied to similar domestic products. This means that

---

2 In *Commission v. Italy*, Case 24/68, [1969] ECR 193 at 201, the European Court said that any pecuniary charge imposed unilaterally on goods by reason of the fact that they cross a frontier, and which is not a customs duty in the strict sense, constitutes a charge having equivalent effect. The European Court has, however, introduced a limited number of exceptions – for example, reasonable payments to cover checks on goods where they are required under Community law or international agreements.

Panel 20.2 Taxation of imported products

EC Treaty

Article 90 [95]

No Member State shall impose, directly or indirectly, on the products of other Member States any internal taxation of any kind in excess of that imposed directly or indirectly on similar domestic products.

   Furthermore, no Member State shall impose on the products of other Member States any internal taxation of such a nature as to afford indirect protection to other products.

imports must be subject to the same tax regime as similar domestic products. Even if the products are not sufficiently similar to be regarded as "similar" for the purpose of the first paragraph, they may still be caught by the second paragraph. This prohibits indirect protection of domestic products. Even if the imported product is different from the domestic product, there may still be a competitive relationship between them. In certain circumstances, consumers might buy the import instead of the domestic product. For example, wine and beer are different, but if a Member State that produces a great deal of beer but little or no wine were to impose a much higher tax on wine than on beer, it could deter consumers from switching to imported wine from domestic beer. This might constitute an infringement of the second paragraph of Article 90 [95].

Whether there is a sufficient relationship between the two products to trigger the application of the second paragraph of Article 90 [95] is a question of fact. In one case decided in 1980,[3] the United Kingdom argued that, in the UK, wine and beer were consumed in different circumstances. Beer was a popular drink consumed mainly in pubs, while drinking wine was rather unusual and special – a view more justified in 1980 than today. The European Court nevertheless held that Article 90 [95] was applicable, since one must consider possible future trends as well as the present situation. The increased popularity of wine in the UK since this case was decided lends support to the court's point of view.

Even if one concludes that the two products are in a competitive relationship, it is not always easy to decide whether the tax system affords indirect protection. How, for example, should one compare the rate of tax on wine and beer? Should one look at the total tax for a given volume of the two drinks? It could be argued that this would be unfair to beer. Since it has a lower alcohol content, it is often consumed in greater quantities. Another possibility would be to compare the tax on a normal serving. In the proceedings before the European Court, the UK Government argued that beer was normally served by the pint and wine by the glass, though it could be argued that wine is in fact served by the bottle. It might be thought that the best indicator would be the tax as a percentage of the normal selling price, though it would not always be easy to know what the normal selling price was. In the case against the United Kingdom, the European Court preferred to compare the tax on the two products relative to their alcohol content, though it admitted that this was not a perfect test.

---

3 *Commission v. United Kingdom*, Case 170/78, [1980] ECR 417.

This problem is further illustrated by our next case.

European Union
Humblot (French Road Tax case)
COURT OF JUSTICE OF THE EUROPEAN COMMUNITIES
Case 112/84, [1985] ECR 1367

Facts

At the time of this case, there were two kinds of road tax applicable to cars in France. They both depended on the horsepower (CV) for tax purposes. One tax (the "differential tax") rose progressively with increases in CV up to 16 CV. The other (the "special tax") was at a flat rate and applied to all cars over 16 CV. It was much greater. In 1981, for example, the highest rate of differential tax was FF1,100, while the special tax was FF5,000. All French-manufactured cars were under 16 CV. All cars above 16 CV were imported.

Mr Humblot bought an imported car rated at 36 CV. He brought proceedings in France claiming that he should be refunded the difference between the top rate of the differential tax and the special tax. The French court referred the matter to the European Court.

Judgment

12. It is appropriate in the first place to stress that as Community law stands at present the Member States are at liberty to subject products such as cars to a system of road tax which increases progressively in amount depending on an objective criterion, such as the power rating for tax purposes, which may be determined in various ways.

13. Such a system of domestic taxation is, however, compatible with Article 90 [95] only in so far as it is free from any discriminatory or protective effect.

14. That is not true of a system like the one at issue in the main proceedings. Under that system there are two distinct taxes: a differential tax which increases progressively and is charged on cars not exceeding a given power rating for tax purposes and a fixed tax on cars exceeding that rating which is almost five times as high as the highest rate of the differential tax. Although the system embodies no formal distinction based on the origin of products it manifestly exhibits discriminatory or protective features contrary to Article 90 [95], since the power rating determining liability to the special tax has been fixed at a level such that only imported cars, in particular from other Member States, are subject to the special tax whereas all cars of domestic manufacture are liable to the distinctly more advantageous differential tax.

15. In the absence of considerations relating to the amount of the special tax, consumers seeking comparable cars as regards such matters as size, comfort, actual power, maintenance costs, durability, fuel consumption and price would naturally choose from among cars above and below the critical power rating laid down by French law. However, liability to the special tax entails a much larger increase in taxation than passing from one category of car to another in a system of progressive taxation embodying balanced differentials like the system on which the differential tax is based. The resultant additional taxation is liable to cancel out the advantages which certain cars imported from other Member States might have in consumers' eyes over comparable cars of domestic

manufacture, particularly since the special tax continues to be payable for several years. In that respect the special tax reduces the amount of competition to which cars of domestic manufacture are subject and hence is contrary to the principle of neutrality with which domestic taxation must comply.

Result: the special tax was contrary to Article 90 [95] EC.

Quantitative restrictions

Simply prohibiting customs duties and taxes having an equivalent effect is not enough. Otherwise, Member States could impose a total ban on imports of specified goods from other Member States, or (less drastically) allow in only a limited quantity. If a Member State passes a law saying that only 1,000 bottles of Scotch whisky can be imported each year, this will protect the domestic spirits industry just as effectively as a law imposing a heavy duty on whisky. However, since the whisky would not be subject to any customs duty or discriminatory taxation, there would be no infringement of the provisions previously discussed. For this reason, the EC Treaty includes provisions prohibiting quantitative restrictions on imports and exports. These are to be found in Articles 28 [30] and 29 [34] EC (Panel 20.3).

Articles 28 [30] and 29 [34] prohibit all provisions limiting – for example, by volume or value – imports of goods from one Member State into another. They also prohibit an outright ban on particular goods, whether in terms of an import/export ban or as a ban on the possession or sale of the goods.

However, in some ways these provisions go too far. They could, for example, outlaw a national ban on the sale of drugs, if the drugs were legal in another Member State. This would mean that if one Member State legalized cannabis, all other Member States would have to do the same. To prevent this, Article 30 [36] (Panel 20.3) permits national measures on the grounds specified in it, provided the measures do not constitute a means of arbitrary discrimination or a disguised restriction on trade. Thus, a prohibition on the sale of drugs could be covered by public morality, public policy or the protection of the health or life of humans.

It will be appreciated that the meaning of these provisions leaves considerable scope for judicial interpretation. We shall now see how the European Court has set about doing this.

> *European Union*
> **Procureur du Roi v. Dassonville**
> **COURT OF JUSTICE OF THE EUROPEAN COMMUNITIES**
> Case 8/74, [1974] ECR 837

Facts

Mr Dassonville imported Scotch whisky into Belgium from France. Under Belgian legislation, the whisky had to have a certificate of authenticity issued

Panel 20.3   Quantitative restrictions

EC Treaty

Article 28 [30]

Quantitative restrictions on imports and all measures having equivalent effect shall be prohibited between Member States.

Article 29 [34]

Quantitative restrictions on exports, and all measures having equivalent effect, shall be prohibited between Member States.

Article 30 [36]

The provisions of Articles 28 [30] and 29 [34] shall not preclude prohibitions or restrictions on imports, exports or goods in transit justified on grounds of public morality, public policy or public security; the protection of health and life of humans, animals or plants; the protection of national treasures possessing artistic, historic or archaeological value; or the protection of industrial or commercial property. Such prohibitions or restrictions shall not, however, constitute a means of arbitrary discrimination or a disguised restriction on trade between Member States.

to the importer by the UK customs authorities. Because Dassonville had not imported the whisky directly from the UK, it would have been extremely difficult for him to have obtained the certificate. So he sold the whisky without it. A criminal prosecution ensued and he claimed that Community law gave him a defence. The Belgian court referred the matter to the European Court.

Judgment

5. All trading rules enacted by Member States which are capable of hindering, directly or indirectly, actually or potentially, intra-Community trade are to be considered as measures having an effect equivalent to quantitative restrictions.

6. In the absence of a Community system guaranteeing for consumers the authenticity of a product's designation of origin, if a Member State takes measures to prevent unfair practices in this connexion, it is however subject to the condition that these measures should be reasonable and that the means of proof required should not act as a hindrance to trade between Member States and should, in consequence, be accessible to all Community nationals.

7. Even without having to examine whether or not such measures are covered by Article 30 [36], they must not, in any case, by virtue of the principle expressed in the second sentence of that Article, constitute a means of arbitrary discrimination or a disguised restriction on trade between Member States.

8. That may be the case with formalities, required by a Member State for the purpose of proving the origin of a product, which only direct importers are really in a position to satisfy without facing serious difficulties.

Result: the Belgian requirement of a certificate of origin was contrary to the Treaty.

Comment

In this case the court adopted a wide interpretation of what constitutes a quantitative restriction. In addition to provisions that impose quotas or lay down an outright ban on products, it was also held to cover provisions that merely hinder imports. Moreover, it is enough if they do this directly or indirectly, actually or potentially. Since the Belgian rule made it easier to import Scotch whisky directly from the UK than to buy it in France after it had been imported into that country, it discriminated between different channels of trade. This, the court held, brought it within the scope of the second sentence of Article 30 [36] (see Panel 20.3), thereby making it irrelevant whether or not it came within the first sentence.

The wide meaning given to quantitative restrictions can have bizarre consequences. For example, it has been argued that the law that used to apply in the UK prohibiting shops from opening on Sundays (the Sunday trading legislation) was contrary to Article 28 [30]. The argument was that if shops could not open on Sundays, fewer goods (of all kinds) would be sold. Some of these goods would have been imports from other Member States. Therefore, the Sunday trading legislation hindered imports – directly or indirectly, actually or potentially. Initially, the European Court was unwilling to reject such arguments out of hand,[4] though subsequently it did so.[5]

> **European Union**
> **Rewe-Zentral AG v. Bundesmonopolverwaltung für Branntwein**
> (Cassis de Dijon case)
> **COURT OF JUSTICE OF THE EUROPEAN COMMUNITIES**
> Case 120/78, [1979] ECR 649; [1979] 3 CMLR 494

Facts

Cassis de Dijon was a fruit liqueur produced in France. In Germany, there was a law that such liqueurs had to have a minimum alcohol content of 25 per cent. All German liqueurs had such a minimum alcohol content. Most French liqueurs had a lower alcohol content. Cassis de Dijon had an alcohol content of 15–20 per cent. The result was that Cassis de Dijon could not be sold in Germany. Proceedings were brought in Germany to challenge this ban, and a reference made to the European Court.

Judgment

8. In the absence of common rules relating to the production and marketing of alcohol . . . it is for the Member States to regulate all matters relating to the production and marketing of alcohol and alcoholic beverages on their own territory.

Obstacles to movement within the Community resulting from disparities between the national laws relating to the marketing of the products in question must be accepted in so far as those provisions may be recognized as being necessary in order to satisfy mandatory requirements relating in particular to the effectiveness of fiscal supervision, the protection of public health, the fairness of commercial transactions and the defence of the consumer.

---

4 *Torfaen Borough Council v. B&Q plc*, Case C-145/88, [1989] ECR 3851.
5 *Stoke-on-Trent City Council v. B&Q plc*, Case C-169/91, [1992] ECR I–6635; [1993] 2 WLR 730.

[The German Government had put forward two arguments to justify its ban. First, it argued (rather surprisingly) that the requirement of a minimum alcohol content was necessary to protect public health. It said that drinkers could get addicted to alcohol more easily by drinking alcoholic beverages with a low alcohol content than with a high alcohol content. The European Court had no difficulty in rejecting this argument. Germany's second argument was based on consumer protection. It said that drinks with a low alcohol content obtained an unfair advantage because of the high tax on alcohol. The court rejected this argument as well. It pointed out that it would be a simple matter to require that the alcohol content be displayed on the bottle. The consumer would then know what he was getting. The court continued as follows.]

14. It is clear from the foregoing that the requirements relating to the minimum alcohol content of alcoholic beverages do not serve a purpose which is in the general interest and such as to take precedence over the requirements of the free movement of goods, which constitutes one of the fundamental rules of the Community.

In practice, the principle effect of requirements of this nature is to promote alcoholic beverages having a high alcohol content by excluding from the national market products of other Member States which do not answer that description.

It therefore appears that the unilateral requirement imposed by the rules of a Member State of a minimum alcohol content for the purposes of the sale of alcoholic beverages constitutes an obstacle to trade which is incompatible with the provisions of Article 28 [30] of the Treaty.

There is therefore no valid reason why, provided that they have been lawfully produced and marketed in one of the Member States, alcoholic beverages should not be introduced into any other Member State; the sale of such products may not be subject to a legal prohibition on the marketing of beverages with an alcohol content lower than the limit set by the national rules.

Result: the German rule was contrary to the Treaty.

Comment

The interesting thing about this judgment is that it was not based on a finding of discrimination against goods from other Member States, though it could perhaps be argued that indirect discrimination did in fact exist. Once it was shown that the rule had the practical effect of hindering imports from other Member States and that there was no justification for it, the court concluded that it was illegal.

Though perfectly reasonable on the facts of the case, this judgment could give rise to anomalies, since it requires the court to decide whether national measures adopted without any protectionist intent are justifiable as being in the general interest. In the next case, we shall see how it has responded to this problem.

European Union
Keck and Mithouard
COURT OF JUSTICE OF THE EUROPEAN COMMUNITIES
Cases C-267 and 268/91, [1993] ECR I-6097

Facts

French legislation prohibited shopkeepers from selling goods at a loss.[6] It seems that its purpose was to prevent supermarkets driving small shopkeepers out of business by undercutting them until they went bankrupt. Keck and Mithouard were charged with infringing this legislation. Their defence was that the legislation constituted a quantitative restriction on trade contrary to Article 28 [30]. The French court made a reference to the European Court.

Judgment

12. National legislation imposing a general prohibition on resale at a loss is not designed to regulate trade in goods between Member States.

13. Such legislation may, admittedly, restrict the volume of sales, and hence the volume of sales of products from other Member States, in so far as it deprives traders of a method of sales promotion. But the question remains whether such a possibility is sufficient to characterize the legislation in question as a measure having equivalent effect to a quantitative restriction on imports.

14. In view of the increasing tendency of traders to invoke Article 28 [30] of the Treaty as a means of challenging any rules whose effect is to limit their commercial freedom even where such rules are not aimed at products from other Member States, the Court considers it necessary to re-examine and clarify its case-law on this matter.

15. It is established by the case-law beginning with "Cassis de Dijon" . . . that, in the absence of harmonization of legislation, obstacles to free movement of goods which are the consequence of applying, to goods coming from other Member States where they are lawfully manufactured and marketed, rules that lay down requirements to be met by such goods (such as those relating to designation, form, size, weight, composition, presentation, labelling, packaging) constitute measures of equivalent effect prohibited by Article 28 [30]. This is so even if those rules apply without distinction to all products unless their application can be justified by a public-interest objective taking precedence over the free movement of goods.

16. By contrast, contrary to what has previously been decided, the application to products from other Member States of national provisions restricting or prohibiting certain selling arrangements is not such as to hinder directly or indirectly, actually or potentially, trade between Member States within the meaning of the *Dassonville* judgment . . ., so long as those provisions apply to all relevant traders operating within the national territory and so long as they affect in the same manner, in law and in fact, the marketing of domestic products and of those from other Member States.

17. Provided that those conditions are fulfilled, the application of such rules to the sale of products from another Member State meeting the requirements laid down by that State is not by nature such as to prevent their access to the market or to impede access any more than it impedes the access of domestic products. Such rules therefore fall outside the scope of Article 28 [30] of the Treaty.

Result: the French legislation was not contrary to the Treaty.

---

6 There were certain exceptions, such as goods that had reached their "sell-by" date. ·

Comment

The European Court obviously thought that things had gone too far. In its enthusiasm to uphold free trade, it had laid down rules that appeared to make
illegal a vast range of perfectly legitimate trading rules. So, it performed something of a U-turn. As a result, *Cassis de Dijon* now applies only to national rules
laying down requirements to be met by the goods themselves. Such rules are
prohibited, irrespective of whether or not they discriminate, unless they can
be justified by a public-interest objective taking precedence over the free movement of goods. On the other hand, national rules restricting or prohibiting
particular selling arrangements are not regarded as quantitative restrictions
provided they apply equally to domestic products.

Possible justifications

We have seen that Article 30 [36] permits Member States to justify quantitative
restrictions if they are necessary on one of the following grounds:

- public morality;
- public policy;
- public security;
- the protection of health and life of humans, animals or plants;
- the protection of national treasures possessing artistic, historic or archaeological value; or
- the protection of industrial or commercial property.[7]

The Member States have a limited discretion, subject to Community law, to
decide what is necessary to achieve these objectives.

However, national measures that seek to achieve them must not come within
the proviso in the second sentence of Article 30 [36]. They must not be a means
of arbitrary discrimination or a disguised restriction on trade. If they are,
they cannot be justified by Article 30 [36]. Thus, even if a national measure
was intended to achieve one of the specified objectives, it would still not be
permitted if similar measures did not apply to domestic goods. For example,
imported goods cannot be restricted on the ground that they are pornographic
(and therefore contrary to public morality) if national legislation does not
prohibit domestically produced pornography.[8]

The European Court has also held that national measures cannot be justified
on the basis of Article 30 [36] if the same result could have been achieved by
less restrictive means.[9] This is an application of the principle of proportionality,
a general principle of Community law.[10] Thus, a national government cannot
justify a restriction on the ground that it is necessary to protect public health,

---

7 Industrial property is patents, and commercial property is trademarks.
8 *Conegate v. HM Customs and Excise*, Case 121/85, [1986] ECR 1007.
9 *Commission v. Belgium*, Case 155/82, [1983] ECR 531 (para. 12 of the judgment).
10 According to this principle, the burdens imposed by governmental measures must not be out of
proportion to the benefits.

if public health could be equally well protected by a measure that had a less restrictive effect on the free movement of goods.

The result is that it is rather complicated to determine whether a national measure is contrary to the Treaty as a quantitative restriction or a measure having equivalent effect. First, it must be decided whether the measure falls within Article 28 [30]. This may depend on whether the measure concerns requirements to be met by the goods themselves (and consequently is covered by *Cassis de Dijon*) or whether the measure concerns selling arrangements (and is therefore governed by *Keck*). If it does fall under Article 28 [30], it may still be justified under Article 30 [36]. To determine this, it must be decided whether the measure is necessary to achieve one of the objectives specified in Article 30 [36]. If it is not, Article 30 [36] cannot apply.[11] Even if it is, it will still not be justified if it is discriminatory or disproportionate.

Harmonization directives

The result is that, in certain strictly defined circumstances, trade barriers may still be permitted under Community law. One way of solving this problem is for the Community to enact harmonizing directives that lay down common rules to achieve the objective in question. If all Member States apply the same restrictions, there will be no barrier.

Our next case shows the effect of such directives. Unlike the cases previously considered, it concerns a ban on exports (Article 29 [34]), rather than imports (Article 28 [30]).

> **European Union**
> **The Queen v. MAFF, ex parte Hedley Lomas**
> **COURT OF JUSTICE OF THE EUROPEAN COMMUNITIES**
> Case C-5/94, [1996] ECR I-2553

Facts

The UK Government was concerned about cruel methods of slaughtering cattle in use in some Member States. In an attempt to meet such concerns, the Community had adopted a directive in 1974.[12] The directive, which was supposed to be the first step towards a general Community policy against cruelty, required Member States to ensure that animals were stunned before slaughter. In Spain, the government gave effect to this by adopting legislation making stunning obligatory, but there was no provision for any penalty if stunning did not take place.

On the basis of information obtained from various sources – including an animal welfare organization in Spain – the UK Ministry of Agriculture concluded

---

11 Para. 8 of the judgment in *Cassis de Dijon* suggests, however, that national measures necessary to satisfy certain other requirements, such as the fairness of commercial transactions or consumer protection, may fall totally outside the scope of Art. 28 [30].
12 Directive 74/557, OJ 1974, L316, p. 10.

that the directive and the Spanish legislation were being ignored in a significant number of abattoirs in Spain. Some abattoirs did not even possess stunning equipment. It therefore banned the export of live cattle to Spain.[13] The ban, which was put into effect by refusing to issue licences for the export of live cattle to Spain, entered into force in April 1990 and was based on Article 30 [36] EC. The UK considered that it was necessary on grounds of public morality, public policy and the protection of the health and life of animals. Although the UK had no proof that every abattoir in Spain was violating the directive, it considered that there was a significant risk that animals exported to Spain would suffer.

An Irish company called Hedley Lomas, which exported live cattle from England, challenged the ban.[14] It brought proceedings in the English courts and a reference was made to the European Court.

Judgment

17. The refusal by a Member State to issue export licences constitutes a quantitative restriction on exports, contrary to Article 29 [34] of the Treaty.

18. Article 30 [36] of the Treaty allows the maintenance of restrictions on the free movement of goods, justified on grounds of the protection of the health and life of animals, which constitutes a fundamental requirement recognized by Community law. However, recourse to Article 30 [36] is no longer possible where Community directives provide for harmonization of the measures necessary to achieve the specific objective which would be furthered by reliance upon this provision.

19. This exclusion of recourse to Article 30 [36] cannot be affected by the fact that, in the present case, the Directive does not lay down any Community procedure for monitoring compliance nor any penalties in the event of breach of its provisions. The fact that the Directive lays down no monitoring procedure or penalties simply means that the Member States are obliged, in accordance with the first paragraph of Article 10 [5] and the third paragraph of Article 249 [189] of the Treaty, to take all measures necessary to guarantee the application and effectiveness of Community law . . . In this regard, the Member States must rely on trust in each other to carry out inspections on their respective territories . . .

20. A Member State may not unilaterally adopt, on its own authority, corrective or protective measures designed to obviate any breach by another Member State of rules of Community law . . .

21. The answer to the first question must accordingly be that Community law precludes a Member State from invoking Article 30 [36] of the Treaty to justify a limitation of exports of goods to another Member State on the sole ground that, according to the first State, the second State is not complying with the requirements of a Community harmonizing

---

13 Meetings were then held between the Chief Veterinary Officer of the United Kingdom and his opposite number in Spain to devise a procedure to ensure that animals exported from the UK went only to abattoirs certified by the Spanish authorities as operating in conformity with the directive. Once this procedure was in place, the UK lifted the ban.

14 Hedley Lomas had specified a particular abattoir in Spain as the destination of the animals and the UK Government had no proof that this particular abattoir was guilty of unnecessary cruelty. However, it would probably have been impossible to make sure that the cattle in fact went there.

directive which pursues the objective which Article 30 [36] is intended to protect but does not lay down either any procedure for monitoring their application or any penalties in the event of their breach.

Result: the export ban was illegal.[15]

Comment

This case shows that the effect of a harmonization directive is to remove the possibility of justifying national measures on the basis of Article 30 [36]. From the point of view of animal welfare, the result was ironic. The directive, which was supposed to help animals, in some ways made things worse. If there had been no directive, the ban might have been justified under Article 30 [36].

Conclusions

It will be seen from the cases considered in this chapter that it is extremely difficult – probably impossible – to remove all barriers to trade. They exist even within a unified country like the UK. However, we do not notice them because we do not think of them in these terms. For example, a ban on beef because of BSE may benefit pig producers in one part of the country at the expense of beef producers in another. Nevertheless, we accept these things as long as the objective is reasonable. In the Community, we also have to accept certain barriers. The problem is to decide which are reasonable.

Further reading

Oliver (Peter) assisted by Jarvis (Malcolm), *Free Movement of Goods in the European Community* (Sweet and Maxwell, London, 4th ed., 2003).
Weatherill (Stephen) and Beaumont (Paul), *EU Law* (Penguin Books, London, 3rd ed., 1999), Chapters 13–17.
Wyatt & Dashwood's European Union Law (Sweet & Maxwell, London, 4th ed., 2000), Chapters 12–13.

---

15 Hedley Lomas had asked for damages against the UK. The English court asked a further question on this point, and the European Court gave a ruling that supported Hedley Lomas' claim.

21

The common market – II

A common market is more than a customs union. In addition to free movement of goods, it requires free movement of labour, free movement of capital and payments,[1] free movement of services and the right of enterprises to establish themselves in another Member State. We shall first examine the free movement of persons.

Free movement of persons

The free movement of labour requires that workers from one Member State be allowed to move to another Member State in order to work. The idea is that workers from countries of high unemployment, or low wages, will move to countries with low unemployment or high wages. In Member States where wage levels are high, this will diminish labour shortages and bring wage levels down, or at least prevent them from rising so fast. In Member States with low wage levels, it will lessen unemployment and thus increase wage levels. Overall, it will tend to even out wage levels and thus put manufacturers in all Member States on a more equal footing. It will also benefit the workers.

This, at least, is the idea. In practice, various factors make the system operate less perfectly. For example, some workers may prefer to remain in their own country even if they are underpaid, rather than live in a country where they cannot understand the language, where the climate is cold and wet and the people seem unfriendly. The result is that, while there have been migrations from, for example, Italy to Germany, there are still significant differences in wage levels between the North and the South of the Community. In most Member States, moreover, immigration from outside the Community is greater than that from within the Community.

The right of enterprises to establish themselves in another Member State (right of establishment) means that companies and businessmen must be allowed to move to another Member State to set up a branch, or even to establish their main or sole centre of operations. This raises many issues, but it includes

---

1 The abolition of restrictions on the free movement of capital and payments is laid down in Arts 56–60 [73b–73g] EC. These provisions have lost most of their importance with the end of exchange controls and the introduction of the euro.

the right of businessmen to migrate, and the right of at least their key staff to go with them. In so far as the latter are employees, they will be covered by the right of free movement of workers, since any employee, regardless of pay or status, is regarded as a "worker" by Community law. In so far as they are self-employed, they will benefit from similar rights granted by other provisions in the EC Treaty.

Free movement of services means that individuals and companies providing services – lawyers, accountants, stockbrokers, doctors, software consultants, advertising agencies, banks, airlines, road-transport undertakings, insurance companies and many more – should be allowed to seek clients, customers or patients throughout the EU, irrespective of the Member State in which they are based.[2] This too raises many issues, but again it includes the right of individuals (both providers and receivers of services) to travel – this time on a temporary basis – so that the service may be performed.

It will be seen from this that the establishment of the common market required rights of free movement to be granted to various categories of persons: employed persons, self-employed persons, providers of services and receivers of services. Moreover, in the years since the common market was established, immigration rights have come to be regarded as more than a matter of economics. The whole purpose of the Community has been redefined to make it more than just an economic organization. Social policies are now seen as objectives in their own right. Immigration rights have social, as well as economic, purposes. The benefit to the individual migrant is considered an end in itself. As a result, further categories of persons were given the right of free movement: retired persons, students and persons of independent means.

This move towards social objectives, which was undertaken to make the Community more appealing to ordinary people, has been highlighted by the establishment of Community citizenship, a concept introduced by the Treaty on European Union. This amended the EC Treaty to create a new Part, entitled "Citizenship of the Union". The first provision in this Part, Article 17 [8], states in its first paragraph:

> Citizenship of the Union is hereby established. Every person holding the nationality of a Member State shall be a citizen of the Union. Citizenship of the Union shall complement and not replace national citizenship.

Having created this new concept, the drafters of the Treaty wanted to give it some content. One of the ways in which they tried to do this was to link immigration rights to citizenship. This was done in Article 18 [8a]. Its first paragraph provides:

---

2 The difference between the right of establishment and the right to provide services may be illustrated by the following example. Assume that a firm of accountants based in England wants to do business in France. If it simply advertises in France and sends people over there on temporary assignments for particular clients, it will be claiming the right to perform services in France. If, on the other hand, it sets up an office in France, and carries on its French operations from there, it will be claiming the right of establishment in France.

Panel 21.1   Principal Community measures on free movement

Legislation under the EC Treaty

Directive 64/221[1]	restrictions on exercise of public policy proviso
Regulation 1612/68[2]	right to find work
Directive 68/360[3]	employed persons (workers)
Regulation 1251/70[4]	right of employed persons (workers) to remain on retirement
Directive 73/148[5]	self-employed persons and providers/receivers of services
Directive 75/34[6]	right of self-employed persons to remain on retirement
Directive 75/35[7]	public policy proviso: right of self-employed persons to remain
Directive 77/486[8]	schooling for children of employed persons (workers)
Directive 90/364[9]	persons of independent means
Directive 90/365[10]	retired persons
Directive 93/96[11]	students

Note: Some of these provisions have been amended. Up-to-date versions may be found on CELEX, Lexis or Westlaw.

[1] OJ (Special Eng. Ed.) Series I, 1963–1964, p. 117.
[2] OJ (Special Eng. Ed.) Series I, 1968 (II), p. 475.
[3] OJ (Special Eng. Ed.) Series I, 1968 (II), p. 485.
[4] OJ (Special Eng. Ed.) Series I, 1970 (II), p. 402.
[5] OJ 1973, L172, p. 14.
[6] OJ 1975, L14, p. 10.
[7] OJ 1975, L14, p. 14.
[8] OJ 1977, L199, p. 32.
[9] OJ 1990, L180, p. 26.
[10] OJ 1990, L180, p. 28.
[11] OJ 1993, L317, p. 59.

> Every citizen of the Union shall have the right to move and reside freely within the territory of the Member States, subject to the limitations and conditions laid down in this Treaty and by the measures adopted to give it effect.

Reading this provision gives one the sensation of first being lifted up and then dumped down. The first half suggests that a new, universal right of free movement is being created, while the second half seems to indicate that the pre-existing law applies as before. In fact, the European Court has applied the provision to extend the rights of Community migrants,[3] but it has so far stopped short of laying down a universal right of free movement.[4] So we still have to consider the specific rights granted to specific categories of persons by specific provisions of Community law. The latter include Treaty provisions and Community legislation. All such provisions appear to be directly effective.[5] A list of the principal legislative measures under the EC Treaty is set out in Panel 21.1.[6]

Employed persons (workers)

The right of employed persons ("workers" in Community parlance) to migrate to another Member State to get a job is laid down in Article 39 [48] EC (see Panel 21.2). This gives the following rights:

3 See, for example, *Martínez Sala*, Case C-85/96, [1998] ECR I-2691; and *Grzelczyk*, Case C-184/99, [2001] ECR I-6193.
4 On the effect of Art. 18 [8a] as regards immigration controls at the frontier, see *Wijsenbeek*, Case C-378/97, [1999] ECR I-6207.
5 Since immigration rights are always asserted against the State, only vertical direct effect is in issue.
6 Citations to the Official Journal are given in this list. They will not be given in footnotes below. In any event, it is advisable to use CELEX, Lexis or Westlaw, since they incorporate amendments.

Panel 21.2   Free movement of workers

EC Treaty

Article 39 [48]

1. Freedom of movement for workers shall be secured within the Community.

2. Such freedom of movement shall entail the abolition of any discrimination based on nationality between workers of the Member States as regards employment, remuneration and other conditions of work and employment.

3. It shall entail the right, subject to limitations justified on grounds of public policy, public security or public health:

(a) to accept offers of employment actually made;
(b) to move freely within the territory of Member States for this purpose;
(c) to stay in a Member State for the purpose of employment in accordance with the provisions governing the employment of nationals of that State laid down by law, regulation or administrative action;
(d) to remain in the territory of a Member State after having been employed in that State, subject to conditions which shall be embodied in implementing regulations to be drawn up by the Commission.

4. The provisions of this Article shall not apply to employment in the public service.

- the right to accept offers of employment in another Member State;
- the right to enter another Member State for this purpose;
- the right to reside in the new Member State in order to work;
- the right to remain there on retirement.

These rights are fleshed out by Directive 68/360 and Regulation 1612/68. Additional rights conferred by these measures include the right to leave a Member State in order to work in another Member State,[7] and the right to be given a passport or identity card by the Member State of which the migrant is a national.[8] On entering another Member State, the migrant can show either of these documents. No visa may be required.[9]

The right to enter

It is clear from the terms of Article 39 [48] EC that the right to enter another Member State was intended to apply only after the migrant had already found a job. The phrase "for this purpose" in Article 39(3)(b) [48(3)(b)] refers back to sub-paragraph (a), which talks of accepting offers of employment "actually made". However, when the drafts of Directive 68/360 and Regulation 1612/68 were before the Council in 1968, a declaration was made by the Member States and recorded in the Council Minutes[10] which reads as follows:

> Nationals of a Member State as referred to in Article 1 [of the directive] who move to another Member State in order to seek work there shall be allowed a minimum period of three months for the purpose; in the event of their not having found employment by the end of that period, their residence on the territory of this second State may be brought to an end.
>
> However, if the abovementioned persons should be taken charge of by national assistance (social welfare) in the second State during the aforesaid period they may be invited to leave the territory of this second State.

Directive 68/360 does not itself grant the right to enter another Member State in order to look for work, but national legislation passed to transpose it into

---

7 Directive 68/360, Art. 2(1). A Community migrant also has the right to return to his own country: *Singh*, Case C-370/90, [1992] ECR I-4265.

8 Directive 68/360, Art. 2(2). Countries, like the United Kingdom, which do not have identity cards must issue a passport.

9 Directive 68/360, Art. 3.

10 Since Council meetings were held behind closed doors and Council Minutes were not published, the existence of the declaration would not have been publicly known had it not been leaked and published by a press agency: see *Europe*, 30 July 1968, p. 5.

national law did so.[11] It is probable, therefore, that the declaration was intended to record an agreement that the right would be granted by national law, and was not intended to constitute a direct source of rights or to indicate the correct interpretation of the implementing measures.

In our next case, the European Court considered its effect.

European Union
Antonissen
COURT OF JUSTICE OF THE EUROPEAN COMMUNITIES
Case C-292/89, [1991] ECR I-745

Facts

Mr Antonissen was a Belgian national who entered the United Kingdom. He was convicted of drug dealing and sent to prison. On his release, the UK Government wanted to deport him. He claimed rights as a "worker" under Community law. This in turn raised the question whether a person allegedly looking for work should be regarded as a "worker" in terms of Community law.[12] The English court before which proceedings had been brought made a reference to the European Court asking whether a Community migrant can be deported if he has not found work within six months, the three-month period under the Council declaration having been extended to six months by the United Kingdom legislation.

Judgment

9. [I]t has been argued that, according to the strict wording of Article 39 [48] of the Treaty, Community nationals are given the right to move freely within the territory of the Member States for the purpose only of accepting offers of employment actually made (Article 39(3)(a) and (b) [48(3)(a) and (b)]) whilst the right to stay in the territory of a Member State is stated to be for the purpose of employment (Article 39(3)(c) [48(3)(c)]).

10. Such an interpretation would exclude the right of a national of a Member State to move freely and to stay in the territory of the other Member States in order to seek employment there, and cannot be upheld.

11. Indeed, as the Court has consistently held, freedom of movement for workers forms one of the foundations of the Community and, consequently, the provisions laying down that freedom must be given a broad interpretation . . .

12. Moreover, a strict interpretation of Article 39(3) [48(3)] would jeopardize the actual chances that a national of a Member State who is seeking employment will find it in another Member State, and would, as a result, make that provision ineffective.

13. It follows that Article 39(3) [48(3)] must be interpreted as enumerating, in a non-exhaustive way, certain rights benefiting nationals of Member States in the context of the free movement of workers and that that freedom also entails the right for nationals of Member States to move freely within the territory of the other Member States and to stay there for the purposes of seeking employment.

---

11 For the United Kingdom, see the Immigration Rules for Control on Entry (EEC and Other Non-Commonwealth Nationals), HC Paper 81 of 1972/73, para. 52.
12 His drug dealing did not count as work since it was illegal.

14. Moreover, that interpretation of the Treaty corresponds to that of the Community legislature, as appears from the provisions adopted in order to implement the principle of free movement, in particular Articles 1 and 5 of Regulation No 1612/68 . . . which presuppose that Community nationals are entitled to move in order to look for employment, and hence to stay, in another Member State.[13]

15. It must therefore be ascertained whether the right, under Article 39 [48] and the provisions of Regulation No 1612/68, to stay in a Member State for the purposes of seeking employment can be subjected to a temporal limitation.

16. In that regard, it must be pointed out in the first place that the effectiveness of Article 39 [48] is secured in so far as Community legislation or, in its absence, the legislation of a Member State gives persons concerned a reasonable time in which to apprise themselves, in the territory of the Member State concerned, of offers of employment corresponding to their occupational qualifications and to take, where appropriate, the necessary steps in order to be engaged.

[The court then considered the effect of the Council declaration. It said that the declaration could not be used to interpret either Directive 58/360 or Regulation 1612/68, since neither of them referred to it. Consequently, it had "no legal significance". After rejecting other arguments, the court concluded as follows:]

21. In the absence of a Community provision prescribing the period during which Community nationals seeking employment in a Member State may stay there, a period of six months, such as that laid down in the national legislation at issue in the main proceedings, does not appear in principle to be insufficient to enable the persons concerned to apprise themselves, in the host Member State, of offers of employment corresponding to their occupational qualifications and to take, where appropriate, the necessary steps in order to be engaged and, therefore, does not jeopardize the effectiveness of the principle of free movement. However, if after the expiry of that period the person concerned provides evidence that he is continuing to seek employment and that he has genuine chances of being engaged, he cannot be required to leave the territory of the host Member State.

Result: it would not be contrary to Community law for the United Kingdom to deport a Community national who has not found work within six months of entering the country, unless he provided evidence that he was continuing to seek employment and had a genuine chance of finding it.

Comment

In this case, the European Court granted Community migrants greater rights than the framers of the Treaty had intended. Although it purported to pay no attention to the Council declaration, it must surely have been influenced by it, though it changed the strict three-month time limit to a more flexible period.

---

13 Editor's note: Art. 1 provides: "Any national of a Member State shall, irrespective of his place of residence, have the right to take up an activity as an employed person, and to pursue such activity, within the territory of another Member State . . ." Art. 5 provides: "A national of a Member State who seeks employment in the territory of another Member State shall receive the same assistance there as that afforded by the employment offices in that State to their own nationals seeking employment."

It will be remembered that the second paragraph of the Council declaration says that a migrant who has not found a job may be deported if he claims social welfare. The court did not indicate whether this represents the law.

Perhaps the most important aspect of the case is the statement in paragraph 11 that Community provisions will be interpreted in favour of the migrant. This, together with the statement in paragraph 13 that the Treaty provisions merely represent minimum rights, sets the tone for later cases. For this reason, the Community rules summarized below should not necessarily be regarded as indicating the full extent of Community rights.

The right to reside

A migrant who has found employment[14] gains the right to reside. Unless the job was merely temporary, this will continue unless and until some event occurs which results in his losing it. Voluntary unemployment – being able to work but choosing not to do so – may be an example. Involuntary unemployment[15] (and the need to claim welfare benefits) will not necessarily result in the loss of the right, though it may do so in certain circumstances.[16]

The right to remain

An employed person who retires on grounds of old age or incapacity resulting from illness or an accident may remain in the country of immigration if he fulfils certain minimum residence requirements.[17]

Self-employed persons

The category of self-employed persons covers businessmen, professional persons, traders, craftsmen and anyone else who earns his living without working for someone else. If such persons wish to establish themselves in another Member State in order to carry on their activity, they have the same immigration rights as employed persons.[18] In their case, it was clear from the beginning that they could enter the country before establishing themselves in their business or profession.[19]

Providers and receivers of services

Providers and receivers of services have temporary immigration rights that last as long as is necessary to provide or receive the service.[20]

---

14 The European Court takes a wide and generous view of what constitutes employment. Part-time work, even if it is so poorly paid that recourse to social welfare is necessary, will be enough, provided it is effective and genuine, not purely marginal and ancillary. See *Levin*, Case 53/81, [1982] ECR 1035; and *Kempf*, Case 139/85, [1986] ECR 1741.
15 A person is involuntarily unemployed when he wants to get a job but is unable to do so.
16 See Directive 68/360, Art. 7.
17 Art. 39(3)(d) [48(3)(d)] EC and Regulation 1251/70.
18 The relevant Treaty provisions are Arts. 43 [52] *et seq.* EC. The relevant legislative measures are Directive 73/148 and Directive 75/34 (right to remain).
19 Directive 73/148, Art. 1(1)(a).
20 See Arts. 49 [59] *et seq.* EC and Directive 73/148.

Other persons

As we saw above, Community legislation grants immigration rights to three categories of persons who are not economically active.[21] They are students, retired persons and persons of independent means. In all three cases, the legislation makes the rights conditional on the fulfilment of two requirements:

- the person concerned must have sufficient resources to support himself without recourse to social assistance; and
- he must be covered by medical insurance.

However, persons who have immigration rights on some other basis – for example, employed persons who have obtained the right to remain – will not necessarily have to fulfil these requirements. Moreover, even those who do not fall into some other category may in certain circumstances be able to obtain social welfare.[22]

Family rights

Persons enjoying Community immigration rights may bring their families with them, even if the family members are not Community citizens.[23] Family members thus have derived rights that cover largely the same ground as those of the person on whom they are dependent. They are entitled to work or engage in self-employed activities.

Immigration control

Most of the Member States have concluded a series of agreements, known as the Schengen Agreements,[24] under which they have undertaken to abolish border controls among themselves. Countries with land borders have always found it difficult to prevent unauthorized persons slipping across the frontier. Many continental countries have, therefore, relied mainly on controls operating after entry – for example, compulsory identity cards and an obligation on all persons to register their addresses with the police – in order to keep out illegal immigrants. It was not, therefore, such a big step for those countries to abolish border controls. Being an island, Britain has been better able to control entry to its territory and has traditionally relied on border controls, rather than controls after entry. Identity cards are unknown and there is no obligation on citizens to register their addresses with the police. For this reason, the United Kingdom did not become a party to the Schengen Agreements.

The Schengen Agreements have now been integrated into the EC Treaty.[25] Article 14(2) [7a(2)] EC states that the internal market (which the Community

21 Directives 90/364, 90/365 and 93/96.
22 See, for example, *Grzelczyk*, Case C-184/99, [2001] ECR I-6193.
23 These rights are given by the Community legislation mentioned above.
24 Listed in an annex to the Protocol integrating the Schengen *acquis* into the framework of the European Union, a protocol to the Treaty of Amsterdam.
25 This took place under the Treaty of Amsterdam: see the Protocol integrating the Schengen *acquis* into the framework of the European Union.

is required to establish) "shall comprise an area without internal frontiers in which the free movement of goods, persons, services and capital is ensured in accordance with the provisions of this Treaty".[26] Article 62 [73j] requires the Council to adopt measures "with a view to ensuring, in compliance with Article 14 [7a], the absence of any controls on persons, be they citizens of the Union or nationals of third countries, when crossing internal borders".[27]

These provisions, however, do not bind the United Kingdom. A protocol to the Treaty of Amsterdam, the Protocol on the application of certain aspects of Article 14 [7a] EC to the United Kingdom, states that neither Article 14 [7a], nor any other provision of Community law, precludes the United Kingdom from establishing such controls on its frontiers as it may consider necessary to verify the right to enter of Community citizens. Thus the United Kingdom can still impose immigration controls to ascertain which would-be migrants are Community citizens and which are not.[28]

The public policy proviso

All the Community provisions granting immigration rights are subject to an exception, usually called the "public policy proviso", which permits Member States to limit those rights on grounds of "public policy, public security or public health".[29] However, although this gives national governments a certain discretion, it is subject to restrictions imposed by Community law. In particular, it cannot be used to exclude general classes of persons. Article 3(1) of Directive 64/221 provides that the public policy proviso can be invoked only on the basis of the personal conduct of the individual concerned.[30] It must, therefore, be applied on a case-by-case basis. There must be an assessment whether the migrant's exclusion or deportation is justified by something he did. This is true even where he is convicted of a crime. There can be no rule that conviction for a particular kind of crime automatically results in deportation. There must be a determination that the particular action of the individual in question is such that his continued presence in the country would be contrary to public policy.

The directive also grants the migrant certain procedural rights. Article 6 provides that he must be informed of the grounds on which the decision was taken, unless this would be contrary to national security.[31] Article 9 provides that there must be a right of appeal to an independent authority against a decision to deport a Community migrant. Thus a Community citizen suspected

---

26 On the effect of this as regards border controls, see *Wijsenbeek*, Case C-378/97, [1999] ECR I-6207.
27 Internal borders are borders between one EU Member State and another.
28 However, a Community citizen who enters the country illegally cannot be deported solely on the ground that he has not gone through immigration control.
29 See, for example, Art. 39(3) [48(3)] EC, set out in Panel 21.2 (workers). On the right of establishment, see Art. 46 [56]. This also applies to services: Art. 55 [66] EC.
30 This provision does not apply to action taken to protect public health.
31 This was the right in issue in the *Cohn-Bendit* case discussed in Chap. 10.

of terrorist connections cannot be deported simply on the say-so of the Home Secretary. The immigrant has a right to submit his defence in person, though this may be restricted on grounds of national security.

Conclusions

It will be seen from the above that today Community law comes close to granting a general right of free movement to all Community citizens.[32] The main (possibly, the only) exception concerns so-called "welfare tourists" – persons who go to another Member State specifically in order to live on welfare. They cannot support themselves and have no intention of working. They want to be supported by the taxpayer. Although there is no clear statement from the European Court to this effect, they are probably outside the scope of Community law. If this were not so, the Member States with the most generous welfare benefits might experience a surge of migrants from countries where the benefits were less good. "Welfare tourists" must, however, be distinguished from persons who migrate for a legitimate purpose, but also need social welfare. They may well be covered by Community law.

Non-discrimination and the right to work

A right of free movement would be insufficient in itself to create a common market if Community migrants were denied the right to work on the same terms as nationals of the State concerned. Community law therefore grants them a right to equal treatment in the field of employment.[33] For employed persons, this is found in Article 39(2) [48(2)] EC, set out in Panel 21.2, above. It is further elaborated in Regulation 1612/68. Similar rights are given to self-employed persons and providers of services.

Community law, however, goes further than simply granting equality in employment. Partly because it is believed that a Community citizen would otherwise be less likely to exercise his rights of free movement, and partly because (as we saw above) social goals are seen as objectives in their own right, Community law also grants equality rights in other areas. Thus Article 7(2) of Regulation 1612/68 provides that a Community citizen working in another Member State must be given the same "social and tax advantages" as national workers. There has been much litigation on what this entails.

Article 12 [6] EC lays down a general ban on discrimination on grounds of nationality. It applies beyond the employment area but nevertheless operates only within the scope of the Treaty. This is why, for example, the right to vote in national elections may be reserved for citizens. Article 12 [6] is also subject to

---

32 It is of course subject to the public policy proviso.
33 These rights are not subject to the public policy proviso.

exceptions specifically laid down in the EC Treaty. One such exception is Article 39(4) [48(4)] EC (Panel 21.2, above). This states that the rights granted by Article 39 [48] do not apply to employment in the public service. Article 45 [55] EC lays down a similar exception with regard to self-employed persons and providers of services.[34] In a series of decisions, the European Court has, however, restricted this exception to public-service positions that entail a degree of discretion or policy making.[35]

The European Court has held that these provisions apply not only to direct discrimination – discrimination specifically on grounds of nationality – but also to indirect discrimination. The latter is discrimination which is ostensibly based on some other ground, but which brings about the same result in practice. Discrimination on the ground that the person concerned was previously resident in another Member State would be an example. However, while direct discrimination is always illegal if it falls within the scope of the relevant provision, indirect discrimination is permitted if it has a genuine purpose that is not inconsistent with Community law.

Our next case is an example.

> **European Union**
> **Groener v. Minister for Education**
> **COURT OF JUSTICE OF THE EUROPEAN COMMUNITIES**
> Case C-379/87, [1989] ECR I-3967

Facts

Mrs Groener was a Dutch citizen living in Dublin. She had a temporary post as a part-time art teacher at a college of marketing and design in Dublin. She applied for a permanent, full-time post at the college. Under Irish law, permanent, full-time teachers in public educational institutions are, except in certain special cases, obliged to have a knowledge of the Irish language. Since she lacked a certificate of proficiency in Irish, Mrs Groener had to sit an examination in Irish. The standard required does not seem to have been high. Nevertheless, she failed. This meant that she could not be appointed to the post. She challenged this in the Irish courts, claiming that the language requirement was contrary to Community law, since it discriminated against citizens of other Member States. Irish citizens normally learnt the Irish language in school, while citizens of other Member States are unlikely to have any knowledge of it. In particular, she argued that Article 3(1) of Regulation 1612/68 (Panel 21.3) precluded its application in her case. The Irish court referred the matter to the European Court.

---

[34] This is extended to services by Art. 55 [66].
[35] See, for example, *Commission v. Belgium*, Case 149/79, [1980] ECR 3881. For a summary of the earlier cases, see Handoll, "Article 48(4) EEC and Non-National Access to Public Employment" (1988) 13 ELRev. 223. See also Castro Oliveira, "Workers and Other Persons: Step-by-Step from Movement to Citizenship – Case Law 1995–2001" (2002) 39 CMLRev. 77 at 97–98.

Panel 21.3 Linguistic requirements for employment

Regulation 1612/68

Article 3

1. Under this Regulation, provisions laid down by law, regulation or administrative action or administrative practices of a Member State shall not apply:

- where they limit application for and offers of employment, or the right of foreign nationals to take up and pursue employment or subject these to conditions not applicable in respect of their own nationals; or

- where, though applicable irrespective of nationality, their exclusive or principal aim or effect is to keep nationals of other Member States away from the employment offered.

This provision shall not apply to conditions relating to linguistic knowledge required by reason of the nature of the post to be filled.

Judgment

18. As is apparent from the documents before the Court, although Irish is not spoken by the whole Irish population, the policy followed by Irish governments for many years has been designed not only to maintain but also to promote the use of Irish as a means of expressing national identity and culture. It is for that reason that Irish courses are compulsory for children receiving primary education and optional for those receiving secondary education. The obligation imposed on lecturers in public vocational education schools to have a certain knowledge of the Irish language is one of the measures adopted by the Irish Government in furtherance of that policy.

19. The EEC Treaty does not prohibit the adoption of a policy for the protection and promotion of a language of a Member State which is both the national language and the first official language. However, the implementation of such a policy must not encroach upon a fundamental freedom such as that of the free movement of workers. Therefore, the requirements deriving from measures intended to implement such a policy must not in any circumstances be disproportionate in relation to the aim pursued[36] and the manner in which they are applied must not bring about discrimination against nationals of other Member States.

20. The importance of education for the implementation of such a policy must be recognized. Teachers have an essential role to play, not only through the teaching which they provide but also by their participation in the daily life of the school and the privileged relationship which they have with their pupils. In those circumstances, it is not unreasonable to require them to have some knowledge of the first national language.

21. It follows that the requirement imposed on teachers to have an adequate knowledge of such a language must, provided that the level of knowledge required is not disproportionate in relation to the objective pursued, be regarded as a condition corresponding to the knowledge required by reason of the nature of the post to be filled within the meaning of the last subparagraph of Article 3(1) of Regulation No 1612/68.

Result: the requirement of a knowledge of Irish was covered by the last subparagraph of Article 3(1) of the regulation and was consequently not contrary to Community law, provided it was applied in a non-discriminatory manner and with due regard for the principle of proportionality. It was for the national court to ensure that this was the case.

---

36 This is a reference to the principle of proportionality, a general principle of Community law. Under it, burdens must not be imposed on the citizen that are disproportionate to the aims pursued.

Panel 21.4 Freedom of establishment

EC Treaty

Article 43 [52]

Within the framework of the provisions set out below, restrictions on the freedom of establishment of nationals of a Member State in the territory of another Member State shall be prohibited. Such prohibition shall also apply to restrictions on the setting up of agencies, branches and subsidiaries by nationals of any Member State established in the territory of any Member State.

Freedom of establishment shall include the right to take up and pursue activities as self-employed persons and to set up and manage undertakings, in particular companies or firms within the meaning of the second paragraph of Article 48 [58], under the conditions laid down for its own nationals by the law of the country where such establishment is effected, subject to the provisions of the Chapter relating to capital.

Article 48 [58]

Companies or firms formed in accordance with the law of a Member State and having their registered office, central administration or principal place of business within the Community, shall for the purposes of this Chapter, be treated in the same way as natural persons who are nationals of Member States.

"Companies or firms" means companies or firms constituted under civil or commercial law, including co-operative societies, and other legal persons governed by public or private law, save those which are non-profit-making.

Comment

This case shows that conflicts can arise between perfectly reasonable national objectives and freedom of movement within the Community. A requirement that art teachers be proficient in the Irish language has the effect of excluding foreigners from such posts. Since the language of instruction in the college was English, there was no practical need for it. Nevertheless, a rule that the requirement did not apply to foreigners, though a possible solution, might be regarded as discriminating against Irish people, as well as undermining the policy as a whole.

Free movement (establishment) of companies

We have already considered the rights of individuals who want to establish themselves in a business or profession in another Member State. Here we shall look at the position concerning companies.

Except in the case of family members, free movement rights for individuals are limited to nationals of Member States. How does this apply to companies? The answer is found in Article 48 [58] EC (Panel 21.4). This states that a company is to be accorded the same rights as an individual who is a national of a Member State if it was formed under the law of a Member State and has either its registered office, its central administration or its principal place of business in a Member State.

Incorporation (formation) of a company is the process whereby it is created and granted legal personality separate from that of its shareholders. Legal personality is the capacity to have legal rights – for example, to own property, enter into contracts or engage in litigation. While individuals are naturally endowed with legal personality, corporate legal personality is bestowed by the law. Each legal system has its own rules for the incorporation of a company. If these are followed, the company will come into existence. If the legal system in question is that of a Member State, the first requirement is met. Normally, one of the requirements for incorporation is that the company must have a registered office in the country under the law of which it was incorporated. So the second requirement will usually be the automatic consequence of the first. The requirements concerning the central administration[37] and the principal place of business[38] are alternatives. They could apply in those rare cases in which the registered office is not in a Member State.

If the company satisfies these requirements, it is entitled to freedom of establishment under Community law. Our next case provides an example.

European Union
Centros
COURT OF JUSTICE OF THE EUROPEAN COMMUNITIES
Case C-212/97, [1999] ECR I-1459 (Full Court)

Facts

Mr and Mrs Bryde were Danish citizens resident in Denmark. They wanted to set up a company. If they had incorporated it in Denmark, they would have been required to put up DKK200,000 (approximately £20,000) share capital. This was the minimum permitted by Danish law. Instead, they incorporated the company in England. Under UK law, there is no minimum share capital. The company has to have a registered office in the United Kingdom, but UK law does not require that the company should own the premises or operate from there. All that is needed is an office, identified as the registered office of the company, where legal documents can be served. A friend of Mr Bryde's agreed that his home could be the registered office.

Having set up the company, the Brydes wanted to establish a "branch" in Denmark. Since the company did no business in the United Kingdom, the "branch" would in fact have been the central administration and sole place of business. They applied to have the "branch" registered in Denmark. The Danish Companies Board (the "Board") refused. They maintained that the Brydes' purpose in incorporating the company in England was to evade the requirements of Danish law. These requirements were laid down in the public interest to protect creditors and prevent fraud. The Board would have been prepared to register the "branch" if the company had carried on business in England. Since it did not, the Board argued that the matter had no Community element: it was a purely domestic matter, internal to Denmark.

37 The place where the central administration is situated is the place where the most important decisions concerning the company are made.
38 The place where the principal place of business is situated is the place where the most important economic activities take place. This will usually be the same as the central administration, but this will not always be so. An example is a mining company that has its head office in London but carries out all its mining activities in Chile. Its central administration will be in England and its principal place of business in Chile.

The Brydes brought legal proceedings in Denmark and a reference was made to the European Court.

Judgment

17. [I]t should be noted that a situation in which a company formed in accordance with the law of a Member State in which it has its registered office desires to set up a branch in another Member State falls within the scope of Community law. In that regard, it is immaterial that the company was formed in the first Member State only for the purpose of establishing itself in the second, where its main, or indeed entire, business is to be conducted . . .

18. That Mr and Mrs Bryde formed the company Centros in the United Kingdom for the purpose of avoiding Danish legislation requiring that a minimum amount of share capital be paid up has not been denied either in the written observations or at the hearing. That does not, however, mean that the formation by that British company of a branch in Denmark is not covered by freedom of establishment for the purposes of Article 43 [52] and 48 [58] of the Treaty. The question of the application of those articles of the Treaty is different from the question whether or not a Member State may adopt measures in order to prevent attempts by certain of its nationals to evade domestic legislation by having recourse to the possibilities offered by the Treaty.

19. As to the question whether, as Mr and Mrs Bryde claim, the refusal to register in Denmark a branch of their company formed in accordance with the law of another Member State in which its has its registered office constitutes an obstacle to freedom of establishment, it must be borne in mind that that freedom, conferred by Article 43 [52] of the Treaty on Community nationals, includes the right for them to take up and pursue activities as self-employed persons and to set up and manage undertakings under the same conditions as are laid down by the law of the Member State of establishment for its own nationals. Furthermore, under Article 48 [58] of the Treaty companies or firms formed in accordance with the law of a Member State and having their registered office, central administration or principal place of business within the Community are to be treated in the same way as natural persons who are nationals of Member States.

20. The immediate consequence of this is that those companies are entitled to carry on their business in another Member State through an agency, branch or subsidiary. The location of their registered office, central administration or principal place of business serves as the connecting factor with the legal system of a particular State in the same way as does nationality in the case of a natural person . . .

21. Where it is the practice of a Member State, in certain circumstances, to refuse to register a branch of a company having its registered office in another Member State, the result is that companies formed in accordance with the law of that other Member State are prevented from exercising the freedom of establishment conferred on them by Articles 43 [52] and 48 [58] of the Treaty.

22. Consequently, that practice constitutes an obstacle to the exercise of the freedoms guaranteed by those provisions.

23. According to the Danish authorities, however, Mr and Mrs Bryde cannot rely on those provisions, since the sole purpose of the company formation which they have in mind is to circumvent the application of the national law governing formation of private limited companies and therefore constitutes abuse of the freedom of establishment. In their submission, the Kingdom of Denmark is therefore entitled to take steps to prevent such abuse by refusing to register the branch.

24. It is true that according to the case-law of the Court a Member State is entitled to take measures designed to prevent certain of its nationals from attempting, under cover of the rights created by the Treaty, improperly to circumvent their national legislation or to prevent individuals from improperly or fraudulently taking advantage of provisions of Community law . . .

25. However, although, in such circumstances, the national courts may, case by case, take account – on the basis of objective evidence – of abuse or fraudulent conduct on the part of the persons concerned in order, where appropriate, to deny them the benefit of the provisions of Community law on which they seek to rely, they must nevertheless assess such conduct in the light of the objectives pursued by those provisions . . .

26. In the present case, the provisions of national law, application of which the parties concerned have sought to avoid, are rules governing the formation of companies and not rules concerning the carrying on of certain trades, professions or businesses. The provisions of the Treaty on freedom of establishment are intended specifically to enable companies formed in accordance with the law of a Member State and having their registered office, central administration or principal place of business within the Community to pursue activities in other Member States through an agency, branch or subsidiary.

27. That being so, the fact that a national of a Member State who wishes to set up a company chooses to form it in the Member State whose rules of company law seem to him the least restrictive and to set up branches in other Member States cannot, in itself, constitute an abuse of the right of establishment. The right to form a company in accordance with the law of a Member State and to set up branches in other Member States is inherent in the exercise, in a single market, of the freedom of establishment guaranteed by the Treaty.

28. In this connection, the fact that company law is not completely harmonized in the Community is of little consequence. Moreover, it is always open to the Council, on the basis of the powers conferred upon it by Article 44(2)(g) [54(3)(g)] of the EC Treaty, to achieve complete harmonization.

[The court then considered whether the refusal to register could be justified on the ground that it was necessary to protect creditors and prevent fraudulent bankruptcies. It said that in certain circumstances national measures restricting fundamental freedoms, such as the freedom of establishment, could be justified. However, the relevant conditions were not fulfilled in the present case.]

35. First, the practice in question is not such as to attain the objective of protecting creditors which it purports to pursue since, if the company concerned had conducted business in the United Kingdom, its branch would have been registered in Denmark, even though Danish creditors might have been equally exposed to risk.

36. Since the company concerned in the main proceedings holds itself out as a company governed by the law of England and Wales and not as a company governed by Danish law, its creditors are on notice that it is covered by laws different from those which govern the formation of private limited companies in Denmark . . .

[The court then pointed out that there were other ways open to Denmark to prevent fraud where it was established that, by incorporating the company abroad, the persons concerned were in fact trying to evade their obligations towards creditors.]

Result: the Board's refusal to register the company was contrary to Community law.

Comment

This case shows that the European Court takes freedom of establishment seriously.[39] It is one of the cornerstones of the common market. For this reason,
the (perfectly reasonable) concerns of the Danish authorities were overridden.
It might be thought that this shows a stricter attitude than the *Groener* case.
However, the court was careful to point out that other measures were possible
to protect creditors and prevent fraud. Such measures might be acceptable if
they passed a four-fold test.[40] They must:

- be applied in a non-discriminatory manner;
- be justified by imperative requirements in the general interest;
- be suitable for securing the attainment of the objective; and
- not go beyond what is necessary in order to attain it.[41]

The Danish solution of totally denying recognition went too far. It infringed the
last requirement. Moreover, as the court pointed out, the Danish authorities
were prepared to register foreign companies if they did at least some business
in the country of incorporation. However, the need to protect creditors and
prevent fraud would be just as important in this case as in the case where the
company did no business in the foreign country. So the Danish solution could,
in any event, solve only part of the problem.[42]

Further reading

Castro Oliveira, "Workers and Other Persons: Step-by-Step from Movement to
    Citizenship – Case Law 1995–2001" (2002) 39 CMLRev. 77.

Green (N.), Hartley (T. C.) and Usher (J. A.), *The Legal Foundations of the Single European
    Market* (Oxford University Press, Oxford, 1981), Chapters 8–12.

Weatherill (Stephen) and Beaumont (Paul), *EU Law* (Penguin Books, London, 3rd ed.,
    1999), Chapters 18 and 19.

Wyatt & Dashwood's European Union Law (Sweet & Maxwell, London, 4th ed., 2000),
    Chapters 14–16.

---

39 For a later judgment, also by the Full Court, reaffirming *Centros*, see *Überseering*, Case C-208/00,
5 November 2002.
40 See para. 34 of the judgment in *Centros* (not set out above).
41 This shows that the thinking behind the exceptions to the free movement of goods (discussed in the
previous chapter) applies here as well.
42 For a detailed discussion of the background of the *Centros* case with particular reference to
comparative private international law, see Stephan Rammeloo, *Corporations in Private International Law*
(Oxford University Press, Oxford, 2001).

Index